This is the first full-length study in English of the political and strategic influence of one of France's most controversial military leaders, General Maurice Gamelin (1872–1958).

Gamelin was reviled by many of his contemporaries and denigrated by two generations of historians as 'the man who lost the Battle of France' in 1940. Here Gamelin is reappraised in the context of the unstable civil-military relations and national decline during 1935–40 when he had major responsibility for French security. The author bases his account on hitherto inaccessible primary sources in France and Belgium, as well as on public and private archives in Britain and the USA. The evidence reviewed, including Gamelin's private headquarters' diary, provides the basis for a revision of the earlier hostile portraits of the general. The author argues that less attention should be paid to the campaign in France in 1940, by which time Gamelin's role was that of an inter-allied co-ordinator and senior adviser to the Franco-British Supreme War Council. Rather, he suggests that great credit is due to Gamelin for his success in holding together the pre-war civil-military consensus, and for rearming France by 1939.

The Republic in danger

The Republic in danger

General Maurice Gamelin and the politics of French defence, 1933–1940

Martin S. Alexander

Published by the Press Syndicate of the University of Cambridge
The Pitt Building, Trumpington Street, Cambridge CB2 1RP
40 West 20th Street, New York, NY 10011–4211, USA
10 Stamford Road, Oakleigh, Victoria 3166, Australia

© Cambridge University Press 1992

First published 1992

Printed in Great Britain at the University Press, Cambridge

A catalogue record for this book is available from the British Library

Library of Congress cataloguing in publication data

Alexander, Martin S.
　The Republic in danger: General Maurice Gamelin and the politics of French defence, 1933–1940 / Martin S. Alexander.
　　p. cm.
　Includes bibliographical references and index.
　ISBN 0 521 37234 8
　1. Gamelin, Maurice Gustave, 1872–1958 – Military leadership.
2. Generals – France – Biography.　3. France. Armée – Biography.
4. France – Politics and government – 1914–1940.　5. France – Military policy – History – 20th century.　6. World War, 1939–1945 – France – Prisoners and prisons. I. Title.
DC373.G27A44　1992
944.081′5′092 – dc20　91–39965 CIP

ISBN 0 521 37234 8 hardback

wv

For Rosalie

When the Republic is in danger the word 'Republican' changes its meaning. It regains its old significance, historic and heroic.
(Léon Blum, 12 February 1934, reported in *Le Populaire*, 13 February 1934)

Contents

Acknowledgements   page xi

Introduction: Maurice Gamelin, the defence of France and the decline of the Third Republic — 1
1 The making of a republican general — 13
2 Gamelin and the rebirth of German power — 34
3 First responses: defence versus détente in the Laval era — 56
4 The Popular Front, the army and politics — 80
5 The road to rearmament: Gamelin, Daladier and Popular Front defence policy — 110
6 Gamelin and air support of the army — 142
7 Gamelin, the Maginot Line and Belgium — 172
8 Gamelin, Yugoslavia and the eastern alliances: assets or embarrassments? — 210
9 Men or material? Gamelin and British support for France — 236
10 Czechoslovakia, Poland, the Soviet Union: from appeasement to war — 279
11 Gamelin and the fall of Poland — 314
12 The Twilight War: military stagnation and political conflict — 348
Conclusion — 378
Appendices
   (1) Diagrammatic organisation of the French high command — 404
   (2) Distribution of the four-year armaments programme of September 1936 (*Le programme de 14 milliards*) — 406

Notes — 407
Bibliography — 518
Index — 557

Acknowledgements

Historical research involves much labour of a solitary kind – traditionally in archives and libraries but also, and increasingly, in front of microfilm readers and computer terminals. Its successful completion and publication depends on these resources; but also owes itself to the cooperation and forbearance of colleagues, fellow scholars, friends and family. My obligations are great: they extend over some fourteen years of research and writing on modern France. It is a source of immense pleasure, therefore, to be able to thank the many individuals and institutions whose courtesy, encouragement and assistance has facilitated my work and, into the bargain, made it extremely agreeable.

In the first place, pursuing historical inquiry against a background of cutbacks of British university budgets in the later 1970s and 1980s, I have been dependent upon a variety of benefactors for funding. Initially, as a graduate student at St Antony's College, Oxford, I was grateful for assistance from the Department of Education and Science of the United Kingdom; the Université de Paris IV (Sorbonne) which awarded me a research studentship in 1977–8; the Educational Trust of ICI Limited; the Countess Eleanor Peel Trust; Oxford University's graduate studies' committee and the Oxford University Zaharoff Travel Fund. In addition, I owe thanks to the Franco-British Council which financed two further years in Paris as one of its research fellows from 1980 to 1982, and to the Taittinger company which, through the generosity of its president, Claude Taittinger, provided valued salary supplementation. As lecturer in modern history at the University of Southampton, I have been generously supported by that University's Committee for Advanced Studies. At Yale, where I was privileged to spend the academic year 1988–9, I received a fellowship from the John M. Olin Foundation and a grant from the John D. and Catherine T. MacArthur Foundation.

Just as the impecunious university historian requires the money of others, so he or she also depends heavily on the cooperation of archivists and keepers of records. I am delighted, therefore, to record my appreciation for the invaluable help of the staff of the Public Record Office in London, at Portugal Street as well as at Kew. It is a pleasure, likewise, to be able to extend thanks to Raymond Teichman, chief archivist, and his staff, at the Franklin D. Roosevelt Presidential Library, Hyde Park, New York; John Taylor, of the military records branch, United States National Archives and Records Administration, Washington DC; Mme F. Collet of the Archives de l'Assemblée Nationale, Paris; Mme Chantal de Tourtier-Bonazzi of the Archives Privés at the Archives Nationales, Paris; Janine Bourdin, Marie-Geneviève Chevignard and Nicole Faure of the Fondation Nationale des Sciences Politiques, Paris; Generals Robert Porret, Jean Delmas and Robert Bassac, successive heads of the Service Historique de l'Armée at Vincennes, along with their hospitable counterparts at the Service Historique de l'Armée de l'Air, the late General Charles Christienne, and General Lucien Robineau. For their counsel and scholarly comradeship, I should also like to record my gratitude to Colonels Michel Turlotte and Henry Dutailly, successive chiefs of the Section d'Etudes of the SHAT, as well as to Dr Patrice Buffotot, now of the Institut Politique Internationale et Européenne at the Université de Paris-X (Nanterre), and Dr Patrick Facon, *directeur de recherches* at the SHAA. For unstinting help in locating documents and providing encouragement at Vincennes, I am delighted to thank Jean Nicot, who placed his immense knowledge of the holdings of the French military archives at my disposal. My thanks are also owed to Mme Combe, president of the SHAT *salle de lecture*, and to her efficient and good-humoured reading room staff.

In Belgium, it was a particular pleasure to experience the friendship and guidance of the country's leading scholars of the inter-war period: Jean Vanwelkenhuyzen, director of the Centre de Recherches et Etudes Historiques de la Seconde Guerre Mondiale in Brussels; Professor Jean Stengers of the Université Libre de Bruxelles and Emeritus Professor Jacques Willequet. For their assistance in making available unpublished Belgian documents I am grateful to Mme F. Peemans, archivist at the Ministère des Affaires Etrangères et du Commerce Extérieur, to Ambassador Maes, the ministry's minister-plenipotentiary, and to Cdt A. Servais of the Service Historique des Forces Armées Belges.

Sources for this study have been found in private hands almost as often as in the public domain. For their gracious permission to consult and quote from collections in their possession or under their oversight I am pleased to acknowledge the late Brigadier George Davy; General Sir David Fraser; Lady Kathleen Liddell Hart and the Trustees of the

Acknowledgements

Liddell Hart Centre for Military Archives, King's College, University of London; the late General Sir James Marshall-Cornwall; the late Paul Gamelin; Mme Hélène Lucius; François Paul-Boncour; Mme Paul Reynaud; Pierre Uhrich; Lieutenant-Colonel Jacques Uhrich; Edouard Weygand; the US National Archives and Records Administration (for the papers in the Franklin D. Roosevelt Presidential Library at Hyde Park, New York).

In the course of my work numerous individuals gave unstintingly of their time in answering my inquiries and I should especially like to thank Bernard Blanchard, the late Sir Ronald I. Campbell, Henri Culmann, General Michel Gouraud, Brigadier Cyrus Greenslade, Dr Louis Guillaumat, the late Major-General Sir Francis de Guingand, Pierre Huré, Alistair Horne, General André Martin, Jean Panhard, Guy Petibon, Raymond Beulaygue and Christian Dumont (of the Société de Constructions Mécaniques Panhard et Levassor), Georges Potut, the late Professor John M. Sherwood and Jean-Raymond Tournoux.

Good cheer and constructive criticism has sustained me during what has been a long and complex endeavour. For their wit and wisdom, I am especially indebted to my mentors, colleagues and friends: R. A. C. Parker of The Queen's College, Oxford; John C. Cairns, formerly of the University of Toronto; Peter Dennis, professor of history at the Australian Defence Force Academy, Duntroon; Bill Murray of La Trobe University, Melbourne; Brian Bond, of the War Studies' department, King's College, London; John Gooch of Lancaster University; and, at the University of Southampton, George Bernard, Edgar Feuchtwanger, Brian Golding, Nick Kingwell, Tony Kushner, John Oldfield, Stevan Pavlowitch, John Rule, Kevin Sharpe, John Simpson and Paul Smith.

In Paris I was advised by that outstanding anglophile among modern French historians, Professor François Crouzet, at the Université de Paris IV (Sorbonne). I was also privileged to attend the research seminars convened at the Sorbonne by Professors Jean-Baptiste Duroselle, Philippe Bonnichon and Georges-Henri Soutou. François Bédarida, also, as director of the Institut d'Histoire du Temps Présent, gave valued guidance. The enlivening conversation and warm hospitality of my friends Maité and Robert Frank, Jacqueline and Georges Soutou, France and Maurice Vaïsse, Elizabeth du Réau, Jace Weaver and David Watson made working visits to Paris as much a pleasure as a scholarly necessity.

At Yale I fell deeply into the debt of Paul Kennedy and Henry Ashby Turner Jr (who graciously elected me to a visiting fellowship of Davenport College, of which he is Master). My 'fellow Olin fellows', John

Morgan Dederer and Saki Dockrill, were the most helpful as well as hospitable companions for a novice in the sometimes curious ways of the USA. William Hitchcock, David Hermann, George Andreopoulos and Hal Selesky exemplified the generosity and scholarly quality for which Yale is renowned. To Piotr S. Wandycz I owe thanks for sharing his unrivalled expertise on the complexities of inter-war east-central Europe. More generally, I am grateful to the history department at Yale, and especially to the secretaries, Gerri Cummings, Betsy McAuley, Haynie Wheeler and Florence Thomas, for unfailingly facilitating my research.

Numerous friends and fellow scholars have unselfishly set aside their own projects to debate my interpretations of inter-war France. For their constructive comments on draft chapters of this work I thank Professor Philip C. F. Bankwitz, formerly of Trinity College, Hartford, Connecticut; Professor Robert J. Young of the University of Winnipeg; Dr Nicole Jordan of the University of Illinois at Chicago; Dr John Morgan Dederer; and Professor Dr Klaus-Jürgen Müller of the Universität der Bundeswehr, Hamburg. To my former student at Southampton, Nick Crowson, I extend my heartfelt thanks for coming to my rescue at the eleventh hour with assistance in gathering in a crop of references and bibliographical citations required to complete the manuscript.

I am grateful also for the encouragement and dedication shown by my editors at Cambridge University Press, William Davies and Sheila McEnery.

The last but greatest acknowledgement is to my family, for their love and practical assistance over the years. It is a delight to be able to thank my parents, Barbara and David Alexander, who encouraged me to follow Clio's call, as well as my wife, Rosalie, for her devotion, companionship and good-humoured sense of perspective. For her, too, this is the culmination of a journey, for she has travelled with me without complaint down the long and winding 'road back to France, 1940'.

Introduction: Maurice Gamelin, the defence of France and the decline of the Third Republic

Military defeats and national crises have repeatedly rocked France in modern times. They have made for a quarrelsome marriage between the French state and its defence services. The career of Maurice Gamelin, from his entry to St Cyr as an officer-cadet in 1891 until his dismissal as commander-in-chief of the French armies in May 1940, epitomises the traumatic nature of the French civil-military relationship. From Dreyfus to Dien Bien Phu, the history of the French armed forces has been bedevilled as much by ill-judged forays into politics as by military misfortunes.[1]

The present study seeks to present a favourable reinterpretation of the customarily maligned Gamelin. It endeavours to focus attention more than hitherto on Gamelin's positive contribution to French national security and political-military cooperation in the approach to the Second World War. In order to situate and understand Gamelin's place in modern French history it is, however, necessary not only to meet the man, it is essential to be introduced to the issues which he both confronted and, historically, represented. For this, some acquaintance is required with the background of civil-military relations under the French Third Republic and some familiarity needed with the attendant historiography.

As a young lieutenant, taking the Ecole de Guerre staff course at the close of the 1890s, Gamelin witnessed at first hand the travails of the French officers of the 'Dreyfus generation'. After the retrial and eventual acquittal of Dreyfus, the Radical-led government of Emile Combes (1902–5) attempted a purge to republicanise the French army hierarchy. In this process it was a soldier who functioned as Combes' military collaborator – to employ an epithet more usually applied pejoratively to the politicised officers of 1940. General Louis André, Combes' minister of war, had the task of manipulating the careers of the French army's officers according to reported political preferences and confessional convictions. André arranged politically biased promotions for those deemed to possess a 'republican' outlook on the basis of notorious secret files, the *fiches*. These dossiers contained the gossip and rumour that André garnered from informants – many of them freemasons – about the tastes and tendencies of every officer qualified for advancement. By this unashamedly partisan purge, the canker of political interference entered the heart of the French military corps. It was in this outwardly apolitical but inwardly disaffected body that Gamelin took up the profession of arms.[2]

Almost fifty years later, the military humiliation of May 1940 became Gamelin's personal calvary. At that moment of military defeat and national crisis, Gamelin discovered how imperfectly his own example of soldierly subordination to the regime was embraced by the officer corps that had been trained and educated under his authority in the 1930s. At its moment of greatest trial, the Third Republic was subverted by its own military guardians. Chief among the Republic's conservative pallbearers was a clique of officers which had proven impervious to Gamelin's demand that the regime be obeyed and respected throughout the army.[3] These uniformed political opportunists shamelessly converted the moment of their own deepest discredit as military professionals into the realisation of their political fantasies. What Charles Maurras termed the 'divine surprise' of 1940 was to drape a spurious legitimacy – the legitimacy of the desperate remedy for a desperate situation – over naked anti-republicanism. From France's military defeat there emerged, under Vichy, a cynical assault on the rights of labour, the lives of Jews and other minorities and on the very continuation of democracy. A key part was played by conservative officers in bringing about the reactionary order that unfolded in France from 1940 to 1944 – an order which wreaked a belated and vicious vengeance on the Dreyfusards.[4]

The triumph of the military and political authoritarians at Bordeaux in June 1940 signified the wreck of the compromise with the Republic to which Gamelin had devoted his career. However, during the death agonies of the regime, Gamelin found himself reduced to impotence. By dismissing him, on 19 May 1940, France's democratic civilian leaders had gratuitously signed the death warrant of the Republic. In its desperation to bolster morale, the government of Paul Reynaud was misled into restoring to high command none other than Gamelin's own predecessor at the head of the army, General Maxime Weygand. Conceived with the best of intentions, to stiffen French military resistance to the panzers, Reynaud's action inadvertently released a reactionary political revolution that swiftly gathered an unstoppable momentum. Weygand did not simply declare the battle of France to be lost; he also refused both to resign and to participate in exploring armistice terms with the Germans. For Gamelin's successor insisted that the cease-fire and termination of hostilities with Germany in June 1940 had to be negotiated not by the military command but by the government. The entire burden of the defeat was to be laid in this way on the political leadership. It was they whom Weygand and the military conservatives held culpable for France's calamity. Unmistakably, this was an echo of the fabrication by German officers of the 'stab in the back' legend surrounding the armistice of 1918 – a legend that purported to show how Germany lost the First World War not on the battlefield but at the hands of peacemongering politicians, the so-called 'November criminals'.

In 1940, Weygand strove not to find ways of continuing the French war effort alongside Britain but, rather, to block every bolt-hole for the civilian authorities whom he condemned for negligent attention to French security after 1919. The Fall of France was an unimagined opportunity for Weygand to help install a government that would dig the grave of the Republic which he regarded as responsible for preparing the catastrophe. In place of the *Troisième*, Weygand sought the establishment of an alternative and authoritarian regime – one predisposed to promote soldierly values of honour and obedience, to revive French chauvinism and to restore a disciplined patriotism. To expedite the last rites of the old regime, the Republic was stained with the discredit of national defeat.[5]

Under Marshal Philippe Pétain, the embodiment of a 'military view of the country's future' and hero of happier experiences for the French army, the military reactionaries played a full part in the adventure launched at Vichy in July 1940. Their objective was nothing less than the remodelling of the state, in a quest to retrieve the values of the Old Regime. Driven by obsessive anti-republicanism among the ranks of its conservative commanders, a part of the French officer corps prostituted itself into differing degrees of collaboration with its conquerors. Yet it was Gamelin who was singled out among the military leaders of the Third Republic. He was compelled to stand trial publicly, before the Vichy regime's supreme court. In the spring of 1942, at Riom, he was formally arraigned for a professional failure to prepare France for the war of 1939, and for responsibility for the subsequent débâcle.[6]

Gamelin was haunted by the hypocrisy of this indictment. Faced by an unholy alliance of accusers, he kept his own counsel. He despised the compact reached at Vichy between political opportunists such as Pierre

Laval, Adrian Marquet and Jean Ybarnégaray on the one hand and, on the other, a cabal of his own pre-war military subordinates that included General Louis Colson, the chief of army staff from 1935 to 1940, and General Charles Huntziger, commander of the Second Army at Sedan in May 1940. After a short statement at the outset of the Riom trial, Gamelin retreated into a studied and dignified silence throughout the remainder of the hearings.[7]

Yet, even for this, he encountered criticism. There were those who argued that his refusal to speak out allowed the case for the defence of the inter-war military leadership to fall by default. In contrast to Gamelin, the general's civilian codefendants – who included two former prime ministers, an ex-air minister and a former secretary-general of the war ministry – vigorously protested their political and executive competence. They deployed documents and called witnesses to insist that they had energetically and effectively discharged their governmental duties in rearmament and war preparation. Léon Blum, prime minister in 1936–7 and again in March–April 1938, defended his record with especial success. So, too, did Edouard Daladier, minister for war and national defence between 1936 and May 1940, as well as prime minister himself from April 1938 till March 1940.

Neither of these statesmen sought to shift blame onto Gamelin (although they did not shrink from criticising other beaten generals, some of whom had become pillars of the Vichy regime by the time of the Riom trial). Nonetheless, as the hearings unfolded in the full glare of the collaborationist press between February and April 1942, the early flush of enthusiasm for Pétainism had already faded except among hardcore Vichyite zealots. Middle and junior-ranking army officers, scattered throughout France in enforced retirement from the 100,000 man army that the Germans had allowed Vichy, disliked the way the civilians had wriggled off the hook at Riom. Some soldiers felt that Gamelin should have spoken up on behalf of the army of 1939–40 – for their comrades who had, for the most part, fought bravely with whatever equipment they had possessed, for those who had been killed, and for the several hundred thousands who had been captured and still languished in German prisoner-of-war camps in 1942.[8]

Such criticism served only to disclose how seriously Gamelin was misunderstood by his contemporaries. Had he chosen to speak out at Riom, Gamelin would have aligned himself with the discredited political leaders of the Third Republic – leaders whose 'guilt' was predetermined in a process that had degenerated into a show trial. Gamelin did not prepare a case – even in his own mind – to defend and excuse his own defeated and demoralised subordinates. Rather, Gamelin's wartime reflections on the débâcle actually reinforced the thoughts that he had experienced about the disaster at the moment of his dismissal on 19 May 1940. As time passed, he became increasingly persuaded that much of the responsibility for its own failure and for France's consequent humiliation lay with the French army itself, and in particular with its general officers. Dismissive of the jurisdiction of the Vichy judges, Gamelin was equally contemptuous of the pre-war and wartime politicisation that he had seen occurring throughout the French armed forces.

Gamelin's standpoint reflected his mixture of disdain and detachment towards the hurly-burly of recriminations whilst the war remained in progress. His composure had, indeed, been an object of comment from the very moment he was relieved of high command. The journalist André Géraud, who wrote under the pseudonym 'Pertinax', saw Gamelin on 23 May 1940 and reportedly found him 'very serene', simply 'waiting for the time when he can justify himself'. Alexander Werth, the Paris correspondent of the *Manchester Guardian*, who heard the anecdote from Géraud's wife, cynically wondered to himself: 'How? Presumably by writing two volumes *chez Plon*.' In fact Gamelin wrote three. Drafting them afforded the general his principal source of intellectual distraction during his wartime captivity. Their speedy completion and publication in 1946–7 gave him a head start when the restaging of the Fall of France began in the postwar memoirs.[9]

Gamelin's wartime conduct contrasted sharply with that of his predecessor and successor, Weygand. The latter foolhardily hastened to accept appointment as minister for defence in Pétain's first Vichy government. Yet, by the time of the Riom trial, even Weygand had discovered for himself that defence policy under the yoke of the Nazis meant little except servility to German dictates. Weygand was led into irredeemable discredit in the summer of 1940 by his notorious impetuosity.

Gamelin's intrinsic caution and keen intelligence saved him from falling prey to any illusions about the realities of French partnership with the Third Reich. For Gamelin, therefore, the Vichy experience did not involve any rude awakenings of the kind undergone by Weygand in 1941. After his dismissal, Gamelin had no illusions left to lose. Weygand had been idolised by the French as the custodian of the 'secrets of Foch', the saviour to whom the Allied supreme commander of 1918 had, on his death bed, counselled France to turn if ever it found itself in grave danger. But Weygand proved to be more myth than messiah, when his hour beckoned in 1940. He was a narrow-minded reactionary with little strategic imagination and even less political acumen. He was a king-maker for Pétain, not a king himself.[10] Gamelin was open, perhaps, to the contrary criticism – to the charge of over-caution. But, politically, he possessed a shrewd instinct for self-preservation. Ultimately it was he, not Weygand, who kept faith with the dictum that Foch had taught at the Ecole de Guerre forty years earlier: before acting, 'first learn to think'.[11]

Imprisoned by the Germans in the Schloss Itter in the Austrian Tyrol from 1943 to 1945, along with an unlikely company of erstwhile luminaries of the Third Republic, Gamelin allowed his fellow captives glimpses of the case with which he might have replied at Riom. Three of his companions in captivity kept diaries. One was Daladier. The others were the former French ambassador to Berlin and Rome, André François-Poncet, and Augusta Léon-Jouhaux, wife of the former general secretary of the Confédération Générale du Travail, the French trade union organisation. From these accounts emerges a bizarre tale of the daily regime endured at Itter aboard a real-life ship of fools. In them lies first-hand evidence of Gamelin's dismay at the politics of collaborationist defeatism.

Gamelin had kept his peace at Riom, recounted Mme Jouhaux's journal, because he would have 'found it shocking to see polemics between generals aired in public places'. François-Poncet similarly recorded how, one day in 1943, Gamelin admitted that his taciturnity in the Vichy court room had been intended to avoid any 'escalation of public controversies between the generals'. Silence, furthermore, relieved Gamelin 'from having to indict Pétain and Weygand' for their responsibilities in France's catastrophe.[12] Even in his cheerless incarceration at the fortress-prison of Itter, Gamelin was not able to bring himself to unleash a wholesale condemnation of France's old army – in important respects, of course, his old army – of which many regiments had fought as best they might, and most of whose officers had made no move against the Republic for all of Pétain's and Weygand's example of disloyalty.

Yet, for Gamelin to have stated the verities as he saw them would, he also admitted at Itter, have compelled him to level his own accusations at those whom he felt had failed. He would have felt obliged to round not only on Pétain but on General Alphonse Georges, commander of the north-eastern theatre of operations facing Germany in 1940, and on generals Huntziger and André Corap, the commanders of the Second and Ninth Armies which had suffered the decisive German blows on the Meuse. Noting all this, François-Poncet reflected, more in sorrow than anger, that Gamelin himself appeared forgetful of the old adage: 'Qui s'excuse, s'accuse'.[13]

Gamelin was plainly haunted by the memory of the débâcle,

according to all three Itter diarists. The general betrayed a compulsive need to anticipate reproaches that he imagined might be made against his own conduct. Through the long months of imprisonment his conversation showed that he was repeatedly reliving his pre-war decisions and the steps that had led down the road to 1940.

Rescuing the respect that he felt was the due of his old army would, he felt, require the drawing of distinctions. For there to be saints there had also to be sinners. For the pre-1940 army to be assigned what he regarded as its rightful measure of honour would have demanded that he name military men of high rank among those responsible for the defeat of French forces and the death of the French Republic. In Gamelin's sight, the counterpoint to the acceptance of the innocence of many was the recognition of the guilt of others. At the feet of commanders such as Georges and Huntziger, he would have placed a charge of executing his strategy incompetently. At the door of the French allies he would have laid other charges, specifically the 'poor conduct under fire of the Belgian army'. Also at fault was what Gamelin termed, at Itter, the 'failings of several French divisions' and the inadequate 'spirit of belligerence in the country at large'.[14]

Regaled at Itter with complaints of this type, François-Poncet concluded that Gamelin was guilty of an unseemly and unconvincing exercise in self-exculpation. Subsequently, scholars have endorsed the former ambassador's judgement. Yet, as the solitary soldier forced to stand trial over the fate of France in 1940, Gamelin could hardly avoid being more concerned with redistributing responsibilities than with advancing historical understanding. Moreover, Gamelin redeemed his tendency to assign blame to almost everyone except himself by confining his condemnations within the privacy of the prison. Confused and even contradictory his motives for silence before the Vichy court may seem; yet, in the context of Vichy's search for a scapegoat, Gamelin's very silence lends him more of an air of sadness than selfishness.[15]

In its eagerness to reproach the general for character defects and professional negligence, the Riom prosecution was closely rivalled by Gamelin's associates from within the pale of the Republic. Few who hunted for the *responsables* of 1940 ever let Gamelin out of their sights. Even though they would all be tarred with the same brush by their Vichy captors, there was no solidarity in adversity among the men who presided over the demise of the *Troisième*. Bickering and bitter recriminations predominated. Paul Reynaud, France's prime minister from March to June 1940, lamented that Gamelin was 'a prefect, a bishop, but absolutely not a commander'. It was a view shared by the president of the French Senate, Jules Jeanneney, who described Gamelin as 'a great prefect – but nothing more'.[16]

Nor were historians any more restrained in their censure. After the publication of Gamelin's memoirs, *Servir*, in 1947, A. J. P. Taylor mercilessly condemned him in a review article brutally entitled 'General Gamelin, or How to Lose'. In 1963 the more sympathetic Paul-Marie de La Gorce, in a history of the civil-military relations of the modern French army, could not resist accusing Gamelin of 'traits normally associated with figures of a decadent era'. This theme of decadence – a canker that was imagined to have sapped and corrupted the personalities and institutions of the later Third Republic – was fashioned into something close to determinism by Jean-Baptiste Duroselle's severe and influential study of French external policy after 1932, *La Décadence*, published in 1979.[17] And, five years before that, the Canadian historian John Cairns had justifiably noted that, from 1940 till the early 1970s, 'for Gamelin, it has been something like thirty years of open season'. Hunted and hounded across the pages of academic interpretations as well as berated in more understandably partisan memoirs, the general had 'almost been reduced to caricature: diminutive, soft-handed, puffy-faced ... an endlessly dilatory political soldier, a finally disastrous generalissimo'.[18]

Until recently, then, Gamelin was mocked and condemned when he was not simply dismissed as a superannuated incompetent. Taylor termed him, as long ago as 1947, 'a generalissimo now forgotten', and harboured no doubt that this was how things should remain, leaving all 'controversy ... ended'. Only one semi-biographical study has appeared hitherto, published in Paris in 1976. Yet even this work served only as a reminder of the political and psychological problems presented by Gamelin's lingering reputation as 'the man who lost the Battle of France'. For though the book, *Le Mystère Gamelin*, was at best guardedly sympathetic towards the general, this did not save its author, Colonel Pierre Le Goyet, from becoming *persona non grata* at his place of work as a research archivist in the French army historical service at the Château de Vincennes – location, ironically, of Gamelin's own wartime headquarters in 1939–40.[19]

Notwithstanding these controversies, the later 1970s and 1980s did start to see a current of revisionism flowing in favour of a more dispassionate, balanced and scholarly treatment of the inter-war French high command. Less partisan assessments became more frequent. Re-evaluations occurred not just of the legends, such as de Gaulle, but also of the fallen idols, the sinning soldiers of Vichy. Weygand and even Pétain became subjects of fair-minded and fastidiously documented historical research, rather than objects of prejudiced polemic.[20]

Though still far from becoming the mainstream in its own right, this revisionist current has begun to clear away some of the obscurantist murk which has for so long clouded the view of Gamelin's role between the early 1930s and May 1940. In a context of interpretatively original studies of French foreign and military policies down to the Fall of France, Robert J. Young as well as Jeffery A. Gunsburg have reconsidered Gamelin's aims and conduct. Under both of these heads, they have awarded the general a limited approbation.[21] John Gooch, in a broader examination of European armies in the nineteenth and twentieth centuries, has drawn out the nature of the difficult balancing act which Gamelin had to perform in the 1930s, as he straddled the gulf between his own membership of the officer corps and his respect, not shared by most of his brother officers, for the Republic. Gooch acknowledges, sympathetically, how 'Gamelin alone appeared to bridge the gap between the ideals of the socialists and the conservatism of the generals, and that was both his and his country's misfortune.' Most recently, Douglas Porch has argued that 'Gamelin ... does not appear to be the weak and characterless man of legend. On the contrary, he bent his energies towards keeping a [politically and doctrinally] restive army ... in line.' In achieving this, affirmed Porch, Gamelin demonstrated that he 'had enormous strength ... and great finesse to match. Simply because he was a "political" general and declined to pound the table and shout as had his irascible predecessor, General Weygand, this did not mean that he lacked character. He managed almost single-handed to keep a potential revolt ... in the army under control in the late 1930s.'[22]

Yet these more positive – or at least open-minded – reappraisals of Gamelin have been limited in scope. They have addressed particular facets of the general's actions: his relationship to the Quai d'Orsay and the making of French foreign policy; his part in the development of mechanisation and tank forces in the French army; his dealings with the labyrinthine organisations responsible for collecting and collating intelligence. In his own right, however, as France's most prominent republican soldier and a central player in the drama that was enacted around the theme of French national security between 1933 and 1940, Gamelin has not until now received a full historical treatment.[23]

The present study seeks to give fresh impetus to the flow of revisionism concerning Gamelin. It will aim to elucidate his approach to the challenge of finding satisfactory security for France in the face of perils not simply from external aggression by Germany and Italy but also from self-inflicted wounds – from domestic dissensions and immobilism, from French society itself. This book's objective is as much to convey the difficulties that Gamelin faced as it is to explain why he opted at particular moments for particular ways of addressing French security problems. Above all, it is a serious endeavour to respond to the injunction of John Cairns that history must 'try to consider Gamelin as fairly as it considers every commander on whom finally the sun did not shine'.[24]

A detailed narrative of the Battle of France is not the purpose here. This is not another study which repeats the preference of many earlier writers for dismissing French defence policy and the politics of rearmament as merely a prelude to the *grande roulée*, the 'big show'. The present book seeks to exorcise the ghoulish fascination which the anatomy of France's collapse has so long exerted. It is not a further attempt to explain away the defeat of France – nor, for that matter, the defeat of any of the other powers swept aside by the Blitzkrieg of 1940.[25] What is proposed via Gamelin's vantage point over French defence policy made under the shadow of Hitlerism, is a new insight into the reasons the French felt unable to risk war with Germany before 1939. What is attempted is the peeling back of layers of later indignation towards those who led France from 1935 to 1939, to suggest the reasons why war seemed so unacceptably hazardous in those years. Throughout, this study concentrates on explicating the French position as it appeared to Gamelin at the time. From this approach, a more balanced judgement may be reached as to the coherence of Gamelin's case for choosing the path of resistance at last, when Germany invaded Poland in 1939.

In 1939, it will be argued, France went to war advisedly. At the hastily improvised meeting with the defence chiefs on the evening of 23 August, called because of the stunning news from Moscow that Germany and the Soviet Union had made a non-aggression pact, the French government, of Edouard Daladier, was told that its armed forces were ready to go to war. But it was also told plainly that neither the French army nor air force was yet ready to win that war. Hostilities were engaged over Poland with Gamelin's military colleagues still profoundly uneasy at the incompleteness of Allied support and French armed strength.[26] The present book seeks to avoid excessive intrusion of the events of 1940 into an analysis devoted chiefly to pre-war French defence preparations. Peacetime security policies possessed logics, dynamics, that were legitimately their own. These logics decisively shaped the nature of the war that France could wage in 1939 and 1940; yet they had not been implemented in any certain knowledge that France would have to fight that war, at that time.

Through Gamelin's perspective we may see that the disastrous days from 10 to 19 May 1940, the general's brief shooting war, formed a postscript to the inter-war defence regime in France. This regime, this system, had its pivotal dilemmas and its decision-making located in the 1920s and 1930s. What Le Goyet has termed Gamelin's 'real war', the war of May 1940, has contributed to some important distortions in the historical interpretations of Gamelin hitherto. A. J. P. Taylor was misleading – if at first typically persuasive – when he unceremoniously consigned Gamelin to the dustbin of history. Taylor has hindered rather than helped us to understand modern France and its tangled civil-military crises if he convinces us that Gamelin mattered only from 10 to 19 May, 'the only days of his life which will give him a place in the history books – or at least a footnote'.[27]

In fact, too much attention to the sound of the guns of May 1940 is a diversion from the other wars which Gamelin fought. These wars are arguably of greater significance: the political war with Weygand and the anti-republican right in the officer corps; the resource war waged with the finance, labour and commerce ministries to accomplish an unprecedented rearmament drive; the war over profits and priorities with the munitions manufacturers; the war over defence doctrines with Pierre Cot and the strategic dreamers of the Armée de l'Air.

Gamelin's central part from 1931 onwards in political-military planning serves, in the present study, as a vehicle. It is a means to assist us to understand the methods by which the general sought security for France against Hitler's resurgent Germany. Yet, in key respects, the vehicle which Gamelin and his functions represents proved to be ill-serviced for a journey along a pot-holed path strewn with the hazards of massive rearmament, alliance reconstruction and psychological preparation for total war. Gamelin's effectiveness has, moreover, to be assessed against several criteria. For he found himself not only acting as push-starter, but also as navigator, driver and self-taught mechanic for the rarely roadworthy carriage of the French defence institution.

It is Gamelin's management of the problems of territorial security that bears the chief burden of investigation here. Air power is examined in its military application – but it is examined from Gamelin's standpoint, the standpoint of an officer whose training, experience and instincts placed him closest to the French land forces. Notwithstanding his background, Gamelin still emerges after 1936 – and especially by 1939 – as a commander who possessed a greater awareness than most other soldiers or civilians of the new dangers represented by German military doctrines that combined aviation in the battlefield support of a mobile offensive. Attention is paid to Gamelin's fight against what he estimated to be the Armée de l'Air's obsession with structuring their forces for an independent grand strategic mission. Nonetheless, discussion of air power is kept in proportion, according to its contemporary importance. In French preparations during the 1930s, aviation did not loom as large as in British planning, where views of defence requirements were commonly darkened by the 'shadow of the bomber'.[28]

Through Gamelin the anxieties and the neuroses which were more significant than the menace of air bombardment – and sometimes more paralysing to France – may be clearly discerned. Having been invaded on land in 1914, with near-fatal consequences, and having succumbed in 1870, the French had a special nervousness about war with Germany. War with Germany meant invasion, occupation, devastation of territory. Gamelin had first-hand experience of the more recent of these crises on which to draw, for he had served in 1914 on the staff of Marshal Joffre, then the French commander-in-chief. And the burden of the earlier débâcle bore on Gamelin almost as oppressively, for the humiliation of the Second Empire had forced Gamelin's parents to flee from their home in a Lorraine seized by Germany just two years before Gamelin's birth in 1872.

In the 1930s perhaps only Charles de Gaulle approached Gamelin's understanding of how a deep and swift rupture of her land defences by Germany might again threaten France. The present book, drawing extensively on unpublished sources in the French archives, including Gamelin's daily headquarters journal, rehabilitates the general's approach to the defence of the Republic in the latter's hour of gravest shortages: shortages of allies, shortages of manpower, shortages of manufacturing capacity, shortages of moral confidence. Thus we see Gamelin resist the voracious demands of French air force commanders for resources to build strategic bombers, not because he envisaged no role for long-range air power but because he appreciated that survival depended on the French armies on the ground first holding firm in the opening round of a new war with Germany. Gamelin's difficulty – and the ultimate source of his failings – was not that he missed the nature of the Wehrmacht's threat but that French politics and inter-service selfishness frustrated his attempts to take effective counter-measures.[29]

Throughout his years of high command, Gamelin was hamstrung. The disability under which he laboured was a double one. The first handicap was the blinkered view of erstwhile friendly powers who insisted, until 1939 in the case of Britain and 1940 in the case of Belgium, that to enter an alliance to deter Hitler would simply provoke the aggression that all the democratic powers wished to avoid. Gamelin's second handicap was the dislocated political economy of France herself – a handicap that thwarted the only alternative strategy, that of rearming the Republic sufficiently for it to defy the Third Reich by itself.

1 The making of a republican general

1872 was a year of rebuilding for France, the French army and the Gamelin family. All three were deeply affected by French defeat at the hands of Prussia the previous year – defeat which had wrenched the provinces of Alsace and Lorraine from France, forcing them into a shotgun wedding with the newly unified German Reich. Some eighteen months after the end of this disastrous war for France, Maurice Gamelin was born, on 20 September 1872. His birthplace, however, was not Alsace-Lorraine – the *pays natal* of his maternal relatives, the Uhrichs – but Paris. For the Gamelins, like so many others, had been forced into an exile in their own country as a result of the German annexation of the lands east of the 'blue line of the Vosges'.

Fittingly, under the circumstances, Gamelin's birthplace at No. 262 Boulevard Saint-Germain was situated opposite the French ministry of war. It was a corner of the French capital with which the adult Maurice would become intimately acquainted as his future turned towards the profession of arms. His family's military tradition, together with his parents' nostalgia for Alsace-Lorraine, exerted a powerful influence over Gamelin from the earliest days of his upbringing. Gamelin's mother, Pauline Uhrich, had been born in Phalsbourg, in Lorraine. Her father served as the last French military governor of Strasbourg before the Franco-Prussian War. Zephyrin Gamelin, father of Maurice, was a senior military administrator, a *contrôleur-général de l'armée*. Wounded at the Battle of Solferino, in 1859, he had gone on to a distinguished career in the service of Napoleon III during the Second Empire. The call of the army always rang loudly in the young Gamelin's ears.[1]

Gamelin's juvenile years in the 1870s and 1880s were also those of the Third Republic. Under the canny political charge of the 'Quatre Jules', Ferry, Grévy, Favre and Simon, the provisional but durable regime of Gambetta and Thiers became a sturdy youngster. As it overcame the challenges thrown at it in these decades by the political soldiers, Marshal MacMahon and General Boulanger, it set course to outlast all regimes except the old Bourbons. The republic and the career of

Gamelin, who was to become its favourite republican general, were destined to travel together and to end together.

One of the most important steps taken by the republicans was to overhaul their army. They consciously modelled a replacement for the discredited Napoleonic structures of 1870 on the successful system of the Prussians. Universal military service was established. So too was a permanent general staff and war council, the Conseil Supérieur de la Guerre (CSG). The prestige and attractiveness of soldiering in *fin-de-siècle* France was restored by the revival of professionalism, the lure of *revanche*, and the opportunity for active service in France's expanding colonial territories in Indochina and Africa.[2]

Little by little, the attractions of the military life grew on Gamelin in these years. They were divided between an education in Paris at the Collège Stanislas in the rue du Montparnasse, and holidays with a cloth manufacturer uncle at Estaivres, the Gamelin home town, near the Belgian border in the Nord. As a boy, Gamelin revealed a precocious talent for art and, despite the arrival of a second child, Marguerite, four years Maurice's junior, his parents endeavoured to nurture this to take the place of his awakening enthusiasm for the army. However, the military traditions among both Gamelin and Uhrich forebears, Maurice's passion for history and genealogy, and his exposure to the jingoistic calls for revenge over Alsace-Lorraine proved too powerful. As a result, in 1889, Gamelin entered the army preparatory class at Stanislas. Yet, even as he made his career choice plain, Gamelin was showing why he would become an uncommonly sophisticated and cultured officer. He retained and even deepened his interests in painting and philosophy at this time. These introspective preferences already set him apart from his more rumbustious and gregarious teenage classmates. They hinted at the unique studiousness of his generalship in later life, on which so many would pass comment. Yet Gamelin was no bookworm, for all his love of reading, reflection and learned conversation. As he retorted later to the charge that he became more a savant than a soldier, '[I showed] at the head of the 2nd brigade of *chasseurs alpins* in 1916, of the 9th infantry division from 1916 to 1918, and in the Levant during the 1925–6 rebellion, that it was possible to act as well as to love meditation.'[3]

In October 1891 Gamelin entered the officer training academy of St Cyr. From the beginning he shone as an academically outstanding student. Two years later, at the head of his class of 449 cadets, he graduated as a second-lieutenant of the *Promotion de Soudan*. The class, like most of the *belle époque* vintages, was to be destined for terrible slaughter when its members found themselves assuming command of battalions and regiments in the trenches twenty years later. Despite the losses, however, at least one other member besides Gamelin survived and rose to high rank and some distinction. This was Joseph Dufieux, who became a member of the CSG and inspector-general of infantry in 1937–8. As Gamelin passed out of St Cyr he received the highest commendation in the school commandant's final report: 'no eulogy could be too great ... This man will become a remarkable officer.'[4]

Freshly commissioned, Gamelin was posted to the 3rd Algerian *tirailleurs*, stationed at Bougie in French North Africa, on 1 October 1893. To his first regimental commander the young Gamelin appeared 'so short of stature and callow, almost child-like'. But soon Gamelin was making a name for himself by dint of an exceptional intellect and 'fanatical zeal' in his job. In Algeria, throughout this period, Gamelin displayed the mental elasticity, aptitude for command and inter-personal skills that promised rapid advancement in the years ahead. His next superior officer also found him highly intelligent, well-trained and hard-working. Gamelin was noted for the pride he took in maintaining an immaculate appearance. Evidently he decided from the outset that, to be a good soldier, one should start by looking like a good soldier, and he 'allied a very fine education to an excellent attitude'. An illustrious career was already predicted when he went to Tunisia to broaden his experience by a secondment with the army geographical survey in 1896. In this, as in all that had gone before, he was praised for his commitment and for his aptitude for all types of assignment. Quietly spoken, but a determined and lucid debater, Gamelin was regarded as a straightforward and sympathetic colleague. By April 1898 he was graded in his confidential file as a keen and professional 'young officer of the future' whom it was 'a pleasure to command'.

In spite of the success of this time spent in the Sahara and High Atlas, however, Gamelin was not tempted to follow in the footsteps of Marshal Bugeaud, or of Lyautey and Galliéni in his own era, and make a career as an *africain*, soldiering continuously in overseas France. In his outlook as well as his ambitions, Gamelin was and remained a distinctively metropolitan officer.[5] Throughout the rest of his long career he commanded French forces outside the mainland of France only once more, during his pacification of the Druze insurrection in Syria in 1925–7. Nevertheless, his North African service was a formative influence: it had given him varied and practical experience by the time of his return to France in 1898 to prepare for staff college entrance. That October, whilst he was studying for the Ecole de Guerre, he was confidentially graded as someone 'to be advanced', who had added to his intellectual eminence 'the knowledge of how to command, and how to make others obey him'.[6]

The staff courses which he entered in November 1899 proved to be no higher a hurdle for Gamelin than any earlier test. Eighth in his class when he was admitted, he graduated in second place two years later. A fellow classmate who became a good friend – and was later to be war minister and therefore Gamelin's direct superior in 1934–5 and 1936 – was Louis Maurin. At this time Gamelin's potential was summed up in a mid-term report by the college's deputy-commandant, Lieutenant-Colonel Lanrezac (future commander of the Fifth French Army in 1914), who wrote that:

> Gamelin entered the Ecole de Guerre with a reputation as an ideal officer. He does indeed have an exceptional intellect, lively and open, lucid, methodical, cultivated. He is prompt and certain in his judgments, very well equipped to study the art of war at a sophisticated level, with a profound and solid appreciation of tactics. By nature he is an enthusiast, upright, brisk and decisive, with lots of personality, spirit and stamina. . . . He is exceptionally fitted for staff duty and must surely fulfil his promise as a soldier of the very highest calibre. This is an officer to push.

On 30 December 1901 Gamelin was promoted captain. He took up his first staff posting, with the 15th army corps, on the last day of January 1902. Further appointments followed over the next four years, with the 23rd infantry regiment, the 9th hussars and the 15th *chasseurs à pied*.[7]

Active service was, for Gamelin, no justification for an inactive mind. He continued to read and write, making time in 1905 to produce a short treatise on warfare, published in March 1906 as the *Etude Philosophique sur l'Art de la Guerre*. The book brought him a 'cherished' letter from Ferdinand Foch, the future marshal of France and allied supreme commander in 1918, whose staff college lectures on history and tactics Gamelin had attended. The book made a name for Gamelin as a rather academic and uncommonly studious officer. He came to wonder, in time, whether he had been wise to produce such a work whilst only a junior captain. He learned as the years went by that it had caused jealousies and insinuations behind his back that he was precocious, presumptuous, even arrogant. He wondered later whether he had 'committed a youthful indiscretion' stored up against him by rival officers, by dint of writing this study.[8]

Whether because of this book or in spite of it, Gamelin's career took its most decisive step forward thus far. The 6th infantry division's chief of staff, Colonel Pellé, was seeking a new staff officer in 1906. He turned to Foch at the Ecole de Guerre for a recommendation. 'Go for

Gamelin, serving in the Vosges with the chasseurs', Foch unhesitatingly replied, 'he's one of the very best.'[9] The posting hitched Gamelin for the following five years to the rapidly ascending star of the division's commander – General Joseph Joffre.

Gamelin became Joffre's adjutant. The formal designation fails, however, to convey the full and crucial scope of the job as Gamelin developed it. For, in a role similar to that played for Foch by Weygand after 1914, Gamelin served Joffre as a complex mix of executor, prompt, inspiration, critic and conscience. In these years, Joffre's rise was meteoric. He was promoted in 1908 to head the second corps at Amiens, was advanced again to become chief of the general staff from 1911 to 1914 and then was commander-in-chief of the French armies from the outbreak of war till December 1916. Joffre's success provided the ladder for Gamelin's own steady ascent during this period – one of high sensitivity in civil-military relations following the *affaire des fiches*, the attempt by André in 1901–4 to use his tenure as war minister to republicanise promotions and favour officers with secular persuasions or Masonic allegiances.

Joffre and Gamelin grasped clearly in this period that it behoved ambitious officers to establish impeccable credentials as friends of the 'republic of the Radicals' that had emerged from the Dreyfus turmoil. During the prime ministership of Georges Clemenceau, from 1906 to 1909, a pragmatic consensus was reconstructed between the army and the regime. Under the tough-minded direction of the future 'Tiger', the republic reaffirmed its understanding that France required stability at home and security abroad, and it restated its respect for the legitimate part of the army command in the pursuit of these goals.

At this time Gamelin learnt the importance of looking behind the outward labels of party which were so readily derided in the snap-judgements he heard from fellow officers in mess-room conversation. The more he saw and observed at first hand, at Joffre's side, the less comfortable he felt with the usual military denigration of France's civilian political leaders. The appraisals of the *popote* or mess were, he realized, reached frequently in haste and were superficial as well as supercilious. Gamelin discovered for himself, by meeting politicians in the course of his duties for Joffre, that the innermost motivations and true worth of the ministers, senators and deputies were seldom quite what they seemed on the basis of simple parliamentary affiliation. Many of Gamelin's fellow officers showed an undiscriminating hostility to all Radicals as *hommes de gauche* and Dreyfusards. Gamelin, in contrast, took the trouble to discover that Clemenceau, and many of his colleagues, put on a Radicalism which did not prevent a firm friendship towards the army. Over time, in the case of the 'Tiger', Gamelin grew not just to respect his ruthlessness in defence of French national interests but also to relish his pungent political wit. The latter was memorably exercised in 1917 when Clemenceau, as prime minister, visited the front at short notice and arrived unannounced at the headquarters of the 9th infantry division which Gamelin was then commanding. Hastily calling together his only regiment immediately available for inspection, Gamelin was relieved at the evident enthusiasm shown by his men as they marched past for the prime minister. On the saluting base Clemenceau grinned with pleasure at his reception and asked Gamelin if the popularity was as genuine as it seemed. 'Yes', replied Gamelin, 'for you were the first French leader to say "merde" to the Boches.' 'That's true', rejoined the 'Tiger'; 'I've always liked dropping people in the shit – I started with my wet nurse!' It was an anecdote that Gamelin retold with relish to his staff over twenty years later.[10]

Through Joffre, Gamelin became familiar with other parliamentarians from 1911–16. They were of vividly contrasting political colours, as he recalled to his *cabinet particulier* during the phoney war in 1939. He made a friend 'he said, of M. Maurice Sarraut, "who would have made an excellent president of the Republic", as well as of Albert Thomas, for whom his feelings had been very warm: "I had ties at one and the same time with Tardieu on the right, with Sarraut, a Radical, with Thomas, who was a socialist; that encompassed a very broad parliamentary spectrum."' It was, Gamelin advised his staff in conclusion, 'necessary to know that you have your independence'. At Joffre's side, Gamelin missed no opportunity to cultivate a cross-section of the emerging generation of civilian leaders. Thomas duly became minister of munitions in 1915–17 before going to Geneva in the 1920s as the founding head of the International Labour Organisation. Tardieu became an emissary to the United States in 1917–18 and rose to be prime minister in 1929–30 and again in 1932, when he took a direct hand in promoting Gamelin to the summit of the French military command. Thus these early contacts turned into perhaps Gamelin's shrewdest career investment: an accumulating nest-egg of political patronage.[11]

In June 1911, at the comparatively early age of thirty-eight in an officer corps choked by a peacetime promotion blockage, Gamelin was listed a major. Soon afterwards he left the staff to widen his experience of regimental soldiering. Joffre lamented losing 'the most valued associate that one could conceivably desire'. But, 'in the army's interests', Gamelin needed to 'be helped get to the top as rapidly as possible'. So, between October 1911 and 1913, Gamelin assumed command first of the 14th *chasseurs à pied* at Grenoble and then of the 11th *chasseurs alpins* at Annecy. His administrative efficiency, his imaginative training methods and his tactical acumen on manoeuvres were all singled out for commendation by his brigade general. Already a staff officer of proven brilliance, Gamelin had now attracted attention as 'a first-class troop commander who allows no detail to escape his eye'.[12]

The Bastille Day honours in July 1913 brought Gamelin appointment as a Chevalier of the Légion d'Honneur. That November he returned from Savoie to Paris, where he joined the 3e Bureau (operations) of the general staff. From there, after working on the French mobilisation plans, he was reclaimed by Joffre in March 1914 and placed in the personal military *cabinet* of the chief of the general staff. It was the perfect point from which Gamelin could demonstrate his multiple talents as executive, counsellor and confidant during the desperate days whilst 'Papa' Joffre strove to rally the army and the republic as both reeled under the onslaught of the German drive on Paris in September 1914.

The Battle of the Frontiers and the Marne manoeuvre gave Gamelin a life-long example on which he built his own subsequent style of command. Joffre's imperturbability was consciously copied by Gamelin in the troubled era of his own generalship in the 1930s. In political as well as military storms, patron and protégé alike strove to calm the waters by their serenity, sang-froid and authoritative self-confidence. For Gamelin, promoted lieutenant-colonel in November 1914, his key role in planning the Marne counterattack led to his appointment as Joffre's *chef de cabinet* until August 1915. After that he moved on to direct the operations bureau at Chantilly, Joffre's supreme headquarters (the Grand Quartier Général). There, at GQG, Gamelin had special responsibility for coordinating the offensives in Artois and Champagne in the late summer of 1915. He also witnessed at close quarters Joffre's constant need to conciliate the war minister, Alexandre Millerand, in order to defend the high command's authority in the making of war strategy. The importance of Joffre's possession of a major political patron, in Millerand, during the first two years of the war, was sharply observed by Gamelin and became his formative civil-military education.[13]

In February 1916 the Germans opened their great offensive at Verdun. The onslaught coincided with Gamelin's return to the front to gain wider experience of command in battle. Taking over the 2nd brigade of chasseurs, and promoted full colonel in April 1916, Gamelin found himself involved in the ferocious fighting on the Somme when his troops were deployed to protect the southern flank of the British armies of Sir Douglas Haig. Once again, in this assignment Gamelin's abilities drew warm praise from his superiors. His divisional commander, General de Pouydraguin, applauded his clear-sightedness and acuity of judgement. Gamelin was now noted as a fine tactician and an exemplary infantry leader, as well as a brilliant staff officer. He was rewarded with acting rank of brigadier-general and was given temporary charge of the 168th infantry division in December 1916.[14]

The appointment proved, however, to be almost as brief as the one for which Gamelin left this command when, four days before Christmas 1916, he was summoned by Joffre to return to GQG to become chief of staff. By this juncture Joffre himself was on borrowed time: his authority as commander-in-chief had been eroded by the repeated failure of his armies to break through the German lines on the western front. Throughout the autumn of 1916 the unrelieved trench deadlock gave rise to growing impatience among the politicians in Paris. By December this discontent had become exacerbated by dissatisfaction with Joffre's autocratic treatment of the civilian authorities. The commander-in-chief's enemies by this point lay to the rear of his headquarters rather than across the German lines in front. Government reconstructions had removed the protection of Millerand. This, and the lack of decisive success in the field, left Joffre vulnerable. As the mists and rain of the war's third winter drew in, so the twilight fell on Joffre's career. His dismissal in favour of the ebullient and politically canny General Robert Nivelle at the end of 1916 was a sharp reminder that victory – not merely survival – was expected of France's military leaders. For Gamelin the episode was a salutary lesson in civil-military power-broking and in the importance, in the Republic, of a general avoiding dependence on the fortunes of any one political patron. The intrigues and cabals that brought down Joffre only strengthened Gamelin's determination to place his own political insurance with a broad cross-party syndicate of parliamentarians.[15]

In the war's fourth year Gamelin saw action almost continuously at the front. From April 1917 and the outbreak of the mutinies and morale crisis that made this France's *année terrible*, he had command of the 9th infantry division. As before, his qualities of leadership in the field attracted praise – both from his immediate superior, General Pellé, commander of the 5th corps, and from General Micheler, chief of staff of the reserve group of armies. Still only an acting brigadier-general, Gamelin was recommended by Micheler and by General Paulinier, commanding the 40th corps to which Gamelin's division belonged in January 1918, for corps command.[16]

The war had been appallingly wasteful to France as a whole. But to Gamelin it had brought rewards as well as rapid career advancement. His distinguished services were soon reflected on his uniform tunic by the addition of a dazzling cluster of new decorations and medals. The Croix de Guerre 1914–18, the Croix de Guerre for overseas theatres and promotion to the dignity of officer of the Légion d'Honneur were conferred by a grateful Republic. Friendly governments were as generous as the French in acknowledging Gamelin's accomplishments. From the Belgians came their Croix de Guerre, as well as their Order of Leopold. The USA, not to be outdone, awarded its Distinguished Service Order. In London Gamelin was gazetted a Companion of the Order of the Bath.[17]

By the resumption of peace Gamelin's was a star on the rise in its own right. He had emerged from Joffre's shadow. His career had combined an almost-ideal alternation of staff and command experiences. Unlike his near-contemporary, Weygand (who spent the entire war as Foch's chief of staff), Gamelin had 'taken over direct responsibility for difficult commands' at the front. Unlike Weygand, he 'could not be accused . . . of being but the shadow of a great leader'. From his own observations, Gamelin deduced that the capacity to cope with both aspects of modern officering – organisational work and front-line command – needed to exist 'together in harmony' in a soldier, if he was to be equipped as a 'complete commander'.[18] Certainly Gamelin would not be alone after the disaster of 1940 in labelling Weygand as a general with insufficient experience in the practical handling of troop formations under fire. As one British commentary put it, Weygand was a 'soldier who gained the highest distinction as a staff officer but failed as a commander [because] . . . he never fully recovered from . . . his self-effacement in the service of Foch'.[19]

After the war, Gamelin, for his part, first served overseas. He led France's military mission in Rio de Janeiro from 1919 to April 1925. There he became well acquainted with Italy's ambassador to Brazil, Marshal Pietro Badoglio who was, like Gamelin, to rise in the 1930s to become his country's chief of general staff. The coincidence of Gamelin's and Badoglio's service together in South America left a legacy of mutual regard and even friendship which helped incline both towards building a Franco-Italian military partnership against Germany in the 1930s.

In Brazil, trying to modernise the South American army on European lines according to 1914–18 experience, Gamelin was judged to have done 'well under difficult circumstances'. His success was noticed by General Edmond Buat, then chief of the French general staff. It led to recommendation of Gamelin for further promotion at the earliest possible opportunity, 'in the army's own best interests'. In December 1925, at the early age for those times of fifty-three, Gamelin was advanced to general of division – substantive major-general – in a spectacular leap over a host of rivals of greater seniority who were blocked by the shortage of peacetime commands.[20]

Professional progress always seemed to come early to Gamelin, at each stage of his career. Marriage, however, caught up with him rather late in life. As an uncommonly studious officer, Gamelin may have struck some as the personification of the barrack-room bachelor wedded only to the army. The long sea voyages from Rio to France, however, during periodic leaves in the Brazilian mission, gave him the opportunity to meet the woman whom he eventually married. Eugénie Marchand came from Romenay in the Saône-et-Loire winemaking country in the very heart of France. Although eighteen years Gamelin's junior, she and the general were married, on his fifty-fifth birthday, in 1927, in a quiet ceremony at the mairie of the 7e arrondissement in Paris – appropriately close both to the war ministry and the Invalides where he was to spend so much of his time in the next thirteen years.[21]

Meanwhile, Gamelin continued soldiering overseas, this time in Syria. The territory, part of the final expansion of the French empire, was a mandate of the League of Nations placed under French stewardship in 1919 after the break-up of the Ottoman Empire. In 1925, however, the Levant was in a state of political turmoil. Successive military high commissioners in Beirut had failed to impose a settled political order and tranquil administration on the region. These authorities were responsible not only for governing the Lebanon but also for controlling neighbouring Syria, which had also been taken from Turkey and mandated to the French. Weygand, who had been in charge in Beirut till 1924, had been defeated by the political complexities of the Levantine situation and he had been recalled at the instigation of the Cartel of the Left government formed in Paris under Herriot and the Radicals that year.[22]

Gamelin arrived in Beirut in September 1925 to find that the local situation had deteriorated further. The Cartel's appointment to the high commissionership of General Maurice Sarrail – reputedly the most left-wing and republican officer in the French army – had not forestalled the outbreak of open revolt in 1925 by the Druzes of the Syria hill country. Indeed, a French military outpost at Souieda was under siege from the Druzes and one relief column had been beaten back with heavy losses and enormous embarrassment. It was into this political cauldron that

Gamelin was thrown, called to hazard his glittering career based mainly on European experience. He had much to lose and, it seemed, little chance of renown in what was more of a colonial police action than a mid-twentieth-century war. We do not know what misgivings were in his mind as he laid his plans to suppress the Druzes, but it can hardly have escaped him that the dusty desert foothills of Syria might become the graveyard of his career.

In fact, though the pacification was a protracted operation lasting till 1928, Gamelin turned it into another personal triumph. Not only were the Souieda defenders rescued in a text-book siege relief but the wider and more problematic mission of restoring calm and order to Syria was accomplished. In a series of awkward actions, Gamelin revealed himself as a master of improvisation and adaptability. He successfully overcame wily, well-armed tribesmen, who had severely discomfited his predecessors and was remembered by the British liaison officer in Beirut for being energetic, 'thorough, cautious and compassionate'.[23] The reward for success came in promotion in December 1925 to be commander-in-chief for the entire French Levant. This appointment, however, signified the downfall of Sarrail, who was recalled to France.

The changeover raised the possibility of bitter recriminations between the generals, for Sarrail was politically well-connected on the left. Moreover, Sarrail was behind Gamelin's presence in the Levant in the first place. For, at the outset of the Druze crisis, when a new operational commander had been required to lead the pacification, Sarrail had rejected several eminent candidates proposed by the French government and simply wired the laconic telegram to Paris: 'GAMELIN. Signé: SARRAIL'.[24] In the First World War, Sarrail had, for a time, been a serious rival to Joffre, a candidate for the supreme command. Indeed, he had been exiled to Salonika to head the French expeditionary corps there in 1915, as a way for Joffre to remove a competitor to a peripheral theatre. Since Gamelin was so closely identified with Joffre, Sarrail may have been suspected of ulterior motives in requesting Gamelin's presence to face the Druzes. In fact Gamelin found Sarrail chastened by his 1914–18 experiences, and Sarrail did not bear a grudge even when he was sent home from the Levant in 1925.

More now drew the two generals together than divided them. Both had a highly developed sense of the part played in the careers of soldiers in the Third Republic by political connection. Both knew that, for better or worse, they had acquired reputations among their professional peers and their civilian superiors as 'creatures of the left'.[25] Therefore, not only did Sarrail show Gamelin his goodwill when the latter arrived in Beirut, he also refrained from intriguing with his political friends against

Gamelin after his return to Paris. In return, Gamelin reached the conclusion that Sarrail was as much the victim of malicious tongues as of his own tendency to wear his convictions on his sleeve. Sarrail, he reflected years later to his staff, was more sinned against than sinner: 'Nobody could have been less prepared than he for the task of solving the complex problems of the Levant; but, stupidity though it was to send him there at all, it was an even bigger mistake to recall him just when he was gaining some success.' In the difficult months after Sarrail's departure for France even the Jesuit Superior of Beirut lamented to Gamelin that he wished 'we still had Sarrail with us' – this of an officer dogged throughout his career by accusations of freemasonry.

With hindsight, Gamelin absolved Sarrail for his passionate emotions and violent temper. He thought it was a case of 'extremism engendering extremism' because of the 'deeply mortifying' ostracism of Sarrail by his own family, devout catholics, when he married a protestant. Gamelin even recalled Sarrail's legendary sharp tongue with some fondness and enjoyed relating how Sarrail – when a senior general in the First World War – once realised just before bedtime that he had gone a whole day without making an enemy, 'so promptly jumped to the telephone and called someone just to chew their ear off!' At bottom, considered Gamelin, Sarrail 'was a "good sort", whom most people never got to know and whose own nature left him open to misjudgment'.[26]

This fair-minded appraisal matched Sarrail's generosity towards Gamelin in the 1920s. In spite of the personal anguish that he must have experienced over his recall from Beirut, Sarrail took pains to commend Gamelin to General Debeney, who had succeeded Buat as chief of the general staff in 1923. The warmth of Sarrail's concluding confidential report on Joffre's former protégé held a symbolic significance in the politics of the higher officer corps. For Sarrail's endorsement of Gamelin removed one of the last remaining political obstacles to the latter's rise to the highest posts – the lingering prejudices of the pro and anti-Joffre camps, the 'westerners versus easterners' feud over 1914–18 grand strategy, in which Gamelin's former chief and Sarrail had stood at the head of the warring factions.[27] More than this, Sarrail's blessing signified Gamelin's entry, once-and-for-all, into the leftist and secular republican tradition of French military politics.

The consequences of this definition of Gamelin's political location were not, however, yet plainly apparent. Gamelin's destined role as a political soldier had still not completely subsumed his career as a professional military commander. In February 1929, the leadership of the 20th corps at Nancy fell vacant. This was the formation which Foch himself had commanded in the battles of August 1914. It was celebrated throughout the army and had won the soubriquet, *Le Corps de Fer* – the Iron Corps. With this elite status, it was the command coveted by every senior general and widely regarded as the most desirable appointment available to a French officer in time of peace. Learning of his nomination to this post, Gamelin looked forward not just to the prestige but also to the fact that he would be able to hold high command in the land of his maternal family. Generals of his rank were obliged to retire at their sixty-second birthday. He had, therefore, at the age of fifty-six, an opportunity to round off his career in Lorraine, guarding France's eastern marches against the Germanic giant that was, in 1929, just starting to stir once again across the Rhine.

Within only eleven months, though, Gamelin's destiny as pupil and inheritor to Joffre again changed the course of his life. Summoned to Paris in January 1930, he learned that the war minister, André Maginot, had chosen him as deputy chief of the general staff. Gamelin was unimpressed. The staff appointment promised the routine of the *bureaucrates en képi* and a daily round filled with meetings and memoranda. Gamelin appealed against the transfer to Pétain, then the army's inspector-general, but was told that the move was the wish of Tardieu, the prime minister, who had served with Gamelin on Joffre's staff in 1915 and remembered his ability. Tardieu intended, it became apparent, that Gamelin should be the general of safe republican pedigree to form a political counterweight to the abrasive and notoriously conservative Weygand. The latter was Maginot's nomination in 1930 to succeed the retiring Debeney as chief of the general staff. Gamelin's balancing role was perceived to be politically essential because Weygand was suspected of doubtful loyalty to the Republic, in Radical quarters, and actually of anti-democratic designs by many socialists and communists. In Tardieu's thinking, the appearance of a 'balanced ticket', through the presence of Gamelin, offered a means to appease the expected critics of the government's choice of Weygand on the left of the Chamber of Deputies. Friendly with parliamentarians of a progressive slant, such as the independent socialist Joseph Paul-Boncour (who himself became prime minister in 1932–3), and the Radical, Maurice Sarraut, owner of the important provincial paper the *Dépêche de Toulouse*, Gamelin had nonetheless avoided being shunned by the right. His conservative associations did not stop with Tardieu. He was linked with Jean Fabry, a former infantry colonel who had been severely disabled on the western front and who succeeded Maginot in 1928 as chairman of the Chamber army commission. Gamelin and Fabry would go on to find themselves working together in the second half of 1935, when the latter was the war minister during the second Pierre Laval government. For Gamelin, promotion to senior general staff responsibility in one of the top half-dozen military posts in the army was the reward for his reputation not only as a proven professional but as an adroit diplomat and congenial colleague. To French republicans he appeared to be the very model of a modern general.[28]

Epitomising the consensual and conciliatory approach to command as he did, Gamelin stood in ever starker contrast after 1930 to the unpredictable and short-tempered Weygand. Because of this underlying disparity it was deceptive when the early months of the partnership between the two appeared to demonstrate that they were going to cooperate 'in complete confidence with each other'. This was actually a honeymoon period. It lasted at least into 1931, for in February that year the two generals assumed still more authority when Pétain was moved to become head of France's air defence organisations (the Défense Aérienne du Territoire). The marshal was replaced as inspector-general of the army by Weygand. Gamelin in turn moved into Weygand's previous post as chief of the general staff. During all this time both officers addressed themselves to uncontentious issues. They had little difficulty agreeing to modernise the army's equipment and to set in hand the eastern frontier fortifications known later as the Maginot Line (for which a first tranche of finance was released by parliament in January 1930).[29]

From June 1932 onwards, however, this harmonious relationship deteriorated markedly. The collapse of a common point of view on pressing military questions occurred in the context of what Gamelin later lamented as 'one of the most difficult' periods of the interwar era for France. In this time a variety of problems that were inherent from a recessionary world economy, deadlocked international negotiations with Germany over reparations and armaments and French demographic stagnation were intensified in the arena of French defence decisions because of the opposed responses that they aroused in Gamelin on the one hand and in Weygand on the other. It became evident that there was scant possibility of reconciling the latter's conception of what constituted minimal national security with the optimistic and internationalist inclinations of the Radical-dominated majority that controlled the Chamber after France's general elections of May 1932.

The stage was set for renewed civil-military conflict. The Radicals and their Cartel des Gauches partners regarded themselves in questions of external and defence policy as enlightened liberal internationalists. Yet in financial and economic matters, in contrast, they preferred approaches that were unashamedly orthodox and deflationist. On the foreign stage the Radicals and their allies were ready to run what a contemporary British prime minister was to term in 1935 in regard to British policy, 'risks for peace'; but the French Cartel ministers stuck steadfastly to the conservatism of seeking balanced budgets at home.[30]

In February 1932, moreover, the long-prepared world disarmament conference at last commenced at Geneva. The opening of the assembly's public sessions excited expectations of reduced levels of military provision throughout Europe, including France. From Geneva there appeared, to internationalists, to be a view pointing towards a system of security for states that would obviate the need for the armed camps and confrontational bloc politics which had been characteristics of the era before 1914. However, 1932 also saw the arrival of the first serious impact in France of the contagious international economic depression that had spread since the Wall Street crash three years before. The decline in tax revenues and customs receipts was a menace to the state's ability to meet budgetary obligations that, by early 1933, the French finance ministry could not ignore. It was, therefore, fortuitous that the Cartel assumed office with an outlook on European international problems that rested heavily on dismantling or negotiating the removal of provocative weapon inventories. For this was a stance on foreign relations and defence that coincided with and was buttressed by the advice of the Treasury and the Bank of France to reduce all categories of public expenditure to compensate for diminishing revenues. Accidental though this timely marriage of internationalist idealism and financial exigencies was, it proved nevertheless to be formative for the shape of French national defences down to 1936. Scaling down the modernisation of the French military arsenal desired by Weygand found favour with the Cartel. It promised to promote congenial conditions for the work of the Geneva disarmers. But, at the same time, such restrictions would curb defence spending and so help address the problem of French budget deficits. The diplomacy of *rapprochement* appeared to offer a convenient way to lower the demands of the French military establishment on a shrunken national income.

By 1933, in short, the wind of financial stringency blew strongly into the political-technical environment at Geneva. From the standpoint of many French military authorities the vista of arms reductions was not so much the sunny idyll that it may have appeared to statesmen wishing to grab the credit for a world with fewer weapons as an arid desert where vital training and procurement funds would be as scarce as water. French soldiers such as Weygand were afraid that it would be an enervating journey on dangerously short rations.

Convinced that the French army would wither and face emaciation, threatening its ability to serve as the vigorous sentinel of national security, Weygand became an increasingly embittered and injudicious adversary of the Cartel governments. As a lifelong anti-Dreyfusard and germanophobe, his brand of forthright patriotism was utterly out of tune with the optimistic spirit and willingness to make concessions over French armed strength that imbued many Radicals and socialists. During 1933–4 the policies of the Cartel therefore encountered obdurate opposition from Weygand. He estimated that his responsibility for discharging the army's duty to guarantee the integrity of French territory could not be met if Cartel policies were implemented. To Weygand the proposed economies in public expenditure, directed at military maintenance and training allocations among other targets, menaced the peacetime cadre's role as skeleton for the general mobilisation of the nation-in-arms in case invasion was threatened. For ministers – especially Daladier, in 1933 – it seemed prudent to postpone calling up a fraction of the conscript class. This would, in the reckoning of ministers, leave a residue or reserve of manpower, liable for service later, to fill out under-strength contingents in the 'lean years' of 1935–9, twenty years after the low birth rate experienced during the First World War.

But to Weygand this precaution – which stood to cut 10 per cent from conscripted establishments during 1933 and 1934 – hazarded too great an immediate diminution of the army's strength with the colours in favour of unproven requirements in the future (when, coincidentally, Weygand himself would be retired). The reports from French intelligence agents and the warnings of the army's 2e Bureau about the growing extent of secret German rearmament were, for Weygand, grounds enough to fear a present danger. They drove him into acrimonious dispute with politicians whom he felt were too credulous, too prone to lower France's guard, in pursuit of conciliation with Germany.

Gamelin, on the other hand, strove with patience, tact and steely determination to mend the civil-military fences during Weygand's four fraught years at the head of French land forces. Gamelin was every bit as watchful and wary towards the Germans as Weygand. But he rejected the latter's aggressive and confrontational approach to disagreement with the civilian authorities over the scale of defence efforts required in 1934. Unlike Weygand, Gamelin remained convinced of the receptiveness of politicians such as Herriot, Paul-Boncour and Daladier to persuasion, evidence and reasoned argument. In something akin to a self-appointed mission, Gamelin set out to distance himself from Weygand's angry exchanges with the government, which he estimated to be counterproductive. Instead he took onto his own shoulders, virtually alone, the burden of preventing a civil-military separation.[31]

All the while Gamelin nevertheless sought to re-establish a political priority in favour of raising the provision of resources to the army. It was his methods and not his objectives in regard to strengthening national defence that differed so sharply from Weygand's. Where the style of the latter was overtly confrontational, Gamelin's was conciliatory. He believed that politicians were likely to be won round to the military's viewpoint if they saw the generals working loyally with them rather than picking fights. He feared that if the high command 'sulked' over decisions it disliked it ran the graver risk of ministers simply bypassing processes of civil-military consultation altogether and fixing future policy on their own. More than once, in the turbulent months of 1933–4, Gamelin accused the 'intransigent' and 'prickly' Weygand of disloyalty to the government. More generally, observing Weygand, he worried that by excessively frequent and intemperate protests a top commander might become 'a pain in the neck and ... exhaust his credit' with the civilian authorities.

Gamelin found this one of the most uncomfortable periods in his whole career. He felt himself 'jammed in' between his military superior and a succession of ministers whose patriotism and good intentions he respected. Above all, Gamelin took away from this quarrelsome time an unshakeable determination to leave the government at all times the master of its own decisions. Weygand's mistake, he was convinced, had been to push politicians beyond the limits of their patience.[32] Gamelin had, 'thanks to his always having refused to identify himself with any political party and to his ... quietly forceful manner', in contrast, succeeded 'in resisting all attempts at political interference in the army; [yet] at the same time he ... retained the full confidence of his political chiefs'.[33]

On 21 January 1935 Weygand reached the age of sixty-eight and was compelled to retire. To take his place there was 'little doubt ... that the choice [would] fall on ... Gamelin', noted the British military attaché in Paris.[34] Since the previous year Gamelin had been the acknowledged 'crown prince' of the high command, as it was put by the war minister at this time, Louis Maurin (a retired general himself and a former inspector of army motorisation). Even so, the transition was not quite trouble-free.

A vociferous minority, a mixture of parliamentarians and a few emboldened subordinate officers, objected that Gamelin was unacceptably 'in tow to the politics of the left'. It was scurrilously suggested in the right-wing fringe press that he had Masonic connections.[35] Moreover

Weygand, who had commended Gamelin five years before as a 'colleague of peerless value', had completely soured. By 1935 he 'looked on Gamelin as a man eternally seeking a compromise and always ready to bow to the decisions of politicians, even when they went against the interests of the army'. Conservatives thought for a moment that they might deny Gamelin his last promotion. Pierre Taittinger, a Republican Federation deputy for Paris, founder and financier of the authoritarian Jeunesses Patriotes and an organiser of the 6 February 1934 demonstrations on the Place de la Concorde that forced the resignation of Daladier's Cartel government, demanded an extension of Weygand's service by special decree. But too many of Weygand's political bridges had already been burned for this view to find a majority. On 18 January 1935 a regular decree instead appointed Gamelin vice-president of the CSG, inspector-general and commander-in-chief designate. At the same time he was reconfirmed as chief of the general staff. No-one since Joffre, his own mentor, had combined these posts or enjoyed such extensive authority.[36]

Eager for security – indeed, increasingly paranoid about it – the French focused their yearning henceforth on Gamelin. Symbolically he inherited the supposed sagacity of the triumphant generalship of November 1918 when, on that winter's day in 1935, he moved his files into the office at 4 bis, Boulevard des Invalides, the office of Foch, Pétain and lately of Weygand. The dark moments when Gamelin would know nothing but disparagement as a 'beaten chief, a disqualified leader' still lay more than five years into the future.[37] In 1935 Gamelin, who came to be called the 'cool and wise counsellor to his government', was confidently expected by observers to soar above the challenge ahead of him and 'evolve something really useful out of the present French military organisation'.[38]

With the easy self-assurance that had become his stock-in-trade, Gamelin dispensed with Weygand's offer to acquaint him at first hand with the agenda awaiting him at the Invalides. Gamelin told Weygand that he would undoubtedly find such a briefing of interest but that he preferred to come fresh to the dossiers himself. 'You know me', he added, 'I'm a strategist.' 'Evidently so', retorted Weygand tartly, as he reflected on his successor's more subtle and successful manoeuvres on the battlefields of politics.

Yet Gamelin was much more than an experienced field commander who had also shown himself adept at the art of political accommodation. He was a flexible and thoughtful professional, a cultured man who had made a serious study of art, history and Bergsonian philosophy. The antithesis of the archetypal military philistine, Gamelin was regarded as the personification of the educated soldier. He was polished, charming and clever. This was felt by foreigners as well as by Frenchmen. Brigadier T. G. G. Heywood, who had been British military attaché when Weygand retired in 1935, wrote in the *RUSI Journal* in 1938, after Gamelin's further promotion to chief of staff for national defence, that he (Gamelin) 'possessed the gift . . . of inspiring trust in his subordinates' and for winning the 'affectionate devotion' of those who worked with him.[39]

Among outside observers, the British found Gamelin 'extremely amiable'. He was described as a well-travelled officer, 'modern in his military views'. He was credited with a lucid and elastic mind, allied to an 'active, intelligent, practical' personality. Although he did not speak English, the British Embassy in Paris took pains to emphasise the cordiality of his relations with English people.[40]

Gamelin's unusually good standing in the eyes of French civilian leaders not only attracted British comment but also drew attention from the Germans. In place of the 'rude, aggressive' Weygand, noted the writer Friedrich Sieburg in the *Frankfurter Zeitung* in the spring of 1935, Germany was to be faced with the 'attractive, patient, correct' Gamelin. The Germans, suggested Sieburg, would find him less doctrinaire, less a prisoner of political prejudices. Weygand, readers in the Reich were reminded, had never shaken off the 'burden of hatred' that he had borne throughout the 'tragi-comedy of the disarmament and humiliation' imposed at Versailles. As Foch's former chief of staff, he was the enduring personification of French nationalistic triumphalism. Weygand, 'l'homme du 11 novembre 1918', both in his own mind and in German sight, censured the politicians who had governed France in the 1920s for allegedly 'betraying or at least emasculating' a victory bought with the blood of the French army. As Sieburg shrewdly concluded, he was one of a body of Frenchmen who found 'scarcely bearable the disproportion between the grandeur of victory [in 1918] and the moral and intellectual despair witnessed in France in the years that followed'.

Where a penchant for reprisals and further retribution was ascribed to Weygand, Gamelin was estimated to be a 'partisan of a *modus vivendi*'. Regarded as reasonable as well as realistic, Gamelin would, Sieburg wrote, neither allow himself 'to be seduced by romantic nonsense about a Franco-German military alliance nor be blinded by the hatred which in some French people would delight in keeping Germany subjugated for ever'. Sieburg thought two salient points were indicated by Gamelin's elevation at the beginning of 1935. The first was the ending of the domination of French defence policy by the 'strategy of movement', the strategy of adventurism, favoured by Foch and Weygand. Gamelin's arrival signified that the bell had tolled for French preventive war projects, such as German observers had attributed to Weygand in 1933. The second supposition was that, in all essentials, Gamelin could be counted on to maintain a watchful policy towards the Reich. Gamelin was not expected to offer grounds for any new hope of Franco-German reconciliation; but nor was he likely to want relations between the two countries to be kept on a knife-edge of tension and rumours of war.

Gamelin was expected to seek the maximum détente that he found compatible with keeping 'the famous "*marge de sécurité*"', the time-honoured basis of French defence policy 'whether expressed through the power of weapons of war themselves or through military collaboration with other nations'. Like his mentors in the secular-republican school of French generalship, Joffre and Sarrail, Gamelin was a military professional who had not degenerated into a militarist. Sieburg expected he would seek a middle course 'between the dreams of the ... internationalists striving for a federated Europe and system of pacts, and the wishes of those who would stay "armed to the teeth" to try to perpetuate the encirclement of the Reich'. And as Gamelin's style of command emerged over the middle-1930s, other German commentators confirmed the accuracy of Sieburg's assessment. As was noted in the *Berliner Tageblatt* in early 1938, when Gamelin was nominated to still wider responsibilities as chief of staff for national defence, he counselled his officers never to act impulsively. Never, it was observed with satisfaction, had he done anything to heighten the risks of war.[41]

Most astute of all, however, was the recognition even among outsiders that Gamelin took on the highest posts in the army without the burden of the 'age-old' baggage of 'distrust of French military men for the political institutions of their country'.[42] As Colonel Kühlenthal, the German military attaché in Paris, put it in 1937, Gamelin was the exceptional French general 'who was accepted by politicians because he did not arouse their suspicions or give rise to the belief that he was making himself too powerful'.[43] Therefore, whilst Gamelin identified internal as well as external dangers to the republic as he assumed charge of the nation's territorial security, he was no pessimist. He considered that he was facing a defence that had been compromised but one not yet in crisis; and he believed that the hurdles confronting him were neither immediate nor insurmountable. Surveying the muscle-flexing of the Nazi regime beyond the Rhine in early 1935, Gamelin harboured no illusions that determination, hard work, the devotion of greater resources to the military and unity of purpose between soldiers and civilians would be demanded if the standing and the security of France were to be maintained. The Reich, reported French intelligence services, was redoubling its programmes of military reconstruction and would obviously not remain for long confined in the shackles of Versailles. To Gamelin it appeared once more (as he would express it near the outbreak of the war), that 'the duel between France and Germany' – whether waged diplomatically or militarily – 'was one more time going to determine the fate of the world'.[44]

2 Gamelin and the rebirth of German power

As Gamelin prepared to assume responsibility for French security in late 1934 his concern was to maintain the established order in Europe. France was committed to upholding this status quo since it had been the leading architect of the 1919 treaty arrangements. In its own right, France was a territorially satisfied and 'mature' power whose outlook was defensive not revisionistic. Hitler, by contrast, displayed a concern from the outset of his rule to alter the status which the former Allies had imposed on Germany. His rhetoric was as unsettling as his early steps towards remilitarising German society were sinister. It was for Gamelin to ponder how far Hitler intended to execute – rather than merely rant about – an expansionist foreign policy and how far Hitler's ambitions for the German armed forces stretched.

Yet, in the opening months of Gamelin's tenure of command, French military modernisation was not so much influenced by developments in Germany as by pre-existing French concerns. The start of Gamelin's mandate was dominated by exertions to establish his own agenda with the CSG, the war ministry and the general staff. Since 1932 Weygand had sought to defend the army's basic structures against measures by the Cartel des Gauches which were, in his eyes, injurious to the ability of the military forces to protect France. However, these campaigns had caused Weygand to concentrate excessively on preserving the army's organisational and numerical establishment. He had, comparatively, neglected its weaponry, munitions and vehicle replacement programmes.[1] Gamelin thus faced the task of imposing his own priorities on a military bureaucracy busily occupied with the concerns of his predecessor. Gamelin believed that experimentation and investment was urgently required to bring French equipment and doctrine abreast of changing conditions of warfare. This became his agenda. Weygand's insistence on emphasising the army's educative and political role consequently declined in importance.

Gamelin's first mission, as he perceived it, was to deflect his fellow generals away from a fixation with sustaining the army's 'moral qualities' and manpower strength as ends in themselves. In place of these preoccupations, Gamelin wished to generate innovation in operational and tactical concepts, backed by expansion of the supply of the best modern *matériel*.[2] In order to free himself to tackle these issues, Gamelin delegated the routine administration of the army to General Louis Colson, the new chief of army staff, relieving himself from the mundane management of recruitment, quartermastering, personnel and so forth. He consciously set himself to direct the CSG and France's political leaders to study and surmount the challenge of Germany's re-emergence as a military power. As early as the start of 1935 it was evident to Gamelin that this task would be the pivotal issue of his years of command.[3]

Hitler's Germany quite obviously had the potential to threaten France. Yet, as Gamelin was alarmed to note, politicians in Paris showed little urgency over the run-down condition into which French defence equipment had sunk. Lip-service had been paid to the growing security problem when the French government delivered its celebrated note of 17 April 1934 to the British Embassy in Paris. By this, Louis Barthou, then foreign minister, had stated that France had decided that disarmament had foundered and that it 'must place the conditions for her own security in the forefront of her concerns'. Yet Gamelin was uneasy at how little action had followed this declaration. He was unconvinced that France had shifted decisively away from policies of disarmament and reliance on international conferences to a policy of defensive rearmament. He estimated, therefore, that he had to assume a role as 'the breather of new life into the army'.[4]

Down to March 1935 – when Hitler publicly repudiated the military restrictions of Versailles – the remilitarisation of Germany remained clandestine. This increased Gamelin's difficulty in opening the eyes of many French politicians to the impending German danger. The secrecy surrounding Germany's military renaissance had been penetrated by French intelligence from the later 1920s onwards. The military authorities in Paris were well aware of developments beyond the Rhine. But the clandestinity cloaking the Reichswehr's build-up made it difficult before mid-1935 to convince French taxpayers that heavy expenditure on modernising and increasing French armaments was essential.[5]

A further problem for Gamelin was the outdatedness of much of the thinking prevalent inside the French army itself. Strategic and tactical concepts remained rooted in the positional warfare of 1915–18. Pétain and Weygand, in their years of command from 1921–34, had retained an emphasis on the importance of manpower in battles of attrition. This derived directly from First World War experience. They had feared obsessively for French military capability during the 'lean years' of 1935–9. Pétain had favoured the preparation in peacetime of frontier defences – notably the Maginot Line's completion and the stockpiling of equipment to permit field divisions to fight in future from 'prepared battlefields'. The marshal was determined to husband manpower and maximise defensive firepower. *Le feu tue* had become the watchword of the saviour of Verdun. It was banal but compelling to a nation so recently bled white by the carnage of the western front. Weygand's obsession, on the other hand, was to persuade parliament to legislate the reintroduction of two-year military service and to restore annual *grands manoeuvres* so as to expand the mass standing-army. Gamelin thought these concerns somewhat tangential to the questions of modernisation, mechanisation and re-equipment that he judged essential by 1935.[6]

In the face of the German military recovery, Gamelin thought his most pressing priority was to put impetus behind provision to the army of high-quality new weapons and armoured vehicles. He estimated that this – rather than longer service-time – was the optimal way to compensate for the conscript shortage implicit in the 'lean years'. Just before he took over from Weygand in December 1934 the government, headed by Pierre-Etienne Flandin of the conservative Alliance Démocratique, was interpellated in parliament on its policy over army manpower and training. Critics appear to have been briefed by officers close to Weygand, such as the latter's adjutant, Colonel André Laffargue. The episode demonstrated how all-embracing the manpower controversy had become. Gamelin was disturbed that this arousal of passions was obscuring the urgent need for a dispassionate and considered review of the material rather than numerical deficiencies of the army. In his opinion the gravest of the material shortcomings was the modest scale of the mechanised forces projected for the late 1930s under the existing armament plans of Weygand.[7] Gamelin knew he had to relieve the political disquiet about the 'lean years' without shutting the door on an upgrading of weapon and vehicle replacement programmes.

Against the background of this necessity the debate about French military policy was suddenly given a dramatic shift from a purely practical to an ideological plane. The cause was an intervention by a then little-known colonel on the secretariat of the CSDN, Charles de Gaulle.[8] On the same day as the attack in the Senate on Flandin's effectives policy, 17 December 1934, de Gaulle received a letter from Colson that forbade publication in the official *Revue Militaire Française* of an article by the colonel entitled 'How to create a professional army'.⁹ Colson stated that this essay's appearance in a periodical approved by the war ministry 'risked placing a professional army and the national army in conflict in people's minds'. The war ministry was 'resolutely opposed to any such distinction'. It thought it inopportune to allow de Gaulle a platform of an official kind for 'concepts which may ... lead some into contradiction with the views of the minister'.¹⁰

De Gaulle, however, was undeterred by this attempt to muzzle him. Seeking alternative outlets by which to disseminate his controversial proposals, he turned to another man with scant regard for convention – the conservative politician Paul Reynaud, whom he had first met in early December 1934.¹¹ The partnership which rapidly developed between de Gaulle and Reynaud was essentially a marriage of convenience. De Gaulle had made an idiosyncratic analysis of the condition of France. All around him he thought he saw decaying national vitality and cohesiveness. He deduced that a revolutionary structural change in the organisation of the army offered a way to revive French patriotism and rebuild French security against the danger embodied in Nazi Germany. Reynaud welcomed de Gaulle's theories with enthusiasm. A former minister for the colonies and minister of justice, Reynaud had been out of office since June 1932. He was a political loner, a maverick who adopted unfashionable ideas and who had not troubled to build any significant personal following as a power-base in the Chamber of Deputies. He seized on de Gaulle's ideas with alacrity, grasping how they offered a cause that was bound to attract widespread publicity and might resuscitate his waning political career.¹² Reynaud was a gifted orator. He had the means to put himself back in the public eye through his advocacy of de Gaulle's inventive programme of military reorganisation. De Gaulle was delighted at Reynaud's interest: the former minister could speak out and attack the orthodoxies of the high command in a way not permitted to a subordinate serving officer.

De Gaulle's proposals have been intensively studied by scholars of French civil-military relations, strategic planning and foreign policy.¹³ Only brief reference need be made to their content here, therefore, before their impact is investigated on Gamelin's efforts to strengthen French security. De Gaulle envisaged two parallel paths of development for the army. The first demanded a massive expansion of mobile automotive forces and their permanent peacetime establishment as a trained and homogenous shock force. The second was the manning of this battle group or 'ready force' solely by professional career soldiers. This was to be the *armée de métier*. Such ideas had first been publicised by de Gaulle in books in 1932 (*Le Fil de l'épée*, The Edge of the Sword), and 1934 (*Vers l'armée de métier*, Towards the professional army). In these works de Gaulle alleged that successive reductions in the duration of conscript service, excessive concentration on fixed frontier fortifications in the late 1920s and early 1930s and, finally, expenditure cuts in 1932–4 had diminished the army's combat readiness to the extent of putting in doubt its capacity to guarantee French territorial integrity in wartime.[14]

Had de Gaulle's arguments and Reynaud's associated critique confined themselves to issuing a clarion call for urgent military re-equipment with emphasis on armoured and motor vehicles, they would have gained the endorsement of Gamelin and Colson.[15] Instead they aroused the irritation of these and many other senior generals. Even more seriously, they intensified political distrust of the expansion of French armoured forces. This antagonism and suspicion combined to impair the army's ability in the long term to match Germany's build-up of tank forces and evolution of accepted and understood mechanised warfare doctrine. Paradox though this was, the propagation of de Gaulle's ideas produced an effect opposite to the one their author intended. Their dissemination and the controversy they generated weakened the army in the short and the medium term, too, by activating political and doctrinal brakes on the development of French mechanised forces in 1935, 1936 and 1937.

The first thing that caused dislike and distrust was de Gaulle's immodesty. In spite of the striking imagery with which his publications promoted the case for massed tank forces, de Gaulle's notions about mechanisation were not in themselves original. General Jean-Baptiste Estienne, known to some as the 'father of the French tank force', had pioneered the use of armoured combat vehicles in 1916–18. Estienne, together with General Joseph Doumenc and Colonel Pol-Maurice Velpry, had written studies during the 1920s in which the strategic employment of heavy armour in division-sized formations had been examined and advocated.[16] Gamelin and Colson knew these studies and held the qualifications of their authors in high esteem. Gamelin pointedly recalled to the post-1945 parliamentary investigating commission that 'having taken on General Doumenc as deputy chief of the army staff . . . I was sure he would concern himself with achieving this development.'[17] Yet de Gaulle failed to make any acknowledgement of his debt to these earlier and contemporary students of mechanisation within his own army. Moreover, his own writings on the subject were – in the sight of the hard-nosed professional military readers he most needed to influence – coloured by an unnervingly optimistic and romanticised vision of the nature of modern war.[18]

Thus de Gaulle's arrogance tended to harden attitudes that were destined to obstruct the advance of mechanised forces in the French army. But an even more important gift to the opposition was de Gaulle's irrelevant claim that mechanisation and professionalisation were synonymous – were part-and-parcel of an army's successful modernisation. 'At root', as Gamelin correctly stressed later on, 'it was the connection . . . made between the question of large armoured units and the question of the career army which certainly proved detrimental in parliament and in a section of military opinion to the creation of tank divisions.'[19]

De Gaulle's published predictions about armoured offensives merited closer general staff attention than they received. For they warned of the perils in an early rupture of the French defensive front. Such a rupture, de Gaulle prophesied, might destroy the preparations for an extended coalition war waged from superior economic strength which was judged the only means for France to prevail in another conflict with Germany.[20] These warnings were overlooked, however. This was because of the controversies stimulated by de Gaulle's addition of a poorly aimed broadside against the army's training, the inclusion of reservists in its major mobilised formations, and on the politically sacrosanct republican tradition of the nation-in-arms.

Many senior and influential soldiers thought it unnatural, unnecessary and impracticable to try to marry the concepts of *métier* and mechanisation. De Gaulle actually provided ammunition to those who were unenthusiastic to start with about the large-scale development of armour. Among these officers two generals stood out: the inspector of infantry in 1935–8, Joseph Dufieux (a former St Cyr classmate of Gamelin), and the inspector of cavalry, Robert Altmayer. These men favoured retaining tanks under the control of their traditional arms – and strictly for their close support.[21] Both Reynaud and de Gaulle justified the latter's call for the professionalisation of the personnel of the proposed armoured force by citing the increasing technical sophistication of tanks and the spread of complex accompanying equipment for signalling, support and logistics. Their argument was admitted by the general staff to be partly valid in respect of vehicle maintenance and operation of wireless apparatus, for which skilled men were required whose training could not be perfected even under two-year conscription.[22] Patently, however, it was absurd to claim that the cooks, quartermasters, drivers and supporting infantry of an armoured force also had to be career soldiers.

Yet it was to a controversy at this level that what should have been a doctrinally fruitful reappraisal of the composition and battlefield role of mechanisation descended. The problem lay squarely with the insistence of de Gaulle and Reynaud on the universal use of professional personnel. In January 1935, prompted by de Gaulle's report that French intelligence had discovered Germany's establishment of her first panzer divisions, Reynaud launched the colonel's ideas onto the national political stage.[23] They appeared during the Chamber debate of 15 March 1935 over the application of article 40 of the 1928 military recruitment law. Use of the article restored two-year military service in the French army. This was done in part to offset the imminent manpower shortfall of the 'lean years', in part to demonstrate attention to French national security in the light of Germany's public re-establishment of an airforce on 11 March.[24]

In Reynaud's 15 March speech were contained all of the much-criticised facets of the link made between mechanisation and professionalisation. Reynaud alleged that 'for a part of our army, the motorised part, specialisation is as necessary as in the airforce and navy . . . The mistake of the general staff is its desire to obtain only the greatest possible number of units all organised on the same footing . . .'. The second part of this accusation was unnecessarily provocative: it ignored the creation by Weygand and Gamelin of specialised motorised infantry, mechanised cavalry and fortress divisions.[25]

More serious, however, was the onslaught on the army's existing recruitment and composition. For to counter this required a protracted, enervating and mostly sterile exchange of memoranda and employment of precious time within the bureaucracies of the staff and the *cabinets* of the war ministers. As an illustration, as late as July 1936 the mere fact of a change of incumbent at the rue Saint-Dominique was sufficient to trigger a new inquiry into the issue and to require a whole new refutation of the need to fill mechanised units with career soldiers. On that occasion Colson, supported by Gamelin, advised the incoming minister, Edouard Daladier, that: 'There is no justification for staffing certain large formations solely with long-service personnel. If it is essential to employ specialists to service . . . expensive armoured vehicles . . . it is, in contrast, unnecessary to be a career soldier in order to become a fighting trooper or lorry driver.'[26]

On 15 March Reynaud in the event attracted insufficient support to prevent parliamentary approval of Flandin's extension of military service through article 40. But he returned to the attack soon afterwards, employing the same formulae as before in tabling a private member's bill for military reorganisation. The bill again urged concentration of the French army's mobile elements into just seven divisions. It lightly side-stepped the complex but crucial problems posed to the high command by responsibility for securing the vast territorial expanses of three distinct theatres: north-east France, south-east France and French North Africa. It ignored the question of how a mobile corps, which Reynaud and de Gaulle proposed to concentrate in just one place in peacetime, could function as, in the bill's expression, 'the cadre-school of the nation-in-arms'. The conscript recruits who required instruction would, in their several hundred thousands, be inevitably dispersed in the training camps throughout the length and breadth of France.[27] Rather than address these matters, Reynaud simply reiterated the essence of his speech, repeating that 'technical development' imposed specialisation and that 'From this stems, for the mechanised part of our forces, the requirement for technically-capable and therefore professional personnel . . . .'.[28]

Gamelin, in contrast, thought the consideration of an all-career army anachronistic. Perhaps it might have been viable had it been created in the early 1920s as a means to preserve the Versailles system (when it would have faced a Reichswehr of only 100,000 men without armour or air support). But, Gamelin contended with good reason, a small professional army could not be trusted to guarantee French security in the radically altered and more dangerous circumstances of the mid-1930s. As Gamelin admitted, he was much influenced by Germany's restoration of conscription in 1935. He knew, moreover, from the French service attachés in Brussels and Berlin, of the campaign in 1935–6 to extend military service in the Belgian army and of the German decision in August 1936 to prolong the period of conscription in the Wehrmacht to two years.[29]

In view of all this the senior generals closed ranks to pronounce an all-career army unattainable as well as undesirable. For Reynaud's interventions neglected the central difficulty of recruiting and retaining the legions of professionals demanded under his schemes. According to Gamelin it would have been impossible to obtain enough recruits for all-professional tank and motorised divisions in addition to the 106,000 career soldiers that the 1928 laws structuring the French army required for fortress garrisons, training cadres and the skeletons of the reserve infantry divisions formed on mobilisation by recalling the time-served conscripts of earlier years from their civilian occupations.[30] Over many months this analysis was disputed by de Gaulle and Reynaud. Each offered their own variations on recruitment statistics. This distracting and profitless paperwork continued to take up general staff time right down till late 1936 when, with Daladier at the war ministry, the judgement of Gamelin and Colson was conclusively endorsed.[31]

Whilst the technicalities of Reynaud's proposals consumed the attention of the generals, the politically contentious characteristics that were associated with a professional army provoked an outcry in parliament. This should not have surprised: suspicions of the professional military lay deep in the psyche of most French politicians who thought the officer corps harboured dangerous anti-republicans. This paranoia stretched back through the era of Weygand, an undisguised and abrasive conservative, the Dreyfus affair and the Boulanger episode to the Republic's infancy in the 1870s. These underlying phobias translated themselves, in the context of the mid-1930s, into antipathy towards development of autonomous armoured forces. The latter, it was felt, might become 'an army apart from the nation' instead of an army that was part of the nation. Tanks were feared as 'aggressive' and in every sense 'offensive' weapons and there had been much attention to imposing upper limits on their size and power during the Geneva disarmament conference in 1932–3. The SFIO leader, Léon Blum, used his speech in the 15 March 1935 debate to urge fresh overtures to Germany. He wished to seek an amicable settlement of differences rather than have recourse to rearmament. He described de Gaulle's professional army as a concept too 'praetorian' and potentially anti-democratic to be approved by a democratically elected parliament. Indeed the history of French civil-military relations was so troubled that ideas redolent of the image of tanks commanded by anti-republican generals clattering onto the boulevards of Paris were unacceptable to all except a handful of extreme-right deputies.[32]

Reinforcing this political distaste for professionalisation were the indications from military sources to parliamentarians of the general staff's great anxiety about the recruitment and training difficulties likely to inhibit a redistribution of available resources of career soldiers. Consequently the Chamber army commission rejected Reynaud's private member's bill in June 1935 on the grounds, as its president Jean Fabry put it, that the 'mission of training the army as a whole cannot be left ... like this'.[33] For most deputies such reasoning was probably a convenient fig-leaf: it spared them from exposing their innermost political fears regarding a professional force.[34]

The rebuff of the de Gaulle–Reynaud projects by army and parliament alike nevertheless occurred against a backdrop of a reappraisal of the Franco-German military balance. Politicians as well as army leaders participated in the work of evaluation. But a consensus was slow to emerge within either group – let alone between them. Weygand, for his part, delivered a valedictory overview or *bilan* to the CSG on 15 January 1935, just as he retired. This had a stridently alarmist tone to it.

Handing over to Gamelin, Weygand remained as obsessed as ever about the effectives question and troubled by what he perceived to be trends towards reducing units in the French interior to lifeless skeletons, low on morale and deprived of relevant training. He alleged that the army had become like a body whose starvation was apparent in its emaciated limbs and extremities.[35]

To be sure the problem of the *années creuses* was serious. Compared to an average annual conscript contingent of 240,000 men, one estimate in March 1935 projected a decline to a yearly mean of only 139,000 between 1936 and 1940. The detailed projection is shown in Table 1.1. Once allowance was made for the medically unfit, it was feared that the usable yearly contingent might shrink to a mere 116,000 in each twelve-month period of this quinquennium.

Table 1. *The annual French army conscript intake in the* années creuses

1936	149,000
1937	117,000
1938	126,000
1939	146,000
1940	150,000

In early 1935 Pétain joined the debate. He threw his prestige into a call for conscripting 280,000 men into the army each year. These interventions helped persuade parliament to apply article 40 of the 1928 recruitment law. This step, added to a lowering of the age of incorporation of the conscripts to twenty, was expected to bring improvements by the spring of 1937.[36] Nonetheless, Weygand's and Pétain's anxiety about manpower was voiced against a background of German military expansion. French intelligence in early 1935 estimated that the Wehrmacht would have some 500,000 trained troops by mid-1936. Another French concern was that their fighting power was nearly all on display in the 'shop-window' of the eastern frontier regions: the security of France was protected by a thin crust of army units with little in depth of any quality behind them. This worry was not without justification, for every regiment of the five divisions stationed in western France had been reduced from three battalions to two. Another sign of weakness was the deployment of eleven native North African battalions to France between 1933 and October 1935.[37]

What was Gamelin's reaction to these difficulties? Though not complacent, he was less vociferous than Weygand or Pétain. Just like Reynaud, however, he was eager to switch priority into modernising the army's equipment. Again like Reynaud, he believed qualitative improvement in armoured and artillery forces was the way to counter Germany's quantitative superiority. But Gamelin was certain that improvements had to be sought within the existing organisational and recruitment frameworks. Otherwise, he feared, they would fail to attract the political support needed not just to gain initial impetus but also to maintain the sustained priority they would need for timely completion. Calibrating exactly how far to alarm the politicians in order to get them to release resources for rearmament was a fine judgement for Gamelin in the first half of 1935.[38]

In this calculated and deliberate 'use of fear', as it has been termed in the slightly different but related context of French response to the air threat, Hitler provided some help by announcing his goal of a thirty-six division army in March 1935. In a brief for the Haut Comité Militaire (HCM), a week after the 15 March Chamber debate, it was argued that Germany's existing army was a 'shock instrument adapted for mounting a surprise assault'. Pétain's and Maurin's re-equipment programmes would require time to bring new weapons into service. Levels of material in all three services were alleged to be insufficient for France to consider waging war in Europe in 1935 or 1936. The committee was warned that most of France's mechanised equipment was obsolete. German intentions were judged all the more suspect because her military material was undergoing rapid and secret development behind 'a near-impenetrable veil'. Most menacingly of all, French intelligence had identified German endeavours to manufacture synthetic oils – evidence, surely, of plans to employ 'a large mass of motorised equipment'.[39]

The 22 March 1935 HCM meeting revealed that Flandin's government was alarmed by French strategic vulnerability. The prime minister said he feared a surprise attack on Alsace before the completion of the Maginot Line. He stressed the need for France to be 'ready' – politically and economically as well as militarily. In Berlin, he contended, 'the madmen' had 'gained the upper hand' around Hitler – an assessment with which the foreign minister, Laval, concurred.[40] The latter said events strengthened his belief in the importance of removing Italo-Yugoslav tension and broadening the Franco-Italian understanding reached in his own Rome negotiations with Mussolini that January.

Laval was supported by the minister of marine, François Piétri, and the air minister, General Victor Denain – even though they knew that the 'idiosyncrasy of its policy' made Italy's help in any Franco-German crisis 'necessarily . . . uncertain'.[41]

These arguments in support of a gamble on Mussolini's good will rested on rational if cynical appraisals of French options in the first part of 1935. A member of the Stresa front – a great power concert with Britain and France – and of the League of Nations at this time, Italy had a thirty-eight division army and appeared to be a mature and militarily significant supporter of the international order. There was some sense, therefore, to Gamelin's and Denain's entry into military talks with Italian army and air chiefs from May to September 1935.[42] Both the outward respectability and the resources of the Italians gave them an appeal to the French leaders in office at this time.[43]

Yet the allure of Italy in Paris also resulted from the unattractiveness of the British. With Germany openly rearming, French leaders found comfort neither in Whitehall's mood nor in its military capacities. British envoys in Berlin such as Colonel Thorne, then military attaché, reported to London that they were reassured 'categorically' – in this case by General von Reichenau, chief of the Reichswehr ministry staff – that Hitler's reorganisation of the army was a final step. It was not, Thorne reported, a prelude to changes in the Rhineland demilitarised zone that 'might be considered to alter the treaty status'.[44] British military intelligence was unruffled by the increase of Hitler's army in 1935, advising that it did 'not [think] . . . a peace strength of thirty six divisions is excessive in view of the strategic position of Germany, the length of her frontiers and the armed strength of neighbouring powers'. The foreign office in London ascribed to the German generals a belief that the growing technical character of warfare made conscripts 'unsuitable for . . . offensive operations'. The German switch to obligatory service was expected to 'certainly mean a considerable reduction in efficiency as compared with the long-service voluntary army previously possessed'.[45]

This British equanimity was reported to the Quai and the generals in Paris by the French envoys in London – Charles Corbin, the ambassador, and Robert Voruz, the military attaché. The French saw that German initiatives were not judged sufficiently dangerous by the British to warrant the latter opening defensive talks with France. Just as evident was British military incapacity for land operations in Europe. Maurin, as war minister, warned colleagues at the January 1935 HCM meeting that Britain's was merely 'a parade-ground army'.[46] French strategists had to assume that it would not count in the foreseeable future in the continental military balance.

Therefore the French continued to court Italy. On paper Italy possessed imposing and immediately available military forces.[47] Until the attack on Abyssinia in October 1935, it was an attractive alternative to Britain in the sight of Gamelin, Denain, Fabry and Schweisguth. These French defence chiefs were obsessed with what Germany intended to do and with the steps France might take to baulk her. As Maurin stated in April 1935 – according to Britain's military attaché in Paris, France was concerned because 'Germany had hitherto been surrounded by a wall of paper [the 1919 and 1925 treaties]; within that . . . she had grown and provided herself with formidable military means . . . [making it] impossible to foretell with any accuracy in what direction the armed forces of Germany would move once the wall . . . was completely torn down'.[48]

Imagery of this type was, of course, a further example of the conscious 'use of fear' by French leaders – this time to direct British attention to Europe's threatened territorial stability. For, in 1935, French intelligence was piecing together an uncommonly accurate estimation of German intentions as well as capabilities. From this data Gamelin and Georges were drafting something close to a timetable of likely German initiatives and were using this to strengthen their case for obtaining greater resources for French defence.[49]

Notwithstanding the withdrawal of France's last Rhineland garrisons in 1930, there was no shortage of information reaching the French high command about Germany's clandestine military build-up between 1930 and 1935. French awareness resulted from the investigations – both overt and covert – of their army's office of intelligence assessment, the 2e Bureau, headed down to 1935 by Colonel Louis Koeltz and from 1935 to 1940 by Colonel Maurice Gauché. These were reinforced by the surveillance conducted by the French army's secret service, the Service de Renseignements et de Contre-Espionnage (SR), headed from 1928 to 1934 by Lieutenant-Colonel Edmond Laurent (later sent by Gamelin to Belgium as military attaché in 1937–40), from 1934 to 1936 by Colonel Roux, and from 1936 to 1940 by Colonel Louis Rivet.[50] Via the informants, spies, cryptography and listening posts operated by these agencies the French obtained extensive knowledge of the German evasions of Versailles.

The precision of much of the French information suggests that many historians have greatly overstated the supposed delapidation of French policy and intelligence analysis in the 1930s.[51] Of course the integration of intelligence into diplomatic deliberations on the one hand or decision-taking on the other was not perfect. An example of weakness may have been the slender linkage between the war ministry and the Quai d'Orsay. This depended on a solitary liaison officer, Colonel Paul de

Villelume, from 1935 to 1938. Only in May of the latter year was this connection reinforced when a weekly liaison committee was established under the chairmanship of one of Gamelin's deputy chiefs of the army staff, General Henri Dentz, an intelligence specialist. This finally brought Quai officials and senior figures from the defence ministry together on a regular basis.[52]

Nevertheless, the shortcomings often attributed to the previous system must not be exaggerated. Schweisguth's daily diary – kept whilst he was deputy chief of army staff with responsibility for intelligence and liaison with France's allies between April 1935 and August 1937 – abounds with reports of Villelume's work in army-Quai coordination. As a busy go-between, Villelume provided a connection that in practice belied accusations that the foreign ministry and the military did not communicate with one another.[53] On the intelligence side, too, the civilian and military resources were not working in isolation from each other. Both the published *Documents Diplomatiques* and the archives plainly show that French service attachés routinely briefed their ambassador or head of mission. The specialists whom France maintained in her embassies and legations were not troglodytes labouring secretively behind closed doors, each studiously shunning contact with his colleagues. On the contrary, French military attachés collaborated closely with the economic experts alongside them in order to gain as comprehensive an intelligence picture as possible. Good cooperation existed in Berlin between François-Poncet, ambassador from 1931 to 1938, and General Georges Renondeau, his military attaché.[54] This was matched – perhaps bettered – by the first-class work of the French envoys in London. There a well-oiled machine served the head of the embassy at Albert Gate in Knightsbridge. The ambassador to the Court of St James from 1933 to 1940 was a seasoned diplomat, Charles Corbin, whose urbanity, cultivation and social position enabled him to move comfortably among the milieux of Whitehall and the clubland of Pall Mall. Alongside Corbin, the French military attachés were officers of great discretion and wide experience: General Robert Voruz, posted to London from 1929 to 1936, and his successor, General Albert Lelong, a personal nominee of Gamelin.[55] Beside these observers were other specialists whose work deepened the French knowledge of military, political and economic conditions in Britain. The industrious and long-serving assistant military attaché, Colonel Cuny, was one; others included the financial and commercial attachés, Emmanuel Monick and Méric de Bellefon, and the counsellors of embassy, Roger Cambon and Roland de Margerie (both scions of renowned diplomatic dynasties).[56]

Men of this calibre on the spot served to ensure that there was no shortage of sound intelligence and advice reaching policy-makers in Paris. The accomplishments of French envoys – civilians and servicemen alike – deserve to be recorded. Noteworthy, too, was the considerable consultation that occurred in Paris itself between the military and the Quai. The latter received frequent briefings from the defence ministry's liaison officer, Colonel de Villelume. From time to time, too, the secretary-general himself, Alexis Léger, conferred with Gamelin and other senior generals.[57] Furthermore, the foreign ministry benefited directly from the intelligence obtained through military attachés – even though the latter were soldiers on secondment with temporary diplomatic accreditation, rather than members of the diplomatic corps in the strict sense. As Colonel Jacques Minart, an officer in Gamelin's *cabinet* during the phoney war, explained: 'military attachés could communicate with Paris only via the intermediary of our diplomatic representatives abroad. Their reports went to the Quai d'Orsay. The minister of national defence was apprised of them by this channel alone.'[58]

The general staff, then, had neither first nor exclusive sight of the reports filed by its own military observers. Despatches submitted by the attachés were conveyed by diplomatic pouch to the foreign ministry – and only thereafter forwarded to the 2e Bureau. Not surprisingly, the relationship between the high command and the diplomats was subject to change. Cooperation between the two bodies appears to have undergone a serious deterioration just before and during the early stages of the war. By the time the conflict began, Gamelin was expressing jaundiced views about the Quai. Perhaps he was seeking a scapegoat for France's failure to construct a multilateral eastern front to support Poland in the summer of 1939. At any rate he complained to his *cabinet* on 18 September 1939 that the Quai was

not organised to work [effectively]. Our most distinguished ambassadors write out their own telegrams, the embassy secretary doing no more than to encode them. Their mornings are spent drafting reports to their minister and their evenings in attending receptions ... Moreover, and as a result, they neither know how, nor have the ability, to work quickly and so are always behindhand and pre-empted by events.[59]

Additional grist to the mill of Gamelin's criticism was provided that month by a former French ambassador to Turkey. This diplomat, visiting Vincennes, volunteered an extraordinary tirade against his old service. An ambassador of France, he claimed, was 'characteristically an isolated individual in a country he often barely knows. For six months he's out of his depth; after a couple of years he knows it like a high school student; after three years like a graduate.' This critic thought that ambassadors had too narrow a range of contacts and travelled too little. Much of their reporting amounted to little more than a digest of the local press. 'One is tempted to ask: "And what do *you* think?" The military or naval attaché, charged with watching several countries, gets around and is thus far more knowledgeable than the diplomat.'[60] Evidently Gamelin – at any rate by the phoney war – shared this disillusionment with the work of the French foreign service.

Yet it would be misleading to assume that the making of French external policy was bedevilled *throughout* the 1930s by a lack of regard and absence of coordination between the general staff and the Quai d'Orsay. There are many instances – not least during the early months of Gamelin's command in 1935 – of the different French agencies performing and cooperating smoothly in their collection, appraisal and exchange of intelligence about Germany. French officials at this time were neither unduly alarmist nor blindly complacent. They did not at first exaggerate the revisionist intent of Hitler's policy, or the readiness of German military power; but nor did they underestimate or ignore them.

In April 1935 Léger's British counterpart, Sir Robert Vansittart, permanent under-secretary at the Foreign Office, heard that the French general staff 'consider Germany will be ready for serious aggression by the spring of 1936'. This, he minuted, might 'be an exaggeration; but it will only be a slight one'.[61] German capabilities were adduced with uncommon accuracy. In February 1935, for example, the Belgian ambassador in Paris, Baron de Gaiffier, reported to Brussels a talk he had had with Gamelin, in which 'the generalissimo [said] he did not believe Germany about to commit immediate aggression but had his fears for the spring of 1936'.[62] Similarly, when the French staff analysed the implications of Germany's return to conscription in March 1935, Gamelin 'estimated that the danger was greater for 1936 than for 1935 and that the alarm signal would be when Germany denounced the demilitarisation of the Rhineland'.[63] Three days after this the head of the 2e Bureau, Colonel Koeltz, warned Britain's military attaché that 'by next year Germany would probably be in a position to make war if she wished'.[64]

In part, warnings of this ilk were issued in order to concentrate the minds of other Locarno signatories on the formulation of a common response in case Hitler attempted a territorial revision in the west. A major French aim was to achieve prior diplomatic coordination with the British and the Belgians. It was to this end that Laval, then French foreign minister, gave an *aide-mémoire* on 23 March 1935 to Anthony Eden, the British minister for League affairs. The French note evaluated possible German initiatives. It was 'highly desirable', it estimated, that the governments which were concerned with the Rhineland's status should not be surprised by a German coup but should, rather, 'know in advance how they would react in such a circumstance'.[65] Such French *démarches*, added to British intelligence, were not without results. Evaluating the drift of Franco-German relations, the Foreign Office estimated in July 1935 that Hitler 'would not be averse to remilitarisation' if there were the slightest sign that the other Locarno signatories 'did not intend to honour their obligations'.[66]

Gamelin's attention to the Rhineland question was, however, not simply a ploy to engineer improved Anglo-Franco-Belgian solidarity. His concern grew from a belief that Hitler was operating to a more-or-less defined design or plan for revision of the entire 1919 settlement. It was a belief that was fed by French intelligence. The French had obtained indications that Hitler would seek to expand southwards and eastwards. They concluded that this objective would compel him to seek an early improvement of German military security in the west. French intelligence offered projections based on their information as to the pace of Germany's military revival. This suggested a timetable in which the spring of 1936 appeared to be the moment Hitler would choose for an attempt to eliminate the demilitarised zone. In May 1935 the peacetime strength of the German army was believed to be twenty-one infantry divisions, two cavalry divisions, two independent cavalry brigades and one light armoured division. This force was known to be expanding swiftly towards a target of thirty-six divisions: officer training schools were being enlarged to produce the cadres required for the new forces. In mid-1935 the French credited Germany with the means to field their twenty-one regular divisions after only four days of mobilisation, reinforced with another thirty-five reserve and *ersatz* divisions after a further eleven days. Before the year ended, French intelligence believed the mobilisation time for the German regulars had been cut to just three days, greatly worsening the danger of an *attaque brusquée* on the French–Belgian frontiers and incomplete Maginot Line.[67]

In spite of their concerns, however, the French did not panic. All in all, Georges told Britain's military attaché, Germany was not reckoned capable before 1939 of launching a full-scale attack in the west akin to the invasion of 1914.[68] The 2e Bureau predicted that Hitler's ambitions in the east would absorb him for several years in building a hegemony over central Europe and the Balkans. This perspicacious estimate was pressed by Gauché, after he succeeded Koeltz as chief of the 2e Bureau in 1935. Such views tended to direct the attention of Gamelin, Georges and Schweisguth to the need to find alternatives to the Rhineland as a route to French friends in eastern and south-eastern Europe. One result was the concern shown by French military leaders in 1935–6 for the friendship of Italy – a country which French strategists thought might function as a 'land bridge' and link to the Yugoslavs, Czechs and Poles. With these projects in view, Schweisguth was working by September 1935 with the chief of the operations bureau, Colonel Louis Buisson, to explore French options in case Germany forced the issue over the Rhineland.[69]

The French courtship of Italy that ensued was a remarkable affair. In twelve short months it progressed from a whirlwind romance and an impassioned honeymoon to an embittered estrangement on account of Mussolini's attack on Abyssinia. The liaison, almost surreptitious in the beginning when Laval visited Rome in January 1935, flowered into a public embrace once Laval became prime minister in June 1935.

The story of the political *rapprochement* has been recounted elsewhere. What is of concern here is the strategic dimension.[70] The chief architect of this was Laval's war minister, Jean Fabry. An inveterate opponent of communism, Fabry was not the least troubled by associations with fascist Italy. Having arrived at the rue Saint-Dominique, he enthusiastically set about encouraging the Franco-Italian diplomatic coupling to bear progeny in the shape of defence accords. Fabry was a distinguished war veteran who had lost a leg whilst leading his regiment on the western front in 1915. In 1919 he entered national politics, securing election to the 'horizon blue' chamber on the list of the *bloc national*. Veteran and *mutilé de guerre*, Fabry epitomised the conservative and fiercely germanophobic character of that assembly. Until defeated in 1936 by a Popular Front socialist, Fabry held one of the seats for the 10e arrondissement of Paris. A member of the Democratic Alliance, one of the two mainstream conservative parties (whose luminaries included Tardieu, Flandin and Reynaud), Fabry built his reputation as a 'constant speaker on all questions connected with security and national defence'.[71] From this platform he advocated repressive policies towards Germany and the maintenance of a strong French defence posture. He advanced his views equally trenchantly in the columns of his own newspaper, *L'Intransigeant*, a journal of obdurately conservative persuasion. By 1935 Fabry had become a self-appointed 'friend of the army' and had inherited the mantle of that other celebrated *mutilé* of the war, André Maginot. Indeed it was Maginot whom Fabry succeeded in 1928 in the presidency of the Chamber army commission – and, as this group's minutes demonstrate, he employed this forum to become chief conservative defence spokesman.

By June 1935 he had become as natural a selection for the war ministry as Maginot himself had been seven years before.

Fabry's appointment was greeted with high hopes inside the general staff. The new minister was expected to inaugurate an era of civil-military reconciliation and steadfast priority for a strong defence. Indeed Fabry's nomination was the object of eager lobbying by the former chief of the general staff, General Marie-Eugène Debeney. Senior officers looked forward to an end to the conflicts of the Cartel years and the disappointing drift experienced under Pétain.[72]

Gamelin found, however, that Fabry was exasperatingly inconsistent. On the one hand, he actively promoted the liaison between the French and Italian armed forces that had been developing since the start of air staff discussions in May 1935 between General Denain, the French air minister, and his Italian counterpart, General Valle. On the other hand, Fabry proved to be irresolute when required to battle against the finance ministry and procurement executives to win resources and priority for the re-equipment of the French army.

On the first count, the Franco-Italian strategic courtship produced Gamelin's visit to Rome in June 1935, and an agreement with Badoglio, chief of the Italian general staff, for planning to exchange a French corps to north-east Italy with an Italian corps to Belfort in the event of a crisis between France and Germany.[73] This arrangement pleased senior French officers: it promised a means to combine French, Italian and Yugoslav forces in a cordon of containment to the south of Germany. More enticingly still, the accord offered means of relief to the French military at a time when they foresaw their strategic balance *vis-à-vis* Germany tilting in favour of the Reich. For the more cordial relations with Rome seemed to present an opportunity to Gamelin 'to withdraw practically all the troops from the Franco-Italian frontier, and in addition ... to withdraw practically the whole of the North African troops from Tunis and Algiers'.[74] Field Marshal Sir Archibald Montgomery-Massingberd, British chief of the Imperial General Staff, visited France in August 1935 as a guest of Gamelin. The latter claimed to his visitor that the Franco-Italian understanding would enable him to strengthen French forces facing Germany by fifteen or sixteen divisions in the event of general mobilisation.[75] This estimate may, of course, have been intentionally inflated: Gamelin wished the British to be in no doubt as to the store the French army set by its better relations with Rome. Internal calculations by the general staff in Paris suggest that they thought the agreement with Italy worth an extra ten divisions for the French order-of-battle opposite Germany.[76] Irrespective of the exact size of the force capable of redeployment, it was clear that France stood to make major military gains from friendship with Mussolini. This prospect – together with the impending completion of the Maginot Line – explained for Montgomery-Massingberd the 'much greater atmosphere of confidence amongst all the French officers . . . as regards the danger of attack from Germany'.[77]

Thus the outbreak of the Italo-Abyssinian war late in 1935 had far-reaching consequences for French military confidence and for the Franco-German balance of power. In the space of a few weeks in October and November that year, Gamelin saw the shattering of his great design to contain German revisionism – a design that had sought to couple the numerous standing forces of the Italians with the imperial and economic long-war resources of the British. For Gamelin on a practical level, as well as for Laval and Fabry at a level of political affinities, the autumn of 1935 was a season of gathering gloom and dashed hopes. British observers remarked on the visible discontent of French leaders whose schemes lay in ruins. In August Montgomery-Massingberd had told Lord Halifax (then secretary of state for war), that 'from a [French] military point of view, any break with Italy on account of Abyssinia would be most unwelcome'. From his talks with Gamelin the British field marshal had concluded that the 'attention of . . . senior French officers' was 'concentrated on the German menace' and that the 'question of what Italy likes to do in Abyssinia looms very small indeed'.[78] The war that erupted in east Africa proved mortifying not just to Laval and his Italophile statecraft but also to the calculations of the French defence chiefs.

In June 1935 French officers were affably exchanging plans with their counterparts in Rome. By November, however, French military leaders were conferring urgently over the measures that might need to be taken against Mussolini if the war of words over the latter's aggression in Abyssinia were to degenerate into a war of bombs and bullets. Confronted by a rapidly deepening antagonism between Britain, with her strong League sympathies, and Italy, the French were forced into an agonised choice. As Gamelin reflected, Italian assistance would be valuable to the security of France; but that of Britain was essential.[79]

With extreme reluctance the French defence authorities agreed to accede to Britain's request that repair facilities in French ports be made available to the Royal Navy. Under subsequent pressure the French went on to consent to the use of French maritime bases for British naval operations against Italy. After great heart-searching the French naval staff agreed to divide the Mediterranean into French and British zones of maritime operations. In vain did Badoglio – aghast at the danger of conflict with France and Britain – tug at French military loyalties by sending Gamelin a personal telegram that reaffirmed the validity of the June accords and pledged Badoglio to resign rather than make war on France.[80]

The need to choose between Italy and Britain disappointed Gamelin. He had hoped to have his cake as well as eat it. Having been forced to give up the short-lived special relationship with Rome, the general was determined to exact concessions in return from the British. The naval conversations initiated over security in the Mediterranean presented Gamelin with just the opportunity he desired: he decided to bargain them against a resumption of staff talks with the British army. As a further argument with which to lead the British in the desired direction, the French generals chose to stress the interdependence of land, sea and air forces in modern strategy.[81]

To encourage this way of reasoning to sink into the minds of the British – and also because they genuinely feared provoking Italy any further – Gamelin, Colson and Schweisguth played for time. They emphasised French military unpreparedness. They sought to encourage the British to drag out diplomatic *démarches* to Rome, to remain flexible and defer a descent down into the abyss of war.[82]

As this crisis in Anglo-Franco-Italian relations ran its course at the close of 1935 the dominant mood among French statesmen and service leaders was one of frustration. They were exasperated by their powerlessness in the face of the disintegration of the strategic edifice which they had so ingeniously fabricated earlier in the year. The impotence experienced by Gamelin as well as by Laval was, of course, a reflection of underlying French national weakness. Discontented with the behaviour of the British, French leaders nevertheless felt insufficiently strong to shun Britain altogether. The French navy, for instance, urgently needed to conclude arrangements with the Admiralty in London for the case of a Franco-German war. Yet, when the naval conversations occasioned by the Mediterranean crisis resulted in an Anglo-French naval agreement in January 1936, the latter made no mention of Germany. In relations between Paris and London it was the British who dictated the agenda in 1935.[83]

At the turn of 1935–6, France was undergoing a severe loss of confidence. Intelligence informed Gamelin that Italian military formations in Europe were being depleted by the despatch of their cadres and equipment to Abyssinia and Libya. It warned, too, that a political *rapprochement* between Mussolini and Hitler lay on the horizon and that European preoccupations were receding into second place on the agenda of the Duce.[84] To make matters still more worrying, there was scant satisfaction for Gamelin in the meetings held in Paris, on 9–10

December 1935, when the French and British army and air staffs met at last. As the senior envoy from the war office on the British team later recollected, 'Gamelin stood me an excellent lunch at Drouant's, but it was clear that nothing was going to happen.'[85]

The year 1936 promised to be difficult and dangerous for France. Gamelin expected it to bring the German remilitarisation of the Rhineland. After a year in the loneliness of high command, Gamelin had taken the measure of the task before him and drew breath to face the challenge. What comes through in the general's outlook at this time is his quiet resolution. As Montgomery-Massingberd had observed, there was a 'determination to make . . . France secure against attack and, on General Gamelin's part, a fixed purpose to supply . . . [his] army with the best modern equipment he can get'.[86]

The struggle ahead of Gamelin involved, on the one hand, an endeavour to match the progress of German rearmament. Yet, on the other hand, it demanded all-out effort to repair relations with Britain. Gamelin grasped the importance of building upon the fragile foundation represented by the Paris meetings of December 1935 – 'a resumption of talks [as he said to his senior staff] whose development could be very useful *vis-à-vis* Germany'.[87] After twelve months of constructing castles in the air with the Italians, Gamelin had reluctantly concluded that there was nothing for it but to rebuild the *entente*. Gamelin now had a policy: he would present the French army confidently to outsiders, avoiding 'giving the impression that it could not or would not do anything'. His objective was, in the short term, to 'give the British an impression of our military strength and our good will'.[88] Gamelin had resolved to depict France as a partner who could do as much for Britain as Britain could do for her. On learning, at a Haut Comité Militaire meeting on 21 November 1935, that Laval had been using both the ambassador in Berlin, François-Poncet, and an unofficial emissary, the right-wing businessman Count Fernand de Brinon, to explore the basis for an appeasement of Germany, Gamelin broke angrily with the advocates of accommodation. In a note written during a sleepless night after the meeting, the general expressed his anguish and disgust for politicians prepared to go cap in hand to do deals with Hitler. Such cravenness, he thought, was demeaning, unworthy of France. Its perpetrators were not fit to wear the mantle of Clemenceau and Poincaré.[89] With a policy that set such store by France strengthening herself, Gamelin had to ensure that 1936 marked the commencement of French rearmament.

3   First responses: defence versus détente in the Laval era

Laval's policy in 1935–6 rested on economics that were rigidly conceived and rigorously enforced. Drastic deflation was initiated by across-the-board axing of public expenditure and imposed by decree-laws. This crude tool was wielded to try to hew away France's worsening budget deficit and stiffening economic inertia. The armed forces had seen, from the proposals over which Flandin had lost office, that new military procurement would get no immunity from Laval's cuts. The ground had been laid for acrimony over defence credits to break out once more between generals and politicians. But this time the latter were of the right rather than the left. For many defence chiefs this disintegration of a sympathy previously taken for granted between the military and political conservatives raised new and uncharted hazards for security policy. Senior officers viewed with alarm the breakdown of a traditional consensus. Nor was their anxiety eased by Gamelin's own unusual coolness towards the political right, his reputation as a particularly 'republican' and left-inclined general.[1]

Before Flandin's ministry fell in May 1935, the battle-lines over curbs on military spending were drawn. The government, in April, approved outlays of 481 million francs in the remainder of that year. This, though, drew on the special account extracted from parliament by Pétain and Maurin in October–November 1934 and voted in January 1935. By May it was being argued by controller-general Pierre Guinand, the civil service head of the war ministry secretariat responsible for administering the department's budget, that 500 million francs would be 'more than sufficient' for the army for the rest of that year.[2] To the soldiers, Guinand must have appeared – just when German rearmament had become overt – to be playing a Trojan horse role inside the rue Saint-Dominique for the parsimonious functionaries of the finance ministry. By 25 May he had induced Maurin, a retired general and sometime inspector of motorisation, not only to cut the army's immediate expenditure in 1935 from the approved 481 million francs to 400 million but also to permit new armaments allocations to take the full brunt of this economy. Finally the minister agreed to extend the re-equipment effort over three years, 1935 to 1937, to ease the annual financial burden, despite the price of entailing an additional twelve-month delay in the complete provision to field formations of urgently needed new-generation tanks and artillery.[3]

The war ministry's daily diary, an informative and inside source, illuminates the struggle over military credits and armaments priorities waged during Laval's government. The chief protagonists were the finance minister, Marcel Régnier, enthusiastically supported by his prime minister, and the general staff. The diary reveals that Fabry, for all his credentials as a defence expert in the conservatives' political circle, quite failed to stop the axe of financial stringency from damaging seriously the pace and breadth of the army's re-equipment programme after June 1935.[4]

Naturally the generals at first hoped that Fabry would secure a restoration of the army's prestige in the country, matched by a renewed sense in the cabinet of priority for the urgent fulfilment of its procurement plans. Gamelin for his part had already opposed Maurin's acceptance of the deferment to the end of 1937 of the existing re-equipment programme's completion. In early June 1935 there were deceptively heartening signs when Schweisguth noted that Fabry, too, intended to seek the necessary finance before conceding reductions in new equipment orders. On 12 June Fabry wrote to Régnier proposing immediate confirmation of the three-year expenditure timetable, so that the war ministry could at least place contracts with manufacturers. The next day, however, a dark picture of impending budgetary and currency disaster was painted to a meeting of the cabinet by Régnier and Laval. The latter emphasised the requirement to retrench, eliminate waste and postpone public works programmes, to 'redress the economy'. This marked, for the army, the beginning of a fight to fund their re-equipment plans which dominated the rest of 1935.[5]

Increased spending for the new military systems conflicted directly with Laval's policy of 'sound finance'. The start given to the army's new programme by Pétain's and Maurin's opening of special armaments credits in July and November 1934 (confirmed during Flandin's government), was checked as Laval tightly controlled all expenditures, including those in the defence sector. Facing a government deficit for the 1935 fiscal year of over 10 billion francs, Laval strove to avoid worsening this by extending existing defence contracts and set his face adamantly against opening new ones.[6] This policy had a two-fold effect for the war ministry. Firstly, during the life of Laval's government it ensured a continuation of conflict over implementing military programmes. This conflict disrupted civil-military relations and poisoned discussion of strategy as well as armaments policy. A persistent failure to evolve long-range coherence between France's foreign policy and its strategic capabilities was this discord's most serious product.[7]

The second consequence of Laval's economic approach, for the defence sector, was felt in the medium term, between Laval's resignation in January 1936 and the announcement of the Popular Front's rearmament plan, the first truly meriting the name, on 7 September 1936. This consequence was the stagnation, in some areas real decline, of military output from French industry in that timescale – something itself deriving from defence procurement's considerable lead-time from specification configuration, through tendering and prototyping, to trials, production and delivery. Laval's insistence on minimising commitments of finance significantly delayed contract signatures from mid-1935 until at least the end of 1936. Total defence expenditures in 1935 absorbed 22 per cent of aggregate state spending. In 1936, despite the continued rise of German power and the deterioration of previously good relations with Italy, the proportion (excluding the Popular Front allocations which were not felt before 1937), had grown only to 24 per cent.[8] The period was, as a result, characterised by uncooperative practices in military-industrial relations which slowed up receipt of equipment and eroded general staff self-confidence. This was in turn reflected in advice to the Quai d'Orsay urging accommodating policies rather than risky resistance to the dictator powers. The impact of budgetary policy of Laval's kind on French military-industrial resources showed itself in businessmen's extreme wariness towards government. As Maurin, restored to the war ministry in the Albert Sarraut government that succeeded Laval's in January 1936, insisted in March 1936, whilst justifying supplementary armaments finance to the deputies:

above all we must overcome this inertia . . . which is so understandable among our industrialists. These businessmen see their order-books full up to a given date. This applies now for assault tanks. The orders . . . run out in August and it is wholly natural that we advise them that these orders will be extended . . . But the credits envisaged for 1936 for this, allowing for the funding deferred, have . . . been revealed as inadequate.[9]

Underlying the damage done by Laval and Régnier to the rhythm of armaments' production was the practice of waiting until all previously voted funds were absorbed by industry and then treating extensions of contracts individually. This meant that funds flowed in drips and dribbles, not as a steady stream. Such a system was to delay the completion of the army's programmes by necessitating the extension of delivery schedules into 1936. Not only this, but under Laval 'the military credits in the 1936 budget which he had voted a few days before his government's fall were actually planned to be lower than those of the previous year. The rearmament process was, by this, slightly interrupted.'[10]

Laval's policies first forced a 270 million franc cut on the army's three-year re-equipment programme sanctioned by Flandin. This was, because of Fabry's intervention, admittedly less than the 300 million reduction desired by Régnier. On 18 June, however, after talks between Laval, Piétri, the minister of marine, and representatives from the war and finance ministries, it was decided that not only should the army's re-equipment be extended but that no accompanying three-year funding plan would be presented to the Chamber. Instead, the government opted to open any 'indispensable new credits' at an unspecified future date, if required. This manoeuvre reduced criticism of Laval in the Chamber during the infancy of his administration. Yet its practical effect was to suspend the millstone of short-term contracts with uncertain renewal clauses around the necks of the general staff and their industrial suppliers. As Gamelin warned the consultative committee for armaments, 'the industrialists only manufacture for us if they know that they will be paid without abnormal delays'.[11] Worse was to follow for the generals.

On 21 June 1935 the full cabinet met, approving the decisions taken by Laval and senior colleagues three days before. These had confirmed an immediate expenditure of 500 million francs in 1935 and 600 million as a first tranche of the 1936 expenditure, together with an undertaking to open a further 400 million franc credit after August 1935, to ensure continuity of orders. But the attendant legislation, presented to the Chamber on 24 June, ran straight into heavy cross-fire from the parliamentary commissions. For four days ministers suffered sniping over the scale and necessity of these allocations. Before the Chamber's army and finance commissions, Fabry argued that the offensive strength of the Germans made funds for new equipment 'indispensable if we are to assure our security'. Interviewed by the same finance commission on 27 June, Régnier had to account for the use made of *all* national defence credits voted since 1920. He had to assure the socialist deputy Jules Moch, who sought strict controls on alleged profiteering by arms manufacturers, that the finance ministry would scrutinise all future military expenditure 'vigorously and rigorously'.[12]

Following these inquisitions the government's Bill was returned to the

Chamber for debate on 28 June. The left had carefully laid an ambush for Laval. They were buoyed up by the surge in confidence given them through preparing their enormous Rassemblement Populaire in the capital on Bastille Day, a fortnight later. Laval sensed quickly the hostility which talk of sizeable new military credits had aroused at the time of his appeals for an acceptance of austerity during the attempt to deflate rapidly back to budgetary balance (condemned already as 'the decree-laws of distress' by the left). The Palais Bourbon rang to emotionally charged speeches as the socialists, Radicals and communists drew strength from their agreement to seal a political pact for a 'Popular Front' with which to make common cause in fighting the Chamber elections due in April–May 1936. One weather-vane indicating the prevailing political wind was the demand that Laval faced from the socialist deputy and future minister of labour, Paul Ramadier, for checks on the 'merchants of death' and for an 'effective control to prevent the return to scandalous profiteering in arms'. Under such attack Laval took the line of least resistance and, with parliament dispersing on 30 June for the summer recess until early October, withdrew the legislation without hazarding a vote on its passage.[13]

On 2 July Laval's cabinet met again. The majority of ministers expressed their 'wish to speed up the squeeze on public expenditure'. Gamelin was taken by surprise and only learned of these developments after his return to Paris from Rome, where he had gone on 25 June for talks with Badoglio, the Italian chief of staff. Wrong-footed on this specific instance, Gamelin grasped that crucial policy on military funding was being made without any professional military input.[14]

Against this backdrop of talks with Italy and deflationary economics, Fabry, Colson and Guinand met in early July to formulate a fresh request for credits of 960 million francs to assure equipment orders into 1936. Laval's economic policy, however, militated against their aspirations. At a cabinet meeting on 9 July Laval confirmed that, beyond the outlay of 600 million francs in 1936 previously agreed, 'no other credit will be allowed until parliament resumes its sittings, except in the event of exceptional circumstances'.[15] Furthermore, on 24 July the government bowed again to left-wing pressure by instituting a special tax on the profits of firms working on defence contracts. In August, during an extraordinary cabinet meeting at the Elysée Palace, chaired by the president of the republic, Albert Lebrun, still more decree-laws for the 'economic renovation' of the country were adopted, avowedly designed to achieve 'the moral cleansing of business and the protection of savings'.[16]

Meanwhile, discussions progressed between Guinand and Régnier over the war ministry's annual regular budget estimates for 1936. These meetings revealed that Régnier wanted to cut the army's allocation by another 600 million francs in addition to the 650 million reduction which the estimates already incorporated over those of the year before. Fabry succeeded in moderating the savagery of these further cuts but could not stop the prolonged crisis over defence financing eroding morale in the general staff, exacerbating the difficulties of evolving a coherent ordering policy for new equipment. The episode undid much of the fragile improvement in civil-military relations which had been effected since February 1934.[17]

For the high command, therefore, successive centre-right governments had failed to restore the army's prestige as an unchallengeable national institution. They had equally neglected to shelter it from financial buffetings. At least one general later alleged that the end of the Cartel era had merely marked the start of a 'truce' between the soldiers and the civilian authorities in the former's continuing struggle to preserve the army's capabilities as the nation's military and moral defender.[18]

Connected to the question of credits in 1935–6 was the equally important issue of industrial difficulties in military equipment procurement. Armoured vehicle and artillery production revealed these problems most acutely. Manufacturers were reluctant to produce military material for which payment might be substantially delayed because of Régnier's financial controls. A similar disincentive was the question mark which Laval's policies placed against contract renewals. Renault, as an example, hesitated to invest in modernising or increasing mass production plant for military output. Despite the growing menace from German rearmament and the ever more threatening tone of Nazi rhetoric about territorial expansion, French industrialists continued to have sound business reasons in 1935 to deem enlargement of their productive capacity for civil markets a more profitable investment outlet than expansion of their military capacity.[19] Laval's foreign policy, with its sympathy towards Italy and attempted negotiation of an understanding with Germany in the autumn of 1935, encouraged this investment preference. Warlike output would hardly sell readily if diplomacy and peaceful *rapprochement* prevailed. 'It seems', it has been noted regarding military aircraft manufacture, 'that . . . the constructors were loath to invest sizeable sums, fearing a collapse of orders the moment when . . . an international détente came about.'[20] Evidence from the army's tank and vehicle re-equipment programmes suggests that it, too, paid heavily for lack of coordination between service requirements and entrepreneurial interest.

The gravest consequence was the spectacular time-lapse which opened up between rearmament credit allocations and receipt of new equipment by units. This gap in the procurement cycle particularly influenced the assessments which Gamelin offered to the government of France's combat readiness in 1937, and in 1938 during the Sudeten crisis.[21] In respect of tanks and armoured machine-gun carriers, this time-lag in delivery became chronic. At its root was the shrinkage of the military-related capacity in French industry. This had occurred through the contraction of new equipment expenditure in the army budgets of the later 1920s and early 1930s. 'If you want an active industrial sector, and especially an active metallurgical industry', reflected Henri Germain-Martin (finance minister in 1934–5) later, 'it must have a substantial customer base . . . The "absenteeism" of orders from the army was therefore the cause of the prolongation of the crisis.'[22] When the army, in the space of a few months in 1935, took decisions which generated comparatively large orders, every military vehicle manufacturer except Renault, and Hotchkiss to a lesser degree, was faced with contracts too technically demanding for their factories whose machine-tools were decrepit or insufficiently accurate, and whose assembly lines were too small. The orders placed during 1935 alone, by the war ministry, were enough to absorb the shrunken capacity of France's armaments industries. Laval's deflationary policies left no place for costly state subsidies to expand that capacity, even in such a strategic sector.[23]

The nature and seriousness of the problems struck the soldiers when new equipment was presented for evaluation. Thus, although numerous companies had submitted prototypes after the CSG's decision in March 1934 to order new generation infantry-support tanks (to replace the obsolete 1917 Renault FT model), trials at Vincennes Camp in spring 1935 were problem ridden. The Hotchkiss tank had design faults. The models from Batignolles and from Forges et Chantiers de la Méditerranée (FCM) suffered prototype production delays and could not even be tested in the intended competition. Therefore, as Schweisguth noted, although the army favoured giving several firms simultaneous orders, 'Renault, alone, is in fit shape to deliver immediately in a significant quantity.'[24] The consultative committee for armaments placed a contract on 9 April 1935 for 200 R.35 tanks. But it had to withhold ordering a similar number from the other manufacturers because of the unavailability of proven prototypes. A further 600 anti-tank guns were added to an order for over 800 passed by Pétain, which was more satisfactory. On the other hand, heavy tanks, where immediate needs were estimated at 50 Chars D2 and 70 Chars B1 (the best armed and armoured in the world), also presented acute problems. Only three B1 prototypes existed in June 1935, despite recognition of the design's unexcelled quality, and an order placed at the end of 1934 had been for just seven of the type. Such hesitancy by the soldiers had given the producers no incentive to set plant up to make more and to introduce mechanised methods. Thus delivery remained slow, the complexity of the design necessitating costly individual construction of each tank by skilled labour. They remained the Rolls-Royce of armoured vehicles.[25]

Equally disturbing for the soldiers was the news, conveyed by Gamelin to the consultative committee, that for the April order of 200 R.35 tanks 'we must reckon with at least a year's lapse between letting the contract and taking the first deliveries of series production'.[26] This delay, affecting the army's combat-readiness, was partly the result of the soldiers' hesitation in 1933–4 about adopting a particular tank type for infantry support. Histories of the Renault firm demonstrate that the war ministry's armaments' production directorate inadequately grasped the company's need to possess assured long-term orders before investing substantially in new machine-tools and before converting capacity tooled for car, lorry and bus manufacture to armoured vehicle output. Although Renault resisted the depression's effects on the automobile market more sturdily than Citroën (who required a major financial rescue in 1935), they were nonetheless facing stiff competition from Peugeot, their other principal rival. Gamelin and Fabry therefore had to re-establish the war ministry as a worthwhile customer in Renault's eyes, since '... [down] to 1935 low budgets, doctrinal confusion and the army's reluctance to make large purchases of what would soon be obsolete or at best worn-out equipment kept orders for specialised military vehicles small'.[27]

Indeed Renault, having withstood the civilian market's recession, was planning to consolidate its relative commercial strength in the spring of 1935 by trimming prices, modifying its product range and attacking new or temporarily lost markets. Its automobile output for 1935 surpassed that for 1929 by 8 per cent. Furthermore, despite the economic difficulties of the period, new plant for civil production was constructed in the first half of the 1930s, in addition to development at the main Billancourt factories. Simultaneously Renault entered aircraft manufacturing. This commercial diversification, allied to comparative financial and product soundness, strengthened Renault during negotiations with the war ministry over implementing the army's re-equipment programme.[28]

Through the winter of 1934–5 Renault successfully resisted a government campaign to make the firm move its military production away from Paris to Le Mans (where they already had a commercial vehicle factory). In particular the war ministry endeavoured to persuade Renault to transfer tank manufacture to Le Mans. The generals feared for the vulnerability of France's defence-related industries which, concentrated in the Paris suburbs, presented inviting targets for the Luftwaffe in the event of Franco-German conflict.[29]

Renault, however, marshalled business reasons to justify its unwillingness to cooperate with the ministry's plans for this decentralisation. The firm doubted that military orders would continue to grow sufficiently in 1935–6 to warrant the disproportionately heavy capital investment required to build the Le Mans plant. Renault estimated that 50 million francs would have to be spent on new machine-tools alone before Le Mans could manufacture tanks. The total investment for the relocation was costed at 90 million francs (15 million less than the value of the April contract for 200 R.35 tanks), according to an 11 May 1935 report to Colson by General Bloch-Dassault, the director of armaments at the rue Saint-Dominique.[30]

After considering these difficulties, the generals agreed on a final appeal to Renault. Yet they did not offer military funding to assist the company's move. On 14 May war ministry officials met Renault directors, but the latter reaffirmed their commercial interest in developing on concentrated sites in south-west Paris. The Le Mans tank project was abandoned.[31] Among this episode's revealing aspects is the fact that this outcome to discussions over a pivotal part of France's preparations to sustain a long war – the diversification of the geographical siting of the nation's military vehicle assembly plants – occurred without parliamentary consultations. Indeed there does not even appear to have been any inter-departmental government debate on the issues involved. Only in March 1936, almost a year later, did Germany's unilateral remilitarisation of the Rhineland provoke agitated parliamentarians into extended interrogation of rue Saint-Dominique technicians about France's flawed strategic readiness. Only then was there an airing within the walls of the Chamber and the Palais du Luxembourg of the questions raised by Renault's refusal to leave Paris.

Even then, before the Chamber army commission on 18 March 1936, Maurin, then war minister again, only alluded to the continued concentration of Renault's military capacity in the capital within a general statement on industrial decentralisation. 'There must, moreover, not be', the minister contended, 'under the pretext of decentralisation, the re-establishment of concentrations in the interior around certain towns which would be even worse protected than Paris – in the region of Le

Mans, for example.' This was an ingenious – although at first sight believable – camouflaging of the real reason for what Maurin admitted to be 'a very unsatisfactory situation for the factories ... from the standpoint of an air attack ... and one very difficult to improve in any substantial degree'. Buttressing his statement by legitimate reference to the difficulties that regional shortages of skilled labour created for relocation of war industries, Maurin left the Palais Bourbon without the army's conduct of dealings with its equipment suppliers being investigated.[32]

One week later, however, before the Senate's army commission, Colson and Engineer-General Paul Happich (successor as director of armaments to Bloch-Dassault), were aggressively questioned on the specific issue of the siting of Renault's tank factories.[33] This revealed the reasons for the failure of decentralisation. In the process a routine hearing of military technicians became an ultimately influential inquiry into the underlying causes on the production side of the strategically crippling slowness of the renovation of the French army's mechanised equipment. Above all, what emerged was the previously overlooked importance of the links between a long-range guaranteed rearmament plan, concomitant guaranteed orders and funding, and the expansion of the manufacturing base on which scheduled completion of such a plan rested. The war ministry was insufficiently concerned about these problems. Its complacency was exacerbated, it is now clear, by the distracting activities of the professional army lobby, as well as by disputes over re-equipment priorities between Gamelin and the inspectorates of infantry, cavalry and artillery. This neglect of an army equipment strategy worthy of the name, and industry's resultant inability swiftly to increase its military production when requested, was recalled before the post-1945 parliamentary investigation by Germain-Martin, the former finance minister. 'The navy had its armaments programme', he reflected, 'but when did the war ministry come along with one? Not until 1935–36 ... Down to mid-1935 ... I found their indecisiveness, sectional rivalries and administrative pettiness quite heartbreaking.'[34]

More seriously, however, there was clear identification in 1936, for the first time, of the neglect of the link between planning, contracts, funding and expanded manufacturing capacity as a pivotal cause of the army's chronic impoverishment in modern equipment actually with units. The Senate learned, whilst inquiring about why firms would not decentralise, that disincentives to dispersing production were intimately tied to disincentives to invest in expanding capacity. This discovery was, in turn, to fashion an environment favourable to nationalisation as the means of harnessing France's productive possibilities to the speediest fulfilment of the army's rearmament requirements. It was Henri Chéron who got to the heart of government handling of industrial decentralisation and expansion by provoking an exchange on the Renault case with Happich, Colson, and fellow senators Jacquy, Jean Neyret and Eugène Le Moignic:

M. CHÉRON: ... ninety percent of our assault tank production lies within range of enemy air bombing. What is the answer?
GENERAL COLSON: ... We must get the industrialist in question to decentralise his factory's location.
M. CHÉRON: Has he been asked to do this?
GENERAL HAPPICH: He is asking for compensation payments in the order of one billion francs ...
M. CHÉRON: You are risking depriving yourselves at a stroke of your source of tanks ...
GENERAL HAPPICH: M. Renault owns sites at Le Mans, but we have never been able to get agreement from him to move a part of his workshops and relocate them at Le Mans ...
M. CHÉRON: When one is in charge of national defence ... you do not 'seek to get agreement', you issue orders. You are facing a real national peril ...
GENERAL HAPPICH: This is first and foremost a governmental question. I should add that we are engaged in a search for other firms to manufacture for us in future ... the Laffly company has declared itself ready to relocate to Laval. We shall do everything in our power towards this goal.
M. JACQUY: There are doubtless other automobile factories in appropriate sites which would expand if you gave them contracts.
M. NEYRET: ... But put yourself in these businessmen's shoes. You are asking them to build a factory, to commit considerable funds, and yet they are not sure afterwards of having any orders, or face delayed payments from the state of a severity that their cashflows cannot sustain ...
M. LE MOIGNIC: ... Parliament has a responsibility for this state of affairs. If the army and navy could let contracts regularly the programme would unfold smoothly and one could obtain decentralisation. But the orders go in fits and starts ... and then dry up altogether.[35]

What most impressed the senators was the way in which France's lack of governmental economic *dirigisme* was adversely affecting armoured vehicle production, and thus military preparedness.

For the first time, non-socialist politicians were demanding that private industrialists be compelled to conform to policy decisions deemed essential on national security grounds. Asked whether withdrawal of contracts could be tried in order to force Louis Renault to decentralise, Colson retorted that the threat would be no more than an empty bluff because 'He is the only one who can produce our tanks.' It seems likely that this exchange in the army commission converted the

Senate in sufficient numbers to its otherwise surprising cooperativeness, in August 1936, in ratifying the Blum–Daladier legislation which nationalised selected armaments' manufacturers.[36]

Back in 1935, however – and indeed until after the approval of the September 1936 Popular Front rearmament programme – army equipment output was confined within limits determined by existing capacity in defence-contracted companies. This was because 'the state had put the cart before the horses, by reserving the major part of its expenditure for purchases . . . rather than for the renovation of the industry . . .' From this concentration on financing defence orders, rather than on financing the preparation of a war economy, it followed that rearmament funds voted on a year-to-year basis were not absorbable in the same time-scale by the manufacturers. Thus for the air ministry especially, but also for the army, 'the deferment of part of their credits from one year to the next became very significant from 1935 onwards . . .'. Régnier even successfully used the argument that previously voted funds remained partly unspent, during the December 1935 army estimates discussions, to reduce the war ministry's allocation for 1936.[37]

An escape route from this financial-industrial bottleneck, which was threatening strangulation of expansion of vehicle and weapon output, was fast becoming vital. Fabry perhaps perceived one. In his memoirs he commented that 'Possibly the orders . . . still appear small in size . . . [but] they corresponded to the productive capacity of France's armaments factories.' In August 1935, therefore, he set aside his ideological antipathy to collectivist economic measures and reopened, through Guinand, a study originally commissioned by Daladier in 1933 of the benefits obtainable from nationalising certain armaments' producers, specifically Schneider and Brandt. But, possibly because Fabry had no personal belief in state ownership, or perhaps because of the cost of the project and compensation to affected firms, no action followed this study.[38] Clearly, therefore, the motivations behind nationalisation legislation when it came, in August 1936, were at least as 'industrial' as they were ideological. In this, as in other respects, the Vichy-organised Riom Trial investigations of 1940–2 distorted the record. The Pétainist authorities deliberately suppressed the evidence that existed of widespread support before the Popular Front for state control over troublesome sectors of defence equipment manufacture. This support indeed was strong among socialists and communists, but it also extended far beyond the doctrinaire left into the heartland of the French centre-right.[39]

In relations between the war ministry and Renault, the second half of 1935 confirmed that the balance of power remained tilted firmly in favour of suppliers. The wishes of the directorate of armaments manufacture still struggled to make an impression. Having rejected the dispersal into provincial towns of its military plant, Renault built a new armoured vehicle design bureau and assembly line sited deliberately across the Seine from Billancourt, at Issy-les-Moulineaux. The inadequacy of rival firms' military vehicle capacity meant that even the orders for R.35 tanks failed to strengthen the army's bargaining power when disputes arose over in-production cost overruns and delivery delays. As before, the cause lay in Laval's refusal to court parliamentary defeat by tabling legislation to ensure long-term credits for the defence equipment programmes. Only such guarantees would have attracted the investment of reduced private profits into non-commercial productive capacity, new tooling and automated assembly lines. However, neither the general staff nor the war ministry analysed other firms' lack of interest in challenging Renault for military orders in terms of investment incentives.[40]

When the armaments consultative committee next met, on 24 June 1935, Bloch-Dassault reported encouragingly on progress of anti-tank weapon output; 320 of the new 25mm guns had been issued to the infantry, whilst delivery of the remainder of those ordered was anticipated by the year's end. Approval was also given to the artillery inspectorate to test a powerful new 47mm weapon for distribution to divisional commands. The armoured vehicle situation, however, remained disturbing. The army planned to possess a backbone of 1,500 modern light tanks and 100 heavy tanks by the end of 1936, under the Pétain–Maurin programme. But, reported Bloch-Dassault, although Renault could produce 300, rather than the original 200, of the first batch of infantry tanks, Hotchkiss alone had capacity to take a portion of the rest of the order and compete with Renault. The subsequent phases of this programme fell foul of additional delays after Laval, on 21 June, confirmed Maurin's postponement of the entire re-equipment plan's completion into 1937. These industrial and financial constraints thus limited the contracts issued at this juncture for tracked carriers for the infantry of the 20 'active' divisions on the peacetime establishment, together with 30 B1 tanks, 100 cavalry tanks of a new design (the powerful S.35 from the Schneider subsidiary, SOMUA), to re-equip the light mechanised division, and the 300 R.35s.[41]

Fabry also sought at this point to solve the disadvantages stemming from Renault's growing stranglehold over armoured vehicle construction. Although lacking a true monopoly, the extent to which the Billancourt firm was capturing the military market emerged through its success in adding the contract for new cavalry scout and combat machines, the *automitrailleuses de reconnaissance* (AMR) and *automitrailleuses de combat* (AMC) to the June 1935 order for the R.35 tanks. Despite Laval's practice of reducing public spending further, which kept these orders 'precariously balanced and subject to costly modifications', Renault's business with the state agencies expanded. Indeed it saw an 80 per cent increase, including the army but excluding aviation, between October 1934 and 1936. The allegedly high prices charged for these military contracts hardened Fabry's insistence that Hotchkiss receive orders and so blow a wind of competition around Renault.[42]

Whether Renault was profiteering unjustifiably in its military work remains unclear. Certainly, from the army's standpoint, Bloch-Dassault was sensible in advising in January 1936 that 'we should not give ourselves up, bound hand and foot, to a single supplier whose prices, in peacetime, cannot be disputed . . .'.[43] Yet Renault's problem was that small orders, which they had received for so long, had discouraged investment in the military vehicle lines in their factories. Furthermore, brief production runs served to keep unit costs high and prevent economies of scale. The individually constructed B1 tanks cost about 2 million francs each. As early as 1932 the company had explained to the war ministry that the unit price of its AMCs could be lowered from 192,000 to 181,000 francs if 200 were ordered, rather than merely 50 as the army was then envisaging.[44]

Concerning the adoption of the Hotchkiss H.35 or the R.35 tank, the controversy between the ministry and the firms overpricing was complicated by the infantry inspectorate. They preferred the robust simplicity of Renault's design over the superior speed, sophisticated engine (allegedly breakdown-prone), and longer radius of action of the Hotchkiss. To obtain a tank deemed by the infantry to be more serviceable to rapidly trained conscript crews, the R.35 was favoured even though it cost twice the price of its rival. The cause, then, of the Renault prices about which Fabry complained was to be found partly in decisions taken inside the army itself.[45] But this outcome was also partly a product of the Renault directors' business strategy. For, in 1934, the firm sought to enlarge its share of the military vehicle market, as well as the commercial vehicle market, by price cutting. To this end it rebuffed overtures from rivals for a market share-out of a cartel kind that would have greatly favoured Renault's share in return for restoration of higher price levels. Meanwhile Renault offered the army reductions of 35 and 40 per cent on military vehicles. This, in the first half of 1935, all but excluded other manufacturers from war ministry contracts. It was, for the Billancourt firm, a successful 'sectoral effort in price cutting (and respect for delivery schedules) on production destined for the army ...'.[46]

However, in the autumn of 1935 Fabry detected that Renault's dominant position as France's largest tank manufacturer was being exploited in the company's interests and against those of the military. It was a realisation which dawned slowly. In June 1935, replying to Lucien Besset's demand in the Chamber army commission 'that there be guarantees of priority for defence orders placed with private industry', Fabry confidently retorted that 'the assuring of this priority was something which the economic crisis brought about by itself'.[47] Subsequently Fabry's attitude to Renault hardened as tank and armoured carrier prices gradually rose, even during the fulfilment of agreed contracts. The company defended the increases by citing in-production modifications demanded by the military inspectorates. At the rue Saint-Dominique the conviction gained hold that Renault was maintaining production levels that suited their factory organisation and labour relations, at the expense of agreed contract completion rates. Bloch-Dassault investigated this suspicion. In January 1936 he concluded that 'in a general way all Renault equipment comes off the lines late, compared with schedules; these delays are sought by Renault, since it is seeking to stretch out its orders ... in order to facilitate the utilisation of its workforce and its machine-tools'. By late February 1936 the feeling that military suppliers were not acting sufficiently 'patriotically' in their defence work had spread to the Senate.[48] There, a month before Chéron's probe into Renault's refusal to decentralise tank assembly, Senator Palamède de la Grandière complained that:

the factories working on national defence contracts have ... a tendency to hold back their production of war-like stores for the slack periods when they have no other orders. What we need is the opposite situation, one in which national defence work takes priority ahead of private industry's orders. The war minister can act on these matters and reduce the delays ...[49]

Through personal initiatives by Fabry, measures had in fact begun during the autumn of 1935 to combat these industrial holdups. First, in September, convinced of 'the necessity of giving Renault competition', Fabry over-rode the infantry inspectorate's dissatisfaction with the H.35 design and ordered the opening of contract negotiations with Hotchkiss. The resulting order, for series production of 200 H.35s, was placed on 4 November. This decision meant that numerous similar light tanks were in service by 1937–8. There was a consequential rise in maintenance costs through non-standardisation of spare parts. The army gained, however, by ensuring that private firms besides Renault possessed armoured vehicle production capacity when massive expansion of rearmament targets occurred in September 1936. Fabry's initiative was the first phase in the important long-term process of maximising French industrial capacity by dividing military orders among many companies, instead of perpetuating a system which had permitted Renault to expand and all but monopolise output of automotive war material.[50]

Secondly, in October 1935, Fabry arranged the first of two meetings with Louis Renault himself. This initiative aimed to eliminate the misunderstandings clouding relations between the company and the army. However, in his talk with the industrialist Fabry heard an account of these relations that was seriously at variance with that offered by the generals. Renault argued, firstly, the need to limit the number of firms producing almost identical tank types if private investment in mass-production assembly plant was to occur, 'because of the significance of the associated expenditures on installation and tooling'. He also attributed delivery delays to interference by the military inspectorates. They sought design improvements after prototypes had been approved and put into production.[51] This problem, though, was only admitted officially in 1936. Then, replying to Senator de la Grandière's accusation 'that the officers from the various branches come to the factories demanding improvements . . . in the course of manufacture', Maurin, then war minister, confessed that 'the statements of officers regarding modifications . . . have given arguments to the constructors for justifying their delays'.[52]

Most severely criticised by Renault, however, was the army's armaments and technical studies section (the SAET), and its head, Engineer-General de Sablet. In November 1935, during his second meeting with Renault, Fabry heard allegations that the army demanded the submission of an excessive variety of different prototypes before approving mass production of any design. This represented a 'regrettable dispersion of effort', Renault argued.[53]

Meanwhile Fabry was also concerned with the condition of the artillery. This, the other chief area in which progress towards re-equipment with modern material was deemed deficient, brought the minister into conflict with Gamelin. Friction first appeared on 11 September. In a war ministry meeting, then, Fabry voiced his dissatisfaction with the 'worrying situation' in artillery output, Schneider having just revealed a fourteen-month delivery period for their 105mm cannon. This, added to the problems encountered in placing orders for the infantry-support tanks, led him to propose to reduce credits for Char B construction in order to concentrate resources elsewhere. Gamelin, a supporter of the heavy battle-tank programme, immediately resisted this. Fabry, undeterred, renewed his assault on the necessity and urgency of the Char B programme later that month, after the director of artillery, General Piquendar, reported that no ordnance existed with which to equip the heavy artillery batteries theoretically attached to corps headquarters on mobilisation. Convinced that these guns should have highest priority, Fabry conceded the need to proceed with Chars D construction but advocated the complete suspension of the manufacture of the B tanks, allegedly 'too heavy, too costly and impossible to produce by mass-assembly'.[54]

Civil-military discord was, by this proposal, brought anew to a climax at the armaments consultative committee's 3 October 1935 meeting. As Gamelin's record reveals, the minister's plans were implacably opposed by the military experts. Bloch-Dassault, 'statistics in hand', supported Gamelin's thesis that although a renovation of the artillery was 'attractive', 'the important thing remained the re-equipment of armoured vehicle forces, where the Germans were on the way to stealing a substantial march on us'. With Dufieux, and more unexpectedly Carence, the inspector of artillery, backing Gamelin, Fabry's recommendations were rebuffed and he left the meeting with 'the worst possible impression' of the committee's work. The minister's 'long-standing camaraderie' with Gamelin could not disguise the thwarting of the political chief of the army by the concerted opposition of the technicians.[55]

On the same day as this meeting, 3 October, however, Italy opened the invasion of Abyssinia. As international crisis loomed to the forefront of the concerns of French defence authorities, the country's long-term unpreparedness for facing hostilities exercised an increasing influence on Laval's conduct of foreign policy. Of special impact was the dawning understanding of inadequacies in military equipment deliveries and in the levels of stocks of war stores. For Laval had heard, at Haut Comité Militaire meetings on 23 January, 22 March and 5 April 1935, that French military readiness lagged dangerously behind the pace of German rearmament. Fabry emphasised that the Abyssinian affair compounded French strategic vulnerability.[56] Firstly, the crisis underlined the impracticability of France foregoing close relations with Britain. For it demonstrated that Italy, for all its attractiveness as a military collaborator, was simply not reliable as a political partner. Secondly, Abyssinia obliged Laval (against his and Fabry's inclinations), to participate with Britain on 18 November 1935 in imposing limited economic sanctions against Italy. Applied to conciliate Britain as much as to placate Herriot's pro-League of Nations wing of the Radicals – on whose votes Laval depended for a Chamber majority – the sanctions jeopardised the future of the 27 June Gamelin–Badoglio defence convention. They equally called into doubt Mussolini's continuing intention to cooperate to preserve Austria against German annexation. Distasteful though he found it, Laval was inexorably impelled, by France's weakness, towards elevating friendship with Britain above friendship with Italy.[57]

Linking Franco-Italian relations and French military inadequacies, as issues, was the renascent power of Germany. In this, again, differences about ways to enhance French security led to tensions between Gamelin and his political superiors. For Fabry had his gaze fixed firmly on the usefulness of the understanding with Badoglio for the integrity of France's north-eastern frontiers. He was, throughout his tenure of the war ministry in 1935–6, 'formally opposed' to any sanctions directed against the Italians.[58] Gamelin, however, disputed Fabry's analysis of the shifting strategic balance (though not disagreeing with the minister's assessment of the British army as only 'a derisory source of succour' in a European conflict's opening stages). Nevertheless, Gamelin regarded a cohesive Franco-British accord as the prerequisite of durable security for France. Writing later he stressed that 'whatever the significance of our relations with Italy, all that mattered compelled us to maintain solidarity with London. For us Italy was important; Britain was essential.' He did not accept that temporarily expedient agreements with Mussolini justified policy that might dissuade the government in London from supporting France, politically and militarily, in negotiations with Germany, either over revision of the Rhineland's demilitarised status or over armaments' limitation.[59]

French sources indicate, however, that, in the autumn of 1935, behind their command's assured mask for outsiders, lurked deep-seated disquiet about the manner in which Laval was confronting Germany's growing power. Schweisguth's diary reveals that by mid-September staff studies were under way in Paris to examine responses to a German reoccupation of the Rhineland. What disturbed Gamelin most was the conclusion of Laval that France's economic difficulties, the industrial constraints hampering French defence renovation, and the developing Mediterranean crisis justified fresh diplomacy designed to achieve general settlement and détente with Germany.[60] Gamelin, for his part, viewed international and domestic trends as compelling reason for new and more determined government intervention to clear away rearmament bottlenecks that he regarded as prejudicial to national security. On 18 October Gamelin and Georges warned Fabry that the Italo-Abyssinian conflict threatened to force on France a clear choice between partnership with Britain and the understanding with Mussolini. Not only this, they cautioned, but the diversion of attention to Africa might offer Hitler a favourable opening for action on the Rhine. Intelligence sources, wrote Gamelin later, 'already showed us that the General Staff in Berlin was studying the possibility of reoccupying the demilitarised zone'.[61]

Laval's and Gamelin's efforts to align foreign and defence policy at the close of 1935 were characterised by diametrically opposed analyses of the measures required by France's vulnerable military and economic condition. Laval's diplomacy at this time seemed illogical to Gamelin. The latter's memoirs reflect this through their defensive stance over the impact of professional military appreciations on the conduct of French foreign policy from 1935 right down to 1939. For never were Gamelin's views on French external relations more completely set aside than during the last months of Laval's 1935–6 government. At no other time did the general's oft-cited skills as a *bureaucrate en képi*, his supposed powers of accommodation and persuasion, so signally fail to influence France's civilian leaders.[62]

Most dismaying for Gamelin was his inability to convince politicians of the army's current rather than future unpreparedness. Fabry contended that preserving the arrangement with Badoglio was the key to covering short-term French deficiencies. To this extent he endorsed his prime minister's foreign policy of indulgence towards Mussolini. Gamelin, however, insisted that fascist Italy's driving forces were too nationalistic, too unpredictable, for France to rely on such technical accords. Badoglio's signature and word might be his bond, 'But', Gamelin subsequently reflected, 'he was not the master – no more than I, in fact.' Fabry therefore remained obsessed with strengthening war material stocks for distant future hostilities. At the 3 October armaments consultative committee meeting the minister alleged that, concerning stockpiles, re-equipment was two years behind schedule. Reports were thus commissioned on the production levels of shells at Brandt and on the size of the army's reserves of munitions. Yet, simultaneously, protestations that structural and weaponry deficiencies rendered 'the peacetime army . . . incapable of conducting an effective operation, or even a gesture of any value', were suppressed.[63]

On 17 October, in an armaments planning discussion, Fabry repeated that 'the commander-in-chief designate . . . is acting within his purview in wishing to accumulate equipment in order to win the first battle in a war, but I, as minister . . . have to think about the replenishment of munitions for all this weaponry in order to permit the subsequent conduct of operations'. This criticism of the soldiers' preoccupation with resisting the initial shock of war assumes ironic overtones indeed with regard to the thesis that the weakness of French planning in the 1930s for a protracted conflict lay in failure to ensure that an attritional strategy was not nullified by catastrophic early defeat of the kind which struck in May–June 1940.[64] What Gamelin was striving to secure was direction of rearmament priority to the sharpening of the peacetime army's operational pre-mobilisation readiness. Hence at another war ministry meeting, on 6 November 1935, he again argued for concentrating 'the greatest effort on the manufacture of equipment and weaponry rather than on the augmenting of stocks of munitions'.[65]

In the Haut Comité Militaire on 21 November Gamelin was overruled about relative priorities for funding these two types of warlike stores. As the general's record shows, Fabry asserted that 'Germany possesses a formidable potential for war. We must not sacrifice stockpiles and manufacturing power in favour of equipment for the army. It is important that we remain capable of extending and lengthening a war.' A 'saddened' Gamelin perceptively noted in the margin on his account: 'As if the opening clash, above all else, is not what shapes the subsequent course of the conflict. Both questions naturally are important; but what if we lose that first battle!'[66]

This Haut Comité meeting marked a turning point in the extended skirmishing between Fabry and Gamelin over allocations of rearmament resources. It was evidence of the vortex of failure into which Laval's foreign, economic and defence policies had sucked one another. For the prime minister used this gathering not simply to justify his stance towards the Italo-Anglo-Abyssinian entanglement, he also employed it to propound his strategy towards the Third Reich: a search, firstly, for a declaration from Hitler of peaceful intentions, and then a general Franco-German détente to generate commercial cooperation and arms limitation agreements. This policy had been prepared by initiatives in Paris and Berlin since October 1935. Ironically, however, it was still-born even as Laval tried to explain it on 21 November. For, that same day, in Berlin, André François-Poncet, France's ambassador, met Hitler, and the German Führer made plain his utter rejection of French foreign policy, both in the eastern Mediterranean and in Europe.[67] To the Haut Comité Laval asserted that, dealing with Hitler, 'we must not set out wearing an importunate demeanour . . .'. In practice, however, it was just this position from which French initiatives derived.[68] As Laval's most recent biographer sums up, 'His failure reflected, above all, the enfeeblement of France.'[69]

Contemporary remarks show that Gamelin perspicaciously grasped the way in which this debilitation was of Laval's own making. Postponement of parts of the defence expenditure programme inherited from Flandin and Maurin, Régnier's cuts in the 1936 estimates, and Fabry's steering of priority towards artillery and munitions had combined to retard Gamelin's ambition of a more immediately combat-efficient peacetime standing army. At the same time, France's stagnant economy denied Laval any trade-led *rapprochement* with the Reich. This double weakness hamstrung foreign policy initiatives. It increased French reliance on Britain. It drained away the military's confidence in the political recipes of French centre-right politics. Gamelin derided Laval's inconsequential, unrealistic and unworthy initiatives: 'Perhaps one day we shall be able to arrive at an understanding with Germany; but let's do it with our heads held high once our defence equipment programme is completed.'[70]

Soon afterwards, on 22 January 1936, Laval was forced from office, deserted by Herriot's section of the Radicals who wished to mark their disagreement with Laval's readiness to offer *de facto* recognition to much of Italy's conquest of Abyssinia. In Herriot's decision a key consideration was the wisdom of adopting an electorally popular stance on foreign policy in readiness for the Chamber polls scheduled for 26 April and 3 May. Sarraut's government, which acted as a caretaker from Laval's resignation until the election, became introspectively preoccupied by the jockeying for domestic political advantage.[71] Defence for a time was dismissed to the shadows.

Thus Germany's reoccupation of the demilitarised Rhineland, on 7 March, was astutely timed to draw maximum benefit from French politicians' distraction from military matters by electoral manoeuvres. Recent ex-ministers as well as those in office under Sarraut had received ample advance warning from the military professionals of the probable imminence of German action. Yet no political leader in Paris before the 7 March coup so much as spoke or wrote about – still less tabled a parliamentary debate on – the issue of using force to evict German troops undertaking a remilitarisation. The strategic question was simply ignored by politicians until after the event when, in practice, all debate was academic. Discussion over the strategic value of the Rhineland to France, and allegations that March 1936 was the 'magnificent opportunity' by which the French might have checked German territorial expansion, occurred only in the context of post-coup diplomacy which sought substitute security through Franco-Anglo-Belgian military staff talks and joint planning. Given the French army's 'gradualistic attitude' to re-equipping for future hostilities, the episode of the Rhineland reoccupation was irrelevant. It was 'a manufactured crisis with a predictable outcome. It figured in no sense as a turning point of the 1930s'.[72] It is in this perspective that must reasonably be judged Gamelin's refusal to be required to shoulder the responsibility for the selection and implementation of policy. This, Gamelin correctly insisted, both in March 1936 and afterwards, was entirely the business of the government, the prerogative of the politicians.[73]

The March interlude did bring favourable consequences for French defence procurement. It impelled the release of extra armaments credits, through the constitution of a special borrowing facility, the *Fonds d'armement, d'outillage et d'avances sur travaux*, to extend the war ministry's extra-budgetary account of 500 million francs allocated on 31 December 1935. Nonetheless this piecemeal easing of the rigidities of 'sound finance' offered only a distant prospect of redressment of French defensive unpreparedness.[74] Colson and Bloch-Dassault cynically commented, emerging from their February 1936 interrogations by the Senate and Chamber army commissions, 'that these parliamentarians are . . . in showing themselves interested in questions of equipment . . . concerned only with protecting themselves in case of a worsening of the situation abroad'.[75]

Military-civil relations as well as military-industrial relations were thus coloured by scepticism and mutual mistrust as France approached its elections. Laval's and Régnier's policies had generated doubts in the general staff's highest echelons about parliament's good faith towards restoring the nation's defences to what soldiers regarded as thorough effectiveness. A number of armaments' manufacturers, Renault pre-eminent among them, had conducted themselves so as to have entrenched among the military a deep disenchantment with France's private defence industries. Consequently these military leaders became blinded to their own aggravation of the problems of the businessmen. Such myopia permitted Gamelin later to ascribe not to the demands of a peacetime economy but to implicitly sinister 'errors' the fact that, after 1918 'we French had completely given up our means of production . . . [so that] when we wanted to start up our [re-equipment] effort again in 1935 and 1936 we first, and before anything else, had to regenerate this productive base. It was this which ensured that our effort, commencing in 1935 and intensified in 1936, only produced its returns in output at the end of 1938 and beginning of 1939.'[76]

These coincident phenomena of military-civil and military-industrial friction received their final twist in a reorganisation of the armaments' directorate. This Fabry implemented just three weeks before leaving the war ministry. Central to the new order was the replacement of Engineer-General de Sablet, whose administration had, according to Fabry, 'betrayed numerous weaknesses . . . and was . . . quite lifeless' and whose personal role had been 'deficient'. The nominated successor was Engineer-General Paul Happich. But above all it was the fact that the changes were made by Fabry at Louis Renault's personal prompting that gave them special significance.[77] For it was not the promotion of Happich that troubled the army's senior ranks (who in any event appreciated his proven accomplishments as a specialist in weaponry development). Rather, it was the manner of his appointment. For this was an elevation rooted in external – and far from disinterested – interference. It exacerbated the irritation already well documented by senior generals towards Renault. Most important of all, it hardened sentiments in the Staff favourable to vigorous and sweeping state intervention in the private French arms industries, as the method to end the dominance of specific firms perceived to be impeding the defence forces' most rapid re-equipment.[78]

One final point must still be emphasised if Gamelin's personal actions from mid-1936 onwards, regarding the earliest possible refurbishment of the standing forces, are to be understood. This is that doctrinal disunity among senior soldiers went on exercising a measurable braking effect on rearmament. One example would be the protracted disagreements, until Dufieux's retirement in 1938, over the role, structures and even at times the necessity of autonomous heavy tank formations. This discord characterised all decision-taking on the comparative priority to be accorded to heavy tank production. A second instance was the effective rearguard action against structural and doctrinal modernisation waged by defenders of horsed cavalry. This was in the teeth of advocacy by Gamelin of the expansion of the light mechanised formations to a corps of three divisions. It flew in the face of studies favourable to the corps' creation by Schweisguth and General Jean Flavigny, commander of the first light mechanised division and a contender that only such formations offered the power 'to engage the enemy attack', leading him to 'insist on these units' defensive value'. This was no Gaullien adventurism but a solid and experienced tank professional's evaluation for France of armour's crucial counter-attack potential. Yet the traditionalists were still so influential that Altmayer, the cavalry inspector, insisted that operational roles attributed to the cavalry would only be performable by horsed units. Enough others followed this line to cut in half Gamelin's proposed increase from one to three mechanised divisions when the CSG decided the issue on 29 April 1936.[79]

This was an unhappy postscript for Gamelin to the shock to French security of the previous month's Rhineland incident. Objectively Gamelin knew that the 7 March coup had brought German concentration centres thenceforth forward from behind a buffer to the very edge of the Franco-Belgian frontier. The acrimonious military-industrial discussions made plain just how far France still was from the capacity to launch and rapidly achieve a thorough-going renovation of her defence equipment. And, not least, Gamelin understood by spring 1936 just how far there was to travel before the military authorities themselves would present an undivided and forward-looking front on the types of equipment they wanted and the operational framework for its use. On Gamelin's problem of a complacent and superficial view by successive ministers, Fabry and Maurin, of the facility to attain close cooperation on design and output with private manufacturers was overlain a further related difficulty. This was the tendency of each traditional inspectorate – the infantry, cavalry and artillery – to defend its own existing structure and budgetary allocations as holy writ inscribed on tablets of stone. Hence, faced by a rising tide of debate over the future shape of armed forces, they gratefully (but for Gamelin most unhelpfully) invoked slow equipment production to explain away their own deferment of experiment and innovation.[80]

At this juncture, May 1936, such interdependent and stagnation-inducing features of the military-industrial relationship persuaded Gamelin, and some of his senior associates, to welcome the arrival of the Popular Front as the lifting of a siege. Specifically, for the defence of France, Gamelin welcomed the Popular Front's penchant for reinforcing state authority over industry. Closer government direction of the activities of the chief weapons-producing firms seemed to carry the greatest chance of a speedy breakout for the army from rearmament bottlenecks in prototype adoption, investment strategies, plant location and labour force shortages. With the left victorious in the 3 May second ballot of the election, common interests thus fashioned an alliance of expediency on defence issues. The security of France, at home as well as abroad, had become an urgent concern by early summer 1936. It was as high on the agenda of Léon Blum's incoming Socialist–Radical government as it was pressing in the preoccupations of Gamelin.

4   The Popular Front, the army and politics

On the rue de Varenne outside the Hôtel Matignon, office of the prime minister, the Gardes Mobiles snapped into salute as Gamelin arrived on 10 June 1936 for his first official encounter with Blum. The Popular Front had been in office for just four days. Only two nights before, in the same buildings, Blum had negotiated an economic and social settlement to end the strikes and factory occupations that had crippled French industry since mid-May. This had been an exhilarating but nerve-stretching beginning to what Blum called his 'exercise of power'. Resistance to the left and its reforming social programme appeared to be in disarray. 'A great many entrepreneurs', Gamelin reflected, 'had lost their heads and panicked.'[1] The conservative parties were wounded by their electoral defeat and had turned in on themselves to seek reasons for their setback. With business bosses as cowed as the political right, the army appeared to be the only quarter from which could come a repression of the workers' carnival. In the heightened political temperature of Paris in that turbulent summer of 1936, a great question hung over whether the military would cooperate with France's first Socialist-led administration.

The doubts hung heavily as Gamelin strode through the Matignon courtyard to meet Blum. Noticing the clerks and orderlies working calmly inside the offices, Gamelin contrasted it with the continuing tension outside, which he later attributed critically to the 'criminal demagoguery of the "Popular Front"'.[2] In a spacious ground-floor drawing room Blum awaited the general. Barely acquainted, the new prime minister sought to break the ice by remarking that he and Gamelin had roots in common, both being born in Paris in 1872. Immediately the well-briefed and elegantly tailored Jewish lawyer and essayist from the Marais charmed Gamelin, appealing instantly to the general's tastes for intellectualism, philosophy and literature.

This meeting, so early after the elections and with the Popular Front facing a crowded domestic agenda, reflected Blum's recognition of the menacing European situation in the aftermath of the German remilitarisation of the Rhineland. Faith in France's military apparatus had been dented by Hitler's easy success, whilst scepticism had been stirred over France's ability to help her friends to Germany's east: Poland, Czechoslovakia and Romania. As Daladier, Blum's defence minister, conceded in July 1936, the French 'attitude to the events of 7 March had shaken the Little Entente'.[3] It seemed imperative to Gamelin to agree quickly with the Popular Front a high priority for reinvigorating France's defence effort.

This invitation to hold talks with Blum so soon was encouraging for Gamelin; hearing the prime minister's views proved unexpectedly reassuring. The discussion was marked by candour as well as cordiality. Gamelin left with the conviction that he could broach anything to Blum with absolute frankness. He had told the prime minister that, although he felt no affinities towards marxism, he considered himself to be a soldier 'with a social conscience'. He stressed that he hoped the government would insulate the army from political commotion. Blum, according to Gamelin, 'emphasised his favourable feelings towards the military, of his concern for national defence . . . "You must not . . . be afraid of the socialists; I guarantee that they now grasp the gravity of the circumstances in which Europe finds herself".' In return Gamelin promised that his soldiers would observe a proper neutrality towards politics. The army, he said, was unperturbed by initiatives to extend social justice to the workers. It had, he insisted, 'to lie completely outside the class struggle'.[4]

Behind this affable encounter, recalled in Gamelin's characteristically smooth style, how easily did the French army accommodate the installation of a leftist government in 1936? To answer the question an analysis is required of attitudes in an officer corps, perhaps an entire army, that was sitting on the sidelines, behaving according to an apolitical tradition. No contemporary survey exists, however, of the moods of the 28,500 officers in metropolitan France and its empire in 1936–7. Sources such as memoirs and journals encourage a close focus on the ideological dispositions of the senior ranks, the generals and marshals (of whom two First World War veterans, Pétain, the 'Hero of Verdun', and Louis Franchet d'Esperey, were still living). But there are limitations inherent in this approach. For one thing, thoughts about military insubordination – still less plans for insurrection – are few and far between in the diaries and correspondence of serving officers. These men, if not quite military Vicars of Bray, nevertheless had pay, promotions and pensions to restrain their political prejudices. Most colonels aspired to retire as successful generals, not as disgraced putschistes. Discretion, therefore, tended to be the better part of political foolhardiness. Yet how far may the army have kept quiet towards the left despite itself? How prevalent were grumbles? Was hostility – or simply indifference about one more change of government – the predominant military sentiment towards the Popular Front?

Gamelin himself was crucial to the general staff's transition without outward protest from serving the centre-right ministries of Flandin, Laval and Sarraut in 1935–6, to working thereafter with the left. Gamelin was not restricted, as in quite opposite ways generals like Sarrail and Weygand had been, by ties to one set of political patrons drawn narrowly from the left or the right. On the contrary, he had since before the 1914 war expressly cultivated support right across the classic parliamentary divide. His friends and allies formed a wide circle that encompassed Tardieu, Maurice Sarraut and Paul-Boncour. For progressives, as well as for orthodox conservative parliamentarians, Gamelin was recognisably and reliably republican. His style was, irrespective of a government's colour, to construct and defend a political-military consensus behind a strengthening of the defence effort. His rare combination of authority as both commander-in-chief designate and chief of the general staff had been conferred in 1935 by Flandin's centre-right ministry. But there was never any suggestion that Blum should diminish this in 1936–7. Evidently the left's approval of this status quo reflected the comfort which Gamelin gave the Popular Front by his particular approach to exercising command. It seems worth repeating the insight of Germany's military attaché in Paris in 1937 that Gamelin enjoyed the confidence of politicians 'because he did not arouse their suspicions or give rise to the belief that he was making himself too powerful'. Gamelin had succeeded in convincing all parties of his absolute loyalty towards France's legitimately elected regime and its institutions.[5] Blum and Gamelin had more than just their Parisian origins in common; they shared a powerful sense of constitutionalism.

The politics of Popular Frontism as such undeniably aroused Gamelin's private distaste. He deplored what he felt was its polarisation of an already divided French society – a tendency from which the Front sprang, but which it seemed to Gamelin also to exacerbate 'by introducing its dangerous ideology'.[6] However, Gamelin's unease at the installation of SFIO ministers was tempered by the new government's large contingent of experienced Radicals. Yvon Delbos, deputy for the Dordogne, became foreign minister. Radicals also took over all three military portfolios. The post with greatest influence – as well as responsibility – fell to Daladier, Gamelin's political ally since 1933, who combined the deputy prime ministership with the ministry of national defence and war. Daladier was then fifty-two, the son of a Carpentras baker. He was a politically experienced and reflective *petit bourgeois* from the Midi, known as the 'Bull of the Vaucluse', for which he had been a deputy since 1919. With a distinguished 1914–18 war record, in which he had been commissioned from the ranks, Daladier was also an academically trained historian. An educated parliamentary survivor, he remained fiercely proud of his Provençal roots. He was to stay at the rue Saint-Dominique continuously, through five governments, from when the Popular Front took office until 18 May 1940. The bonds formed through their collaboration during the effectives clash with Weygand in 1933, their temperamental compatibility and the sheer length of their tenures made the Gamelin–Daladier partnership the central human element in French defence policy after June 1936.[7]

Politicians to the left of the Radicals were excluded by Blum from sensitive defence posts. Moreover, the PCF supported the Popular Front only in parliament, refusing any share of offices. It practised instead a self-proclaimed role from the sidelines as a 'ministry of the masses'. Ostensibly, at least, this secured military secrets from communist purview. Blum's intention was to keep Gamelin's confidence by alleviating fears of security risks inside the political *cabinets* of the service ministries. In the case of the air ministry under Pierre Cot, however, this may not have been achieved, despite the marginalisation of openly declared Communist Party militants. The equanimity with which Gamelin viewed the Popular Front was born of his practised partnership with Daladier, whose patriotism and political astuteness he respected. By 1936 Daladier had proven his credentials in Gamelin's eyes as a bulwark between the army and the anti-militarist left on the one hand and the conspiratorial right on the other.

Not all soldiers shared Gamelin's sang-froid, however, even if vilification of the Popular Front was usually expressed openly only by retired officers. One example was Weygand, who complained about France's military condition in October 1936 in the *Revue des Deux Mondes*. He censured the left for allegedly infecting the country with anti-patriotism. For him the primary school teachers, the *instituteurs*, mostly CGT and SFIO stalwarts, were indictable:

Certainly [he wrote] the majority of the French love their army . . . but the cult of the motherland and military duty face dedicated adversaries whose poisonous propaganda is all-pervasive . . . Many of these adversaries belong to the state education service . . . What sort of soldiers may we expect to emerge from *their* schools?

Only restoring 'patriotic education', argued Weygand, would lay the foundation required for reconstructing sufficiently solid French defences. Similar antipathy to the teachers was expressed by Pétain who sought appointment as education minister in Gaston Doumergue's 'national union' government after the February 1934 crisis, before finally agreeing to take the war ministry.[8]

Such diatribes from army elders indicated their prejudices against the left. But what explains the active cadre's readier toleration of Blum? The latter's speeches and journalism suggested, after all, that he would emasculate the armed forces if he ever attained power. As the US assistant military attaché in Paris observed, 'Without governmental responsibility his [Blum's] main thesis was disarmament at any cost, and on many occasions in the Chamber he showed himself a strong partisan of the reduction of France's military expenditures and consequently her means of defense.'[9] Blum was given the benefit of the doubt by serving officers. Was this because by 1936, the memory of the Dreyfus crisis was confined to harmless pensioner generals in the plays of Jean Anouilh and the apartments of the 7th arrondissement? Or was a wider malaise reflected in the public criticism among retired officers of the direction in which the republic was travelling? The evidence available suggests that two attitudes existed side by side.

On the one hand, there was the case of the general staff in Paris and the officer corps stationed in metropolitan France as a whole. Here Gamelin was able to enforce his insistence that the army accept changes in the civilian regime. His personal authority and prestige was enough to hold the line. By 1936 Gamelin was, after all, in his sixth year as chief of the general staff and his second as vice-president of the CSG. Time had enabled him to set the tone he required not just in the *Etat-Major* but also among the field officers he met during annual exercises and inspections at the great military camps like Larzac in the south, Coëtquidan in Brittany and Bitche in Lorraine. At home, then, Gamelin was able to deliver the political neutrality – or at worst the political taciturnity – that he insisted be shown to the Popular Front as the legally elected government. 'With rare exceptions the army staff . . . refrained from judging government policy. Under . . . Gamelin this respect for absolute discretion on matters of politics – domestic or foreign – became . . . dogma.'[10]

In adopting this approach Gamelin appears to have set greater store in dispelling neuroses among his officers and calming their suspicion of the left than he did by any enthusiasm for Blum. Gamelin's main objective was to avoid piling up fresh internal problems. He already faced enough external difficulties from Germany as well as from France's reluctant allies and partners.

Demonstrating an iron will, therefore, Gamelin resolved to prevent a new outbreak of civil-military confrontation. To achieve this aim he had to enforce a disciplined silence and circumspection throughout his officer corps. The job was not straightforward. Discretion did not come as second nature to officers who had been encouraged by Weygand's loose tongue to express criticism of France's political leadership. But, without a strictly 'correct' response to the election of the Popular Front, Gamelin foresaw a further deterioration of the already problematic conditions under which he was trying to maintain French security. He had to calculate the best way of building upon Blum's concession at their 10 June meeting of the need for stronger national defences. His choice was characteristic: he opted to dust off and reutilise the *grande muette* tradition of the officer corps.

Though Gamelin and Blum quickly fashioned a satisfactory working partnership, it would be mistaken to conclude that they became bosom friends in 1936–7. The general's conciliatory attitude whilst Blum occupied the Hôtel Matignon arose from a hard-nosed assessment of what was best for the defence effort, not from any conversion to Popular Frontism. Gamelin's example was intended to send a personal signal about the discipline he expected throughout the armed forces. In private, however, Gamelin's and Blum's opinions of each other were marked by serious reservations. As the general subsequently confided to his personal staff, he considered Blum 'a bogus or sham intellectual'. Blum for his part said he thought 'Gamelin is intelligent but limited.'[11]

In any case, Gamelin's grip on his officers was not always as firm as he wanted. Across the continent, as well as in the colonies, distance from Paris emboldened officers hostile to the left. Advocates of *rapprochement* with fascist Italy – such as the military attaché in Rome, General Parisot – viewed the Popular Front with consternation. Parisot's deputy, Captain Maurice Catoire, vented in his diary his horror at Blum's election: 'a catastrophic result . . . and a triumph for Moscow'.[12] By late June the agenda of French diplomacy had been politically reordered, dropping friendship with Mussolini. Delbos and Cot were instead concerned to revitalise cooperation with east-central Europe. The Popular Front foreign minister spent much of the summer of 1936 touring the Little Entente capitals. Catoire thought this a 'lamentable' external policy, 'in tow to our domestic politics and prey to their vacillations'.[13] Nor was the Popular Front held in any affection among the ambitious military proconsuls in the French empire – to judge by the fealty readily given the Republic's Vichyite successors by Generals Noguès and Dentz, in North Africa and Syria, as well as by Admiral Decoux in

Indochina.¹⁴ But it was perhaps unavoidable that Gamelin had little control over the politics of subordinates who enjoyed the liberties and alternative political environments offered by service abroad.

Within France itself, serving officers seldom flaunted political prejudices. For most, an overriding concern for their careers induced this circumspection. The central exception was de Gaulle. His long-running campaign to overcome the snubbing of his professional army proposals in 1935 was more inflammatory than ever in the circumstances of 1936. De Gaulle betrayed the fact that some officers held blatantly opportunistic political attitudes, regardless of Gamelin's pledge to Blum of an apolitical army. Unavoidably, in the agitation that preceded the 1936 elections, French military chiefs were drawn into contingency planning in support of the security services, the police and gendarmerie. General staff officers were first consulted by an 'apprehensive' Paris prefect of police, Roger Langeron, during the leftist assembly in the capital on Bastille Day 1935. Fabry, responsible as war minister for the military parade on the Champs Elysées early that day, reflected ruefully that the Parisians, 'so patriotic in the morning, were singing the *Internationale* by the afternoon'.¹⁵ Again, the military authorities appear to have identified Daladier as their political champion inside the Popular Front. Many people readily recalled the public order crisis of February 1934. It was reckoned that Daladier – forced to resign during the 1934 troubles – should prepare against any repetition of political riots. To some the gravest danger appeared to be that of an outbreak of serious disorder during parliament's recess; Daladier was therefore urged to keep a list in his pocket with 300 signatures of deputies and senators, as was constitutionally required to compel an emergency recall of the legislature.

In September 1935 Colson and Schweisguth discussed the 'steps needed to strengthen the Parisian garrison with a view to maintaining order'. Six additional battalions of troops would be required to hold open two secure corridors, 'one to Versailles and one to Vincennes, across the proletarian "red belt"'. But Gamelin, quite characteristically, thought that this was an overreaction. He would allow only one extra colonial regiment as reinforcement to the permanent garrison in the capital.¹⁶ As Britain's ambassador to France observed in 1937, Gamelin was 'a man of quite remarkable . . . sang-froid'. Manifestly, he was no latter-day Gallifet, set on increasing the political temperature by provocatively raising the army's profile in the working-class suburbs in any way redolent of the Commune crisis of 1871.¹⁷

In May 1936 the factory occupations that seemed to herald a 'red spring' in France reached their greatest extent. Frightened industrialists, surprised at the suddenness and size of the workers' protests, urged government action to evict the strikers by means of the courts, the police and the troops. Sarraut, a caretaker without a mandate, understandably equivocated. He feared to acquire the unwanted stigma of a prime minister with blood on his hands (as had been Daladier's lot after the deaths in 1934). Nevertheless the situation was deemed sufficiently unstable that by late May the army was again drawn into consultations. Schweisguth recorded that Colson had been called to see Sarraut about the factory takeovers. He found Langeron claiming that the workers could not be ejected because their action was peaceful and not causing any disturbance to public order. 'That attitude', said Daladier, 'was how the fascists prepared their seizure of power in Italy.' Yet, in spite of this plea against passivity, the meeting adjourned without deciding upon any action. This was a problem to be left to the Popular Front: 'It was agreed to refer it to Blum.'[18]

In contrast to such deference to the new political majority, de Gaulle articulated an authoritarian personal view of the implications for the army of what he predicted would become a slide into chaos. He had alerted Reynaud that the economic, political and moral crisis was spreading. In his opinion this increased the likelihood of a collapse of internal security. De Gaulle wondered how 'in the mounting tumult (Popular Front or right-wing leagues)' to prevent a 'situation of anarchy, perhaps of civil war . . . ?' He denigrated the police and the Garde Mobile: '15,000 family men scattered the length and breadth of the land'; he doubted their capacities if disturbances 'broke out simultaneously in Paris, Lyon . . . Lille, Limoges . . . and in the countryside'. The army, he asserted, had fulfilled the duty and function of supporting the maintenance of order during crises since time immemorial; 'but how can we expect this of it when its units are now all composed of voters or natives?' For de Gaulle a professional army was as necessary by 1936 because of imminent insecurity in metropolitan France as it was required by tension abroad.

The conditions which generated a Popular Front government that sympathised with Gamelin's aim for an expanded defence effort also gave de Gaulle unexpected extra fuel to get his broken-down career army schemes back on the road. There they could once more cause political jams to hinder Gamelin's own movement of the army towards enhanced capabilities and enlarged strength.

In September 1936 de Gaulle was invited secretly, during a second and calculated CGT strike campaign, to meet Camille Chautemps, minister of state in Blum's government, senator for the Loir-et-Cher and leader of the conservative wing of the Radicals. Chautemps, de

Gaulle reported to Reynaud, seemed very well disposed, 'even greatly stressing . . . the importance that my specialized corps would assume in current and future public order problems (both at home and in North Africa)'.[19] It is hard to dispute Guy Chapman's conclusion that, however exemplary a Frenchman after 1940, de Gaulle was 'a bad officer, undisciplined and disobedient . . .' who risked splitting the army.[20] It is equally difficult to avoid judging the former prime minister Chautemps ruthlessly ambitious, scheming and disloyal, an insincere Popular Frontist and a most dangerous viper for Blum to have lurking in his basket of ministers.[21]

Nevertheless such support for de Gaulle was untypical of most parliamentarians. Inside Blum's government, and within the democratic right, most shared Gamelin's condemnation of the separate professional army. Roger Salengro, Socialist deputy and mayor of Lille and interior minister from June to November 1936, politically responsible for internal security, spoke publicly for the Popular Front's commitment to improve French defence against German remilitarisation. From the ranks of Blum's senior colleagues, only the pacifist Paul Faure, SFIO secretary-general, opposed rearmament. The official Radical view came from Daladier. In the Chamber in February 1937 he was 'unable to agree with those . . . who demanded a career army or . . . specialist corps of armoured divisions' because it was essential to preserve a proper balance and proportion between the army's various components.[22] Daladier was here remaining true to his pre-Popular Front position governing the relationship which he sought between the army and the populace. This was a relationship that he had characterised in 1927 as one 'requiring from our citizens only such sacrifices as truly are indispensable, and thereby winning the support of everyone called on to bear the burdens . . .'. Daladier, in essence, set himself as a watchdog for taxpayers and conscripts alike against excessive military impositions.

Besides his key role in rearmament, Daladier had a central place in the evolution of French military relations with Britain and Belgium. These countries were courted by Gamelin for help in the direct protection of France by virtue of their geographical proximity and assumed congruence of security interests. Daladier's sojourn at the rue Saint-Dominique until 1940 provided welcome and unusual continuity of political direction for French commanders. Gamelin, discontent fresh in his mind at Fabry's and Maurin's procrastination towards his re-equipment priorities and call for stronger ministry controls over defence suppliers, valued Daladier's confidence and support. He found Daladier refreshingly 'attracted by the idea of moving towards a planned economy'.[23] In return, Daladier regarded Gamelin so highly as to consider awarding him a marshal's baton in 1938 and to shield him, right down till 19 May 1940, against attempts, especially by Reynaud, to remove him from the supreme command.[24] Gamelin's leadership personified, for Daladier, France's destiny of military grandeur. It was most remarkably expressed in a paeon before the Chamber army commission in early 1938:

> The commander-in-chief ... is a man directly descended from that dynasty of great military leaders that France possessed during the last war. He is not only outstandingly open-minded ... but is admirably cultivated and is, I believe, a man with all the intellectual and moral attributes which may rightly be required of one on whom such grave responsibility is to be placed.[25]

In sum, Daladier's chief difference from Fabry and Maurin was his readiness to trust absolutely in Gamelin's appraisals of French defence preparedness. His method was to give his political approval to projects in their outline stage and thereafter to leave Gamelin with a wide latitude over detailed formulation and execution. Compared to his predecessors in the conservative governments of 1934–6 (who were all, of course, senior retired officers themselves), Daladier seldom interfered in technicalities. Perhaps – since he had never risen higher than his First World War field promotion to infantry captain – he regarded himself as insufficiently experienced. Perhaps he felt unqualified to challenge the uniformed professionals about up-to-the-minute military science with which he had not kept abreast. Provençal politician that he was, Daladier preferred to rely on his nose for the concerns of the rank-and-file *poilu*. His instincts were those of his old comrades who had formed the backbone of France's effort in the trenches.[26]

Yet the long rein which Gamelin was given by Daladier was dictated at least as much by circumstance as by choice. With his duties as leader of the Radicals, Daladier was frequently bogged down in the internal affairs of the party. From April 1938 onwards, he was increasingly criticised for accumulating so many functions that he discharged none of them with the thoroughness they demanded. This was the period in which he added the prime ministership to his burdens, without relinquishing his responsibilities for the war ministry and national defence. It was all an excessive load for one individual. Slowly but surely, the excellent working relations between Daladier and Gamelin deteriorated as the former took on work in more and more areas that distracted him from the duties required of him at the rue Saint-Dominique. As early as 1937–8, Gamelin registered his irritation at finding his minister often unavailable to consider defence business because he had prior party commitments or public engagements.[27]

Daladier was far from being the only civilian leader whose distraction from affairs of national security by the day-to-day demands of politics and government irked French soldiers. Just like Gamelin, de Gaulle also experienced the burial of critical questions of military policy underneath the avalanche of ministerial and party business, such as when he was summoned to the Matignon in the late summer of 1936 to discuss his *armée de métier* project with Blum. During their talk, recalled de Gaulle, 'the telephone rang ten times, turning Léon Blum's attention to trifling parliamentary and administrative questions. As I was taking my leave . . . he made a weary gesture. "You see", he said, "how hard it is for the head of the government to concentrate on the plan you are outlining when he cannot spend five minutes thinking about the same thing."' Blum as Popular Front prime minister was not, however, directly responsible for the conception of French strategy, for the coordination of the fighting services or for the execution of armaments programmes. Daladier, as the minister for national defence and war, was.[28]

Symbolically, at least, Daladier sought to signify publicly that questions of military preparedness and national security were to be placed right at the centre of the concerns of the government by continuing to work from his offices at the rue Saint-Dominique – instead of moving to the Matignon – when he himself became prime minister after April 1938. This, however, was window-dressing as far as the problems with an efficient management of the many demands on his time and concentration were concerned. The more time passed and the more he began to fret about France's own defensive shortcomings, the more exasperated Gamelin became with Daladier's irresolution and vacillation, as well as with the easy-going toleration of the prime minister for interruptions from security affairs. The process of disenchantment was gradual. The damage it did to the morale of the senior French generals and to efficient military management was felt fully only after September 1939. Even then, Gamelin and his staff found it possible, albeit briefly, to recapture the good old days by getting Daladier out to Vincennes for a lunch or meeting where, for a few hours, he could escape the intrigue and gossip of Parisian politics. As Gamelin's adjutant noted in respect of one of these occasions that presented itself in October 1939, Daladier appeared to enjoy the chance of conversation over a long lunch with the officers, 'his genial straightforwardness putting everyone at ease'. He seemed to have lost none of his intellectual clarity or good sense and 'imposed himself by his serious, attentive and considered attitude, not by putting on an authoritative air' or standing on ceremony. The staff noted approvingly that he remained a good listener who 'never sharply contradicted' his interlocutors, and a keen observer of the reactions of Gamelin's officers to his own propositions. By the time he took his leave, Daladier was 'very relaxed'. It 'appeared to do him good to find himself among soldiers', concluded the adjutant; 'We said this to the general.'[29] Such interludes, however, offered only temporary relief to a civil-military relationship in decline. As with so much else that proved wrong with the politics and administration of French military policy by 1939–40, the fall of Daladier's stock as a defence chief gradually added an increasingly important dimension to Gamelin's problems.

Another cause of unease in 1936–9 was Daladier's lack of concern at his feeble position as defence and war minister. He possessed merely 'coordinating' authority – not command – over the navy and air ministries. Britain's observant military attaché, Beaumont-Nesbitt, perceived that this was 'no ministry of national defence as such, only a committee for producing a coordinated solution of certain definite problems'. Reynaud exercised no such English restraint, caustically condemning Daladier's arrangements of June 1936 as simply 'a label stuck on an empty bottle'.[30] Despite his nominally enlarged responsibilities, therefore, Daladier 'was only a glorified minister of war'. His 'reluctance to tighten the defence organisation was also the result of political considerations': there were 'strong groups in the Chamber which did not want the Air Force and the Navy to lose their autonomous status'.[31] In addition to this requirement to accommodate political lobbies and special interests – so characteristic of the 'Republic of Pals' – there was a more unconscious but nonetheless important influence that militated against establishing a unified direction of the armed forces in France. This, of course, was the innate reluctance of republicans to concentrate military power in any one person because of the temptations that it was believed this might arouse for such power's constitutional misuse. Daladier, moreover, was such an archetypal republican himself that he was not the man to try to lay aside this ancient taboo – especially in 1936–7, when he and his Radical party had to show sensitivity to the fears of praetorianism amongst their SFIO partners in government.[32] Both for personal reasons and for historical-systemic ones, therefore, Daladier rested content with maintaining the status quo of independent but loosely coordinated service ministries under his own rather informal purview. By this arrangement he averted the worried interpellations from parliamentarians that might have been levelled if one man was totally in charge. Also avoided were fights over autonomy and authority with his fellow ministers for the air force and navy. Finally, with a fragmented administration of defence, Daladier himself retained great power. Committees, departments, bureaus and directorates ultimately had to come to him for arbitration of their disputes.

These problems, though they were serious, were not the end of the difficulties arising from Daladier's complacency over the shortcomings of inter-service cohesion. For further friction and ineffectiveness resulted from the failure to create a real national defence staff. Indeed, until January 1938 and the extension of Gamelin's remit to the realm of defence coordination, Daladier relied entirely on goodwill to lubricate the meshing of the three separate service commands. Yet this *ad hoc* system was condemned – immediately after the March 1936 crisis – both by the prime minister of the day, Sarraut, and Pétain, as a 'complete and utter shambles'.[33] As late as February 1937 Daladier reiterated to parliamentarians his belief that the 'idea of a single generalissimo in time of peace had more drawbacks than advantages'. He thought that no one person 'could be asked to accept such crushing responsibilities'.[34] Instead of empowering a strong tri-service defence supremo, Daladier contented himself in 1936–7 with improvisation to address issues as and when they turned into problems. Thus he delegated to Gamelin such aspects of defence policy as the prioritising of the land forces' rearmament, the pursuit of military diplomacy with the Belgians, and the lobbying of the British to build a field army suited for a continental role. This display of political confidence in a general had not been witnessed in France since the Millerand–Joffre duo's heyday in 1914–15. Yet Gamelin's authority in this regime was not systematised or given formal structures. It depended upon the preservation of a delicate and personality based equilibrium between a small group of like-minded individuals. It kept Gamelin without the power, outside the army, to run French defence his own way. Moreover, these vulnerable and circumscribed arrangements survived even the broadening of Gamelin's title to the grandiose style of chief of staff for national defence in January 1938.

The altered form left the substance unchanged. Gamelin was enabled to counsel and coordinate air force and navy policies. But he could not command, nor did he control. Long tradition ensured that the ministry of marine guarded its independence zealously. Although the French army was the senior service, the admirals were successful before 1940 in denying it any tangible expression of this standing. Encouraged by the political and financial favour shown the navy in the 1920s and early 1930s – when it had been expanded by Georges Leygues, several times minister of marine – the influential parliamentary lobby that supported them was mustered by the mariners in defence of their autonomy. The successive chiefs of the naval staff between 1933 and 1940, Admirals Georges Durand-Viel and François Darlan, were at least as adept as Gamelin at courting political patronage. Daladier was all too aware that 'unifying the command under Gamelin would provoke a nasty fight' with Darlan and the civilian champions of the navy.[35] Gamelin himself maintained professionally correct relations with Darlan, nothing more, reflecting later that the admiral 'was the epitome of intelligence, alive and open to all problems; but ... he was hardly a man bothered by scruples'.[36]

The air force, for its part, was just as uncompromising in guarding an independence that its officers – not unjustifiably – thought remained precarious. But the navy was defending centuries of custom, whereas the air force was a newcomer (an air ministry having been created only in 1928). French aviation's fight for a life of its own displayed all the vigour of the growing and adventurous youngster in the 1930s.[37]

Gamelin had restricted authority over these sister services. As Britain's military attaché devined, the general was empowered 'to lay down ... within certain limits – the roles to be assigned to the navy and air in time of war'.[38] Budgets, procurement, training, promotions and most crucial facets of naval and air policy in peacetime were, however, subject to nothing more compelling than 'coordination' by Gamelin. This remained unchanged even when the general was named chief of staff for national defence on 21 January 1938. None disputed the confidence of Anthony Eden, then British foreign secretary, that this promotion was 'a wise step'. But Phipps, the British ambassador in Paris, who observed the telling Gallic distinctions between style and substance, warned perspicaciously that it remained 'to be seen what success will attend these ... measures' since similar steps in earlier years had 'not proved effective'.[39]

A further problem stemmed from Daladier's toleration of organisational confusion and personal animosities within the defence bureaucracies. His own confidence in Gamelin was offset by tensions and by tortuous lines of command. There was no systematic endeavour to define and delimit responsibilities in a logical and universally understood manner. In theory, both in the war ministry and in the wider domain of national defence, the role of the secretariat at the rue Saint-Dominique 'was to execute the command's directives as approved by the minister'.[40] This was how the secretariat's function was formulated according to decrees cited by Robert Jacomet, the functionary who succeeded Guinand as secretary-general at the ministry in September 1936 and remained at the head of the defence civil service till the Fall of France. In practice, the hierarchy did not operate in the straightforward way implied by Jacomet. An ideally vertical chain of command was rendered circuitous by Daladier's complaisance towards a multitude of bureaus and study groups, and his failure to upbraid military personnel who sought to obtain decisions by back-stairs intrigue. Neither uniformed officers nor civil administrators were shown unambiguously where their duties lay or to whom they ultimately answered. At best the consequence was delayed decision-taking. Often the results were even more damaging: the exacerbation of institutional rivalry, the fomenting of private jealousies and distrust, the obscuring of an objective and unbiased perspective on the overall French defence requirements. One example was the preparation of industrial mobilisation for war. This agency, of growing importance as the economic dimensions of conflict assumed increasing significance in the light of 1914–18 experiences, was placed under the CSDN secretariat of General Louis Jamet, instead of answering to Jacomet. Moreover, through Jamet, it depended not on the minister for national defence and war, but on the office of the prime minister.[41] Not until Daladier returned to the Matignon in April 1938 did this amount to one and the same thing. Muddle of this sort helps explain why the law for the organisation of the nation in time of war was not passed, despite sixteen years of deliberation, until July 1938 – and why, as will be discussed in this study's final chapter, the French move onto a war footing in the autumn of 1939 was marred by mismanagement and disorder.[42]

A second difficulty arising from the defective structures for making French security policy was the gulf between the lavish staffing available to Daladier and the skimpy resources given Gamelin. The former was supported by a bevy of bureaucrats, in addition to the Radical party functionaries who ran his political office. Daladier, moreover, possessed a military *cabinet* which attended to defence and war department business. Gamelin, in contrast, had only a handful of officers to conduct studies for him or to execute and follow up his directives. Heading Gamelin's small office was his *chef de cabinet particulier*: at first General Emile Ricard, in 1935–6, then General Joseph Jeannel, and finally Colonel Jean Petibon after 1937. In support – besides clerks, telephonists and messengers – were just two adjutants. One of these, Major François Huet, was responsible for maintaining the daily diary or *journal de marche* of Gamelin's headquarters. It is this revealing source – only portions of which appear to have survived Gamelin's death and the Gaullist return to power in 1958 – that yields many of the present study's insights into the inner workings of French defence policy down to May 1940.[43]

When war broke out in September 1939, Gamelin's headquarters transferred from 4 bis, Boulevard des Invalides to the Château de Vincennes on the eastern edge of Paris. His staff remained under Petibon's direction, but was expanded to meet Gamelin's increased responsibilities as commander-in-chief of French land forces and chief of staff for national defence. Sections of the *cabinet* were established to deal with questions of national defence, inter-allied liaison, and the north-eastern theatre, facing Germany. These branches or sections were headed, respectively, by Lieutenant-Colonels François Guillaut, Olivier Poydenot, and Henri Simon.[44]

This enlarged staff was never available to Gamelin during the years of peace, however. Consequently, as his burdens became more onerous in the later 1930s, Gamelin grew increasingly reliant on his closest confidant and longest-serving aide, Petibon. Severely wounded as a company commander at Verdun, Petibon first served Gamelin when he was posted to the staff of the latter's 9th infantry division in 1917. Thereafter the two were never separated for very long. Petibon was on the mission which Gamelin led to Brazil from 1919 to 1925. He took the staff course at the Ecole de Guerre from 1926 to 1928, whilst Gamelin pacified Syria, and then became assistant professor of tactics at St Cyr. After general staff and regimental service in the early 1930s, he rejoined Gamelin's personal *cabinet* in 1936 as a major.[45] Soon afterwards this 'hard-looking, hard-driving officer whose arrival at a colonelcy at the age of forty-five was considered precocious in the French Army', was appointed Gamelin's *chef de cabinet* and appeared to have laid the basis for a glittering career. In due course the war saw his advancement to brigadier-general, but the débâcle of 1940 dispelled his chances of higher honours.[46] He slipped into an obscurity only relieved momentarily by what Gamelin acknowledged to be 'an important role in the Resistance'. The latter occurred when, in November 1942, commanding the 151st infantry regiment in Vichy's armistice army, he helped obstruct the dash of the panzers for the French fleet at Toulon as the Germans invaded the previously unoccupied south of France.[47] At the war's end Petibon retired from the army, all but forgotten.

From 1936 to 1940, however, Petibon's role was of the greatest significance. No-one was closer to Gamelin in these years. At one and the same time he functioned as military secretary, sounding-board and screen against unwelcome intruders. His intuitive rapport with Gamelin was uncanny. Indeed it was so complete that in 1938 Britain's military attaché in Paris, Colonel William Fraser, described him as the general's 'mouthpiece' in dealings with visitors. Envoys from foreign nations as well as French politicians discovered that requests for an interview with Gamelin often led no further than a meeting with Petibon. It became gradually more difficult for everyone except Invalides insiders to fathom Gamelin's intimate thoughts about French military politics and defence strategy.[48] Indeed it became the practice of the *cabinet* as a whole – its style set by Petibon – to work with 'extreme freedom', as a one-time member later recalled. Gamelin's officers increasingly acted in the general's name, according to what Petibon directed on the basis of his long experience of the way Gamelin looked at issues.[49]

Since Gamelin's burdens were growing steadily, it was vital that he avoided enslavement by the army's mundane business and the self-reproducing paperwork of modern military bureaucracy. The *cabinet* played a key part in shielding Gamelin. As a result it became more jealous of its privileges, its influence and its familiarity with the private confidences of its master. In return Gamelin gave wide discretion to his personal staff – in part because he was too busy to do otherwise, in part as a testimony to their loyalty. As one of the three section heads of the enlarged *cabinet* at Vincennes in 1939–40 has remarked, Petibon had a brilliant and flexible mind. 'But, like "The Boss", he was rather secretive and, although always very conversational, never actually told anyone any more than he wanted to say.'[50] Completely trusted, Petibon was also completely dependable. Gamelin paid warm tribute to his 'quick intelligence, his industriousness, his thorough professional knowledge, as regards both regimental and staff work' and had 'nothing but praise' for his 'all-round loyalty, in every situation'. An *éminence grise*, Petibon's understanding with Gamelin replicated the latter's own association with Joffre a generation earlier.[51]

However, much else had changed radically between the *belle époque* and the later 1930s. Defence policy could not be effectively conducted as it had once been by a general and a tiny band of trusted intimates. Air power had brought a whole new dimension – and a complex technologically specialised one at that – to warfare. Communications had become complicated, the burdens on staffs heavier. For all the capabilities of Petibon and the modest-sized *cabinet* at his disposal, the small personal staff was no longer enough to provide Gamelin with the outreach of a management team worthy of the name. Yet, without an instrument of this sort, Gamelin lacked the means to develop his own ideas or to promote and exert his own influence, in the places where defence policy was implemented.

No inter-service unified national defence staff – drawn from army, navy and air force personnel – was ever established to help Gamelin enforce and oversee 'coordination' after he was named chief of staff for national defence at the start of 1938. A reformed high command was only once floated, in principle, in an endeavour to address the problem of Gamelin's emasculated authority beyond the army. That was in June 1937. The initiative suggested that the commander-in-chief in French North Africa and resident-general in Morocco, General Auguste Noguès, return from Rabat to head the metropolitan army. Then, in the outlined reorganisation, Gamelin was to be appointed executive generalissimo, in command over all three services. As before, however, the forces favouring the status quo prevailed over pressures for change. The army general staff continued to report to its old chief, Colson, through three deputy chiefs of staff and four bureaux (training, intelligence, operations, transport and supply). Meanwhile the navy and the air force – the latter by vigorously lobbying Daladier – successfully defended their autonomy.[52]

Far from promoting integration, inter-service politics was tending at this time to exaggerate the rivalries between the French armed forces. Under Daladier's government, formed in April 1938, the colonial ministry, at the behest of its ambitious political chief, Georges Mandel (*chef de cabinet* to Clemenceau in 1917–19), established its own control over the forces stationed in the French empire overseas. A decree in May 1938 created a chief of staff of colonial forces, with membership of the CPDN, equal in official standing with Vuillemin and Darlan and, in practice, as free as these service leaders from any orders from Gamelin. In the face of these trends to increase the number of independent and coequal French military chiefs, it was little consolation to Gamelin that in 1938 he acquired access in his capacity as chief of staff for national defence to CSDN secretariat resources because these 'in no way became, as would have been logical, a national defence staff'. It was a further demonstration of the justification of Gamelin's complaint that, each time he mooted reform, 'the extension of the authority of the chief of staff of national defence met immense resistance'.[53]

This ongoing weakness in Gamelin's position was exacerbated by the competitive and antagonistic relationship in which he found himself in 1936–7 with General Victor Bourret, head of Daladier's military *cabinet*. A 'political general ... of little or no worth', in a British assessment of the late 1930s, Bourret had an importance that was out of all proportion to his formal rank as a brigadier-general.[54] His influence was great. It stemmed from the fact that Daladier was obliged as a result of his heavy party political commitments to delegate much of the executive business at the rue Saint-Dominique to his personal military staff. Not only was Bourret alleged to be a born intriguer with an abrasive personality, but he and his subordinate officers in the *cabinet* formed a 'screen interposed between the minister and the command'.[55] Gamelin found that these intermediaries restricted his own personal contact –

and indeed that of all the CSG generals – with Daladier. Reported to be not just a collaborator of Daladier but also one of his friends, Bourret had an intellectual quality and 'down-to-earth good sense' that Gamelin privately recognised. Indeed, Bourret was deemed able enough to be appointed to command the Fifth Army in Alsace during the phoney war and the Battle of France. As Gamelin admitted to his own staff in late 1939, subordinate officers who had previously been Bourret's 'hardened detractors' grew to admire him as a commander, where they had been hostile to him as a uniformed politician.[56]

Notwithstanding these more mellow appreciations later, Gamelin discovered in the mid-1930s that Bourret was instrumental in erecting an almost-impenetrable labyrinth of political and military aides and advisors around Daladier. Gamelin not only found this an obstacle to obtaining decisions swiftly, he also observed how, in his view, it corrupted the proper processes of policy. For, he complained, it encouraged officers who were denied regular lines of access to their political authorities to engage in practices such as lobbying backbench parliamentarians who were reputed to have the ear of the minister and planting stories with newspaper editors or military correspondents. These devices to gain a hearing, these resorts to middlemen in the corridors of power, were all too much part-and-parcel of the 'Republic of Pals'.[57] They were nevertheless the antithesis of the disciplined, loyal and hierarchical structure of command to which the military were trained to respond. Gamelin was on firm ground in worrying about the adverse effects that the practise of such habits could have on the discipline and unity of his officer corps. The trouble was that he was not in a solid position from which to preach on the issue, since it was widely rumoured that he had helped his own career to flourish, and had advanced causes dear to his own heart, by shrewd use of just such networks as these among press men and parliamentarians. There was, therefore, a certain credibility problem in Gamelin trying to prescribe a code of conduct for the officer corps when he was suspected of not having observed it scrupulously himself.[58]

The direct cause of the problem – the presence of Bourret in the rue Saint-Dominique – was eased in March 1937 when a transfer brought in a new chief for Daladier's military *cabinet*. The replacement was General Jules Decamp, a 'discreet and capable' officer in the view of another member of Daladier's staff in 1938–9, the Quai d'Orsay trained Jean Daridan. In spite of the change, however, Gamelin complained that through 'force of habit and their self-sustaining momentum', the intrigues and irregular communications between senior military figures and politicians continued to compromise open and trusting civil-military relations. Yet Gamelin seemed to remain oblivious – or sublimely indifferent – to the encouragement that his own example gave to the very conduct that he criticised.[59]

The last but not the least of the flaws in the higher command structure was the distrustful relationship that existed between both Daladier and Gamelin on the one hand and General Georges, Gamelin's most senior subordinate, on the other. Much of the trouble stemmed from Georges' pedigree: he had risen within Weygand's entourage. In the late-1930s Gamelin suspected Georges of heading an unofficial coterie of officers who retained attachments to Weygand and the French political right and who were indifferent, at best, to Gamelin's appeal for republican loyalty. Later, Gamelin took Georges to task for possessing 'the soul of a chief of staff, not that of a wartime leader'. However, in spite of his lack of experience in operational high command – excepting a short time in charge of a corps in Algeria in 1932 – criticisms of Georges rarely surfaced before the campaign of 1940.[60] Less debatable was the fact of his conservative connections. These dated back to his service under Foch, alongside Weygand, in 1914–18, through a spell as Pétain's chief of staff during the Rif War in Morocco in 1925–6, to a term as Maginot's *chef de cabinet militaire* in 1929–31. It was at the instigation of yet another right-wing war minister, Fabry, that Georges was appointed deputy to Gamelin in mid-1935.[61]

Within the army, however, the limitations on Georges tended to mirror those which frustrated Gamelin's own aims towards the other services. As Gamelin's deputy or *major-général*, Georges' authority derived only from specific delegation by Gamelin in order to oversee a particular task or programme. A relationship such as this could function effectively only if oiled by complete trust and a near-intuitive sense of his chief's thinking on the part of the subordinate. Such a rapport existed between Gamelin and Petibon. It was conspicuously absent in the case of Gamelin and Georges. In practice Gamelin delegated little of importance, since he knew that at the close of 1934 Georges had been Weygand's nominee, instead of himself, to succeed Weygand as vice-president of the CSG and commander-in-chief designate. Gamelin realised that to deny Georges full knowledge of what was going on was to deny him a chance to be an alternative locus of power in the high command.[62] Gamelin's staff consequently tended to leave Georges ill-informed, so that he had 'great difficulty keeping abreast of matters' as Schweisguth noted. Georges himself felt inadequately briefed by Colson and yet, from this position of semi-ignorance, was charged with chairing the important commission that modernised and codified operational doctrine and produced the *Provisional Instruction on the Handling of*

Large Formations of 1936. As Schweisguth recorded in May that year, Georges bewailed 'how false a position he [Georges] was in; he deputizes for ... Gamelin as the army's inspector-general instead of replacing him as chief of the general staff when he himself is away on inspections; he's thus forever finding that he's not in the picture'.[63]

Daladier's dislike of Georges aggravated these problems from June 1936 onwards. The minister's long-running disputes with Weygand over military policy in 1933–4 left a legacy of suspicion towards Georges. Even an easing of tensions between Georges and Gamelin by 1939 failed to change Daladier's outlook. When, that January, Gamelin urged Daladier to promote Georges at last to the CSG vice-presidency and leave Gamelin himself to concentrate on national defence planning and negotiations with allies, Daladier took it askance. Indeed, he contrived to avoid Gamelin altogether for a month afterwards. When, finally, Gamelin cornered Daladier in February 1939 at an Elysée reception and pressed for a decision, the prime minister (as he had by then become) adamantly refused to consider Georges for more extensive powers, saying: 'He will not have your calmness and independence ... and I do not share your confidence in his military ability.'[64]

Thus a series of initiatives intended to create workable and comprehensible lines of command foundered on personality conflicts and political suspicions. The failures were, however, owed more to poor man-management than to malevolent or conspiratorial intentions. Blum, surely, was justified in his phlegmatic view of the military institutions that France possessed in 1936–7, for whose political dependability he had Gamelin's assurances. Yet, at the same time, he was wise to fear a lurch in a Gaullien direction. Blum had denigrated the idea of forming a separate career army as proposed by Reynaud in the 1935 debate on two-year service because he believed such a corps would be 'praetorian' and opposed to a French republicanism rooted in a *levée en masse* of citizen soldiers.

Blum considered that some of France's 'important military leaders' were of 'more than doubtful' loyalty to the Republic. He had in mind Pétain as well as Weygand and he worried that a great many more junior officers 'were suspect'. He was anxious about what would become of the rank-and-file – whom he extolled as the 'sons of our soil and our cities ... the salvation of our free institutions' – if they were ever 'turned over to [command by] a blindly obedient praetorian elite'. For the SFIO leader astutely recognised that the question of professionalisation was a red herring in relation to a strictly technical military reform such as an expansion of mechanised forces. Gamelin and other generals such as Jean Flavigny (the first commander of France's prototype light mechanised division), concurred with Blum that de Gaulle and Reynaud 'allowed or even caused a fearful confusion'. Since they argued as if 'the armoured divisions ... had to *become* the army ... it followed that our effective military power would be placed in the hands of a professional army and no longer in the hands of a national army, an army of citizens'.[65] Neither de Gaulle nor Reynaud, according to Gamelin, had taken sufficient precautions to forestall this suspicion. Nor were the two views reconciled when Blum himself interviewed de Gaulle at the Matignon in the late summer or early autumn of 1936. Blum merely restated his confidence that Daladier's and Gamelin's military programmes would meet the technical demands put forward by de Gaulle, without carrying the latter's political provocativeness.[66]

Military hostility to the Popular Front was not, therefore, commonly manifested. But when it was it revived serious phobias: it opened the cupboards of the Third Republic onto one of its most feared skeletons. Among the bogeymen, besides Weygand, Pétain and de Gaulle, there was the retired General de Castelnau who was a bigoted clerical and 1914–18 army commander, nicknamed 'the booted Capucin'. It was de Castelnau who, after the Spanish Popular Front's election in February 1936, coined the expression 'Frente Crapular'. Nonetheless we remain, as Jean Lacouture cautions, 'short of information about the army's state of mind'.[67] Blum grasped that the SFIO's support for internationalism and arms reductions in the 1920s and early 1930s hardly banked him much credit with which to open his account with the generals. Politicised right-wing officers may have been few, but they made a disproportionate commotion in the press and in salon society. It was hard, then, for a nervous and governmentally inexperienced left to exorcise the spectre of a military menace to their policies, particularly once the Spanish military rebels of 18 July took on the personification of superficially similar ghouls south of the Pyrenees. Even Gamelin later candidly conceded that 'in their hearts and their heads the sympathies of our soldiers favoured Franco'.[68]

Was much menace posed, therefore, by the secret right-wing organisations discovered by the authorities in 1937, the *Corvignolles* cells and the Cagoule or CSAR (Comité Secret d'Action Révolutionnaire)? The former was an officers' network, clandestinely coordinated by Major Georges Loustaunau-Lacau, one of Pétain's staff. *Corvignolles*' objective was to prepare in country-wide garrisons for immediate counter-action (even without war ministry directives) in the event of indications of a communist coup in France. Allegedly the organisation could count on 10,000 officers, one-third of the corps, had it decided to move. Loustaunau claimed success in eradicating pacifist literature from the barracks and in negating what he asserted was a PCF-inspired subversive campaign directed at conscript other ranks. Yet by February 1938 Loustaunau had been uncovered by an informant, disciplined and placed on the inactive duty list. The CSAR was a different kettle of fish. It was civilian controlled. It had service connections only with a handful of officers of ultra-conservative persuasion – mostly retired reactionaries such as General Duseigneur and Marshal Franchet d'Esperey. The former was a one-time air force officer; the latter a legendary anti-Bolshevik who bankrolled the CSAR to the tune of 1 million francs from his personal fortune.

Loustaunau conferred occasionally with the CSAR leaders. But the two networks differed crucially in nature and intent. *Corvignolles* was dedicated to eradicating communist and anarchist influence from the army's depots and camps. It conceived of a military defence of the regime as a last resort against a left-wing coup. The CSAR, by contrast, was *itself* an actively subversive organisation. It not only intrigued against the Popular Front but it worked to undermine the Republic. Loustaunau was dismayed to learn of CSAR approaches not only to d'Esperey but also to Colonel Georges Groussard (a former member of Georges' staff), and to senior serving generals of the CSG. These last contacts also embarrassed Gamelin during 1937. Indeed the latter was obliged to secure assurances under oath of honour from fellow CSG members that there was no anti-regime plotting among them. The indignity was even inflicted on the inspector of infantry, General Joseph Dufieux, even though he was a former classmate of Gamelin from the St Cyr promotion of 1893.

Notwithstanding these alarms, however, *Corvignolles* remained free from CSAR infiltration. Loustaunau, for his part, distinguished between his own defensive counter-coup network and the conspiratorial designs of the Cagoulards to install their own right-wing regime. The cells, secrecy and suspicion of this episode reveals an officer corps that was ill-at-ease with itself in the ideologically charged socio-political culture of France in the 1930s. Nevertheless it remained a corps of which it has been convincingly demonstrated that 'definite antiregime plans did not exist in the Command'.[69]

During the Popular Front there was no organised challenge from the officers to Blum's government or to the Republic as a whole. It is fair, however, to turn the coin over and inquire whether the officers for their part perceived a threat from the left. Did the French high command concur with a judgement by the British foreign office in September 1936 that 'the spirit and morale of the army is infinitely more healthy than that of the capital or of the civilian population generally'?[70]

Without doubt it was an aim of French spokesmen to reassure foreigners – and especially the sought-after allies such as the British and the Belgians. Senior French officers kept up a confident appearance in order to maintain faith abroad that France retained the ability to defend herself and assist her friends. In this vein Gauché, the head of the army 2e Bureau, affirmed that France was 'not in the state of decay' that she was 'often thought to be by outside observers. Let them only scratch [her] . . . and see'.[71] Outside observers, when given the chance to judge for themselves, tended to share this conclusion. The US military attaché attended French manoeuvres near Aix-en-Provence in September 1936 in which about 38,000 troops participated. 'Approximately fifty per cent', he reported, 'were reservists drawn to a large extent from communistic areas in and around Marseilles. I was [however] particularly impressed with the esprit of the troops.' He added that other military attachés with whom he spoke 'were all of the opinion that the morale of the troops was very high and that there was little possibility of Communism having a foothold . . . although French officers also stated that constant efforts were being made by the Communistic leaders to break down or undermine the morale'.[72]

In fact military service was regarded as one of the key educative experiences undergone by young Frenchmen. Throughout the *Troisième*, conscription had been valued by the regime as a republicanising influence. It was perceived as an institution for the inculcation of social discipline and the taming of extreme political opinions.[73] In this respect, little had changed since 1891 when this function of military service had been articulated in print by Hubert Lyautey – later famous as the 'pacifier of Morocco' – in his celebrated article, 'Du rôle social de l'officier'.[74] The system still appeared to function as republicans desired during the Popular Front. The American military attaché reported that 'undoubtedly some Communistic propaganda and theories are spread amongst the enlisted personnel *but on the whole the draft each year is soon weaned away from these undermining influences*'. His British counterpart spoke in 1937 with a close confidant of Gamelin, André Pironneau, who edited the conservative newspaper *L'Echo de Paris*. The journalist felt that 'the majority of men joining the army with extreme political views lose the latter rapidly'; despite sometimes re-adopting them back in civilian life, after completing their term of conscription, they nonetheless made 'excellent soldiers'.[75]

Naturally there is evidence of paranoia among the officers about pacifist and anti-militarist literature finding its way into the barracks. But this fear was more widespread among conservative politicians and self-appointed 'friends of the army' than it was within the serving officer corps. For example, on only his second day in Laval's government as war minister, in June 1935, Fabry took pains to tell his *cabinet* of his 'decision to fight communism in order to restore confidence to the line officers'. A sworn enemy of the Popular Front, Fabry lost his Paris seat in the Chamber to an SFIO candidate in 1936, which served only to increase his hatred of the left even though he subsequently gained a Senate seat in a by-election that November. 'A decent man, but a political operator', in Gamelin's unforgiving assessment, Fabry was an officer-turned-politician. His concerns situated him closer to Colonel de La Rocque's Croix de Feux and veterans and rightists of the Parti Social Français than to the general staff.[76]

In the ferment of 1936 some left-wing tracts which regimental commanders regarded as seditious inevitably reached rank-and-file soldiers. But proven instances where troops were incited to acts of insubordination were very rare. Neither Gamelin nor Daladier was seriously perturbed. Addressing the Versailles federation of the Radical Party on 28 June 1936, the minister for national defence and war took care to emphasise the close cooperation and common positions that unified the Popular Front government and the armed services. Danger to the military, insisted Daladier, arose solely from forces beyond the political pale – from the 'enemies of the Republic' engaged in 'their old game' of social and institutional destabilisation. Just three weeks into office Daladier was publicly pledging major improvements for the defence services. From these beginnings arose the rearmament programme of 7 September 1936.[77]

As far as reconciling the left to a military build-up was concerned, it was helpful that the external danger had now become so apparent and proximate to the French political community. The perilousness of France's international situation helped bridge the traditional misunderstandings and suspicions between the army and the left-wing parties because it drove them together in a common recognition that major new military procurements were urgently required. Indeed the Popular Front's readiness to undertake a defence effort for the army alone of 14 billion francs over four years, beginning in September 1936, dwarfed anything previously contemplated by French conservative administrations. It represented a crucial show of intent and realism to the French generals. It also re-established the credentials of the republican left as the heirs to the Jacobin and Gambettist tradition of patriotic defence. In this fashion the Popular Front was spectacularly able to trump a usual ace card of the right – the claim to be the party of strong defence.[78]

From this time, too, Daladier and Gamelin consolidated the army's internal stability by taking steps to enhance its unity, raise its morale and rekindle a sense of mission. The army was shown that the government and public at large appreciated it once again. For his part, Gamelin sought to modernise the management of personnel questions, encouraged by the feel possessed by Daladier for the cares of the rank-and-file.[79] In the spring 1936 factory occupations, Gamelin was uneasy about anti-militarist literature targeted at his non-commissioned officers, 'seeking to foment a real revolution and tempting them by saying: "Come with us and you'll be the officers tomorrow."' This disquiet found an echo that autumn when the US military attaché reported French officers admitting 'that there were opportunists among both officers and non-commissioned officers who would follow any line of political trend that would seem to enhance their own prospects'.[80] In truth, however, the extreme left itself saw little hope of inciting either the conscripts or the cadres to an insurrection. Indeed an anarchist newspaper, in a discussion of ways of fighting fascism in April 1936, referred to the 'barrier of republican feeling . . . among the forces of law and order'. The overall moderation and apoliticism of the military offered as little solace to the revolutionary left as it did to the conspiratorial right. Blum had been told at his 10 June meeting with Gamelin that politics had to be kept out of the army in return for keeping soldiers out of politics. For the most part the bargain was preserved.[81]

In November 1936 Daladier successfully met one of his stiffest political tests. This occurred over revolutionary proposals to democratise the army. The plan originated in the Chamber army commission where it was tabled by Robert Lazurich of the SFIO and Marcel Gitton of the PCF. It demanded a democratically organised citizen-soldiery. Its model was Jean Jaurès's scheme of 1913 for a patriotic militia. Lazurick and Gitton proposed to admit trade unionists to the CSDN. This would have afforded communists access to highly secret strategy documents and to the arrangements for converting France from a peacetime regime to a war economy. The deputies also sought to replace conscription with para-military instruction and to create in every barracks a *cercle des soldats* affiliated to the CGT – a trade unionising of the rank-and-file. To this Daladier countered that it was impossible to reconcile the rights enjoyed under the law by trade unions in civilian society with the necessities of military discipline. The latter, he reminded his colleagues, had to be based on strict subordination within a hierarchy and on obedience, without dispute, to orders from superiors. Daladier refused to entertain 'illusory promises which neither I nor others could keep without compromising national security'. He had the scheme defeated in committee by reminding the army commissioners from the SFIO and

PCF that they too were 'supporters of a government for whose decisions they had to take their full share of responsibility'. And this episode was, it appears, the closest Gamelin found himself to the nightmares that periodically ruffled his outward serenity so long as France had a government 'obedient to a socialist imperative'.[82]

Happily for Gamelin, Daladier retained in 1936–7 not just a satisfactory rapport with the military – other ranks as well as officers – but also a legacy of credibility with the parties of the left. Certainly in 1939 – and probably earlier too – he was anxious to inculcate in young officers a greater sense of civic consciousness. To Gamelin 'he cited Jaurès's idea: "The army should be linked to the elite of the nation." Instead of two years at Saint-Cyr, future officers ought to spend twelve months at university and only their second year at the academy.'[83]

Beyond this, Daladier possessed a solid political power-base. His extensive support among Radicals contrasted with the weak parliamentary position of the erratic mavericks such as Reynaud and Mandel, or the professional soldiers-turned-politicians such as Fabry and Maurin. The Radical Party under Daladier's command remained a major parliamentary force in both the upper and lower houses. Even reduced by their casualties in the 1936 elections, there were still over one hundred Radical deputies in the Chamber in the Third Republic's sixteenth and last legislature. The Radicals remained powerful and at least pivotal – still the makers and breakers of governments if no longer automatically their leaders. Last but far from least in this connection, Daladier himself had personal political skills of a singular potency. His was an appealing blend of patriotism and provincialism; his was a taciturn manner broken periodically by an innate eloquence of a rough-and-ready kind that spoke for the common man. Above all, Daladier had the gift of a sixth-sense for what the popular mood would tolerate, for what was politically possible at a given time.[84] According to Colonel Georges Raquez, Belgium's military attaché in Paris, Daladier was 'the only one' of the ministers for the French armed services in 1937 to exhibit 'a forceful personality capable of being a great leader'.

Attending the debates in the Palais Bourbon in January–February 1937 on the year's defence budget, Raquez described Daladier as 'of the three ministers for the [French] armed forces, [having] far and away the greatest technical mastery of his area of responsibility'. Daladier was 'the heavyweight in debate, the one to place his points above party politics, the one with the most "national" perspective ... the least evasive when answering questions'. Unlike Cot and Gasnier-Duparc, Daladier struck Raquez as someone with 'the air of a statesman' about him.[85] Daladier knew how to maximise this asset. He traded on it to obtain unusually broad support for his policies. Most remarkably, he achieved the previously unknown feat of shepherding the 1938 army estimates through the Chamber without opposition. The watching British military attaché ascribed this triumph in part to Daladier's deft parliamentary performance; but he also felt that 'credit . . . [was to] be given to the personal prestige of the minister', who was judged 'within the army and outside as one of the most capable and energetic . . . whom France has had for many years'.[86]

Relations thus remained stable between the Popular Front, parliament and the professional officers. This state of affairs owed much to the pledge Blum gave Gamelin in June 1936 that the left would attend responsibly to the requirements of national defence. Blum was important in this. He gave sufficient assurance that he and his ministers – though not all his grassroots militants – understood and shared the anxieties of the generals about French strategic vulnerability. The US assistant military attaché in Paris put his finger on the shift that had occurred by October 1936. 'A further change of attitude', he reported, 'can also be noted when one considers M. Blum's utterances on various military questions prior to his assuming office and those since he became Premier . . . Whilst still voicing his desire to maintain peace, he has not hesitated, in view of the German decision [to extend conscription], to augment the number of professional soldiers . . . and to increase considerably the budget for national defense.' 'Responsibility', as the American put it, had 'evidently caused a change in the attitude of M. Blum. It would appear that after all is said and done he is a Frenchman first and a militant socialist afterwards.'[87] This was indeed evidence of a pragmatism that Gamelin could recognise and admire.

If Blum was important to this live-and-let-live formula for civil-military relations, Gamelin was crucial. He upheld his reputation as an inoffensive republican with a wide gamut of political friends. His style disarmed Blum as effectively as it had Tardieu before him. Indeed his style itself became one of the pillars on which the civil-military consensus rested. The army remained insulated from France's socio-political disorders of 1935–7. By keeping the army on one side Gamelin relegitimised the high command in the eyes of a suspicious SFIO and Radical leadership. This was no mean feat after the hostilities of the Weygand years. France's officers stayed, in the main, plainly anti-communist. In spite of this, however, Gamelin managed to keep them obedient enough to the apolitical tradition of *la grande muette*. In 1936–7 this enabled him to bring about a successful cohabitation with the moderate governing left – a cohabitation given its example by the *ménage à trois* of Blum-Gamelin-Daladier.

Inevitably, however, there was an inherent fragility in reliance upon such a personality based formula for civil-military harmony. As Lacouture has expressed it, the problem was that 'Daladier's authority was generally admitted. But to what would this have amounted if the president of the Radical Party had been pitched out into opposition?'[88]

Too much turned on the partnership between Gamelin and Daladier. Too much depended on the patronage of this one minister towards one general. By the late 1930s the duumvirate had grown synonymous, inside and outside France, with the French defence effort. By 1939 the pairing had become something very close to an institution in its own right. At one level this was a remarkable accomplishment for the two men. But it was not healthy. Ultimately it disguised more than it could achieve. The rearmament and military preparation which Gamelin and Daladier achieved were impressive enough by 1939–40 that they obscured the continuing absence in France of the institutions needed for success in modern war. As the phoney war made plain, Gamelin's relationship with Daladier was no substitute for a well-established ministry of armaments and a unified high command.

Before the crisis of 1940, it can be concluded that the French army lacked the well-spring for a political intervention of the type essayed by its Spanish counterpart (also in response to a Popular Front government). It has been asked whether the political discipline imposed by Gamelin on French army officers had negative consequences, however. Did it preserve obedience at the cost of stifling professional innovation? Did it prevent new military ideas from hatching? Did it impose a technical and tactical conformity that proved fatal in 1940? Did it deny advancement to able and imaginative younger commanders?[89] It seems difficult to establish any convenient connection of this sort. Some but not all of the military reformers and innovators detested the Third Republic; some but not all of the doctrinal diehards were republican loyalists. Neither 'camp' had any monopoly on forward thinking, nor on political discontent. Nor, for that matter, was the situation in Spain at this time a clear-cut struggle between military rebels and civilian republicans. By no means all the officers of the Spanish army rose against the Frente Popular. Moreover it should be remembered that those who did rebel in Spain had not experienced a Dreyfus affair to restrain them. In France, after all, the political partisanship betrayed by the general staff over Dreyfus had cost the army much of its autonomy. It had helped bring about the 'Republic of the Radicals' which had then staged a purge of the officer corps in which – significantly – the young Gamelin was rising during the 1900s.

Gamelin and his contemporaries remembered this uncomfortable civil-military experience undergone at the time of Dreyfus. These men knew better than to oppose the regime so long as it responded by heeding the military's analysis of French security interests. In the 1930s the apoliticism of the French officers was maintained by Gamelin; but it was not guaranteed. It was not an absolute allegiance; it was merely conditional. It could extend to toleration of the electoral triumph of the French left. But it could not, as 1940 demonstrated, survive the military triumph of the Germans. The latter was a catastrophe which demolished the reputations – and with them the authority – of Gamelin as well as Daladier. The shock was too much for the discipline of the malcontents among France's higher commanders. After Gamelin's authority had been smashed the putschistes and Pétainists could impute the disaster to the regime – and specifically to the Republic's allegedly poor war preparations. So started the pernicious but persuasive myth that the Popular Front, during its summer of 1936, sowed the seed of the German harvest four summers later. This became an alibi for a France bewildered by its defeat.

5 The road to rearmament: Gamelin, Daladier and Popular Front defence policy

In mid-1936, for Gamelin and Daladier, anxieties over the inadequacies of French policy-making machinery were secondary compared to their alarm about the lethargic pace of France's military re-equipment programmes. German armaments, the French believed, were still increasing remorselessly. As Blum assumed office the CSDN secretariat counselled that it had become indispensable to extend Laval's 2,629 million franc military refurbishment programme of 21 June 1935, then in progress. For Jamet's officials had uncovered a disturbing gap between the army's estimated needs in mechanised material and the quantities already supplied or ordered. Of the 140 Chars B required to constitute an agreed strategic reserve, half were not yet on order. Moreover contracts had only been awarded for 700 of the R35 and H35 light tanks, for 30 infantry-support battalions, against the 1,500 required.[1]

Daladier confronted the army's equipment deficiencies when, on 26 June 1936, he chaired the very first meeting of the new CPDN (the Haut Comité Militaire's successor). He emphasised the Blum government's determination to apply centralised methods to resolve inter-service disputes. Long-range planning was to be sought to calibrate the needs of each of the armed forces to a target of an integrated national security policy. Needing to defend France 'without faintheartedness', the government proposed to address immediately what Daladier called the 'agonising question' of industrial mobilisation. It would seek a complementary relationship between the three services' equipment programmes, balancing the degree of urgency of each's production requirements 'and the total financial resources allowed for national defence.' Gamelin for his part urged the release of credits, the shifting of manufacture 'onto a war footing, especially for tanks' and the 'tooling-up of the defence industries'. He aimed at early formation of two tank divisions equipped solely with Chars B, a third light mechanised division and motorisation of ten of France's twenty standing peacetime infantry divisions.[2]

In the absence of Cabinet minutes, the bargaining and brokerage by which Blum's ministers arrived at the scope, priorities and pace of the Popular Front's four-year rearmament plan of 7 September 1936 elude appraisal. The resulting 14 billion franc army programme was distributed, by agreement on 30 October 1936, as shown in Table 2. By this massive initiative the Popular Front, elected amidst euphoric social anticipation, set the foundations to do more for guns than for butter.[3]

Table 2. *Allocation of the 14 billion franc programme of September 1936*

1937	1938	1939	1940
2,642 m. frs.	4,571 m. frs.	3,642 m. frs.	3,133 m. frs.
18.9 %	32.6 %	26.0 %	22.4 %
(of 14 bn. total)			

Meanwhile Daladier brandished before the CPDN the instrument selected to cut through the production problems and delivery delays which had plagued re-equipment in 1934–6: enforced nationalisation of selected war material manufacturers. This would 'confer on the state a direct means of action over preparations for industrial mobilisation', affecting the air force and army.[4] For the latter the painful experiences in 1935–6 of attempting to expedite development and output of military vehicles at Renault and Hotchkiss predisposed Gamelin and Colson to support Daladier. Initially Gamelin, Daladier and the defence ministry's secretary-general, Robert Jacomet, envisaged state share-holding in selected firms, to exert leverage rather than assume overall control. But outright physical expropriation became the preferred formula once Jacomet, after inquiries, reported that the 'political tide' was 'running in favour of nationalisations'. State takeovers would elicit from parliament the money required 'without quibble' whereas finance for any other approach would be 'much less easily' forthcoming.[5]

Gamelin at first seems to have been unsure about nationalisation. He cannot but have heard it blowing in on the wind. For since the early 1930s the air had been noisy with political clamour from the left against 'offensive' armaments in general and profiteers from trade in weapons, the 'merchants of death' or *marchands de canons*, in particular. In Britain the period saw the issue probed by a Royal Commission on the Private Manufacture of Arms under the chairmanship of the cabinet secretary, Maurice Hankey. In France a bill aimed at securing state control over the trading and production of weapons, backed by Pierre Cot, was among the Popular Front's earliest initiatives. On 10 June 1936, the same day as Gamelin saw Blum at the Matignon, Britain's military attaché was told by Petibon (doubtless speaking for Gamelin) 'that the general staff would have preferred to have gone on as they were . . . with a combination of state and private armament works . . . [but] on the whole the change would be more one of name than of fact so . . . they faced the future without misgiving'. Once draft legislation was in preparation by late June, Gamelin saw that the proposals were indeed for a future mix of government-controlled plants and private enterprise. He was reassured by Jacomet's argument for pragmatism and Daladier's restrained intentions towards takeovers of army equipment suppliers. When the minister named specific targets for nationalisation – Renault and Hotchkiss – it was to stress that he wanted possession of their military vehicle departments alone, not the wholesale expropriation of these companies. Daladier declared himself opposed to takeovers of firms only a small part of whose turnover was generated by defence orders. He also pledged compensation for share-holders in affected companies.[6]

Discovering, in his first month back at the rue Saint-Dominique, alarming inadequacies in French defence readiness, as he told the Chamber's army commission on 1 July, Daladier found himself at one with most senior commanders. His inquiries reassured him about the quality of the reservists available by mobilisation, the 'fighting mass of Frenchmen' in whom he anticipated would be rekindled in another emergency 'that enthusiasm we saw in 1914'. But Daladier shared Gamelin's disquiet at the shortage of modern equipment for the troops. Nationalisation was to remedy this, and only Bloch-Dassault among leading military figures questioned the policy, alleging that it would exacerbate production delays by increasing industrial costs and reducing profit incentives through state underwriting of business. For Daladier, though, Goering's appointment at this time to direct Germany's four-year plan for economic self-sufficiency was both model and warning. It demonstrated the 'grip of the army over German economic activity' and underlined how French army equipment deficiencies threatened to 'crumble' France's defences. War stocks, Daladier impressed, could not 'just be improvised'.[7]

By 8 July the war industries' nationalisation bill was before the

Chamber commission. Daladier explained to deputies that, although the legislation would confer broad powers on the defence ministers, his personal objective was to enable the state to underwrite particular industries which lacked either the means or the determination to modernise. No firms likely to be the object of nationalisation were named, since it was intended – as with much Popular Front legislation – that this be an outline law (*loi-cadre*) enabling case-by-case decisions over relevant companies by each service ministry. Reassured, the army commission approved the bill on 15 July and it received the Chamber's assent two days later. The Senate then inserted a clause defining war material and also struck out the possibility of combining state and private shareholdings to create mixed companies. The bill became law on 11 August 1936.[8]

Which businesses were nationalised, and with what effects on production and equipment supplies to the French forces? Allegations around these questions underlay the case against the defendants tried by Vichy's supreme court at Riom from 1940 to 1942. There Blum, Daladier, Gamelin, Jacomet, Guy La Chambre and Cot (*in absentia*) were indicted for supposedly applying domestically divisive 'class politics' in an irresponsible way when France required national unity and a common purpose to prepare against external peril. In fact the political enemies of the Popular Front deployed the criticisms of nationalisation characteristic of Riom as early as the 1937 Senate debate on the army budget. Fabry, the former war minister under Laval, condemned state takeovers as a cosmetic pretence at rearming. 'Our whole society', he asserted, 'the minds of the elites as much as the hands of the workers, has been crippled, paralysed . . . and instead of distributing new tools the government has been buying up buildings.' Fabry ignored the Senate's own responsibility for limiting the nationalisation to compensated but outright takeovers. Yet Gamelin and Daladier unsuccessfully sought the mixed enterprise formula which, retaining private incentives on some scale in every arms producer, might have generated higher investment in modern plant.[9]

It seemed, to industrialists, that nationalisation decrees appeared 'like so many revolutionary summonses' through the winter of 1936–7. Yet, related to the total of firms engaged on defence orders, sub-contracts and component supply, takeovers were few. All told, the air ministry took possession of twenty-eight plants, the navy just two and the war ministry only nine (these coming from just seven separate companies). The army's nationalisations included Renault's armoured vehicle design and assembly centre at Issy-les-Moulineaux, on 28 October 1936; Brandt's munitions' works at Chatillon and Vernon, together with Schneider's artillery factories at Le Havre and Le Creusot, all taken over on 31 December 1936, and the Levallois-Perret Hotchkiss small-arms and tank plant. Daladier's commitment that only enterprises in which defence work predominated would be affected was honoured: on nationalisation, on 18 May 1937, the Hotchkiss-Levallois military output represented three-quarters of turnover, whilst the firm's two other factories, at Clichy and Gennevilliers, were left untouched.[10] Nonetheless, gross misrepresentation of these government takeovers has persisted in the historiography of France's politico-economic and military experiences of the 1930s. Even Henri Michel's study, written with access to Riom archives, private papers and the documents of major ministries, has criticised the takeovers for responsibility for the 'big black mark' of the 'long delays incurred before this enormous industrial machine could function fully'. But, though unquestionably there was disruption (to achieve long-term good) in the aviation sector under Cot, the war ministry nationalisations were far too limited in number and scope to be capable either of creating or removing industrial bottlenecks affecting army equipment delivery rates.[11]

By no imaginable yardstick were the businesses that fell to rue Saint-Dominique management an 'enormous industrial machine'. The 9 nationalised plants contrasted with 600 private factories that Daladier reckoned in November 1936 to be doing war department work. The sector taken over seems even more minuscule compared to Jacomet's account that working in some form for the services, directly or as sub-contractors, component or material suppliers, were 6,000 concerns in 1936 and over 11,000 by 1939 (figures closely corroborated by later scholarship on Daladier and industrial mobilisation). Likewise the expropriated sector for the army was small if measured by the labour employed at the plants: 311 workers at the smallest at Issy (ex-Renault), and only 3,033 at the largest, the ex-Schneider Le Havre-Creusot factories, with an overall total of just 9,243 employees. Finally, measured by costs, the nationalisations were modest. For the war ministry takeovers 200 million francs in all was budgeted. Renault accepted a 3 million franc indemnity for losing Issy and there, Jacomet recounts, subsequent investment of just 44 million francs of public money produced a tripling of Chars B and D2 output. Global public investment in the plants expropriated by the three armed services down to September 1939 was 450 million francs – about one twenty-fifth of the *annual* budget of the war ministry alone.[12]

In return for such modest outlay the French armed forces enjoyed substantial benefits in relation to the limited terms of the takeovers. The army gained research and construction facilities of its own, conferring independence from private weapons-system designers. Particular satisfaction was obtained from ending Renault's near-monopoly about which so much ill-feeling had arisen in 1935–6. By 1940 most combat vehicles were scheduled for replacement by state-produced and designed models.[13]

The expropriations were most attacked, however, not on financial or production statistics but on assertions that they 'poisoned the atmosphere' between business and government. Fabry, in the Senate in 1936, alleged that a 'wave of laziness' was sweeping away France's entrepreneurial spirit. He contended later that in juxtaposing industrial restructuring with the start of the four-year rearmament programme Blum 'got the brake and the accelerator mixed up'. Being impressionistic rather than statistical this criticism – predictably prevalent in businessmen's Riom depositions – became self-perpetuating and is thus commonplace in the polemical literature.[14]

But this case against the nationalisations was thoroughly subjective. A representative exponent was the industrialist Raoul Dautry, chairman of a railway company until Chautemps' mergers of 1937 to form the state-run SNCF, and recalled from retirement by Daladier to head the ministry of armaments belatedly established in September 1939. Dautry criticised the takeovers for their supposed 'psychological damage', which consisted of distracting the creative imagination of businessmen and their research departments away from rearmament problems. He was still more forthright in attacking what the expropriations represented:

Whereas for politicians they were a symbol of state control, for entrepreneurs they were an emblem of the dispossession of the rights of private property; because of this perception . . . the industrialists who could have worked for the army were slow to step forward for fear of becoming 'merchants of death' and being one day themselves menaced with nationalization . . .

Yet Dautry was as unable as others to sustain these contentions with documentary proof. Moreover, he expressed the conclusion, regarding the war ministry's takeovers, that they were of scarcely any significance industrially because they were so limited. It could not be said, he recognised, 'that by the coming of war nationalisation had had any very serious direct ill effects'.[15]

Rather, for military equipment, the ill effects were located in what Dautry termed the 'thousands of factories' throughout France working indirectly for the defence effort as sub-contractors and suppliers. Problems in these plants were not those of disorder induced by clumsily executed statist restructuring. They were disruptions by unresolved industrial strife in 1937–8 that had been removed neither by the June 1936 Matignon agreements nor by the subsequent Popular Front collective contract and compulsory arbitration legislation. They were difficulties caused by political preference for leaving undisturbed the balance between military and civil production in the French economy, so as to maintain exports to offset increasing inflows of militarily essential raw materials. They were acute shortages of skilled workers in engineering, optics and metallurgy.[16]

The Matignon agreements and subsequent laws of June–July 1936, improving workers' conditions by a forty-hour week, paid holidays and wage increases, have been often enough in the historians' gaze. Their focus, however, has conveyed a distorted image of the French industrial world of the later 1930s, the heroic episodes of the Blum government's debut 'pushing into the shadows the conflicts that followed', disguising the fact that the era was characterised 'more by social guerilla warfare spreading with each passing day than by the spectacular . . . flare-up of the Popular Front's beginning'.[17]

In the case of war material manufacture there was serious industrial disruption in 1937–8, in addition to orders delayed by the dislocation of June 1936. A report from the technical bureau that month to Daladier warned that the 37mm anti-tank gun, of which 500 were on order for Maginot Line forts, would not meet its January 1937 delivery date because the 'recent strike movements' had 'completely halted all production'. The stoppages were reportedly 'even more damaging' in armoured vehicle manufacturing. Of 70 Chars B demanded by the armaments' consultative council in April 1935, just 15 had been delivered by July 1936. Delays of two months were attributed to the June 1936 strikes in regard to R35 and H35 tanks ordered in September and November 1935. Falling productivity because of the forty-hour week was identified as a further problem. Daladier was told that 'however zealous in the future the workforce in factories engaged on defence jobs . . . the alteration of the working week . . . can only entail a serious slowdown and, consequently, fresh delays in armaments' manufacture.'[18]

But though the forty-hour legislation interacting with labour shortages was to be French rearmament's long-run handicap, Gamelin's and Daladier's first appraisals of the September 1936 programme's progress betrayed worry about strikes in defence-related industries. Paul Happich, director of armaments at the war ministry, was later convinced that the programme 'might even have been completed ahead of time', through developments in production processes, 'had it not suffered the impediment of the social upheavals of 1936 and the following years'.

Serious stoppages occurred throughout Daladier's tenure at the rue Saint-Dominique. More than 50,000 workers were on strike in nine different months between July 1936 and April 1938, when Daladier became head of the government and allied himself with the 'bosses counterattack' against workers' assertiveness. Notwithstanding this picture of unrest, however, after 1936 with its major strike-waves in May–June and September, the weapon and military vehicle plants were rarely hit by direct stoppages. Instead these businesses were chronically affected by disputes among their vital component suppliers and sub-contractors (Dautry's 'thousands of factories' across the length and breadth of France). Especially disruptive stoppages in metallurgy in the 1936–7 winter led Daladier in November 1936 to seek powers against the organisers, declaring that 'strikes in the past had meant considerable delay in provision of materials essential to the army. In future they were not going to be tolerated.' He would 'never admit the right to strike' for the labour force in defence work. However, his call for draconian measures was resisted by Blum and Chautemps. They, with little success, sought industrial peace by collective bargaining mechanisms and compulsory labour arbitration. By the spring of 1938 the unrest in metallurgy had broken out anew.[19]

The impact of industrial strife among suppliers, as it characteristically hindered army equipment delivery, is best illustrated through particular firms' experiences. The Panhard et Levassor company manufactured the highly regarded AMD 178 armoured car. It was a small, independent family concern, chiefly engaged in motorcar, lorry and bus assembly at its factories in the Paris suburb of Ivry-sur-Seine. In 1936 it had a labour force of about 3,000. Because its military work represented only a small part of turnover Panhard was not nationalised. Its only army contract in 1936 was for thirty of the AMD 178s, a very small job even for this size of firm. Yet delivery of the completed order, placed in May 1935, was delayed until November 1937. The cause of the problem was partly strikes and factory occupations by Panhard workers from 29 May to 15 June 1936, again on 12 October 1936 and from 5 to 19 November. But this was not the main difficulty, according to Paul Panhard, the chairman. He cast responsibility on 'strikes at our suppliers' which stopped Panhard's work so that production, 'which had not got back between the ... strikes to a regular rhythm', was still not normal in January 1937.[20]

Panhard's case implies that suppliers' strikes and specialist labour shortages created a chain reaction of hindrances that led to continual inability to meet delivery schedules. The first order of Panhard

Table 3. *Letting and completion of contracts for Panhard AMD 178s*

Date of order	Number of vehicles	Contracted completion	Actual completion
11 Aug. 1937	80	July 1938	Feb. 1939
31 May 1938	35	Apr. 1939	Dec. 1939
31 May 1938	40	June 1939	July 1939
14 Sept. 1938	4	Dec. 1938	July 1939
17 Sept. 1938	40	Sept. 1939	Apr. 1940
17 Sept. 1938	80	Dec. 1939	Nov. 1939
9 Dec. 1938	24	May 1939	Dec. 1939

Table 4. *Scheduled and actual deliveries of Panhard AMD 178s*

	Total scheduled for delivery	With the Army
By mid-May 1938	79	30
By end-Sept. 1938	110	60
By end-Jan. 1939	133	105
By end-Aug. 1939	292	217

armoured cars received by the army on or ahead of schedule was placed in June 1939 and delivered in the spring of 1940. With only one exception contracts placed from 1937 until June 1939 were completed late (see Table 3). Equally instructive is a tabulated comparison of the number of these vehicles contracted for delivery, against those in the army's hands. To take the critical dates of the May 1938 German–Czech war scare and partial mobilisations, the Munich crisis, the early 1939 rumoured German threat to Holland, and the German–Polish crisis which triggered World War Two (see Table 4). At every point the French command was between approximately 20 and 40 per cent short of its field requirements when asked to advise Daladier on the country's state of war readiness. Small wonder that Daladier received cautious counsel and proceeded prudently in each of the 1938–9 emergencies.[21]

From the French rearmament standpoint it is noteworthy how crucially the army's late receipt of equipment occurred through factors beyond Panhard's control. That firm had a strike-free year at Ivry in 1937. Yet the potential benefits were then dissipated by the army itself. For, after the original contract for thirty AMD 178s of 27 May 1935, it was not until 11 August 1937 that interest in the weapon was confirmed by placement of a second order. The cavalry branch, recipients of the vehicle, insisted naturally on rigorously testing the design before reordering. But they inexplicably took six months between receiving a first batch of seventeen AMDs in February 1937 from the initial order to signing the renewal contract. Such a long delay during testing forced Panhard to mothball the AMD assembly track in 1937 on completion of the only order placed. The firm was also deterred from taking the risk of expanding its AMD production capacity as an act of faith in its excellent design because of the army's tardiness in paying for the 1935 order; 100 million francs from that was still owing to Panhard in September 1936. When assembly restarted in February 1938 the army had missed the settled period of labour relations, and a fresh strike halted output in April 1938 'preceded and followed by a period of disruption'.[22]

A further recurrent problem bedevilling rearmament was the interference (identified and condemned by Louis Renault and General Maurin in 1935–6) caused by the inspectorates' fussy mania for improvements. Daladier restated the difficulty in May 1937: 'the unending modifications to our equipment, much more than any fault of the manufacturers, cause the delays that we are experiencing. The army's inspectors ... are excessively set on attaining perfection.' Even two years later, in the anxious days of spring 1939, constructors like Panhard were still suffering from the myriad overlapping officialdoms of the armed forces whose movement was sometimes glacial, so slow as to be almost imperceptible. These were services, as Dautry put it, that had 'bureaucratised themselves ... between 1919 and 1936 when little had been demanded of them, and which had not been revitalised' thereafter. The consultative armaments' council's lack of a secretariat or investigative powers denied Gamelin any instrument, as he lamented in 1937, to use against 'the malign influence that our protracted administrative formalities exerts on the rate of arms production'. An instance where he tried personally to cut through red tape involved his support of a general staff complaint to Jacomet about receipt of 264 Lorraine infantry carriers. These had obtained staff approval on 17 October 1936 but, though manufacture had begun on 13 November, the firm had not received its formal contract from Happich's directorate until 29 April 1937. Thus for over five months the manufacturer had needed to buy materials without, for want of the contract, credit from the banks. Eventually unable to accept such burdens, the company had halted production, leaving Gamelin angry about the 'repercussions of this situation for the commander-in-chief's summer manoeuvres' in which the vehicles in question were to equip two mobile battalions.[23]

Defence-contracted companies thus had to contend with an ivory-towered military incomprehension of the business imperatives demanding cost-effective employment of plant, capital and labour. But more than this, Panhard and similar enterprises experienced their chief problems with suppliers and firms to whom secondary but vital assembly processes were devolved. These businesses and their raw material suppliers, notably the steel foundries, suffered strikes when Panhard did not, in the 1937–8 winter, with knock-on effects. Steel hull castings arrived belatedly and turret deliveries were plagued by irregular supply from the builder, the Atelier de Construction de Rueil, between spring of 1938 and summer 1939.[24]

These rearmament bottlenecks retarded the modernisation of French military thought about the operational doctrine for mechanised forces and their organisational structures. At the level of grand strategy the log-jams conditioned Gamelin's assessment of the degree of security that he felt able to guarantee for France and her allies with such seriously under-equipped forces. Industrial problems often occupied senior officers' time. The generals' concerns are especially illuminated by the CSG meetings held on 14 and 15 October 1936 to consider the September rearmament programme. For tanks, as for Panhard armoured cars, the difficulties were uncovered chiefly in the secondary assembly and component factories. Of the R35 tanks assembled no fewer than 280 were without turrets and armament, with this essential equipment not expected until April 1937. But part of the trouble with the turrets and guns lay a stage further back, with optical sight and range-finder manufacturers suffering 'persistent deficits' of skilled labour. In addition, tank armour-plate supply to the body assembly plants was below requirements. Dufieux, the infantry inspector, for whose troops these tanks were destined, urged an expansion of the number of factories making armour-plate. More far-reachingly he insisted on 'changes in our methods of production . . . a break with our ponderous administrative habits . . . and action to deal with the state of mind of the workers' whose output he alleged was 30 per cent lower than in the spring of 1936.[25]

But the unavoidable parameter was the policy of successive governments, down to September 1939 and Dautry's installation as armaments' minister, to permit no significant diversion of non-military industry into defence work. France rearmed within the framework of a peace economy. On 3 May 1937 the armaments' consultative council heard that at issue was much more than the restricted output from the steel factories supplying munitions' and equipment producers – it was the whole alignment of the economy endorsed by the rue de Rivoli and the ministry of commerce and industry. Happich told the meeting that production of more weapons-grade steel would be frustrated by the steelmasters' chamber, whose strictly commercial outlook 'did not take sufficient account of the higher interests of national defence'. The industry in eastern France, Happich claimed, enjoyed the chamber's favour but produced inferior quality steel, and the defence ministry's secretariat under Jacomet was requested to take up cudgels with the businessmen on the army's behalf.[26]

However Jacomet's efforts to assist the generals foundered on a wider consensus of interests among powerful politicians. For, in the view of the finance ministers of 1936–8, Georges Bonnet and Paul Marchandeau as much as Vincent Auriol in Blum's first government, France's civilian economy required strengthening. Maintaining and preferably increasing exports of civilian products was argued to be crucial to allow government expenditure from the trade account on rearmament. Stockpiling against the demands of the attritional war that French planners anticipated had received priority since 1935. Diversion of capacity manufacturing for export markets was impracticable in the eyes of the influential finance ministry mandarins like the secretary-general, Yves Bouthillier. As it was, France's foreign exchange account was under strain to purchase raw material imports, especially of oil and coal bought respectively in dollar and sterling prices with a franc weakened after September 1936 by devaluation. The politics of financial husbandry rather than military neglect of the problem of high-grade metals determined that France 'had done little' to increase her steel or armour-plate resources and 'had not sought to get help from abroad'. Basking in the approval of the ministries that supervised the economy, many French manufacturers continued to develop their commercial markets ahead of their defence work. Renault, between Munich and the outbreak of war, was preoccupied with overhauling Citroën and Peugeot, both of whose car outputs in that period surpassed those of the Billancourt firm. Indeed it has been said that, from 1938 on, Louis Renault 'thought of nothing other than developing his precious car production and to this end pronounced himself a pacifist, resolutely pushing aside everything that was not automobile orientated from the concerns of the Renault group'. Certainly war material manufacture, even on 1 September 1939, accounted for a mere 18 per cent of total Renault production.[27]

Unavoidably, this continuous lag of vehicle and weapon deliveries behind the forecasts of 1936 eroded Gamelin's confidence. It also delayed expertise among the staffs, from the brigades in camps like Mourmelon and Mailly in Lorraine to the officers at the academies of Saumur and the Place Joffre, home of the Ecole de Guerre and the Centre des Hautes Etudes Militaires. Training at every level suffered from postponements or reductions of scale and duration. Such constraints left field officers unpractised in implementing the 12 August

1936 *Provisional Instruction on Tactical Employment of Major Units*, the work of the commission set up in 1935 under Georges. For too many officers this manual remained an academic treatise rather than a working tool, even though it codified coherent doctrine drawn from technical developments affecting land warfare since its predecessor's appearance in 1921. Such was the impact of deprivation of equipment for major exercises in 1937 and 1938, which alone would have made the modern operational prescriptions second nature to French field commanders by the coming of the war.[28]

Instead, of the formations encompassed in the 'prodigious effort to motorize the French army' pledged by Salengro, Blum's interior minister, in reply to Germany's re-establishment of two-year conscription on 24 August 1936, only the seven motorised infantry divisions trained for 'missions of a strategic or tactically urgent character' were ready in 1939. Motor equipment for the other thirteen divisions in which the infantry was organised in peacetime suffered as a result of this specialisation. The infantry lost out to the competing requirements of expanding the original single light mechanised division into three, and the creation of an experimental heavy armoured division. Yet, since one supporting battalion of tanks was scheduled for each of these thirteen divisions, in which by 1937 'the troops refuse to contemplate making an attack without tanks', the poverty of the supply of equipment was by default reducing half of France's standing army to a purely defensive capability. As early as October 1936 Gamelin warned his generals that their large infantry units scarcely understood how to employ armour and should be equipped with tanks. But by this time the R35 and H35 machines ordered for the infantry were being diverted, at the rate of half of output, to the expanding light mechanised divisions which had outstripped availability of their own S35 cavalry armour. Sustaining simultaneously all of the re-equipment programme of the French army, especially as Gamelin expanded cavalry armour and heavy tanks in reply to intelligence on German developments, was quite beyond France's economic resources.[29]

The experimental heavy division formed in November 1936 was a notable casualty, or at least a semi-invalid. It remained provisionally structured and equipped *ad hoc* until December 1939. To create it at all Gamelin had to prevail over CSG resistance from Dufieux of the infantry, as well as Generals Prételat and Dosse, by stressing that France needed a 'powerful . . . instrument . . . for counterattack in force . . . a weapon stronger than the panzer division'. Then the 1937 experimental armoured manoeuvres at Mailly revealed to the supervising tank specialists, General Besson and Colonels Charles

Delestraint and Louis Keller, that the Char B alone met the need for equipment impervious to German anti-tank guns. But Char B production was 'hopelessly slow'. Just two battalions existed in 1937 and still only 132 tanks, in four battalions, when the war came. Acute underinvestment prevented modernisation of the artisanal construction methods used on them. They were the coach-built limousines of France's armoured force, with all the merits of quality and drawbacks of scarcity that this implied.[30]

Perhaps the Char B's biggest misfortune was to arouse Daladier's antipathy. Like Fabry in 1935, he disparaged the tank as disproportionately costly and configured for 'aggressive' offensives or breakthroughs, supposedly inappropriate to republican France's status as a defender rather than a disturber of the European order. General Velpry, the tank inspector and a renowned innovator with armour, vainly pleaded the Char B's case in 1936 as a 'master of opposing anti-tank systems'. An enthusiastic Char B colonel directly lobbied Daladier for ten battalions of the type, but without success. The experimental division therefore trained with equipment acknowledged to be unsuitable. Part of it, the 507th regiment, was led from late 1937 to late 1939 by de Gaulle. He followed his politicking in Paris by learning practical lessons the hard way, for the first time, about trying to work R35, D2 and Char B tanks together. Reports of the three designs' incompatibilities circulated, enabling the heavy division's opponents to use CSG meetings in December 1937 and December 1938 to press Gamelin to disband it into small combat groups. Gamelin, however, stood by the plan to build up a four or even six battalion heavy division, emphasising the merits of concentration as well as the value of creating divisional staff experience and an *esprit de corps*. He conceded only that operational circumstances might compel the Chars B to have to fight as separate brigades.[31]

Especially allowing for his lack of personal tank experience, 'Gamelin was undoubtedly one of the French generals most favourably disposed to the offensive organisation of the army through the use of mechanical power'. But the disproportion between resources and requirements under which he laboured 'hit you between the eyes', as Besson put it.[32] For example the 1937 trials at Sissonne camp revealed so many unsatisfactory features in the R35 that re-equipment of the infantry support battalions with the D2 was mooted. But production of this tank had to be abandoned, after only forty-five had been finished, because it was drawing off special steel and turrets needed even more pressingly for SOMUA cavalry tanks. Gamelin would not have required Pierre Mendès-France to tell him that running an army, like running a government, enforced very hard choices indeed.[33]

Cavalry mechanisation was deemed of the highest priority. The Maginot Line did not cover France's left flank. There Gamelin, supported by General Massiet, the cavalry inspector, as well as René Altmayer and Flavigny, commanding the two light mechanised divisions, wanted mobility to permit 'penetration into Belgium'. Three light mechanised divisions were Gamelin's objective, 'by virtue of their radius of action and speed of intervention'. But inadequate Panhard and SOMUA production kept the second of these divisions under strength throughout 1938, whilst the third division was formed in 1939 only by the expedient of equipping it with modified H35s designed for work with infantry. These material shortages in the autumn of 1937 were followed a year later by cancellation of the main manoeuvres as the Sudeten crisis occasioned a partial French mobilisation. Gamelin's plans to get his new formations familiar with tactics and combined-arms work in corps-scale mechanised exercises were thereby completely dashed in the last two summers before the war.[34]

In these circumstances it was unhelpful that in 1937 Reynaud reopened the professional army question. The speeches and book published that year by which he did so suggest that he neither understood nor was interested in the considerations that led the generals to reject his schemes. The authorities firstly feared dislocation of the 'proper balance and proportion between the various component parts of the army'.[35] Secondly, it was apparent to many that de Gaulle's and Reynaud's obsession with all-career forces stemmed from politically motivated analysis of alleged French decadence and not from ascertained military need. In technical capability the army reflected the general population, in the view of Daladier's *cabinet*. It denied the relevance of the professionalisation issue to doctrinal and material modernisation. In even the most sophisticated tank a commander and driver alone needed to be long-service personnel. For the rest the staff could not imagine difficulties in training drivers from conscripts in a country then possessing over 1 million automobiles. Moreover Reynaud entirely relied on de Gaulle's appraisal of whether it would be possible to recruit enough new professional soldiers to fill their proposed seven all long-service divisions. De Gaulle treated this socially and economically complex problem quite superficially, tendentiously assuring Reynaud that the additional men for a reconstructed army would be queueing up among the jobless, just waiting to be recruited, simply because the mid-1930s was a 'time of chronic unemployment'.[36]

But labour market conditions were actually quite inauspicious for an expanded professional military corps. It was strictly correct, whilst Reynaud campaigned for more career soldiers, that France witnessed chronic unemployment. At the depression's worst, in February 1935, there were 545,500 unsuccessful registered applications for work in France. Two years later, despite palliative public works measures by the Popular Front (considerably reduced from initial intentions because of the scale of rearmament expenses), the figure was still 441,200 in February 1937. But the total of workers registered with the labour ministry for placement in jobs fell by over 16 per cent between March 1935, the time of the great army debate in the Chamber, and February 1937, the occasion of Reynaud's final drive in print and in parliament for the career corps. The lines of the jobless were thus shortening all through the very time when de Gaulle simplistically suggested that they offered a grand army of potential recruits.[37]

The general staff, meanwhile, learned that the Popular Front's partial reflation of the economy had stimulated an upturn in industry's hiring of labour, especially marked in 1937. They appreciated that this made military recruitment of large numbers of specialists, or of men seeking to learn technical skills through the army, an unrealistic objective. Indeed, responding to a request by Daladier for a study of Reynaud's proposals, Colson stressed in July 1936 the struggle to maintain the statutory 106,000 career soldiers required to train the conscripts. This trend against the army as a profession amongst ordinary soldiers was in part a result of improving civilian employment under the Popular Front, in part a product of the impossibility of providing all the men with promotion to senior non-commissioned rank. This latter problem fomented disillusionment and a steady haemorrhage of soldiers refusing to re-enlist; 70 per cent were not signing up to re-engage at the completion of a term of professional service. But it was estimated that 1 billion francs would have to be added to the 1937 army estimates to improve pay, pensions and barracks sufficiently to attract enough re-enlistments and new recruits to allow expansion of the career cadres. However, with budgetary priority directed to new equipment, it was necessary 'to maintain continuous drives for new recruits' to preserve the army's professional backbone.[38]

Yet re-equipment, like recruitment, was dogged by keen shortages of personnel – in this case of skilled engineering workers. Scholarly attention has highlighted this problem's relevance to Britain's rearmament difficulties in the 1930s, but has hitherto overlooked the issue's significance as a headache for French defence planners.[39] The papers of the Chamber's army and labour commissions clearly reveal, however, that a major blockage to rapid expansion in manufacture of armoured vehicles, weapons and munitions was the persistant deficits of qualified workers in engineering and metallurgy.

Concern over availability of specialist labour, required if armaments' producers were to fulfil rapidly multiplying defence contracts, first surfaced in early 1936. The difficulty then raised for Gamelin and Maurin, then the war minister, was of finding large enough numbers of surplus trained men outside the Paris region to allow decentralisation of military manufacturing as an aid to safety against aerial bombing in a war. What emerged was the existence of a severe shortage of skilled labour in the provinces. This hardened the disinclination of companies to accede to government wishes that defence work be taken to Brittany and southern France. Metallurgical firms, supplying weapons' producers in Paris like Renault, Panhard and Hotchkiss, were often already provincially located. There, they reported, spare labour for expansion was scarce or altogether unavailable. Full employment in provincial metallurgy before the rearmament drive made the whole issue of expansion 'delicate', warned one member of the Senate's army commission from the Lot-et-Garonne in the south-west (an area into which relocation of defence industries was sought). Higher output in the industry before the Depression had rested on usage of temporary immigrant workers, many of them Italians. Yet 2 million such visitors had been repatriated since the early 1930s, consequently 'posing a particularly serious labour problem for our war industries'.[40]

Even more alarming was the discovery by Happich and Gamelin in 1937 that the Parisian industrial suburbs – Issy, Rueil, Billancourt, Levallois, Courbevoie, Aubervilliers and Bagnolet – were also quite devoid of any reservoir of skilled workers. The realisation hit French rearmament plans severely. For these districts, dominated by light engineering and vehicle assembly, had been thought easily capable of absorbing large new defence contracts. In March 1936 Maurin had believed that in Paris 'intelligent, specialist ... workers can be found easily', that double shift working might be difficult in many of the provinces but straightforward to arrange in the capital. There were, after all, many jobless in Paris and its surrounding hinterland. But, as de Gaulle had done with recruitment, French defence chiefs fell into the trap of regarding the Parisian unemployed as a labour pool. They failed to give close scrutiny to the characteristics of this supposed reservoir of talent. For in fact the bulk of this imagined 'workforce' was composed of unskilled men and workers no longer employable in munitions and military vehicle work because of advanced age, infirmity or obsolete skills.[41]

Therefore even as French rearmament got under way it became the victim of the measure of success which attended Blum's boost of purchasing power and public works between September 1936 and October 1937. That period saw steadily falling unemployment along with renewed buoyancy in both internal French trade and exports. The armed services found themselves forced to compete in an economy actually containing very little slack waiting to be taken up by defence orders. In these conditions the skilled labour shortage for military-related industries quickly became acute as firms rapidly hired the small reserve of tool-makers, turners, welders and fitters previously without work. Moreover it was difficult to offset the scarcity of skilled men by more overtime working or night shifts. These options were prohibitively expensive, in the view of many bosses, because of the special payments required under the forty-hour legislation and collective contracts of the Blum reforms. Yet the French service ministries, and the anxious generals in particular, were so eager to expedite rearmament by 1937 that money seems unlikely to have been an obstacle if entrepreneurs had come back to Jacomet and Happich to insist on more finance to cover their higher wage bills. The evidence is rather that businessmen, dismayed by the workers' gains of 1936, quickly evolved a conscious strategy of revenge designed to restore patronal power, trim back trade union rights and 'discipline' the workforce. These bosses had no intention of rendering their objective, of rolling back 1936, harder to attain by entrenching working practices and overtime payment in what they feared might easily become an exemplary defence sector. There is no sign that Gamelin and the other military authorities awoke to the subtleties of an employers' campaign which from late 1936 to late 1938 effectively subordinated national security to entrepreneurial interest.[42]

Only gradually did it dawn on the war ministry, as 1937 wore on, that the enormous finances allocated in September 1936 to rearmament were not of their own accord going to inspire the required upturn in munitions, weapons and vehicle output. As Colson later admitted, the scheduling of four years' worth of expenditure by the 1936 plan permitted the army 'to go far beyond the provisions previously limited to the then current financial year, as regards equipment orders'. This theoretically allowed for an expansion of the pace of production, but 'in practice this could be achieved only within the limits set by the working regime in the factories'.[43]

Moreover labour shortages, like strikes, were most serious not in nationalised armaments concerns but in medium-sized private engineering firms that supplied the former with machine-tools and components. By 1937, because of the huge increases in the armed forces' demands for equipment of every kind from bayonets to bomb-sights, the labour problem was emerging in the basic trades underpinning the entire rearmament effort. The 3 May 1937 armaments consultative council addressed itself wholly to the manufacturing crisis. It warned Daladier that essential military material of all sorts was not appearing according to the rearmament plan's timetable because of the 'restricted capacity of existing steel foundries and inadequate output of some metallurgical plants . . . the reaching of maximum levels of production in the cordite factories' and the skilled labour crisis in the optics industry. As the limited quantity of unemployed with serviceable skills was absorbed, the root of the crisis was uncovered. 'No real effort had been authorised', as Edmond Miellet, chairman of the Chamber army commission said in 1939, 'to develop apprenticeship colleges.' Behind France's labour difficulties lay her chronic dereliction in the 1930s of education and training for the modern world of technically skilled work.[44]

Economically liberal France left apprenticeships as the domain of the private entrepreneur, guided by the free market. State intervention to plan the labour side of the economy was virtually unknown, even under Blum. Thus an official study of the lack of qualified workers at Creusot in 1939–40, corroborating Miellet's discovery, emphasized the labour shortage's origins in general French demographic weakness and specifically in 'the apprenticeship crisis'. In 1939 there were only fifteen state-controlled apprenticeship and retraining centres in the whole of France. Before the war what limited government action occurred was directed at reskilling the unemployed but not at youth training.[45] The policy was endorsed by successive ministers of labour, Jean Lebas (under Blum), André Février and Paul Ramadier (under Chautemps until January 1938, and Daladier until August 1938 respectively). These ministers were all from the SFIO. They felt a strong personal duty, stemming from the expectation and trust vested in their party by workers in 1936, to wage a war on France's chronic unemployment with perceptible success. Blum's general stimulation of demand was one means towards this goal. But these labour ministers hoped to promote retraining so as to match the workforce more to anticipated future uptake in newer industries than to the fickle cyclical revivals of sectors experiencing underlying decline.[46]

Resistance to this political priority by both the general staff and some Chamber labour commissioners in 1937 enjoyed scant success. From the former quarter Gamelin warned Blum as early as July 1936 of how reduced output would hinder the army's attainment of improved combat-readiness. Once the generals had appraised the consequences of the forty-hour legislation Gamelin made another representation, to Daladier, to address the labour crisis, in January 1937. It was the 'undoubted disturbance' to the industrial economy by what they termed the 'brusque application' of the Popular Front's social legislation that perturbed the generals.[47] From the labour commission, ministers were warned about retrained workers subsequently becoming unemployed again or encountering domestic impediments too great to permit them to move to jobs in another part of France. The building of new factories in towns with particularly high unemployment was urged. But the SFIO politicians – the largest group in the commission as in the Chamber itself – maintained a majority behind the policy of retraining. They succeeded in pressing Ludovic-Oscar Frossard's objection that 'making the requirements of national defence coincide with the specific needs of certain regions' was just impossibly contrived and difficult.[48]

Throughout 1937 the target of the generals over the labour bottleneck was Daladier. He was believed to be the minister most receptive to the staff's conviction that pre-May 1936 output would be resumed only 'when sufficient specialist workers are trained to allow either shift work in existing factories, or the fitting out of additional plant'. The soldiers also sought exemptions from the forty-hour legislation by May 1937 for 'certain industries' engaged in defence work. Gamelin and Happich, by this juncture, had outpaced Daladier in attention to the growing problem of delayed fulfilment of military contracts. Gamelin understood, by this time, that hold-ups further back in the industrial processes needed to be tackled. He asked Jacomet to support the general staff's demand for exceptions to the forty-hour week in the steel and optical industries since the latter, specifically, was 'unable to find . . . any extra qualified labour'.[49] However, these military proposals fell foul in the second half of 1937 of the anxiousness of Chautemps, his finance minister Georges Bonnet and the labour ministry to appease organised trade unionists. By the negotiation of a *Statut Moderne du Travail* they aspired to complete Blum's work at the Matignon agreements and re-establish stable industrial relations. Their overriding preoccupation was for an economic quiet life at home and, with exports boosted through a second currency devaluation on 3 July 1937, the revival of France's economic competitiveness in civil exports abroad. It was hoped that these approaches would create rising prosperity, inducing full cooperation from labour and thereby avoiding compulsory changes to working practices in the defence industries. But these aspirations foundered on the rocks of continuing industrial disruption and a return to rising unemployment between September 1937 and February 1938. National finances remained precarious, Bonnet having to estimate a public borrowing requirement of 27 billion francs in his 1938 budget and increase taxation by 8 billion francs at the start of that year.[50]

Parliament's acquiescence in the expansion of both public indebtedness and the burden of taxation reflected its awareness of the deterioration by early 1938 of France's international security. Through the briefings by Gamelin, Happich and other senior military figures to the army, navy and air force commissions of the Chamber and Senate, politicians were conscious of France's slippage in rearmament relative to the progress of Germany. In January 1938 Chautemps briefly resigned, before reconstituting a new government from which most Socialists were excluded. Even this realignment, however, failed to allay French anxieties about their insufficient defensive preparedness. Heading public concern was the extreme vulnerability of French aviation, where Cot's policy of decentralising and nationalising the engine and airframe industries had – for all its strategic farsightedness – alarmingly reduced output and air force strength by 1938. The removal of Cot, changes in the air staff and a new air rearmament plan betokened attention to the problem in the spring of Hitler's Austrian Anschluss.[51]

The fresh air rearmament scheme, termed Plan V, was also the first beneficiary of a new mechanism for financing the French defence effort. This was burgeoning by 1938 on a scale that seemed about to burst completely out of the regular channels which existed, through ministerial budgets, to pay for state defence contracts. Whilst French industry was struggling to absorb the expanding demand for armaments on the footing of peacetime economic organisation, this was ceasing to hold true for French finances. On 5 March Chautemps established, within the treasury, a separate drawing fund for defence investments. Designed to operate for two years, this Caisse Autonome des Investissements de la Défense Nationale possessed an annual drawing power of 11.2 billion francs, funded by gilt-edged issues. It marked the shift of French rearmament financing from a predominantly tax-based to a predominantly borrowing-based regime. Whereas loans, and special accounts off the balance sheets of the service ministries, had covered only 14.7 per cent of defence expenditure in 1935 and 45.4 per cent in 1936, the proportion had become 53.6 per cent in 1938.[52]

It was in no sense a financial straitjacket, therefore, but the familiar and chronic 'crucial problem ... of restoring national production' which impinged, throughout 1938, on the attainment of the armed security which Gamelin sought.[53] This manufacturing issue needed to be addressed by action on the skilled labour shortages and the forty-hour working in defence-sector firms. An approach of this sort could be attempted only if the Radical Party moved rightwards, as it had in 1934, to jettison the remnants of Popular Frontism and ally with conservatives. Decree powers and the support of the Senate might then permit the tackling of rearmament bottlenecks by coercion rather than by consensus. But Chautemps's negotiations in March 1938 in this direction with the crucial centre-right Democratic Alliance led by Flandin, the former prime minister, were fruitless. Blum then tried to resurrect the conciliatory approach in a brief second government that lasted only three weeks, until 8 April. His strategy in attacking the production problem involved combining cooperation or brokerage with bosses and unions and a dramatic extension of government economic management. The recipe required a tax on capital, together with exchange controls. On the other side, Blum met Léon Jouhaux, CGT secretary-general, and Ambroze Croizat, the metallurgists' leader, and secured unionised labour's 'willingness to contribute actively to the organisation of the country's defence, of its independence and of its liberties'.[54] This transitory government, it seems, was French labour's final chance for partnership in the adoption of an approach to the problem of the skilled workforce in the defence industries. But it seemed 'too interventionist and "left-wing"' for the Senate, which for the second time refused Blum decree powers and, as before in June 1937, provoked him into resigning his government.[55]

With Daladier's move into the Matignon in April 1938 a new rigour, a fresh priority for defence needs above democratic niceties, became apparent. The return to office of right-wingers like Reynaud, to the justice ministry, and Clemenceau's old lieutenant Georges Mandel, in charge of the colonies, was indicative of the harder edge which the new prime minister wished to apply to cutting through obstacles facing rearmament. More symbolically still, Daladier not only kept to himself the departmental responsibility for national defence and war but emphasised his priorities by continuing to conduct all his governmental duties from the rue Saint-Dominique instead of moving his office to the Matignon.

The new regime's face was first bared by Daladier's acquisition of the decree powers refused to his more left-wing predecessor. On 24 May 1938 edicts were published which permitted the forty-hour legislation to be suspended, subject to labour ministry inspection, at selected defence-contracted plants. Initially Daladier hoped for voluntarily negotiated extensions to working hours. But business resisted, on grounds that low profits made overtime pay for the first five supplementary hours worked unjustifiable. Croizat's metallurgists in return demanded basic wage increases as their price for considering such unremunerated overtime. Daladier sought a compromise by constituting an inquiry in July 1938 to seek to compose the differences between both sides over means to raise output in the defence industries. But agreement remained unattained by late August, the workers contending that unemployment's renewed upward trend offered labour resources that should be tapped before any breach was made in the forty-hour law. Such objections, Daladier was advised by the inquiry's officials (mostly military engineers), were a political ploy in defence of the 1936 social settlement. He was urged by the engineers to 'impose governmental authority' and take the defence sector out of the ambit of the Popular Front's economic arrangements.[56]

The stage was set for an autumn of socio-political confrontation. Daladier, one eye on the worsening German–Czech antagonism over the Sudetenland, grew ever more nervous in late summer 1938 about French strategic capabilities. Organised labour grew increasingly anxious at the prospect of a government-backed socially repressive bosses' offensive, masked by appeals for solidarity and sacrifice in the cause of national security. Not only, as has been seen, had Daladier resisted the Lazurich–Gitton initiative of November 1936 to let the CGT into military camps, he had extended his opposition to any right to strike in factories completing defence orders. To labour Daladier was an object of distrust, the architect of a creeping militarisation of the economy. In a speech on 21 August 1938, Daladier squarely placed responsibility for private industry's inadequate or delayed supplies to state arsenals on the forty-hour legislation and the allegedly intransigent defence by workers of their sectional interest in it.[57] Daladier announced the institution of a forty-eight-hour week immediately 'in businesses in which there is any national defence interest'. Shocked at such blatant use of special decrees to undermine a reform enacted by the still-extant 'Popular Front Chamber', two cabinet ministers, Ramadier and Frossard, promptly resigned; deputies from the Socialist and Republican Union, both men were independent of the SFIO but broadly supportive of Blum. Replaced at the ministries of labour and public works respectively by Charles Pomaret and Anatole de Monzie, their departures served only to tighten further the grip of Daladier and the armed forces over the style and destination of French state policies. At the same time the partial mobilisation from 22 to 30 September 1938 only uncovered 'further unbelievable lacunae' still bedevilling the provision of French munitions and armaments.[58]

If Daladier's cautious statesmanship in the Munich crisis owed much to his impression of catastrophic French weakness in aviation, the prime minister, along with Gamelin, was appalled at the further dismaying reports on the condition of fortifications and equipment manufacture which the partial mobilisation threw up. In October Camille Fernand-Laurent, for the Chamber's army commission, produced a devastating indictment of Happich's armaments directorate. This, it was recommended, required restructuring by the establishment of a separate industrial service to manage the nationalised factories. The service needed a businessman at the helm, not a *bureaucrate en képi*. In this question of armaments, concluded Fernand-Laurent, the state was powerless 'unless it had the support of private industry, reorganised and encouraged afresh'. Complete cooperation had 'with the utmost urgency' to be re-established between the armaments' producers and the whole 'of the country's creative resources'.[59]

Yet Daladier only reiterated his rejection of Gamelin's request for the creation of a centralised ministry of armaments. From 1936 onwards Gamelin had proposed such a ministry. He insisted again following the September 1938 mobilisation. But Daladier rebuffed the plea once more, just as he had taken the idea no further than to talk about it in generalities when it surfaced in April, at the time he formed his government. Gamelin sought the establishment of this ministry to revitalise, oversee and pull together the disconnected administrative and political machinery charged with equipment and munitions' provision. In the run up to Munich Daladier was apparently 'on the point of taking a decision' with regard to Gamelin's plea. Yet, inexplicably, he cold-shouldered the whole initiative on undisclosed grounds of 'personality questions'.[60] Politics, it must be supposed, again prevailed over military need. The 'Law for the organisation of the country for time of war', enacted on 11 July 1938, gave Daladier a case against the necessity for a new technical defence post at cabinet rank. The prime minister himself was charged, by this legislation, with general supervision of national security. But Daladier was already so personally committed by his responsibilities as head of the government as to leave him neither time nor energy to convert his extensive theoretical powers in this law into the required unrelenting attack on the many logjams in French war preparation. Gamelin was left frustrated. He grew increasingly short of patience with his now overburdened and often inaccessible one-time confidant.[61]

Instead of investing an experienced service minister or businessman as an armaments' supremo in November 1938, Daladier resumed his neutralisation of trade union privileges. His new hammer of the workers was Reynaud, moved to replace Marchandeau as finance minister. Advised by young economic technocrats, including Alfred Sauvy and Michel Debré, Reynaud embarked on an aggressive application of liberal market economics designed quickly to restore a strong French economy. This was to be a 'fourth arm' of defence to deter any further German expansionism. Jacques Rueff, a Reynaud aide and later mastermind of the Fifth Republic's currency revalorisation of 1958, recorded how Reynaud 'completely changed the atmosphere' surrounding French economic planning under Daladier. 'Resignation was replaced by the will to succeed.'[62]

Gamelin was informed by Daladier on 12 November 1938 that 25 billion francs, as well as the country's maximum industrial effort, would be directed in the year ahead to meet the combined rearmament requirements of the three services. The price, Reynaud had persuaded the prime minister, was to be paid by industrial labour. Decrees to this effect were published that same day. They slashed overtime pay rates at a stroke, made refusal of overtime working in the defence-related economy punishable by forfeit of paid holidays or by loss of pay in lieu of notice of dismissal. Moreover, they menaced with imprisonment anyone charged with inciting opposition to the new overtime regime in the defence sector. In their turn the trade unions interpreted these decrees as a manoeuvre to smash their role in the organisation of industry. For them the offensive by Reynaud seemed shamelessly vindictive. It appeared to strengthen the barrier that the employers' confederation had laid across the path down which business, government and workers had previously travelled towards the establishment of a national labour-dispute regime, a *Statut de la Grève*. This had been designed to make it obligatory for employers to shut any factory affected by an official ballot-sanctioned stoppage of work and apply binding arbitration procedures. Such reforms had been very much in the spirit of the now vanished Popular Front. To the unions the policies pursued by Reynaud seemed like the deliberate encouragement of a *revanche du patronat*, a bosses' revenge. In some desperation, on 30 November 1938, the CGT tried to reverse the tide by calling a national general strike against the decrees. This was a recourse to the heroic and almost mythological weapon of French revolutionary syndicalism. But the gunpowder of the labour leaders was damp after long neglect and preference for a corporatist-style of brokerage with governments. The strike was so feebly supported that the protest collapsed after only one day.[63]

Reynaud and Daladier were rather more embarrassed by well-informed criticism in the Chamber's labour commission in December of their claim to have set the government to attain a strictly economic objective. This goal was ostensibly the improvement of the output of military vehicles and munitions. But Gaston Monmousseau, a communist deputy for Saint-Denis and trade unionist from the railwaymen, reiterated the conviction of the workers that Reynaud's motive was political rather than economic in wanting overtime paid at standard wage rates whilst skilled men remained unemployed. Monmousseau argued that it had 'quite bluntly' to be stated that 'in all this the government's aim is to drag us back to the situation that prevailed prior to June 1936'. The minister of labour, Pomaret, was told that, for any given industry, the extension of the working week in one part of France might be offset, from the trade union viewpoint, by redundancies and short-time working elsewhere. It was said that unemployment, as the government was tackling the problem, was not sure to be reduced, merely redistributed. Such arguments impressed Pomaret. He continued to contend that overtime at normal pay rates was much discussed but little practised. Nonetheless, he pledged not to permit it so long as there were qualified labourers without jobs.[64]

Pomaret's concession in fact raises doubt whether the confrontational rhetoric which embellished the Reynaud–Daladier decrees of late 1938 was as commonly translated into effective policy as some have supposed. Did Reynaud and Daladier really leave 'much less' to the market? Did their 'massive spending on rearmament, and economic mobilisation ... after Munich' really demonstrate 'that the old liberal era was over'?[65] Certainly Daladier's exceptional powers were extended by parliament until 30 November 1939 after the German seizure of Prague, in March, had violated both the Munich accord and Bonnet's agreement of 6 December 1938 with Ribbentrop on future Franco-German consultation. Fresh decrees granted to Daladier on 20 March 1939 retained all conscripts indefinitely with their units. They also permitted the recall of reservists without reference to parliament and created a production directorate to implement the recommendations of an inter-ministerial production committee established in 1938. Most controversially of all, one of these new decrees extended a sixty-hour week to all factories directly constructing defence equipment. It was measures like these that provoked the swingeing allegation that the '[Radical] party and ... parliament abdicated to Daladier who was, in this respect, the precursor of Marshal Pétain'.[66] Yet the indictment seems misleading. For whatever doubts they cast on the quality of democracy in the late Third Republic, the decrees scarcely touched the elements of national life most crucial to accelerated defence preparedness.

The forty-hour law did undergo significant derogations under the new regime. But these were specific to closely defined areas of industry. It was not until September 1939 that powers were taken to direct labour generally. It was the outbreak of the war itself that activated controls over men in reserved trades, as laid down by the July 1938 legislation. Before the start of hostilities the blueprint drawn up by Reynaud was, as even his clerk of works, Sauvy, later confessed, 'certainly not to give France a war economy ... but simply the means to produce rather more wealth'.[67] The plan was to restore a high level of exports to help offset imported materials drawn from the sterling and dollar zones. Chiefly this meant coal and oil, in which France was gravely deficient in her own right. For all their posturing and their undeniable prejudices against the CGT, Reynaud and Daladier subscribed as dutifully as all earlier French governments to a balance in the economy between civil production, especially to export, and armaments. Economic equilibrium, Reynaud reasoned, would restore business confidence. And, indeed, in 1939 capital that had sheltered abroad since the Popular Front did at last return. Not only this, but the franc's value hardened and French leaders grew more confident that their country would enter a war with a resilient economy. None of this, however, meant that Reynaud, a doctrinaire opponent of state planning, intervened to point industrial recovery specifically towards a war economy.[68]

The Daladier decrees, therefore, only marginally utilised available labour more intensively. Moreover, Pomaret hesitated to sponsor the training of cohorts with special skills for the defence factories, lest he succeeded only in storing up trouble ahead. He feared the political difficulties that would have to be faced in making armament workers redundant once the equipment programmes were completed. Pomaret remained receptive, therefore, to the trade union demand for further searches for labour among the existing unemployed. There was, in this, a striking similarity with the concerns of the Amalgamated Engineering Union in Britain at the same time. The British engineers feared that an ephemeral arms-fed boom would be followed by a slump, as after the First World War. On both sides of the Channel the output of munitions was constrained by debates about means to avoid severe unemployment for skilled men in excessively expanded industries, in the event that diplomacy eventually accommodated Germany peacefully. In France, consequently, there was no turn towards the alternative sources of labour: diversion from civil production and expansion of training.[69]

In March 1939 the Chamber's labour commission, with its left-wing majority, was incited by Lebas, Blum's old minister of labour, to reject the forty-hour extensions in defence industries. The commissioners were overridden immediately afterwards, once Daladier obtained his additional decree powers on 20 March. Yet the deputies still found Pomaret sympathetic to selecting economically blighted regions for defence work. He had always thought, he asserted, 'that it was necessary to give military contracts to these areas'. And again, in Britain too, similar pleas came from certain businessmen, engineering union officials and the Treasury, that defence orders be deliberately placed, or subcontracting be encouraged, in regions with jobless workers.[70] One argument for this approach, Pomaret disclosed in June 1939, was that sixty-hour working had caused a counter-productive increase in industrial accidents with tired workers. No solution, evidently, was free from drawbacks of some sort. A ministry of labour inquiry showed that unemployment among skilled men by the summer of 1939 was indeed so low as to foreclose immediate expansion of engineering from that quarter. Contrary to the myth so dear to the left, there was 'never a great surplus of [skilled] manpower waiting [in the wings] ... for its re-employment'.[71]

Meeting the needs of a greatly expanded arms' industry for suitable workers was not, therefore, something that France could achieve without Daladier and Reynaud adopting a new policy to retrain and redeploy labour in substantial strength out of civil manufacturing industry. A strategy of this kind, however, conflicted with Reynaud's aim of rapid restoration of French finances. By May 1939 he was declaring that France already was 'from the point of view of finances, on a war footing'.[72] His objective, equally sought by Bouthillier, the senior civil servant at the rue de Rivoli, and by Daladier, was to create the largest war chest he could in as short a time as possible.[73] The first step to this was to reverse earlier outflows of gold to support the franc from the exchange equalisation account. This had been needed to defend the fixed exchange rates with sterling and the US dollar under Franco-Anglo-American currency arrangements of September 1936. Preservation of the franc's value was therefore sought under Reynaud not by defensive sales of gold but by a new emphasis on exports, trade surplus and improved foreign exchange holdings. Constantly haunting the minds of ministers responsible for France's defence economy was the US Johnson Act's denial of dollar credit facilities to debt defaulters. France, liable to this sanction because of suspending repayment of certain 1914–18 loans, had to prepare to purchase raw materials, machinery and perhaps future armaments from the USA in a war in 1939 or 1940 entirely on a cash-and-carry basis. For this, exports needed to be buoyant, the currency sound, and exchange and gold reserves considerable. The USA's rejection, between February and April 1939, of an offer by Daladier and Reynaud of 10 billion francs in gold and cession of strategic French Caribbean or Pacific territories, in return for release from the Johnson Act, made attainment of this capability a still higher priority.[74] The paradox of Reynaud's policy, noted a fellow cabinet minister in May 1939, was that, whilst its author 'reckoned another war inevitable', its recipe for long-term financial provision categorically precluded adopting any further measures of strategic economic preparation in the short term.[75]

The foregoing investigation of the Daladier government's concerns in 1938–9 demonstrates just how completely French functionaries and politicians trusted the existing strength of Gamelin's army to preserve military security. Not until 1939 itself did Gamelin grasp and belatedly address this problem of complacency. Reynaud and his advisors watched output rise on average by 20 per cent in early 1939 in coal-mining, chemicals, construction, steel and textiles. They congratulated themselves that 'despite a heavy burden from rearmament' their policy had, 'in very difficult conditions', effected the most rapid recovery ever known to the French economy.[76] Neither Reynaud nor Daladier was willing to borrow heavily to pour money into rearmament in 1939 without heed for future economic resilience and international competitiveness. In 1939 itself the only heavy new expenditure on war material involved aviation. This exception, by CPDN decision of 5 December 1938 to seek purchase of 1,000 combat aircraft from the USA and the expansion in June 1939 of the air force's Plan V recovery programme, spoke for Daladier's personal perception of French air weakness at the Munich crisis. It indicated his readiness to loosen Reynaud's tight purse-strings at least in respect of countering a feared knock-out blow from the skies.[77]

Aside from this exception for aviation, discussed further below, French political leaders prepared their country's defences in a consciously chosen regime of limited sacrifices, limited efforts. Central to the approach of Daladier, Pomaret, de Monzie – and Reynaud to a lesser degree – was their doubt about when and even if war would occur. An excessive supply of munitions workers was not risked so long as the slenderest prospect persisted of reaching a diplomatic détente with Hitler. Nor was financial frailty to be chanced whilst possibilities were pursued of an international accommodation; for this might open avenues of opportunity for a reinvigorated French economy, geared for civilian manufactures, to drive into profitable export markets in and beyond Europe. The approach of Reynaud and Bouthillier sought for France a strong position among the trading powers if peace were preserved. At the same time it aimed at foreign confidence in the economy so as to allow a war effort to be sustained if conflict came. For all the financial sense of the strategy, it neglected the continuing competition for labour between firms in civil trades and those in manufacturing munitions. Furthermore, by rehabilitating liberal market economics, it made politically less possible any assumption of government powers – even under the March 1939 decrees – to conscript workers into armaments.[78]

Thus, if Daladier's and Reynaud's financial conservatism applied no appreciable brake in itself on French defence preparation this was overwhelmingly because of the persistence of the chronic labour crisis. Industry simply lacked the means to convert money into munitions. Armament factories nationalised under rue Saint-Dominique direction in 1936–7 had not been enlarged by 1938 (in contrast to expansion and reorganisation effected by this stage in the aviation industry by virtue of the originally disruptive activism of Cot and his air staff). And by 1939, with Reynaud's market economics in the ascendant, the acceleration of arms output became treated like any other economic objective. In this way no different from porcelain or perfume production, the munitions manufactures so essential to the safety of France became treated like any civilian consumable, to be a function of private business decisions, which the government would push only by the most general and traditional capitalist mechanisms of constraining state indebtedness and encouraging lower interest rates. Such an extraordinarily relaxed approach to economic management in France during Europe's last summer of peace reveals the deep impregnation of the dogma of the extended or attritional war, the *guerre de longue durée*, into official and political consciousness. The government's perspective in Paris, as its gold reserves worth 87 billion francs in February 1939 rose to 92 billion worth by July, already betrayed the same complacency that 'we'll win since we are the stronger' as did Allied phoney war propaganda posters of the succeeding winter of bitter illusions.[79] For the government – although not for Gamelin and the defence services – this dogma had drugged and dulled all sense of danger to France from early and irreversible military disaster.[80]

In 1939 Gamelin's disquiet at the relative unreadiness of his ground forces was as great as ever. Yet, except with regard to urgent reinforcement of aviation, in which Daladier had assumed direct personal interest, ministers thought only of the long term. Their concern was with how extended a war would be, and with France's position at the end of it among the winners. Too late, Gamelin changed his approach and began emphasising critical deficiencies which might jeopardise even a strategy for survival, let alone for victory. Only in March 1939 did he alter his expressed 'scepticism' about the menace from blitzkrieg or an *attaque brusquée* against France, conceding that he 'now believed that it could become dangerous'.[81] In essence, Gamelin was caught in a dilemma of his own making. He, along with every other senior general, admiral or air force commander in France, subscribed to the blueprint of attrition and fully mobilised industrial war as the only strategy offering a chance to France and her friends to prevail in a war with Germany. Indeed Gamelin and his colleagues not merely agreed with the blueprint but were themselves its very authors. But the requirements, especially the economic requirements, to sustain the strategy were incompatible with embarkation on an unrestrained emergency programme in 1939 to shore up the field forces that would have to withstand the opening blows of a new war.

And by mid-1939 serious deficiencies were evident in Gamelin's ground forces, just as in 1938 they had been exposed in French aviation. There were shortfalls of lorries and vehicles sufficient for Colson and Gamelin to speak in the CSG of a 'crisis of military transport'.[82] Likewise the continuing low output of heavy tanks had denied Gamelin any opportunity to plan a date for the disposition of the two heavy armoured divisions into which he had, since 1936, aimed to group the Chars B. The 'Provisional notice on conditions and methods of employing large armoured units' approved by Gamelin on 16 December 1938 remained uncirculated because of the unavailability of tanks and other equipment.[83] In June, July and August 1939 average monthly output of many key armaments remained pitifully small: just 18 Panhard AMD 178 armoured cars, 12 S35 and 10 B1 tanks, 7 25mm anti-aircraft guns. The air chiefs, General Vuillemin and La Chambre, the minister, warned when the war started, that at least six more months with minimal operations would be needed before the Luftwaffe could be faced with anything like parity.[84] But less understood among Parisian politicians was that France's armoured divisions projected in 1936–7 also remained hopes on a distant horizon and that, more widely still, Gamelin and his army felt quite unready for more than a 'wait and see war', a *guerre d'attente*.

Gamelin was quite late in ringing these alarm bells about the French army. But it is not apparent that if he had sounded an earlier alert this would have carried any more clearly to the governments between 1936 and 1939. With every French defence service – indeed all of French society – suffering disruption in 1936–8, he might have been simply dismissed for crying wolf. Gamelin was unimpressed by the results of Weygand's bad-tempered alarmism during earlier troubled times for the military. It is 'perfectly clear that he hesitated between forcing the government's hand and an unwillingness to encourage dangerous illusions'. By 1939 Daladier, formerly a close collaborator and reliable support, was visibly distracted more and more from the army's concerns by pressing issues of diplomacy and domestic government. This exposed Gamelin, in what he knew was an unsympathetic environment, to his own unusually developed conscience about the burden represented by responsibility for keeping French frontiers inviolable. He could, he appreciated, be pilloried by politicians for being either too cautious, or too bold, if fortune were to gainsay his appraisal of French readiness for war. Gamelin was alive all along to a potential fate as a scapegoat for ministers hesitating to shoulder their own responsibility for foreign and defence policy formulation. He was 'quite intelligent enough to realise that his opinions might be treated as decisive arguments'.[85] In 1939, probably too late, he fell back onto the professional's cautious position of articulating genuinely held personal unease about the capabilities of his forces. But with Weygand, habitually so pessimistic, offering a public eulogy of the army as 'stronger than at any moment in its history', in a speech at Lille in July 1939, Gamelin's protests were sceptically received.[86] For Reynaud, irredeemably prejudiced by de Gaulle against the 'bemedalled sexagenarians' of the army command, Gamelin became increasingly despised for a defensiveness that the cocksure minister considered almost defeatist.[87] For Sauvy, Reynaud's advisor, the army's pleas of unpreparedness served to confirm his cynical suspicion that the military were 'never satisfied because they *never* reckon they have sufficient . . . equipment'.[88]

Partly perhaps by his own making, Gamelin had become a victim of a separation between the military and political authorities in France. By an almost imperceptible widening of the gulf in 1938, this separation in the civil-military relationship had become the irretrievable breakdown in 1939 from which came the acrimonious divorce of 1940. The relationship in 1939 was crumbling because it was no longer founded in a shared understanding of its purpose. Political leaders, so obsessed with having an economy that would hold out in the future, were deaf to entreaties to act urgently so that the French armed forces might hold out in the present. Instead, Reynaud's confidence spread through the government. He insisted that finances were recovering, that the burdens of belligerence were to be shared with Britain under Neville Chamberlain's agreement to joint defence planning in March 1939, that manpower would begin increasing after the end of the 'lean years' in October 1940. Weygand's Lille encomium in these circumstances simply silenced the last politicians mindful that if Hitler 'put his momentary superiority to advantage quickly' it would 'be no use . . . being strongest in the long term'.[89] Gamelin, for his part, was left the unhappy lot of defending France with tools which he feared might break even as he tackled the task. He had, however, built his career and his relationship with the politicians around constitutional correctness. He was unable, therefore, in 1939, to put his doubts about France's defensive readiness above a whole lifetime's 'scrupulousness about respecting the superior authority of the political arm'.[90]

6 Gamelin and air support of the army

The German application of air power in conjunction with their ground offensives in 1939–40 ensured that the Vichy court at Riom in 1942 investigated not only the deficiencies of France's preparation for war on land but also the shortcomings of French aviation. Pétain's prosecutors inculpated both France's air ministers of the 1936–40 period: Pierre Cot (who had fled to the USA and was tried *in absentia*), and his successor, Guy La Chambre (who had also found safety in America but who elected to return to Europe and face his accusers). However, Vichy allegations of the underestimation of air power before the war were not confined to these one-time incumbents of the air ministry. The accusation was also levelled at Gamelin.[1]

As preparations for the wartime trial gathered pace, the general found that the hollowness of his pre-war authority over French aviation was no protection against the charge that he had failed to take sufficient precautions against the Luftwaffe and, in particular, against the part which it had played in combination with panzer forces in securing German victory in 1940. Testifying in the pre-trial examinations, in early 1941, the one-time conservative deputy of the Republican Federation, Edouard Frédéric-Dupont, opened this dossier against Gamelin. The former parliamentarian asserted that, in July 1939, as part of a Chamber army commission deputation, he had been briefed at Mailly camp by Gamelin.

I asked about air power [claimed Frédéric-Dupont] for I was worried about the inadequacy of our aviation. But General Gamelin responded that 'Air forces will not accomplish what some military writers claim to foresee for them in the next war. The flare-up of air activity will very quickly be damped down by attrition of equipment and especially by attrition of aircrews. Aviation, like a straw fire, will swiftly burn itself out'.[2]

From Frédéric-Dupont to J.-B. Duroselle, an influential current in the historiography of the war of 1939–40 has contended that deficient Allied air rearmament, exacerbated by neglect of tactical air support of ground operations, went far towards causing the French military defeat of 1940. Modern historians have confirmed, through research into the comparative orders of battle, that the Germans did enjoy numerical preponderance in air forces during the Battle of France. French, Belgian, Dutch and British air strength on the continent simply did not match the quantities of Luftwaffe aircraft in the western operations. There is, it is true, some persuasive evidence that the French air force performed creditably in combat, in 1940, in spite of its daunting disadvantages in communications, ground control systems and available numbers of first-class aircraft. The French probably had a larger proportion of very highly trained and proficient pilots and aircrew than did the Germans. And undoubtedly their aircrews contained many men of lion-hearted courage, undaunted by the unfavourable numbers against them. The casualties and aircraft lost in combat in Luftwaffe-Armée de l'Air encounters indicate that, when given any sort of a fighting chance, French aircrews exacted a fearsome toll on their opponents.[3]

Yet none of this prevented even a relatively charitably disposed writer such as Le Goyet from reproaching Gamelin for 'not having managed to secure a rational organisation for French aviation' in French national strategy, for 'not knowing that he should impose a firm operational doctrine' and for 'not understanding some of the lessons of recent wars, notably concerning the intervention of air power in the land battle'.[4] This chapter seeks to uncover what Gamelin thought and said about French air power before 1940, to determine what efforts he made to provide for air support to his armies for their mission of defending France and to question the applicability of Le Goyet's criticisms.

Germany's numerical advantage in the air may not, in practice, have been as overwhelming as it appeared at the time to Allied land forces who sourly complained that the skies always seemed to be empty of Allied aircraft. But the Luftwaffe's numerical superiority was considerable enough to leave a sense – even after revisionist historians have had their say – that the Armée de l'Air in 1940 could do no more than make the best of a bad job. This perception has, in turn, kept the focus of most works that treat French air power's shortcomings in the Battle of France on the air rearmament race of the 1930s. Counting aircraft and analysing the reasons why the French fell calamitously behind in the race has been fashionable; examining the French debates over the function of military aviation and over the latter's relationship to the army has not.[5]

It has been commonplace to emphasise how the French air force was chronically under-strength and unsuitably equipped from 1934–5 until its incomplete recovery in 1939–40.[6] Contemporaries, just like many historians, found Allied air deficiencies entirely explicable by reference to the French air industry's crisis of design and production by 1936–8 – a crisis whose ramifications were aggravated by Britain's refusal during the phoney war to commit the RAF unreservedly to a continental campaign. Consequently it has been suggested that Allied thought, and especially French thought, regarding the usage of military aviation was crisis-ridden and ineffective.

However, through a closer investigation of Gamelin's pre-war attention to military aviation it is possible to elucidate the successes as well as the shortcomings of the French defence authorities in the face of the air threat in the later 1930s. In the main what emerges is that inter-war reflections about military employment for air power fell victim to a paradox in the ways of thinking about all future warfare at that time. For most European politicians and defence staffs acknowledged that the 1914–18 conflict signified the advent of 'total industrialised war'. The fingers of future wars were expected to reach out and close their grip around civilians as well as combatants. Financial resilience and economic strength, a new 'fourth arm of defence', had acquired an importance for war winning perhaps greater than human bloodshed. On the other hand, however, a classical soldierly view persisted – at times seemed even to flourish anew – of combat as a distinctive and specialised affair peculiar to those elites engaged in the professions of arms.

The former of these appreciations predominated in the forums of civil-military planning which proliferated between the wars, like the French Haut Comité Militaire or the CSDN. It flourished, too, in the forcing houses of strategic thought in Paris, like the inter-service Collège des Hautes Etudes de Défense Nationale, the CHEDN, established under the naval theorist Admiral Raoul Castex in 1936 on the model of Britain's Imperial Defence College, and the army's own 'school for marshals', the Centre des Hautes Etudes Militaires.[7]

But the latter idealisation reflected a military craving for a bygone age of 'simple soldiering'. It attracted officers whose ambitions extended no further than their regiment; it appealed to those spared from wrestling at the war ministry with the political complexities of conscription or with the niceties of inter-service and inter-allied coordination. Indeed studies of military thinkers or 'makers of strategy' easily overlook the simple truth that the bulk of all officers' experience lay in garrison or camp routine. At this level the profession of arms expressed itself through perfecting separate skills and distinct doctrines. At this level the separate services conceptualised themselves as independent institutions, guarding the land, sea or air as their private preserve.[8]

In France, as elsewhere, the interdependence of the military services was only slowly perceived. This was neither surprising nor uncommon. Throughout the armed forces of Europe, combined-arms operations tended to occur as offspring of expediency rather than of prescribed peacetime policy. If a new understanding dawned after 1936, with the founding of Castex's college, it was nonetheless slow to break. It was 1936 before even de Gaulle first glimpsed the new interconnections. At last, from his vantage point on the CSDN secretariat he wrote that he could no longer imagine 'an army today winning the battle on land if subjected to air interdiction'. This indicated the 'inter-dependence henceforth . . . between the diverse components that comprise what we call military force'. Likewise Reynaud, though favourably receiving de Gaulle's recommendations for expansion of French mechanised contingents since 1934, was still sufficiently orthodox in 1937 to state in parliament that 'air power may wreak destruction, air power may reconnoitre; but air power does not conquer ground and cannot hold onto it'.[9] With de Gaulle's circle only hesitantly perceiving the interrelationships between military forces it is not surprising that they were scarcely noticed by regimental colonels on provincial bases, their horizons bounded by a six-monthly drill cycle with reluctant conscripts rather than by lofty ambitions to meld three rival service doctrines into a coordinated national strategy.

The deficiencies discernible in the French army's outlook on air power appear less blameworthy in the light of the subject's treatment in the mid-1930s by officers who have often been lauded by later writers as the military prophets of the age. De Gaulle in mid-decade showed no special clairvoyance towards military applications of aviation. His *Vers l'Armée de Métier* of 1934 offered no doctrine of air–armour coordination. In spite of working until 1937 in the relatively sophisticated milieu of Paris, free from the intellectually suffocating routines of a provincial barracks, de Gaulle's depiction of armoured operations was one-dimensional. He did not seriously look higher than the ground beneath his tanks' tracks. He argued, as has been discussed earlier, that larger mechanised forces should be grouped into divisions capable of ambitious and semi-independent manoeuvre. Each de Gaulle division, however, was to have only a small air component. Moreover he envisioned these air elements solely for the missions undertaken by aviation in 1914–18. An integrated air observation group was recommended, to reconnoitre as the 'eyes of the force', as was an artillery spotting component. One regiment of reconnaissance aircraft and one of fighters were to belong to the mechanised army's general reserve. No level bombers, dive-bombers or assault aircraft were proposed. There was no doctrine of tactical air attack in support of the tanks.[10]

Combined tactics of this sort – replicating the air–armour methods of what became known as German blitzkrieg – were advocated by de Gaulle only *after* he had digested the reports of the Wehrmacht's operational successes in Poland in 1939. Not till his memorandum of January 1940, addressed to Gamelin, Weygand, Georges, Daladier and Reynaud, did de Gaulle finally prophesy the capability of 'massed armour supported by massed aviation'. Only in 1940 did de Gaulle prescribe both elements of a remedy to German methods: 'Massive counter-attack by ground and air squadrons launched against an opponent . . . more or less disorganised and disrupted by . . . defensive lines.' But by early 1940, contrary to pro-Gaullist mythology, identification of the indispensable features of successful defence against an air–armour attack was not a wisdom on which de Gaulle held any monopoly. Indeed, in addressing Gamelin, de Gaulle was preaching to the converted. As this study's penultimate chapter explains, Gamelin was well-informed about the German methods used against the Poles and personally strove to impress on his subordinate generals the need for countermeasures. Indeed his headquarters journal records him instructing, as early as 14 September 1939, that 'the fight against the enemy's aviation be prepared most urgently and thoroughly, with the object of ensuring that Germany's air force, emboldened by its success in Poland, receives a good drubbing when it first tries conclusions against us'.[11]

Earlier in the 1930s, however, Gamelin was more circumspect in his estimation of military aviation. This caution over an untried arm was understandable and unexceptional among contemporary senior army leaders. Nevertheless it had serious consequences for the approach that was gradually evolved towards both air defence and air–army cooperation. For one thing, neither Weygand nor Gamelin saw any need to establish an army air command or corps under their own control. This was an oversight which greatly eased the growing pains of the infant French air force by relieving it of any need to fight from birth, against an army air component, for resources of finance, personnel and industrial capacity.

Founded as an independent service in 1928, the early autonomy of the Armée de l'Air was decidedly tenuous.[12] Not until 1933 did the air force achieve any degree of security. For in that crucial year France not only saw the arrival at the air ministry of Pierre Cot, a dynamic and imaginative young Radical, but it also witnessed the establishment of an air staff, a Conseil Supérieur de l'Air (equivalent to the army's CSG), and an aviation-officer training academy, the Ecole de l'Air. This removed young air force officers from the influence of army instructors. These institutions represented the trappings of a distinct third service. After 1933, the air force possessed at least respectability, if not full equality, vis-à-vis the army and the navy.[13]

Cot's appointment to the Boulevard Victor was crucial in another respect. For he was enthusiastically – even fanatically – predisposed towards the grand strategic role for airforces. He shared the vision sketched in the 1920s by the Italian air power prophet and theoretician, General Giulio Douhet. The future which Cot imagined was one in which aircraft waged their own offensives and counteroffensives. Their role would be one of deterrence in peacetime, by spreading fear of air bombardment, and of long-distance attack, in wartime, against an adversary's reserves, communications and factories.[14]

Consequent on French government changes in the early 1930s it was not Cot, however, but his successor, General Victor Denain, a retired chief of air staff, who began French air rearmament. In 1934 Denain launched Plan I. This scheme proposed to equip a French air force of 1,010 front-line aircraft, with 20 per cent reserves, within two years. The programme would, it was claimed, 'provide France with an air force of quality' whose first-line squadrons would provide a 'permanent safeguard' for French security.[15]

These developments laid out an opportunity to fashion a tri-service approach to national defence in France. Embodied in an independent air force and ministry, the arrival of the air dimension could no longer be dismissed by the French land forces. However, this also meant fresh difficulties for French army commanders. In particular, it was harder after 1933 for generals, such as Gamelin, who were receptive to the implications of more capable military aviation, to press successfully for army air assets. Furthermore, the formulation of coordinated air–land operational doctrine became, in practical terms, a prerogative of the independent air force staff. After 1933 any demands by army generals for air forces under their own control required tough inter-service and inter-ministerial bargaining with a partner service. The Armée de l'Air had graduated to the status of actor in its own right, jealous of its own prerogatives and claimant to all the roles which aviation aspired to fulfil. It was no longer possible when Gamelin took charge of the army in 1935 to treat the air force generals as auxiliaries – still less as subordinates.

Gamelin's difficulties in obtaining an air policy that was flexibly balanced between ground-cooperation aviation and strategic aviation stemmed more from the army command's attitudes than from the fixed ideas of the air ministry. Responsibility for the French army's dilatoriness in reappraising battlefield air–army cooperation during the 1920s rested, in the main, with the army generals themselves. Before 1931 aviation's tactical functions were envisioned in traditional and circumscribed frameworks – principally those of reconnaissance and artillery observation. The chief of the general staff from 1923 to 1930, Debeney, was a soldier of orthodox outlook who paid little attention to the potentialities of military air power. Debeney and the general staff under his direction placed priority on fortifying eastern France with what became the Maginot Line. Moreover (perhaps presaging de Gaulle's unadventurous prescriptions for air–army combinations in the mid-1930s), even the proponent of mechanisation and 'father' of French tank forces, General Jean-Baptiste Estienne, was conservative about establishing a tank–aviation tandem. He argued, in 1931, that by their 'technical and psychological affinities' armour and aircraft might achieve 'fruitful collaboration' in providing frontier security, joint reconnaissances, harassment and pursuit of a retreating opponent.[16] Conceived in these terms, however, this was still not an innovative or unorthodox delineation of how air forces might transform or revolutionise land warfare. Crucially, this conservatism in the upper reaches of the French army left little in the way of Cot when he and the 'strategic school' among French air commanders took the Armée de l'Air off onto an independent course in the mid-1930s.

Prior to that – and in particular prior to the initiation of French air rearmament with Plan I of 1934 – the French army's generals might have established their own air command, subordinated to the land forces and under their outright control. After 1933–4, however, any such ambitions on the part of rising army generals such as Gamelin, Héring and Giraud were destined to encounter fierce political and air force opposition. For Cot's greatest single achievement, by the yardstick of French aviators, was to have deprived the French war ministry, after 1933, of its proprietorial rights over the Armée de l'Air. Cot at this period overstated the point reached in air power's evolution when he claimed it could win a war by itself. Nevertheless, the energy with which he espoused the cause of the Armée de l'Air had decisive institutional and political repercussions for the structuring of French defence in the later 1930s. After 1933, and especially after Plan I, the technical, doctrinal and organisational shape of French aviation was determined independently by the air staff officers, air ministry officials and air industry bosses. Equipped by Cot with the institutional and political paraphernalia of autonomy, the Armée de l'Air, and through it French air power theoreticians, were securely protected against the re-emergence of predatory ambitions in the later 1930s, among the more 'air minded' circles in the army leadership, including Gamelin.[17]

Indeed, some indication of the reappearance of a desire for army paramountcy showed itself in 1935. In March of that year Germany announced the official reconstitution of an air force. This overt air rearmament confirmed earlier French intelligence that Germany had secretly acquired military aviation, in contravention of Versailles. A fear gripped French politicians, the press and air force chiefs that the Luftwaffe was being formed to enable Germany to terrorise an adversary's cities and civil population and knock out its industries. These Frenchmen imputed a Douhetist air strategy to the Germans.[18]

Quite a different utilisation of German aviation was, however, postulated by French army leaders. In March 1935, Maurin, the war minister, raised the danger to the Chamber army commission of a 'surprise attack' by mobile ground forces with air support 'against an inadequately defended sector of our frontier'. Maurin's prophecy foretold what became familiar later as blitzkrieg:

We should suffer a rapid ... breakthrough by armoured and motorized units moving through the breach at hitherto unknown speed and dislocating our mobilization centres whilst the enemy air forces ... sealed off the battle-zone to prevent the arrival of our reserves ... These operations need not, moreover, stop portions of the enemy's aviation from fulfilling the strategic role of air power by trying to destroy our aircraft on the ground, strike our supply depots ... and sow panic in our ranks.

Perceptively forecasting what later became a short-war strategy, Maurin argued that Germany would need to avoid a stalemated offensive with no prospect of obtaining a decisive and rapid victory. Germany's requirement for swift success if it took the risk of starting a conflict would, Maurin believed, prompt it to use aggressive and mobile methods to seek victory 'in a few weeks'.[19] Just as the army's 2e Bureau was forecasting to Gamelin, the French air intelligence service predicted that Germany would be sufficiently rearmed by the summer of 1936 to tempt the Nazi leaders to use military options.[20]

Maurin was not alone in experiencing these anxieties. Georges shared his worries. In May 1935 Colonel T. G. G. Heywood, Britain's military attaché in Paris, reported that Georges was 'convinced that the Germans would employ the bulk of their air force in close cooperation with their ground forces and not, as many people thought, in intensive warfare on the civil population'.[21] Gamelin himself evaluated air power's potentialities at this juncture with characteristic circumspection. He proposed that the prioritisation of French aviation's wartime missions would depend on the particularities of the conflict, the topography of the theatres of operations and the comparative strengths and objectives of the protagonists. For France, he said to the CPDN in late-June 1936, it remained imperative that any attack across the north-eastern frontier be stopped 'in its tracks'. If this type of offensive were launched against France, Gamelin argued that all of the Armée de l'Air would need to be deployed 'in direct liaison' with defending ground forces.

Gamelin also believed that the French air force ought to be subordinated to the army high command during the three-week mobilisation and concentration of the armies. Here, thought Gamelin, the air force's capability for near-instant war readiness suited it to shield the army's move from a peace to a war footing. In this phase Gamelin wanted control of air assets to lie with the commander-in-chief of land operations, who would reassign aviation to the air force when he no longer required it. In a war which began with no menace to French territorial integrity, Gamelin recognised that the fight for air superiority would 'take precedence'. All along, however, Gamelin's priority was to safeguard metropolitan France. This was the sanctuary of the air force just as much as it was the home base of every other component of the French war machine. Gamelin was quite free of prejudiced opposition to grand strategic employment of French aviation. But he was convinced that the Armée de l'Air had an obligation, first and foremost, to protect national mobilisation and prevent violation of the home frontiers.[22]

Gamelin's outlook may best be described as an 'open-minded orthodoxy'. His insights into how air power might transform warfare possessed a remarkable breadth and liberality considering how little first-hand acquaintance Gamelin had with aircraft. His conceptions were realistic in view of the modest performance of aircraft in the late 1930s (and even in the early years of the Second World War). Gamelin was no military reactionary. He sought to avoid, not to provoke, the politicised brawl that broke out between army commanders and the evangelists of strategic air power. The latter constituted themselves into a fanatical band of acolytes around their messiah, Pierre Cot, during the minister's second coming to the Boulevard Victor from June 1936 to January 1938.

Cot's strategic thought was, like his concern for the long-range projection of military force by a bomber air arm, a function of his left-wing politics. He was just forty years old when Blum made him air minister. An outspoken partisan of collective security, Cot harboured some uncommonly left-wing views for a member of the centrist Radical Party. The US air attaché in Paris, in his report on the nomination in June

1936, underlined the reputation for controversy:

> It is probable that M. Cot's appointment will be received with favor in aeronautical circles as his previous record is good and he is popular with aviators ... However it should be remembered that M. Cot was Air Minister at the time of the February 6, 1934 riot, and that he is reputed to have been in favor of having troops fire on the crowds massed on the Place de la Concorde – a fact which is, of course, held against him by the Right's partisans.[23]

Already regarded as a political maverick, Cot belonged to a rising group of comparatively youthful and prodigiously talented Radicals that also included Pierre Mendès-France and Jean Zay. These men had been among the 1928 and 1932 intakes elected to the Chamber of Deputies. Their progress since had been meteoric. The world economic depression served as the chief formative influence both on their decisions to enter national politics and on the content of their political agendas. Though described by contemporaries as a distinctive group within the Radicals (they were labelled 'the Young Turks'), they were never as united as this tag suggested. Indeed they were, in practice, more a collection of brilliant individualists than a cohesive faction with a common programme. Their political ideas were characterised by diversity rather than by homogeneity.[24]

Cot, for his part, envisioned the use of national planning, state intervention and the taking of industries into public ownership on a scale so lavish that it far exceeded contemporary socialist or communist proposals. His objective was to stimulate French economic recovery and to force through a vast extension of social justice by the redistributive action of the state. All of these young Radicals aimed to relegitimate the Republic by transforming it into a social-bourgeois regime. But only Cot was also concerned to refashion French foreign and strategic policy. In his bid to accomplish this he selected two immensely controversial instruments: on the one hand closer co-operation with the Soviet Union, and, on the other, the creation of a grand strategic air force.

Ever since he had visited the Soviet Union in September 1933, Cot harboured a burning ambition to promote closer Franco-Soviet relations. He wished to recreate the traditional Franco-Russian squeeze on Germany by means of a Franco-Soviet military partnership. This combination, he believed, would probably deter the expansionism of Nazi Germany. Even if it did not, it would act as a barrier to keep that expansion within the bounds of central Europe. Cot sought to build upon the Franco-Soviet treaty of friendship that Herriot that concluded in November 1932 and which Laval had developed by diplomatically linking France to the Soviet Union through the mutual assistance pact of May 1935.[25] Cot was perhaps the first and the most consistent senior

French politician to advocate the pact's conversion into a full-scale military alliance. After his return to the air ministry in June 1936 Cot sought to bring this alliance about by urging Gamelin and the other uniformed service chiefs to embark upon staff talks and joint planning with the Red Army. Faithful to the canons of collective security, Cot endeavoured to achieve tighter bonds between France and her east-central European associates – Czechoslovakia, Romania, Yugoslavia and Poland – as well as between them and the Soviet Union. From 1933 until 1939, even after losing ministerial office, Cot argued for a militarily integrated 'eastern front' or eastern combination in order to baulk Hitler's designs for *Lebensraum*.[26]

Cot's return to the air ministry in June 1936 afforded him the opportunity to steer both the Armée de l'Air and France's geo-strategic policy along the lines of his personal agenda. He knew that Gamelin's land forces, even rearmed, would not possess the reach to contribute directly to Czech, Romanian or Polish security. Only the air force promised a means to buttress the delapidated structure of eastern alliances. Therefore, asserted Cot, French engagements in the east, contracted in the 1920s, demanded the augmentation of its strategic aviation. French intelligence, Cot reminded the CPDN in late-June 1936, indicated that the Germans planned to fortify their frontiers with France. This would 'block French armies . . . and in these conditions the air force alone will be able to undertake offensive action'. For Cot, the possession of a large and long-range bomber arm offered two ways in one of strengthening French security: it would provide deterrence and it would also make available a power of reprisal. No longer, Cot reasoned, were these capabilities possessed by Gamelin's land forces – with or without their own aviation component. Cot contended that his aircraft might go where Gamelin's tanks could not: to eastern and Balkan Europe, using air power to conduct an aggressive strategic defence of France's friends.[27]

In spite of Gamelin's essential catholicity towards the future relationships between the defence services, a conflict between the army and the air force became unavoidable once Cot gave his air-power philosophy this crusade-like fanaticism. For Cot, by mid-1936, aviation no longer offered merely a means for projecting French military strength east of French frontiers, where no land operations could reach. It also represented a way to raise the status of the air ministry and advance his own career.

In obtaining air staff support, Cot was more the beneficiary of institutional self-interest than of a conversion among the air force officers to his leftist politics. French air commanders were worldly-wise about the advantages of deploying bolder arguments and fresh assertions in an endeavour to win a larger slice of defence resources. In conditions of tri-service competition (initially for credits, later for industrial capacity and scarce skilled labour), the air staff was ready to join Cot in his exaggerated claims that aviation had become a war-winner in its own right.[28]

Cot began his 1936–8 tenure at the air ministry by attending to some incomplete details of the air force's command and training structures. To the existing Conseil Supérieur de l'Air he added an air staff college, the Ecole de Guerre Aérienne, and an academy for senior air commanders, the Centre des Hautes Etudes Aériennes. To direct his ministerial office he appointed two key figures. One was a charismatic rising star of the prefectoral corps, the 37-year-old Jean Moulin, later a legendary leader in the wartime Resistance and a torture victim of Klaus Barbie. The other was Jean-Henri Jauneaud, high-priest of strategic aviation and, at forty-four in August 1936, the youngest general in the French air force.[29]

To transform their strategic dream into policy, Cot, Moulin and Jauneaud first had to renovate France's 'anarchic and artisanal' aviation industry.[30] The enterprises engaged in airframe and aero-engine manufacture required drastic reorganisation. In mid-1936 Cot told fellow ministers and military chiefs that he believed France still possessed a 'modest margin of superiority' in air strength over Germany. But, he warned, this advantage would be 'reversed from 1937 onwards and German aeronautical power will be double our own in 1938'. The Blum government responded to these bleak predictions by authorising a restructuring of the aviation industry, under the guise of satisfying left-wing demands for controls over the so-called 'merchants of death' arms manufacturers.[31]

The speed and the scale of Cot's air industry reform owed much to the acute sense of responsibility felt by the Popular Front towards their electors. Paris was a place of frenzied governmental activity as Blum's ministerial teams laboured over legislation throughout July and August 1936. Working through the usual weeks of summer recess, the deputies and senators of the left drafted bills, accommodated amendments and enacted laws at an unprecedented pace. One was the 11 August nationalisation of selected munitions and aircraft industries. This enabled Cot to take twenty-eight aviation factories into state ownership. This, in turn, gave Cot the control he needed to proceed to decentralise aircraft manufacture away from Paris. In the closing months of 1936 and early part of 1937 aero-engine and airframe plants around the capital were closed and literally dismantled. Then, in an unprecedented industrial *déménagement*, entire companies were transferred to the south and south-west. Toulouse, Marseille and Bordeaux replaced Paris as the centres of the French aircraft industry. An imperative of Popular Front political ideology – the left's curbing of the private arms manufacturers – was satisfied at the same time as the vulnerable concentration of the air industry in Paris was eliminated.[32]

Cot and his *cabinet* evolved other reforms, remodelling the air force structures and the air force command. The last found expression through decrees that lowered the upper age-of-service limits in each rank. Most of the generals of the air council were taken unawares and sidetracked into early retirement after September 1936. Pujo's successor as chief of air staff, General Philippe Féquant, was a confidant of Cot and shared his vision of the Armée de l'Air's development into a grand strategic arm.[33]

But French air rearmament was still working to the target of only 1,010 front-line machines set by Plan I. Cot therefore pressed his fellow ministers for larger-scale and more rapid refurbishment of the air force. For Gamelin the proximity of German concentration areas suitable for a westward offensive was sufficient justification, after the Rhineland's remilitarisation, for massive increases in army procurement. For Cot, however, his sights extended beyond this essential but unambitious securing of the metropolitan base. In the air minister's case it was the European-wide ramifications of the fascist menace which motivated him. His commitment to the active resistance of fascism made him a zealot for the air force. The long arm of Armée de l'Air bombers was the means by which Cot envisioned packing punch into an aggressively anti-fascist French foreign policy.[34]

Thus Cot campaigned vigorously, during and after the 26 June 1936 meeting of the permanent committee of national defence, against circumstantial and temporary subordination of air units to the army. To oil committee wheels he stated himself 'entirely disposed to assist the war ministry'. In reality Cot conceded nothing to his army rivals. Air power was not, he insisted, 'a mere ancillary'; it had matured to equality with the army and navy. It had become a 'major actor in its own right'; indeed, he claimed, it would in future warfare command centre-stage. To divide the air arm would be to enfeeble it; decisive results would be accomplished only by concentration. In urging further expansion of the air force, Cot rested his argument almost entirely on untested assertions about its grand strategic potential.

Gamelin, responding to Cot, offered a less grandiloquent but empirically proven perspective. A substantial part of French air strength in a future war would, he argued, still be required for reconnaissance and observation where it had proven its worth in 1914–18. Rapid battlefield intelligence could in future, contended Gamelin, come only from the air. Consequently, at least during a war's first phase, he wanted aviation to 'be under the orders of the commander-in-chief of the armies on the ground'. Early in a conflict Gamelin felt 'unable to conceive of the air force pursuing its own disconnected and independent action'. Cot retorted that he could admit the assignment of aviation to 'support a land army yet without being entirely detached to it'. But he was adamant that there had to be one single and self-contained air force. He accepted that aviation had a part to play in cooperation and ground support. Its primary purpose, however, remained the accomplishment of a grand strategy of its own. For this he implored the CPDN for a 'great effort of reinforcement and expansion'. This meeting in June 1936 – for all the ritual conciliatory punctuation – showed the French defence policy-makers how different were the emerging army and air force doctrines and how competitive were the resource demands of the two rearmament programmes.[35]

Quickly the disrupted French air industry demonstrated that it was chronically unable to keep the second and third Armée de l'Air expansion programmes on schedule. On paper the schemes did not appear unduly ambitious. Plan II, which Cot inherited and for which the Blum government approved additional credits at Rambouillet on 6–7 September 1936, set a target of 1,500 first-line aircraft. Plan III, heavily influenced by Cot and Jauneaud, was a November 1936 scheme for 2,400 first-line aircraft to be completed by June 1940. But aircraft production levels made a mockery of these ambitions. In the last quarter of 1937 the average output of French aircraft had declined to just forty machines per month. In January 1938 it sank even lower, to a mere thirty-five aircraft. This was caused in part by the relocation of the aviation industry, in part by the introduction of new types of all-metal aircraft, whose complex construction and requirements in skilled labour Cot had underestimated.[36]

In 1936–7 France experienced a dismayingly rapid decline from sufficiency to inferiority of air strength *vis-à-vis* Germany. There had been a cautious confidence among the French military about the air balance just before the Popular Front took office. Gamelin, Georges and Schweisguth concurred with Pujo in April 1936 that the observation squadrons were then well-equipped, the bombers sufficient and only the fighter force inadequate. The army chiefs did not disagree that, 'viewed overall', France retained 'temporary superiority over the Luftwaffe'.[37] Even in July 1936 Cot's already-cited assertion that the Armée de l'Air still had a 'modest margin' of advantage was not contested.[38] When this disappeared, partly because the industrial reforms engendered such short-term disruption and partly because the French were badly behind in the technological revolution coming over aircraft types in 1937, a scapegoat was required and Cot fitted the part.

Objectively, the French aviation problem in these years was endemic rather than the result of Cot and his policies. France was not ready to compete successfully with Germany in any short or medium-term air arms race. Germany enjoyed the decisive advantage of already possessing an appropriate aero-engineering industrial base upon which, at any rate in a two to five-year time scale, it could outbuild France. Cot showed some grasp of this, for he drew the imbalance in manufacturing capacity between French and German aviation to the CPDN's attention in July 1936. Attaining Plan II's target of 1,500 first-line aircraft, would, he warned, still leave the Armée de l'Air numerically inferior against an expected Luftwaffe strength of 2,500 or 3,000 aircraft. Worse, argued Cot, a French air strength of 1,500 would be a ceiling above which it would be purely academic to plan. Even were unrestricted credits opened in 1936 it would, he said, be 'impossible to build beyond this figure of 1,500 aircraft because of the inadequacy of [French] industrial capacity'.[39] Shortages of skills and modern machine tools could not be overcome merely by voting credits and making wishes. The impediments encountered by the army at this time in its armour and artillery modernisation thus were also encountered in air force programmes. Yet the snags proved more awkward for Cot than for Daladier. 'In respect of aviation', Gamelin conceded later, 'even more than on the ground, we were very severely restricted by our available "industrial power".'[40]

Yet the air ministry exacerbated its own problems, failing to collaborate with the army's procurement offices in pursuit of shared solutions to common difficulties. On their own, Cot and his inner circle successfully identified the vulnerability of France's aircraft factories because of their concentration around Paris. They also appraised for themselves the dearth of skilled aero-engineering labour reserves in the capital. They thus based the relocation of aircraft manufacturing on sound arguments and had a rational project for a strong aircraft industry in the long run. But in other respects the reforms were executed too hastily and dogmatically. For instance, the air ministry underestimated the difficulties that the aeronautical companies would suffer because of the paucity of suitably skilled workers resident in Toulouse and the other sites where the industry was relocated. Nor was there any tapping of the experience of the army (whose artillery inspectorate, for example, knew the southwest through twenty years of administering the huge munitions plant at Tarbes). In military-industrial policy, therefore, as in the formulation of integrated defence strategy or combined-arms doctrine, French efforts were hampered by inter-service animosities. The outcome was a rearmament drive in which military programmes proliferated in competition with each other, instead of in a cooperative and prioritised overall plan.[41]

Moreover, in 1937, under the patronage of Cot and the direction of Féquant, French air chiefs attended less to the problems of the aviation industry than to the production of blueprints for grand strategic air war. Flesh had to be put on the bare bones of the dogma of an offensive role for French air power within what was termed the 'aerial battle'. This was set about with a will by the men of the reconstituted Conseil Supérieur de l'Air: Generals Vuillemin, Aubé, Mouchard, Houdemon, Keller, Têtu and d'Astier de la Vigerie. These were ambitious officers, who sought advancement through expanding the size and status of their service. But the real powerhouse of ideas inside the Cot regime was the precocious General Jauneaud, whom admirers and detractors alike credited as the air force's *éminence grise*. He spearheaded the drafting teams which produced both the mid-March 1937 parliamentary bill to increase French front-line air strength to 1,500 aircraft and the 31 March 1937 *Instruction on the employment of major air units*.[42]

The latter document represented the major statement of the Cot administration's air policy. It was the chief conduit by which Cot and Jauneaud sought to disseminate their doctrine of an autonomous strategy for the Armée de l'Air. The message was direct and uncompromising. French aviation's principal wartime function was to locate and destroy enemy aircraft, and then to attack enemy air bases and communications. The objective was to win air supremacy and thereafter to employ French air power to bombard the aviation industry and other economic assets of the enemy, and, it was presumed, thereby shorten the war. Having codified a doctrine, Cot had the manual to go with the money voted by parliament, as well as men in command who shared his own mode of thought. Though Gamelin was concerned by the questionable effectiveness of a French air force forced into this strategic format, it was not he who brought about Cot's departure in January 1938.[43]

Quite simply, Cot had become a political liability. Indeed, as the humiliating statistics of production from the aviation factories in the final quarter of 1937 emerged, he became a political embarrassment. He was demoted to the less contentious post of minister for commerce after the reconstitution of the Chautemps government in January 1938. A man who was in politics for principles and causes, Cot had neglected to make himself indispensable to his prime minister. Too much the individualist, the maverick, Cot had failed even to make himself the undisputed standard-bearer for the younger Radicals. He had been flamboyant, innovative and publicity conscious. In July 1936 he had initiated the so-called 'popular aviation' movement, to popularise flying and widen its social accessibility, by requiring aero clubs to offer inexpensive pilot training and technical courses. In September 1937 he inaugurated the first 'festival of popular aviation' at Vincennes, the forerunner of the air displays and air shows of later times. Militarily, he instigated Armée de l'Air experiments with autogyros. Inspired by Red Army airborne forces displayed in the 1936 Soviet manoeuvres he established France's first companies of paratroops, deployed with disconcerting effect on the French army in the September 1937 Normandy exercises. But none of this counted when the storms of criticism broke over the retarded rearmament of the air force. Not having practised the *politique politicienne* of the 'Republic of Pals', Cot fell because he had too few political allies.[44]

Gamelin did not engineer Cot's downfall. Indeed he was less affected than most army generals by anti-air force prejudice. Nevertheless, he disliked Cot's style and regarded his strategic ambitions for the air force as misconceived. These reservations were not Gamelin's alone. The Belgian military attaché in Paris watched the defence budget debate for 1937 in the Palais Bourbon and reported that:

M. Cot, the air minister, is undoubtedly a man of dynamic intelligence, an orator of remarkable facility and eloquence; he is also a dialectical gymnast of unequalled agility who has succeeded in circumventing the most awkward questions with astonishing adroitness and who excels in turning them [to his advantage]. This does not mean that he cannot have a quite different way of working in the quiet of his office where, it appears, he is prodigiously active ... However the debates leave me convinced that party politics [*la politique des partis*] is no stranger to his ministerial preoccupations, for all that he denies it.[45]

In Gamelin's case, his recorded conversations and writings over ten years attest to the growth within him of a deep-seated conviction that Cot had grievously retarded French air rearmament in the late 1930s. Thus in early September 1938, the British ambassador in Paris reportedly was told by Léger, the Quai d'Orsay secretary-general, that Gamelin deplored 'the ravages made on French aviation by Monsieur Cot'.[46] One year later, soon after the outbreak of war, Gamelin's personal adjutant recorded the general lamenting 'the dreadful damage that M. Cot did' by his 'sabotaging French aviation'. This, Gamelin was quoted directly as saying, 'has now emerged as the greatest gap in our national security ... we are paying the price for two years of mistakes'.[47] At Riom, during the wartime Vichyite show trials, Gamelin of course said nothing publicly about any issue or anybody. But he did contribute testimony in writing to the pre-trial investigating counsel.

Then, in contrast to his balanced and frequently supportive depositions in respect to Blum, Daladier, Jacomet and Guy La Chambre (Cot's successor), his judgement on Cot was unrelievedly critical. In a report that became part of the Blum dossier, for instance, he wrote that the 'harm done, which turned out in fact to be irreparable, was in aviation ... and there the name on everyone's lips is that of M. Pierre Cot'.[48] In his memoirs, in 1946–7, Gamelin explicitly differentiated between the imperfect but acceptable understanding that he claimed he had reached with chiefs of the air staff over circumstantial air assistance to the army, and the inflexibility of Cot. 'This meeting of minds [with the generals of the air force]', alleged Gamelin, 'did not exist' between him and Cot, who 'was the convinced partisan of independence for the bulk of the air forces. No doubt he always paid lip service to the need to turn over to our land armies those air assets that they legitimately claimed. But his saying this was not enough . . .'.[49]

Gamelin's strength of feeling over the difficulty of cooperation with Cot owed something to his awareness in 1936–8 of the German development of the combined offensive air-ground blitzkrieg. Army intelligence in April 1936 identified an increasing emphasis in Wehrmacht doctrine on surprise attack 'by mechanised forces and aviation'. The adaptation of storm troop tactics 'in an up-to-date guise' and German attention to renovating the methods that had restored the power of breakthrough in the spring 1918 Ludendorff offensives were also noticed. A specialised spearhead army, it was judged, would carry the primary offensive responsibility if Germany launched an aggressive war. The attack would be staged jointly by mobile ground units 'as well as by air power'. The French army, at any rate, did not ignore the operational interaction of tanks and tactical aviation.[50]

However, the fixation of Cot, Féquant, Jauneaud and their air staff acolytes on aviation's strategic promise was so firm as to preclude at this time any cooperation to produce a combined-arms doctrine.[51] Indeed the obsession with developing their own air strength into a grand strategic striking force led French air chiefs in 1936–7 to neglect their own intelligence reports. For the evidence of increasing Luftwaffe training in tactical ground support emanated not just from French army intelligence but also from the 2e Bureau of the Armée de l'Air. The latter service (commenting on the German official notice on air warfare), warned of how closely the Luftwaffe was likely to be committed in support of German ground formations whilst breaking an opponent's organised defence.[52] Moreover, in September 1937, at the German manoeuvres, the French witnessed the appearance of the tank/Stuka Ju.87 combination. Through industrial intelligence as well as the information supplied by an able team of air attachés in Berlin (Colonel de Geffrier, aviation-engineer Léon Poincaré and the assistant air attaché, Captain Paul Stehlin), the French air staff knew of Germany's acquisition of assault aviation and dive-bombers for direct battlefield intervention. It was the Armée de l'Air's obsessional pursuit of its grand-strategic dream, not ignorance of the changing threat, which interminably delayed effective French responses.[53]

What influence did the civil war which had broken out on Spain in July 1936 exert on this tussle over the shape of air doctrine between the French services? Like all foreign military intelligence organisations, the French gave the conflict across the Pyrenees close attention. General Armengaud, a former inspector-general of the French air force whom Cot had retired early in 1936, produced a study of the air aspects of the war in 1937. In 1938 an article was published by General Henri Niessel, a former chief of the French military mission to Poland; yet another, *Les Leçons de la Guerre d'Espagne*, by the retired army general Jean Duval, carried an authoritative preface by Weygand. These works wisely cautioned that the scarcity of air resources on both sides in Spain prevented the drawing of conclusions about aviation in a strategic role. In most cases air forces had been confined to operations close to the front, and had commonly been treated as a longer-range form of artillery.[54]

The war in Spain was regarded by the French as too under-resourced and too peculiar a military laboratory for the fashioning of hard and fast rules regarding air power.[55] Indeed it was, counselled Duval, 'very far from unveiling any clear view of the future'. French observers were unconvinced that the improvised and intermittently supplied air forces in Spain were any more reliable a guide to the future of military aviation than were the stylised simulations seen at German manoeuvres. One thing that was noticed, however, was the value of preparatory air strikes on defending troops which it was intended to attack on the ground. This, emphasised Duval, 'had devastating psychological if not material consequences . . . and sowed disorder . . . as well as paralysing troop movements'.[56] For Gamelin, by 1937–8, evidence was accumulating to compel him to treat aviation as a growing threat to a French land strategy premised on the integrity of her frontier defences. Enough signs were emerging, from German exercises and Spanish campaigns, to lead Gamelin to take a fresh interest from 1938 onwards in acquiring more defensive and tactically capable French air power.[57]

But in 1937–8, as the entire Armée de l'Air rearmament fell behind schedule, Gamelin at first inclined to disguise the problem's severity. He did not mask his mounting concern out of any loyalty towards Cot. Rather, Gamelin judged that France might lose much-needed friends and allies, not gain them, if excessive frankness were shown in admitting French military difficulties. He considered that elusiveness and imprecision were likely to be more expedient than candour both for his own diplomacy and for that of the Quai d'Orsay.[58]

Since Britain was estimated to be the most essential of these desired allies, it was unhelpful to the French that accurate knowledge was possessed in London about the Armée de l'Air's depleted combat strength and disorganised industrial base. The French, furthermore, were unaware that their British interlocutors were so well informed. Plainly, this British intelligence advantage was a handicap for the French in negotiations with the British authorities over cooperation or burden-sharing in air matters.[59] As early as 1934 the RAF staff had expressed concern to policy makers in London about the Armée de l'Air's Plan I, because it had a planned reserve of only 20 per cent above its projected first-line strength of 1,010 aircraft. Such small reserves had caused the British to doubt what post-1945 strategists would term the wartime 'sustainability' of French aviation.[60]

Gamelin, for his part, was too wily to allow the British to ensnare him or factually contradict his reports about the French defensive programmes. Cot, however, more given to boastful self-advertisement, fell foul of the inquisitive British air attaché in Paris, Group Captain Douglas Colyer and the investigations of the British Board of Trade's industrial intelligence centre. On reading a report by Colyer of Cot's claims in 1936 for the results of his personal initiatives in French air policy, a Foreign Office minute scathingly noted that:

Monsieur Cot . . . is . . . talking nonsense when he says that France will be at the peak of her strength this year . . . The truth is that at the present moment of the 1,000 first-line machines, about 600 are obsolete types . . . The industry is in confusion and nothing has [yet] been done to organize it. To those who know France and recall that in 1870 and again in 1914 adequate preparation for war was conspicuous by its absence, these facts are not surprising.[61]

During 1937 the deepening disarray of the French air arm became an open secret inside and outside France. Though Gamelin would not scaremonger, he revealed enough of the difficulties to the British ambassador in Paris, Sir Eric Phipps, in July 1937, that William Strang, the head of the Foreign Office's central department minuted on Phipps's report that 'her [France's] airforce alone is not now a match for that of Germany'.[62] By year's end the evident crisis of production and delivery of aircraft was threatening to escalate into a crisis of aircrew training and punctured air force morale. It was no longer just the self-respect of French aviation but the security of France which was at stake – and which cost Cot the air ministry.[63]

The year 1938 was a time of soul-searching and, ultimately, of constructive new directions for the Armée de l'Air. Many of the problems of the service – though not all – had been found promising and pragmatic solutions by its close. Much credit for the nascent recovery was given by contemporaries to Guy La Chambre, the Chamber army commission's president since 1936, who succeeded Cot on 19 January 1938. Another of the new generation of younger Radicals, La Chambre was not doctrinaire or provocative. He enjoyed the political support of his friend and kindred spirit, Daladier (as well as of Daladier's confidant William Bullitt, the American ambassador in Paris).[64] In the circumstances of his appointment, the choice of La Chambre was reassuring. In the new air minister, France had acquired 'a very good man', enthused Chautemps, the prime minister, to Anthony Eden, Britain's foreign secretary, when the latter visited Paris after the government reconstruction.[65]

Gamelin, too, welcomed the change of administration at the Boulevard Victor – even if it would be a year before tangible signs appeared of reinforced French air strength. In his final reflections on the Battle of France, penned around 1956–7, the general underlined the inferiority of the Armée de l'Air *vis-à-vis* the Luftwaffe right to the end but absolved both General Joseph Vuillemin, the chief of air staff in 1938–40, and La Chambre, 'who, since his appointment in January 1938, had done everything possible to catch up the time that had been lost'.[66] The Cot regime's rhetorical bluster and airy dismissal of practical difficulties became a thing of the past. In its stead appeared a spirit of stark realism and a reordering of the Armée de l'Air's rearmament priorities.

Signs of the new urgency – it should be acknowledged – did antedate the Cot–La Chambre changeover. In 1937 Cot and Féquant visited London for talks with the British secretary of state for air, Lord Swinton. The British agreed to periodic Anglo-French air staff conversations as well as to meetings of air industry experts to seek joint solutions to the impediments to air rearmament on both sides of the Channel.[67] On 20 November 1937 Féquant was instructed to 'take up as a matter of urgency the question of the eventual expansion of the air force'.[68] Cot alerted the CPDN in early December that year to the need for increased expenditures if the Armée de l'Air were to remain competitive *vis-à-vis* Germany and Italy. France, he warned his colleagues, would 'finish up having the weakest aviation because we have given it the most parsimonious of financial allocations'.[69]

It was, however, the alarms from the air force's own commanders, rather than the oratory of politicians, that caused commotion about the state of the service in early 1938. On 15 January Vuillemin sent a written warning to the air ministry – destined for Cot but received by La Chambre because of the mid-month succession – that 'if a conflict breaks out this year . . . the French air force would be obliterated in a few days'.[70] Such blunt language captured immediate attention. In February Vuillemin was appointed chief of air staff. La Chambre responded to Vuillemin's shrill warnings by ordering the preparation of a new and vastly more ambitious air expansion programme. The curtain was rung down quickly – but belatedly in relation to German progress – on the outdated scheme for 1,500 aircraft to which the Armée de l'Air was still working.

From the start, La Chambre signalled his intention to restructure the rearmed air force. Plan II and its offspring had reflected the dominance of strategic doctrine under Cot; 49 per cent of its proposed first-line squadron strength was to consist of bombers. The new thinking, from 1938 to 1940, envisioned a reduced proportion of bombers within a numerically much larger first-line and reserve strength. It also scaled up the air force so that its financing would dominate the rearmament budget. The way forward emerged when La Chambre explained on 16 February 1938, to the aeronautical commission of the Chamber of Deputies, that:

> regarding bomber aircraft, I consider it an error to give no thought to questions of offensives . . . In the initial phase of a war, however, what we'll need above all to do is to put our airspace under lock and key, as we've done for our frontiers . . . I shall continue to have bombers manufactured because we require retaliatory airpower. However, I am not certain that we need aviation with such an offensive character as that indicated in our instruction on the employment of major air units . . . It is not a matter of sacrificing bombers to any god of fighter aircraft. It is a question of our need for a proportionality . . . I must state that I do not accept assertions that fighters are useless; . . . they can contribute to our defences [now] . . . and . . . in the days ahead, they will be our bomber escorts.[71]

As La Chambre argued in February 1938, to a joint session of all the armed services commissions, fighters had increasing importance not just in protecting French cities and industries but for escorting army cooperation missions in the face of enemy interceptors.[72]

Plan V, as La Chambre's programme was designated, was approved by the air council on 15 March 1938.[73] That same day the CPDN also convened. The latter meeting was attended not only by the service ministers and chiefs of staff but by the prime minister (Blum, heading his brief second government) and foreign minister, Paul-Boncour. Lest these politicians not specialist in defence questions doubted the urgency of the air rearmament, Vuillemin reiterated the apocalyptic prophecy that he had rehearsed in January to La Chambre. If obliged to fight the

Luftwaffe for air supremacy (the hypothesis being a Franco-German war caused by Hitler attacking Czechoslovakia), Vuillemin warned that the Armée de l'Air would be 'annihilated in a fortnight'.[74]

Financed by a new special credit of 3,465 million francs (added to the air force's normal budget already allotted for the year), Plan V represented a pointed shift in French defensive priorities.[75] The scheme put the Armée de l'Air in 1938 in receipt, for the first time, of more money than either of the other services. In that year's cutting of the rearmament cake the air force obtained 42 per cent of the finances compared with the army's 36 per cent. This change was accompanied by the resetting of the proportions between the different categories of aircraft *within* the air force. A direct comparison of types between the upgraded Plan II, in force at the end of Cot's ministry, and Plan V illustrates both the expansion wrought by the latter and the way in which La Chambre translated new thinking about the Armée de l'Air's roles into a different force-structure (see Table 5).[76] Plan V also fully addressed the issue of the high aircraft attrition rates that were increasingly expected to characterise air operations. Because of this, not because of any complacency, in September 1938 Gamelin opined (according to a talk with Léger, the Quai d'Orsay secretary-general, reported by Britain's ambassador in Paris), that 'the role of aviation is apt to be exaggerated and that after the early days of a war the wastage will be such that it will be confined more and more to acting as an accessory to the army'.[77]

Table 5. *French air rearmament Plans II (1935) and V (1938)*

aircraft type	Plan II		Plan V	
	target strength	% of total	target	% of total
Bombers	755	49	876	33.4
Fighters	439	29	1,081	41.3
Reconnaissance/ army cooperation	326	22	636	24.3
Air infantry	0	0	24	0.9
Total (first-line)	1,500	100	2,617	100

The projected reserves under Plan V were lavish. The French goal was a rearmed air force with up-to-the minute technology – one able to maintain a near full-strength first-line force in extended air operations entraining heavy losses; 80 per cent first-line reserves (2,122 aircraft) were tabled in Plan V, a four-fold increase over the 20 per cent reserves considered sufficient in Plan I of 1934. As it was formulated in early 1938, Plan V was to be accomplished in three year-long stages, culminating in March 1941. Subsequently, with the increasingly perilous appearance of European relations after the German–Austrian Anschluss, La Chambre had the scheme compressed into the two years from April 1938 to 31 March 1940.[78] La Chambre pleaded that 'the impossible be done' to complete the entire new air programme on this foreshortened timetable.[79] Gamelin counselled, in a note written in mid-March, the desirability of disguising from public (and particularly allied) sight 'the current enfeeblement' of French aviation.[80] A yardstick of how much remained to be done was that the entire aero industry still managed to complete only sixty aircraft in April 1938.[81]

Plan V (itself expanded in June 1939 into 'Plan V renforcé', with a target of 8,500 aircraft), was not a complete about-turn for French air force operational doctrine or equipment. La Chambre had made it plain to the parliamentary commissioners in February 1938 that he was not scrapping bomber aircraft or a French air force with long-range retaliatory capabilities. His purpose was, rather, to give the air rearmament programme a balance. He placed new emphasis on defensive and escorting fighter aircraft and he marginally increased reconnaissance and ground cooperation types. In comparative terms the loser under Plan V was the bomber force. Yet even the bombers were to be more numerous under La Chambre's programme than in earlier ones.

Gamelin was conscious that Plan V represented a significant rearguard success for air staff officers who wished to retain the long-range bombers in the aviation programme. Plan V was the outcome of compromise between Gamelin, the army general staff and the air force chiefs, to raise the priority for fighters and anti-aircraft resources. But it amounted to a relative rather than an absolute switch in favour of these defensive systems. More importantly, it did little to enhance the willingness or ability of the air force to perform ground support roles in which the French army was now interested. Plan V therefore did not relieve Gamelin's growing anxiety regarding the security of French air space and air-land cooperation.[82]

However, Plan V at last furnished the framework of managerial pragmatism, industrial resource-utilisation and almost unlimited finance for a major expansion of the air force and for re-equipment with up-to-date, competitive, aircraft. La Chambre, justifiably, is accorded some credit for these achievements – and particularly for replacing Cot's ideological adversarialism with a functional relationship to the army, navy and industry. Nevertheless, La Chambre was the largely inadvertent beneficiary in 1939–40 of the fruits of Cot's reorganisation of the aviation industry. The chaos and collapse of output that resulted in 1937 from the nationalisations and relocations gave way – indeed actually made possible – the French aviation industry's prodigious feat by 1940 of outproducing the Germans. Not only did francs flow without impediment into orders for new aircraft but so too did workers into the airframe and aero-engine plants. Here a further advantage of the Cot reforms emerged, as mass-assembly in the new factories permitted the employment of more semi-skilled labour. The workforce in the French aviation industry expanded from 35,000 men in January 1938 to 88,000 a year later and to 171,000 by January 1940. Along with this revolution in the manufacturing base occurred a revolution in the modernity and combat-capability of the aircraft emerging from this renovated industry. One landmark was the design of a new generation of swift, heavily armed, single-seat monoplane fighters. The first of these, the Morane-Saulnier 406, flew in prototype in 1938. Though slower than Germany's rival Messerschmitt 109 interceptor, the Morane was ruggedly built and manoeuvrable. Not dissimilar to the British Hawker Hurricane, then entering RAF service, the Morane's attributes quickly endeared it to aircrews and made it practicable to plan to defend French air space. In 1939 the Morane was followed by the outstanding Dewoitine 520, a fighter that outclassed all contemporary Luftwaffe aircraft. And with the LéO 45, new high-performance bombers also made their appearance.[83]

There was a new, though premature, optimism in 1939 about the Armée de l'Air. The emergence, after so long, of competitive aircraft engendered a surge of confidence. In January that year Belgium's military attaché in London reported that 'knowledgeable British circles ... believe numerical inferiority [*vis-à-vis* Germany and Italy] will tend to diminish through the fact that in France they now seem to be surmounting their aeronautical production difficulties, and because the collaboration of French and British aeronautical technical services promises positive results'.[84] The manufacture of aircraft with advanced specifications, along with the expansion of the labour force in aviation manufacturing, has enabled at least one historian to assert that 'it was possible, in the spring of 1939, to talk of a veritable resurrection of the [French] aeronautical industry'.[85]

The return of French air strength from the dead, however, was no three-day miracle. Monthly output levels from the French aviation factories recovered with painful slowness throughout 1938. Most of the aircraft in service (and many that were manufactured) that year remained of obsolete type. It was qualitative as well as quantitative inferiority, combined with the appraisal of the Luftwaffe that he was able to make on an official visit to Germany from 16 to 21 August 1938, which impelled Vuillemin, shortly before the climax of the German–Sudeten crisis, to repeat his warning that the Armée de l'Air was no match for the Luftwaffe. Employing identical language to that used in January and March 1938, Vuillemin restated that, if war resulted, his forces would be unable to sustain more than a fortnight's combat operations.[86] On 24 August, on his return from Germany, the chief of the French air staff was received by Gamelin, who found him 'enormously impressed by what he had been able to observe'.[87] In an influential report which he wrote for La Chambre on 26 September, when faith in settling the Sudeten issue peacefully rested on a knife edge, Vuillemin deployed every argument at his command against – as a specialist historian has put it – 'any premature French entry into a war'.[88] The Armée de l'Air, said the report, could field just 250 fighters, 320 bombers and 130 reconnaissance aircraft against the Luftwaffe.[89] It may be admitted that the willingness of the west's leaders to go as far in appeasing Hitler as to accept the Munich settlement owed itself less to calculations of relative strategic disadvantage than to residual convictions about the opportunity to achieve a general European détente. In the French case, however, Daladier without a doubt journeyed to Munich with what Patrick Facon has called the 'sombre tableau' of French air weakness drawn by Vuillemin and La Chambre graven in his mind. The plight of the Armée de l'Air was not what sent the French prime minister to meet Hitler; but it was probably the most pressing reason for his determination not to return without a settlement.[90]

Despite the far-sighted though initially disruptive industrial restructuring of 1937, the adoption of an air rearmament plan worthy of the name in 1938, and the emergence of up-to-the-minute aircraft in 1939, war in and from the skies remained the Achilles heel of French defence right down to 1940. Allocating insufficient resources – always among the most fraught of managerial functions – therefore remained the principal challenge facing makers of French defence policy from the spring of 1938 till the coming of war. It also remained the chief cause of altercations between the army and air force. Neither Gamelin's ambiguity-ridden appointment as chief of staff for national defence in January 1938, nor Plan V's adoption two months later, subordinated the air force's procurement policy or its strategy. Plan V intended to give the air force a reduced strategic bombing role, not to deprive it of one altogether. Plan V intended to provide an improved fighter defence for the French homeland, but not a secure one. French air rearmament right into the war remained an unsatisfactory halfway house, the product of competing views of its main purpose and of compromise as to the Armée de l'Air's relation to Gamelin's land forces.[91]

The chronic problems that afflicted the air force were, Gamelin did not doubt, the result of the air ministry following its own headstrong inclinations and of the tenuous integration of aviation into national defensive planning. The inadequacy of French air strength, in 1938–9, originated, in Gamelin's estimation, from the late start to French air rearmament. Exacerbating this basic problem, contended Gamelin, was the mismanagement of the aviation industry's modernisation in 1936–7 – a task which the general thought should have been entrusted not to a political ideologue such as Cot but to a proven businessman or a military technocrat.

These handicaps to French air rearmament were, according to Gamelin, complicated further in 1938–9 by the failure of the political authorities to resolve unambiguously the place of the air force in national strategy and within the command structure. And it was indeed the case that French air rearmament, as well as the development of any doctrine for air–ground cooperation at an operational level, was marked throughout by cloudiness over objectives and rivalry over resources.[92] Reynaud, with foresight but little effect, 'begged' Daladier in the 1937 defence budget debates 'not to wait till the bombs are raining down on Paris to ascertain whether the supreme commander [*le généralissime*] will or will not have the disposition of French aviation in his power'.[93] As discussed earlier, however, Daladier was not willing to implement a proposal in 1937 that General Auguste Noguès, the commander-in-chief of French North Africa, return to Paris to head the army so that Gamelin could be promoted to supreme generalissimo over all the services. Daladier was constrained by the powerful parliamentary lobbies that defended the independence of the navy and the air force.[94] His reluctance was doubtless reinforced by his innate suspicion – resulting from his republican political *formation* – of a concentration of offices in the person of any Frenchman in military uniform. Daladier shared as well as shaped the calculation of the Radicals (to say nothing of parties further to the left) that, historically, the more French military chiefs were kept divided and beset by their own rivalries, the less likely they were to challenge their submission to civil authority. Hence Daladier rested content with according Gamelin the grandiose but largely hollow title of chief of staff for national defence in January 1938, which left the general with his functions as army commander-designate.

Unable, as a result of the dualism in his attributions, to pose as an impartial arbiter striving even-handedly after an integrated national defence plan, Gamelin was equally powerless to dictate on the vital issues of doctrine and procurement. The decree that broadened Gamelin's purview was noteworthy for its vagueness. 'As far as the army and air force are concerned', it said, 'he [the chief of staff for national defence] coordinates the studies addressing strategic preparation for war and the establishment of plans for operations and mobilisation.'[95] Gamelin appreciated the acute limitations inherent in drawing the terms of reference of his functions so ambiguously.[96] From March until August 1938 he corresponded with Vuillemin, on occasion acrimoniously, as he endeavoured to gain the authority of command, in at least certain circumstances, over the air force. Each general appealed to his respective political superior and sought to enlist his support – so entangling La Chambre and Daladier in the controversy. Reference to ministerial authority, however, served merely to emphasise the irreconcilability of the army and air force views of the appropriate weighting to be desired between, on the one hand, truly independent air power and, on the other, subordinated tactical aviation, at the completion of Plan V. A decisive resolution of the disagreements was precluded by Daladier's unwillingness to give Gamelin a completely unambiguous promotion. Consequently, resort was made to compromise: at the price of stepping back from direct command of the northeastern theatre facing Germany, Gamelin was empowered to distribute air as well as land forces between different theatres of operations wherever France had interests and military deployments. On this murky definition of attributions the issue of an integrated air–army command was left to rest.[97]

After Munich Gamelin called for statements from all three services on their progress in rearming and their expected states of readiness in 1939. The gloomy report that Vuillemin submitted on 25 October served to confirm France's need to associate itself completely in a political and military partnership with Britain. Only the obtaining of a substantial RAF commitment to France offered a rapid way to remedy French air weakness. But the Vuillemin report also highlighted the urgency for France to acquire alternative sources of combat-serviceable aircraft.[98] On both counts, Gamelin was convinced that absolute priority should be accorded to territorial air defence and to air assistance in his army's mission of securing western Europe. Gamelin supported Daladier and La Chambre when they turned to the United States and its aviation industry, as a short-cut to re-equipping the Armée de l'Air. He endorsed the despatch of Jean Monnet to Washington to negotiate – with the encouragement of Bullitt, the American ambassador in Paris – French purchase of 200 Curtiss P-36 fighters and Glenn Martin bombers.[99] This order was increased to 1,000 aircraft when the CPDN convened on 5

December 1938. At that meeting Gamelin was outspoken against both Vuillemin and Reynaud, then finance minister, in insisting that production at home and purchase abroad be concentrated on aircraft to defend French air space or directly participate in the land battle. 'Our overriding preoccupation', he argued successfully, 'must be fighters; they must have precedence over bombers other than those for battlefield bombing. We need fighters to protect French territory and to protect our armies . . .'.[100]

As the likelihood of a European war increased, Gamelin at least arrived at a clear formulation of the air policy that he wanted for France. He wished to eradicate, root and branch, the impracticable grand strategic air power ambitions still nurtured by sections of the air staff. He wanted unswerving attention to building up the air force's capacity to make French air space impenetrable to hostile bombers. He desired role-specialisation, or burden-sharing as post-1945 terminology would describe it, between the Armée de l'Air and the RAF. With the prioritisation of French fighter aircraft production which Gamelin sought, the Armée de l'Air would have few medium and longer-range bombers before 1940–1. These, however, were to be sought from the British. At one with Gamelin on this, both Lelong, the French military attaché in London, and Jamet, the chief of the CSDN secretariat, sternly contested the switch in the Chamberlain government's priority for British aircraft manufacturing in 1938–9 to fighters designed mainly for UK home defence.[101] From the French standpoint there was much to be said for the allocation of the greater portion of British air assets to the maritime-air and offensive bombing roles, whilst the Armée de l'Air and continent-based RAF fighters shouldered the responsibility for forward air defence of France and Britain – and of Belgium and the Netherlands too, if their cooperation could be won. A distribution of tasks on these lines, formulated with considerable participation by Gamelin in the 1938–9 winter, became and remained right down to the 'rupture' of June 1940 the cornerstone of French thinking about air power's place in western strategy.[102]

It may hardly be doubted that, if French air industry production had not sunk so low or its recovery been so extended, the grand strategic role cherished by Cot and Jauneaud would have been defended more ardently and perpetuated more effectively by the Armée de l'Air chiefs of 1938–40. In this sense, therefore, the French air force's part in national defensive strategy was given practicable and coherent shape by 1939 as a result of the harsh choices that were forced by the crisis of French air rearmament. Almost by accident the makers of French defensive strategy arrived at a cogent and compellingly sensible wish to share the responsibilities and potentialities of aviation with the British. They did so, understandably, from a French national perspective. But the British had their own national perspective – cautious and insular to be sure, but defensible and indeed compelling when viewed simply in its own terms. The resultant compromises once Franco-British staff talks began, in March 1939, ensured that there was no Allied consensus as to the location of their front line in the air. The French naturally were adamant that it was in France; the British were just as dogmatic that it lay over the English Channel.[103] On this critical issue of strategy, as on that of air cooperation with the French armies, Gamelin was not master in his own house. Organisational and command ambiguities, chronic industrial bottlenecks, divergences between allies who took legitimately contrary views of their vital interests: these were the obstacles which proved insurmountable to the elaboration of an integrated and efficient French national defence. Gamelin had discerned the danger from the air, and particularly its potency in support of land offensives. That much was clear, as will be seen later, from his attention to the air–armour combination used successfully by the Germans in Poland in September 1939. That he was comparatively unsuccessful in countering it was because, as one of his obituarists put it, 'weakness[es] . . . and especially that of the air arm, which he had probably no means of remedying, hampered him at every turn'.[104]

7 Gamelin, the Maginot Line and Belgium

Preserving the integrity of the French frontiers was the most fundamental and most difficult challenge that Gamelin had to face in his years of command. Germany's violation of Belgian neutrality in 1914 served as a constant reminder to him that the defence of north-east France was inseparable from the defence of Belgium. Versailles, with its demilitarisation of the Rhineland, shelved the problem of French frontier security. It did not solve it. Gamelin had to calculate that if Belgian independence had been disregarded by Germany once – even when guaranteed by Britain – it might be disregarded again.[1]

French military leaders were consequently faced with choosing between strategies of passive or active defence for their frontier bordering Belgium and Luxembourg. The former option implied the defence of a long line through the Lille industrial basin and across terrain whose high water-table made it impracticable for deep fortifications of the type that became the Maginot Line in Lorraine. The latter option demanded despatch of French divisions into Belgium to help the Belgian army stop a German invasion in the north before it reached France.

This second strategy attracted French defence chiefs because it promised, firstly, a shorter front, economising on French forces, and, secondly, the possibility of incorporating the Belgian army into French defensive strength. Less attractively, it carried the danger that the Belgian army might be overwhelmed at the conflict's outset by a powerful German *attaque brusquée*. Such a situation in turn carried the risk of exposing advancing French reinforcements to an improvised encounter battle on the open plains of central Belgium.[2]

Faced with these problems, French strategists sought to resolve them by combining a strategy of active or forward defence with policies of cooperation with the Belgians. These policies strove to encourage Belgian governments to address their own defence requirements more seriously and endeavoured to ensure coordination of plans between the French and Belgian military commands. At first this coordination was satisfactorily achieved by means of the military accord concluded in

1920 between Marshal Foch and General Maglinse, then chief of the Belgian general staff. Both men favoured the policy that came to be styled 'integral defence of the frontiers'. In that strategy, Belgium's border with Germany and supporting positions like Liège was designed to form the main line of resistance to German invasion.[3]

After 1930, however, the military problem posed by Belgium took on a different form. This occurred in the first place because of the withdrawal of French occupation troops from the Rhineland five years earlier than envisaged at Versailles. The move immediately reduced the protective value of the Rhineland glacis. It was aggravated by the diminished size and combat-worthiness of the French army, following the reduction of French military service to twelve months in 1928.[4] It was then worsened further by the emergence among the Belgian defence authorities of a streak of neutralist or independent strategic thinking. In particular, the chiefs of the Belgian general staff between 1932 and 1934 called into question the wisdom of an 'integral defence of the frontiers'. Aware of clandestine German rearmament, Belgian military opinion came to favour defences 'in depth, stretching back throughout the interior of Belgian territory' and backed by a last-resort 'national redoubt', at the Scheldt, Ghent and Antwerp. A strategy of this kind, unlike all-out frontier defence, offered the advantage of greater strategic flexibility. It took account of several contingencies, 'instead of arbitrarily fixing once and for all the battlefield on which Belgium would put its fate in the hands of the god of war'.[5] On the other hand, this strategy posed a serious dilemma for Gamelin and the French military authorities.

The dilemma was whether the French general staff were to continue to cultivate their Belgian counterparts or whether they were instead to fortify the Franco-Belgian frontier. The latter alternative risked consolidating Belgian inclinations towards isolation. André Maginot, when war minister in 1930, had argued, for instance, that it was 'not possible ... to construct a strong defensive organisation opposite the territory of this friendly nation'.[6] In Brussels, however, the revised Belgian strategy was regarded as realistic rather than isolationist. It appeared to offer Belgium more comprehensive insurance, in the light of the imbalance between Belgian and German military capabilities. Belgian commanders did not want their army to suffer irreparable damage in attempting to implement a strategy of frontier defence against hopeless odds.[7]

In these circumstances the French command adopted plans to reinforce and relieve the Belgian army.[8] By doing this, the departments of the Nord and Pas-de-Calais could also be protected. However, pressure from the politicians of the Nord, combined with a lingering sense of caution, persuaded French military leaders to consider a post-Maginot fortifications programme for the Franco-Belgian frontier.

The fact that such a scheme was never wholeheartedly adopted gave rise to controversy following the Franco-Anglo-Belgian defeat in 1940. Critics underestimated the technical obstacles to the construction of sophisticated Maginot-type works in the industrial region of Lille and in the water-logged lands between Cassel and Dunkerque. Critics also overlooked the inhibiting effects of inflation in construction costs on decisions to embark on large-scale and long-term fortifications. Little notice has been taken of the relationship inside the French parliament between the approval of Maginot Line finance and subsequent attitudes towards other military expenditures such as those requested during 1935–7, by Gamelin, for new artillery, tanks and other armaments.[9] A contemporary critic such as Reynaud sought to have his cake as well as eat it: he attacked Weygand and Gamelin for not opting decisively to extend the Maginot Line north of Luxembourg and Montmédy; yet he also censured them for not creating a heavy armoured corps for a forward manoeuvre defence in central Belgium.[10]

In practice, however, French military leaders always possessed an optimal strategy for the Belgian theatre. It was a strategy derived from their conclusions in 1922 that defence on the Belgian–German border would best give security to France. In the 1930s the French strategic problem in the north was complicated by the need to calculate that construction of the Albert Canal from Antwerp to the Meuse near Liège would not be complete till 1939. The canal, though, was intended to serve as Belgium's principal defence against a German flanking invasion through Holland.[11] Consequently, the intended defensive advance of the French First Army remained a hazardous manoeuvre on account of Belgian vulnerability to an unannounced German mobile offensive.

The germ of the strategic quandary that ultimately confronted the armies of Generals Henri Giraud and Georges Blanchard in the Dyle–Breda manoeuvre of May 1940 was noticed once France's occupation forces evacuated the Rhineland in 1930.[12] Maginot, then war minister, agreed with Weygand and Gamelin on the 'need to establish . . . a "position of insurance" on our frontier which, despite the difficulties, protects our territory and the riches of the Nord as well as possible . . . against a case where the Belgians . . . prove unable to hold their frontier against an *attaque brusquée* until our main forces arrive'.[13]

French assistance to Belgium was always endangered by problems of time and distance. The French reinforcements were confronted with a 200 kilometre dash to reach the Albert Canal and Meuse. It was essential to make this advance at maximum speed, to bolster the Belgian army before the latter collapsed completely.[14] Though accepting that forward defence was their optimal strategy, Weygand and Gamelin were anxious to possess a *ligne d'arrêt* in case Germany attacked Belgium so suddenly that French assistance arrived too late. 'The building of fortifications along our northern frontier', explained Gamelin later, 'was, therefore, to be presented only as a "fallback" position.'[15] Such defences, organisable in peacetime on French soil, were conceived as a backstop onto which the French army could retreat if disaster overtook Belgium.[16]

Gamelin neither pressed – nor subsequently claimed to have pressed – for sealing the northern French frontier with fortifications. Nevertheless, he and Weygand were, in the early 1930s, perturbed about the risks to which France had been committed by the fortifications policy decisions taken in 1927.[17]

These decisions were the outcome of a protracted series of CSG meetings between December 1926 and October 1927, which reviewed the results of the preliminary studies undertaken by the Commission de Défense des Frontières. The task of that body had been to propose the regions to be fortified and to differentiate between defences to be constructed in peacetime and defences whose creation was to be left until a conflict broke out. In its turn, the CSG decided to protect Alsace by strongpoints along the natural barrier of the Rhine; to defend the industries of Lorraine by two discontinuous fortified zones, the Région Fortifiée de Metz and the Région Fortifiée de la Lauter, which became the heart of the Maginot Line. The CSG decided to secure the northern frontiers by advancing French troops to positions inside Belgium.[18]

These principles determined that the French frontier defences would be characterised by static positions in the north-east and by a considerable reliance on mobility in the north. It has to be emphasised that the manoeuvre into Belgium was not cast offensively. Rather, it was designed to secure superior defensive positions, avoiding the heavily populated border cities of Lille, Douai and Valenciennes. Moreover, an advance into Belgium offered the French the prospect – which was obviously not publicly discussed – of transferring the war onto someone else's soil.[19]

Nevertheless, consideration was given to one further option for the defence of the north – that of the provision of French finance to permit heavy fortification of the Belgo-German frontier. In Paris as well as

Brussels there were advocates of a French subsidy to underwrite a programme of fixed defences in eastern Belgium. This proposal's proponents reasoned that a strongly fortified eastern Belgium – a kind of 'Belgian Maginot Line' – would secure northern France as effectively as a French manoeuvre into Belgium. They contended, furthermore, that fortifications would avoid the political controversy that a strategy of intervention was likely to arouse among the Flemings concerned about Belgian independence and among Belgian socialists who were agitated that France might intend to use her intervention in Belgium as an offensive springboard.

The most eloquent champion of French loans for Belgian fortifications was André Tardieu. French prime minister in 1929–30 when the initial tranche of Maginot funding was committed, Tardieu was again head of the French government in the spring of 1932 during the decisive French debate over northern defence. Tardieu's plan took as its starting point the decision of the Belgians themselves to construct new forts at Battice and Pepinster, as well as at Eben-Emael on the intersection of the Albert Canal and Meuse. Tardieu was keen to give these projects French technical expertise. He also suggested lending Belgium 1 billion francs to help towards the construction of a whole new network of eastern fortifications. These defences would have joined the Maginot Line's western end at Montmédy to an equivalent Belgian line stretching northward to the Maastricht appendix. Gamelin, for his part, was receptive to Tardieu's plan. In August 1932 he recommended that Belgium be exhorted both to extend her Liège fortifications southwards and to build fixed defences around Arlon, in Belgian Luxembourg. Belgian general staff officers and engineers agreed, moreover, to take French advice and in 1932 visited Maginot constructions near Metz.

Between the Tardieu plan and Gamelin's welcome for it there was, however, an important difference of outlook. For Tardieu, subsidising Belgian fortifications offered a means of avoiding the advance of French armies into Belgium and was, furthermore, an alternative to the refurbishment of French ground forces required for such a manoeuvre. For Gamelin, on the other hand, Belgian fortifications were envisaged as a complement to a French strategy based on forward defence. What would doubtless have been a lively dispute between the two men was forestalled by the defeat of the conservatives in the May 1932 French elections and Tardieu's loss of office.[20]

The question of French finance for Belgian fortifications did not surface again until 1934. On this second occasion the initiative appears to have come from Brussels and to have been broached through the

French minister of commerce at that time, Lucien Lamoureux. The latter was responsible for renewing Franco-Belgian customs agreements. Lamoureux found the Belgians keen, because of their troubled economy, to turn the trade talks into a means of obtaining a defence subvention from the French. Since their new fortifications 'served as a sort of ... shield for France', the Belgians argued, according to Lamoureux, that France should 'allow them some economic privileges ... to finance the construction of their fortified line'. Some Belgians apparently went as far as to 'demand that France herself shoulder the cost of building their defence line'. Lamoureux rejected these overtures. He disapproved of the way in which they sought to confuse commercial relations with considerations of foreign and military policy. Yet he also criticised the Belgian importuning of France because of the former's 'undertaking to build an extension of our fortified line in the east'.[21]

This contention was, however, no more than a characteristic French misrepresentation of their neighbour's level of commitment to joint planning. Lamoureux was the victim of an increasingly common French delusion. The fact was that at no point had the Belgians agreed to extend the Maginot Line. They had simply accepted French technical assistance in a limited expansion and modernisation of their defences around Arlon and Liège.[22] Most probably, Lamoureux's judgement of the Belgian approach of 1934 illustrates the poverty of the French imagination when it came to the exploitation of their financial and commercial relations in order to further the objectives of French security policy.

In a second account, however, the progenitor of this still-born attempt at a fortification loan was not the Belgians but Pétain. In this version of events, recounted by General Raoul Van Overstraeten, military advisor to the Belgian King Leopold, a meeting occurred in Paris in December 1935 between Pétain and Count André de Kerchove, the Belgian ambassador to France. During this encounter Pétain claimed to have proposed – whilst serving in 1934 as war minister – to cease defensive work along the Franco-Belgian border. His alternative proposition, it was alleged, had involved 'making over a sum of money, equal to the cost of these works, to the Belgians, to let them continue the Maginot wall without overburdening their budget'. In this account the initiative failed not because of any link to trade negotiations but because the Doumergue government failed to support Pétain.[23]

By the mid-1930s Pétain had become a one-man institution. His position in French society was unique. When the Haut Comité Militaire was formed in 1932 he had been elected – apparently at Gamelin's behest – an *ad hominem* permanent member. He retained this place on the CPDN when that committee was created to replace the HCM in June 1936. No military chief had ever before obtained such a lifetime military sinecure.[24] From about 1934, Pétain's private agenda was starting to rise above matters of narrowly military concern. Along with other conservatives – among them Weygand – he increasingly addressed himself to the fight against the influence of internationalism and anti-militarism among the youth of France. He became a champion of compulsory pre-military training in schools and he sought the education ministry rather than the rue Saint-Dominique when he served in the Doumergue government from February to November 1934.[25] With his susceptibility to flattery and his personification of French military prestige he had become, by 1935, an 'ambitious old man', as Gamelin later described him, taking the first steps down the authoritarian political road that finally led to Vichy.[26]

Pétain's attempt to underwrite a Belgian Maginot Line in 1934 was consistent with his argument – first adumbrated in the fortification debates of the 1920s – that northern France needed to be defended on the forward line of the Belgian–German border. It fitted his doctrine of the superiority of the defensive and his preference for battles offered from prepared positions. It responded, moreover, to his anxiety in the mid-1930s to address the military consequences of French demographic decline by economising on manpower and adopting fortifications as 'force multipliers'. Finally, it met the underlying wish of all French strategists and politicians to transfer the battlefields of a future war away from the blood-soaked soil of northern France.[27] Realising, too, that Belgian politics was increasingly calling into question the feasibility of an interventionist strategy, Pétain's proposal for a fortifications loan to Belgium may have been a cunning marker for the sake of his own place in the historical record.

Partisans in France of lending Belgium the money for eastern fortifications made one further effort to attract French government support. Their attempt occurred after Germany's re-establishment of conscription in March 1935. In the Chamber army commission the war minister, Maurin, was asked about the value attributed to French agreements with Belgium, Poland and the Little Entente. Even though French intelligence ascribed offensive capabilities to the Germans by 1936, Maurin reported that Belgian fortress construction would not then be complete. At this point in the debate a conservative deputy, Charles Reibel, asked whether it would not be a 'wise policy' to advance 'the necessary sums to Belgium' to expedite the completion of her defences. Reibel suggested that her fortifications were 'really non-fortifications' in their existing state of incompleteness and asserted that Maurin's duty was to signal to his fellow ministers the 'evident' French interest in assisting Belgium financially. Maurin declined to reply. He took refuge behind a statement which he had already made, in which he stated that France had always encouraged Belgium to fortify itself and 'counted on the blocking force of their army, together with the divisions that we would send to their rescue'.[28]

The secretiveness of Maurin does not appear to have masked any clandestine continuation of the Pétain–Lamoureux initiatives. It is likely that Maurin was simply loathe to tell an all-party group the details of Franco-Belgian defence contacts whose future was decidedly precarious by the spring of 1935. Talks between Gamelin and General Cumont, then the Belgian chief of staff, were set to take place in April. Belgian unease about close relations with France was known to Maurin, who may have felt that discretion was required in order to avoid jeopardising the coordinated Franco-Belgian forward defence which Gamelin wished to maintain.[29]

The abortive fortifications loan illustrates the exceptional place accorded to the Maginot programme in the overall French defence effort. No other part of the French military programmes ever received the sacrosanct status of the Maginot Line. It is worth exploring, therefore, why the line attracted such cross-party consensus and what were the consequences of this privileged position for French defence priorities.

Politically, the support all around the hemicycle of the Chamber of Deputies for fixed defences may be ascribed to the universal wish among the French to secure their country for evermore against a repetition of the German invasions of 1870 and 1914. Once French statesmen had agreed in 1925–6 that their forces of occupation in the Rhineland would be evacuated by mid-1930, it was essential to make provision for the long-term security of the eastern frontiers.[30]

It has sometimes been asserted that the French eastern fortifications, being such a capital-intensive project, mortgaged the future of French defences. It is claimed that the fixed defences closed down other, arguably more forward-looking, options and swallowed vast appropriations that might more fruitfully have been invested in motorising and mechanising the army and in creating a modern air force and air defence system.[31] None of this is self-evident, however. Perhaps the negotiations over a fortifications loan to Belgium in 1934 hint at the vulnerability of projects that fell outside the sacred Maginot programme. Maurin's refusal in the army commission to debate the proposition that it might be 'good politics' to underwrite Belgian defences may reflect the unwillingness of mid-1930s French governments to pour additional funds into concrete at a time when their intelligence showed Hitler moving towards panzers and strategies of mobile war.[32]

On the other hand, the argument that the main fortifications of the Maginot Line diverted French military appropriations away from more important development of land and air forces is untenable. The fixed defences erected along the eastern frontiers may appear to have been expensive. But they actually cost no more than half of the sum originally budgeted for the army's rearmament programme of September 1936.[33] Politically, these fortifications enjoyed near-unanimous approbation. They were endorsed by parliamentarians of the left and centre as much as they were supported by those of the right. The enthusiasm shown for the barring of the French borders by Painlevé, Briand and Blum was matched by the warm embrace it received from Paul-Boncour and Daladier, the welcome it got from Poincaré, Tardieu and Fabry.

The consensus in favour of fortifications opposite Germany was a function of its time. To contend that the francs poured into this concrete and steel were misdirected is to overlook both the strategic and political purposes of the programme. On the former count, the French generals were intent, quite sensibly, on protecting the economic resources of Lorraine, shielding the army's two-week-long mobilisation and gaining a force-multiplier to counteract German numerical advantages. On the latter count, fortifications in the east were so politically attractive that no other significant defence programme stood any chance of winning parliamentary approval in the 1920s and early 1930s.[34]

The concrete and cupolas of the Maginot Line were products of the Geneva era. The preparatory sessions in readiness for the world disarmament conference which opened in February 1932 were already in progress when the first tranche of fortifications expenditure was obtained by Maginot from the French parliament on 14 January 1930. Against this background the French generals – Gamelin, Weygand, Pétain and the rest – embraced the concept of the Maginot Line not simply because they believed in its strategic utility but because they understood that they would get nothing else in its stead. In the era of disarmament there was no chance of securing extra expenditures to procure new armour, artillery or aircraft. Building the Maginot Line was attractive to the French public – it appeared that their country was engaged in what late-twentieth-century strategic analysis would have termed 'defensive' or 'non-provocative' defence. The fortifications were the only new military burden that a war-weary France would agree to shoulder, little more than a decade after Versailles. Gamelin understood this. He realised that requests for re-equipment of the French ground or air forces, rather than for defensive fortifications, would have been scattered on the wind in a storm of domestic indignation and international outrage.[35]

As French governments showed their readiness to invest in fortifications in the early 1930s, Gamelin and Weygand decided to make a virtue of necessity. Both understood that new fortifications were better than no new defence expenditures at all. Moreover, conscious as they were of the accelerating pace of technological change, Gamelin and Weygand were wary of demanding an unnecessary and premature rearmament programme which would face the threat of early obsolescence. Prior to Hitler's public announcement of German rearmament in 1935, the fortifications were the only programme of capital investment in French defence which was politically acceptable.[36]

It seems unlikely, therefore, that the opportunity-cost of the Maginot Line was in any way detrimental to army or air force equipment.[37] If the Maginot funds had not gone into fixed defences, it is probable that they would have been lost to the military services altogether. There was no choice to be made in the early 1930s between concrete and cavalry tanks, nor between barbed-wire and bombers. Indeed no alternatives were presented. If they had been, they would have juxtaposed civilian projects, such as Tardieu's proposed investment in 1930 of 5 billion francs in modernising public utilities, against the fortifications.[38]

In any case, a by-product of the construction of the Maginot Line – and one hitherto neglected by researchers – was the assistance which this huge public works programme gave to the slump-hit local economies of Alsace and Lorraine. The fortifications generated thousands of new jobs, not just in the building and transport industries but also in a more diffused way, in the steel works, railway shops and artillery manufacturers of half a dozen departments bordering Germany, from Montmédy to Mulhouse. The erection of the Maginot Line sheltered entrepreneurs as well as their employees from the chill winds of the Depression. Since it brought immediate prosperity as well as longer-term security to the Moselle, the Meurthe-et-Moselle and the Bas-Rhin, it was small wonder that the Maginot Line was as enthusiastically supported by labour leaders and left-wing politicians as it was by germanophobe conservatives.[39]

The securing of the east by fortifications and the north by forward defence was Gamelin's way of fashioning a defensive strategy that promised France the greatest chance of territorial inviolability. Nevertheless, three problems continued to worry Gamelin in the mid-1930s.

The first was the reported weakness of the Belgian army, a force whose ability to hold the Meuse until French assistance arrived was much in doubt. In 1932 the CSG noted with concern that, after a four-day mobilisation, Belgium could put only six divisions in the field, supported by six more divisions in static garrison duties. Gamelin warned the CSG that third-line Belgian units were envisaged but that the Belgians had 'told us nothing precise about this'. More generally, Gamelin was alarmed that Belgium was 'very vague' about its war plans. What the French feared was that their First Army, intervening in Belgium, might be caught in an encounter action against a German offensive that had already smashed the Belgian defences.[40] A sprawling and formless action of this sort was the complete antithesis of French operational doctrine, which emphasised methodical and carefully prepared battles under a centralised command and control. The dreaded encounter battle in central Belgium conjured up a vision of chaos – a negation of the French concept of generalship.[41]

The second point that disturbed Gamelin in 1935 was the coincidence between the delays that were emerging in the refurbishment of the French and Belgian armies and the delays in the completion of the Maginot Line itself. Something of a myth was taking shape in 1935, as the French and foreign press reported extensively on the construction of the fortifications.[42] Indeed, this was the point at which the defences came to be popularly baptised as the 'Maginot Line'. It was 'more or less during 1935', recalled Gamelin, 'that the habit spread of using this designation. Its generalisation coincided with the inauguration of the monument to "Sergeant Maginot" at the roadside from Verdun to Douaumont.'[43]

Yet before 1936 the fortifications neither fulfilled the role as a barrier to guard Alsace-Lorraine nor released active field divisions for service on the Belgian border or in the Mediterranean. For French strategists not only faced the difficulty of securing the northern frontier, they also had to meet defensive commitments on the Swiss and Italian borders, in North Africa and the Near East. On the Rhine Gamelin was concerned that 'down to 1935 there was only a series of widely-spaced casemates'.[44] The Maginot Line proper, in Lorraine, took many years to complete. Meanwhile, Gamelin subsequently remarked, the existence of the fortifications construction sites was 'more of a hindrance than a help, since they created areas . . . unusable for the defence at the very places that were important'.[45]

As late as August 1935 the progress of the Lorraine programme was arousing anxiety. Maginot's financial law of January 1930 had allocated 2,734 million francs from 1930 to 1934 to build the Metz and Lauter fortified regions. This was a lavish investment when compared to the 1,091 million francs provided over the same period for all the other sectors, including the north, Alsace, the Jura, the Alps and Corsica. Nevertheless, technical difficulties and cost-overruns were underestimated. The serviceability of the heart of the Maginot Line had to be postponed. General Georges, Gamelin's deputy, was troubled in late-1935 that the Saar's prepared inundations were not ready for use.[46] Another problem was the unexpected difficulty encountered in raising the cadre garrisons for the defences, the *frontalier* battalions, designed to be recruited from the local population.[47]

No problem was as intractable, however, as that of the northern frontier. Local discontent was aroused once it emerged that the French command did not intend to construct Maginot-style defences immediately in front of the cities of Lille, Roubaix and Douai. As General Ragueneau said when the CSG met on 28 May 1932, the French military frontier in the north was 'in reality located at the Belgo-German border'. Even should France fail to obtain Belgian assent, it was affirmed that 'invasion of that country by Germany will be sufficient authorisation for us to make our advance'.[48]

As Gamelin repeated in a confidential memorandum of January 1934, 'to be able to use Belgium's appeal to shift the war off our own territory ... would be a benefit in its own right'. An early appeal, during a period of international tension foreshadowing an outbreak of war, would afford France 'more advantageous defensive positions and the assistance of Belgian forces that would still mostly be intact'.[49] In 1935 Maurin candidly restated this to the Chamber army commission, arguing that France should prepare to give rapid support to the Belgians

in such a way as to distance the war from French soil and – since Belgium's unhappy destiny down the centuries has cast her as a battleground – ensure that this clash of arms does not occur over our towns of the Nord which have suffered so much or in these northern departments with their ... enormous resources of coal, benzol and ... militarily vital economic activity.[50]

The commitment to forward defence in Belgium remained. But Gamelin was uneasy in the mid-1930s about the practicalities of the strategy. He was, specifically, worried by the reported development of mobile forces and doctrine in the German army. Belgium's open ground, north and east of Brussels and the Dyle river, invited a mobile attack. Though he did not question the principle of defending inside Belgium on forward positions, Gamelin felt that France ought to 'take precautions to protect the frontier [with Belgium] against all eventualities'.[51]

The divisions over a northern strategy reached their climax in these

CSG meetings of 28 May and 4 June 1932. Ostensibly at issue was the use to be made of a 250 million franc credit which the Senate had recommended be put at the government's disposal for northern defences.[52] In practice it was the means of defending the whole Franco-Belgian theatre that was at issue. For the first meeting, the agenda papers proposed to invest the funds in three strongpoints (*môles de résistance*). These were at Maubeuge, Condé-sur-Escaut and the Monts de Flandre. Recalling the vulnerability of Joffre's armies in northern France in 1914, Gamelin obtained priority for the defences at Maubeuge.[53] The agenda also emphasised – probably at Gamelin's instigation – that the 'defence . . . of the north must be based *entirely on movement* . . . by our armies into Belgium'. It stressed, too, that the Franco-Belgian frontier's defensive organisation was intended to facilitate the French manoeuvre 'to support the Belgians on their own territory'.[54]

Pétain, however, opposed even the limited compromise implicit in the provision of backstop strongpoints inside France. Unable to attend the 28 May CSG, he submitted a written protest against further discussion. The means of defending northern France had, he claimed, been satisfactorily discussed in 1926–7.[55] He persisted in his view that the French armies should seek to offer defensive battle on forward lines deep inside Belgium. For the French even to toy with plans to hold lines inside their own territory would, said Pétain, be to forgo a crucial 'opportunity for close collaboration' between the French and Belgian nations.[56]

In Pétain's absence, on 28 May 1932, his arguments were taken up and elaborated by generals Guillaumat and Ragueneau. The lean years were looming, observed the former. If France constructed northern fortifications, 'Who', he wondered, 'shall we put in this new wall of China?' A 'wall of France', was, he argued, 'a dream financially . . . and could become a danger militarily', leading 'to the subordination of all our war planning . . . to existing or intended fortification'.[57] Pétain, for his part, proposed in writing that the available credits be switched away from fixed defences on the ground and into the acceleration of French air rearmament. This, however, was not an issue within the remit of the CSG and army command.[58]

The Pétain proposals and the disunity that they revealed among the military chiefs was symptomatic of a 'certain intellectual disarray' among French defence policy makers.[59] Piétri, then the defence minister, indicated to Gamelin his awareness that the generals appeared to be harbouring a 'hostility to the system of fixed defences that enjoys favour in parliament'. The episode was one further indicator of the fragility of the French civil-military consensus.[60] Gamelin wanted some fortified strongpoints behind the frontier with Belgium to provide insurance in case a manoeuvre into Belgium went awry. He was placed in an uncomfortable position, therefore, by the refusal of Pétain, the army's most prestigious leader, to endorse his plans.

For their part the politicians, Piétri, the prime minister, Tardieu, and the newly elected president of the Republic, Albert Lebrun, felt unqualified to impose a decision of their own over the divided military council. As civilians they were perplexed to be faced with the unusual spectacle of 'military chiefs [who] could not reach prior agreement among themselves'.[61]

The impasse was not a situation to which the republican civil-military framework was accustomed. Nor was it one for whose resolution it was structured. For it was not within the purview of the French civilian defence authorities to make military strategy – still less to arbitrate between different operational plans. It was the task of the politicians to determine the grand-strategic objectives of national policy. It was the task of the military leaders to identify the optimal means of attaining them. Of course, ministers from time to time made common cause with groups of generals. Daladier had sided with Gamelin, Maurin and Carence in 1933 over the scheme to postpone a part of the conscript callup in order to establish a manpower reserve for the 'lean years' of 1935 to 1939. But such combinations were the expression of political tactics in a pluralistic democracy.[62] They were accepted in relation to questions of organisation and administration. In the realm of strategy, on the other hand, not even those politicians such as Reynaud who claimed some knowledge of defence matters pretended to possess decision-making competence. Rather, until 1940, France's uniformed leaders remained without challenge in their own domain. The confidence that they enjoyed among the French civilian authorities, in parliament and with the press, is comprehensible only in the context of the world before the Fall of France. It was a world in which, to adapt Foch's aphorism, French generalship was not yet peopled by *chefs battus, chefs disqualifiés*.[63] Set against these pre-1940 behavioral norms for civil-military relations, the French command's inability in May 1932 to agree strategy for the northern frontier caused bewilderment among the government. Ministers present at the CSG meeting fell into 'painful silence' in the face of the military indecision.[64]

On 4 June the CSG reconvened, following an attempt to restore unity among the generals through a compromise. The basis of this was that the soldiers settle for advising that the 250 million francs for equipment be spent on the army's manoeuvre divisions. Gamelin, however, estimated this compromise to be misconceived. He did not deny that new tanks, anti-aircraft guns and anti-tank artillery were needed urgently. But he deplored the unwillingness of his fellow generals to concentrate on programmes that accorded with the preferences of parliament. As on so many occasions, Gamelin saw no purpose in the military command wilfully provoking a dispute with the civilian authorities. Securing what was currently obtainable, and planning to procure other resources at a more propitious moment, remained Gamelin's preferred political strategy.

In 1932 what concerned Gamelin was not the alternative ways of enhancing French defences, but rather the question of timing. Unlike many of his colleagues, including Weygand, Gamelin sought to harness the prevailing political tide – not swim against it. Since fixed defences were something on which parliament was willing to spend money, Gamelin judged it inopportune to look this gift horse in the mouth. In any case, a limited construction of fixed defences in northern France was attractive to Gamelin and Weygand on strategic grounds. Such fortifications would usefully serve as a fallback position, a safeguard behind the plan to assist Belgium with a forward defence.[65]

As the options were tabled before the CSG on 4 June 1932 it was apparent that the vote would be a close one. In the event, by just seven votes to six, Weygand and Gamelin were defeated. The CSG preferred to commit the French army to a precipitate dash into Belgium, irrespective of the circumstances of the moment, and without the security of even modest fall-back positions inside northern France. No other CSG decision was reached so narrowly throughout the interwar period. Moreover, because fortifications were such a long-term engineering undertaking, never was so consequential a choice made. The repercussions affected French and British strategy right down to May 1940: they left no alternative but to risk a forward defence of the Belgian–French theatre.[66]

The decision of the CSG left Gamelin without any insurance against failure to reach Belgian lines before encountering attacking German forces. It obliged him to strive, instead, to obtain sufficiently close cooperation with the Belgian general staff to reduce to a minimum the hazards inherent in the strategy of forward defence. Franco-Belgian relations, as a result, became dominated from 1932 to 1940 by efforts from Paris to gain acceptance for a pre-emptive French advance, before a declaration of war, to positions inside Belgium.[67]

Gamelin never lost sight of the perils associated with this policy of cooperation. Weygand, too, remained deeply uneasy. He inserted into the record of the 4 June 1932 CSG meeting that the council's decision required him to 'reserve . . . entirely the prerogatives conferred on him by his personal responsibility as commander-in-chief designate'.[68] It was an endeavour to retain a vestige of choice in the matter of defending northern France where, in reality, none now existed.

A major problem for Gamelin and the French command was posed from this juncture onwards by Belgian domestic politics – a factor largely outside the French military's control. Some Belgians – particularly the Walloons of eastern Belgium who were most exposed to the German threat – supported standing defence arrangements with France. Their political champion was Albert Devèze, Belgian defence minister from 1932 to June 1936.[69]

A lawyer and a deputy for Brussels, Devèze was president of the Belgian liberal party in the 1930s. He was a politician of substance and a notorious francophile. Though a partisan of military accords with France, Devèze caused great problems to French planners. As far as the latter were concerned, he was less than helpful in his enthusiasm for the erection of French fortifications along the border with Belgium. Devèze regarded such defences as a deterrent – one which might convince the Germans that there would never again be any strategic profit in seeking to launch an attack on France across Belgian territory. As a French CSG note recorded, Devèze favoured the organisation of the French northern frontier because he thought that 'multiplication of lines or obstacles ... would discourage an adversary from attacking via Belgium'.[70]

French fortifications' policy on the northern frontier was, therefore, central to discussions in Belgium about foreign and defence policy. French military attachés in Brussels, General Chardigny, General Riedinger and Colonel Laurent, reported the growth of Belgian discontent over the 1920 defensive accord.[71] Ever since its signature the Belgian foreign ministry had sought a complementary military arrangement with the British. This would have reduced Belgian political dependence on France.[72] In Belgium there was considerable anxiety about the implications of French obligations in eastern Europe, towards the Little Entente, Poland and, after the Franco-Soviet mutual assistance pact of May 1935, Russia. Belgian politicians and officials increasingly feared that the Germans might regard Belgium as a party to French external policy. They were disturbed that Belgium might, as a result, be dragged unnecessarily into a future Franco-German war. Gradually, therefore, Belgian opinion hardened into a conviction that the 1920 military accord represented an unacceptable mortgage on Belgian independence.[73]

The debate in Belgium was not just about defence but about the wider question of Belgium's situation in the European state system. On the issue of strategy the Belgians divided into two schools. Devèze was the leading advocate in the 1930s of a group that argued for defence of Belgium's eastern frontiers, supported by close military collaboration with France. But the alternative plans, based on defence in depth, possessed more influential supporters. One was General Emile Galet, who had been *aide-de-camp* to King Albert during the First World War and then chief of staff from 1929 to 1932. Another was General Raoul Van Overstraeten, the opinionated and ambitious personal liaison officer and counsellor appointed to King Leopold III in 1934.[74]

This emergence of two distinct and opposed strategic schools closely mirrored – and also further complicated – the political and linguistic divisions in Belgium. Defence in depth meant resistance in the western parts of Belgium, where the population was Flemish. 'Furthermore', as the historian David Kieft has remarked, 'the concept "defence in depth" implied the immediate abandonment of a Walloon province.'[75]

The linguistic considerations greatly complicated the task of strengthening Belgium's defences. It was easier for the factious Belgians to concur about the need for stronger defences than it was for them to agree on what to do about it. The Walloon provinces in the east and south-east felt most exposed to German invasion. Not surprisingly, their representatives favoured peacetime military arrangements with France and detailed Franco-Belgian staff talks to secure French intervention in the event of German aggression.[76]

But Flemings feared that standing arrangements of this sort would infringe Belgian sovereignty. They refused to vote increased military expenditures essential to the modernisation of the Belgian armed forces until they were convinced that the money would serve Belgium alone. They sought a strategy entirely disconnected from that of the French – one directed, instead, towards improving Belgium's prospect of becoming an internationally respected neutral in any future war. Many of these Flemings aspired to model Belgian policy not on the solidarity shown the Allies by King Albert in 1914–18 but on Holland's status as a non-belligerent. Since the Flemings had grown to around 60 per cent of the Belgian population by the 1930s, their views were heard ever more stridently. Endorsing the Flemings was the socialist anti-militarism of the Parti Ouvrier belge. This set its face against any increases in military credits or conscription. The combination of Flemings and socialists was an increasingly formidable obstacle to the maintenance of Belgian military ties with France.[77]

For their part, French statesmen and soldiers did not doubt that a Franco-Belgian defence arrangement was needed at least as much as it had been in the 1920s. They sought, therefore, to redefine the 1920 accord, to make it the basis for detailed and regular Franco-Belgian staff meetings. The problem with this was that close cooperation between the staffs would have compelled the disclosure to Gamelin of the Belgian mobilisation timetable and order of battle. Such arrangements were to carry a concomitant pledge that France would earmark most of her mobile forces for a defensive manoeuvre into Belgium. Such intimate strategic links to France were, however, precisely what the Flemings and Belgian socialists had disliked in the original accord. Devèze therefore encountered stiff parliamentary resistance to his threefold policy of modernising the Belgian field army, constructing additional eastern fortifications and pre-arranging the provision of French assistance.[78]

Most inflammatory to the Flemings and Belgian socialists was Devèze's proposal to extend military service to eighteen months. Emile Vandervelde, leader of the socialists, thought that Devèze and the French were in collusion. Their objective, he suspected, was to reduce Belgian forces to a role as the subordinate left wing of the French army.[79]

By early 1936 the controversy over strengthening the Belgian army had deepened into a full-scale political crisis, because of the general election that the Belgian government had to face that summer. On 15 February 1936 the Belgian prime minister, Van Zeeland, travelled to Paris. He explained to Flandin, then French foreign minister, that the Foch–Maglinse accord had become a millstone. The Quai d'Orsay was reluctantly advised by the French high command that it was essential for French diplomacy to accommodate Belgian concerns in the interests of securing the enactment of Devèze's military reform bill.[80] As a result, the French invited Fernand Van Langenhove, secretary-general of the Belgian foreign ministry, to negotiate the abandonment of the military accord. Whilst Van Langenhove was in Paris, on 27 February, the link between the agreement and the Belgian army reforms was rammed home by the defeat of the first reading of Devèze's bill in the Belgian parliament.[81] Not even the publication of the letters of 6 March between the French ambassador in Brussels, Jules Laroche, and Van Zeeland, abrogating the agreement, was sufficient to mollify the groups which opposed Devèze.[82]

In the resulting stalemate – exploited by the Germans to remilitarise the Rhineland – an escape was sought through the submission of the bill to an all-party parliamentary commission for amendment. The commission held a series of meetings, against a backdrop of a violent electoral campaign that was inflamed by Flemish nationalists as well as by the anti-parliamentary rhetoric of Léon Degrelle's fascist movement, the Rexists. In the election, held on 24 May, the moderate parties emerged badly mauled. This exacerbated the problem of securing sufficient parliamentary support for the Devèze bill.[83]

Furthermore, when the second Van Zeeland government was formed, in June 1936, there was no place in it for Devèze himself. He was excluded in favour of a new defence minister, General Henri Denis. The change was expressly intended to appease the Flemings and depoliticise the formulation of Belgian military policy. Denis was a cautious and uncontroversial officer. An artilleryman, his promotion to the ministry from command of the 3rd corps at Liège owed everything to the respect in which he was held as a technician and nothing at all to any political experience. At first the French were gratified by his appointment. Schweisguth formed a 'good impression' of him – a view corroborated by the French consul at Liège who reported that Denis was 'very francophile' and convinced that 'tight-knit Franco-Belgian military cooperation was . . . indispensable'.[84]

Denis's military programme, however, brought forward in the autumn of 1936, was too similar to that of Devèze. It failed to still the political discontent. This obliged Leopold himself to intervene. On 14 October, in a subsequently notorious move, the king read a declaration to his ministers which asserted the complete freedom of action of Belgian external policy. Belgium's foreign and military postures, said Leopold, were to be directed 'not at preparing to wage a war, more or less victoriously, within a coalition, but at keeping war away from our territory altogether'. The objective of Belgian statecraft was declared to be the positioning of Belgium outside all future conflict.[85]

Without this much-publicised declaration it is unlikely that any Belgian army reorganisation could have been accomplished. Nevertheless, the pronouncement caused deep dismay among the French who overreacted and complained, particularly in the Paris press, about desertion by an 'ally' (which, of course, Belgium never was).[86]

In some alarm, the CSG met to assess the implications of Leopold's speech for the French First Army's mission of intervention in Belgium.[87] Then, in late November, two secret rendezvous were made between Van Zeeland, Paul-Henri Spaak, the Belgian foreign minister, Blum, Chautemps and Delbos. At these meetings the French were told that there was no alternative to their acceptance of Belgian independence. This, and this alone, could save the Belgian military reform bill and enable a stronger Belgian army to play a full part in the future in covering the forward defence of northern France. Van Zeeland, it was added, had to be able to announce French recognition of the new Belgian stance in order to reconcile Belgians to the costs of refurbishing their army. The French realised that they could do no more than make a virtue of necessity. On 2 December 1936 Van Zeeland declared that Belgium had withdrawn from the Locarno frontier guarantees of 1925.

Immediately afterwards, placated by the change to their country's formal status, the Belgian parliament enacted the military reform bill.[88]

On 24 April 1937 Belgium's exit from the European system that had been constructed on the basis of the post-1918 peace arrangements was sealed by a declaration from the French and British governments. This statement formally released Belgium from her Locarno obligations to render assistance to France or Germany if either suffered unprovoked attack by the other. The statement also reaffirmed the Franco-British intention to assist Belgium if she were to come under attack. Belgium remained the recipient of an unwanted guarantee.[89]

This status left Belgian diplomats uncomfortable. They still feared that their neutrality might be tainted in German eyes as a result of this residual Franco-British expression of interest in insuring its observance.

French strategists were even more worried, however. Belgium's shift into independence made it problematic whether Franco-Belgian defence preparations could continue to be coordinated. Belgium's international realignment greatly diminished the value to Gamelin of the military arrangements reached previously with the Belgian general staff. In the early phases of military talks, under the accord of 1920, the French had sought to prepare the logistical and operational minutiae of their deployment onto the Albert Canal and the Meuse. Conversations on these terms were agreed in October 1934.[90] The Belgian concern was to discover whether French assistance would reach Belgian forces in time to stave off their annihilation. The meetings occurred in Paris on 21 and 22 November 1934, between Gamelin, Weygand and General Cumont, then the chief of the Belgian general staff. The French found Cumont preoccupied with Belgium's northern flank, facing south Holland. He feared a German 'irruption' across the Netherlands, to fall upon the Belgian army's rear.

Gamelin concurred that northern Belgium and southern Holland were potentially crucial.[91] In mid-January 1935, whilst Gamelin was taking over responsibility for French military planning, Cumont stressed again, to the French military attaché in Brussels, that his chief fear was of a German flanking attack through Limburg and southern Brabant. In response, Gamelin sent his deputy chief of staff for inter-allied liaison, General Lucien Loizeau, to Brussels. There the French general learned that Cumont expected to require four French divisions to reach the Albert Canal by the fourth day of operations if the threat of the flank attack through Holland was to be parried. Gamelin, for his part, conferred with his senior staff in mid-March 1935. It was agreed to prepare to advance a screening force between Arlon, in the Ardennes, and the

Meuse, and also to deploy five divisions to operate on the Belgian army's left flank.[92]

The latter units were to constitute the French First Army, earmarked in 1935–6 for General Henri Bineau. A *polytechnicien* and, since 1933 the director of France's 'school for marshals', the Centre des Hautes Etudes Militaires, Bineau enjoyed a reputation as one of the French army's shrewdest strategists.[93]

In outline, the French plan of operations was decided when Cumont visited Gamelin on 5 April 1935. Gamelin emphasised the importance of the earliest possible Belgian appeal for support if an intervention was to stand the maximum prospect of success. He was anxious that the Albert Canal be reached by the First Army without a fight through enemy advance parties on the way. Reaching and relieving the Belgian defenders would have to be accomplished by the active formations of the First Army because reservist divisions would not reinforce the manoeuvre until the ninth day of a conflict. Cumont agreed to facilitate the intervention by arranging the supplies and lines of communication required for the French with the Belgian road and railway authorities. This less glamorous but no less essential element of Franco-Belgian planning was put discreetly into place when French 4e Bureau officers visited Brussels in July 1935.[94]

Further consultations took place in September 1935 when Belgian officers – including Van Overstraeten – attended the French manoeuvres in Champagne. The exercises took the form of an elaborately choreographed presentation of French military power, intended to impress not just the Belgians but also the chief guest, Marshal Badoglio, the Italian chief of staff. Regarding the Belgians, the French goal was to reassure the visitors that they had chosen wisely in linking their defence planning with that of France. Gamelin had correctly discerned the need to impress Van Overstraeten. He assigned his own adjutant, Petibon, to accompany and escort King Leopold's confidant. As Van Overstraeten recollected, Petibon eulogised the 'unified doctrine and noteworthy skills of command' present in the French army. Showing off the DLM, France's first armoured division, Petibon boasted that the unit was five years ahead of German panzer developments.[95]

The warm glow radiated by these cordial late-summer encounters rapidly cooled, however, as 1936 saw first the Belgian abrogation of the military accord of 1920 and then Leopold's declaration of an independent Belgian foreign policy. The French command in general, and Gamelin in particular, took these adjustments with very bad grace. Initially Gamelin ordered that the Belgians be reminded that they had a 'greater interest than us [French] in not remaining passive bystanders'.[96] Then he added the menace that French forces would 'only enter Belgium if they'll find themselves with a good line to hold when they get there'. In February 1936 Georges warned Belgium's military attaché in Paris that what French strategists sought was a 'pre-established military agreement'; without this, he threatened, French troops 'would be unable to intervene beyond the Scheldt'.[97] This was tantamount to saying that France would permit the Germans to occupy four-fifths of Belgium in the event of another war, unless arrangements to take the place of the 1920 accord were first fashioned with the Belgian generals.

As 1936 wore on the French became ever more cagey as to whether they would automatically assist Belgium militarily in a future crisis. To an extent, French policy was a bluff: it was a calculation to try to exert pressure on the Belgian foreign ministry and government. In part, however, the ambiguity that now entered the discourse of French military spokesmen was required in order to cloak some confidentiality around French planning. Gamelin could no longer dismiss the neutralists among Belgian policy-makers; their hour had come and they qualitatively changed the nature of Franco-Belgian relations as 1936 wore on.

Briefly, after the reoccupation of the Rhineland by Germany, it appeared that the French might be able to use Britain as a cement to repair the rapidly fracturing Franco-Belgian rapport. British, French and Belgian ministers, meeting in London, agreed on 19 March 1936 that tripartite discussions could take place between their military staffs.[98] Dismayingly, for Gamelin, the British dimension to these arrangements swiftly proved to be chimeral. Schweisguth, paying a semi-official exploratory visit to London from 17 to 23 March discovered from France's military attaché that the War Office had a negligible influence over British defence policy. The British generals, reported the French attaché, retained their service's traditional concern that the Low Countries should remain free of great power control; they dreamt of building a British field army as the powerfully equipped heart of a Dutch-Belgian disposition. But this was quite hypothetical: as the chief of the Imperial General Staff, Sir Archibald Montgomery-Massingberd, told Schweisguth, 'there was no British [field] army' ready for any such mission, nor did the British government intend to prepare one.[99]

On 15 and 16 April 1936 Schweisguth revisited London, this time as chief French delegate to the tripartite military talks with the British and Belgian general staffs agreed on 19 March. The April meetings confirmed how little Britain could offer to any discussions about the ground defence of western Europe. General Sir John Dill, then the director of military operations at the War Office, stated that a field force would consist of just two ill-equipped infantry divisions. After returning to Paris, Schweisguth reported this to Raquez, the Belgian military attaché. The latter was pointedly told – for the information of the Belgian government – that British support would be 'minimal and tardy'. That of France, by contrast, remained 'allocated and available'.[100]

Apprised of the military situation, Cumont's successor as Belgian chief of staff, General Edouard Van den Bergen, journeyed to Paris to confer with Gamelin on 15 May 1936. Gamelin insisted again that it would be essential for Belgium to make an immediate appeal for a French defensive intervention if they wanted effective assistance against German aggression. Van den Bergen, as an inveterate francophile, needed no persuasion on the issue. He agreed that a German attack would probably feature a sweep through southern Holland. The French and Belgian armies were to plan to make their main defence on the Meuse and the 'shelter of the Liège-Albert Canal breastplate' against the 'growing . . . peril . . . presented by the panzer divisions'.[101]

During this deceptively harmonious phase of planning, Schweisguth was accompanied by operations and logistics specialists from the French army staff on a visit to Belgium in mid-July 1936. In addition, a reconnaissance of the Sambre and Meuse position was conducted by General Dufieux, the French army's inspector of infantry. Schweisguth himself returned to Belgium at the end of July, inspecting Belgian lines at Antwerp, Liège and in the Ardennes. This detailed liaison greatly increased French familiarity with Belgian defensive preparations. An optimistic report to Gamelin at this time described how Belgian officers seemed 'converted to a close collaboration with the French army'.[102]

Such a conclusion was not untrue, as far as it went. Belgian officers harboured few illusions about the prospects – even after their own army's modernisation – of defeating a German attack by themselves. To keep a sizeable part of Belgium unoccupied, in the event of a German invasion, they knew that they required French support.

On the other hand, French observers such as Schweisguth and Gamelin gravely misjudged the amount of influence that sympathetic Belgian commanders were able to exert over Belgian foreign policy. Politicians in Brussels were markedly less deferential towards their generals than were their French counterparts towards Gamelin. Neither the Belgian parliamentarians nor the Belgian public held Cumont or Van den Bergen in the esteem, even awe, which their opposite numbers in France reserved for Gamelin, Weygand and Pétain. Senior officers in

Belgium were not public figures; they did not enjoy the prestige and national prominence of the French *grands chefs*. The radically different standing of the military in the two countries required Gamelin to experiment with new ways to maintain an accommodating Belgian defence posture once Belgium had embraced the policy of independence. Thus it was that clandestinity and covert cooperation became the hallmarks of Franco-Belgian military relations after the autumn of 1936.

The new approach was not long in emerging. On 15 October, before a hastily convened CSG the morning after Belgium's declaration of the policy of independence, Gamelin put a brave face on the turn of events. Belgium's 'return to neutrality' did not, he said, 'just inconvenience us; it [also] frees us from a burden that was becoming increasingly onerous'. Henceforth, it appeared to be 'no longer possible to undertake firm commitments'. France would only 'enter Belgium if circumstances lent themselves to this'.[103] Within a week, however, Gamelin realised that he was deceiving himself with such fighting talk. It was not possible, in practice, to renounce the strategy of forward defence in the north. The French Popular Front government was at this point still striving to maintain the impetus of its social reforms. It had, nevertheless, consented on 7 September to the army staff's long-sought rearmament of the field forces and had approved a four-year plan to cost 14 billion francs. Gamelin sensed that the high command had already received an unexpectedly sympathetic hearing from Blum. He understood that there was no further scope in which to seek a major new fortifications programme for the Franco-Belgian frontier. Gamelin concluded that he had no choice but to coax and cajole the Belgians into resuming military cooperation. His approach was to alternate the use of the carrot and the stick. 'We won't alter our concentration plans', he instructed the French army operations staff; 'but we won't make promises any more either.'[104]

The French now began to apply indirect pressure on the Belgians by means of the British. Gamelin judged – correctly as it transpired – that the British were as concerned as ever about the security and independence of the Low Countries. He also perceived that the Belgians were more trusting towards the British than they were towards the French. From this, Gamelin deduced that it could be advantageous to sow doubt in Whitehall as to whether the French were to be relied on to intervene in the event of a German attack on Holland or Belgium. Schweisguth's talks in London in March and April 1936 offered evidence that the British remained alarmed about the threat of German submarine and air bases becoming established on the Dutch–Belgian coast. Furthermore, Schweisguth had learned from his War Office contacts that the British lacked any means to make their own military response to this menace.[105] British interests, along with British military incapacity, strengthened the French hand when it came to negotiations with the Belgian general staff about the practicalities of assistance to Belgium.

In late October 1936 the French made their first move in this new game. According to Britain's military attaché in Paris, Petibon threatened 'that the French general staff would have ... to reorganize French war plans ... and in the changed circumstances these would be kept secret from everyone'. Such calculated vagueness by Gamelin's adjutant was surely intended to make the British reappraise their policy of non-engagement in defence of Holland, Belgium and France.[106]

A combined Franco-British approach to the problem of Belgian neutrality was not the only scheme hatched in Paris as French military chiefs pondered how to escape the embarrassment into which Leopold III had plunged them. An alternative particularly favoured by Daladier was to re-examine the feasibility of a strictly defensive posture all along the French frontiers. On this issue Gamelin and Daladier did not, for once, see eye to eye. Gamelin, for his part, 'after 1935, when he became generalissimo-designate, placed his major emphasis on increasing the defensive capabilities of the Maginot Line'.[107] This led to investment in upgrading the eastern section of the line in 1936–7 so that it formed a hinge 'in order [as Gamelin wrote] that we might eventually "mass on the left flank" where there were open spaces in which to manoeuvre'.[108]

Daladier's return to the war ministry in 1936 obliged Gamelin to reformulate the arguments in favour of a defensive intervention in Belgium. The speech by King Leopold had revived the attraction to Daladier of settling for a 'fortress France', behind a continuous border barrier from Switzerland to the Channel. Over territorial security Daladier was the heir to Painlevé and Maginot. As prime minister and war minister in 1933 he had tried to initiate a scheme of fortifications behind Belgium. This project had been reduced, when Pétain was at the rue Saint-Dominique in 1934, to works around Maubeuge and Valenciennes.[109] But Daladier's enthusiasm for the continuous front had remained undimmed. It was the gut-instinct of the ex-infantryman of 1914–18. In Daladier's sight the shift of policy in Belgium amply justified a defensive recasting of French plans.[110]

On 21 October 1936 Daladier urged on Vincent Auriol, the finance minister, the need to extend the Maginot system south to the Jura and north to the Channel. To begin the latter programme, Daladier sought 360 million francs.[111] From 28 to 31 October he toured the northern frontier in company with Gamelin and General Antoine Huré, the inspector of military engineering. In part his aim was to identify the sites for the first phase of a new defensive line; in part it was to indicate to the northern *départements* that the government was concerned about its security. 'We shall', said Daladier at Cassel on 31 October, 'protect the important industrial areas of the north . . . We shall establish the defence of Flanders . . . and make certain that the north will never again be invaded and occupied. Our frontier will be inviolable.'[112]

The pledge was not only politically incautious, it contradicted established French strategy. Gamelin's adherence to a plan of intervention into Belgium remained cogent. He was able to see that Daladier's revived passion for a new defensive line along the Franco-Belgian border was the child of instinct rather than of reason. Daladier had many qualities – but mastery of defence economics, still less of public finance, was not one of them. A patriotic populist in the Jacobin mould, Daladier was wholehearted in wishing to spare France the horrifying devastation of another war on its own soil.[113] But Gamelin appreciated the impracticability of what Daladier had so lightly announced. Though Daladier may not have read it before his northern tour in October, his papers contain a June 1936 operations bureau report that revealed how behindhand was the modest programme of defensive works approved in 1932–3. In the fortified sectors of Maubeuge and the Scheldt only 30 per cent of the artillery positions and 70 per cent of the casemates were serviceable.[114]

This unsatisfactory progress had a number of causes. The first was the low priority for fortification on the northern frontier until the crisis in relations with Belgium in 1936. The second, and a consequence of the first, was the low level of investment in the northern French defensive works. Just 113 million francs were allowed to the combined Rhine and Franco-Belgian sectors in the first tranche of funding in 1930. The additional work agreed in 1932–3 received only part of 292 million francs devoted to fortifications in the army's special credit of 1,275 million francs obtained in July 1934 by Pétain.[115] A third reason for the slowness of the work was the incidence of labour stoppages in the era of the Popular Front. Nor was this a problem that disappeared as soon as Blum secured the Matignon agreement in June 1936, for Schweisguth recorded in July that there were further 'serious interruptions . . . and continuation of strikes at the fortification construction sites'.[116] Finally, there was the perennial problem of the unsuitability of northern France for deep concrete emplacements because of the high water-table, the mine workings and the proximity of the very same industries which French strategy desired to protect.

These difficulties were neglected by Daladier in late 1936. He had declared at Cassel that 'the line must be completed where the gaps exist' in northern France.[117] Gamelin was, however, dismayed at the mismatch between this ambition and the enormous economic redirection that would be required to make it a reality. The original Maginot Line, he knew, had absorbed over 5 billion francs down to 1936 and remained incomplete. It would run to a total cost of between 6 and 7 billion francs by 1939. The more complex works discussed by Daladier for the Franco-Belgian frontier would, Gamelin estimated, have cost an additional 10 to 15 billion francs.[118]

Without costing his proposals, Daladier was challenging the entire basis of French strategy for the defence of the northern border. He was questioning Gamelin's plan to sanctuarise northern France by conducting its defence far in front of its border with Belgium. He was ignoring the economic vice in which French public finances, along with the existing social and military programmes of the Popular Front, were being squeezed.

Gamelin offered an alternative, based on realism, to Daladier. He accepted the improvement of prepared inundations around Dunkerque and a strengthening of the Monts de Flandres – but only as strongpoints to reinforce the security of a defensive manoeuvre. In mid-October he had repeated to the CSG that, owing to the adjacent border, Lille could only be protected by an advance at least onto the Belgian Scheldt. As discussed earlier, Leopold's policy declaration of 14 October made Gamelin more circumspect about implementing a forward defence; but it had not overturned the rationale behind the strategy.[119]

This review of the French northern defence plan in practice produced an ill-supervised and incomplete spread of fixed positions bordering Belgium. Nowhere was the spectacular achievement of the Maginot Line replicated. Daladier's ambitions represented a 'vast programme' for which, Gamelin later reflected, 'we were only able to obtain ... credits in dribs and drabs'.[120] In the first and second military regions, headquartered at Lille and Amiens and bearing responsibility for the border with Belgium, only 94.5 million francs were provided for supplementary defensive works in 1937 and 39.1 million francs in 1938. This was a minuscule investment in comparison with the expenditure in Lorraine earlier in the 1930s.[121]

Had Gamelin's heart been in a Maginot Line extension in the north, he would have lobbied to obtain more credits for it. Gamelin, after all, did not shirk the fight to re-equip the army in 1935 and 1936. The fact was that his concerns lay elsewhere by 1937. He was more concerned to eradicate the armaments production bottlenecks; to expand the mechanised forces;[122] to establish secret military coordination with Belgium's general staff in order to circumvent the declared Belgian foreign policy.

On this last count, Gamelin was increasingly attracted to the fashioning of a special relationship with Van den Bergen, his Belgian counterpart. Moreover, Gamelin was not convinced that France could spare the financial resources both to build up her conventional forces and greatly extend the fortifications. Gamelin sought more armaments and more 'punch' for his army, not more concrete. His approach to the Franco-Belgian sector is elucidated by his one-time *chef de cabinet*, General Ricard, who said of the modest scale of works behind Belgium in 1939–40 that to obtain 'effective protection for this part of the front would have demanded an effort truly disproportionate to our means. In this region fortifications could only be planned to augment . . . the defensive combat power of the main fighting corps to be deployed there.'[123]

In March 1938 the Anschluss prompted Gamelin to request that Daladier seek additional funds for fixed defences. The object, however, was only to erect additional 'permanent fortified "strongpoints"'.[124] It was not an alternative to forward defence in Belgium. It remained as true of Gamelin as it had previously been of Weygand that he 'couched his defence of permanent fortifications in terms of providing a backstop for a French advance across the Belgian border'.[125] The long-standing reasons why the French army preferred to reach forward positions were as valid as ever. The Belgians understood this – even if they did not like it. In October 1936 their ambassador in Paris had relayed rumours to Brussels that the French forces might no longer leave their own frontiers. The threat was immediately dismissed by Belgian neutralists as an empty bluff. Van Overstraeten, for instance, reiterated France's interest 'militarily, in shifting the battlefield off her own soil, as far in front [of her own frontiers] as possible'.[126]

By December 1938 Gamelin was aware of the disparities between the state of progress of defence works on different sectors of the French borders. This warning was sounded by General Gaston Prételat, responsible for the Maubeuge-Givet-Mézières region. Prételat had toured these defences. He signalled deficiencies in the Maginot Line itself.[127] He also drew attention to 'the Ardennes gap from Maubeuge to Sedan, [where] there was still no real defensive organisation apart from a few light blockhouses'. The area subsequently became the stage for the German breakthrough in 1940, alleged Prételat later, because it 'ranked bottom' of Gamelin's concerns.[128]

It is the case that Gamelin never attached priority to fortifying the Ardennes. But it is not the case that he lacked a defensive plan to protect the centre of his front. On the contrary: for Gamelin and most makers of French strategy between the wars, the Sedan–Ardennes sector was intended as a pivot or hinge, to link the forward swing of an army concentrated on the border with Belgium to the westward extremity of the Maginot Line. Gamelin was only the latest in a succession of distinguished French commanders who reasoned in this way.

French thinking about this sector was not primarily concerned with halting a German offensive through the Ardennes massif. Rather, it focused chiefly on utilising the area as a hinge for the defensive advance of the French left flank onto positions inside Belgium or for a counterattack into the flank of a German sweep through Belgium. The possibility that the Ardennes might be the main axis of a deadly blow against France was not seriously entertained by the successive heads of the French army.[129] The authority for this outlook came from Pétain. In answer to Senate army commission questions about security behind Luxembourg, Pétain gave the subsequently notorious pledge in 1934 that the Ardennes were 'impenetrable so long as we make special provisions in them. We therefore consider this a zone for demolitions . . . We should erect blockhouses there.' He concluded by reassuring the parliamentarians that even if an enemy launched an attack through this sector he would 'be pincered as he leaves the forests. This is not, therefore, a dangerous sector.'[130] Nobody contested Pétain's judgement. Indeed, this litany's recitation by one general after another established a faith to which Gamelin subscribed in his turn. In 1937 he justified his opposition to a Meuse *département* senator who was seeking extra credits to fortify Sedan. The 'experience of past wars', argued Gamelin, showed that the 'Ardennes has never favoured large [military] operations'.[131] Much was expected of the Meuse as an impassable defensive barrier. Yet little was done to site artillery to support the natural features. Late in 1935 a visiting Belgian staff officer found casemates under construction from Givet to Monthermé to be 'few in number . . . and indifferently built'.[132]

Moreover, not only was the Meuse insufficiently fortified, it was also inadequately garrisoned. In 1935–6 the divisions deployed in the sector were charged with holding 40 kilometres of front each – three times the distance prescribed by French defensive doctrine.[133] In the CSG on 15 October 1936, discussing Belgium's announcement of neutrality the previous day, Prételat suggested that the Ardennes and Meuse were vulnerable to the 'danger of an *attaque brusquée*' that would 'initially encounter only absurdly [few] peacetime effectives' defending it. Yet only minor artillery redeployments were made to meet this threat.[134] Gamelin was satisfied that a German adventure in the Ardennes, after attrition from demolitions and Belgian delaying action, could be stopped by the 'bastions of Sedan and Montmédy' and by the 'formidable obstacle' of the Meuse.[135]

The justification of this sector's light defence was supposed to be the existence behind the centre of the Franco-German front of a substantial mechanised reserve. Such a force was to represent the conjuncture in Gamelin's thinking both about territorial security and rearmament priorities. A powerful armoured corps, trained in the methods of sealing-off and counterattack (*opérations de colmatage*) to defeat a breakthrough, was to be concentrated in encampments near Laon, Rheims and Châlons-sur-Marne until required. The force was to be capable of moving to crush any rupture of the front on the Meuse, or of deploying north or south against a German outflanking manoeuvre. The French army's operations bureau had formulated the principles of a mechanised riposte in June 1936. It prescribed that 'hostile armour penetrating our fortified front . . . demands that we prepare to establish large tank units . . . commanded by generals who familiarise themselves in peacetime with their employment . . . Four new units would constitute the battle corps . . . to make the maintenance of the integrity of our fortified system absolutely dependable.'[136]

As the 1930s closed this concept of mechanised counterattack came to bulk ever larger in French defensive strategy. It was the corollary to the gradual waning of Gamelin's interest in developing further fixed defences. The EMA appreciated that the method would be most decisive if applied against both flanks of an enemy penetration at once. Map exercises, manoeuvres and war games confirmed that counterstroke was the optimal role for tank forces on the defensive. The French command concluded that tank developments favoured the defender, furnishing him with the tool to restore a defensive front swiftly and securely. Since the 'possibility of an enemy incursion could not altogether be eliminated', the French recognised their need to 'be in a position to retake lost ground . . . by means of large specialised units of the armoured division type'.[137]

A capacity to restore the front's integrity rested, however, on possession of an organised and trained mechanised reserve under central control. This was the *masse de manoeuvre* concept. Establishing it was Gamelin's goal when he prioritised weapons like the Char B and the SOMUA S.35 cavalry battle-tank in the 1936–9 rearmament programme. To make the doctrine operational it was necessary to form the unit at its heart – the Division Cuirassée de Réserve. To be effective in war this type of formation required peacetime training; it had to have its permanent commanders and cadres and it needed familiarisation with combined-arms tactics.

Yet, as has been seen, the establishment of DCRs was greatly delayed. First, in 1936–7, their creation slipped behind as bottlenecks worsened in mechanised vehicle and armour-plate manufacture. Later, in 1937–8, brigade-strength heavy tank manoeuvres were postponed – in the former year because vehicle shortages prevented the units being formed, in the latter because the Sudeten crisis obliged a partial mobilisation of the active army in the main exercise season.[138] Furthermore, with the honourable exceptions of Gamelin and Héring, the CSG remained hesitant and half-hearted about concentrating tanks and mechanised infantry into DCRs.[139] Even Prételat, anxious though he was about the Ardennes, resisted the experimental formation of such divisions, asserting that it would be 'enough to constitute a few brigades of heavy tanks that will be distributed when required'.[140]

The risk along the Meuse and in the event of battle in Belgium was therefore greater, by 1938–40, than Gamelin had envisaged. The unexpected slowness in building a mechanised manoeuvre reserve increased the danger. To try to supplement the output of French industry, Gamelin turned towards Britain after 1936. He pressed the British – as is discussed later – to prepare a small armoured expeditionary corps to fill this worrying gap in the French order-of-battle. The second source of unanticipated risk in the frontier defence plans based on both the Maginot Line and a forward defence in Belgium was the fact that the Belgians clung adamantly to their policy of independence.

Gamelin sought to overcome this problem by developing his own military diplomacy with the chief of the Belgian general staff. He sought, in this way, to by-pass the official Belgian foreign policy by means of clandestine and confidential agreements with the Belgian army. He strove to continue joint planning, to share intelligence and coordinate the logistical aspects of the advance of French forces in the event of German attack.[141]

In pursuing secret military collaboration with the Belgian command, Gamelin sought to retain the substance of a defensive alliance in spite of losing the form. The task was one calling for delicacy as well as discretion. The lynchpins of the effort were, on the one side, the French military attachés in Brussels and, on the other, Van den Bergen, the Belgian army's chief of staff.[142] In 1936, as has been outlined, Gamelin took full advantage of the fact that Belgium's abrogation on 6 March of the 1920 military accord with France did not prohibit Franco-Belgian staff cooperation under the auspices of Locarno.

But after the affirmation of Belgian independence in October 1936 the basis of cooperation became fragile and unusually personalised. From the French standpoint, everything was gambled on the good offices and influence of Van den Bergen. The latter had been well-liked by Gamelin when the two had met in May. He was candid to Gamelin about his dismay over the increasingly unyielding neutralism of Leopold and his senior advisors such as Pierre Van Zuylen, director of political affairs at the Belgian foreign ministry, and Van Overstraeten, Leopold's military counsellor. During the winter of 1936-7 the French military attaché in Brussels, General Georges Riedinger, assured Gamelin that Van den Bergen was ready to assume personal responsibility for continuing regular but under-cover exchanges with the French army. By an act of private defiance the Belgian chief of staff was willing to circumvent the official external policy of his king and his government. Van den Bergen was reportedly sceptical that Germany would ever respect Belgium merely because the Belgian government had publicly disavowed ties with France. He was said to have no faith that Germany would respect Belgian integrity if German strategists ever again saw advantages in crossing Belgium to strike at France or to threaten Britain. Van den Bergen bore responsibility for preparing a military defence of Belgium in case the policy of independence should ever fail. Consequently, he judged it his duty to maintain military arrangements with the French army – the only army able to help Belgium in a meaningful way.[143]

Van den Bergen's motives in continuing to collaborate with Gamelin were an admixture of francophile sentiment and national strategic calculation. Unlike most contemporary Belgian leaders, Van den Bergen adhered exclusively to military considerations. He set aside the complexities of Belgian domestic politics in identifying a policy for Belgian security. His reasoning was probably instinctive, for he was not a politician but a military professional. At any rate, his cooperativeness appeared to be sufficiently reliable that it encouraged Gamelin to take the risk of working covertly with him, instead of recasting French defence plans in favour of a positional defence on the Franco-Belgian frontier. This was a critical calculation. It was a point of no-return in 1936-7, when Gamelin decided to ignore Daladier's call for a new fortifications effort and a static deployment along the border with Belgium.

Gamelin's choice of secret cooperation with Van den Bergen meant that France was making a hazardous wager: Belgium's chief of staff had henceforth, in a war crisis, to be able to overcome the reluctance of the Belgian government to admit French troops so as to present a combined and continuous front to the Germans. The risk was that Van den Bergen might not prevail. Then, with a German invasion under way, the French forces would have to dash into Belgium and take the chance of an encounter battle in a bid to prevent the Belgian resistance from collapsing. It was the dilemma that was never resolved and which still confronted the Allies in 1940, leading some of the best French divisions to rush headlong into the trap embodied in the German offensive through the Ardennes.[144]

Thus Gamelin's adherence to a defensive intervention into Belgium proved to be crucial. Yet the bet was not made impulsively or impetuously. Rather, it was a calculated risk taken in the hope of a great reward. Gamelin was playing for the removal of the war zone far forward of French soil, for shorter lines and for the incorporation of the twenty-two divisions of the Belgian army to redress French numerical inferiority. In electing to seek these advantages, Gamelin kept company with Pétain and Weygand and, more distantly, with Maginot himself. Daladier's was the isolated opinion.

The secret coordination with Van den Bergen was a highly sensitive mission. It fell chiefly to Riedinger's successor as military attaché in Brussels, Colonel (later brigadier-general) Edmond Laurent. A *polytechnicien* and artilleryman, Laurent was assigned to Belgium in July 1937. Fifty-two years old, with great experience in intelligence work, he was hand-picked by Gamelin and given the exacting job of forming a personal conduit to the Belgian chief of staff.

Laurent's specialisation in intelligence had commenced in 1918 when he was posted as chief of the 2e Bureau of the inspector-general of artillery. This led in 1921 to his appointment to the German section of the general staff's 2e Bureau, where he was commended for his 'extensive knowledge, appetite for work and receptive intellect'. His qualities were such that he was selected in 1928, whilst still a major, to take charge of the army's Service de Renseignements (SR). As chief of secret intelligence for the following six years Laurent drew praise from many quarters. General Guitry, assistant chief of the army staff at the time, recorded at the end of 1931 that Laurent was an 'officer of the foremost value' whose performance was admirable in the 'very oppressive and delicate task' of secret intelligence. Soon Laurent's qualities caught the eye of Gamelin, who noted that he had 'to be allowed to get ahead as soon as possible'.

Laurent's nomination as attaché in Brussels in 1937 followed tours in command of artillery regiments and attendance at the CHEM, an academy then under the direction of General Bineau. Though the evidence is inconclusive, it may be that Bineau recommended Laurent for the posting to Belgium, since Bineau was an expert on the problematic strategy of intervention, having in 1935–6 been commander-designate of the army charged with the mission.[145]

From his arrival in Brussels in August 1937 until after the outbreak of war in 1939, Laurent was a privileged and self-effacing intermediary between Gamelin and Van den Bergen. For much of this time he was the sole channel of communications to Gamelin for the clandestine exchanges about military reorganisation, concentration and war movements mooted inside the Belgian defence ministry. In the main he was obliged to lead a highly irregular Jekyll and Hyde existence. Ostensibly, he performed only the routine functions of any military attaché, attending exercises, social functions and ceremonial occasions. Yet alongside this overt role he undertook secret contacts with Van den Bergen that would, had they become known, have caused uproar among Belgian politicians and a first-class Franco-Belgian diplomatic row.

With Laurent playing the part of the indispensable Figaro, the *billets doux* of this furtive military courtship slipped back and forth from Brussels to Paris. Driving a cart and horses through the policy of independence, Van den Bergen kept Gamelin abreast of modifications in Belgian mobilisation and operational planning; the French army engineer corps was enabled to furnish technical assistance in the construction of the Belgian outpost line in the Ardennes and in the incorporation of the latest Maginot Line technology in the new Belgian forts near Liège. In June 1937 Schweisguth – disguised as a civilian tourist – was enabled to reconnoitre the Belgo-German and Dutch–Belgian frontiers. False identity papers were provided in 1937 and 1938 for Laurent, variously disguising him as a travelling salesman and as a Walloon parliamentarian, so that he was able to investigate off-limits Belgian military installations.[146]

Laurent's unique status during more than two years of undercover Franco-Belgian cooperation is attested by the trust he won from Van den Bergen. The Belgian chief of staff was hazarding his career by collaborating so extensively with Gamelin.[147] By confiding in Laurent as intermediary he gave the attaché an unparalleled position. Strikingly enough, no other Belgian officers became privy to the secret exchanges. Knowledge of them was withheld from Belgium's military attachés in Paris, Colonels Georges Raquez and Maurice Delvoie. It was also hidden from Van den Bergen's assistant chiefs of staff and from the head of the Belgian army's 2e Section (intelligence).[148] Fearful of leaks and the political furore they would create in Belgium, Van den Bergen lived in constant fear of 'indiscretions'. As Laurent alerted the French 2e Bureau in December 1937, Van den Bergen believed 'that my reports are destined solely for the sight of the General, Vice-President of the CSG [Gamelin]'. The Belgian chief of staff was sensitised to the semantics of his illicit trade, instructing Laurent to speak of 'conversations' with him, never of 'communications' from him.[149] In March 1938 Van den Bergen even showed himself ready to act against other Belgian officers whose conduct threatened to arouse unwanted interest among Belgian politicians in high command activities. Thus he quashed attempts by General Jamotte, the Belgian army's francophone director of munitions, to remain in post beyond his mandated retirement age. Laurent reported that, with Jamotte's departure, France had 'lost a friend because he showed his friendship too energetically and *too publicly*'. When Jamotte then warned Laurent that France should distrust Van den Bergen, the attaché reflected that he was 'unable to disabuse our friend by telling him of the substantial conversations I'm having with the chief of staff'.[150]

How successful was Laurent's mission? As informant and confidant he undoubtedly accomplished a great deal. Without the confidences divulged to Laurent the French EMA would not have obtained a continuous updating about the defensive plans of the Belgian army. Gamelin was immeasurably better informed about Belgian political tendencies and military preparedness by 1939 than if he had not established this special means of communication with Van den Bergen. Gamelin expressed his appreciation of Laurent by noting in the attaché's confidential dossier at the close of 1938 that he had 'succeeded very well at the SR' and was 'rendering the best of services in Brussels'. Colson added to this same report that Laurent seemed 'very suitable' for promotion to brigadier-general (a distinction he obtained a year later). Dentz, the assistant chief of staff who coordinated the 2e Bureau, SR and attachés in 1938–9, recorded that Laurent was 'succeeding to perfection' as military attaché, had shown skill in winning the confidence of the Belgian command and was 'very up-to-date about Belgian military questions, as well as about the army's and the country's *mentalité*'. The sensitive communications with which he had been entrusted showed the high regard Van den Bergen had for him. His despatches in an era 'pregnant with internal as well as external incidents' were praised for their 'perspicacity and sound judgements'.[151]

Laurent's achievements were, however, offset by serious shortcomings. The attaché's special relationship with Van den Bergen kept Gamelin better informed about Belgian military affairs than the Belgian government intended; yet, ultimately, there were severe limitations on what a technical collaboration of this sort might accomplish. It could facilitate the preparation of a French intervention. But it could not oblige the Belgians to invite French forces to their aid early enough in a crisis to eliminate the risk of an encounter battle. The appeal for French assistance remained a decision for the Belgian government. It was a decision over which Van den Bergen, let alone Laurent, had no control. The success of Laurent's mission did not, therefore, reduce the magnitude of Gamelin's wager that the Belgian government would revert from neutrality to a full-scale political and military partnership with France.

When, in September 1939, Belgium clung steadfastly to non-belligerence, Gamelin was dismayed. His strategic calculations were gravely discomfited. His embarrassment reflected the seriousness of his misjudgement of Belgian political resolve. It also betrayed how far he had overestimated Van den Bergen's influence – or at any rate, how much, as a result of Laurent's reports, he had erroneously attributed political power and not simply goodwill to his Belgian counterpart. Evidently the wish that Belgium would rejoin the Allies was father to the thought.[152]

The revelation of the extent of French miscalculation over Belgian policy in September 1939 provoked a storm of intemperate language from Allied military leaders. Gamelin wrote to Daladier on 1 September that Belgian neutrality hugely strengthened the German lines protecting the Ruhr and the Rhine valley. The Belgian stance, said Gamelin, played entirely into German hands. It increased their security in the west and reduced the Allied means of deflecting Wehrmacht resources from Poland.[153]

The realisation that Allied hopes of a pre-emptive invitation to move to the Albert Canal and the Meuse were illusory prompted bitter recriminations among the frustrated French and British. Delvoie, the Belgian military attaché in Paris, reported on 8 September that, at the French war ministry, he met his British counterpart, Colonel Fraser,

who told me how much Belgium's position was hampering the Allies. We fought for you in 1914, he said. If Hitler were to be victorious, what will become of you? If the war drags on long, what will become of you in the ruins of Europe? ... Your neutrality prevents us even from easily overflying the Ruhr basin. It prevents or terribly handicaps us from attacking Germany. Because of it the war risks being extended, for we shall not negotiate so long as Hitler remains in power.[154]

Three weeks later, at the beginning of October 1939, the Belgian attaché reported another talk with Fraser. This time the British attaché said that if events led Belgium to appeal to the Allies, the latter would 'not want to expose themselves to an encounter battle with the Germans'; therefore they would 'await them on a chosen battlefield'. Fraser was, in Delvoie's view, seeking to intimidate Belgium into joining the Allies by implying that it would otherwise be left to fend for itself against Germany. This, estimated the Belgian, was pure bluff. It did not correspond with what he had been told by Gauché of the 2e Bureau; the latter had said 'that the 4e Bureau had, for certain, calculated the rate of intervention by French troops for our benefit'.[155]

Correctly, Delvoie discerned an embitterment towards Belgium because of its decision to stand aloof from the conflict. 'Colonel Fraser has said to me', he reported to Brussels on 3 October, that 'after the war it is probable that the victorious Allies will have to take steps *vis-à-vis* the small powers so that they can no longer obstruct the military arrangements of great powers who are fighting at one and the same time on their own behalf and on behalf of the small powers'.[156] This 'sort of threat for the future', as it was termed by Belgium's counsellor of embassy in Paris, characterised the fulminations directed at Belgium after September 1939.[157]

Gamelin had imagined that the shock of war would jolt the Belgian government out of its neutralist trance. This expectation went unfulfilled. His gamble that cooperation with Van den Bergen might compensate for Belgium's uncooperative external policy had failed. With a war on his hands, Gamelin had not obtained the politico-military solidarity on which he had counted as a consequence of Laurent's liaison with Van den Bergen. Nor had any worthwhile extension of fixed defences along the Franco-Belgian frontier been undertaken. The persistence of Belgian neutrality after September 1939 signified nothing less than the collapse of French hopes for a secure defence of the Allied northwestern flank.

Angry as well as impotent, Gamelin joined in the censure of the Belgians. By their non-belligerence they had, he exclaimed to his staff on 21 September, neutralised the French army's prospects of threatening western Germany and thus were 'responsible for the obliteration of Poland'. Retribution would overtake Belgium, prophesied Gamelin. He added that Belgium was only an 'artificial construct designed, at its inception, against France'; it was 'fragile, having no solid basis either in a long tradition or in any natural frontiers'.[158] In an even more ill-tempered outburst on 9 October 1939, over lunch with Reynaud at Vincennes, Gamelin described the neutrals as 'fearful or merely opportunistic', likening them to 'terror-stricken spectators' at the gladiatorial contest between France and Germany:

Among them the Belgians play a baleful role being thoughtless and short-sighted, mediocrities, traders whose perspectives have been distorted by business; they are, in large measure, to blame for the crushing of Poland; they seriously hampered Franco-British action when they could have facilitated it in many ways – through clearing their air-space for the passage of British aviation, through shortening our front-line to enable a greater threat to have been posed [to Germany] during the Polish campaign, through making action easier against German fortifications that are less powerful on their frontiers than on ours.

Belgium had acquired the status of the 'major culprit' in Gamelin's eyes. In what approximated to a transfer of the subliminal guilt and fear which his strategy's disintegration must have bred in him, Gamelin conjectured that Belgium would 'pay by becoming a battlefield or by splitting asunder if she ever turned towards Germany'.[159]

Anger, however, could not disguise failure. Throughout the 1930s Belgian security and its domestic political ramifications had been analysed far too superficially by French strategists and political leaders. Gamelin was as much to blame as any of his colleagues in this regard. Belgium had consistently and disastrously been examined through a prism of French interests and French circumstances. From defective analysis and large doses of wishful thinking resulted a fragile strategic policy. Gamelin deluded himself that covert technical arrangements fashioned with Van den Bergen might suffice in lieu of a reconstructed Franco-Belgian political agreement. The rejection of the obvious alternative – a Maginot Line extension to the Channel – was based on such major economic and engineering objections that it demands the respect of the historian today. To this extent, therefore, it may be that Gamelin's gamble on Belgian behaviour in wartime was the only course that France could take. Possibly Gamelin and the French governments of the middle and later 1930s indeed faced an insoluble dilemma over their northern frontier. Possibly, right down to the disaster in 1940, there was no way for them to escape the 'risk . . . that Belgium would call for France's help at the last moment, too late to entrench the defence at . . . the Meuse and the Albert Canal. Hence the entire security of France rested finally on the arrangements of a neighbouring state which was too weak to defend itself.'[160]

8 Gamelin, Yugoslavia and the eastern alliances: assets or embarrassments?

French policies towards east-central Europe between the wars have generated a vigorous historiography. The policies remain highly controversial. France has been accused, at least implicitly, of patronising east-central Europe when it was of use to her in the 1920s and then failing to protect the region when it became a target of German expansionism in the following decade. French inter-war governments stand under a cloud of suspicion. It is a suspicion that they pledged promises which they had neither the intention nor the ability to keep. It is a suspicion, too, of undertaking obligations which they could not fulfil. French military leaders are said to have encouraged strategic fantasies that, in reality, they had neither the armaments nor the doctrine to make effective. French bankers and businessmen are indicted for pursuing a 'poor man's imperialism', mixing parsimonious investment and selfish economic exploitation, with the connivance of successive French governments.[1]

Yet, in appraising French conduct it must be remembered that France's motive for engagement in eastern Europe after 1919 was to improve her own security against Germany. This reasoning inspired all the French geo-strategic machinations in the region during the 1930s. The 'system' with which the French replaced their pre-1914 ally, Russia, did not come about instantaneously. Nor was this 'system' any sort of smooth-sided monolith. This much has been demonstrated by modern historians.

What France possessed by late 1927 with Warsaw, Prague, Bucharest and Belgrade was not a 'system' at all. It was a loose network. It was a diplomatic construction of uneven and unequal linkages. It was a Heath Robinson contraption of untested and incomplete foreign policy engineering. For one thing, no militarily integrated alliance between Poland, on the one hand, and the Little Entente of Czechoslovakia, Romania and Yugoslavia on the other, was ever forged. Furthermore, after the 1926 coup in Poland that installed the regime of Jozef Pilsudski, there was a virtual suspension of the cooperation between the French and Polish general staffs. It is a mistake, therefore, to exaggerate the coherence, consistency or completeness of French relations with their eastern allies.[2]

Scholars have paid considerable attention to Franco-Polish and Franco-Czech relations. Diverse in character and multi-faceted, they were an important 'element in the diplomatic game and even an object of military planning'.[3] In contrast, surprisingly little has been done to explore dealings in the 1930s between France and the Balkan states, Yugoslavia and Romania. This chapter seeks to make good this oversight in relation to contacts between Paris and Belgrade, by addressing the place given by Gamelin to Yugoslavia in defensive planning against Hitler's Reich.[4]

The Franco-Yugoslav relationship possessed a strategic significance in its own right (most especially in 1935–6, during French *rapprochement* with Italy). But it also constituted a case study of a great power–small power relationship. The features of the dialogue between Paris and Belgrade raise questions about the wider military diplomacy practised by Gamelin. How far, for example, did distance from the Franco-German border – with which Gamelin was obsessed – exacerbate difficulties in French-allied relations? What influence did Gamelin seek to exert over engagements contracted before he became responsible for the French army in 1931? Can patterns be discerned in Gamelin's reactions to the challenges which allies mounted to his military diplomacy? What may be made of Gamelin's special reliance, when dealing with Belgrade as when dealing with Brussels, on liaison between the French military attachés and the high command of the allies? Did Gamelin and his associates consider employing economic assistance, or arms sales and cessions, to create extra leverage behind an 'eastern front' strategy?

In so many of these areas, Yugoslavia offers an instructive example of the way French policies evolved. It was, geo-strategically, one of France's most promising allies. Yet, judged by economic and military resources, it was also one of the poorest. A treaty of guarantee and security of 11 November 1927 allied Yugoslavia to France. The accord had been renewed in 1932. In spite of this treaty, however, Franco-Yugoslav defence cooperation rested on an *ad hoc* basis. It was not founded on any military convention. This was a contrast to French relations with Romania and Czechoslovakia, as well as with Poland. In these three instances staff accords or exchanges of military letters existed.[5] This was natural: the value of east-central European allies to

France was, after all, the former's ability to menace the German rear in case of a breach of Versailles and a threat against France. Gamelin, along with many but not all other influential Frenchmen, cynically sought to confront Germany 'with a second political-military front in Europe'. This front, 'with all its infirmities and imperfections', lay in eastern Europe, along a north–south axis running from Poland to Yugoslavia. Throughout eastern Europe and the Balkans, however, the French wanted this front without either paying the full price of friendship or openly naming their game. What 'was needed was allies who would go to war for France but who would not make France go to war'.[6]

Before the early 1930s the French did little to promote useful cooperation between their general staff and those of their eastern allies. A flurry of Franco-Polish meetings occurred from 1922 to 1924, following the secret agreement for defensive exchanges appended to the 1921 Franco-Polish treaty. But contacts were attenuated at the wish of both parties during the Locarno era. The French military presence in Poland was reduced. All that remained were advisors such as General Louis Faury, commandant of the higher war college in Warsaw for eight years (and whom Gamelin recalled from retirement in September 1939 to lead the French liaison mission to Polish headquarters).[7] Franco-Czech military coordination was more deeply embedded. A French mission was stationed in Prague from 1919 onwards. It was led first by General Pellé, then by General Mittelhauser and finally, after 1926, by General Louis Faucher ('Notre Faucher' as the enthusiastic Czechs termed him).[8] These officers, judged the French army staff, 'added weight to [French] influence in Prague' during the inter-war decades.[9] The Czech officer corps was more openly francophile than those of the other eastern allies. The size and duration of the French mission in Prague laid the basis for a Czech army with methods and mentalities similar to those of the French. In the 1920s, moreover, the Czechs seemed geographically well placed to aid France, for the Bohemian salient jutted threateningly into Saxony and Silesia.

Yugoslavia, too, was well placed to assist France. The French were, however, slow to appreciate this. They remained evasive in 1928 when the Yugoslavs first sought to open staff conversations. Until 1933–4 the French judged Italo-Yugoslav antagonism to be too deeply entrenched to make a southern strategic partnership feasible between Paris, Rome and Belgrade.[10] The French at this time considered that sufficient strategic coordination with Yugoslavia was accomplished by the posting of military attachés in Belgrade. French coolness particularly disappointed King Alexander of Yugoslavia. A devoted francophile, Alexander sought a military mission from the French general staff in 1930. His wish was to be placed on a par with Czechoslovakia. The French, though, maintained that a mission of theirs in Belgrade would offend the Italian government at a time when France desired closer relations with Rome. The snub added injury to insult. For Alexander smarted over the omission of a French military arrangement in the treaty with Yugoslavia of 1927.

Instead of a military mission the French reinforced their service attaché in Belgrade with four field-grade military advisors, in March 1931. These French officers faced a formidable task. For they had to try to coax and cajole the Yugoslav army into adopting modern methods of warfare. One of this quartet was Colonel Antoine Béthouart. For him the posting marked the start of almost seven years in Belgrade, first with the staff academy and later, between 1934 and 1938, as military attaché himself. Béthouart became more intimately aware than anyone of Yugoslavia's political and military situation. By the later 1930s he had an unrivalled knowledge of the country and its army. He also acquired decided views of his own about the position Yugoslavia should be accorded in French external policy and grand strategy. Just like military attachés elsewhere – and not just French ones – he learned the difficulty of singing in harmony with the tunes of his hosts as well as with those of his masters. Yet his expertise made him an unusually important factor in Franco-Yugoslav relations for most of the decade.[11]

The military attaché in Belgrade – like his counterparts in Warsaw, Brussels and London – was a key instrument in furthering French influence. As a soldier-diplomat, Béthouart was an ambassador for Gamelin. He was, too, the eyes and ears of the war ministry and of the 2e Bureau. In the absence of a French military mission in Belgrade it was upon Béthouart's shoulders that fell the responsibility for fence-mending after King Alexander was assassinated in France at the start of a state visit in October 1934. A seasoned Yugoslav expert by this date, Béthouart had actually been at the side of Alexander on the quay at Marseille and had witnessed the murder at close hand. Furthermore, his posting to Belgrade as attaché in 1934 had resulted from an express request to the French army by the Yugoslav king.[12] With a background – just like Gamelin – of service in the elite *chasseurs alpins*, Béthouart was reckoned to be a rising star in the French officer corps. Supported in Belgrade by just one assistant attaché, responsible for surveillance of Italy, Béthouart's 'vital services' required tact and no little skill, and were paid handsome tribute by Gamelin.[13]

From his post at Belgrade and from his diverse contacts in the Yugoslav army, Béthouart provided a generally accurate assessment of this ally's strengths and weaknesses. It was apparent that Yugoslavia's political volatility and geographical location gave it vulnerabilities as well as opportunities in about equal measure. Nature had endowed the country to pose to Germany – or Italy – a considerable threat in wartime. This, in peacetime, afforded Belgrade a significant diplomatic bark; its domestic dissensions, on the other hand, together with its shortage of industrial–military resources, deprived it of a corresponding military bite. Béthouart, beginning with his first report to the Yugoslav and French war ministries in November 1931, candidly outlined the weakness of Yugoslav military muscle, a weakness not immediately apparent if solely measured by numbers on paper. His earliest impression in fact was of the disproportion between the modest size of the Yugoslav population (about 12 million) and its peacetime standing army of sixteen infantry and two cavalry divisions. The French peacetime army was, after all, organised around only twenty infantry divisions from a population 39 million strong. But the French army was backed by a sophisticated reservist system which could triple its infantry strength after mobilisation. In contrast the Yugoslav forces had few reserves: their mobilised strength of twenty-two divisions being only four divisions more than their peacetime army.[14]

Exacerbating this crisis of manpower were even more significant internal problems; in fact, it quickly became evident to Béthouart that the 'value of the Yugoslav army depended completely on the internal political situation'. He saw that for the most part the Yugoslav officer corps was incapable of providing a strong foundation on which to build an army. Officers were ill-trained, and generals were promoted above their abilities. Yugoslavian poverty and her underdeveloped industrial base caused a shortage of modern military equipment, a situation the French might have remedied had they been more concerned and had Yugoslavian internal politics been more settled. On the other hand, Yugoslavia's diverse ethnic population and the failure of the government to assimilate and integrate its non-Serb nationalities, particularly the Croats and Slovenes, into its military caused no end of problems. Even as early as 1931, Béthouart feared the portents that reconciling the nationalities 'was not the road' that the Yugoslav government had chosen to travel. An alternative direction, towards a 'smaller but truly national, loyal, well-equipped and trained army' sustained by 'reliable allies', appealed to Béthouart. Yet this ideal army encountered not only the obstacle of stubborn and unteachable Yugoslav generals but also the reluctance of France itself, 'far away and unwilling to guarantee its military support'. Béthouart wrote retrospectively that he had 'neither the competence nor the authority' to try to alleviate the 'terrible political handicaps' crippling the Yugoslav army, although in his posting in Belgrade as an attaché from 1934 to 1938 he personally strove to persuade Paris to shoulder greater responsibility for Yugoslavia's protection.[15]

By the mid-1930s, however, Béthouart had few illusions remaining about either the extent of Yugoslavia's weaknesses or the low regard in which it was held as an ally in Paris. Without 'urgent reforms', he reported, the Yugoslav army faced 'intellectual death'. Serb-Croat antagonism prevented the fashioning of a cohesive and modernised military instrument. This may be seen when, in March 1931 and again in November 1933, King Alexander pressed Béthouart for Weygand to visit Yugoslavia. Although he had travelled to Prague in 1933, Weygand remained either unwilling or unable to make a similar gesture of support to Belgrade, perhaps because current French foreign policy favoured better relations with Italy.[16]

Gamelin's own views on the military capabilities of French allies at this time emerge in a cautiously worded memorandum which he framed in January 1934. He argued that France's own forces required to be re-equipped to 'enable them to attack Germany (after not too great a delay) in order to relieve Poland and Czechoslovakia' or to attack Italy 'if required to relieve an endangered Yugoslavia'. On the other hand, Gamelin was already becoming interested in the attractive possibilities that would emerge for France – and indirectly for the eastern allies – if a *rapprochement* were effected with Rome. On their own, said Gamelin, the eastern allies would not 'directly' be able to give France 'any effective aid'. Romania and Yugoslavia, he asserted, were making 'no serious progress in respect of their armaments'.[17]

Gamelin's doubts about the help France might expect reflected the generally held French appraisal of the military worth of their eastern allies by the mid-1930s. In the HCM in January 1935 Pétain reminded his colleagues 'that they should not count too much on any external cooperation'. Laval, then foreign minister, objected, countering that Czech and Romanian assistance 'in particular' – and especially the former – was understood to represent 'something substantial'. Did policy-makers 'really have to envisage France standing alone', he inquired. This, replied Pétain, was indeed the prospect.[18]

Soon events proved the marshal correct. In March, just two months later, Germany re-established conscription and openly proclaimed air rearmament. Reactions by the generals of the CSG varied, but Mittelhauser spoke from his central European experience to venture that the Czechs had now lost confidence in France and, with the Yugoslavs, would increasingly look for support to the Soviet Union. An HCM memorandum was equally pessimistic. It attributed a surprise attack capability to Germany's regular forces. It also noted that the 'immediate assistance' to France from most of her friends would 'necessarily be precarious'. Czechoslovakia's location and 'valued [military] assets' would not even divert German offensive resources, it was feared, because of the paralysing threat against Prague from Hungary, Austria and perhaps also Poland.[19]

In January 1935, however, Laval's visit to Mussolini was perceived as the foundation for a Franco-Italian entente. The bulk of France's military leadership welcomed this in view of their gloomy prognostications about the value of east-central Europe.[20] In their enthusiasm for the possibility of a new strategic liaison, the French command decided to look afresh at how it might help its Balkan friends overcome their military weaknesses. In April 1935 Gamelin talked in Paris with General Samsonovici, the Romanian chief of staff, whilst Béthouart reported in preparation for the visit to France in June by the military chiefs of all three Little Entente states. In the late summer, after Gamelin had concluded a military accord with Badoglio in Rome, the Czechs, Romanians and Yugoslavs came to France once again.[21]

These extended consultations represented a major stocktaking with the Little Entente. Gamelin's object was to familiarise the allied generals with the latest French strategic thinking and with an assessment of Germany's military renaissance. The visitors were treated to the largest staff exercise conducted by the French since 1918. The more important purpose, however, was to convert the allies to the thinking behind the agreement that Gamelin had reached with Badoglio. This provided for joint action to keep Austria independent of Germany. Plans envisaged transporting three French divisions across northern Italy to operate against Germany on the Yugoslav frontier in exchange for Italian deployments at Belfort. Gamelin knew that in order to effect such schemes he had to dispel Yugoslav distrust of Italy, which was suspected in Belgrade of harbouring hegemonic ambitions in the Balkans. The French corps linking the Italians and Yugoslavs was aimed at securing a partnership for which Belgrade otherwise had no enthusiasm.[22]

In October 1935 Gamelin sent his adjutant and confidant, Petibon, along with Schweisguth, deputy chief of staff responsible for liaison with foreign armies, to the Romanian manoeuvres. These officers returned not just with information from Bucharest but, from talks with the Yugoslav delegation at the exercises, with a heightened sense of the military weaknesses of Yugoslavia. The Romanians wished to re-equip themselves with French armaments. The Yugoslavs were exposed for their equal or greater dearth of modern material and for their outdated doctrine.[23]

Paris was perturbed by these appraisals. As the Abyssinian crisis in late 1935 turned the Franco-Italian alliance into a frosty animosity, Gamelin was obliged to re-evaluate Yugoslavia's potential as a strategic partner. The possibility of Franco-Italian conflict rendered Yugoslavia more vulnerable. On the other hand, the alteration of European alignments potentially raised Yugoslavia's strategic utility to France by offering a means of projecting French force to menace southern Germany and Austria as well as by constituting a threat to Italy. The question was whether or not France was prepared to devote sufficient resources of her own to modernise the Yugoslav armed forces to the extent required – and to give the Belgrade francophiles reason enough for fidelity to the French alliance.

By 1936 parts of official Paris recognised France's need to act vigorously to restore lost influence in east-central Europe. Daladier, restored to the rue Saint-Dominique in Blum's Popular Front government, moved swiftly to alert the CPDN that French inaction over the Rhineland remilitarisation had 'shaken the Little Entente'.[24] Efforts to revive France's reputation in Yugoslavia began that May with a visit by the aged and long-retired Marshal Franchet d'Esperey. Although afflicted by arthritis, d'Esperey received an enthusiastic welcome from both the crowds in the street and from a Yugoslav press nostalgic for the liberation of the Balkans in 1918. Honoured with the rank of *voivode*, or marshal, of the Yugoslav army, d'Esperey was fêted as the living – if infirm – embodiment of privileged Franco-Yugoslav relations. He visited Prince Paul, regent since Alexander's assassination, as well as Stojadinović, the prime minister, and Marić, the former chief of staff who had become war minister. However, once back in France, d'Esperey wrote to warn Gamelin that he had detected signs of Yugoslav intimidation in the face of Germany's international renaissance. France, he advised, urgently needed to mount an energetic diplomatic and military response if it were to reassure its Balkan friends.[25]

The summer of 1936 was, however, as will be discussed later, devoted principally to French initiatives to reactivate their strategic cooperation with Poland, whose size made it appear the most readily usable eastern counterweight to Germany.[26] In October 1936, however, Gamelin turned his attention again to Yugoslavia. An opportunity to pursue the strategic dialogue was presented by the visit of the Yugoslav war minister, Marić, to unveil a monument at Marseille to the late King

Alexander. Once more Franchet d'Esperey was called upon, highlighting his function as a catalyst of Franco-Yugoslav cooperation. Gamelin, however, now turned to possibilities of future military collaboration. He profited by Marić's presence and took the Yugoslav minister on a tour of the French eastern frontier fortifications. The success of the visit marked a step forward in the strengthening of Franco-Yugoslav relations.[27]

Throughout 1937 the French worked industriously to develop their military cooperation with Belgrade and to reinforce what their intelligence said was a decrepit Yugoslav war machine, seriously run-down even for a defensive role. As Béthouart wrote in April 1937 to Gauché, head of the 2e Bureau in Paris, Yugoslavia had arrived 'on the agenda'. According to Béthouart the problem facing France was only in part concerned with Yugoslavia's enfeebled military capacity. An equal source of alarm, he suggested, was presented by the doubts sown among the Yugoslav political leadership as to the reliability and direction of France's own policy. Ninčić, a former Yugoslav foreign minister, had confided his fears that the Prince Regent was working towards a *rapprochement* with Germany. But what most concerned the French attaché was what he termed Prince Paul's 'inordinate preoccupation with the communist peril'. The Regent's fixation, feared Béthouart, was no longer confined to Yugoslavian politics; it had spilled over to take the form of distaste for a France that had ratified a pact with the Soviet Union and elected a communist-backed Popular Front government.[28] What Béthouart reported was the same disquiet that the advent to power of Blum had aroused among other friends of France. As France adopted a more cooperative attitude towards the Soviet Union, from the mutual assistance pact concluded when Laval visited Moscow in May 1935 to Blum's overtures for staff talks in early 1937, anti-communist politicians and officials in countries such as Belgium and Yugoslavia responded by seeking to restore their own freedom of action. Belgian leaders did not want their country 'towed like a trailer behind Popular Front France'; likewise, the Yugoslav government of Stojadinović sought to avoid entanglement in possible quarrels between the Soviet Union or France and Germany.[29]

Just as in Belgium, the orientation of the Yugoslav politicians was differentiated by the French general staff from the attitude of the Yugoslav military command. The latter, reported Béthouart, was 'every bit as anti-Soviet as the Prince [Paul] but has kept its confidence in us, or at least in our army'. The Yugoslav generals were expected to be able to block any change in their country's foreign policy inimical to France, and the attaché did not judge the Regent sufficiently powerful to prevail against the army. Thus France had to retain the confidence of the Yugoslav generals 'without which the game here will be up for us', argued Béthouart. He urged that cooperation be bolstered by expanding joint officer training programmes through greater Yugoslav use of the French staff college and by secondments of French officers to Yugoslav units. He also recommended increasing the number of visits to France and Yugoslavia by each country's commanders, including Gamelin himself.[30]

In the summer of 1937 the French seriously addressed Béthouart's proposals. There was no doubt that Yugoslav officers who had attended French military academies had benefited from their experience. But Béthouart warned that the returning Yugoslav officers often found their special skills ignored by their conservative superiors. Secondments of the French to Yugoslavia had produced even greater disappointments. According to a report from the attaché in July 1937, French officers attached to the Yugoslav artillery and engineer corps had been able to influence reforms, but the infantry, around which the Yugoslav army remained organised, had resisted French influence. Béthouart's main source was Commandant Molle, a respected officer whom the attaché had personally picked from his own old regiment of *chasseurs alpins* for secondment with the Yugoslav school of infantry. Molle painted a bleak canvas of an army that had undergone hasty expansion after 1918 and was consequently officered by men whose 'intellects and general culture' were 'utterly inadequate' for senior command. The French general staff was warned not to expect that a handful of its own middle-rank officers could foster innovation throughout the mass of the Yugoslav army. Molle argued that a beneficial transformation demanded that every Yugoslav officer preparing to serve as a Yugoslav school of infantry instructor be enabled to train in France. He urged that France shoulder a part of the burden of expense that this would entail. Béthouart supported these recommendations, adding that it was 'stupefying' to see how the 'Yugoslav infantry manoeuvres in 1937 just as it used to in 1912'. He closed with the warning that unless France was ready to commit money and men to the task, there was 'no great hope of ... improvement in the Yugoslav army's value'.[31]

When Daladier was apprised of these reports he concluded that the history of the secondments of French officers made their continuation 'useless' if seen from a purely military viewpoint. He offered, however, to continue the existing policy if the Quai d'Orsay 'thought it desirable from a political perspective' (although he demanded diplomatic support in such a case, through Quai intervention that would alert Belgrade to its army's 'basic failings').[32]

From Béthouart's position it did not appear that the maintenance of secondments would, in itself, be sufficient to halt a drift away from France on the part of Yugoslav leaders. Increasing German and Italian military power was, the attaché reported in February 1938, becoming 'strongly impressed' on Yugoslav public opinion. Creating fear in some quarters, arousing admiration in others, it was a factor 'which, however one looks at it, works in favour of the fascist states and against France'. As a countermeasure Béthouart asked permission to promote lectures about the French army and he sought authority to release French military films and non-classified data to Yugoslav audiences.[33]

In the event, these pleas proved enough to preserve the French policy of secondments in Yugoslavia, though the French authorities on the spot knew that any dividends would be reaped only in the long term. It was this distant goal, said Béthouart's successor, Colonel Merson, in 1938, that had to sustain those 'representing the French army here in thankless times'.[34]

There was, meanwhile, a clear understanding in 1937–8 of the danger of German influence gaining the upper hand. Indeed, whether measured by political or commercial criteria, the balance of foreign influence inside Yugoslavia had for some time been tilting away from France. In part the cause was the loss of King Alexander, who had steered a francophile course with what Béthouart called 'unshakeable fidelity'. Prince Paul, as well as Stojadinović, the prime minister after June 1935, was markedly less cordial towards France. Béthouart warned that Stojadinović was shifting Yugoslavia 'towards a policy of neutrality, in imitation of Poland and Belgium'. Citing the 'lamentable' spectacle that France had presented to its friends during the February 1934 crisis and subsequent ministerial instability, the attaché argued that it was understandable if his country 'inspired less and less confidence in her central European allies'.[35]

The process of Balkan realignment, in a sense unfavourable to France, had been gathering momentum since 1936. The Laval–Fabry strategy of Franco-Italo-Yugoslav cooperation against Germany had been undermined by Italy's breach with western Europe over Abyssinia. Subsequently Italy withdrew from the League of Nations, paving the way for the Rome–Berlin Axis of 1936. Not only did Gamelin's southern strategy founder as a result of these changes but, in November 1936, Mussolini himself offered to begin talks with Belgrade for an Italo-Yugoslav agreement, a pact which would build upon an earlier Italo-Yugoslav economic accord. In moving in these new directions

Stojadinović was attracted by the prospect of securing long-term peace in the Adriatic region. He pained the French by stating, according to Béthouart, that this result would give Yugoslavia more security than the 'support of an enfeebled France'. And in due course an Italo-Yugoslav pact was signed in Belgrade in March 1937 by Ciano, Mussolini's foreign minister.[36]

The pact did not stop Yugoslavia entering or maintaining other diplomatic partnerships. Nevertheless, it dealt French authority in the Balkans a heavy blow. It was an irony not lost on the French that Italo-Yugoslav cooperation, for which the Quai d'Orsay and Gamelin had laboured in the face of Yugoslav suspicions in 1934–5, had come about because of Axis diplomacy. The French understood that in 1937 the Italians, and the Germans too, had gone far towards seizing the political initiative in Yugoslavia – and, increasingly, in the Balkans as a whole. Even the visit that Stojadinović paid to Paris in 1937 could not disguise the change.[37]

In the case of Germany, her penetration in Yugoslavia was most apparent in the commercial sphere. Here, too, argued Béthouart, France had been a poor servant on its own account. Since the early 1920s it had enjoyed a near-monopoly in supplying Yugoslavia's automobile and aircraft markets. Yet in spite of advice to do so from Béthouart and Emile Naggiar, Roger de Dampierre and Raymond Brugère, the successive French envoys in Belgrade, the French authorities had failed to make France a significant market for Yugoslav exports. Since Yugoslavia's economy was a mix of an excessively large agricultural sector and an under-capitalised industry, it was becoming industrially underdeveloped by the 1930s. Stojadinović, who had served as finance minister before forming his own government, was particularly alert to Yugoslavia's trade imbalance. It therefore did not surprise the French envoys in Belgrade, although it did displease them, when, in June 1936, Hjalmar Schacht, the German economics minister, visited Yugoslavia. He brought an offer that was simple but seductive. Germany proposed a trade accord by which it would purchase, *en bloc*, the entire Yugoslav annual harvest. German payment was to take the form of transfers of machine-tools and manufactures. A wholesale extension of the Reich's sway over Yugoslavia, through a close meshing of the German and Yugoslav economies, stared France in the face.[38]

In June 1937 the German drive for greater influence throughout the Balkans was stepped up through a region-wide tour by Hitler's foreign minister, Neurath. The streets of Belgrade were 'bedecked with swastika flags' in the German's honour, whilst Stojadinović praised the development of 'fruitful collaboration' and 'close friendship' between Yugoslavia and Germany. Moreover, he claimed that this policy was agreeable to Yugoslavia's other allies. As Béthouart pointed out, this was untrue.

To console his interlocutors in the French war ministry, Béthouart assured them of the 'discontent in Yugoslav military circles at the external policy of their government'. The Yugoslav generals were depicted as being a dependable support for 'traditional' Franco-Yugoslav friendship, against the vicissitudes of the Yugoslav politicians. This suggestion from Béthouart resembled the way in which, at just this time, the French attachés in Brussels were encouraging Gamelin to treat Belgium's generals as a better guide than *their* government to the long-range direction of Belgian policy.[39]

In the Yugoslav case, the judgement of France's attaché was not surprising. For, in June 1937, he had been assured by the Yugoslav chief of staff, General Nedić, that a difference had to be drawn between the expedient twists of Yugoslav foreign policy and the fundamental francophilia of popular instincts. Weak, impoverished and poorly armed Yugoslavia, said Nedić, had, in the short term, to avoid war and reach accommodations with powerful and threatening neighbours. The day after this conversation Béthouart spoke to the war minister, Marić, who had just visited Prague. The Czech army had impressed the Yugoslav and the latter's optimistic tone again reinforced Béthouart's belief that Yugoslavia's soldiers offered a 'resistance to the *politique d'abandon* of the country's present government'.[40]

Back in Paris the analysis by the 2e Bureau of the trends apparent in Neurath's Balkan tour revealed deep French disquiet. A German political-economic drive for eastern European hegemony, a 'veritable "Drang nach Osten"', was discerned. Neurath's visits to Sofia and Budapest were interpreted as a design to isolate Czechoslovakia and to prepare a Hungarian–Yugoslav pact that would remove any teeth from the Little Entente altogether. The analysis judged that, of all the German initiatives in east-central Europe, it was their activity in Yugoslavia which was 'far and away of most significance for France' and demanded full attention. On top of this was the rebuilding of Mussolini's respectability in the Balkans, by means of the March 1937 Italo-Yugoslav pact. French intelligence warned that the Little Entente was 'losing cohesion' and that, 'whether or not concerted', the Germans and Italians were 'becoming the dominant element' throughout the region. Such developments menaced 'the results of fifteen years of French . . . policy'.[41]

Language as alarmist as this, from the intelligence bureau as well as from attachés, had the intended effect of alerting Gamelin. Special importance was suddenly attached to the visit, planned since spring 1937, of the Yugoslav and Romanian chiefs of staff, Generals Nedić and Sichitiu, to the French summer exercises to 'impress' them and show off French strength.[42] Gamelin's programme for his guests, from 13 to 20 July 1937, was calculated to dazzle them with the magnificence of the Bastille Day in Paris as well as to impress them by a display of mechanised units at Mailly Camp in Lorraine. Moreover, because of the success of Neurath's sojourn in Belgrade, Gamelin understood that the visit of the Yugoslav and Romanian generals to France needed to pass off as a *tour de force*. And, when it was suggested that Gamelin return Nedić's visit by attending the Yugoslav manoeuvres in September, the French seized the invitation with alacrity. Yugoslavia was no longer merely 'on the agenda', as Béthouart had put it as recently as April. It was being wooed in a manner that was peculiarly and passionately French.[43]

In early July, before Nedić's arrival, Gamelin received a detailed intelligence dossier to brief him about the Yugoslav. At fifty-four, Nedić was ten years his host's junior. He had wide European experience through service as Yugoslav military attaché in Bulgaria, in France from 1922 to 1923, and in Italy from 1928 to 1929. He had served as deputy-commander and then commander of the Yugoslav air force from 1929 until 1936 and succeeded Marić as Yugoslavia's chief of general staff in September of 1936. Perhaps his greatest attribute in French estimation was his 'readiness to show his francophilia' in Belgrade. The French intended that he become their anchor, to stop or at least slow down the perceived drift of Yugoslavia away from French influence.[44]

From the moment Nedić arrived in Paris, therefore, Gamelin rolled out the red carpet for him. The Yugoslav party, which included Béthouart and the French-trained head of Yugoslav military intelligence, Colonel Popović, was met by Colson and Gamelin in person. Sparing no expense, the French lodged Nedić and Sichitiu in the most luxurious hotel in Paris, the Crillon. And, from the outset, Gamelin deftly used his press contacts to flatter the visitors. *L'Echo de Paris*, edited by Gamelin's friend André Pironneau, extolled the trip (in words possibly suggested by Gamelin) as 'testimony to the solidarity' between the French and Yugoslav armies – a 'solidarity whose significance deserves to be signalled in present circumstances'.[45]

Throughout the week of their stay the visitors were treated to a programme demonstrating French past and present military glories. In addition to the ceremonies and receptions in Paris, it included attendance at the Mailly manoeuvres, visits to Verdun, Metz and Strasbourg and inspections of three Maginot Line forts. Calls were paid on France's luminaries of the past – notably Pétain and Franchet d'Esperey – and talks conducted with present leaders. The meeting with d'Esperey was attended by a French intelligence officer, who reported the conversation afterwards through Colson to Daladier himself. D'Esperey had cautioned Nedić about accepting help from 'tricksters the Germans' in developing Yugoslav war industries. It was the Hungarians who came in for the most vehement hostility from Nedić, who expressed fears that the Little Entente as a whole remained threatened by Hungarian ambitions.[46]

This visit by Nedić and Sichitiu, successful through the French judged it to be, nevertheless only represented a first step towards restoration of France's reputation in east-central Europe. More needed to be done. Consequently, in September 1937, Gamelin accompanied General Syrovy, the Czech army's inspector-general, along with a Polish delegation, to the main French manoeuvres in Normandy. Also present were Britain's secretary of state for war and Field Marshal Sir Cyril Deverell, chief of the Imperial General Staff. The latter reported afterwards his 'conviction' that the manoeuvres 'were subservient to an ulterior aim – the dominant desire to impress . . . the need for those present to cooperate with France'.[47]

Immediately after this, on 20 September, Gamelin himself travelled to the Yugoslav manoeuvres, the most elaborate and most important organised by Belgrade up to that time, and thence on to Romanian exercises. Accompanied by Petibon and by Dentz (who had succeeded Schweisguth as deputy chief of staff responsible for intelligence coordination), Gamelin was playing for high stakes. The question was whether France could retrieve the diplomatic and political initiative in the Balkans. Gamelin's mission was the first attempt to accomplish this aim.

What the commander-in-chief saw and heard confirmed that Yugoslavia was, in large measure, the weakest link in France's rusting chain of eastern alliances. Gamelin observed for himself that three years of reports by military envoys and intelligence had been all too accurate in this regard. The situation seemed restorable in Romania where the welcome for Gamelin was warm and the army showed signs of labouring 'strenuously' to improve itself. In Belgrade, however, Gamelin encountered a 'troubled atmosphere' and noticed evidence of the political opportunism of Stojadinović. The latter, himself scheduled to visit Paris in October 1937, was estimated to be concerned only to exploit Gamelin's tour to 'improve his own "press" in France'. Sensing the precariousness of the French position among the Yugoslav government, Gamelin used talks with Prince Paul and Marić, the war minister, to reiterate that France was 'faithful in her friendships' and would be found equally 'faithful to her commitments'.[48]

In practice, however, Gamelin came away deeply disturbed by what he had observed. Militarily, the Yugoslavs remained deficient in armour, anti-tank weapons and organised defences on their Italian frontier. They seemed insufficiently aware that, in twentieth-century industrialised warfare, individual soldierly valour 'was no longer enough'. Marić had shown the efforts under way to create arms-assembly workshops. But Gamelin was afraid that the expense of creating a modern armaments industry on the required scale was too much for limited Yugoslav resources. Politically the signs appeared to be even less encouraging: French prestige was evidently devalued and Stojadinović 'no longer inspired . . . confidence'.[49]

French anxiety mounted further when, just as the Quai d'Orsay was preparing in November 1937 to receive the Yugoslav prime minister, the latter journeyed to Rome. There, in early December, Stojadinović told Ciano that he opposed French plans to reshape relations with the Little Entente into an all-round defensive bloc. Furthermore, he announced that he was cancelling Yugoslavia's direct engagements towards Czechoslovakia. This was all most alarming to the French not just because the Yugoslav prime minister was soon to visit Paris but because the French foreign minister, Delbos, was himself preparing to tour east-central Europe.[50]

This December 1937 mission by Delbos may have had differing degrees of significance in respect to the different countries visited. In Prague it may have been an empty – even misleading – gesture of friendship. At least this can be argued by the acceptance of Delbos and Chautemps, his prime minister, in London at the end of November 1937, of British leadership to press the Czechs into concessions to Germany in order to prevent any conflict arising from the Sudeten question.[51] The appearance of Delbos in Belgrade, however, may not have been with a clearly defined agenda, but it was nevertheless important. For the French generals, especially, the initiative of the foreign minister was a welcome source of support for the labours of French military diplomacy.

The need for these fresh *démarches* was emphasised in the most vigorously phrased report Béthouart ever sent across Gauché's desk. Forwarded to Colson's office on 13 November 1937, this report argued that the manoeuvres attended by Gamelin had proven the Yugoslav army's lack of progress. Seven years of French assistance had 'neither matched our expectations nor repaid our investment'. Béthouart advised a review of whether it remained opportune to continue aiding

Yugoslavia at all. This, the attaché recognised, required a decision by the government. Nevertheless, he asserted, forceful action at both the political and military levels was necessary if Yugoslavia were to be kept in the French orbit.

The agenda that Béthouart suggested be recommended to the Yugoslavs for reform of their armed forces was dauntingly extensive. France, he urged, had to insist that more experienced Yugoslavs fill secondments and that these officers be empowered to promote changes on their return home. The greatest problem, containing an irony not lost on Béthouart, was that of the sclerotic and hidebound Yugoslav high command which, nevertheless, was the most reliable political support for pro-French policies. In an uncharacteristically patronising phrase, indicative of his mounting frustration, the attaché recommended that the French general staff prepare the alterations that it would wish 'to propose, *even to impose*' on its Yugoslav counterpart.[52] Delbos' visit to Belgrade was regarded as an important opportunity for the application of French government pressure to encourage the Yugoslav reforms. As French military intelligence in Paris argued in a note dated 21 November 1937, the foreign minister's mission offered a chance to 'convince the Yugoslav government that without a reconstruction of its army all help from France is doomed in advance'. Furthermore, it was observed, the continuation of French military assistance, if the Yugoslav government failed to express its readiness to help, would be justifiable only on specifically political grounds. Evidently these warnings sufficiently impressed Daladier that he spoke personally with Delbos about the issues at stake, before the latter left for Yugoslavia.[53]

The success of the foreign minister's stay in Belgrade was reported afterwards in decidedly ambiguous terms. Three commercial agreements were signed during the visit, whilst the communiqué after the talks with Stojadinović spoke of their place in the 'tradition of Franco-Yugoslav friendship'.[54] But a 'very well placed' French informant in Belgrade remarked that the reception for Delbos in the Yugoslav capital was marred by preventive arrests and widespread street disorders. Apparently Yugoslav policy was to be understood by the French as a cause of violent and divisive conflict.[55]

It was, in fact, extraordinarily hard for Gamelin and French intelligence to arrive at any clear view of the results of Delbos' eastern tour. Pessimistic reports of a decline of French influence were offset by indications of some revival of confidence. Béthouart, most strikingly, began to show a renewed optimism. In contrast to the disheartened tone of his autumn despatches, the report he sent Paris on 21 December ventured that success was attending France's two-part diplomatic counteroffensive through, first, the mission of Gamelin, then that of Delbos. This report, which reached Gauché, Colson and Georges, highlighted the francophilia of Yugoslavia's war minister, Marić. He had told the French visitors that he expected Italy to resume its hostility towards his country and that he therefore sought to prepare a *couverture* facing the Italians and capable of two or three months' resistance, along with the development of Yugoslav war industries. In these sentiments Béthouart claimed to detect evidence of the benefit of Delbos' mission and the basis for a more 'confident view' of future Franco-Yugoslav relations, driven forward chiefly by greater military cooperation. Paris should, he urged therefore, maintain 'and, if possible, extend' its assistance to Belgrade.[56]

French intelligence remained, however, more cautious than Béthouart. There were too many signs that Yugoslav external policy had become shifty and opportunistic. The 2e Bureau 'did not think' the hope of enhanced military cooperation 'justified any prediction as to general future policy towards France'. It suspected Stojadinović of resorting to an expedient search for good terms 'with as many powers as possible' and surmised that Yugoslavia was not so much returning to the French fold as pursuing a '"wait and see" policy'.[57]

Confirmation of the Yugoslav government's quest for amicable relations with Germany was not long in coming. In mid-January 1938 Stojadinović visited Berlin. He assured Hitler of Yugoslavia's abstention from pacts directed against the Reich. In return the German leader disavowed any territorial ambitions in the Balkans, expressing only a wish for greater economic outlets in south-east Europe. Many former tensions in Yugoslav–German relations, declared Stojadinović publicly, had arisen from a tendency in Belgrade to view European politics 'through French spectacles'.[58]

Stojadinović's statement sharply refocused the minds of the French on the fragility of Yugoslavia's loyalty towards France. Raymond Brugère, the French chief of mission in Belgrade since late 1937, accepted Béthouart's advice that France needed to promote her own interests more aggressively. In February 1938 Brugère began the campaign himself, by expressing his 'astonishment' to Stojadinović at the latter's germanophile declarations. When the Yugoslav leader retorted that friendship with France remained his policy's 'fundamental element', Brugère asked for evidence. More open defence cooperation and a greater place for French business in equipping Yugoslavia's war industries were cited as ways in which Stojadinović could show his sincerity.

Since Yugoslavia's government was endeavouring to remain on the fence at this time, it was alarmed by the candour and toughness of this French language. Neither Stojadinović nor Prince Paul wished to alienate the French completely and close down Yugoslavia's balanced position between the fascist and democratic camps. They therefore hastened to assure Brugère that Franco-Yugoslav relations still 'amounted to an "alliance"'. The Regent undertook to reinforce military cooperation. Meanwhile, Marić spoke to Béthouart and restated Yugoslav fidelity to traditional friendships. He emphasised his belief that, in the event of European war, the two countries would 'undoubtedly' be 'on the same side of the barricade'. But, in the interim, Yugoslav defensive resources were so inadequate as to require a temporary accommodation with the Axis. Yugoslavia would, said Marić, 'speak up' again and rally openly to France and Britain once it was militarily and industrially prepared.[59]

For Béthouart, the extension of general staff and industrial cooperation were the touchstones by which to estimate Yugoslav 'sincerity' and 'loyalty' in 1938. In the former area a major initiative occurred before the close of the attaché's eventful posting. This was the coordination of Franco-Yugoslav intelligence. A link of this sort had been mentioned first in July 1937 when Popović, head of the Yugoslav military intelligence section, accompanied the Nedić mission to Paris. Popović then sought Gauché's assistance and that of the 2e Bureau and Service de Renseignements to modernise the Yugoslav army's intelligence capability. Schweisguth, responsible at that time for military liaison and assistance, offered three forms of help: conferences between the intelligence assessment chiefs; sharing of information (with France concentrating on Germany, Yugoslavia on Italy); and training for the rudimentary Yugoslav agencies. Gauché, however, warned against France expecting too much from links of this sort. The 'greatest' and perhaps the only beneficiary, he cautioned, would be Belgrade. France was, he judged, unlikely to receive more than 'perhaps . . . fragmentary and uninterpreted' information on Italy. Popović apparently showed no interest in Germany. Moreover, the linkage was likely to embarrass Yugoslavia if its existence leaked out; the Yugoslav military attaché to Paris, Colonel Glišić, was anxious, according to Gauché, to keep the partnership 'very discreet'.

Consequently, intelligence cooperation continued to advance at a steady pace. Because of the political sensitivity involved, Gauché and Colson made no move until they received a written request from the Yugoslav general staff to begin the coordination. For the first six months after the Paris talks with Popović, therefore, it continued to be Glišić, Yugoslav attaché in France, to whom communication with the French army was entrusted.[60]

The intelligence link was fully opened in the spring of 1938. In February an invitation was sent to Gauché to visit Belgrade. The 2e Bureau chief was in Yugoslavia from 3 to 11 May. According to a report from Brugère to Georges Bonnet (who, in April, had replaced Delbos at the Quai), encouraging progress ensued. The Yugoslav chief of staff, to Brugère's delight, wanted the most fully developed of several levels of cooperation offered by Gauché. Brugère thought this a sign that his frankness with Prince Paul and Stojadinović in February had been effective. An intelligence link, Bonnet was advised, might prefigure a 'rekindled desire for – secret – collaboration' on wider questions. Far from disguising Gauché, the Yugoslavs insisted that he wear his uniform and appear in public. This appeared as a positive indication that Belgrade was not so intimidated as to seek the cloak of furtiveness around military cooperation. On the other hand, Marić expressly reminded Gauché that the agreement was a technical one, without political obligation and without prejudice to Yugoslavia's necessarily 'accommodating' stance towards Germany. Nevertheless, Brugère felt that the head of the 2e Bureau had pulled off a personal triumph in Belgrade, to France's 'greatest imaginable benefit'.[61]

Within a fortnight Yugoslav-French links were tested by the 'May weekend crisis', when Germany and Czechoslovakia partially mobilised over frontier incidents during the Sudeten elections. According to Brugère, important intelligence was furnished about Hungarian military activity during the alert, without any formal requests that might discomfit Yugoslav policy. The director of political and commercial affairs at the Quai, René Massigli, informed Daladier's military *cabinet* that the arrangements had worked 'very satisfactorily' and that 'nothing but good' from the foreign ministry's perspective could result from intensified military cooperation. The latter promised a way of educating Yugoslavia to a 'commonality of outlook' with France before a really serious European crisis occurred.[62] This interpretation by Massigli was consistent with his personal endeavours to maintain active support of the eastern French allies.

At least some French officials and their ministers had urged the French military chiefs to take at face value the Polish protestations of support which were offered by Colonel Josef Beck, Poland's foreign minister, as a gesture to France at the time of the Rhineland crisis.[63] But by 1938, the advocacy of a *politique de fermeté* such as this had become imprudent on Massigli's part. For, by 1938, French foreign policy was under the direction of Bonnet – and he was not eager to hear arguments in favour of reasserting French commitments to east-central Europe. Massigli soon felt the way the wind was blowing. Before 1938 had closed he found himself exiled to Ankara, as ambassador to Turkey, where he naturally found it harder to make his voice heard as he continued to work against the appeasement tactics of the foreign minister.[64]

In 1938 there was a decline in arms sales, technology transfer and industrial assistance by France to Yugoslavia. This decline largely offset the progress made by Béthouart and Gauché in improving Franco-Yugoslav general staff coordination. Like his counterpart in Belgium that year, Béthouart encountered only caution and introspection among his superiors on the question of supplying French munitions to friendly powers. Gamelin was obsessed with the military balance on the Rhine. He would look no further than the ratios of divisions and the state of the equipment inventories in the French and German armed forces. Moreover, Gamelin increasingly regarded the unsatisfactory statistics of French arms production as a barometer: the lower the output and more delayed the deliveries, the more circumscribed were the strategic options which he was willing to lay before French ministers.

There was, of course, no shortage of precedents nor any lack of contemporary practitioners in the art of cutting the coat of strategic counsel according to the cloth of military readiness. The near-collapse of French aircraft production in 1937–8 undermined the morale of La Chambre and Vuillemin and percolated out from them into the wider reaches of the government, where it sapped the self-confidence of Daladier. The Munich crisis most starkly showed this process at work. The delays in the completion of French arms programmes reinforced the ingrained reluctance of commanders to release equipment that reached the French factory gates – let alone French combat units. Only a supernatural visionary could, in these circumstances, have relinquished equipment to refit the army of a small and distant ally. The improbability of such altruism was evidenced by the conspicuous absence of spokesmen arguing for such a policy to be applied even to help as close a friend as Belgium. It has been justly remarked that the neglect of a 'sustained effort to strengthen the military capabilities of the allies ... through systematic and large-scale material aid was striking'.[65] But it cannot be said to have been a surprise.

There is, perhaps, a case for saying that, in a Europe-wide perspective, French policy on this question of assistance with armaments and technology for friendly powers was stingy and short-sighted. But, at the time, no greater vision was apparent on this issue in the policies of Britain or the United States. Viewed from the Hôtel Matignon, or the rue Saint-Dominique, France appeared beleaguered. Ministers and generals responsible for French security would have been irresponsible, if not irrational, had they proposed to divert the inadequate output of

French defence industries into the direct protection of foreigners – even friendly ones. It is understandable, therefore, that French arms cessions were rare – and usually consisted of obsolete material when they did occur. The impediment to timely procurement of new French weapons remained one of industrial bottlenecks, not financial emasculation. Nothing that French military envoys did, in Prague, Belgrade or Brussels, was enough to counteract this 'France first' policy over French rearmament. The policy was too powerful, too pervasive – too natural. 'The role of military representatives abroad was beneficial in smoothing differences but could not be of decisive importance.'[66]

The French army's place in the diplomatic and economic dimensions of Franco-Polish-Czechoslovak relations has undergone a meticulous scholarly appraisal. But the Paris–Belgrade dialogue in general, and Franco-Yugoslav material and financial dealings in particular, have been neglected hitherto. Béthouart, at the time, was outspokenly critical of the scant sympathy or comprehension in Paris for Yugoslav economic weaknesses. The trouble was that Gamelin did not become significantly aware of these problems for himself until the autumn of 1937 when he visited Yugoslavia. Even then, he may not have understood fully the severity of Yugoslavia's shortcomings and the scale of French effort needed if they were to be redressed.

French reluctance to sell arms or grant production licences was an obstacle with some history to it in the 1930s. It was first met by the Yugoslavs when Marić, then chief of the general staff, submitted a list of munitions desired from French suppliers during the Paris meetings of June 1935. Faced by requests for new Brandt mortars, and modern light tanks, as well as for older anti-tank guns and ammunition, the French generals hesitated and said the request had to be presented formally through the Quai d'Orsay. In the case of the old equipment, the Quai found the war ministry willing to cede less than 10 per cent of Yugoslav requirements. In regard to new weapons, no objection was raised to the acceptance of the orders as long as adequate financial terms were fixed.

In practice, Yugoslavia's problems in making payment were as great an obstacle as French under-production to a Franco-Yugoslav military alliance. Yugoslavia's deepening economic quagmire had led to a negotiated moratorium on her repayments for equipment supplied under a 300 million franc French credit of 1924. In spite of the inability of Belgrade to finance her military requirements, in early 1935 the French consented to a further loan of war material itself, with a book-value of some 10 million francs. Also in early 1935 Brandt signed a 25 million franc contract to supply 300 mortars and their ammunition, offset against twelve years' worth of Yugoslav tobacco exports to

France. Further negotiations, however, stalled completely, in respect of the material sought by Marić that summer. Shortage of Yugoslav foreign exchange, remarked French intelligence, 'ruled out' any 'normal commercial transaction'. What was at issue was a matter for the French government: whether, in its own financial difficulties which were creating rising pressure for devaluation of the franc, France could 'financially underpin' Yugoslavia.[67] In effect, French inability to support the even more seriously ailing Yugoslav economy set the real parameters for Franco-Yugoslav strategic collaboration. As Gamelin and his colleagues learned during 1936–8, France's manufacturing crisis provided the clear and negative answer to the question of whether France could meet the strategic challenge to its interests at this time by use of industrial or financial instruments.[68]

What Béthouart sensed most, as he completed his attachment in 1938, was not so much a failure as a fragility to the cooperation that he had helped rebuild with Yugoslavia. In February 1938 French intelligence was reminded of the mixed blessings resulting from the French, Czech and Romanian pacts with Russia. For the Yugoslav government remained convinced that these accords increased, and did not diminish, the risks of European war. The Yugoslavs again stated that their own conduct would be entirely calculated according to the circumstances of the moment if hostilities arose from the Moscow connections of France or the other two members of the Little Entente.[69] In May 1938 Béthouart reported growing concern in Belgrade at German aggressiveness since their Anschluss with Austria. The attaché added that he observed Yugoslav disillusionment, albeit 'terribly late in the day', with Stojadinović's tightrope walk between the western and fascist blocs. Whether playing political, economic or military cards, warned Béthouart, the Germans appeared to possess all the strong suits in the Balkan poker game.

To preserve Yugoslavia's independence required staunchness from the Yugoslavs themselves and 'effective help from outside'. On the former count the French feared that a demoralised ruling clique in Belgrade had sapped the fortitude shown by the Serbs in 1914. Béthouart nonetheless thought that the Franco-Yugoslav intelligence agreement showed how devices existed for removing the tarnish from Franco-Yugoslav relations. Even though they could not instantaneously rebuild Yugoslav military power, Béthouart urged that these devices be utilised. In the first place, he argued, French assistance offered the only means to make possible Yugoslav resistance to German entreaties. Secondly, further French vacillation appeared likely to condemn Yugoslavia to a reluctant absorption into the German–Italian camp –

into 'vassalisation'. This would protect Germany's south-eastern flank and give it a 'free hand' throughout central and eastern Europe.[70]

Why was so little done to follow Béthouart's advice? One explanation lies with the structural economic problems of France. These prevented it rearming as fast as Gamelin and Daladier wished in 1937–8. Perhaps it was true, as Pierre Cot had suggested to the CPDN in July 1936, that 'One has a hold on a country once one has penetrated it industrially.'[71] But France at this time lacked sufficient military-industrial power even to meet the direct and pressing needs of its own defence. It cannot, therefore, be accounted strange that it refused – or reduced – commitments to become the arsenal for the nations of eastern Europe. France understandably remained 'more interested in what her allies could do for her than in what she could do for them . . . alliances not [being] charities'.[72]

The failure or refusal of the French authorities to pick up a tune from calls to action heard from envoys like Béthouart can also be explained in terms of the dynamic nature of French external policy. French government advisors on defence and strategy were, certainly, inward-looking to a fault. The ministry for war and national defence, under Daladier's long tenure, seldom looked outside 'worst case' analyses, rarely questioned its own timidity. Yet the high command was not a monolith. Colson and Schweisguth mourned the brief 1935 alliance with Italy. Georges, too, was a conservative whom Daladier classed as a Weygand protégé and distrusted accordingly. Yet there were counsellors who advanced alternatives: General Lucien Loizeau, deputy chief of staff during 1935–7, who heatedly argued against Colson and Schweisguth in favour of a full military alliance with the Soviets, following his attendance at Russian manoeuvres in 1935; General Henri Giraud, military governor of Metz from 1937 to 1940 and commander of the Seventh Army in the Battle of France, who told Britain's military attaché in Paris in September 1936 that he thought active French support for the Little Entente was 'really crucial' (even if he denounced the Franco-Soviet pact as of 'no benefit at all').[73] Gamelin himself held views somewhere in the middle: no enthusiast for the Soviet Union, he was, nevertheless, not an advocate of French withdrawal from the east either – as his favour for the Poles revealed. Gamelin's discomfort throughout these debates on the eastern engagements arose from his discernment of every side to the French dilemma. He understood both the scale of French military unpreparedness and the risk of politico-strategic collapse if it were admitted. The result was a policy towards the east during 1937–9 that posterity has not considered honest.[74]

Yet military cloth with such variegated hues as these was inevitably tailored, as strategic advice, into a coat of many colours. It is not surprising that French diplomacy too, during 1937–9, failed in assuming any uniform or unvarying pattern. The suggestions of envoys such as Brugère and Béthouart, it must be recalled, were not the garb in which Bonnet wished to clothe French foreign policy as he strove to keep France at a safe distance from the developing crisis over the Sudetenland. Béthouart's pressure for France to reassert itself economically and militarily in Yugoslavia was unavailing, therefore, not just because France had insufficient means to follow his counsel. His exhortations were set aside at least as much because senior foreign policy-makers did not wish to hear them. Indeed the close of Béthouart's term in Belgrade overlapped with Bonnet's (partly coded) articulation of a policy of disengagement from east-central Europe. As against this, it might be reiterated that it was in June 1938 that Massigli, who was among Bonnet's most senior officials at the Quai d'Orsay, supported the Belgrade envoys' recommendations for a deeper rather than shallower commitment to Yugoslavia. Perhaps the most that may be concluded from these contradictory indications is that, in mid-1938, the French strategic policy debate remained alive and appeasement not quite unchallenged.[75]

By the year's close, however, the effects of French fear and forfeited self-confidence on relations with their eastern allies were undisguised. The insistence of Vuillemin, the chief of air staff, on three separate occasions – in January, March and August – on the incapacity of French aviation was the strongest single consideration that prodded a reluctant Daladier down the road to Munich.[76] The dishonour of the September 1938 settlement was never something that Daladier tried to deny. He was dismayed by the blindness to the French capitulation shown by the crowds which hailed him as a peacemaker when he returned to Le Bourget airport. But the popular reaction was not one which he had any difficulty understanding. Faced by the spectre of apparently imminent war, Daladier reflected, as Anatole de Monzie (one of his cabinet ministers) understood, 'the hesitations within the soul of France herself'.[77]

The fear of the destructiveness of aerial bombing reinforced Daladier's attraction in 1938 to the 'fortress France' configuration to defence that had first tempted him two years earlier. The intuition he felt for his compatriots' hopes and fears, ordinarily his strength as a domestic politician, was Daladier's weakness when he needed to be a statesman of strong nerve. A chill had overtaken the French, at least from about 1936, at the possibility of having to wage another war. This was not only understood and indeed shared by Daladier, it was an object of concerned comment from France's friends and allies. If the Rhineland had been one illustration, the elaboration of the policy of non-intervention in Spain's civil war even by a French Popular Front government was another.[78] The British ambassador in Paris by the autumn of 1936 reported it to be the 'reliable' opinion of French people that their country was 'unlikely to obey a call to arms in the future unless the frontiers of France are actually invaded'. He thought it certain that on any future issue 'on which Frenchmen are called to sacrifice themselves for their allies [the government] will have to ... convince this country that its own future is at stake'. The envoy's perceptive conclusion was that it was 'problematical' whether direct military assistance would be offered to the Little Entente unless French territory itself was also violated.[79]

In Gamelin's own case it was not until after Munich that a recovery of purpose and confidence reappeared. But by December 1938 he was counselling that France endeavour to stiffen the resolve of the remaining free European nations to defy Germany. His memoranda and his talks with ministers became informed by a sense of forthcoming fundamental struggle: one concerned with morality and ideology even more than with a balance of power. He wrote at the turn of the year that it was France's continuation as a great power that lay at issue in the months ahead.[80] Complementing these sensibilities – but indicative of the continuing French cynicism – was the energy which Gamelin devoted in the first half of 1939 to refurbishing plans for a *guerre ailleurs* – a war on another front to be waged by French allies, a war by proxy.[81] Gamelin grasped, however, that this design could no longer be fashioned out of the old arrangements in the east. For, as Britain's military attaché in Paris, Colonel William Fraser, noted at the end of 1938, 'the Little Entente' had 'ceased to have any military possibilities, at any rate in the early stages of a war'.[82] Gamelin's belated determination to establish an eastern rampart therefore brought his focus back to Poland, his favourite eastern ally since 1936 and one whose capabilities he seemed almost wilfully to overestimate. It was thus from an unrealistic starting point in 1939 that Gamelin attempted no less than a ground-up construction, against a ticking clock, among the frightened and suspicious states in eastern Europe that still remained independent of the spreading Nazi hegemony.[83]

9 Men or material: Gamelin and British support for France

By 1938 it was apparent in Paris, to politicians, military chiefs and diplomats alike, that the worsening European crisis was beginning to close in on France itself. Throughout the previous year the threats posed by the fascist powers seemed comparatively distant or at any rate indirect. French intelligence had been indefatigable in monitoring the steady and relentless build-up of Germany's military preparedness. But, during the extended lull since the remilitarisation of the Rhineland, Hitler had made no further expansionist move. Indeed Germany, as well as Italy, had become involved and discomfited in the unexpectedly long civil war in Spain.

Yet the French and British had managed to confine the Spanish conflict – albeit precariously – by cooperating to fashion the policy of non-intervention, as well as through the Nyon conference and the policing of Spanish coastal waters by the French and British navies. Despite the fears at its outset, the civil war had not dragged Europe as a whole down into the dark abyss of a continental war. This was, by the start of 1938, no mean achievement for the authorities in Paris and London. Europe was not free from war, still less from the prospect of war in the future; but most of Europe still remained at peace. Hitler, judged French intelligence, was going through a phase of consolidation. The French themselves had not stood idle in 1937, however. Rather, the year had witnessed some attempts to mend broken diplomatic fences and pursue *démarches* to improve France's position. There had been a deliberate decision to meet the challenge of Belgian neutralism by developing deeper and covert cooperation between Gamelin and senior Belgian military chiefs; there was the belated but bold attempt by Gamelin and Béthouart, supported by the mission of Delbos, to restore French influence in the Balkans, through liaison with the Yugoslavs. One senses that French leaders, during the course of 1937, retained a good deal of faith in themselves and in their ability to redress a perilous but not hopeless international and strategic situation. This was the last year in which there were clear instances of France acting independently, exercising policy options entirely of its own choosing, demonstrating some belief in its own capacity to control or at any rate substantially shape the shifts in the European distribution of power.

In all this, no little part was played by the sense of detachment that was still commonplace in Paris. The threats evident throughout 1937 were, in a French perspective, in the middle distance rather than near at hand. Democracy in Spain was under attack; the independence of Austria and the territorial integrity of Czechoslovakia looked liable to imminent menace. But these were not direct dangers to France itself. By the end of 1937, however, the chill wind stirred by a Germany that was once again preparing to move was making itself felt in Paris. A whole range of indicators in December 1937 came together ominously, to suggest that the European crisis was entering a different phase, and one directly dangerous to France.

In the first place, reports from Belgrade after Delbos' visit there in December 1937 soon made it plain to the French that the outward success which attended the foreign minister in Yugoslavia was not going to translate into an unequivocal Yugoslav resumption of full alliance with France. Secondly, the talks in London on 29–30 November 1937 between Delbos, the French prime minister Chautemps, Chamberlain and Eden revealed the narrow limits to British readiness to uphold any Czech or Austrian firmness in the face of German claims in central Europe.[1] Thirdly, the British review of their own defence and rearmament priorities, in the report by Sir Thomas Inskip, minister for coordination of defence, was approved by Chamberlain's cabinet on 22 December 1937. It reaffirmed – indeed made yet more pronounced – Britain's preponderant concern for home and imperial defence and its relegation of assistance to friendly continental countries to the lowest of its priorities.[2] Finally, the close of 1937 was a bleak time for France's own defensive programmes. Gamelin was confronted by mounting delays in re-equipping virtually every category of his ground forces, with particularly acute shortages in the key tank and artillery armaments, whilst the air force's expansion and modernisation was stalled because of the manufacturing crisis in the aeronautical industries.

Was it, Gamelin had to wonder, time for the French authorities frankly to confess their military shortcomings and plead for the British to provide their defensive security? Ever since the *entente cordiale* of 1904, France had enjoyed a special relationship with Britain and had benefited from Britain's concern to preserve a European balance of power. The resulting Franco-British security relationship was – and indeed remains – complex and marked by defence interests that at best may be described as circumstantially convergent.³ This was as evident in the 1930s whilst the two powers sought common ground on which to cooperate, as it was in 1940 when defeat and the lure of armistice to some French leaders rent the powers apart.⁴ With its maritime-imperial interests and obligations around the globe – and being an island-nation off the European continental shelf – Britain lacked a natural affinity with French perspectives.⁵ In particular, Britain could share French strategic concerns about the menace of the German army only grudgingly. Without land frontiers the British simply could not feel as threatened as the French by the increasing size and offensive power of the revitalised land forces which Hitler was building after 1935. Traditionally Britain looked to maintain its home defence as well as its imperial territories and communications by naval power. To this priority was added, in the early 1930s, considerable attention to aviation as the new dimension of war from the skies threatened a different means of bypassing Britain's maritime security. On wholly natural and sensible grounds, the British continued to attach least importance in their defence planning to their army; the French, for reasons every bit as sound, continued to attach greatest importance to theirs.

Thus the overlap, the commonality, between French and British grand strategies, was bound to be extremely circumscribed. This had been so even before the First World War. Then the British attached far more value to their naval agreements with the French of 1912–14 (assigning fleet responsibilities for the Mediterranean and Channel theatres according to mutually convenient deployments) than to the arrangements reached in those years between the respective army general staffs to enable the operation in France of a small British Expeditionary Force (BEF) of five or six divisions.⁶ The French, however, once Joffre reshaped French mobilisation and concentrations by his introduction of War Plan XVII during 1911–14, set great store – much criticised by subsequent commentators – by the presence of these British land forces on their left flank in the event of Franco-German hostilities.⁷ In the light of the fundamentally dissimilar French and British geo-strategic concerns and priorities, the actual pattern of close and massive-scale Franco-British military cooperation on the western front during the First World War was highly misleading. The deployment in France of vast and eventually conscripted British armies, supported by imperial divisions from Australia, New Zealand, Canada,

South Africa, India and elsewhere, was a wildly inaccurate gauge for the French as to the course that British governments intended their foreign and defence policies to take after 1918. In sum, the unparalleled extent of the partnership between France and Britain between 1914 and 1918 was not generally regarded by the British as the creation of a precedent.

It was in this sense, as much as from a humanitarian standpoint, that the 1914–18 conflict was so widely felt in Britain in the 1920s to have been the war to end all wars. Hence, as the first postwar decade gave way to the second, the era of Gamelin's responsibilities in France, the divergences in geo-strategic interests between France and Britain appeared to policy-makers in London to be more significant than the remaining matters of common concern. At best, partnering each other more or less petulantly to try to preserve the Versailles settlement and to make the League of Nations work, France and Britain made uncomfortable bedfellows.[8]

At first sight, against this background of so fragile a political understanding, it was paradoxical that Franco-British relations were marked at the military level by a strong carry-over of the comradeship and friendliness that had been forged between the two armies in the fires of battle during 1914–18. Yet this was perhaps not so surprising. The immensity of the military effort which Britain and its empire had made in France during the First World War, and the heavy loss of life that British forces suffered, impressed the French. The grimly beautiful and immaculately maintained imperial war cemeteries that sprang up throughout Flanders, Artois and Picardy moved the French and reminded them in permanent fashion of the sacrifice of manhood which the two Allies had borne together in common cause. The battlefield tours run by the instructors at the British army's staff college at Camberley, for the rising officers who would form Britain's military chiefs of the future, were matched by the visits organised by the British Legion and similar veterans' groups in order that war widows and old comrades could pay homage at the gravesides of fallen friends or family. The ties between the French and British armies, and more significantly between the officer corps, thus survived not just the conclusion of the First World War but the subsequent vicissitudes of the two countries' peacetime relations. Particularly between the field grade officers and the generals, experienced professionals who knew and respected their own kind when they met them, strong and enduring bonds remained in place during the early 1930s.

The evaluations which at this time were made by the French and British general staffs of the quality of each other's army were, however, strikingly asymmetrical. In the broadest sense, before examining the appraisals that the two armies formed of one another, it should be noted how the attention of historians to these questions has been conspicuous in the main by its absence. The part played by intelligence gathering and intelligence analysis has, it is true, ceased to be the 'missing dimension' – as once it was – of the scholarship devoted to the history of diplomatic relations and strategic planning. Indeed, with illuminating consequences for our understanding of issues of modern foreign relations, security policy and war itself, intelligence history finally has been brought out of the closet.

Breaking away from sensationalism, spy stories and mole-hunting, the 'new intelligence history' has earned for itself a cloak of respectability. This has resulted from the subject being practised by reputable academic scholars and propagated within specialist journals established especially for the genre. Yet the research undertaken in this 'new intelligence history' has thus far, with few exceptions, attended to uncovering and interpreting the efforts of nations and their intelligence agencies at investigating potential adversaries – at 'knowing one's enemies'. Very little, to date, has been done to examine what might be termed 'assessing one's allies (or friends)'.

Any attentive search of the diplomatic and military archives of the French, British, Belgians, Germans, Americans and no doubt others demonstrates very quickly, however, that considerable energies and extensive resources were expended by all the powers before the Second World War on surveillance, or at least observation, of friends and allies. That this should have been so – and remains so with rather rearranged combinations of nations today – is perhaps unremarkable. Choices in defence and diplomacy have, after all, historically contained an allowance for perceptions about friends and allies, just as they have taken account of evaluations of potential adversaries. Two of the most obvious and important national security decisions that any power can take are, on the one hand, the contracting and renunciation of alliances and, on the other, the entry into a war or the adherence to neutrality or non-belligerence. In the case of both these options or decisions, the balance is as likely to be tipped one way rather than the other by calculations about the powers who are with you as it is by estimations of those who are against you. Possibly these considerations have appeared to be so obvious that most writers about Franco-British relations in the appeasement era have simply left them aside, taken them for granted. Yet, for whatever reasons, historians have been shy about extending their researches into French and British policies to include an inquiry into the military and strategic appraisals that each nation explicitly made about the other. This must be undertaken, however, if the particular cooperation that Gamelin sought from Britain between 1935 and 1940 is to be understood.

The first point that should be noted is that the French, in Gamelin's time, expended a prodigious effort in documenting British political developments and national policies in general, and in compiling continually updated dossiers on Britain's strategic capabilities in particular. The French missions in London in the 1930s were staffed by highly trained, experienced and carefully selected diplomatic, commercial, financial and military experts. The envoys and attachés posted to the French embassy at Albert Gate in Knightsbridge furnished Paris with copious and comprehensive reports. Every conversation with a representative of Britain's armed services, political class or business community was swiftly relayed to the appropriate quarters in the Quai d'Orsay, rue Saint-Dominique or rue de Rivoli. Moreover, the attachés of the French armed forces supplied their 2e Bureaus with regular despatches which closely and continuously monitored the vital functions of the corresponding British service. These reports were usually compiled fortnightly, and more frequently in times of acute international tension or abnormal internal change (such as the modifications in men and methods effected by Leslie Hore-Belisha at the War Office, in the closing months of 1937). Supplementing these despatches was the annual report on the host country. These, in the case of French civilian and military envoys in London, were astonishingly compendious *tours d'horizon*, often more than two hundred pages long, that ranged far beyond a narrowly defined remit of military affairs. They joined detailed accounts of the country's political evolution over the previous twelve months with a sectoral analysis of economic performance, budgetary policy, events in colonial and other overseas territories, and foreign relations.[9] The redoubtable research, as well as the liaison, undertaken by the French military missions and military attachés makes it absolutely accurate to label these officers as 'soldier-diplomats'.[10]

The result was that the French general staffs and particularly the army general staff under Gamelin (which had the largest network of attachés), received copious reports concerning virtually all aspects of the countries in which they had representatives. To these essentially open sources of information and evaluation was added the intelligence obtained clandestinely, and channelled through Rivet's Service de Renseignements. In sum, Gamelin and his fellow defence chiefs in the navy and air force appear to have had networks at their own disposal which kept them as well, perhaps better, briefed about Britain – its leaders' policies, its outlook towards France and Germany, the state of its military forces – than the Quai d'Orsay itself.

On 15 January 1935, six days before his sixty-eighth birthday, Weygand delivered his 'last testament' before the CSG and bowed out from the high command.[11] Gamelin's unchallenged tenure, as commander-in-chief designate as well as chief of staff, had begun. What were relations like between the French military and their British counterparts, and how did Gamelin envisage using the entente with Britain to strengthen the security of France?

At this mid-point in the 1930s, the French army command's relationship with its opposite number across the Channel was as cordial as its expectations of the British army were low. Just two days after Gamelin moved into the saddle, at the HCM meeting on 23 January 1935, Pétain gloomily asserted that Britain's forces were so weak as to be of no worthwhile help for French defence. The marshal doubted even that the RAF represented a fighting force of any use to France. General Maurin, then the war minister, concurred. 'British help', he opined, 'would at the present moment be less than was provided in 1914. The British army has not made any progress. It's for show, for the parade ground.' Pétain repeated his belief that there were no really reliable or militarily powerful friends for France anywhere in Europe and that, in its diplomacy and strategic planning against the mounting German threat 'too much store was not to be set on external cooperation'.[12]

It had not always, indeed not for long, been thus. In the late 1920s and early 1930s the British army had been admired by the French as a supremely professional and even progressive force. In particular, French observers were greatly impressed by the lead that the British showed in pioneering a return to mobile operations, in searching for means to restore the possibility of breakthroughs and decision on the battlefield – in escaping from the static killing matches of 1914–18. The ferment in military thinking and the wide scope for innovation that prevailed in Britain, especially in regard to mechanisation, was envied by the French. Britain's leading theorists, notably J. F. C. Fuller and Basil Liddell Hart, were followed with especial interest. Not only did the British produce some outstanding military thinkers in the 1920s, they also led the way in field trials with experimental mechanical forces. This flowering of theory and practice made a favourable impression on French army leaders.[13] Whereas they spent the 1920s with their gaze fixed firmly on Germany and the possibility of its revival to challenge Versailles (and thus they decided to build the Maginot Line), the British had no immediate and obvious enemy at that time. This permitted some scope for innovation and experimentation by progressive officers interested in exploring what tanks and motor transport could do, in a relatively relaxed climate conducive to developing theories quasi-scientifically.

The remarkable British exercises on Salisbury Plain with various combinations of mechanised and motorised units, between 1927 and 1931, were an inspiration and an example to the French army. The forces involved were, at first, miscellaneous and ill-assorted. But lessons were learnt each summer, equipment improved and the trials culminated in the successful manoeuvres of the 1st brigade of the Royal Tank Regiment in 1931. In widely reported exercises, the formation, directed by Brigadier Charles Broad, moved some 180 tanks as a whole and triumphantly concluded the exercises by traversing several miles in dense fog before emerging as if by clockwork to parade past the army council's watching dignitaries. Equally important for the reputation gained at this time by the British army as a leader in experiments with mobility was the publication in 1929 of the 'Purple Primer', the first official manual on mechanised warfare. This was the booklet *Mechanised and Armoured Formations*, by Broad (its more popular title deriving from the colour of its covers). At the core of Broad's thinking was the conviction that tanks should be employed chiefly to exploit their firepower and shock action in attack and that they should preferably be used in independent formations.[14] Britain, reported France's military attaché with undisguised admiration, was 'at the head of the nations that have undertaken modernisation ... through the use of mechanisation ... which will assure her of rapid and decisive results in the event of hostilities'.[15]

To the fore in evincing interest in the experiments of the British army in the early 1930s were Weygand and Gamelin. Both generals saw in military modernisation of their own forces the way to offset the three emergent threats to French security at this time. These threats were, first, the growing evidence of clandestine German military stockpiling in contravention of Versailles; second, the accession to power of National Socialism in Germany, with its aggressively revisionist foreign ambitions; and, finally, the diminishing prospect of a verifiable arms control agreement issuing from the Geneva disarmament conference, where deadlock was resulting from German insistence on 'equality of rights'. Weygand, though a political reactionary, was receptive to the benefits to be gained from the French army's adoption of modern technology and greater mobility. He had initiated a programme, sustained by Maginot whilst the latter was war minister in 1930, to motorise seven of the twenty active peacetime infantry divisions. Gamelin supported this faster introduction of mechanical equipment to counterbalance the army's impending reduction in size with the onset of the 'lean years' for the conscript contingent, twenty years after the First World War. Weygand's invigorating spirit was apparent in the re-introduction in September 1930 of corps-scale manoeuvres for the first time since 1918. They indicated, according to the previously critical British military attaché, 'the transition of French military mentality from an undue tenacity to the methods of trench warfare ... to a more vigorous policy of instruction on modern lines and especially directed towards solving the problems connected with a war of movement'. Although the formations involved were handicapped by the absence of half-tracks that French industry had failed to deliver, the British attaché realised that Weygand and Gamelin were progressively transforming the French army. He was impressed 'by the improved methods of movement and concealment of tanks which had hitherto usually been puerile', and concluded that the French command had 'really woken up' to the ways in which land war could be made a mobile affair once again.[16]

The combined effects of hopes for disarmament and the onset of the Depression meant, however, that both Britain and France slipped back in their military modernisation in the years from 1932 to 1935. The experimental mechanised force in Britain was disbanded. This was partly to be explained by the belt-tightening imposed by the Treasury on the War Office in the wake of Britain's 1931 sterling crisis. Partly, however, it resulted from the increasing caution of Field Marshal Sir George Milne in the latter part of his tenure as chief of the Imperial General Staff from 1926 to 1933. When, in that last year, he handed over to Field Marshal Sir Archibald Montgomery-Massingberd there were still only 4 established tank battalions compared with 136 infantry battalions in the British army; furthermore, just 2 out of 20 cavalry regiments had converted to mechanised equipment. The traditional military conservatives had regained the ascendancy.[17]

The problem for French military leaders was that this loss of impetus, innovation and inspiration across the Channel occurred at the precise moment that France's own need for alliance support was becoming plain. Financial retrenchment after 1931 had imposed a straitjacket on the War Office and left the British regular army, as well as the Territorials, living from hand to mouth.[18] As the British general staff struggled to keep a professional army worthy of the name in 1932 and 1933, their French counterparts noted with growing dismay the decline of the forces which they had admired only three or four years before. Throughout 1933, 1934 and 1935, the despatches from General Robert Voruz, the French military attaché in London, and from Major Cuny, his assistant, formed a lengthening tale of woe for their readers in the 2e Bureau and in the French war ministry. They amounted to a dispiriting catalogue of belt-tightening, creeping conservatism, foreshortened experimentation and still-born initiatives.[19] To Weygand and Gamelin it became apparent that the British army had been relegated by the British government to a threadbare service, the lowest priority for the extra funds which were committed to remedying the 'worst deficiencies' of Britain's fighting forces following the investigations of the Defence Requirements Committee in 1933–4.[20] Over and above these shortcomings, the reports from Voruz and Cuny in 1934 warned French military chiefs that the poor pay and unattractive conditions of service in the regular and Territorial forces were creating a crisis of recruitment throughout the British army. Re-enlistments were slumping; new recruits were not coming forward in the required numbers. In almost every branch of both armies, it was correctly reported, units were suffering from the manpower shortage and some had been skeletonised in order to maintain others – usually sister battalions of the same regiment – near to regulation strength.[21]

French attitudes to the decline of the British army changed quite dramatically as a function of mounting nervousness about the scale of German remilitarisation. Thus, in January 1934, Gamelin observed what was occurring in Britain with a mixture of disappointment and relaxed dispassion. He expressed himself with equanimity when reporting that the 'initial assistance of English land forces would be of secondary value' in any combined Franco-British operations to defend France. What mattered, he felt, was for France to be able to rest secure in the knowledge that it had Britain's resources to rely on for the long and arduous haul to victory if another war with Germany ever came about. Gamelin and his colleagues at this stage were confident that French armies were capable of *defending* France. It was for the phase beyond that, for going on to win a war, that they recognised they would need what Gamelin called the 'highly valued eventual British assistance from the political and moral . . . the maritime and aerial points of view'.[22]

By June 1934, however, it was becoming plain to the leading French generals just how intractable were their difficulties in refurbishing their own army on the scale and at the speed that they considered the German threat demanded. As has been discussed earlier, Pétain's tenure of the war ministry after the 6 February crisis proved to be no more satisfying to Weygand and Gamelin than the previous left-centre administrations. Pétain was uncomfortable in the world of parliamentary compromise and cut-and-thrust, and seemed to lose much of his self-confidence once put in charge of the executive direction of a great government department. At any rate he obtained only modest increments in funding for the army and betrayed a dyed-in-the-wool conservatism towards the newer manifestations of military power, such as armoured forces and motorisation. He appeared to Gamelin to be uncomfortable in his role as minister and essentially negative in his influence. Weygand, for all that he shared Pétain's right-wing political outlook, was also disillusioned by the marshal's performance at the rue Saint-Dominique. It marked no more than a 'truce', as one officer put it, between the command and the civilian authorities in the tussle over the size of resources devoted to the army.[23] Yet the generals had harboured the expectation that Pétain, as a professional soldier, would reverse the Cartel's compressions and increase the money, material and men available to the army.

Against this background of disappointment with Pétain, it was disconcerting for Weygand to see for himself, on visits to Britain in the summers of 1933 and 1934, the accuracy of French attaché reports on the British army's loss of the momentum of reform. The armoured manoeuvres which Weygand watched at Sandhurst and Tidworth in June 1934 were particularly discouraging in the light of the exciting and inventive activities which the British had been undertaking not long before. After talking to Montgomery-Massingberd and to General Sir Cyril Deverell (who was to succeed the former as chief of the Imperial General Staff in 1936), Weygand 'shook his head and went away', according to another senior British officer, 'hoping that we really had something better than what he was shown'.[24] The trouble was that, by this point, they had not.

As Gamelin approached the start of his own single-handed direction of French military policy, he was left in no doubt by the French general staff's antennae in London of the twin obstacles in the way of British military aid to France. The first was the technical one of the British army's enfeebled condition. The other was the powerful political aversion in Whitehall and Westminster to any repetition of the sort of continental military commitment made in 1914–18, at the eventual cost of over 700,000 British lives.

Paradoxically, the problem that was to dog Gamelin throughout his years of command, in respect of securing a British expeditionary corps or 'field force', was that the British found it hard to take French needs seriously. Few strategists in Whitehall, and even fewer Treasury officials, found anything persuasive in arguments made in 1934 for expending resources to equip a continental field force. German rearmament was still on a comparatively modest scale. French land armaments remained overwhelmingly preponderant and certainly well able to defend

Men or material?

France itself, along with neighbours such as Belgium. It was not open to the French to protest that they had lost the edge over Germany which they would require for offensive operations, should they be needed, to respond to German aggression against the Little Entente or other eastern allies of France. The British had always looked with distaste on these French entanglements, regarding them as a form of neo-imperialistic aggrandisement even in the 1920s. Nobody on the Defence Requirements Committee, or in the circles around it in London, had a convincing case to offer for reinforcing the British army in 1934–5 – still less for configuring it to become an expensively equipped and highly mechanised corps destined to operate as an adjunct to the French. The money recommended for the British army by the committee was halved, after consideration by cabinet sub-committees, by the end of July 1934. The secretary of state for war, Lord Hailsham, conceded that the British army had been demoted to the 'Cinderella . . . of the forces'.[25]

As Gamelin clearly understood, none of this helped French security problems. In particular, none of this helped Gamelin find a solid and long-term alternative source of military support to the increasingly self-willed Belgians. None of it helped him as he sought means of overcoming the growing threats of the 'lean years' to the size of the French army, and of the defective French munitions industry to its refurbishment with modern, technologically advanced combat material. Gamelin learned what an uphill battle he would face if he wished to persuade the British to devote more resources to forces that could support France. His informants were British officers themselves, as well as the French envoys in London.

In the former category, Gamelin enjoyed a professional understanding and a 'close friendship' with Montgomery-Massingberd.[26] In 1933 the latter was taken on a tour of the Maginot Line construction sites, shown the limited amount of new material entering French army service and told of the cancellation in 1932 and 1933 of all French manoeuvres above divisional level, as part of the Cartel's budgetary economies.[27] No doubt Montgomery-Massingberd assured Gamelin of his own belief that Britain ought to maintain an army trained and equipped at least to deploy to the Low Countries to shield the Channel ports, in the event of another war with Germany. But he would also have explained how little influence this view had in the British Committee of Imperial Defence and among ministers, where there was a fixation with air defence of the British isles and naval modernisation against Japan. With army funding slashed, the British general staff were under orders to configure their army unspecifically, as a 'general purposes' force able to intervene in theatres as varied as the Far East, Egypt or Europe.

However candidly Montgomery-Massingberd outlined the remit of British military preparations to Gamelin at first hand, the scant succour that the French army could expect from Britain was spelt out unambiguously by French envoys in 1934–5. In April 1934 the military attaché in London underlined that Britain's army had 'as an objective to respond to the complex and contradictory tasks of colonial as well as continental warfare. The regular army is unable to prepare itself for one single type of war.'[28] Then, just as Gamelin was preparing to succeed Weygand at the close of 1934, the attaché warned that British land forces could not be counted on to participate even in operations in defence of metropolitan France itself. The operations of a strictly land-based nature, he reported, 'would be entrusted to Britain's eventual allies, the British expeditionary corps cooperating only under exceptional circumstances'. Furthermore, 'all the opinions' that the attaché had been able to gather indicated that the field force's use would never again be 'in the manner of 1914'; if a continental intervention was again forced on the British, they would 'not juxtapose or mix their expeditionary corps with an allied army' but would 'choose a separate ... theatre where Britain would enjoy sole mastery'.[29] Shortly afterwards, in April 1935, the French assistant military attaché confirmed the growing obsession of British leaders with 'aerial and naval threats hanging over the metropolitan [United Kingdom]'. He urged that it be recognised in Paris that this preoccupation, added to Britain's need to mobilise imperial resources before embarking on a major war, might keep Britain on the sidelines – at least initially – if France clashed with Germany.[30]

The political and psychological reluctance of the British to give any undertakings that might limit their freedom of action in the event of a crisis on the continent had not been grasped sufficiently in Paris until this time. Too much had been read by the French into the British signature of the Locarno treaty, as one of the guarantor powers, in 1925. Just as French diplomatists and defence chiefs had slipped lazily into regarding the military convention with Belgium between 1920 and 1936 as an alliance (because it suited French interests), so they tended, with the passing of the years, to treat Britain's undertaking at Locarno as a guarantee of armed support – even though the British had always refused to hold staff talks that would have been essential to give a guarantee any military meaning. In both instances French attitudes are to be explained by the familiar, but in these cases dangerous, habit of the wish becoming father to the thought. It was this self-induced misunderstanding that accounted for the extent of French surprise when Britain took fright in 1934–5 at proposals to hold staff conversations and discuss how British defence reorganisation might be coordinated with French defensive shortcomings. Weygand, during his June 1934 visit to Britain, got the frostiest of receptions when he argued that, to dissuade Germany from policies that might result in war, Britain ought to issue an unconditional declaration of military solidarity with France. His suggestion that the rise of tensions on the continent justified Anglo-French military staff consultations of the pre-1914 variety likewise fell on stony ground. The British were chary of ties that might involve them in conflict between third parties. They quite reasonably did not want their foreign policy made, or its options constrained, by decisions in Paris, Prague or Warsaw. Even the mere presence of Weygand in Britain was denounced in some British press quarters as a painful reminder of unwanted killing matches. The 'memory of . . . secret talks before the war', complained the *Daily Herald*, 'is still too near home for Englishmen' – a remark which the French military attaché took pains to report to Paris.[31] Nor, even a year later, after the reintroduction of conscription and an airforce in Germany, had this resistance diminished. Then, in May 1935, the now-retired Weygand, paying a private but authorised visit to London to stress France's heightened security anxieties, found that the British government 'was still opposed to the French and British staffs working together in order to conclude "arrangements of the 1912–14 sort"'.[32]

Gamelin, responsible for trying to meet the German danger by this point, now found himself face to face with the recurring dilemma of his stewardship of French military policy. He could ring loud alarm bells and indicate a precipitate decline or delapidation of the French armed forces, in the hope of shocking allies and friends into changing their own strategic dispositions so as the better to assist France. This, however, carried a problem of credibility in 1935–6 – not so much because the French army was thought to be problem-free but because the German peril could not be portrayed convincingly as beyond France's capacity for containment and response. Alternatively, Gamelin could maintain a low-key reaction, taking care not to over-dramatise the situation, and work discreetly behind the scenes to win a more sympathetic hearing in London, and elsewhere among French allies, for the claim that France alone could no longer risk a war to uphold the 1919 status quo. This carried some risk too: that Britain and the allies would mistake – or prefer to interpret – such *sang-froid* as continuing underlying self-confidence. In this case the danger was that French pleas would not be taken seriously at all and that no helpful shifts in diplomacy or defence policies would be forthcoming, whilst all the while the Franco-German power balance steadily swung further in the Reich's favour.

In the spring and summer of 1935 Gamelin chose the second of these two courses, and with his colleagues put a brave public face on the French strategic situation. Privately, in the January meeting of the HCM, Pétain had bleakly forecast (as we have seen) that French strategists should thenceforth frame their plans solely on their estimations of what France could do for itself, all the allies and friends being allegedly too vulnerably located or too disarmed to count for much. It was interesting, therefore, that official spokesmen adhered to a bullish attitude in their pronouncements at this time, even under questioning from the well-informed critics of the Chamber army commission. These parliamentarians were not in the same league as gullible journalists perpetually chasing a good story and turning only occasionally to the more exotic aspects of defence, such as the installation of the Maginot Line's underground railway or the unveiling of a new tank. The commissioners took national security and the welfare of the army extremely seriously. Almost all of them had arranged with the leaders of their parliamentary groups to be nominated to the army commission because they wanted to be – because they had an enthusiasm for and sincere interest in the condition of French defences. Many, as we have seen, had extensive military experience in their own right, as was the case with Maginot, the commission's president before he became war minister in 1928, and Fabry, the president in 1935. Commissioners were too knowledgeable to be dismissed with platitudes from the ministry or general staff. Indeed, more often than not, they were accustomed to being taken into the confidence of the army commanders, who appreciated the potential value of their support to secure the voting of credits in the face of the more uncertain sympathy for the military in the massed rank-and-file of the full Chamber.[33]

On 21 March 1935, Maurin, who was then war minister, met the Chamber army commission in the wake of the parliamentary debate six days earlier which had endorsed the *de facto* return of the French army to two-year military service. Pierre Taittinger, Republican Federation deputy for Paris, champagne tycoon and founder of the proto-fascist Jeunesses Patriotes, seized the occasion to lambast the government for complicity in the decline of France as a European power. France's international position, contended Taittinger, was far less strong than in 1914. In regard to relations with Britain, he suggested, a time of 'disappointing discoveries' had been reached.[34]

There was, no doubt, a considerable validity to Taittinger's observations. He had been on the army commission for a number of years and was well connected. Strongly anglophile, he not only visited Britain on business but was, until the Fall of France in June 1940, a leading light on the Anglo-French parliamentary committee. This organised fact-finding tours, exchanges and liaison between Westminster and the Assemblée Nationale. Taittinger was also closely identified with Weygand's policies in 1933–4, sharing the general's right-wing political disposition and even lobbying, in December 1934, against Maurin's wish to promote the republican Gamelin to succeed to the combined posts of commander-in-chief designate and chief of the general staff.[35] It may have been this antipathy between Gamelin and Maurin on the one hand and Taittinger on the other that accounted for the lack of candour from the war minister in reply to the commissioner's hostile questions in March 1935. Whatever the motive, Maurin airily dismissed Taittinger's warning that Britain no longer had the ability to send five first-class battle-worthy divisions to aid France in an emergency, as it had done in 1914. The 'question had changed aspect', he responded; Britain was 'pushing her aviation at the present moment' and he argued that the build-up of the RAF had become 'the greatest guarantee of peace in Europe'. France, he told the parliamentarians, should take heart from such positive developments and not dwell upon the different forms of assistance furnished in the past in different circumstances. It was vital for France to appear self-assured in order to justify and sustain the leadership of its alliances. 'If they know that we have confidence in ourselves', he concluded, 'the others will come to us.'[36]

Such robust views were held with far less conviction, however, behind closed doors in the rue Saint-Dominique and the Invalides. The spring of 1935 witnessed the appearance of the skilled labour shortages and deficient productive capacity in the engineering industries that, from then on, acted as a severe brake on French rearmament. This was especially a cause of concern for those, like Gamelin, anxious to strengthen the French army by putting the accent on modern equipment rather than on increased mass. As a result, doubts grew in Gamelin's mind about whether France could afford to acquiesce passively in British strategic policies which placed such low priority on building a land force fitted to help France hold its own in a continental struggle with Germany. Hitler's first panzer divisions were established in 1935, and French intelligence knew it. Yet France still had just the solitary light mechanised division (DLM) constituted in 1933, and only three prototypes of the heavy Char B. If there were to be an arms race in mechanised and tank forces, the omens were not favourable to France's chances of staying level, let alone of pulling ahead.[37]

Britain, however, was credited with large reserves of appropriate industrial capacity. Some strategists in Paris, Gamelin to the fore, decided that they should press the British to apply this resource rather more to restoring Britain's lost primacy in mechanised forces than to air and naval building programmes. French military diplomacy *vis-à-vis* Britain now aimed to convince the British to fashion a small but highly mobile and hard-hitting field force. It wished for armoured divisions trained and equipped to function as the insurance policy for the French front, to counterattack and eliminate any breakthrough by hostile mobile formations seeking a quick decision to pre-empt the full development of French power by the mobilisation of the nation-in-arms. British fears of a repetition of the raising of mass armies, as had been required in the First World War, were thus to be allayed. This time, against the new German threat, French generals like Gamelin and Maurin would put their emphasis on asking the British only for what the French army was finding it could not create by itself: a mobile armoured reserve corps.

There were signs that this would henceforth be the French goal in defensive cooperation with Britain when the military leaders convened in Paris the very day after laying the smokescreen about French self-reliance before the army commissioners. The briefing dossier for the HCM meeting on 22 March 1935 alluded to the peril of a German *attaque brusquée*. This menace was said to arise from the 'notable advantage' attributed to Germany at the outset of a conflict, by virtue of the 'number and quality of her elements capable of immediate action'. The value of the defensive assistance of British air squadrons and ground forces 'from the very first days' was underlined, to support the conclusion that French policy needed to apply itself 'above all' to the task of 'organising ... the immediate support of England'.[38] French envoys, it was urged, needed to grasp every opportunity to persuade British officers, officials and politicians not only to confirm the permanent establishment of the British army's solitary tank brigade but also to forge ahead with further mechanisation. 'Our immediate support by British armoured brigades ... would appear to be indispensable', advised one French general to Reynaud in April 1935 at the time of the distraction from de Gaulle's *armée de métier* scheme.[39]

Amongst their military counterparts in London, the British general staff, there was some sympathy for Gamelin's concerns. In their annual review, in April 1935, the British chiefs of staff restated their support of 'close and friendly' relations with France. British interests, they added, could not all be secured by the RAF and navy; 'the integrity of the Low Countries' was said to be 'of greater importance than ever ... and the Army must be prepared in conjunction with the French to attempt to deny those countries to German invasion'.[40] But the British government remained unwilling to embrace the implications of the military recommendations, on account of the political unpopularity of renewed continental commitments and the need to prioritise the British rearmament programme so as neither to overspend nor overstretch Britain's modest armaments industry. Moreover, when every allowance has been made for problems of resources and politics, it must be said that the British army's leadership in the mid-1930s was unimaginative and unsophisticated. Montgomery-Massingberd was not a keen supporter of tanks and armoured warfare; indeed he detested J. F. C. Fuller, who was edged into retirement as a major-general in 1933, and he obstructed the advance of other progressive senior officers. Furthermore, though it was an article of faith for the British general staff to say that Britain had to prepare to deny the continental Channel coast to an enemy, little definite idea existed as to the operations that an expeditionary force would conduct if it was sent to north-west Europe. Critics, such as the astute chancellor of the exchequer, Neville Chamberlain, who had his hands on the purse strings of rearmament, were able to starve the army of money and manufacturing capacity so long as the War Office failed to produce a rationale for larger land forces as persuasive as those produced by the Admiralty and air staff for their services.[41]

Many British observers and government advisors thought it more cost-effective to encourage measures that would deter Germany from ever again attacking the Low Countries, rather than invest in forces to aid the French meet the attack if it happened. It was, though not expressed in such modern terminology, a crude preference for a policy of deterrence over one of defence or war fighting. Thus the British began to favour the fortification by the French of their frontier with Belgium, continuing the Maginot Line as far as the waterlogged terrain allowed and preparing inundations and minefields in the lowest-lying areas. Colonel Heywood, the British attaché in Paris, reported, for instance, late in 1934, that France planned to rush their one DLM and three motorised divisions onto advanced defensive lines in Belgium in the event of German aggression there. Correctly, he added that the lighter positions which France had begun constructing on its border with Belgium since mid-1932 were in the nature of a back-stop, a second line. Britain, he judged, had an interest in encouraging the French to develop this frontier line more seriously because the additional obstacle it would represent 'will make the Germans hesitate to repeat the out-flanking movement . . . so successful in 1914 and may induce Germany to attack France on the battlefield selected and prepared by the latter on the north-east frontier' (the Maginot Line).[42] Implicit in this argument was the corollary that such a canalising of Germany's offensive options in the west would enable the French army to cope on its own. This would obviate the need for British intervention altogether. As Sir Esmond Ovey, Britain's ambassador in Brussels, added in a paper about Belgian security a month after Heywood's report: 'If the French defended their own frontier from Metz ... on to the sea, there seems to be no valid reason why the German ... should see any advantage whatever in invading Belgium.'[43] Furthermore, the British foreign policy experts were untroubled by the reconstruction of his forces that Hitler carried out in 1934–5, crediting this as a defensive measure and Germany's generals 'with the belief ... that in a modern army conscripts are unsuitable for ... offensive operations'. Germany's adoption of compulsory service in March 1935 was therefore interpreted not as a harbinger of aggression but as the onset of 'a considerable reduction in efficiency as compared with the long-service voluntary army she has hitherto possessed'.[44]

With such views prevalent in British policy-making circles in 1935, the French began to appraise the magnitude of the task facing them. As France's military attaché in London warned, much of the army in Britain was little more than a base depot to service imperial garrisons. Moreover, the government had decided against compensating for numerical weakness either by massive infusions of modern equipment or by expanding the Territorials. Therefore, Gamelin was told, any British field force deployed to Europe in the foreseeable future would be only a third as strong as the BEF of 1914. 'This regrettable situation', the attaché emphasised, 'does not appear to be due for improvement over the next few years.'[45]

Gamelin now realised with crystal clarity that getting the British to do for the French army what it could not do for itself would be a two-fold challenge. In the first place, there was going to be the problem of convincing them to commit, arm and train a field force for continental service at all. Secondly, there would be the problem of inducing them to shape this force in the image of French requirements, as a homogenous corps of powerful armoured divisions for the counterattack role.

To overcome British abhorrence of a continental commitment and to get them to divert some of their rearmament effort from their other services to the army was to engage Gamelin's energies and diplomatic skills for the rest of the decade. In pursuit of his goal he knew that he had to convince the British authorities that European defence could not simply be left to his own army. Therefore, along with his senior subordinates, he set about characterising the nature of Germany's military threat in a different way. His objective was to sow doubts in London as to the correctness of supposing that German aggression would take the form of strategic air bombardments accompanied by a limited war of position on land. Instead, Gamelin and other French defence spokesmen began peddling the line that, even in the west, Germany would initiate a war by a lightning mobilisation and menacing ground offensive. General Georges, reported Britain's military attaché in Paris in May 1935, affirmed that 'the Germans would employ the bulk of their air force in close cooperation with their ground forces and not, as many people thought . . . on the civil population'.[46] This was only the first of many French statements that were designed, during 1935–9, to impress on the British the increasing probability of Germany attempting a knock-out offensive through the Low Countries in the opening stage of a war, with the goal of defeating Holland, Belgium and France and catching an insufficiently prepared Britain at its mercy.[47]

Throughout 1935–6, therefore, Gamelin was walking a tightrope. He was endeavouring to frighten Britain into raising priority for fitting out a mechanised field force and earmarking it for deployment in France, concerted through staff talks with Gamelin's own officers. At the same time he was striving not to suffer the by-product of adverse publicity about French military deficiencies. For the latter, he appreciated, might see his tactics backfire and reinforce the inclination of many British politicians, and some military leaders, to steer clear of all involvement with the French. He had to avoid making France appear too vulnerable. Yet at the same time he had to spread just enough of a suggestion that the swift intervention of a powerful, mechanised British corps might be essential to help the French army keep the continental Channel coast secure and German air bases at arm's length from Britain.[48]

Meanwhile Gamelin had to advise the French governments on the implications of deteriorating great power relations in Europe as 1935 wore on. He did so in the full knowledge of the poverty of support that could be given by Britain if war threatened. The British army's 'assistance immediately, and even after several months of war, would be almost nil', he reported in July 1935 to Fabry (Maurin's successor as war minister). This consideration underlay Gamelin's enthusiasm for the benefits of Italian friendship as a strategic makeweight against Germany – benefits expressed in the June 1935 Rome accords with Badoglio.[49] In his outlook on Italy's Abyssinian aspirations in the late summer and autumn of that year, Gamelin displayed the qualities of a cynical *realpolitiker*. He argued, in his memoirs, that France had no vital interests in Abyssinia and, as a great imperial power, could not adopt a stance of anti-colonialism to deny Mussolini's wish for territory overseas. He was candid in confessing that he thought France should have endorsed Italian expansion in East Africa if Mussolini had contrived an annexation under a cloak of League of Nations approval. Furthermore he was quite unabashed in asserting that the French would probably have turned a blind eye to a carve-up behind some legalistic fig-leaf from Geneva. 'What did the form matter so long as you get the basis as you want?', he admitted saying to Badoglio when the Italian chief of staff was in France attending manoeuvres and having meetings in Paris in September 1935.[50]

This opportunism by Gamelin was complemented by the Italophile connivings of Fabry and, of course, Prime Minister Laval. Montgomery-Massingberd, Gamelin's guest for a second visit to the Maginot Line and the 1st DLM in August 1935, discerned the balancing act that the French were trying to sustain. Any 'break with Italy on account of Abyssinia would be most unwelcome', he reported to the secretary of state for war, Lord Halifax, 'and . . . Monsieur Laval will get that advice . . . The attention of General Gamelin . . . is obviously concentrated on the German menace . . . and what Italy likes to do in Abyssinia looms very small indeed.'[51]

Mussolini's heavy-handed aggression in East Africa in the winter of 1935–6 in the event forced Gamelin off the fence. As the general later conceded, 'Whatever the importance of our new relations with Italy, it was imperative for us to maintain solidarity with London. Italy was important for us; England was essential.'[52] In the short term, the British were militarily weaker than the Italians; they could be of less immediate help to restrain Germany by a show of force. But if France even suspected that it might again have to wage war against Germany, Britain would be an indispensable partner in a way that the mercurial Mussolini and the fragile Italian strategic economy could never be.[53]

Given the rising French concern about Germany, it was in the nature of an opportunity for Gamelin when the possibility of conflict with Italy brought the British knocking on doors in Paris in search of strategic support. The British sought, and obtained, naval and military conversations between November 1935 and January 1936.[54] In these a precautionary coordination was arranged between French and British forces in the Mediterranean, against the danger of Italy's Abyssinian war escalating into a wider conflict. The French met a number of requests of importance to the British – notably in regard to opening their bases and port facilities. The talks between the air force and army delegations, held in Paris from 9 to 12 December 1935, were devoid of benefit to France in the short term. Britain restricted the agenda to the Mediterranean crisis and to precautionary planning against Italy. General Sir Ronald Adam (who, as deputy director of military operations, headed the War Office team at the talks), believed till his last years that the meetings were 'valueless' and that Gamelin 'stood me an excellent lunch but it was clear that nothing was going to happen'.⁵⁵

This, however, was an excessively negative judgement. For one thing, the British departed reassured about the security of their fleet bases and territories in the Near East, *vis-à-vis* Italy. Furthermore, from Gamelin's perspective, French cooperativeness towards Britain in the Mediterranean was reckoned to be a lever by which to improve France's bargaining position on the issue of real concern in Paris – German rearmament. The Abyssinian affair had forced London to consent to military consultations, albeit of limited scope. These were regarded as a significant gain by the French, even if their remit did not yet extend to the defence of north-west Europe. Gamelin welcomed any strengthening of military cooperation with Britain, irrespective of its source. The 'resumption of staff talks', Schweisguth reported him saying, could 'be very usefully developed *vis-à-vis* Germany'.⁵⁶ The growing likelihood of Hitler attempting to remilitarise the Rhineland in 1936 was what French strategists intended to use to induce the British to broaden the compass of the consultations.

Hitler's coup in the Rhineland on 7 March 1936 overtook the rather leisured pace of French military diplomacy on this question. The French were not ready when Hitler made his move; in his timing, the dictator literally stole a march on them. Evidently, Gamelin and his associates had seriously overestimated how long they still had in early 1936 in which to persuade the British of the need to formulate a common response to a German ultimatum or violation. Neither the French generals – Gamelin, Georges, Schweisguth – nor the foreign policymakers such as Flandin and Léger had finally determined what they wanted from Britain at the moment the crisis materialised.⁵⁷ The correspondence about the eventuality of a remilitarisation that passed between Flandin, the foreign minister, and Maurin, the war minister, in February 1936, indicates that the French government and its senior counsellors thought they would have until after the French parliamentary elections in April–May before Hitler acted.⁵⁸ The British, too, showed no urgency during the first two months of the year as they unhurriedly considered whether to meet the French to agree how to react in the event of remilitarisation.⁵⁹

In pursuing their diplomacy with London in such dilatory fashion the French authorities in general, and the Quai d'Orsay in particular, were negligent. It was not as if a timetable that proved to be approximately accurate in regard to German moves had not been estimated by French military chiefs. In February 1935, according to a conversation reported to Brussels by Belgium's ambassador in Paris, Gamelin was 'experiencing fears with respect to the spring of 1936'.⁶⁰ From September 1935 onwards the Service de Renseignements and 2e Bureau of the army were specific in advising of signs of German activity preparatory to remilitarisation.[61] In addition, in many circles including the general staff and retired commanders like Weygand, the Chamber's ratification of the 1935 Franco-Soviet mutual assistance pact (which occurred on 27 February 1936) was expected to be seized by Hitler as a pretext to move on grounds of 'encirclement' of Germany.[62] It is customarily argued that a reason the French were nevertheless taken partly unawares on 7 March was that ministers had only one eye on the international situation, the other being on the domestic electoral campaign against the surging support for the Popular Front.[63]

As far as it goes, this interpretation has some force. Undoubtedly Flandin was concerned with the fortunes of his party, the Democratic Alliance. (This was in the middle of a reorganisation and membership drive that he had instituted to halt its decline after its poor showing in the 1932 elections.)[64] The Radicals were divided amongst themselves: some, including Albert Sarraut, the caretaker prime minister, were in office in coalition with the centre-right, whilst the bulk, under Daladier, were bidding to win power after the elections in conjunction with Blum and Thorez.[65] All this is familiar ground in accounts of the Rhineland episode and explains why the French political class was badly placed to have a clear foreign policy at the ready or even to improvise decisively after Germany moved.[66]

The equanimity shown by Gamelin, however, was born of quite different considerations. Study of the French military documents makes it apparent that he all along discounted any recourse to force to turn German troops back out of the demilitarised zone. He did stay true to his belief that political decisions – and the acceptance of war most of all – were not in his resort. As Schweisguth noted him remarking in one of the meetings between generals during the crisis, the soldiers had not to 'set themselves against virile decisions', only to oppose 'madcap solutions'. Characteristically, he declined to add any definition of his own of either contingency.[67] It seems most plausible to infer from his statements and behaviour that Gamelin never estimated there to be more than an outside chance that Sarraut's government would order him to march French soldiers in to clear the Rhineland after a German *fait accompli*. His own counsel, as is well known, helped make the government's selection of a military riposte quite unlikely, for he advised that the army could not risk any action unless the government decreed general mobilisation. Furthermore, he estimated that if the Germans resisted a move to turn them out of the Rhineland the result would be a lengthy war in which the military stalemate would require full-scale

British assistance to bring about Germany's defeat. This was an unappealing vision of 1914–18 all over again.[68] As a deliberately discouraging army staff memorandum put it four days after Hitler's coup: 'a deep penetration into the Rhineland, where we would run into not just the forces that are there but very quickly into the main weight of the German army, would necessitate the action of several armies, that is to say, the total mobilisation of our forces'. By a notorious inflation of numbers, counting labour corps, SA and state police as combat forces, the French army staff concocted a German strength in the reoccupied zone of 295,000 men or some twenty-one or twenty-two infantry divisions.[69]

It was hardly surprising that Sarraut, Flandin and the majority of other ministers opted to temporise and meet the German remilitarisation with talk rather than force. It is apparent that Gamelin never believed any other French reaction to be realistic. He had therefore played his part, through the pessimistic language of his military appraisals, in ensuring that his own prophecy became self-fulfilling. A close examination of the French documents substantiates this reading by revealing how, from before the onset of the crisis, Gamelin had decided to use remilitarisation to draw Britain into a closer and more permanent defence arrangement with France.[70] The affair, and particularly the politico-diplomatic talks whilst Flandin was in London, between French, British, Belgian and Italian ministers from 10 to 19 March, was therefore treated by Gamelin and the other French military chiefs as an exercise in obtaining long-term compensation from the British, not in inflicting any instant retribution on the Germans.[71]

Since Gamelin regarded the Rhineland's reoccupation as both inevitable and unopposable he viewed the event itself as not so much a crisis but more an opportunity. What mattered, he judged, was that it should not pass without France gaining some advantage in exchange for the lost demilitarised zone. The specific form of compensation that was desired is evident from the records of talks between the French military leaders. Gamelin told Schweisguth that Britain's military attaché had come to ask in mid-February what cooperation would be desired from the British in the event of remilitarisation. Gamelin had apparently replied that he would want to see a battalion of British troops sent to Metz, whilst Colson wished to get the British linked into the French air early-warning system. Study of what economic sanctions would most be felt by Germany was also proposed.[72] Gamelin developed this objective of securing a continental commitment from London in a further meeting with Georges, Colson and the French air and naval chiefs on 19 February. He noted the desirability of securing a 'permanent' standing deployment of British soldiers on France's north-east frontier, so 'that any German aggression would be directed not just against us but also against England'. Behind Gamelin's thinking must have been the time-honoured argument that Britain could not but commit itself to the hilt in future, if the life of a single British grenadier were taken on the continent. Though, in the longer term, Gamelin wished the British to constitute a particular type of small and powerfully armoured field force, he understood that the crucial first stage was to wring the commitment of troops to France in principle out of the British government.[73] The goal of the French military – as the army's 2e Bureau put it on 18 February 1936 – was the construction of an 'Anglo-Franco-Belgian bloc whose massive solidity would be compensation for the loss of the Rhenish "no man's land"'.[74]

But, in spite of warnings received from their envoys in London, French generals were still underestimating the depth of British opposition to substantive defence commitments in Europe. (Georges had some inkling, for he minuted cautiously, on the 2e Bureau's 18 February note, that 'everything rests on the willingness of England to tie herself to France'.)[75] Voruz, the military attaché in London, drove home the magnitude of France's problem in a despatch of 11 March. This stressed the unsympathetic British press reaction on the morrow of the reoccupation. The papers, he reported, censured the way in which Germany had acted; but their main concern was the need to pick up the pieces and rebuild good relations with Hitler, not to upgrade the *entente* with France.[76]

Suspicion that the British would not oblige France by a show of enthusiasm for new strategic arrangements had been voiced already in the improvised meeting of the CSG called by Gamelin on 9 March. The general warned his colleagues at that early juncture, noted Schweisguth, that he had the 'Impression of great reticence on the English side.' He agreed that the earliest possible resumption of Franco-British staff talks should be a French objective. Later that day Schweisguth was told by Petibon – who had met the military attachés of the Locarno powers – that the British attaché was showing 'the least sense of urgency'.[77]

In view of these unpropitious omens, Gamelin sent Schweisguth to London from 17 to 23 March to talk directly to British military chiefs and make a first-hand assessment of the prospect of gaining a greater level of British military support. His discoveries, however, were not encouraging. Voruz, as well as the ambassador, Corbin, estimated that British forces would refuse to be integrated 'under any circumstances' into a French deployment plan; they were more likely to be prepared as the 'core of a Dutch–Belgian disposition' because of the War Office's emphasis on the significance of the Low Countries to British security.

There were, anyway, only two British infantry divisions available and Montgomery-Massingberd told Schweisguth 'General Gamelin knew full well that it is more than a five-minute job to create an army.' Heywood, who had just been relieved after three years as military attaché in Paris, tried to comfort Schweisguth by asserting that francophile sympathies were strengthening in the British army. Voruz, however, quickly dampened any optimism by reminding Schweisguth that this was irrelevant: 'the English soldiers have no political influence, in contrast to the sailors; but the trouble is, the Admiralty is generally anti-French'.[78] Disheartened by these discoveries, Schweisguth wrote on his second day in London to warn Colson that it was 'certain' that France had reached 'a grave crisis in relations with England'.[79] Schweisguth asked Corbin if Franco-British staff talks could be obtained by reminding the British of France's cooperativeness three months earlier, during the Mediterranean crisis. The ambassador thought this might be possible, 'but not straight away: the British soldiers see the German danger clearly; but their politicians don't yet'. Only the improvement of London's air defences through access to the French early-warning network appeared likely to elicit immediate British interest.[80]

This mission's meagre results were partly offset by Flandin's success in the negotiations which he was pursuing simultaneously with British, Belgian and Italian ministers, also in London. Out of these talks the French foreign minister got British and Belgian assent on 19 March to the convening of trilateral military conversations, in the context of the pursuit by the diplomats of a replacement treaty of guarantee for the western German frontiers (a 'new Locarno' as it was termed). The accord, Flandin pompously claimed in describing his accomplishment in the Chamber of Deputies, 'marked a decisive stage in post-war Franco-British relations' and a 'notion of complete solidarity' to 'permit . . . the banishing of the hideous spectre of war'.[81] In the light of Britain's coolness towards commitments, the agreement that staff talks were to occur may have represented what one scholar has called the 'least adverse compromise' available to France.[82] Flandin's claim, however, was absurdly hyperbolic and was probably a self-advertisement calculated to improve his prospects in the impending elections. The reality was that France had obtained a precarious temporary basis for consultations with the British and Belgian armies, and one which forbade her interlocutors from going into the question of integrated plans that would entrain political commitments. On the same day as Flandin's speech in parliament, Petibon suggested to the new British attaché in Paris, Colonel Beaumont-Nesbitt, that neither the French general staff nor

French opinion would be ecstatic about Britain's concession because 'confidence in the efficacy of treaties, even between allies, had been seriously weakened' by the Rhineland affair. 'It had taken 13 days of argument and discussion' to arrive at the scarcely risk-laden response of a declaration censuring Germany for an illegal treaty infraction. Gamelin himself spoke to the British attaché, trying to continue his double-sided campaign of stressing France's need of firmer British help to contain Germany without giving an impression of French powerlessness. He underlined the importance of impressing on the Belgians the need for 'a serious military effort on their part' and he warned that if France and Britain did not present a 'firm and united front' it 'would mean that in a few years' time we should see the Anschluss followed by the subjugation of Czechoslovakia, followed in turn by that of Poland'. On the other hand, he 'did not think that Germany had any intention of attacking France . . . France was too big a mouthful to swallow'.[83]

The Rhineland episode did not, in short, alter the underlying pattern of Franco-British defence relations. Cooperation remained confined to highly circumscribed contingencies and stayed a matter for the discretion of the British government. Nothing had been done to overcome the crisis of confidence among French political leaders as to their country's ability to police and contain the expansionist will proclaimed by Hitler and his associates. Nor, in a narrower technical sense, had Gamelin made any progress towards convincing the British to invest rearmament resources in establishing an armoured field force to address the deficiencies in the upgrading of France's own forces. The British Statement Relating to Defence published in March 1936 merely reiterated that the British army had a multiple role and reaffirmed that neither its organisation nor its equipment would be specifically configured for continental warfare.[84] French envoys in London reported this discouraging news to the army staff in Paris, independently of Schweisguth's mission to Britain.[85] Questioned in the Chamber's army commission, on 18 March, about the state of Britain's army Maurin, the war minister, admitted that the forces that Britain could put into Europe in the foreseeable future would be 'greatly inferior to what she gave [us] in 1914'.[86] Observing all this with a mixture of sadness and anger from his retirement, General Debeney, a predecessor of Gamelin, wrote to Schweisguth to commiserate with the difficulty of his task as he prepared to return to London for the tripartite staff talks, in mid-April 1936. 'You've certainly become our Franco-British man', sympathised the former chief of the general staff, 'but . . . to set any store by signatures after the March experiences is truly a derisory idea.' He criticised Flandin for naïveté and expressed a fear that, in London, Schweisguth would have a 'hard task', finding the British 'profiting from these delusions, sincere or otherwise, to run a trade in their practical and effective collaboration'.[87]

The talks in London between the military delegations, on 15–16 April 1936, were indeed as hollow from the French viewpoint as sceptics had feared.[88] According to one British participant, Schweisguth frustratedly likened them to 'a football match with the referee continually blowing for offside'.[89] The British strictly limited the agenda to technical questions about military orders-of-battle and logistical facilities. Substantive matters, notably possible deployment zones and operational missions in the event of a war against Germany, remained taboo. The British were determined not to let the French suppose they had got the equivalent of a military guarantee, on the strength of which they could take a stand against Germany of their own – but not Britain's – choice and timing.[90] The British declined to mortgage their diplomatic freedom to France. They feared, as their ambassador in Paris put it two weeks before the staff talks, that the 'fundamental *military* policy' of France was 'still defensive' but that this did 'not necessarily preclude the possibility of a military adventure for political needs'.[91] The French military attaché in London perceptively advised that British opinion distrusted the occurrence of the talks. For the '"man in the street" such conversations . . . signify war in a short while', and were consequently treated by the British government not as a step towards an integrated Anglo-French defence but as a political gesture – a lever with which to exert greater diplomatic force for good behaviour from Germany.[92]

Out of the April meetings the French got nothing more than a sporadic continuation of exchanges of military information of a technical kind, through the channels of the military attachés. In early May 1936 Voruz held discussions at the War Office about port and railway requirements in France if the British field force were deployed to Europe. The 'great goodwill' shown by the British officers, General Sir John Dill, director of military operations, and Colonel Sir Ronald Adam, his deputy, did not blind the French attaché to the fact that this was but a 'first contribution to what would necessarily be a long drawn-out job'.[93] At the end of that month, in Paris, Beaumont-Nesbitt furnished Schweisguth with an order-of-battle for the only two divisions available in Britain to serve as a field force.[94]

A great difficulty for Gamelin's objective of getting the British to fashion a mechanised counterattack force was that leading military thinkers in Britain, such as Basil Liddell Hart, *The Times*'s military correspondent, were themselves opposed to a European role for the British army. Likewise, most British generals were unenthusiastic about offering to help pull French military chestnuts out of fires that the British felt had been started by French politicians and diplomatists in parts of Europe where Britain had no vital interests. Liddell Hart was the most prolix advocate in 1936–9 of what became known as the policy of 'limited liability' (the commitment of the fewest possible troops, and ideally none at all, to a European alliance). His views coincided with the convictions of Chamberlain, and technical advisors to the British government such as Lord Weir, a Glaswegian businessman and engineering industry specialist. These men, who together formed an articulate and politically influential caucus especially once Chamberlain became prime minister in May 1937, insisted in prioritising a limited British rearmament effort in favour of RAF strategic bombers and naval building as a deterrent to aggression. In general, and through Liddell Hart's writings and lobbying in particular, they believed that the defensive had acquired an intrinsic superiority in modern land warfare. This conviction, allied to the numerical size of the French army and the completion of the Maginot Line, suggested to them that Gamelin had little need of the small contribution that Britain could make to fighting on the ground in a new continental conflict. Liddell Hart presented an argument which dovetailed conveniently with the home defence focus of Baldwin's and Chamberlain's governments in 1936–8, asserting that the defensive was so much more an advantageous posture on land that victims of aggression were unlikely to be beaten so long as they avoided unwisely essaying offensives themselves.[95] Liddell Hart influenced Chamberlain directly through at least one of his books at this time, and indirectly through the hold he gained over Chamberlain's new secretary of state for war, Hore-Belisha, to whom he supplied unofficial but oft-heeded advice from mid-1937 to mid-1938.[96]

The only straw at which Gamelin could clutch in 1936 was the evidence of the British general staff's wish to retain contingency plans to deploy two British divisions into the Low Countries in order to try to keep the Channel coast and Dutch–Belgian ports secure from Germany. Even on this count, concerning an area which it advised remained of vital interest to British security, the War Office counselled in July 1936 that a 'definite commitment to France and Belgium . . . would be most dangerous'. To all of these friendly European nations, it was to be 'made clear that the despatch of the force could only be decided upon by the government at the time'. The British general staff, mindful of responsibilities in the Middle East and elsewhere, argued for a rearmed and powerfully equipped force, with full reserves, but still one with flexibility, 'not tied down to . . . France and Belgium but prepared to operate anywhere'.[97] Not only did British ministers wish to retain full freedom in their diplomacy, British soldiers wished to remain unentangled in Gamelin's plans. It does not appear to have occurred to the War Office that uncovering the details of those plans, and then seeking modifications to correspond more closely with British instincts, might have been a sufficiently worthwhile objective to have justified entry into fuller staff talks.[98]

The British therefore remained remarkably ignorant of the strategy as well as the specific shortcomings of Gamelin's armies. The War Office conjectured, quite erroneously as we have seen, that 'without our intervention there is little doubt that France would abandon Belgium to her fate' if Germany attacked westwards. The British general staff accordingly reasoned that they might need a well-armed corps to intervene and bond together French and Belgian armies retreating on divergent courses under a German Schlieffen-style offensive. They also believed that what the French and Belgians deemed vital was the despatch of a British corps as a symbolic gesture of political solidarity to refashion the previous war's alliance.[99] It was more than just British staff exercises that, in Liddell Hart's critique of September 1937, were 'still running on 1914 tram-lines'; it was the whole British way of thinking about French strategic requirements *vis-à-vis* Germany.[100]

Gamelin must have been frustrated by British obduracy and incomprehension of the real need in his army for assistance to overcome the bottlenecks impeding its own strengthening of mechanised forces. Nevertheless he grasped that British fixation with the Low Countries could be turned to French advantage, if he allowed the British to think that he no longer possessed the right type of French units with which to bolster Belgian and Dutch defences. On 15 October 1936 – the day after Belgian 'independence' was proclaimed – Gamelin argued to a CSG meeting that the Belgian change of course disadvantaged Britain more than France because it increased the risk of Germany seizing bases along the Channel. U-boats operating from Belgian ports, together with the 'aerial danger suspended over London', advised Gamelin in a memorandum on 16 October, might induce the British to upgrade the priority of a field force capable of deploying quickly to shore up Belgian defences.[101] It thus became Gamelin's tactic to try to shake the British by suggesting that France might have to leave Belgium naked. (Privately, Gamelin knew that the Belgians did not alter their plans and decide to withdraw away from France, towards Antwerp, Ghent and Bruges, until February 1937. But he left the British to fret about the threat to their own interests if French and Belgian planning remained uncoordinated.)[102]

Throughout 1937 the deepening production crisis in the French armaments and metallurgical industries made it clearer still to Gamelin and other French defence planners that there was a need to gain a promise of support from a British mechanised force. Gamelin began the year by disclosing the French army's re-equipment problems to Alfred Duff Cooper, then Britain's secretary of state for war, when he visited Paris in early January. The minister agreed to send British armoured warfare specialists to discuss French deficiencies. On 27 January, as a result, General Sir Hugh Elles, who had led the tanks in their first use *en masse* at Cambrai in 1917, and Colonel Giffard Martel, assistant director of mechanisation in the War Office, travelled to Paris to see the tank specifications which the French staff recommended for a British force.[103]

The Quai d'Orsay was enlisted to make the same case to the British through diplomatic channels. Delbos, the foreign minister, and Pierre Viénot, his under-secretary, told Anthony Eden, the British foreign secretary, that Britain's 'most useful' contribution to reinforcing the military security of western Europe would be to build a 'small but powerful and mechanized force even if there were only two divisions of it'. Eden reportedly learned that France needed the addition of a 'concentrated striking power rather than a mass'.[104] The War Office, however, quickly betrayed its coolness towards a specialised configuration of this sort for Britain's army. On 29 January 1937 an assistant to General Haining (Dill's successor as director of military operations and intelligence), was sent across Whitehall to tell the Foreign Office that:

the French military authorities aim to get us committed to assisting them in case of need to the extent of two armoured divisions. If Anglo-French staff conversations were to be held we should doubtless be faced with this request. Whilst, however, it would no doubt suit the French very well indeed that we should have two armoured divisions . . . it would not necessarily . . . be to our advantage . . . Armoured divisions cost enormously more money than infantry divisions and . . . would no doubt be very well adapted for operations in France but not for operations in other parts of the world, yet our commitments there . . . are very great.[105]

Haining's deputy conceded that the French had begun to call in unison for Britain to prepare a mechanised corps of intervention: in addition to the requests in this sense by Gamelin to Duff Cooper and by Schweisguth to Elles and Martel, there had been identical approaches by 'senior French officers' to Britain's military attaché in Paris as well as by General Albert Lelong, whom Gamelin had hand-picked to replace Voruz as French military attaché in London, in June 1936.[106] Nevertheless, he urged the Foreign Office to ignore these representations. The senior officers of the British general staff, under the unimaginative leadership of Field-Marshal Sir Cyril Deverell (chief of the Imperial

General Staff, April 1936 to December 1937), remained wedded to rebuilding an old-fashioned infantry-based army for 'general purposes'.[107]

The War Office found a surprising and influential ally for its resistance to French entreaties. This was Sir Robert Vansittart, the long-serving permanent under-secretary at the Foreign Office. Vansittart had consistently preached watchfulness of Germany, even before Hitler's advent to power. He was friendly and sympathetic towards French defensive concerns – indeed deplored by many British officials and ministers for being too francophile. He cannot have wished to do anything at this time to set back the cause of French security. Yet, however unwittingly, this is what he brought about by adding his voice to those who opposed Gamelin's wish that Britain prepare a small armoured field force. The advocacy of such a direction for British rearmament by Delbos and Viénot was to be dismissed (he advised Eden) as misguided if not mistaken; the Frenchmen were 'two novices ... without any pretence at being qualified to speak on matters such as these'. The foreign secretary objected: 'But it now appears that the view of French ministers is shared by the French general staff, if not by ours.' Undeterred, Vansittart rejoined that this had to mean that France wanted two mechanised divisions *in the first instance* without prejudice to other assistance on land *as well*'. He added that he thought it 'academic' to discuss an armoured corps: he understood that Britain would not be manufacturing enough tanks 'even for our limited *all-round* purposes, by 1939, let alone for two mechanised *divisions*'.[108] Vansittart was eager enough to raise priority in British rearmament for military aid to France – he had been preaching for years that the two countries had inseparable strategic interests in reining in German ambitions. But the under-secretary was no military specialist and was unaware of the very specific deficiencies in the French army's modernisation which Gamelin sought a British corps to fill.[109] Quite ignorant of the damage that he was doing to the country he wished to help, Vansittart gave Gamelin an even harder row to hoe by lending his voice to the War Office conservatives who opposed the project of a mechanised field force. Vansittart was a diplomat, not a strategist; he still measured military power more by quantity than quality. As he said to Eden, after Reynaud lamented Britain's 'practically non-existent' military power in December 1936, Reynaud meant armies rather than navies and air forces, 'a fresh sign ... that the French ... will always count on us for a *substantial supply of ground troops*'.[110] Like the War Office, Vansittart had a 1914–18 frame of mind on this question, reiterating in February 1937 that infantry was 'still the dominant factor'.[111]

By this time, January–February 1937, the British chiefs of staff had obtained better intelligence about Gamelin's plans. They admitted to being 'credibly informed' that France would rescue Belgium, in the event of German invasion, by intervention with nine divisions 'on condition that a British Field Force were despatched to the Continent'.[112] The problem for the War Office's hope that this would raise the priority for rearming the British army was, however, that Chamberlain asked how a British intervention requiring two weeks to transport and deploy could reach the battlefield soon enough to affect the outcome in Belgium. The British generals stuck stubbornly to a request for re-equipping five regular and twelve Territorial divisions so as to be capable of European service; but they had no answer to Chamberlain's searching questions as to the missions and role of such an army, and so failed to divert British defence priority away from air forces, home air defence and warship construction.[113]

There were a few who got the message that the French 'really only wish for two mechanised divisions as our total land contribution' (as Oliver' Harvey, then Eden's private secretary, minuted in February 1937).[114] But they were not numerous enough, nor did they speak with the authority of recognised military experts. Most importantly, their pleas to heed what Gamelin was requesting were too inconvenient to Chamberlain and the air and navy lobbies in Britain who had nailed their colours to different rearmament masts – and who had an ill-concealed dislike for France anyway.

The more time passed, however, the more the growing German menace and the continuing stagnation of French rearmament made it important for Gamelin to be able to look forward to including a British mechanised corps in his troop inventory. He therefore continued his campaign to get Britain to regain its position of the early 1930s as a leader in armoured warfare. Schweisguth was sent to Britain again, in March 1937, to try to put pressure on the War Office to make changes to their programmes. Meeting with Duff Cooper, the assistant chief of the French army staff emphasised that, since the minister's January visit to Paris, Gamelin had decided to accentuate development of armoured forces. Schweisguth then talked to Deverell and Haining about tanks but found them 'very embarrassed . . . seemingly without a well-defined programme for the choice of equipment or the organisation of future units', and facing difficulty in obtaining funds. Schweisguth left with the impression that though France was encountering bottlenecks in tank output, it had nevertheless a great lead over Britain in the modernity of designs, in prototypes and in firm doctrinal concepts for mobile warfare. More technical missions, he suggested to Colson and Gamelin, should 'very discreetly' be sent to Britain to share French advances for the benefit of the British army. On the bigger question of a pledge of British military support in the first place, this mission left Schweisguth no more sanguine than a year before, at the time of his two visits to London after the Rhineland reoccupation. Ambassador Corbin, he reported, said the British still feared that 'a technical military agreement with us . . . would lead to an obligation of a political order', and he concluded gloomily that personal contacts with Britain's generals would remain 'as cordial and easy as official conversations would be . . . difficult'.[115]

Through the spring and early summer of 1937 Franco-British exchanges were continued discreetly. They were confined, however, to divulgence of technical information and did not extend to war planning or strategic coordination. An officer from the operations and intelligence directorate of the War Office visited Paris in mid-April and received a memorandum from Schweisguth with a suggested table of organisation for British mechanised formations.[116] In May, just after Hore-Belisha became Britain's war minister, Reynaud travelled to London to talk to him and Vansittart. He re-emphasised to them how 'England . . . with her professional army could, in case of war, bring extraordinarily powerful support to the allies by creating an armoured corps.'[117] But, when Daladier visited Britain from 21 to 24 April to fulfil engagements in London and Manchester the opportunity was not taken to press the British further on the question of reorganising their army rearmament, even though he held meetings with the British service ministers as well as with Chamberlain and Eden.[118] (Daladier, it will be recalled, was at this time more preoccupied with his favourite personal project of extending French frontier fortifications behind Belgium – whose neutrality the French and British governments guaranteed in a joint declaration on 24 April 1937 – than in promoting British rearmament.)

With hindsight, it appears that Gamelin and his associates were ineffective political tacticians in 1937–8 and made no progress towards persuading the British to reorder their defence programmes so as to be able to fill France's shortfall in mechanised counteroffensive capabilities. An important reason for the frustration of Gamelin's wishes in this sense was the power of British official and ministerial circles favouring a cautious approach to British rearmament – balancing improvements in armed strength against retention of a vigorous domestic and export economy. Compounding this concern to keep 'business as usual' in the British economy (a particular priority for Chamberlain and his Treasury officials), was the resolve to put the air force and air defence at the top of British defensive planning. What Chamberlain and most of his senior advisors wanted was an RAF that had a strong enough bomber force to deter Germany from aggression, and some effective defences by fighters, anti-aircraft batteries and the new radar detection system which was becoming a realistic operational asset in 1937. These were sensible security concerns for British leaders at this time. They would, on their own merit, have weighed heavily against prioritising an army to deploy on the continent to bolster the French or Belgians.[119]

But British perceptions of France gave a further twist to the underlying reason why Gamelin's search for support from a British mechanised corps went so unrewarded. In 1933–5 the British authorities considered, with a great deal of justification, that the French army remained vastly superior to the German, whether gauged by quantity and quality of officers and men or by equipment and weaponry. By 1936–7, when the balance was swinging in favour of the Reich because of its earlier start to rearmament, the British government adopted a more-than-usually disdainful attitude to France. This arose out of the distaste for the Popular Front and the leftist direction taken by French politics in the Blum era among the conservative bourgeois and aristocrats who predominated in official and ministerial ranks in London. The disparagement of France for having chosen to be governed by the Popular Front served only to reinforce British inclinations to look out only for their own direct interests in couching defence policy – and to strengthen the prevailing belief in Whitehall that Britain had to take command in dealing with the whole series of problems looming from Hitler's European ambitions. Sir George Clerk, the British ambassador in Paris, painted a bleak picture of the decline of France as an international force after the election of Blum's first government, finding 'singularly little comfort . . . in the present internal situation'. He conjectured that 'for the time being' France was 'reduced . . . to the status of "quantité negligeable" in the councils of the nations'.[120] The prejudices of British envoys and ministers against the Popular Front permeated assessments at this time. Gamelin's army was often described as an isolated rock standing in a sea of political and social turpitude, as when the British military attaché warned Whitehall in mid-1937 – actually after Blum's replacement by Chautemps – that:

cooperation and agreement between the component parts of the state are . . . conspicuously lacking. It is true that General Gamelin occupies a special position in the councils of the government and that the French army appears to remain unaffected by the conditions prevailing throughout the country but the best military advice must remain a dead letter if the government is powerless, or the people unwilling, to accept it.[121]

Though these reports might have rung alarm bells for the British, giving them pause for thought about the risks they were running in neglecting the preparation of a mobile European field force, they did not. Instead the unpalatable domestic conditions in France, and the social ferment so distasteful to British conservatives, were instrumental in bolstering the British policy of cold, reserved detachment from continental entanglements.

The rest of 1937 and 1938 was a barren time for Gamelin's search after British military cooperation and commitment. It did not help to have Chamberlain in 10, Downing Street, after May 1937. The new prime minister had no innate warmth for France but brought to British foreign policy a burning conviction that he, personally, could negotiate a peaceful resolution of German grievances with Hitler.[122] Though he continued British rearmament he brought a cost-accountant's searching gaze to bear on its expense and return. Neither on grounds of sentiment nor hard military evidence did he see any reason to strengthen Britain's preparations to be able to help French land defences. Chamberlain's aim, executed by his successor as chancellor of the exchequer, Sir John Simon, was to control British rearmament expense tightly and avoid setting back the recovery of Britain's civil trade and industries from the depression. A ceiling of £1,500 million was placed on defence expenditure for the quinquennium from 1937 to 1941. It was reaffirmed that there was to be no increase in the British army's programme in the foreseeable future. Without a reordering of British rearmament priorities, there was no place in such a strictly regulated defence programme for production of greater numbers of tanks and other up-to-date equipment for mobile war on land. When British rearmament was reviewed in the autumn of 1937 by a committee led by Sir Thomas Inskip, the minister for co-ordination of defence, it was determined that 'cooperation in the defence of the territories of any allies Britain might have in war' was to be the last of four roles assigned to the army. Home security of the British Isles, protection of imperial communications and the defence of overseas dependencies were deemed to be more pressing missions than preparation to assist Gamelin and the defence of France or Belgium.[123]

Within the British general staff, some doubts emerged about the wisdom of leaving the French without support. Deverell, who attended French manoeuvres in Normandy in September 1937, was dismayed to see that the 'first-line transport of infantry battalions still consists of . . . carts drawn by horses or mules'. He noted with concern that the R.35 tanks had 'very slow speed, poor cross-country performance, insufficient armour and would be considered by us as not satisfactory'.[124] In the War Office it was correctly judged that Gamelin had the 'ulterior aim' in the exercises of desiring 'to impress in every way possible the need for those present to cooperate with France'. Likewise, scepticism was voiced for almost the first time about the security provided by French frontier fortifications, the British general staff minuting on the report Deverell filed after his visit to them that:

regarding the strength of the Maginot Line it is essential to bear in mind that . . . a purely defensive role must . . . succumb to succeeding offensives . . . provided sufficient force was concentrated against it. Any defensive position, no matter how strong, could be broken . . . In the next war the use of air power should enable that break to be complete and beyond repair.[125]

Deverell's estimate – shared widely among senior British army officers – was that a need for British military intervention to save France from disaster could not be completely discounted and should therefore receive some preparation and resources out of the British defence programmes. As it was argued by Lord Gort (at this point military secretary to Hore-Belisha and Deverell's replacement as CIGS in December 1937), only the continental deployment of a British army would avert French defeat if a 'troglodyte existence in the Maginot Line' undermined French alertness and enabled armour and air forces to force a breakthrough 'by rapidity, deception and surprise'.[126] This was a pessimism that British military officers had not voiced in regard to the French army since 1930–1. For once, moreover, it was expressed quite brutally – stripped of the laconic understatement that usually characterised British army prose. France, warned the general staff in the light of Deverell's observations, had become 'a nation apprehensive of the future, concerned over its dwindling manpower and its lack of national combination . . . equipped principally with the materials of the last war rather than with those of the next'.[127]

These perceptive warnings went unheeded by British policy-makers, however. It seems hard to believe that they would have dented Chamberlain's assumptions and *idées fixes*, even had they been forcefully argued by the service ministers in cabinet. But the whole question is academic, because the notion of French vulnerability was dismissed out of hand by Hore-Belisha. He, too, had attended the French manoeuvres and toured the frontier defences. Unlike Deverell, however, he returned burning with a blind faith in the prowess of Gamelin's army. He mentioned to fellow ministers at the end of September 1937 that the French were interested in obtaining a contribution to their defence of two British mechanised divisions. But he assured his colleagues that Gamelin's need was imagined rather than real. The French fortifications, he said, were 'virtually impregnable to tanks or any other form of attack' and he supported Chamberlain's refusal to give any undertakings about an expeditionary force. He judged that once French leaders finally grasped 'that we cannot commit ourselves . . . they should . . . accelerate the extension of the Maginot Line to the sea'.[128]

Deverell's warnings were treated as risible alarmism by the secretary of state. The latter concluded that the general's nerve had cracked and his judgement gone haywire when he came 'back from the German manoeuvres with a report that the French could not stand . . . that the Maginot Line would not hold and that the offensive would succeed – contrary to Hore-Belisha's impressions'.[129] The outright hostility to remodelling the British army as a mechanised force for a continental role shown by Hore-Belisha at this time owed much to the advice he was unofficially and irregularly taking from Liddell Hart. The latter had long expressed the view in his books and newspaper columns that British military participation in the battles on the western front in 1914–18 had been the result of misguided departure by Britain's statesmen and generals from what Liddell Hart claimed was a 'traditional' British way in war. This 'way' supposedly involved the conduct of land operations by proxy, through continental alliances, whilst Britain limited her liability to maritime and economic participation – blockading an enemy, whilst acting as the banking house and industrial arsenal of a friendly coalition. Liddell Hart showed no sensitivity to the suspicions of people in Paris that such a policy amounted to a selfish and cynical strategy of 'fighting to the last Frenchman'.[130]

Liddell Hart's influence over Hore-Belisha – and thus on British defence policy and priorities – was as important as his notions about Gamelin and his plans were ill-founded. He believed that the French army under Gamelin was bent on repeating an all-out initial offensive like that of 1914, in the event of war with Germany. He considered also (in the light of First World War precedent), that a British field force would be sucked into such hazardous French operations if it were deployed to Europe to undertake a role coordinated with Gamelin's armies. So far from estimating France to be vulnerable to a rupture of its defences by Germany – let alone to a knock-out blow – Liddell Hart advised that the 'only serious chance of the French resistance collapsing completely' was as 'a sequel to a rash offensive on their own part, and the crippling of their own force in it, as in 1914'.[131] This was a bizarre interpretation of Gamelin's strategic thinking in view of the deep impact in France of the casualties and devastation of 1914–18; the erection of the costly Maginot Line; reliance on short-service conscription and a cumbersome mobilisation of reservists to go to war; and Gamelin's lack of powerful offensive armoured forces. It is to be explained by the fact that Liddell Hart was misinformed about French military doctrine in the later 1930s, on which his intelligence was defective and unreliable.[132] He had quarrelled at the end of the 1920s with Weygand, over questionnaires he sent the latter as part of the research for his book, *Foch: The Man of Orléans* (1931). Weygand had been angered by some of Liddell Hart's interpretations of his former chief's actions in the battles of 1918 and it appears that Liddell Hart was *persona non grata* in high military circles in France after the book's publication.[133] At any rate, Liddell Hart only ever had one perfunctory personal encounter with Gamelin, at the British manoeuvres of September 1937 and the general's policies remained a mystery to him. This did not stop him clinging even years after the war to the belief that French policy might have been defensive 'but the French temperament was offensive and in the army . . . was deepened by its doctrine and training which were still mainly concentrated on offensive action' – a stricture born of ignorance and diametrically opposed to the criticism of insufficient offensive-mindedness in the French army of the late 1930s with which every other commentary on the Fall of France is replete.[134] Liddell Hart's odd conviction that 'Gamelin, in particular, was scornful of what he called "defensive ideas"' played a part in helping to strengthen the hand of anti-continentalist ministers in London.[135] British policy was reaffirmed on existing lines, with precedence for the RAF, the air defence of Great Britain (ADGB) and naval forces, at the end of 1937 and beginning of 1938. As Hore-Belisha, drawing authority from Liddell Hart, put it to Chamberlain, 'our army should be organized to defend this country and the Empire . . . a military prepossession in favour of a Continental commitment is wrong'.[136]

Gamelin did not succeed in shaking this British posture in 1938. The 'year of Munich' saw no progress in preparing a British corps of intervention. When pressed by French ministers in conversations in April, May and September 1938, the British government was able to state only that two infantry divisions were available for deployment in the event that circumstances altered so that a sufficiently important British interest was endangered. These divisions were never a reinforcement on which Gamelin could set any store at all throughout the international tensions of that year. Nor were they any nearer to constituting the type of corps able to serve in lieu of the larger force of French armoured divisions that Gamelin had persuaded the CSG to develop in 1936–7, but whose realisation was many months in arrears because of French industry's deficiencies in labour and productive capacity.

Britain remained non-committal about military support for France from the time of the Anschluss through to Munich. In part this attitude stemmed from Chamberlain's conviction that Hitler's demands could be accommodated, and his appetite for revisions of the post-1918 treaties satisfied, through resolute and fair dealing directly with Berlin. For this reason – given expression in Chamberlain's well-known faith in the possibility of negotiating a 'general settlement' of European national differences – British efforts after the ministerial talks in London with Chautemps and Delbos on 29–30 November 1937 concentrated on pressing Czechoslovakia to make the best terms it could with Germany to eradicate the Sudeten problem. The corollary to this policy was that Britain spent 1938 discouraging the French from utterances and actions that could tend to make Prague obdurate rather than conciliatory towards Hitler. Though these political-diplomatic considerations exercised the chief influence on British responses to Gamelin's campaign for closer Franco-British military ties, other factors reinforced them. One of these was distrust, voiced by senior British generals such as Pownall and Gort, of the security on the French side around any secret military coordination. The War Office, and through them British policy-makers, never shook off a fear that the French would 'leak' news of any Franco-British staff meetings – either deliberately or because of lax security – with the result of angering Hitler and diminishing the likelihood of a successful outcome for Chamberlain's *démarches* to achieve a Europe-wide pacification.[137] Another brake on Franco-British military *rapprochement* was the continuing concern among Britain's military chiefs with their army's responsibilities beyond the boundaries of Europe. Far-flung British interests, it was estimated, demanded flexibility and freedom for Britain's small field force. British generals were ready enough to acknowledge that deployment to France *might* become unavoidable, but were not ready to foreclose their ability to meet other eventualities by guaranteeing that deployment ahead of time. As General Ironside (who would be CIGS in 1939–40) put it in March 1938: 'The French . . . love order in their plans and these . . . often become inhuman and impracticable in consequence. We cannot make hypothetical plans to meet uncertain circumstances.'[138]

Gamelin and the other French military authorities registered these divergent British concerns. 'At the present moment', noted Daladier in the CPDN meeting of 8 December 1937, 'what interests . . . the English is Egypt, Palestine, North Africa and the Near East. It's by this route that it will be possible to bring about the alliance [with them].'[139] They strove to avert the British army's gaze from its imperial commitments, but were rebuffed. The French military attaché in London, Lelong, was told by Hore-Belisha in February 1938 that Britain refused to be 'stuck with the obligation to send an expeditionary corps . . . into Flanders'.[140]

Two days after this conversation, Eden resigned the British foreign secretaryship. This removed one of the few voices around Chamberlain that had preached the symbolic and demonstrative merits for French political morale of permitting the War Office at least to make joint contingency plans with Gamelin, even if these remained non-binding politically.[141] Eden's departure dealt a blow to the French command's aim of leading the British to allocate important rearmament resources to create a mechanised corps of intervention for use in north-west Europe. As Lelong downheartedly reported, all idea of more intimate British army contacts with France were doomed to be 'left to slumber'.[142]

Gamelin was up against the problem that the British government and its defence advisors believed that Hitler still lacked enough military strength to embolden him to push his aggressive diplomacy to the point of war. 'The German general staff are unlikely', estimated Britain's military leaders at the start of 1938, 'to consider that the strength of the German army is sufficient to justify . . . a land offensive before 1939–40'. The French army by itself was judged likely to remain sufficiently powerful to deter the Wehrmacht at least for the rest of 1938 and its fortifications to 'present military obstacles of a strength which make any rapid German or Italian success on land unlikely'.[143] Gamelin was also mistaken in his estimate of how the British would react to his bluff that, unless assured of support from a British mechanised corps, France would not give military assistance to Brussels if Belgium were attacked. For British strategists, including Maurice Hankey, the secretary to the CID, and Gort, had reached the conclusion by 1938 that Britain could best help Belgium not by preparing armoured divisions to join French troops in an intervention after German aggression, but by pressing France to complete the Maginot Line to the sea and so remove the temptation for Germany to repeat a Schlieffen-style attack. Gort judged the Belgian invasion route 'hackneyed and also most unsuited for the employment of armoured divisions owing to the waterways etc.';[144] the chiefs of staff in Whitehall thought that the whole area would be much less vulnerable and dangerous by late 1938 when Belgium's additional eastern fortifications would 'be formidable'.[145] With talks between Daladier, Bonnet, Chamberlain and Halifax (Eden's successor) occurring in late April 1938, Gamelin's assistant chief of staff with responsibility for intelligence sought to play the 'Belgian card' by warning Britain's military attaché in Paris that Germany was near to possessing the capability for a *mobilisation brusquée*; he added, in an attempt to frighten British policy-makers, that he 'did not expect to find the bulk of an attacking German mass . . . opposite France but rather opposite Holland and Belgium'.[146] This left the British unmoved. So, too, did identical scaremongering by Gamelin and Daladier when Hore-Belisha visited Paris on 24–5 April. The British war minister coldly responded by reiterating the 'improbability' of Britain developing mechanised divisions to help secure Belgium 'at the beginning of hostilities'.[147]

In sum, British leaders called Gamelin's bluff in 1938. Whether accurate or not, their own intelligence appreciations led them to conclude that the French army remained sufficiently strong at least for all defensive missions in respect of France and her north-west European neighbours and friends.[148] Nor were they rattled by French talk of abandoning plans for a military intervention to succour Belgium unless a suitably equipped, tank-oriented British force could be relied on to land quickly and lend its assistance to a forward defence in the north. On the former count, Corbin, the French ambassador in London, disconsolately concluded in April 1938 to Paul-Boncour (foreign minister in Blum's brief second government), that 'certain British politicians' judged 'that the French army . . . is the true army of Great Britain'. This complacency was never quite eradicated, the same envoy warning Daladier in October 1939 that the 'English have . . . such confidence in the French army that they are tempted to consider their military support more as a testimony to solidarity with France than as a vital necessity'.[149] On the question of aid to Belgium, the British strategic advisors to Chamberlain were cynical about French reasons for the light defence of their border with Belgium. Some suspected 'that the existence of a gap between Lille and the sea might be a deliberate inducement to compel us to intervene on land'.[150] It was agreed that Chamberlain should press Daladier to undertake to extend French northern fortifications – something which Daladier, always keener than Gamelin on a static, defensive strategy, consented to do in the ministerial talks at the end of April.[151]

It was a serious setback for Gamelin's policy of seeking to make Chamberlain change British rearmament priorities and it showed the limits to Daladier's reliability as an advocate of his high command's causes once he was away from the prompting and support of the French generals.[152] (Daladier's acquiescence in Chamberlain's suggestion that extending the Maginot Line was preferable to expecting British military assistance was probably also motivated by his relief, in his other capacity as French prime minister by the time of the talks, at the British agreeing to assume the diplomatic lead to resolve the Sudeten problem.)[153] In all likelihood, Gamelin's ambitions never stood much chance of success because of the sheer force of the imperatives of home defence and belief in the deterrent effect of air power which animated and shaped British defence policy in 1936–8. Only low-key exchanges of order-of-battle and logistical information, through the intermediary of the military attachés in Paris and London in May 1938, occurred that summer. These contacts, the British restated, were purely to facilitate the technicalities of a move of their only two infantry divisions to Europe and were devoid of political commitment.[154] In vain did Reynaud, also in May, use a visit to Britain to plead that a 60,000 man armoured force was 'the extent and the type of the help' France wanted; in vain did Lelong strive to convince Liddell Hart, in June, that Gamelin 'did not want infantry but simply mechanised troops' especially because of 'their value for counterstroke'; in vain did Gamelin even resort to lobbying King George VI, on the latter's state visit to Paris from 19 to 22 July 1938, as to the 'necessity of Britain as soon as possible constituting . . . some large units of tanks'.[155]

By the time of the September war scare over Czechoslovakia the military diplomacy of the French had drawn only the most limited concessions from Britain: an undertaking to base an RAF bomber force on French airfields in the event of war, agreement to convene naval staff talks, and a commitment for closer on-site liaison with the 4e Bureau by a new section of the British general staff responsible for sea and rail arrangements for the two British infantry divisions in the event of their deployment to France.[156] The measures were peripheral to Gamelin's quest for the British to provide the armoured corps to match the panzers that French factories could not. It was ironic, and symptomatic of two years of frustration for Gamelin, that the French army's partial mobilisation occasioned by the Sudeten crisis not only forced the cancellation, for the second year running, of its own mechanised manoeuvres but also prevented meetings with senior British generals, who were to have been Gamelin's guests at the exercises.[157] Just after the Munich *dénouement*, Britain's military attaché was taken by Gamelin in person to visit mobilised formations in eastern France, including the only full-strength French armoured division, the 1st DLM. The British envoy was left in 'no doubt that he [Gamelin] is of the opinion that two or three divisions of this type would be the most valuable kind of expeditionary force which Great Britain could send France'.[158] But for Britain to have met this need would have required it to believe there had arisen a significant risk of a French defensive collapse. Gamelin could not sell that idea, however, much as he wanted British mechanised divisions, because the British did not believe it – and neither did Gamelin himself.

10 Czechoslovakia, Poland, the Soviet Union: from appeasement to war

The Czechoslovakian crisis of the summer of 1938 was, for the French, a classic example of the way in which their diplomacy of the 1920s brought them unwanted entanglements and dangers of war in the 1930s. Gamelin would not have resisted a decision of the government to fight for Czechoslovakia in September 1938, but he was no enthusiast for it either. His advice to Daladier was, as many scholars have noted, hedged around with caution, and he accentuated the difficulties that would have faced the French military machine.[1] Daladier himself – a veteran of the 1914–18 trenches – was desperate to avoid the need to declare war on Germany to aid Prague. He needed little persuading of the validity of Gamelin's warning that to launch French forces into the Rhineland would result only in 'a modernised battle of the Somme'.[2] He was more relieved than most when the diplomacy of Chamberlain and the last-minute mediation of Mussolini on 29 September 1938 made possible the four-power conference at Munich and the cession of the Sudetenland to Germany without resort to war.

Neither Gamelin nor Daladier, however, took any pride from the capitulation at Munich. Both understood how severely it had dented France's position as a first-rank European power. Both appreciated that there could be no further retreats before Hitler's aggression. The question, after Munich, was not whether to make a stand, but when, and over what issue. Between 15 and 23 March 1939, Hitler destroyed Czechoslovakia, forcibly establishing a Reich protectorate over Bohemia-Moravia, and also annexed Memel. These coups signalled that Germany had resumed its march of conquest. The resumption of expansion catapulted Poland to the forefront of international attention.

At the end of March 1939 the British guaranteed Poland's independence and her territorial integrity. In April similar undertakings were extended to Greece and Romania.[3] The French, anxious to guard their hard-won British alliance, took care to duplicate these commitments by issuing their own guarantees of these east European nations. For France, this period witnessed a cautious but noticeable recovery of confidence. Daladier, in particular, showed a new willingness to assume a resolute anti-German stance.[4] Much of this resurgence in French self-assurance resulted from the British undertaking of 6 February 1939 to give military support to France, Holland, Belgium and Switzerland, in the event of German aggression in the west.[5] It had been consolidated by British agreement to begin staff talks with the French – the opening round taking place between Anglo-French army and air force delegations in London from 29 March to 4 April 1939.

For his part, Gamelin had recognised since the start of the year that 1939 was likely to bring about a direct German threat to Poland's integrity. As a memorandum to Daladier emphasised at the beginning of 1939: 'One cannot too heavily underscore the value [to the German army] of the partial mobilisations it conducted, at the time of the Anschluss and the Sudeten affair, for the training of its troops and cohesion of its units.'[6] The main questions seemed to be when, and under what pretext, the menace would materialise.[7] For all this realisation, however, the nuts and bolts of the political and diplomatic guarantees given in the spring of 1939 were fitted together with comparatively little reference to Gamelin. At two levels, it is true, it would have been redundant for Daladier or the Quai d'Orsay to have pursued detailed consultation with the military commanders concerning Poland.

In the first place, earlier discussions – especially in 1935–6 – had shown that neither France nor Britain had the strategic wherewithal to assist Poland directly if it were invaded by the Germans. This situation of impotence was reaffirmed during the Anglo-French staff talks of April 1939. These meetings examined the general principles of a Franco-British grand strategy in a war against Germany. The report of the talks reiterated that France and Britain lacked the means to help the Poles directly if Germany attacked eastwards whilst maintaining an adequate defensive posture on the Rhine. The French and British acknowledged in their private conversations that they would be unable to go beyond operations designed to apply pressure on Germany's western borders in the hope of distracting some Wehrmacht forces away from Poland.[8]

There was a second reason why Poland was guaranteed without proper consultation of Gamelin and his fellow service chiefs. This was the fact that Daladier's government was convinced that the French high command regarded Poland as a very substantial ally. Daladier had long been conditioned to regard Poland as an asset of the first importance – not least because Gamelin had stressed this very point since 1936. Therefore, by the time of the flurry of diplomatic activity towards Warsaw, Bucharest and Athens in the spring of 1939, Daladier was primed to react vigorously at the slightest suggestion of a German threat taking shape against the Poles. Such a menace, in the prime minister's sight, was a gauntlet which, once thrown down, would have to be picked up. In short, Daladier was conditioned to regard Poland as the very cornerstone of an eastern front against Germany.

Throughout the 1938 crisis, Gamelin himself had spoken of the Poles as holding the key to the European situation. In judging them this important, Gamelin did not disregard Poland's unpredictable national policy over the previous five years, nor their notorious antipathy towards the Czechs arising from the two nations' dispute over their border territory of Teschen. As early as January 1934, when German aggression against Czechoslovakia was quite hypothetical, Gamelin had advised fellow senior officers in Paris that the Czech forces might 'contain' a German attack but that this would be 'very problematic' if Prague was 'not supported by Poland and the Little Entente'.[9] Thus French military planners calculated that any ally in eastern Europe which intended to resist German aggression by force would be unlikely to survive till French operations were mounted against western Germany unless it enjoyed the assistance of the Polish army in the interim. Among the constellation of French regional allies in east-central Europe, Poland's place was that of the polar star. And if Czech–Polish relations had been cordial in 1938, if the two nations had possessed an integrated plan for a common defence, Gamelin would have been more prepared to contemplate a French diplomacy which would have stiffened Czech resistance to German demands on the Sudetenland, even to the point of provoking war. As it was, France was unready for war in 1938, Britain unwilling and Czechoslovakia unsupported. Summoned to London on 26 September 1938 and asked for an estimate of the probable duration of Czech resistance to a German invasion, Gamelin 'was only prepared to say that she could hold out certainly for a few weeks, but perhaps not for a few months'. Not surprisingly, with Daladier's chief military advisor making an assessment in these terms, French confidence was at a low ebb. Just as crucially, in September 1938 there remained other eastern allies still in play. For Gamelin – as the French account of his remarks in London indicates – the French and Czechoslovak armies 'represented the sole forces at the ready' to oppose Hitlerism. They constituted 'the shield for the forces of the entire world'; 'but to win a war [against Germany] they would need to be assisted'.[10] It was the old theme of the need for a grand coalition before joining battle with Germany – a coalition which Daladier's government still had not constructed. Gamelin cautioned bleakly against the risk of shattering the French shield through premature, isolated action. For these reasons, from Gamelin's strategic point of view, Czechoslovakia was ultimately deemed to be expendable.

For Gamelin, Poland's supposed military strength, together with its geographical position, made it crucial to French designs for an eastern bulwark against German aggrandisement. Indeed Poland's importance grew exponentially in the calculations of the French general staff, the more the latter acquired doubts about each of the other eastern allies. None of these allies was regarded as capable of significantly assisting France by the mid-1930s, were France to be the first object of future German aggression. But French intelligence analysts did not believe that Germany's designs – other than for remilitarising the Rhineland – lay in the west. This meant that it was regrettable, but not particularly risky, that none of the eastern allies could directly give France 'any effective help', as Gamelin put it in January 1934. Among them, he estimated, only Poland had the resources to 'play an important role' indirectly if Germany did, after all, menace France; this might be accomplished either by mobilising and retaining major German forces in the east of the Reich where they could not join an attack on France, or by staging a relief offensive into Pomerania, East Prussia or Silesia.[11]

Prospects for Poland if Germany – as was thought more likely – sought to expand eastwards were less sanguine. Poland, judged Gamelin, had no more realistic a chance than any of the Little Entente of 'taking on the Germans without assistance'. The Polish command, it was lamented, had 'cut itself off from French counsel' after its dismissal of the French military mission of General Niessel in 1926.[12] The French were, as in their relationships with so many other friends and allies, torn between their wish to shepherd and guide the military policies and the rearmament of Poland and their fear of the political commitments to which they might be held by the government in Warsaw if the 1921 treaty of friendship were defined more closely and strengthened. Poland was another case, among many that confronted the military chiefs, politicians and diplomatic officials in Paris during the 1930s, where 'what was needed were allies who would go to war for France but who would not make France go to war'.[13]

Though none of these eastern allies fitted this unrealistic and selfish French ideal, Gamelin gave pride of place to Poland. His views on the relatively greater significance of the Poles, compared to the other eastern allies, possessed a consistency from 1935 to 1936 that, by 1938–9, had taken on a distinct appearance of obstinacy. From the moment of the death of the Polish dictator, Josef Pilsudski, in 1935, the French high command sought an improvement of Franco-Polish defensive collaboration. The amelioration was predicated on cooperation with the new inspector-general of the Polish armed forces, Marshal Eduard Rydz-Smigly (whom foreign observers from several countries in Warsaw expected to become Pilsudski's *de facto* successor and new 'strong man' of Poland).[14] Early intimations in this sense were brought back from Poland by Pétain, who represented France at Pilsudski's funeral.[15] By November 1935, Gamelin and fellow senior generals were resolved to 'seek a *rapprochement*' with Poland's high command – and, in particular, to strive for cooperation with Rydz-Smigly, who they estimated was 'becoming preponderant' in Polish national affairs. In deciding to reconstruct the relationship with Poland, despite the continuation of the distrusted and disliked Beck at the Polish foreign office, Gamelin once again wagered that political difficulties could be smoothed or surmounted, provided solid practical cooperation was established between military men.[16] His belief in 1935–6 that he could refurbish Franco-Polish relations by means of deals struck between himself and Rydz-Smigly was another illustration of the heavy reliance Gamelin put on military diplomacy. His ability to press this method on the Quai d'Orsay was also a measure of his influence in French external policy-making. In this sense, Gamelin's cooperation with and from Rydz-Smigly, so extraordinarily personalised in character, paralleled the soldier-to-soldier relationships which he built with the leaders of other friendly armies, and most notably with Van den Bergen of Belgium and Nedić of Yugoslavia.

The wooing of Rydz-Smigly began in earnest in the summer of 1936, when Gamelin and Daladier, encouraged by other Popular Front ministers such as Cot, Delbos and Blum, addressed the future of French prestige in eastern Europe after the remilitarisation of the Rhineland. In April 1936, in an *ad hoc* civil-military conference to take stock of French options, Gamelin asserted that Germany was to be expected to protect itself in the west by constructing an 'unbreachable fortification' system. Notwithstanding this, and the prospect it raised of a stalemated war on the western front between France and Germany, Gamelin ventured that outflanking strategies 'analogous to what was done at Salonika' in the First World War would remain practicable as a means to hurt Germany – 'so long as we have alliances'.[17] The Mediterranean would have to be kept open for French communications with an eastern or south-eastern front formed by such alliances, and this meant no diminution in the central importance of obtaining the full military and political assistance of Britain to neutralise the Italian threat that sat astride Franco-Balkan sea lanes.

France, recognised Gamelin, would have to bear the brunt of a land war against Germany for the first year or two, if another conflict occurred. But victory over Germany, rather than mere French defensive survival, would necessitate military assistance on a grand scale. The 'French [strategic-diplomatic] problem', argued Gamelin in the CPDN in late June 1936, 'was essentially a function of the alliances'. Taking a concrete and none-too-hypothetical example of a prospective danger, he illustrated his contention by pointing out that if Germany ever bullied Prague, 'Poland would be able to come to the rescue of Czechoslovakia quicker than anyone else.'[18] From 1936 onwards, Poland was, for Gamelin, the key to making practicable a military defence not just of Czechoslovakia but of any part of east or south-east Europe placed in danger of dismemberment by Hitler.[19]

It is unclear how far this excessive estimation rested on faulty French intelligence and how far on the neglect of good intelligence. The latter failing was possible in Gamelin's case because of his enthusiasm for Rydz-Smigly at a personal level and because he was reluctant to face the fact that only the Soviet Union possessed the military power to lead successful resistance to Germany.[20]

The credibility of this latter explanation of the delusions inside the ranks of the French general staff is heightened by the desperate wish of French strategists to believe that it was possible to fashion an eastern front without Russian participation. Furthermore, the overestimation of the Poles resulted from the need of the French military chiefs to identify at least one ally in eastern or south-eastern Europe that could act as a regional surrogate for France itself and form the core or nucleus of an eastern front. At bottom the French general staff sought to encourage Poland to assume the leadership and run the risks that the French were not able to undertake on their own account. As an unusually candid internal study from the French army's operations bureau put it in June 1936, when surveying French military requirements: 'direct assistance to our east and central European allies lies outside the compass of this exercise and *is irrelevant to the future configuration of our army*'.[21]

The sheer size of the peacetime Polish army appears to have mesmerised French onlookers such as Gamelin. The Polish active forces looked formidable, at least on paper: a standing strength of 305,000 men, constituting 30 infantry divisions and 12 cavalry brigades, supported by 500 light tanks. On a war footing, after mobilisation of reserves, this force rose to some 50 divisions, making it by some way the largest army in Europe after the French, Germans and Russians.[22] To this potential, Gamelin's grand strategy accorded a position of paramount importance from the summer of 1936 onwards, as a 'zone of manoeuvre' and *clef de voûte* of an eastern anti-German bulwark.[23]

In setting so much store by Poland's military capacities – as well as in exaggerating its leaders' likelihood of unifying a largely incompatible set of east European nations – Gamelin appears to have looked too much at maps and too little at reports from French intelligence. Whereas he consistently belittled, understated and suppressed data favourable to Czech defensive capabilities, he equally obstinately inflated or glossed those of the Poles. The Czechs, however, embarked on a worthwhile overhaul of their military forces long before the Poles began discussing their own deficiencies with Gamelin in August–September 1936. In December 1934, for one thing, the Czechs extended conscript service in their army to two years. This not only allowed longer and more realistic training programmes, it enabled them to raise their peacetime standing force from 148,000 to 165,000 men. Daladier indeed then described the Czechs to French parliamentarians as having 'undertaken a very serious effort since 1934 in every aspect of national defence'.[24] Gamelin, however, remained prejudiced against the Czechs. He valued their military capabilities less highly than those of the Poles, even though France had maintained an advisory mission in Prague, first under General Mittelhauser and latterly under General Faucher, right down to the Munich agreement.[25]

The Poles' position as Gamelin's favourite eastern ally was cemented by his visit to Warsaw in August 1936. The mission offered evidence that Poland's special status in official Paris held firm not simply in the general staff but a good deal more widely among the diplomatic corps. In preparing the ground for Gamelin, the Popular Front foreign minister, Delbos, instructed Léon Noël, the ambassador in Warsaw, to assist Gamelin establish close military cooperation with Rydz-Smigly. Delbos' communication to Noël suggested that francophobe machinations by Beck (for whom there was no love in the Quai d'Orsay) lay behind many of the difficulties then troubling French standing in eastern Europe. The Polish–German pact of 1934 was, almost routinely, cited to the discredit of the Polish foreign minister. As was so characteristic of French leaders, Delbos showed himself blind to Poland's legitimate prerogative to negotiate as it judged best in its own interests; he was likewise apparently dismissive of Poland's predicament in the face of

German rearmament, Soviet malevolence and French vacillation. Delbos was heedless of Polish dilemmas. Polish diplomacy, he complained to Noël, had 'too often given the impression that her government is motivated much more by . . . demonstrating the complete independence of its policy than . . . showing the solidarity of interests between our two countries'.[26] No statement could better have made plain the habit among French politicians and officials of forgetting that their alliances were consenting relationships between adult partners – albeit usually ones of unequal size and longevity – and not a tutelage of the master over unruly pupils. The French too often tried to pursue their policies with reference only to French needs in a quite narrowly conceived sense, rather than to Franco-European ones. Their paternalism – which struck many of their allies as arrogance – was usually counterproductive to the attainment of their goals.

The Gamelin–Rydz-Smigly talks in Warsaw established an amicable and enduring rapport btween the two. Additional discussion with Poland's war minister and army chief of staff, Generals Kasprzycki and Stachiewicz, focused on the prospects for French industrial and financial assistance. Preliminary inquiries in this latter regard had been pursued by two Polish armaments purchase missions to Paris in mid-July.[27] The growing collaboration culminated in Rydz-Smigly's visit to France in the first week of September 1936, when the Rambouillet agreement was signed. Under this accord the French government opened a 2-billion franc military credit for Poland. Part of this was earmarked to enable Polish purchases of equipment from French munitions' manufacturers; part was intended to pay for technology transfers and acquisition of plant to facilitate development of a native Polish arms industry.[28]

The scale of these credit arrangements to strengthen Poland militarily and buttress the position of Rydz-Smigly was a striking testimony to Poland's privileged position in the eyes of Gamelin and his staff. No comparable financial or industrial assistance was ever offered to the Little Entente. It is not, therefore, wholly fair to say, as has the foremost historian of French diplomacy with east-central Europe in this period, that the 'absence of a sustained . . . effort to strengthen the military capabilities of the allies (especially Poland) through systematic and large-scale material aid was striking'.[29] It may, rather, be more accurate to suggest that the shortcomings of French defence industries when called upon to meet hugely expanded orders from France's own armed forces left the authorities in Paris powerless to provide invigorating infusions of warlike stores to their many small allies. Indeed, in such crucial respects as armoured fighting vehicles, the French were so stricken by their own difficulties that they were importuning Britain for help by 1937; certainly they were in no state to dispense largesse themselves.

The Rambouillet agreements, then, represented a substantial commitment to Poland in the context of French rearmament programmes which were themselves only at the beginning, not nearing their end, in September 1936. Poland was more generously treated than any other French ally: Rambouillet represented some action in response to the call made in early 1936 by the French military attaché in Warsaw, General d'Arbonneau, for a large defence loan to Poland to offset the fact that French help, thereto, 'had not been considerable from a financial point of view'.[30] It represented an answer to Weygand's lament, as he handed over to Gamelin in January 1935, that French meanness over economic aid was 'prejudicial' to France's 'higher interests'. 'What', he had complained, 'are some dozens of millions of francs if they could help to eliminate the risk of war?'[31]

Gamelin and French decision-makers appear, however, to have left Rambouillet to stand almost in isolation. They seem to have paid scant attention to Polish defence planning in 1937 and 1938, thus setting themselves up for an unwelcome discovery in the crisis of 1939 that Poland's vaunted military prowess was largely a paper tiger – and just about as intimidating to Hitler. The confused and excessively complicated administrative structures responsible for French rearmament, arms sales and manufacture under licence do not appear to have liaised efficiently with either the top military bodies, Gamelin's *cabinet*, Daladier's office or Gauché's 2e Bureau, or with the department for commercial accords at the Quai d'Orsay. Gamelin himself had too few staff and Daladier too many calls on his time to enable either to keep satisfactory track of Rambouillet. A victim, on the French side, of bureaucratic muddle and oversight, the question of whether Poland actually made any notable gains in military strength between 1937 and 1939 was lost to view. The assumption, it has to be believed, was that it had. The reality was quite the contrary. From their own disillusioning experiences at this time, Gamelin and the French service chiefs should have realised that converting francs into forces would be as slow and problematic a process for Rydz-Smigly as it had proven to be for themselves. The failure of Rambouillet's loans and credits to expand Polish defence industries – most specifically their failure to promote the manufacture of French munitions under licence – testified to the difficulty of bringing about major defence improvements merely by turning financial taps. The puzzlement and surprise of French military chiefs such as General Armengaud, sent as head of a French air force liaison mission to Warsaw in late August 1939, at Poland's weakness at the outbreak of war highlights the inability of these commanders to fathom the complexity and long lead-times that had become part-and-parcel of military procurement.[32] Though there were many French officers and officials reluctant to make large investments in the eastern allies, even those who recommended it showed far too little understanding of the practical obstacles between commitment of funds and attainment of a stronger defence.

The discovery that Poland remained desperately unready to fight off a German invasion in September 1939 seriously discomfited Gamelin and his associates. The surprise that they experienced was not, however, altogether the result of their own illusions or wilful ignorance – important though it was that Gamelin and the army staff did not wish to know about a Poland too weak to function as the key to an eastern front that Gamelin's grand design required by 1939. For the Polish government and military command themselves contributed substantially to the deception. Consciously, deliberately, they chose to mislead the French and British by exaggerating Poland's defensive preparedness. Certainly, with Hitler's speeches reclaiming the corridor and Danzig growing more vitriolic during the spring, the Poles were faced with mounting evidence that German designs would provoke conflict before the year's end. Hitler's denunciation of the 1934 pact after the Anglo-French guarantee was a pointer.[33]

Yet the assurances from London and Paris induced a false sense of security amongst Polish leaders. The latter – from Beck to the military chiefs, Rydz-Smigly, Stachiewicz and Kasprzycki – became overconfident about their prospects of deterring Germany once Chamberlain stated on 31 March that 'in the event of any action which clearly threatened Polish independence, and which the Polish government accordingly considered it vital to resist with their national forces', Britain and France would 'feel themselves bound at once to lend the Polish government all support in their power'.[34] Thereafter, with an assurance that was part self-deception and part boastful *amour-propre*, the Polish authorities forbore to admit the many grave shortcomings in their armed forces – shortcomings that affected their army, which was poorly equipped and inadequately trained; their air force whose airfields were ill-defended and whose aircraft were obsolete; and their fortifications which were too lightweight, too widely dispersed and too often built in the east of the country against the Soviets rather than in the west facing Germany.[35] Partly to live up to their new importance as the favoured eastern partner of the British as well as the French, partly out of complacency, Polish military spokesmen eschewed several opportunities in the spring and summer of 1939 to confess their defensive weaknesses and press for urgent western assistance.[36]

Instead of doing this, however, they insisted on their ability to defend themselves effectively. No inkling was given to Gamelin of the defects that plagued Polish dispositions in the course of his talks in Paris with Kasprzycki from 15 to 20 May, from which came the military protocol outlining the nature and schedule of French assistance in the event of Poland coming under German attack.[37] Nor were Polish military spokesmen any more frank with the British. The latter gained an impression of strength and self-confidence from General Sosnkowski, one of the senior Polish staff officers, when a British services' delegation headed by Brigadier Clayton visited Warsaw in May 1939 – an impression only confirmed by the cheerfulness and robust spirits which General Ironside, the British CIGS, also encountered when he travelled to the Polish capital in July.[38] Yet Sosnkowski subsequently admitted not only that he had misled the British but that Poland's defensive preparedness in the 1930s was hopelessly incomplete and that there had never been a realistic prospect of Poland rearming itself.[39]

In Paris and London, throughout all this bluff and disinformation, there were no eyes so blind as those that would not see. A defensively powerful and adequately self-reliant Poland was progressively factored into Franco-British strategic calculations by the summer of 1939. This helped ease the consciences of Gamelin, Vuillemin and their British counterparts, who conceded during their own staff talks in April that they had no means of bringing any large-scale military assistance or relief to the Poles in the first months of a European war initiated by German aggression in the east.[40] Reports from intelligence sources that did cast doubt on Poland's capabilities to stand like a rock against the German tide – such as the warning from Britain's military attaché in Berlin on 18 March 1939 that 'Germany must be confronted with the problem of a two-front war if the Poles are really to be enabled to put up a show' – were too inconvenient to be taken seriously. They were, therefore, set aside, left to gather dust in the files.[41]

Accepting Polish vulnerability would have required the French and British authorities to rethink their policy in the east. To admit that Poland was not sufficiently strong to bear the weight of being the keystone of an eastern front implied that Poland needed help. The French and British had already decided that their own rearmament was too incomplete to enable them to provide it;[42] nor was Czechoslovakia any longer a factor. This, of course, left the Soviet Union. The Poles, though, had a long history of wars against the Russians and rebellions against their annexations of Polish territories, from the eighteenth century to the twentieth. In the circumstances of the late 1930s, it was especially relevant that the infant Bolshevik state had fought its equally insecure Polish neighbour in 1920, being beaten back from the gates of Warsaw in desperate fighting (during which the Poles had the assistance of a French military mission led by Weygand). Over the remainder of the 1920s and 1930s, Polish–Soviet relations had been at best frosty and more often deep-chilled.

The French knew that Polish–Soviet animosity ran deep, although they appear not to have realised its full consequences for Polish military preparations and war plans. These latter, it has emerged, were directed, to a great extent, against the hypothesis of a conflict with the Soviet Union. This possibility was, indeed, the chief concern for Polish strategists throughout most of the inter-war period. Defensive planning and preparations with a view to surviving a German invasion were, in contrast, a relatively low priority in Warsaw. Polish war plans which foresaw Soviet Russia 'as its main protagonist' went back to the 1920s, according to a leading specialist on the question.[43] Moreover, so far from being replaced in the later 1930s by a shift of emphasis to the security of Polish western frontiers against German expansionism – a shift whose prudence might have been indicated by the Anschluss and the dismemberment of Czechoslovakia – the Poles continued to make ready to fend off the Red Army in the east of their country. Indeed 'this war design was completed in the first part of 1939'.[44] This anti-Soviet configuration to their dispositions and concentration plans was not something that Polish leaders disclosed to the French – any more than they admitted that such additions as they had made to their frontier fortifications had been undertaken not on the borders of East Prussia and Silesia but in the east, facing the Soviet Union.

Both by what it did and by what it led other powers to do, Russia thus played a central part in the ultimate failure in 1939 of the French endeavours to fabricate an anti-German eastern front with any diplomatic or military credibility. The difficulty of bringing about Polish–Soviet reconciliation and cooperation was not stumbled upon by the French, as if by accident, in 1939. Soldiers and diplomats in Paris had known, for years, of the smouldering antagonism and mutual distrust that divided Moscow from Warsaw. But, for reasons of geography and ideology, they had done nothing of consequence to bridge the chasm, even though France served as a common diplomatic denominator with the treaty of 1921 forming a link with Poland and the mutual assistance pact of May 1935 associating France with Russia.

French relations with the Soviet Union had thawed out in the first half of the 1930s. The icy anti-bolshevism of the era of the Russian civil war in 1917–19 had given way to the restoration of diplomatic normalcy with the accreditation of Charles Alphand as France's first ambassador to the Soviet state in 1932. This opening led in quick time to the appointment by Weygand of a military attaché, Colonel Edmond Mendras, to Moscow and to the signing of a Franco-Soviet non-aggression pact in November 1932.[45] The latter, over the succeeding two years, served as the foundation stone for the more wide-ranging commitments implicit in the pact of mutual assistance.[46]

This diplomatic *rapprochement* fell well short, however, of establishing the firm Franco-Russian alliance which had been such a rock in the shifting shoals of European international politics before 1914.[47] Most French politicians, officials and military leaders remained, at best, warily watchful towards Stalin. They harboured suspicions about his volte-face of 1935, when he sanctioned an end to 'class against class' tactics by west European communist parties, including the French one, in favour of constructing Popular Front alliances on the left and centre to support the electoral drives of socialist and liberal parties. Even before Laval visited Moscow and signed the mutual assistance pact, there was little enthusiasm among French political leaders of the right and centre for allowing Marianne a more passionate embrace with the Soviet bear. The geo-political rearrangements in eastern Europe after the First World War argued against making the relationship too intimate. Whilst France retained a common land frontier with Germany of similar length to the border between the two nations in 1914, Russia did not. The recreation of an independent Poland, along with the establishment of the Baltic republics, meant that Germany and the Soviet Union had ceased to have any point of territorial contact after 1919.

Many French strategic commentators argued that a Soviet military alliance was impracticable and therefore made poor political sense from a French viewpoint, in the light of these revised frontiers in the east. Discussing how to react to Germany's reintroduction of conscription and public establishment of an air force in March 1935, the conservative deputy Pierre Taittinger remarked to the war minister, Maurin, that France was 'in a much worse international situation than in 1914' and no longer had the 'great support of Russia' that it had enjoyed at that time. Maurin retorted that the Red Army was spread out to meet commitments over the length and breadth of a vast empire and had to attend particularly to its security concerns in the Far East. Even if it were still admitted that the Russians possessed powerful air and ground forces and had a benevolent disposition towards France, 'where [he asked] would be the point of application for this force?' It was not sufficient for

Russia to have an imposing military arsenal; it also had 'to be able to employ it purposefully' in order to be valuable as an ally of France. In 1914 East Prussia had served as the 'immediate point of application' enabling the Tsar's army to 'render France immense services' by creating a distraction for the German high command on the eve of the Battle of the Marne. Such a direct path by which the Red Army might exert pressure on Nazi Germany no longer existed.[48]

Maurin, though addressing this meeting of the Chamber army commission in his capacity as war minister, was articulating a scepticism about the Soviet Union that permeated most of the French command. This scepticism about the military utility of the Soviet armed forces intermingled with a deep-seated reluctance among French generals to facilitate closer contact between their own army and sources of communist influence – whether it be the newly legitimated PCF, suddenly voting at Stalin's behest for French rearmament credits and depicting itself as a Jacobin party of republican defence, or the newly respectable Soviet military and air attachés.[49] The majority of the French high command opposed any steps that would advance the *rapprochement* with Soviet Russia beyond ratification of the May 1935 pact. Even the ratification – effected by the French parliament on 27 February 1936 – was accurately regarded by French generals as a provocation to Hitler which would be used as a pretext for German remilitarisation of the Rhineland.[50]

Few French generals were interested in building cooperation with Moscow on the foundations laid by Laval's diplomacy. In so far as they welcomed the mutual assistance pact at all, they did so only because they perceived it to be a negative political asset – it kept Germany and Russia apart and left Hitler with one more uncertainty when he came to calculate the future behaviour of the powers to Germany's east.[51] Most of the French officer corps were suspicious and unenthusiastic about the Soviet Union, believing that it had not renounced a long-term goal of destabilising France through the agency of the PCF and the communist trade unions. Some generals, however, were explicitly anti-Soviet and were determined to undermine any effort by ministers to add a military dimension to the *rapprochement* with Russia.[52]

Among the most anti-Soviet generals were Maurin, Colson and Schweisguth. Situated as they were in key positions in 1935–7 – the war ministry and the army staff – at the time when the Soviets showed a great desire for substantive military cooperation, these officers were instrumental in emasculating the Franco-Soviet pact.[53] In 1935–6 they found it convenient to be able to cloak their ideological prejudice against the Soviets in objections of a 'technical' nature. Most obviously, they cited the geographical obstacles in the way of Soviet military action against Germany as grounds for declining to discuss joint defence arrangements with Red Army leaders. When a parliamentary army commissioner, discerning a means of by-passing the absence of Russo-German land frontiers and venturing that France could 'always count on Russia's aviation', asked Maurin if he could tell the deputies about the state of the Red air force, the latter was quick-witted enough to extricate himself with the lapidary response: 'I'm not the air minister.'[54]

Doubts about the military effectiveness of the Soviet forces, even if a route were found by which they could engage the Germans, formed the second long-running objection of French generals to the pursuit of talks with their Russian counterparts. These doubts crystallised into a systematic disparagement of Soviet capabilities after Stalin began to extend his political purges to the high command of the Red Army in 1937. But by at least two years they antedated the show trial of Marshal Mikhail Tukachevski and the elimination of three-fifths of the Red Army's officer cadres. As early as February 1935, prior to Laval's journey to Moscow to sign the mutual assistance pact, a French military mission was reported to have returned from observing Russian manoeuvres with predominantly negative opinions. Whereas it had been favourably struck by the Soviet air force (which it considered had 'raised itself to the first rank in world aviation'), it had been dismayed by the deficiencies of the army leaders whom it adjudged 'totally inadequate in the higher ranks, with colonels and generals of unbelievable ignorance and no general appearing capable of commanding an army'. The mission's report apparently 'made the most deplorable impression on the French general staff'.[55] The anti-Soviet prejudices of French generals were only reinforced by the vulgar and loutish conduct of the Soviet delegation to the main French manoeuvres of 1935, in Champagne in September (the first time Russians had been invited to French exercises since 1914). The Red Army mission, a disgusted Schweisguth noted in his diary, behaved 'arrogantly and indiscreetly ... always ordering whatever was most expensive, fine wines etc. (leaving us a 10,000 franc bill to settle), and having themselves treated as *grands seigneurs* whilst boasting all the while that they were proletarians'.[56]

At the same time, in September 1935, a French mission led by one of Schweisguth's fellow assistant chiefs of staff, General Lucien Loizeau, attended Soviet manoeuvres. Loizeau, however, was one of the few senior French soldiers innately favourable towards the broadening of the alliance with Russia. He had been an important participant in the triumvirate of officers whose support in 1933–4 for the Barthou–Alphand strategy of diplomatic *rapprochement* with the Soviets had overcome outright French military opposition to the transformation of the non-aggression pact of 1932 into the mutual assistance pact of 1935. (The other members of this triumvirate were Mendras, the first French military attaché accredited to the Soviet regime, and Colonel Jean de Lattre de Tassigny, chief of operations to Weygand in 1932–4.)[57] The report which Loizeau brought back positively lauded the capabilities, ingenuity and fighting power of the Red Army. The much-publicised and novel highlight of the manoeuvres was an airborne simulated attack in which 1,000 paratroopers were dropped in two waves in less than eight minutes and were then supported by parachuted equipment as well as by second-echelon air-landed troops and vehicles. Loizeau concluded that the Soviet armed forces had been transformed from a huge but ill-trained mass (the Red Army alone numbering a standing force of some 900,000 according to French intelligence), into a sophisticated, innovative and potent arbiter of international relations in eastern Europe. He recommended that Franco-Soviet staff talks be promptly opened to obtain France the support of this modernised version of the Russian steamroller.[58]

Such advice was anathema, however, to most of the general's colleagues and superiors at the war ministry in Paris. Maurin, who had been unreceptive to suggestions of military collaboration with the Soviet Union, had been replaced at the war ministry by Fabry, a zealous anti-marxist, when Laval became prime minister in June 1935. Fabry explicitly opposed the demand of the Soviet ambassador, Potemkin, during talks in Paris in July 1935, that the mutual assistance pact be given a military dimension. Fabry suspected Stalin of seeking to make Franco-Soviet relations appear provocative to Hitler and of a secret wish to bring about a Franco-German war from which the Soviet Union would benefit by supporting communist seizures of power in a war-devastated Europe.[59] Many of the French general staff gleefully seized on the minister's anti-Sovietism to squash and then suppress the Loizeau report, with its inconveniently enthusiastic appraisal of the Red Army. Loizeau himself was admonished for his pro-Soviet bias in a heated interview on 20 September with Colson, whom he 'displeased' by his 'eulogy on the Red Army'.[60]

Gamelin did not share the doctrinaire anti-communism of generals of the stamp of Colson and Schweisguth. His was a pragmatic view, closer to that of his old friend and *camarade de promotion*, Maurin. He distrusted the long-range political intentions of the Soviet leadership but recognised that, in the *realpolitik* of the military balance in eastern Europe, the Red Army and air force represented factors of prime importance. When Daladier sceptically asked in October 1939, after

Stalin and Hitler had divided a conquered Poland between them, if 'Russia is really a force', Gamelin retorted that 'a mass of 150 million men is always [going to be] a force'.[61] He estimated that Russian military power was growing impressively from 1933 onwards, becoming 'imposing as regards numbers and industrial production' but 'whose value' (as he put it later) 'one was entitled to doubt, as much from an intellectual as from a moral point of view'.[62] The exclusion of the Soviet Union from the various attempts to regulate Europe's affairs by a concert of the major powers – such as the Four Power Pact of 1933, the Stresa Front of 1935 or the Munich conference of 1938 – was 'justified', Gamelin subsequently argued, by the 'dangers of contamination' that would have been presented by 'her intrusion into European politics'.[63]

The era of attempted *rapprochement* between France and the Soviet Union in 1935–7 therefore evinced Gamelin's suspicions but not his intransigent hostility. Unlike Colson, Schweisguth and other conservatives, Gamelin forbore, even when behind the closed doors of the general staff's offices, to propose that the military command attempt to stall or scotch the addition of arrangements for strategic coordination onto the 1935 pact. Compared to many, if not most, senior French officers, Gamelin kept an open mind about the potential for the pact to be enhanced and developed to French advantage. Indeed, after being favourably impressed by his first meeting with Tukachevski whilst both men were in London in January 1936 for the funeral of King George V, Gamelin invited the Soviet marshal and commander-in-chief-designate for talks in Paris the following month, from 10 to 15 February. Notwithstanding Tukachevski's admission that he was in contact with the German army leadership, he and Gamelin agreed that they 'would intensify the relations' between the French and Soviet armies.[64] Gamelin, apparently, viewed such undertakings with equanimity because he considered that the political opposition to any enlargement of the 1935 pact was so deeply entrenched in Paris as to make the authorisation of defence exchanges with Moscow singularly implausible. 'The question of the USSR', he reflected later, 'ran into the prejudices of French domestic politics.' Any proposed *rapprochement*, he also knew, would encounter 'difficulties from the Polish side'. Asked in 1934, by Barthou, to discuss with Weygand the military's view of *rapprochement* with Moscow, Gamelin subsequently affirmed that there was no disputing the continuing potential of Russia as an 'eastern "counterweight"' against Germany. Like Weygand, Gamelin agreed that 'it mattered first and foremost to avoid a Russo-German entente' whose goal would be 'a new partition of Poland', a reordering of central Europe and the transformation of the continental balance of power.[65]

At the level of international politics, then, Gamelin admitted that the 1935 pact had the merit of closing off one avenue by which Germany might seek to obtain an enormous diplomatic advantage – tantamount to a free hand – in east-central Europe. But he was no more prepared than the conservative French generals to countenance all-embracing Franco-Soviet military collaboration. 'We soldiers', he subsequently explained, 'distrusted bolshevism and French communism – fomenters, above all else, of national disintegration. It was important that our new relations with Moscow did not have any repercussion for our internal politics and on the morale of our army.'[66]

The election of the Popular Front government in mid-1936 changed the nature of the political outlook on the Franco-Soviet pact, to the discomfiture of Gamelin (who had expected its parliamentary ratification in February to be as far as politicians would agree to go in an association with Stalin.) The Popular Front brought Cot – a *compagnon de route* since his seduction during a visit to the Soviet Union in 1933 – back to the air ministry. This immediately increased the pressure on the French military commanders to begin meetings with their Soviet counterparts and arrange how the pact's requirements to provide assistance might be implemented.[67] By November 1936 the question had reached the attention of the prime minister, Blum, who proposed to Daladier and Gamelin that secret discussions start in Paris with General Ventzov, the Soviet military attaché.

Blum argued that, with the pact eighteen months old, it was desirable for France to ascertain from the Red Army exactly how it envisaged furnishing military help against Germany.[68] Within the French high command, however, there was a widespread sense that military conversations with Moscow might backfire, by enabling Soviet commanders to pose embarrassing questions about the plans of the French army to render them assistance by means of offensive action against western Germany. To many French generals, it appeared that the more deeply France became involved in reciprocal military arrangements with the Soviet Union, the more it risked an increase in its liabilities rather than an increase in its security. The last thing French commanders wanted to be asked about by any eastern ally was their planning for relief operations against Germany's western frontiers, since they had none worthy of the name. Nor was this a concern confined to the generals. In one meeting at the Palais Bourbon, eight days before the pact's ratification, two deputies who specialised in defence questions, Taittinger and Guy La Chambre (who became president of the Chamber army commission in July 1936), explicitly cited the 'anxiety' of Maurin, voiced eleven months earlier in March 1935, about the absence of Russo-German land frontiers. La Chambre expressed the fear, also, that the pact would result only in the laying of additional military burdens on France, 'particularly in respect of [further increases in] the duration of the conscripts' active service'.[69]

From the Popular Front's election till the spring of 1937, however, the Russians pressed relentlessly for negotiations with the French high command. On 30 June 1936 the Soviet chargé d'affaires in Paris invited Schweisguth to attend the Red Army's manoeuvres near Minsk, that September, as a sequel to Loizeau's visit a year earlier. At the same time, the French general staff began to receive a stream of warnings that their hopes of closer relations with Britain might be jeopardised if a Franco-Soviet strategic convention were concluded, over and above the 1935 pact. The pact itself – as the British clearly intimated – was disliked and distrusted in Whitehall. The indications are that, from this point in time, British frostiness towards Franco-Soviet military arrangements became the mainspring of the behaviour of French war ministry officials on this issue.[70]

At first, during the autumn of 1936, the French strove to steer a middle course. Their fears of losing the Soviet Union into the German orbit led them to suggest to the British that a *rapprochement* with Russia might have considerable 'negative' value. At the French manoeuvres near Aix-en-Provence, in September 1936, the British military attaché, Colonel Beaumont-Nesbitt, was told by his German counterpart, Kühlenthal, that more than 200 panzer officers had undergone illicit training in armoured warfare in the Soviet Union during the years before Hitler's announcement of German rearmament in 1935. French officials, meanwhile, repeatedly warned the British that too much store should not be set on the ideological incompatibilities of Nazism and Bolshevism. These political factors might, it was felt, be outweighed by more opportunistic calculations in Berlin and Moscow. French 2e Bureau sources indicated an urgent German need for access to raw materials that were plentiful in the Soviet Union, such as oil and wheat. Stalin, for his part, urgently required manufactured goods. These were possible pre-conditions for a *rapprochement* between the two dictators.[71]

Arguments such as these were not sufficient, however, to allay British anxieties about the condition of France under the Popular Front. British envoys, such as the ambassador in Paris, Sir George Clerk, suspected that the Franco-Soviet pact had succeeded not so much in keeping Russia and Germany apart but in strengthening the French communists and in destabilising the French army and nation. Already, in June 1936, Clerk had filed a gloomy despatch that warned of a loss of national cohesiveness among the French.⁷² By late September, Blum was struggling to contain a second wave of industrial strikes and factory occupations. Clerk deplored the turmoil and speculated that communist infiltration within the French army had reached levels where the reliability of troops in a strike-breaking role was no longer assured.⁷³

Nobody had a more acute sense of the danger in a British loss of confidence in France than Gamelin. In early November 1936 the French senior commanders received a visit from their military attaché in Britain, General Lelong (an old associate of Gamelin from the mission to Brazil of the 1920s, whom the chief of the general staff had hand-picked for the London assignment). Lelong warned that British policy-makers were divided between factions – one described as the 'Admiralty view', another as the 'City view' and a third as the 'Foreign Office view'. Only the last of these groups had much sympathy towards France (and it was to them that Clerk's discouraging despatches were filed).⁷⁴ The message from Lelong appeared to be that France could not afford to rest on its laurels as far as maintaining support for its policies among British leaders was concerned.

This was the consideration that shifted Gamelin out of his neutrality or disinterest towards the controversy about military conversations with the Soviets. It induced him to join his more conservative general staff officers and lead the latter in dragging their feet to defer the start of meaningful talks. On 7 November, three days after Lelong's visit to report the unpredictability of British support, the French army staff was informed that Blum's government had decided to order talks with the Red Army through the medium of the Soviet military attaché in Paris, as soon as a successor arrived for Ventzov (who had been recalled to Moscow after more than three years in post).⁷⁵ Gamelin, uneasy about the prospect in view but unwilling to dispute Blum's instructions, nominated Schweisguth and Colonel Paul de Villelume, the general staff's liaison officer to the Quai d'Orsay, as the army's negotiators. Beyond this, however, no preparatory steps were taken by the high command, which intended to temporise for as long as possible and avoid substantive discussions.⁷⁶

To reassure London, the French military leaders meanwhile embarked on a carefully orchestrated weakening of the theme of Franco-Soviet *rapprochement*. The new and softer tune was played in perfect harmony by every officer from whom the British heard it. The military governor of Metz, General Giraud, was 'emphatic in his condemnation of the Franco-Soviet Pact', reported Britain's military attaché, declaring that it 'conferred no benefit at all on France'.⁷⁷ The attaché added that Gauché, head of the army's 2e Bureau, had denied that France was in 'the state of decay which she is often thought to be by outside observers'.[78] Clerk, the ambassador, also remarked on the 'marked hostility to the . . . Pact in French high military circles'. He advised London that it seemed to him 'significant' that Franco-Soviet military conversations, 'which it had been expected would shortly take place', were not occurring.[79] In mid-October 1936, via one of Clerk's embassy staff, Gamelin let it become known to the British that he was going to resist military exchanges with the Red Army, so long as he remained chief of the general staff and in a position to do so.[80] By 1937, after talking to the editor of *L'Echo de Paris*, André Pironneau, a 'personal friend' of Gamelin, the British military attaché reported – as he was doubtless meant to – 'that . . . Gamelin was utterly opposed to too close a connection with the Russians'.[81]

Consequently the French command showed no urgency about getting down to brass tacks when, at the start of 1937, a new Soviet military attaché, General Semenov, arrived in Paris. His first two meetings with Schweisguth and Villelume, on 7 January and 2 February, were spun out by the French on questions concerning protocol and terms of reference.[82] Two considerations underlay the reticence of the French negotiators. Neither was altogether new, but each assumed a new importance – or a new plausibility – at this time.

In the first place, Schweisguth's own coolness about enlarging French ties to the Soviet Union had been reinforced by his visit to the Red Army manoeuvres in September 1936, in company with de Villelume, General Vuillemin of the air staff, and other officers. His since-notorious report on the mission estimated that the Red Army was badly under-prepared for a war in the foreseeable future against a front-rank European power. Though it 'appeared to be strong, abundantly equipped with modern *matériel* [and] imbued with an offensive spirit', the Soviet army's shortcomings, according to Schweisguth, included retention of crude cavalry-style tank tactics, a naïve faith in the possibilities of successful attacks even against modern anti-tank defences, and the absence of a native Soviet tank industry to enable a war of attrition to be sustained. Most damningly, however, Schweisguth suggested that the Soviets harboured subversive political motives in their search after a military alliance with France. The Kremlin, he considered, wished to win the faithful friendship of France in part so that Hitler would face the perils of a two-front war if he should decide to mount a German attack on Russia. In part, Schweisguth argued that Stalin wanted the military alliance in order to encourage German paranoia about encirclement and provoke Hitler into war against France – a war at whose end the Soviet Union would triumph as the unopposed arbiter of an exhausted

Europe's destiny. Meanwhile, counselled the general at the conclusion of his report, France ought not to be deceived by the Red Army's propaganda concerning its ability to assist it; its 'conditions of employment against Germany remain[ed] very problematical'.[83]

Loathe, then, to implement the wishes of Blum and Cot for a full military partnership with Moscow in early 1937, the French generals were even more perturbed by the mounting evidence of British discontent about Franco-Soviet *rapprochement*. 'British friendship remained our base', Gamelin put it later, whereas he 'had always expressed reservations about the USSR's power, notably of an offensive nature'.[84] On 8 February 1937, six days after his second round of preliminary talks with Semenov, Schweisguth told the Quai d'Orsay secretary-general, Léger, that the British had been displeased by the Franco-Soviet pact and could be expected to look more askance still at any military accord that further entangled French policies with the interests of Moscow. In reply, Schweisguth was assured that Blum understood this problem of British susceptibilities: he was resisting pressure from both Herriot, among the Radicals, and the PCF to speed up the conclusion of an agreement.[85] On 17 February Blum himself met the Soviet ambassador, Potemkin. He explained that the French general staff wanted an authoritative answer to the question of how Red Army leaders proposed to bring military force to bear on Germany. He particularly feared that the Poles, Romanians and Baltic republics would remain adamantly opposed to the passage of Soviet units across their territories.[86]

To obtain the Soviet high command's official reply, Semenov, the Soviet military attaché, was immediately despatched to Moscow. Daladier explained in his memoirs what then happened. First the Russians returned 'a verbal response: "If Poland and Romania allow passage of Russian troops, action [would be taken] against Germany's eastern frontier. If not, troops would be sent by sea. In both cases, the Soviets would supply war materials and would participate in the struggle between the navies and in the air."' On receiving a report to this effect from Schweisguth, Daladier said he then 'invited him to pursue this useful inquiry further, without hesitation'. It seemed 'especially necessary' to Daladier to probe more deeply into the 'question of Soviet air assistance'. On 19 March a demand for clarification in this sense was put to Semenov. The latter set off the next day a second time, in search of answers in Moscow, announcing that he would return to Paris in early April.[87]

On the 9th, with still no sign of the Soviet attaché's reappearance, Gamelin had a meeting with Daladier. The minister was preparing for a visit two weeks later to Britain, where it was to be expected that he would receive a hostile interrogation about the Franco-Soviet talks. Gamelin now made it plain to Daladier that he objected to military negotiations or agreements with the Soviets if these stood to alienate either the British or the Poles.[88] By the closing days of April the French generals had learned of the attitude in London. Schweisguth noted that Colson had seen the minister immediately after his return on 25 April from Britain, where 'Daladier had been told that France was naturally at liberty to proceed to military conversations with the Soviets' but that Germany was issuing warnings on the matter and that France 'would not have to be surprised at the consequences'. Under these conditions, with the scarcely veiled threat of Britain's withdrawal of diplomatic support, it was decided to suspend the conversations.[89]

All that remained was for the French generals to devise a pretext with which to justify the freezing of the talks to the Russians, when Semenov returned from Moscow. An excuse was fashioned on 27 April between Schweisguth and Gamelin. There it was noted that it had been said to Daladier in London à propos Franco-Soviet conversations: 'Six months ago we would have raised a loud outcry; now we would understand better but, in our view, the matter is still not ripe'. Unsure about citing British objections, therefore, Gamelin proposed instead to kill the negotiations by using his visit to London in May for the coronation of George VI, to take aside the Soviet military representative and tell him 'that the French soldiers were in favour of an agreement, but were unable to admit of Russian interference within the French army, intended to weaken it'.[90]

Stalin, however, spared Gamelin the embarrassment of having to proffer such a contrived excuse. The purges of the Soviet politburo and party cadres which the Russian leader had been pursuing with gathering ferocity during 1936 were suddenly extended, in the spring and summer of 1937, to the Red Army high command. To the dismay of all western observers and envoys in Moscow, Stalin had Tukachevski himself condemned to death before a show trial in early June, on fabricated charges of treasonable dealings with officers of the German army. Besides leading to the death of Tukachevski, the purge of the Soviet army saw the execution of three-fifths of its senior officers.[91] One assumed victim, scarcely noticed in such a fearsome and extensive pogrom, was Semenov, who sent signals announcing his return to Paris first on 5 April, then on the 10th, but never materialized. With the disappearance of the Soviet attaché through whom his subordinates had been conducting the talks to add military agreements to the mutual assistance pact, Gamelin was let off the hook.[92]

The eleventh hour attempt by the French, accompanied by the even more reluctant British, to resurrect a military partnership with Russia in the summer of 1939 was blighted from the outset by Soviet distrust. Indeed, the French game of hard-to-get in 1935–7 made it unavoidable that Stalin should view the renewed approaches by the western powers for an Anglo-Franco-Soviet coalition against Germany in April–August 1939 with suspicion and cynicism.

The cards in the hands of the French and British when they rejoined the Soviets at the table, after two years with only a formal level of diplomatic contacts, were weak ones. They had to importune the Russians for military assistance on behalf of Poland, after giving a guarantee to Warsaw that they were themselves powerless to uphold. Stalin, who could not be directly attacked on land by Germany, possessed all the bargaining chips. This balance of advantage was calculated in itself to turn the Soviets – ostracised by the French and British governments as recently as the Munich conference – into uncompromising negotiators.[93] Over and above this consideration, however, was the fact that the Germans had begun extending their own commercial and political overtures to Stalin, through their ambassador in Moscow, Schulenberg, in the early months of 1939. Suddenly in the unaccustomed position of being wooed by both sides, Stalin was able to await the rival bids, playing the game of a *politique de surenchères*.[94] The omens were inauspicious for the belated Franco-British effort to make Russia the guarantor as well as the arsenal of their flimsy eastern front.

Most crucially, however, even in the spring and summer of 1939, Gamelin and the French defence experts continued to doubt the military value of the Soviet armed forces and to overestimate the military capabilities of the Poles. The French general staff had always thought that a full military alliance with Russia would not be compatible with their existing alliance with Poland. 'It will be necessary to make a choice', as they had forecast in January 1936, shortly before the parliamentary ratification of the Franco-Soviet pact.[95] In showing time and again that they favoured Warsaw over Moscow, the French army's leaders were consistent if perhaps not very circumspect in their judgement. Gamelin himself evidently hoped against hope to fashion a compromise that would avoid the need for a choice. During and after his two rounds of talks with Rydz-Smigly, in August and September 1936, he said he 'tried in vain to make the Poles understand that not just Russian neutrality but Russian assistance was indispensable to them'. But he had, he reflected, only received the reply that the Poles 'detested' their former governors, Russians and Germans alike, and that of these they 'hated the Russians, all the more because they were so distrusted'.[96] The intransigent politics of Polish–Soviet relations thus played a major part in perpetuating Gamelin's plan to make Poland the foundation-stone in 1939 of an eastern front. Yet, at the same time, the ravages inflicted on the Red Army by Stalin's purges provided a means by which French leaders could dress their choice in a persuasive strategic rationalisation. 'From 1937 onwards', Gamelin reflected later, 'Russia was going through a period when her military power was subject to a temporary eclipse.'[97] He convinced himself at least as early as the winter after Munich – and remained convinced down to the short and disastrous campaign in the east in September 1939 – that Poland was a better bet than the Soviet Union as an anti-German bulwark. Right to the end, therefore, it was the resistance of Poland to Germany that Gamelin thought of as a magnet to draw other powers into an eastern front.

Several factors, therefore, combined to stop the French treating the reconciliation of Poland and Russia as a matter of urgency and fundamental importance to the creation of a militarily credible eastern barrier against further German expansion. It was apparent to the French army staff that such a reconciliation would be extraordinarily difficult to effect; moreover, their misplaced confidence in Polish defensive capabilities caused an underestimation of the need to mediate and strive imaginatively and relentlessly to bring it about. In January 1939 the French military attaché in Warsaw, General Musse, sounded the Polish military staff and reported it very hostile to any understanding with the Soviet Union – even one limited to the provision by the latter of munitions and material supplies. Musse advised that, in these conditions, France should 'avoid appearing to press the Poles to make a move towards the Soviets', and wait to see if time brought about a reduction of tensions or an opportunity for an accommodation.[98]

The military attaché – like d'Arbonneau before him – was a convinced devotee of the Franco-Polish alliance as well as an eloquent advocate for it. His repeated expressions of confidence in the underlying fidelity of the Polish leadership towards France, during the recriminations between Paris and Warsaw over Munich and the Teschen affair in September–October 1938, had helped limit that controversy's damage to Franco-Polish friendship. However, Musse showed in his report about Polish–Soviet relations in January 1939 that he shared the prevalent and misplaced view that plenty of time remained in which to work on dispelling the antagonisms dividing the two French eastern allies. This complacency among the government and general staff in Paris – added to the revulsion felt by Chamberlain and British conservatives for supping with Stalin except with a very long-handled spoon – lay behind the fatally dilatory western initiatives to achieve an

Anglo-Franco-Polish-Soviet alliance for mutual and reciprocal defence. It also explains why Germany's much swifter, more cynical and more decisive diplomatic opening to Stalin succeeded in bringing Hitler the spoils of the Nazi-Soviet non-aggression pact signed by Ribbentrop and Molotov on 23 August.[99]

At the beginning of 1939, therefore, there were signs that some French and Polish leaders felt it imperative to reinvigorate the alliance between their countries and put practical measures to deter German aggression at the top of their priorities – even at the price of admitting Soviet participation in Polish defence. General Sikorski, then on the retired generals' list and enduring his personal *traversé du désert*, visited France at this time and – despite some doubt that the Maginot Line might dissuade the French from offensive plans – wrote in his diary that France understood Poland's 'key position'. He judged France 'as ready to fight for Poland as for its own interests. It works the whole time to steady Great Britain. In spite of the affronts it has received from [Beck] it is comparatively faithful.' Back in Poland by the spring, Sikorski continued his earlier advocacy of limited cooperation with the Soviet Union to dissuade Germany from a drive eastwards. In 1937 he had written in his diary that an 'alliance of Poland with Russia, envisaging the march of the Red Army over Polish territory, is unacceptable to Poles'. Yet Poland, he estimated, could 'not reject *a limine* all forms of aid which would in fact be possible in the case of a war with Germany'. He thought, then, that the 'simplest solution would be an understanding with Russia which would ensure us the supply of Russian goods', concluding that to gamble Poland's 'future on the old antagonism between G[ermany] and R[ussia] or on our declaration of neutrality ... would be the policy of an ostrich and would have suicidal consequences'.[100] Most Polish leaders, however, disagreed.

Britain's chiefs of staff, surveying the military balance at the start of 1938, had noted perceptively that it was 'only if Poland is friendly and willing to cooperate that Russian intervention on behalf of France and England could quickly develop into a real menace for Germany'.[101] The unarticulated corollary to this state of affairs was, however, that Polish readiness to be helped by the Soviet Union was also the indispensable requirement before the western powers could align the Red Army as a barrier to a German drive in the east. Most Polish politicians and military leaders remained suspicious, however, that for them to agree to Soviet military assistance would be to swallow a medicine more dangerous than the problem it was supposed to treat. As one Polish official put it, when faced by Anglo-French exasperation at Poland's objection to authorising a right of passage for Red Army forces during the critical summer negotiations of 1939: 'With the Germans we may lose our liberty; with the Soviets we shall lose our soul.'[102]

The shocks of March 1939 – Germany's violation of the Munich accord in annexing Bohemia and Moravia on the 15th and seizing Memel from Lithuania a week later – stirred French military diplomacy, though into a trot rather than a gallop. Following the 31 March guarantee of Poland, Beck held talks with the British government in London in the first week of April.[103] It was agreed that negotiations would proceed to reach a reciprocal and permanent Anglo-Polish accord, eventually to succeed the unilateral assurances given to Warsaw the previous week. On 10 April a French army staff study of the strategical situation reiterated the vital importance of 'obliging Germany . . . to make war on two fronts by forming as important and active a coalition as possible with Poland and eventually Romania, with a view to immobilizing part of the Reich's forces and withholding from Germany the economic resources of Eastern Europe (wheat, oil)'.[104] On 29 April, the day after Hitler abrogated the 1934 Polish–German pact, Gamelin wrote to Rydz-Smigly to propose the resumption of Franco-Polish staff talks. The Poles readily agreed. Their chief of general staff, Stachiewicz, told Musse that a military delegation would travel to Paris to discuss the outline of projected operations and Poland's need for material assistance through another Rambouillet-style accord.[105]

Gamelin, though anxious to shore up both the intention and the ability of the Poles to resist Germany, was embarrassed by the desire of the Polish military chiefs to begin the staff conversations straight away. He claimed later that he 'would have liked, before holding any specific conversation with the Poles . . . to have been able to have had talks with the Russian general staff'.[106] Evidently Gamelin realised that the resistance of Poland or Romania (guaranteed by France and Britain on 13 April) would only be prolonged, in the event of their suffering a German attack, if it was backed by Soviet support – support that Gamelin understood needed to be secured by the western powers because the Polish leaders would refuse to negotiate for it directly. The French commander's conviction in this regard was confirmed once French and British *démarches* in Moscow were in progress. On 19 July Musse reported from Warsaw that the Poles were following Franco-British diplomatic efforts to attach the Soviet Union to the peace front 'with sympathy'. But, warned the attaché, Poland's own position on the overtures to Moscow remained one of 'the greatest reserve': it was not to be expected that Poland would depart from an 'attitude of benevolent neutrality towards a negotiation in which she did not have to become embroiled'.[107] In fact, since he had received a report on Musse's talk of

24 March with Rydz-Smigly, Gamelin knew that the Polish government had refused to join any four-power accord of the kind floated that month by French and British ministers. In approaching the meeting with the Polish military delegation to Paris, therefore, Gamelin was aware that Polish–Soviet cooperation remained taboo, Rydz-Smigly having made it plain that he feared Hitler seizing Polish–Soviet contacts as a pretext for fresh German demands against the Corridor or Danzig.

The Franco-Polish staff talks occurred on 16 and 17 May. They were high-level affairs, involving Gamelin himself, along with Georges, Dentz, Musse (who had travelled from Warsaw to provide first-hand advice) and other army officers, together with Vuillemin of the air force and Darlan for the navy, on the French side. The Polish deputation was led by the minister for military affairs, General Kasprzycki, and also included Colonels Jeklicz, first deputy chief of the Polish general staff, Fyda and Perrinski, respectively military and air attachés in Paris, and Loyko, head of the armaments purchasing commission. The meetings resulted in agreement on measures to be taken by each nation in the event of a German attack on the other. For the French land forces, the main undertaking was to begin offensive action with limited objectives to apply pressure on German forces in the west, beginning after the third day of French mobilisation. This was to be expanded to offensives with 'the bulk' of French ground units concentrated on the frontier with Germany, when the sixteen-day mobilisation process was completed. In the talks, Gamelin clarified this commitment by telling the Poles that about three-quarters of the mobilised French army would deploy in the theatre against Germany and that about half of this would be able to participate in the promised relief offensives. On behalf of the French air force, Vuillemin made the astonishing pledge that he would be able to take 'vigorous action' to assist Poland from the outset of a conflict. In a subsequent meeting with Vuillemin's chief of operations and other officers of the Armée de l'Air staff, the Poles fashioned arrangements in principle that were to enable five French bomber groups (sixty obsolescent Amiot 143s) to fly across Germany to reinforce the feeble Polish air force and operate from bases earmarked around Radom and Lublin against targets in Pomerania.[108] As the counterpart to these undertakings, the Poles agreed to advance against Germany's eastern frontiers in the event that Hitler should attack France in the first instance. The outlines of these commitments were incorporated in a protocol of the talks that Gamelin and Kasprzycki signed on 19 May.[109]

On the French side, these conversations were marked by a lack of candour, no little cynicism and a measure of deception that did no credit to the general staff, the air staff or the foreign minister, Georges

Bonnet. As far as Gamelin was concerned, he had been blatantly misleading in sending Kasprzycki away from Paris believing that, if Poland suffered a German attack, it could count on a bold French relief offensive against the Reich's western frontiers within three weeks.[110] French planning in reality envisaged nothing remotely so ambitious. In consequence of the undertakings given to Kasprzycki, Georges, who was commander-designate of the north-eastern theatre and thus responsible for preparing plans for the land war against Germany, received a directive from Gamelin on 31 May 1939.[111] The document made no mention of any rapid and adventurous advances. Rather, it told Georges to draft plans for a careful, graduated and step-by-step engagement with the German defences in the Saarland, between the Rhine and Moselle. In turn, on 24 July, Georges sent his own instructions to General Prételat, the commander-designate of the army group that would be directly responsible for mounting the operation. These papers emphasised the need for a cautious clearance of the west bank of the River Saar and the Warndt forest, after the seventeenth day of French mobilisation. The orders further prescribed that the Third Army, which would conduct this advance, was then to consolidate, harass the Germans beyond the Saar with its artillery and 'proceed with the offensive supply of its front in order . . . to be prepared for a river-crossing operation which it might later on be called upon to carry out'.[112] Evidently, these were plans for a demonstration in front of the German lines, a gesture. They were not the preparations for an offensive that would require the Wehrmacht to weaken an attack against Poland and redeploy major forces from the east to the west. They did not, therefore, honour the spirit of the Paris talks or the 19 May protocol – even if Gamelin and other French leaders later made tortuous claims that they did conform to the letter.[113]

The conduct of the French air staff and of Bonnet was perhaps even less creditable. In the case of the former, Vuillemin was personally familiar in painful detail with the delays in the re-equipment and expansion of the Armée de l'Air. He had assured La Chambre, the air minister, in January and September 1938 that French air strength would be completely used up by a mere two weeks of combat operations against Germany. In August 1939 he was to confess that his air force's rearmament was still so retarded that a further six months without serious operations and concomitant attrition would have to elapse before the Anglo-French air strength could approach parity with that of the Luftwaffe. When the Second World War finally began, no-one was a more adamant opponent than Vuillemin of the Allies initiating the air war by bombing raids into Germany, so afraid was he of provoking the Germans to retaliate on a scale that the French and British would be unable to match for many months. It was thus misleading for Vuillemin to pledge 'vigorous' action on targets in Germany by the Armée de l'Air, to force the Luftwaffe to withdraw significant forces from an attack on Poland. In mitigation, it can only be noted that the minutes of the talks in Paris on 25–6 May 1939, between delegations under Colonel Karpinski, deputy chief of staff for the Polish air force, and Colonel Bergeret, Vuillemin's chief of operations, spelled out that French air support in 1939 would be conditional upon the prior security of the air space of France, French North Africa and the Levant. They also recognised that the deployment of the five Amiot bomber groups across Germany to Lublin and Radom would depend on their having refuelling facilities at airfields in western Poland – facilities which, in the event, were overrun in the first hours of the German invasion, leaving the project stillborn. Finally, the record of these meetings observed that the French air force expected to be in a condition to provide much more powerful assistance to Poland by 1940, if a confrontation with Germany could be staved off until then. These caveats notwithstanding, it is clear that the Poles went away believing that they would receive serious help from France in the air at whatever point a war came about.[114] As far as Gamelin was concerned in this, he appears to have been privately surprised that, in the existing parlous state of the Armée de l'Air, Vuillemin had spoken to the Poles as unguardedly as he had. Characteristically, however, he raised no protest about Vuillemin's undertaking, and acted strictly by the letter of his brief as chief of staff for national defence – to coordinate but not to command French air and maritime forces.[115]

More to Gamelin's credit was his anger and outcry at the behaviour of Bonnet. The latter put in doubt the meaning of the talks with Kasprzycki by refusing to sign the Franco-Polish political accord that was intended to provide the framework and governmental authorisation for the 19 May protocol. Indeed, the political agreement was supposed to embody and express the reciprocal determination by the French and Polish governments to come to the aid of one another if either were to be attacked by Germany so that it felt compelled to fight back. Gamelin indeed knew that senior Quai d'Orsay officials were busy drafting the political document even as the military conversations with Kasprzycki and his fellow officers were proceeding. The very terms and language of the military protocol – which Gamelin appears to have drafted personally – rested on an assumption that it would draw its authority from and serve as a technical codicil to an inter-governmental agreement. With the conclusion of the latter, which Gamelin did not think was in doubt as the talks progressed, the military document was to be formally termed a 'general staffs accord' – a document representing firm and politically approved commitments in a way that a mere protocol of talks would not.

Predictably enough, accounts differ sharply between Gamelin's memoirs and those of Bonnet as to how and why the political agreement did not materialise at this point. However, it appears from research into Bonnet's conduct in the summer of 1939 that the general was correct to suspect the minister of seeking to evade closer ties between France and Poland.[116] The officials at the Quay d'Orsay did draw up a document in time for signature before Kasprzycki's return to Warsaw. This much Gamelin learned at the time by telephoning the secretary-general, Léger. Bonnet, however, declined to sign. An embarrassed and suspicious Gamelin then sought the arbitration of Daladier, the prime minister. But the latter, he discovered, had left Paris to spend the long Ascension Day weekend in the country and would not return until after the Polish minister's departure. In the circumstances, Gamelin and Kasprzycki signed the military protocol – which remained no more than that, Gamelin adding a prefatory note that its application would depend on the ultimate conclusion of the political agreement at a later date. Aware that the Poles were perplexed and disappointed at what had transpired, Gamelin made a point of saying farewell personally to Kasprzycki at the Gare du Nord, 'in order to ease the impression of uncertainty as to what lay at the bottom of our thinking, that he did not disguise he was taking back from Paris'.[117]

Gamelin found the episode discomfiting and dishonourable. He claimed to be 'ulcerated that the minister for foreign affairs had not acted with greater frankness towards the command' and deplored the deviousness of Bonnet. The latter, according to Gamelin, was wrong to have let the Polish military delegation travel to Paris and hold talks if he had not intended to give the undertakings reached in these the authority of the expected inter-governmental agreement.[118] 'Was this not', Gamelin wondered, 'likely to lead Poland to have only limited confidence in us and to face us one day with a fait accompli?' It was certainly, as he also complained with a nicely sardonic note, 'very difficult' to keep French military conceptions adjusted to a foreign policy 'as versatile as this'. The senior civil servants at the Quai were to be exculpated from the fiasco, according to Gamelin; they were 'in despair' at Bonnet's actions which Gamelin insisted were 'prejudicial to the higher interests of France'.[119]

What Gamelin learned from the whole mismanaged affair was how cunningly and single-mindedly Bonnet still clung to projects for further appeasement in eastern Europe. Whereas by the end of 1938 Gamelin had become persuaded that Hitler's aims at least directly threatened France's reputation and future great power status – perhaps even its independence – Bonnet remained eager to strike deals. His appeasement had not been ended by the evidence of Prague and Memel that Hitler did not keep his bargains. The foreign minister spent the summer months of 1939 in devious and complicated suggestions, inquiries and propositions designed to avoid France becoming involved in a war arising in the east.[120] Gamelin passed it by striving to ensure that France would make aggression against Poland the occasion for a stand and a declaration of war. For him, what mattered was his conviction that the next German attempt to destroy or dismember an independent European nation had to be met by Anglo-French armed force. And the crucial advantages of choosing to withstand Hitler over Poland – or Romania – were, firstly, that Britain would automatically be there too, shoulder to shoulder with France; and, secondly, that the war facing Germany would be a war on two fronts.

In all this it was to Gamelin's credit that his goal was to make an attack by Germany on Poland an occasion for resistance, not an opportunity for capitulation.[121] What was less laudable was his deeply cynical outlook on the strategic plight in which Poland would find itself in the event of this war. Gamelin knew that Polish resistance could do no more than succumb bravely. Nor did he think there was anything that France and Britain would be able to do, militarily, to make a significant impact on a German–Polish outcome. But, as has been shown, he passed over the chance to spell this out to Polish leaders during the meetings in May with Kasprzycki. Instead, he counselled the Polish officers to expedite the construction of as many light fortifications as possible and to adopt a defensive plan that would screen the frontiers lightly and concentrate the main resistance as deep inside Poland as possible. This was sensible advice – though the Polish commanders ignored it on political grounds, and at the insistence of Rydz-Smigly, adhering instead to a suicidal forward defence by three divisions in the Corridor and a deployment of 20 per cent of their army in the east, watching Russia.[122] In accompanying this guidance with the promise of major offensive action after the seventeenth day of French mobilisation, against western Germany, Gamelin was, however, committing a deceit. This was none the more excusable just because the British were party to it[123] – their chiefs of staff having concurred during the Anglo-French military conversations in April and early May that Poland's defeat was not an eventuality that the western powers would be able to prevent but one that they would undo through final Allied victory in the war.[124]

The difference between Bonnet and Gamelin was, then, that whereas the minister wanted to avoid going to war over Poland at all, the general wanted to declare war over Poland so that France would not have to fight seriously until the following year.[125] Gamelin's outlook in this sense is crystal clear, for he came clean with his cynicism in the privacy of talks with his British counterpart, Lord Gort. Meeting in Paris in mid-July 1939, Gamelin told Gort: 'we have every interest in the war's beginning in the east and becoming a general conflict only little by little. We will thus have the time necessary to put on a war footing all Franco-British forces.' The sacrifice of the Poles, continued Gamelin on this occasion, would lead to 'the immobilisation, to our advantage, of important German forces in the east'.[126] But Gamelin continued to overestimate the powers of resistance of the Polish army. He also mistakenly assumed that Rydz-Smigly and Stachiewicz had followed his counsel about adding extra fixed defences and concentrating well back inside the Polish interior. As a result of these misplaced beliefs – reinforced among Anglo-French governmental and military circles by the optimism with which Ironside returned from Warsaw that same month – Gamelin remained over-confident.[127] He considered that Poland would be able to withstand an assault by Germany, alone, for between four and six months, before its organised and effective resistance collapsed.[128] As Petibon and Dentz (deputy chief of army staff with responsibility for intelligence) had reportedly explained it in January 1939, the French command ascribed to Poland 'possibilities of long resistance ... since she has ... room to manoeuvre'.[129] Nor did the Poles, as noted earlier, do anything to dispel this Anglo-French illusion that they would succeed in opposing German invasion with a stalwart and protracted defence. Colonel Szymanski, the Polish military attaché in Berlin, depicted the command in Warsaw in the springtime as 'full of confidence in the spirit of their country and efficiency of their army'.[130]

During this period of the summer of 1939, there were no further Franco-Polish staff meetings to complement and follow up the talks held in May. There was a legalistic justification, in that arrangements and undertakings had been left suspended in limbo by Bonnet's withdrawal of the political agreement. Gamelin claimed later that this was the only correct procedure in the circumstances, for the May protocol, technically, remained shorn of governmental sanction.[131] Contacts continued through the military attachés. But the abbreviated nature of the staff conversations had several drawbacks, of which the most important was that neither the French nor Polish generals learned the nuts and bolts of each other's concentration and operations plans. These had been evoked in only the most general outlines both during the Gamelin–Rydz-Smigly talks in 1936 and in May 1939. The Poles, on the latter occasion, had arrived expecting full details to be requested and were prepared to oblige, their plans being in Colonel Jaklicz's briefcase throughout the meetings.[132]

The French did not ask, however. The only plausible reason can be that an insistence on their part would naturally have led to their interlocutors demanding detail about the French plans. This – since these plans were scarcely worthy of the name and undercut the impression being purveyed of French readiness to attack – Gamelin was not prepared to disclose.[133] This state of partial military coordination continued down to the outbreak of war, neither ally becoming acquainted to any useful degree with the other's intentions. This reticence prevailed even when a French military mission arrived in Warsaw to represent Gamelin at Polish headquarters, led by General Louis Faury (who had been the founding commandant of the Polish war college and was highly regarded by his hosts).[134] Only the conclusion of the Franco-Polish intergovernmental accord could have broken the deadlock. The agreement, however, was not finally signed till 4 September, three days after Germany invaded Poland and one day after France and Britain went to war. To the end, then, Bonnet's readiness to buy peace at any price imposed crippling limits on the Franco-Polish alliance – and it furnished Gamelin with disreputable but nonetheless welcome grounds for not revealing the French relief offensive for the meaningless Grand Old Duke of York gesture that it really was.[135]

In Gamelin's grand strategy of 1939 Poland was not to be rescued. Rather, its resistance was to inflict attrition on the Wehrmacht; secure France from having to face any serious combat before the year's campaigning season was over; and free the western Allies to amass the military and economic resources of their empires to overthrow Germany and resurrect Poland after two or three years of war. The truculent refusal of the Polish government during the Anglo-Franco-Soviet negotiations of May to August 1939 to concede the Red Army a right of entry only made the Polish army's defeat at the hands of a German invasion doubly sure; the signature by Ribbentrop and Molotov of the Nazi–Soviet non-aggression pact on 23 August meant the defeat would also be dismayingly swift. The pact was fatal to Franco-British hope that Polish resistance could be of long duration. But it did not shake Gamelin's resolve over the need to go to war.

When a crisis meeting of military and political leaders was hastily convened in Paris on the evening of 23 August to discuss the meaning of the Molotov–Ribbentrop pact, Gamelin said that it represented Hitler's green light to move on Poland. He also said, unequivocally, that the French forces were ready to go to war.[136] By this he meant that the forces had the strength, training and support of the British to enable them to defend France.[137] His pronouncement was, nevertheless, of central importance in encouraging Daladier to pick up the gauntlet that Hitler's strike against Poland would throw down. Gamelin's positive military guidance and the assurance of British support were decisive in leading Daladier to resist in September 1939 – just as Vuillemin's negative advice and the uncertainty about Britain's position had been decisive in leading Daladier to negotiate a year earlier.[138] Gamelin pressed that Hitler's challenge be opposed at the end of August 1939. Partly this was because he mistakenly believed Poland to be an ally that could give an excellent account of itself for several months; partly because the perils of appeasement after Munich seemed to him to outweigh the risks of war. As he put it in a written submission for his trial before the Vichyite wartime political court at Riom: 'In the end, after the Russo-German entente, if we had given way we were condemned more than ever to recognize the hegemony of Germany over Europe ... [for] to have given way, to have trusted Germany, would have been to become in our turn the "brilliant second".'[139]

11 Gamelin and the fall of Poland

It speedily became evident that France had not gone to war to save Warsaw. Indeed, well before September 1939, the civilians and the military leaders in Paris had quietly disavowed any serious offensive intentions. The French and British both agreed that there should be no 'dash[ing] off ... merely to relieve the Poles'. At their spring 1939 conversations their military staffs had reluctantly concurred that Poland could not be saved by precipitate Allied action.[1] This decision implied that serious fighting on the western front should be deferred – a view that Gamelin endorsed.[2] The independence of the Poles would not be restored, thought Gamelin, by hastily mounted and under-equipped Allied sorties in the war's first weeks. It would be revived instead as the eventual result of carefully planned and lavishly supplied Allied offensives in the closing stages of a long conflict. Gamelin shared the prevalent Franco-British belief that Poland's restoration required a strategy of overthrow. The first stage of this was to be a methodical wearing-down of the Wehrmacht; the second the economic exhaustion of Germany by the long-term squeeze of the Allied blockade; the final stage the removal of Nazism.[3]

Holding these views, Gamelin's first concern in the autumn of 1939 had to be to secure France itself as the base from which to prosecute this strategy of a *guerre de longue durée*. Like his French political superiors and British Allies, Gamelin 'could not envisage Germany's defeat until their enemy had exhausted its reserves and resources'. In the short term 'the primary mission of the army was to prevent defeat'.[4] Gamelin's perception of Poland – a perception that recurred in Weygand's memoirs in respect of France itself – was that in the war's opening phase it constituted the advance guard of civilisation. It was cast as a shield for a global alliance not yet fully alive to the perils of Nazism, let alone fully mobilised. As the head of the French air liaison staff in Warsaw in August–September 1939 told the Poles: 'The battle of Poland was just the first battle of the war ... The Polish army, the first to be attacked, was just the advance guard of the armies of a coalition.'[5]

This was, by any reckoning, a cold-blooded and inglorious western attitude whilst the Polish forces fought literally for their lives as well as for Poland's survival as a state. But was it, as has been alleged, a spurned opportunity to embarrass Germany seriously whilst the Wehrmacht was heavily engaged – even if it was not a realistic chance to rescue Poland from defeat and occupation? Without arguing counterfactually it is hard to insist, one way or the other.[6] What may be said is that, from a French standpoint, the options appeared to be hazardous, complicated and limited. An ill-prepared offensive, however heroic, seemed likely to endanger the future application of a coherent Franco-British grand strategy. Gamelin knew the shortcomings of the French army and air force. He knew, too, about the small size and unarmoured character of the British Expeditionary Force (BEF) which would arrive in France during the first month of hostilities. His headquarters journal demonstrates, day by day, the diligence with which he applied himself to the responsibility of defending France in 1939–40. It also reveals the doubts that he felt concerning the operation of the French mobilisation and the uneven quality of the French army itself. He shared sentiments expressed by one British diplomat in his diary at this time, that the benefits of a quiet start to the war in the west were too valuable to be jeopardised by 'quixotry' or ill-considered offensives for the sake of a gesture to the Poles 'when by conserving our effort we should be able to deal a much shrewder blow later'.[7]

Thus Gamelin's certainty of the strategic correctness of going to war over Poland did not prevent him having deep misgivings about the security of France during the autumn of 1939. As this chapter will show, he paid close attention to the reports about German air–armour methods used to destroy the Polish army. 'When the war begins over here in earnest', he alerted his staff during the deceptively calm first weeks on the western front, 'it will be a very rude awakening.'[8] He did not dispute the formulation offered by the finance minister, Reynaud, on a visit the latter paid to Gamelin's war headquarters in the Château de Vincennes in October, that the 'French army represents the world's final rampart against the predatory forces' of dictatorship and barbarism.[9] The 'crux of things', Gamelin himself said to his aides at this time, was the need to 'make troops such as ours, which are not yet battle-hardened, capable of holding an all-out German onslaught whenever it is unleashed'. Hitler, he warned his subordinates, would not shrink from sacrificing lives and material without limit, to crown his march of conquest with success.[10]

Such illusions as persisted in Paris evaporated swiftly as it appeared that the collapse of Poland would be not just speedy but total. The comprehensiveness of Germany's triumph in the east was unexpected to Gamelin. It was not that he had believed the Poles able to survive indefinitely, but he did express the hope to Rydz-Smigly, via the military mission under General Louis Faury that he despatched on 23 August to Warsaw, that the Poles could 'drag things out'.[11] On 3 September, after the French had transmitted their ultimatum to Hitler to withdraw German forces from Poland, Gamelin remarked to his staff that it was 'now a matter of assisting the Poles to the maximum of our ability and, to this end, of concerted Franco-British action to draw off onto us as much German strength as possible'.[12] Fleetingly, French and British leaders indulged a self-deception that the conflict in the east might continue into the winter – towards the possibility of resistance of between four and six months' duration that Gamelin had attributed to Poland in the summer of 1939.[13]

The short-lived optimism briefly deluded the French that the alliance (and, therefore, a war on two fronts), had a serious future. Colonel Fyda, the Polish military attaché, was received by Gamelin on 1 September. On the 4th, the long-deferred Franco-Polish political treaty, never signed at the time of the May 1939 Franco-Polish military talks, was finally concluded. It put the formal diplomatic seal on the war for Poland in which France was by then engaged. More ironically, it was virtually the final act of Bonnet as French foreign minister before his removal from the Quai in Daladier's government reshuffle of 13 September. On the 8th, Colonel Fraser, the British military attaché, in Paris, buoyantly suggested to his wife that he did not '*think* the news from Poland is really too bad at the moment'.[14]

Throughout the first week of September, whilst Poland fought for its very survival, all was quiet on the western front. French general mobilisation had been decreed at midnight on 2 September. French commanders showed far greater concern that this should be completed without enemy disturbance than they did about making any offensive moves that would provide relief to the Poles. Gamelin's staff were satisfied on 6 September that the 'concentration was proceeding in the best possible conditions. The Germans have not yet sought to trouble it.' Ten days later the Belgian military attaché in Paris, Colonel Maurice Delvoie, reported to Brussels that Gauché, head of the 2e Bureau, had also 'said that French mobilisation was exceptionally well carried out'.[15] The French plan called for a diversionary attack towards the Saar and the Siegfried Line. But first the armies involved – General Condé's Third, General Requin's Fourth and General Bourret's Fifth – had to complete their incorporation of reservists behind the shelter of their own *couverture* units and the Maginot Line.

Air action by the western Allies was another possible way to support Poland and was considered when the British CIGS, Ironside, and chief of the air staff, Sir Cyril Newall, visited Vincennes on 4 September for the first Allied military meeting of the war. Newall, however, was 'reticent' about beginning bombing operations against Germany without prior enemy air attacks on French or British targets. Vuillemin, whose bomber force was less than 400 strong and not yet equipped with the effective new machines like the LéO 45 just appearing from French industry, was equally negative in appraising Allied air capabilities.[16] On 6 September Gamelin's adjutant noted that the 'news from Poland is vague . . . [but] it appears that it is bad: the Poles are in retreat and the jaws of the vice already seem to be closing around Warsaw'.[17] The next morning the French army finally suffered its first casualty of the war, when a soldier in a mobile reconnaissance group near Wissembourg was wounded in the hand. In view of the rather more serious injury being inflicted at the time on France's eastern ally, it can hardly have been surprising that Gamelin was 'bothered incessantly' by Poland's military attaché, 'distraught at the news he was receiving from his country'.[18]

By 9 September the initial Franco-British illusions were dispelled. It was plain that the Poles were experiencing a military disaster. Gamelin ordered the CSDN secretariat under Jamet, responsible for releasing military communiqués to the press, to ensure that the newspapers did not disguise the débâcle. They were 'not to put out any eye-wash, especially regarding Poland which – let's not hide the fact – is finished'.[19] Gamelin also issued orders to Georges, who had assumed the duties of *de facto* command of the front facing Germany and had his Grand Quartier Général (GQG) at La Ferté-sous-Jouarre, about 50 kilometres east of Vincennes (where, in the Château, Gamelin had established his own war headquarters). It was 'to be foreseen', opened the first of Gamelin's 'Instructions personnelles et secrètes' of 9 September, that the Polish army would not much longer be able to sustain open combat against the Wehrmacht. Georges and General Bineau, the chief of staff of the armies, were told to reconsider their precautions in case Germany redeployed major forces to attack the west and in case Italy used Poland's collapse as a pretext to join the enemy camp. In a second 'Instruction', the next day, Gamelin told his subordinates to study what could be done if Belgium called for assistance 'in useful time', and if Holland was attacked and Belgium offered French forces a right of passage to move north to help the Dutch.[20] When, also on 10 September, a Polish military liaison mission under General

Burhardt-Bukacki arrived in France after a circuitous journey via Scandinavia, they found that events had overtaken them. Gamelin and Burhardt-Bukacki observed military protocol by meeting several times, but their encounters could only have the character of relatives exchanging condolences after a family funeral.[21]

The exceptionally hot and dry 'Indian summer' of 1939 had reduced Polish river levels and provided firm cross-country terrain ideally suited to the Wehrmacht's mechanised offensive. The Poles were ruthlessly exposed, militarily, as less the first storey of an imposing edifice of eastern allies than a house of cards which collapsed the moment a blow was directed against it. On 12 September, in the *sous-préfecture* at Abbeville, the Franco-British supreme war council held its first meeting. Gamelin, asked to give a briefing, observed that Poland's organised military operations had virtually broken down. He recommended abandoning the limited French offensive operations in the Saar, arguing that they could no longer affect the outcome in the east. The British representatives agreed that, just as had been envisaged in the Anglo-French conversations between March and May 1939, Poland would have to be resurrected by the eventual Allied overthrow of Hitler's Reich. Meanwhile, Gamelin emphasised that the pressing question was whether Germany would exploit victory in the east by driving on into the Balkans or by transferring the weight of its armies to the west. He thought that the latter was most likely, warning of the 'possibility of a German effort against us, especially through Luxembourg, Belgium and Holland, from October onwards'.[22]

Gamelin was reduced to hoping, from Poland, for last-ditch resistance to win the maximum respite possible for France and Britain. As Fraser, with British understatement, wrote to his wife on 14 September, the war was 'not going well in Poland'; but he thought 'it might still last some time – it depends on the weather'.[23] By the 16th (the day before the Red Army attacked Poland, in keeping with the secret protocol of the Molotov–Ribbentrop pact), Gamelin knew that only a climatic *deus ex machina* could keep the Polish alliance in play. Indeed, since the start of the month, the general had been 'frequently and anxiously checking the barometer', hoping for rain. Wet weather would 'severely handicap' the Germans in the east. Armoured columns and supplies 'would have difficulty moving without becoming bogged-down'.[24] But early on 17 September the Soviets launched their own invasion of eastern Poland. It was the *coup de grâce* for Rydz-Smigly's embattled armies. Four days later, on the 21st, even Fraser's optimism had disappeared; the 'Polish show', he acknowledged, 'is finished to all intents and purposes'.[25] Perhaps Gamelin and his staff felt some qualms of conscience about the way in which they looked to the weather to succour Poland when they, with their ponderous mobilisation and cautious strategy, could not. At any rate such clutching at straws moved Fraser to reflect at the end of September how 'The Jehovah who brings down rain to save his favourites is still the God whom an awful lot of people prefer to believe in, and they were quite baffled as to why he had ordained such a dry summer in Poland.'[26]

Within ten days of the war's outset, then, the Franco-British statesmen and commanders understood that it was not the fate of Poland that demanded their attentions. The first issue that did exercise them was the achievement of security in the west – initially during the vulnerable period of the sixteen-day mobilisation and concentration of the French armies and the move of the British Expeditionary Force to France, and then for the longer term. The second matter was the evident need to learn from the nature of the Polish defeat in order to seek to preclude any similar catastrophe in the west.

On the former count, the fears of the Allies derived from the redoubtable capabilities which they ascribed to the Wehrmacht. Germany was credited, especially by Georges and by Prételat (commander of the Second Army Group that coordinated the modest Saar offensive), with the ability to harass France from the very beginning of the war, even whilst the German–Polish war was still in progress.[27] French intelligence estimated that Germany was fielding between eighty and ninety divisions at the start of September, with about sixty of these attacking Poland. It was also reckoned that a further thirty reserve divisions would be raised in the first three weeks of hostilities.

From this the 2e Bureau concluded that a force of thirty to thirty-five divisions might oppose them in the west from the outset, and that this could rise to fifty or even sixty divisions if the Germans felt it unnecessary to reinforce their initial deployments against Poland.[28] These estimations exaggerated the size as well as the quality of the forces which the Germans deployed defensively behind their Siegfried Line and opposite Luxembourg, Belgium and Holland. Only eleven regular infantry divisions were disposed there by the Wehrmacht on 3 September, although these troops were reinforced by reserve divisions.[29] In one significant respect at least, French intelligence was wise not to underestimate Germany's readiness for operations on two fronts. For the German army had been maintained in a state of continuous mobilisation since March 1939 when parts of it had occupied Bohemia and Moravia. After the spring alert there had been no general stand-down but instead a period of intensive training. This led directly into summer exercises, deliberately concentrated in the Reich's eastern training grounds so as to achieve the maximum intimidatory effect on Warsaw. By August 1939 the German forces, especially those facing Poland, were like a wild dog on the leash, straining with a pent-up ferocity and baying for release. In contrast, the French army had remained at its peacetime establishment until general mobilisation – a sixteen-day process – was decreed on 2 September.[30]

The cautiousness of the French armed forces throughout Poland's destruction sprang from several factors. The first was the long-war grand strategy that had been elaborated in full agreement with the British. This presupposed a defensive opening phase for the western Allies with the minimisation of risk and the husbanding of resources. Victory was envisioned as the result of a long haul and Poland's resurrection as one of the principal prizes. Leaders in London and Paris concurred in rejecting any vainglorious gestures in September 1939 which might erode the capacity of their forces to stay the course and reap eventual triumph. The second cause of the French command's caution was the sheer poverty of their military means in the first phase of hostilities. Until the completion of general mobilisation on 18 September, none of the French infantry divisions raised in metropolitan France was ready for battle. All of the twenty peacetime or so-called 'active' infantry divisions had first to play their part in the amoebae-like self-reproduction that incorporated mobilised reservists and transformed the army onto a war footing. This process involved a three-fold expansion, each peacetime division providing a proportion of its officers, nco's and career soldiers to serve as the commands and skeleton organisation of the A-series and B-series reserve divisions. Whilst the German hammer-blows started to strike Poland, immediately disposable French formations were limited to two light mechanised divisions (with a third under formation), a clutch of colonial and North African infantry divisions and two heavy tank brigades with 130 of the powerful Chars B. These forces, representing the fruits of Weygand's and Gamelin's labours over six years to equip France with hard-hitting mobile units, were themselves still in the process of receiving equipment straight from the factories.[31] Gamelin judged them far too precious a tool to risk blunting in 'premature' aggressive strikes into western Germany. Moreover, such operations would, the general affirmed, have dangerously depleted French ammunition and equipment stockpiles. The munitions 'stocks existing at the present moment', Gamelin advised Daladier on 1 September, 'have been scaled in accordance with restricted financial resources rather than related to real rates of expenditure'.[32] Interestingly Colonel Delvoie, Belgium's military attaché in Paris, who was kept closely informed by Gauché and the 2e Bureau throughout the phoney war, readily accepted, in a 'personal view' that he sent to Brussels on 7 September, that France possessed 'no superiority, for the moment, over Germany' with 'her present forces' in view of the neutrals and the Italians against whom France had also to provide defences.[33] In a more political consideration, Gamelin instructed his staff on 16 September to tell Georges that care was required over 'the delicate position' of the 4th colonial division. It would, he said, 'not do for it to be our Senegalese troops who first experience the shock of . . . tanks and low-flying aircraft'.[34]

A third consideration that dissuaded the French from any initiative at the start of the war was the conviction that German aggression in the east would be matched by extensive Luftwaffe action against the west. This fear gripped Paris as tightly as it did London. French and British alike thought that the declaration of hostilities would instantly be followed by German aerial bombardments against the principal cities and industrial concentrations of the western Allies. The air menace, furthermore, was a divisive issue between the British and French. The former were as convinced that London and the factories of the Midlands lay in the Luftwaffe's sights as the French were that the targets lay in Paris and Lorraine. There was no meeting of minds on the direction of the threat. Nor was there any elucidation from intelligence. This had singularly failed to discern that the aircraft types and training of the German air force had geared it for missions of tactical ground support and interdiction behind an enemy's armies, not for strategic attack on his economic base.[35]

For a time, near paralysis was threatened by this erroneous reading of the German role for air power. As early as 1 September clusters of silvery barrage balloons were floating on the Parisian skyline, as sinister as primeval monsters. Gamelin himself, on 3 September, discounted any immediate German land operations to disrupt French mobilisation but instead warned his staff that an 'air action by them could be serious'. Before dawn on both 5 and 6 September the Vincennes headquarters was awoken and driven into its underground shelters by air-raid alerts. Although these proved to be false alarms, Fraser still thought in mid-September that there was only 'a fortnight at worse or a month before the air war starts on this side'. He considered that a Luftwaffe offensive would be launched as a prelude to an invasion. Indeed he ventured that the air forces might hold the key to events on the French front, believing that the armies would attempt 'no decision until . . . one side or the other' had 'achieved supremacy in the air'.[36]

It is unclear whether Gamelin himself went this far in gauging the significance of possible air operations.[37] He did, however, know about the warning of 26 August 1939 from Vuillemin and La Chambre that had emphasised the need for six more months of all-out aircraft manufacture and the lowest possible level of air operations before the Allies would attain equality with the Luftwaffe.[38] This awareness of their air inferiority served only to reinforce the strategic and operational caution that their long-war grand strategy had already ingrained in Franco-British leaders. The air force chiefs, presiding over the weakest part of the Allied war machine when the conflict began, simply showed the general tendency in particularly exaggerated form. For fear of reprisals neither the British chief of air staff nor his French counterpart wished to escalate the air war beyond dropping propaganda leaflets over Germany in September and October 1939. In setting so much store by non-provocation of the Luftwaffe the air marshals had the full support of Chamberlain and Daladier.[39] When the French military leaders met, as they naturally did at frequent intervals, 'the most reticent among us', Gamelin recalled, 'was always General Vuillemin'.[40] At this stage, however, few doubted that Allied productivity would, given a respite until 1940, eradicate this short-term Allied disadvantage.[41]

French circumspection during the phoney war of October 1939 to April 1940 resulted, too, from a supposition that Hitler would lunge at his eastern and western adversaries in swift succession. Gamelin, more than most, felt that Germany would follow its triumph over Poland by immediately attacking France or the Low Countries. In September he was, remembered an officer of his Vincennes staff, 'persuaded that the Germans would attack France before the winter . . . since they had, by his reckoning, every advantage in seeking a decision before Allied armaments attained their maximum level'. Gamelin's anxieties were intensified by the startling speed of Poland's collapse and by the continuation into October of ideal campaigning weather.[42]

Furthermore, Gamelin was angered and at the same time disconcerted by Belgium's rejection of Allied pleas at the war's outset to renounce neutrality. His policy of clandestinely cooperating since October 1936 with Van den Bergen, chief of the Belgian general staff, had rested on his conviction that the government in Brussels would throw over its independence and join the Allies if war eventuated between the latter and Germany. When, on the contrary, Belgium remained resolutely neutral in September 1939, Gamelin warned Daladier that it complicated Allied strategic problems and 'worked wholly to the advantage of Germany'. Since the Allies sought to enlarge their coalition by attracting neutrals who were appalled by Hitler's roughshod expansionism, French forces, the general remarked, 'will not, because of the moral point of view, be able to move onto their territory unless called in by them'. Belgian neutrality magnified the difficulty of mounting offensive action to distract German forces from eastern Europe. It also aggravated Gamelin's long-standing problem of securely defending northern France. Only by obtaining Belgian cooperation, said Gamelin, would France 'be able to bring to bear powerful relief, certainly effective and relatively rapid, to Poland'. Defensively, in the event of subsequent German aggression in the west in violation of Belgium and Holland, he reiterated French 'interest in advancing to support Belgian forces in their defence of the important obstacles provided by the Albert Canal, Liège, the Meuse'. Accomplishing this defensive advance would give France the benefit of forward air bases in Belgium 'and would distance the war from the French frontiers, particularly from our rich provinces of the Nord'. French strategic assets and interests remained the same as they had been in 1932 or 1936 and Gamelin's refrain, worn though it had become, still rang with common sense. Moreover, in something of a prophecy of May 1940, he warned: 'if the Belgians appealed to us only at the moment when they're attacked . . . we should have to run all the risks of an encounter battle with the difficulty of supporting retreating armies'.[43]

Before the end of September, the return of Wehrmacht formations from Poland to the west was detected by French intelligence. Opinions differed about the significance of the transfers. Did they reflect French success in the limited offensive undertaken by Condé's and Requin's forces towards the Saar, obliging the Germans to reinforce their western defences? Or did the movements herald German preparations for an offensive of their own, to seek swift victory over France before substantial British assistance reached the continent?[44] As early as 9 September Gamelin 'feared Germany's return with all her forces concentrated against us, as soon as the Polish affair is over'. Georges was instructed, that day, to redouble his watchfulness on the borders of Belgium and Luxembourg, whose conquest 'would greatly improve German jumping-off lines against ourselves and Britain'. At the next day's staff meeting, on 10 September, Gamelin repeated orders that Georges and Bineau (the chief of staff of the armies), should attend to the 'possibility of attack' by the enemy's main forces, as well as 'to the contingency of their violation of Belgium'.[45]

In these alerts – which were just the beginning of a tension that gripped the western front until late November – Gamelin and the senior generals of the Franco-German theatre, notably Georges and Prételat, felt that an early German offensive in the west was highly probable. French intelligence chiefs did not.[46] The latter retained confidence in their secret sources and it is worth pausing to review the bases for the unruffled calm displayed during this first phase of the phoney war in the French intelligence bureaux. At the head of the French army's secret agencies was still the vastly experienced and respected Rivet. A month after the outbreak of war, on 3 October, his Service de Renseignement and Service de Contre-Espionnage were redesignated the 5e Bureau (secret services). The reorganisation brought about a sharper division between the SR branch, which was instructed to devote itself more intensively to military intelligence work *vis-à-vis* the actual German enemy, and the CE branch which was told to concentrate not only on counter-intelligence but on diplomatic intelligence, surveillance within France, postal censorship and internal security. The SR, once the war began, worked ever more closely with Gauché and the 2e Bureau in Paris, and with Colonel Baril, Georges' head of intelligence assessment at La Ferté (GQG).[47]

Still firmly in overall control of this modified intelligence organisation was Rivet. To his devoted and fanatically loyal officers he was, simply, 'The Boss'.[48] An intelligence professional down to his fingertips, he let little – especially concerning Germany – escape his personal attention. In 1939–40, as he wrote later, 'the French special services' had 'a margin of good fortune . . . This lay . . . in a network of agents of long-standing, deeply implanted in the German war machine.'[49] Most crucial among these informers, as he had been since he started taking French pay in 1931, was Schmidt or Asché (HE). Still working within Goering's security and intelligence service, the Forschungsamt, still using his business activities to cover his travels to Swiss rendezvous with his French controllers, Schmidt remained an invaluable source. His brother's indiscretions about the campaign in Poland (where he commanded the 1st panzer division) became a French source about the wear-and-tear on the German mechanised forces in the east. These enabled Rivet to doubt their fitness to lead a new offensive in the west straight away. Nevertheless, under the constraints of wartime, Schmidt's communications became sporadic. On 8 September a letter from him reached SR headquarters in Paris. It warned that the Germans had intercepted signals which disclosed the French plan to begin a limited Saar offensive. Rivet noted in his diary that day: 'General Gamelin, advised of this, decided to take no account of it.' Then there was nothing from Schmidt until the end of September, when he wrote about the redeployment westwards of his brother's refitted panzers. After that, Schmidt was silent again until the end of October.[50]

Fortunately the French had other secret sources. The anti-Nazis within Germany were, in Rivet's term, an especially precious 'windfall'.[51] Probably the most informative and certainly the most sensitively placed during the phoney war, when the contact from Schmidt became intermittent, was Colonel Hans Oster, deputy to Admiral Canaris, the head of the Abwehr (military counter-intelligence). Oster was a long-standing opponent of Hitler's regime who had, since 1932, established a friendship with the Dutch military attaché in Berlin, Major Sas. By this informant, backed by the outstation which the French SR maintained in the Netherlands down to May 1940 as well as by the secret intermediary role played by Belgium's military attachés, French intelligence had quite accurate warnings of the numerous alerts about German attack. This was invaluable at the moments of serious invasion scare: in November 1939, January, April and May 1940.[52]

Also starting to show progress in this period were the several and long-sustained efforts by Polish, French and British cryptologists to defeat the Enigma codes so that German signals might be intercepted, deciphered and passed to Allied headquarters quickly enough to assist at operational levels. The arrival in Paris of two of the Polish reconstructions of Enigma machines in July 1939 (one of which was sent to London in August) had been a major benefit of Anglo-Franco-Polish military collaboration in the final weeks of peace. Also provided were copies of the methods by which the team of Polish mathematicians and code-breakers had been striving to break the daily Enigma key. As Poland's armies gave way under the blows of the German invasion in September, the Polish cipher bureau escaped to Romania, whence they reached France on 1 October with two more Enigma machines. With the agreement of General Sikorski, the head of the Polish government-in-exile, newly installed at Angers, the Polish specialists went to join the French code-breakers tackling Enigma. This team was directed by one of Rivet's subordinates, Colonel Bertrand (long responsible for contacts with Schmidt in respect of the spy's communication of blueprints and keys before the war). The group had been assembled when France mobilised in the top-secret and heavily guarded 'PC Bruno', at the Château de Vignolles, 50 kilometres north-east of Paris. This was the French Bletchley Park. It was where the Franco-Polish experts strove throughout the autumn of 1939 to pierce the Enigma intercepts and break back into German codes which had been impenetrable since sporadic decrypts in 1938. The breakthrough was achieved in January 1940, when PC Bruno and Bletchley succeeded in reading intercepts from late October 1939.

Quickly the speed at breaking the intercepts increased. Rivet met Major-General Sir Stewart Menzies ('C'), head of British secret intelligence, in early January 1940. The secret service chiefs agreed that the French should have exclusive responsibility for utilisation of Enigma intelligence by Allied headquarters on the western front. Soon sufficient signals – mostly Luftwaffe traffic but also identifying German ground formations – were broken sufficiently rapidly that on 6 March Rivet informed Gauché and Baril (Georges' intelligence chief) that what the French termed 'Source Z', and the British 'Ultra', was about to become operationally exploitable.[53]

This progress, however (and the greater precision it promised for assessment of enemy intentions), lay months ahead when, in September, Gamelin and Georges first became alarmed about the possibility of imminent German attack in the west. Troop train movements from the eastern theatre towards the borderlands with France, Belgium and Holland were 'very noticeable', as one of Gamelin's staff put it, from 20 September onwards. More and more German divisions were exactly identified by their number or their insignia.[54] The temporary lull in the west, thought the British military attaché in Paris on 25 September, was 'the calm before the storm as the Boche is moving troops across and . . . will most probably try something over here during the next month'. The BEF chief of staff, Pownall, visited Georges at GQG two days after this, finding him 'preoccupied' by indications of 'quite a lot of German formations west of the Rhine'.[55] Gamelin's headquarters, recalled one of its officers, had the impression that the redeployment of major enemy units was greatest from 25 to 29 September.[56] The main task at this point for French intelligence, in Rivet's words, became 'to discern the first signs that would presage a German offensive, whilst still building our picture of the German order-of-battle'.[57]

By mid-October Franco-British commanders credited Germany with sufficient forces in the west to begin a major attack. French GQG reckoned that German redeployments would be completed by 10 October and that 'an offensive in the grand style remained possible at that date'. The French secret services, according to Rivet, 'had no great difficulty in monitoring the constitution of the German [western] front and the progressive arrival of units from the east and from [training] camps'.[58] Six divisions (three mechanised or motorised) were identified between Emden and Bielefeld; twelve (four mechanised or motorised) between Mönchengladbach and Cologne; twelve more between Eupen-Malmédy and Wiesbaden, and guard formations facing Alsace. The whereabouts of some of the panzers was unknown (Schmidt, the spy, not writing till the end of October that his brother's tanks were north of Cologne).[59] Pownall noted in his diary on 12 October that they were 'no doubt refitting in the centre of Germany' but able to 'come up rapidly into line'.[60] The Allied commanders concluded that Hitler had both the capability and the motive to begin his attack. He had established a reputation as a gambler, and a western offensive offered a way to avoid a winter of inactivity and doubts inside Germany about a lengthening conflict. In part the French and British generals reasoned from their own weaknesses. A further winter's work by French and British troops on their defences, thought Pownall, would leave Germany little remaining prospect of success in the west by the spring of 1940.[61]

Western commanders judged that their governments' rebuff, after the fall of Poland, of Hitler's overtures for a negotiated peace would be Germany's pretext to attack westwards.[62] But they still hoped that the front would remain quiet. French intelligence indicated that this hope might not be completely illusory. During September the German generals logically preferred to be permitted to overcome Poland without disturbance. Maintaining only eleven regular divisions to screen France, they had no interest in instigating large-scale military activity in the west. As one of Gamelin's staff recalled: 'we received signals that the high command would view with some scepticism the possibility of taking the offensive on the western front . . . and that the German general staff would view such a project with little favour'. Belgium's military attaché in Paris reported that Gauché told him how German troops were 'blatantly seeking to fraternise with French soldiers, advising them not to get killed for the sake of the British'. Moreover, the German aircraft that had penetrated French air space had not conducted bombing raids. The Belgian attaché had the impression that Germany 'did not wish to poison' her relations with France and Britain, 'to whom she intended to offer peace after Poland was conquered'.[63]

Though the western generals welcomed intelligence that pointed to a continuation of the military stalemate, they were troubled that their governments might show serious interest in Hitler's proposed political compromise. A 'premature patched-up peace' was, for Britain's military attaché in early October, 'the worst thing that could happen'.[64] Anglo-French commanders wished the war to go on through the winter of 1939–40 – albeit at a low level of intensity – so as not to undo the accomplishment of French mobilisation and the unimpeded deployment of the BEF to the continent. They suspected that a German peace offer would be no more than an expedient, a truce rather than a settlement. They feared a German gambit to trick the Allies into a false sense of security out of which, in Pownall's words, they would eventually have 'to start all over again in circumstances that will favour Hitler much better'.[65] It came as a heartfelt relief to the military when the Anglo-French cabinets rejected Hitler's feelers. 'Daladier put it best when he said: "they come to us talking of peace, and their hands are covered in blood",' wrote Fraser, with evident approval, on 9 October. Gamelin was equally resolute. The French position, he said to Bineau on 10 October, was clear: 'We must tell Hitler that we took up arms against you in support of Poland. You have obliterated her and [now] wish to make peace. But we will not bow before your fait accompli and shall remain under arms for as long as it takes [to defeat you].'[66]

Gamelin thought, however, that this steadfastness would provoke Hitler to attack the west. From October onwards, recalled Rivet, the 'imminence of a German offensive weighed upon the Allied front'.[67] Already, in the light of the Wehrmacht redeployments identified in late September, Gamelin had issued a further two 'personal and secret instructions' to Georges, outlining the French switch onto a wholly defensive posture. This was to be 'based on the fortified system', although limited forward defence was prescribed in sectors where the French tactical position made it worthwhile.[68] In the main, however, the result was that, by 4 October, the units of the Third and Fourth armies which had marched out to the Siegfried Line had, Grand Old Duke of York style, marched back again. Only reconnaissance groups and about one quarter of the infantry remained in front of the Maginot defences, in contact with the Germans. At this same date, the first two British divisions also moved into line, near Maulde on the Belgian frontier. By 9 October, defending a 120 kilometre line from the Vosges to Montmédy, the Second Army Group under Prételat had deployed, in addition to fortress garrisons, nineteen field divisions and the high command expected attack imminently.[69]

Late that day, returning from GQG to Vincennes, Major Georges Deleuze, Gamelin's adjutant, reported intelligence that Germany would take the offensive between the Moselle and Rhine, with a diversion around Basle, on the 15th.[70] Throughout the next two nights the front became shrouded in low cloud and the onset of autumnal rains, during which intensified German patrolling was reported along the Moselle–Saar front.[71] Early on 12 October, therefore, Gamelin dictated an order-of-the-day (copied to Gort and the BEF and issued on the 14th): 'Soldiers of France! A battle may begin at any moment on which will again depend, as before in our history, the fate of the *Patrie*. The eyes of the country, those of the whole world, are on you. Lift up your hearts. Use your weapons well. Remember the Marne and Verdun!'[72] All indications, wrote Britain's military attaché to his wife on the 13th, were that 'the Boche may ... attack over here ... before very long now'.[73]

Spending the morning of 14 October at GQG, Gamelin returned to Vincennes around midday, 'preoccupied' by the growing likelihood of an attack. He ordered his staff to expect the battle to be joined within forty-eight hours. Late that afternoon Vuillemin conferred with Gamelin, who then went in to Paris to brief Daladier, Decamp and La Chambre.[74] Meanwhile, that day the Dutch military attaché in Paris, Colonel Evekink, passed his Belgian counterpart and the French military authorities a copy of a general order on 9 October from Hitler to the Wehrmacht command. Possession of this information was one of the fruits of the Sas–Oster link in Berlin. The order instructed the Wehrmacht immediately to recapture German territory in front of the Siegfried Line taken by the French in September. It also directed German forces to be ready to attack through Holland, Switzerland and across the Rhine near Freiburg after French advanced posts were eliminated.[75]

The tension reached its climax on 15–16 October, as Gamelin made preparations to leave Paris for an inspection of the French First Army and the BEF. At Vincennes 'numerous indications maintained the impression that the Germans were preparing something but did not permit any conclusion as to its scale and direction'. Around 9 pm the GHQ of the BEF heard from its representative with Georges, Brigadier Jack Swayne, that 'the show was expected by GQG to start down in the south tomorrow'. Pownall thought it would extend to Luxembourg, but he estimated Allied preparedness sufficient to repulse Hitler with a 'pretty heavy knock if he pokes his nose too far'.[76]

The alert was likewise taken seriously by Gamelin, although he maintained his normal sang-froid. Remaining closely informed of the developing intelligence picture he nonetheless convened the regular meeting of the commanders-in-chief on the morning of 15 October, before leaving Vincennes at midday to lunch at his home on the avenue Foch. Whilst crossing Paris he not only halted at the war ministry for a short meeting with Decamp but also stopped at Notre-Dame. Later, after dining at Vincennes, Gamelin, along with his naval adjutant, Commander Ausseur, Petibon and Captain Huet, drove to the Gare de Pantin to board the commander-in-chief's special train. The next day's itinerary was scheduled to include visits to the headquarters of the First Army at Bohain, the 51st infantry division at Lille, the BEF at Habarcq and the 16th corps at St Omer. Leaving Paris, Gamelin's train travelled as far as La Fère-en-Tardenois where it stopped at the station at 10.30 pm to let the general and his staff sleep before completing their journey to the frontier armies at dawn.[77]

An hour before midnight, however, the local station master received a telephone call for Petibon, from Colonel Revers, chief of staff to Bineau. This bore 'urgent' news: Laurent, France's military attaché in Brussels, had just reported the possibility that the German offensive was to be launched the very next day, 16 October, on the Franco-German front 'with an extension of the attack towards the north'. The intelligence was only classed as medium grade and originated from an agent in Aachen who had overheard German officers' conversation. Nevertheless both GQG and Petibon treated it seriously. Gamelin was awoken and informed. To avoid alarm he decided against an immediate return to Paris. Instead he continued early in the morning of 16 October to Bohain. There he chaired a meeting with Billotte, commander of First Army Group, Blanchard, the First Army commander, and the latter's corps and divisional generals. Throughout the morning Gamelin's staff periodically telephoned GQG, but found the situation on the front to the south-east unchanged. Gamelin consequently continued in mid-morning to visit the 51st division headquarters, before proceeding just before noon to the BEF's 1st corps, where he met its commander, Dill, along with Gort and Pownall. About one hour after this, whilst lunching with the British commanders in the Kergorlay château at Cauroy, where Gort had installed his GHQ, Gamelin heard by telephone from GQG of the start of German attacks on the Moselle. The news seemed to show that the warnings of the previous week had, after all, been well founded. Gamelin decided to abandon his afternoon visits – though not his interrupted lunch. Instead of proceeding to St Omer for a conference scheduled with General Fagalde, commander of the 16th corps, and Admiral Castex, commander of the Channel maritime region, he returned directly to see Georges at La Ferté, before finally rejoining his own staff at Vincennes just before eight that evening. Gamelin discovered that the officers of his *cabinet* had been on continuous alert during his absence but that the dimensions of the German offensive remained unclear. He estimated that the situation would unravel itself over the following forty-eight hours.[78]

On 17 October news of further fighting on the Third and Fourth French Army fronts in Lorraine and the Saar reached Gamelin. But the day's reports left the French uncertain of the significance of the German operations. In the small hours of the morning of 18 October intelligence reported the imminent 'certain entry of the Germans into Belgium and Luxembourg'. This kept Petibon awake and prompted Gamelin himself to spend the whole morning alongside Georges at GQG. The alarm, however, proved to be false. Indeed the day unfolded without any extension of the enemy operations already underway to the south. By the 19th there was a marked easing of the tension. The high pitch of alert which had been maintained by all the Allied units and headquarters for over a week was gradually reduced once it became evident that the Wehrmacht was engaged not in a general offensive but in a more limited objective of clearing its lines all along the front of the Siegfried position.[79] As October drew to a close the onset of torrential rain increasingly waterlogged the western front and convinced a growing body of Allied opinion that the phoney war would continue until the return of fine weather in 1940.[80]

In fact, historical scholarship has demonstrated that throughout October and November 1939 an immense battle of wills was occurring in Berlin between Hitler's wish to mount a potentially decisive offensive and the caution of his generals. In this struggle, which paralleled the 'war of nerves' being endured by the Allied commanders, the Wehrmacht's leaders manifested as great a desire as their Anglo-French counterparts to use the approaching winter for strengthening and sharpening the military instrument under their hand. In the case of the German commanders, they sought a respite in order to train and incorporate the 1939 conscript class, called up just as the war began; they wished, also, to refit divisions that had suffered in the Polish campaign, to reorganise and expand their panzer forces and attend to shortcomings in tactical execution and combined-arms operations revealed during the eastern battles.[81] Yet, from 9 to 15 November, Hitler came very close to prevailing in his wish to launch his westward offensive, even with a strategy of attack through Belgium that the Führer himself recognised might fail to knock out Britain and France and lead only to a stalemated war of attrition. The generals who opposed this risky gamble included Brauchitsch, the army commander-in-chief, Halder, the army chief of staff, and two of the three army group commanders in the west, Leeb and Bock. In spite of a stream of memoranda to Hitler from these officers, emphasising the hazards inherent in mounting a potentially indecisive autumn operation, and numerous face-to-face attempts by Brauchitsch and Halder to dissuade Hitler from his adventure, it was in the end only the intervention of torrential rains which forced the cancellation of Germany's projected November offensive.[82]

The November alert is a much more familiar scare than its October predecessor and only a few salient points need be dwelt on here. First it may be noted that during both alerts the Allied commanders were blessed – as well as cursed – with the superabundant fruits of intensive and even frenetic activity by their intelligence services. The results were predictably mixed and the characteristic difficulty of identifying a clear signal from the cacophonous 'noise' from intelligence sources was all too apparent. Perhaps the extremely accurate conclusions which the west reached about the imminence and direction of a German attack in November were – notwithstanding the German informers serving the

Allies in Berlin – more a product of good fortune than good judgement. After all, every bit as much information had reached the Anglo-French high commands in October. The result was to convince Gamelin, Georges and the British headquarters of the veracity of signs of an impending German onslaught around the fifteenth of that month.[83] Historians have subsequently learned that the German army's OKH staff only produced its first draft plan for a western offensive – and then with extreme reluctance – on 19 October. What the west's intelligence and agents in Berlin had interpreted as a firmly elaborated German scheme of attack can, with hindsight, be seen to have been no more than Hitler's Führer-directive of 9 October that overrode the objections of his senior generals and insisted on the production of a strategy for as early a Wehrmacht drive westwards as possible.[84]

A second point is that German interpretations of the planning of the Allies in this first phase of the phoney war also suffered from uncertainties and disagreements. When, on 27 September, with the Polish campaign still in progress, Hitler told his generals of his wish to attack the west at an early juncture, much of the German army command was severely discomfited. Not only was the OKH staff at this stage without any plan for an offensive against the French and British, but most of the German generals held the Anglo-French armies in high regard and had no faith in the Wehrmacht's capacity to achieve a swift and complete defeat of them. Moreover, the Polish operations had damaged a number of first-line German divisions and revealed deficiencies in tactics as well as in air–ground cooperation.[85] There was, therefore, a wish and an expectation 'particularly in the army', as it was put in October by General Jodl, chief of operations of the OKW, 'that the war would die a natural death if we only kept quiet in the west'. In contrast, Hitler, in his 9 October directive, insisted that preparation be made with all despatch for Germany to move onto the attack against the western powers. The 'passing of every further month', he asserted, represented 'a loss of time unfavourable to the German power of offensive'.[86] Hitler had persuaded himself – in the event quite groundlessly – that the French and British were poised to advance into the Low Countries, where they could have threatened Germany's vital Ruhr industries directly. In part, then, Hitler's concern in ordering his own generals to prepare to move westward had a defensive motivation. But, in part, it arose from his longer-standing conviction that his political ambitions required the early search for a battle of annihilation against his western adversaries. He wished to subjugate France and drive Britain off the continent. Therefore, French leaders were not guilty of hyperbole when they speculated in Wagnerian language about the coming struggle in the west as a matter of the very highest stakes.[87] Releasing his 14 October order-of-the-day, at the height of that month's alert, Gamelin warned his *cabinet* that the 'crux of things is that troops like ours, which are not yet battle-hardened, should be capable of withstanding a full-strength German onslaught. For, in his search for success, Hitler will not shrink from making whatever sacrifices are necessary in men and material.'[88] Gamelin was not mistaken in drawing such grim conclusions about the Führer's desperation and mania for risk, for these were the very traits which at just this time were troubling the German generals.[89]

Another remarkable feature of the autumn of 1939 is the way in which the split between Hitler and most of his generals over the ambitiousness of Allied intentions was mirrored by division in France between Gamelin and Georges – who thought that Germany would attack soon after finishing with Poland – and French intelligence, which expected an extended lull. Down till the end of November, Gamelin betrayed great anxiety about the possibility of an all-out German offensive in the west. As early as 10 September he ordered the French army staff to instruct Georges and Bineau to study the responses that might be made 'if Germany attacked with all her forces en masse, and in the eventuality of the violation of Belgium'. Eleven days later, with Polish resistance crumbling fast, he opined to officers of his *cabinet* that 'on our front we are now in a period of expectation'; the initiative, he accepted, lay with the Germans rather than with the Allies.[90]

By 10 October, when the next turn that the war might take was analysed at Vincennes, Bineau was outlining three hypotheses. First, there was the chance that Hitler would simply bide his time (which, thought Bineau, would damage French home-front morale). Gamelin, however, thought such inactivity was unlikely, because 'Hitler would lose face and because it is not in his nature to wait'. Secondly, the Wehrmacht might attack France and/or Belgium, in spite of having to overcome the handicap of the autumnal rains if they did so. Lastly, there was the option which Bineau judged most probable: 'the operation with the best pay-off, the seizure of Holland without touching Belgium, by which Hitler would gain airfields nearer to Britain, submarine bases on the mouth of the Rhine, the Dutch gold reserves and colonies and, perhaps, the internal disintegration of Belgium'.[91] In this period of early October Gamelin felt so apprehensive that he pressurised the British, with success, to assume responsibility for defending a section of frontier with Belgium with their first corps of two divisions.

Though Gamelin's nervousness was shared by other senior generals, notably by Georges and Prételat, his alarm was far from universal within the French command. A more phlegmatic view was taken by General

Héring, a leading pre-war proponent of constituting armoured divisions and, in the phoney war, the military governor of Paris. Visiting Vincennes on 19 October, he caused Gamelin surprise by venturing that the Germans would 'pursue their peace offensive whilst leaving the front to slumber'.[92] Such composure was prevalent, too, among the French intelligence chiefs.

They, of course, continued to enjoy privileged access to information from inside Germany, thanks to spies and informants such as Schmidt and Oster and the cooperation that was maintained between the French SR and the Dutch and Belgian intelligence services. The proven worth of their sources since the early 1930s gave Rivet and Gauché confidence in the information that they provided in 1939. This led the heads of French intelligence to offer reassurance to Gamelin during the September and October alerts and to advise the maintenance of a high state of defensive wariness in the November scare. Thus, on 7 September, Gauché told Belgium's military attaché in Paris that he knew the Germans to be fitting out their second-line divisions. Since their manpower was reportedly untrained they would 'not be ready until 1940', he concluded. Following a further talk, on 16 September, the Belgian informed his superiors in Brussels that Gauché's view had hardened into a 'belief that Germany would not [that autumn] mount any significant operations in the west and estimated that, if he was correct, France would be able to demobilise a little during the winter'.[93]

Obviously, French intelligence was not entirely privy to the strictures within the Wehrmacht command about the deficiencies that some German units had shown during the operations in Poland. But it was not wholly ignorant of them either. It was aware, for instance, that the Germans were disturbed by the high levels of attrition inflicted on many German divisions even in such a spectacularly successful operation as 'Case White'. 'Our agents inside Germany', recalled an officer of Gamelin's *cabinet*, disclosed 'the rather knocked-about state in which the armoured and motorised divisions returned from Poland. The repairs and replacement of material did not seem as though it could be accomplished before the end of November.'[94] By mid-October the 2e Bureau was sharing its 'high-grade intelligence indicating that [Germany's] armoured vehicles suffered severely in the Polish campaign, some having been destroyed in combat but many requiring serious and protracted repairs'. By 25 October Gauché had concluded that wear and tear tended to rule out an impending German offensive in the west.[95] Rivet likewise sought to exercise a calming influence on the nerves of the French commanders. At the climax of the mid-October alert he visited Vincennes and told Gamelin that he 'did not share the apprehension of General Prételat and GQG in regard to an impending German attack and ruled out the plausibility of the date – 15 October – that had, over the previous few days, been canvassed as the likely start to such an offensive'.[96]

Rivet's confidence arose, in part, because in October–November 1939, as he later wrote, 'our informers depicted [the morale of the German army] as frankly poor, with the exception of the young conscripts and the elite troops . . . The attitude of the reserves betrayed a certain passivity and a persistent apathy.' In late-October Gauché passed intelligence to Belgium's military attaché which indicated that Luftwaffe veterans of the Polish operations, together with front-line ground troops, were receiving home leave. French analysts deduced that these were not the steps that would be taken if the Germans were intending to mount an early western offensive.[97]

At the beginning of November, however, as Rivet subsequently recounted, sources again indicated that a German invasion was imminent. The receipt of new intelligence in this sense is confirmed in the memoirs of Colonel Minart, an officer in Gamelin's *cabinet*. French code-breakers played a part in the build up of this alert. Their decrypt of an intercepted telegram, sent to the Düsseldorf police chief by the head of the Nordrhein-Westfalen SS, revealed these enemy security officers holding a meeting in 'the interest of the decision in the west'. Also, according to Minart, a secret source reported that German squad leaders in units behind the border with Holland had been issued with Dutch currency and Dutch phrase-books. Further indications from neutral countries, revealed in Paris on 11–12 November, affirmed that Hitler had made up his mind to attack.[98]

Rivet, however, remained calm. His most highly valued secret source, Schmidt, had re-established contact with his French controllers at the end of October, after almost a month's silence. From what his brother had told him about his panzer division's refit and redeployment, Asché asserted that Hitler would attack in the west, but not before the end of the 1939–40 winter. On 2 November Rivet noted in his diary that he was 'Summoned by Gamelin who wished to know the value of the intelligence indicating the improbability of a German attack on the western front before the end of the winter.' As the alert nonetheless grew into a full-blown scare, Rivet's confidence in the correctness of his analysis and the reliability of Asché remained unshaken. Indeed, the SR chief recounted, the 'verifications by our agents in the days that followed confirmed that no movement or important regrouping had occurred in the German dispositions'.[99] In spite of the Dutch and Belgian fears, Rivet noted in his diary between 7 and 12 November that there was 'little modification in the west' to enemy deployments and no sign of any tell-tale introduction of armour into an offensively oriented disposition. He took the view that the scare was part of Germany's extended war of nerves designed to strengthen its peace offensive and 'apply influence on the neutrals'.[100]

Gamelin and the French high command did not wholly trust these reassurances from their chiefs of intelligence. In mid-October and in mid-November they whipped themselves as well as their British counterparts (who depended heavily on information from the French), into fever-pitch anxiety.[101] As noted earlier, it remains unclear whether or not Gamelin himself knew the identity and connections of Asché. What is important, however, is that, in either event, Gamelin and Georges felt unable to relax their state of maximum vigilance on account of Schmidt's information and Rivet's faith in it, when this was contradicted by sources which did suggest the imminence of Wehrmacht aggression. To an extent, Gamelin's caution was nothing more than the proper professional response; it was not his duty to gamble with French security when there were indications that his guard ought to be kept high. Yet Gamelin's reaction was as much a result of his ingrained assumptions as of any considered appraisal of the conflicting sources of the moment. As Minart, a first-hand observer at Vincennes recalled, the 'high command could not . . . believe that chancellor Hitler would rest his weapon of war for long'.[102]

Convinced in his own mind that the Germans were on the verge of a surprise attack or coup against Holland or Belgium, or both, Gamelin again unavailingly sought pre-emptive entry for the French First Army and the BEF to move to forward defences alongside the Belgians.[103] Meanwhile, in a decisive reconfiguring of his strategy that cost the Allies dear in May 1940, he overrode the objections of Georges at an Anglo-French command meeting at Vincennes on 14 November and imposed the so-called Dyle Plan on the Allied forces on the left flank. Articulated in Gamelin's Instruction Personnelle et Secrète No. 8, of 15 November, the manoeuvre committed Franco-British divisions disposed north-west of the Givet salient to a cross-country dash to buttress the Belgians on the Namur–Dyle River–Antwerp line, east of Brussels, in the event of a German violation of Belgium. The plan was hazardous for it imposed the advance so long as Belgium appealed for military assistance once under attack, even without pre-emptive entry and in the absence of full-scale Anglo-Franco-Belgian staff coordination. At a stroke, Gamelin threw away his long-standing refusal to risk French divisions in an encounter battle by declaring himself willing, in the middle of a German offensive, to rush towards eastward Belgian defences.[104]

This critical strategical modification, though ratified by the Franco-British political leaders at the supreme war council of 17 November in London, was wholly of Gamelin's making. It was a plan whose uncharacteristic boldness possessed its own logic in the circumstances of November 1939. Firstly, it offered a riposte to a German move to knock out France and secure the Low Countries as a protective glacis for the Reich. Secondly, it promised a way to stabilise the northern extension to the western front on lines that were shorter than the Franco-Belgian border and far forward of the French industries of the Nord. Furthermore, the plan held out the prospect, which Gamelin had favoured since the CSG debates over French northern frontier defences, of incorporating the Belgians into Allied strength. With a mobilised army of twenty-two divisions and rapidly improving capabilities as a result of the post-1936 Belgian military reforms, this was an attractive and not inconsiderable asset to Gamelin. Coordination with Belgium might compensate for Germany's inherent manpower superiority and the modest contribution on land from the British.[105]

The main effect of the onset of winter, however, was to afford the Allies and the Wehrmacht alike a valuable opportunity in which to analyse and disseminate the lessons that each elected to draw from the September campaign in Poland, as well as to improve the equipment and training of their armies and air forces. Williamson Murray has shown how seriously German generals viewed the Wehrmacht's shortcomings against the Poles and how assiduously they sought to enhance their combat effectiveness by critically evaluating the German military performance in the east.[106]

Almost ignored, however, is the considerable effort expended by the western Allied high commands – but especially by the French – in comparable studies of the experiences that emerged from the Polish campaign. Consequently, well before the opposing armies in the west finally settled, in the second half of November 1939, to a winter of respite and refit, they had turned to the education of their forces in the light of the war's first operations.

In the French case, the most senior commanders quickly received extensive and accurate information as to the character of the German methods against the Poles. The French had a number of sources. The first was General Félix Musse, France's military attaché in Warsaw in 1938–9, who remained in Poland and continued reporting to Paris after hostilities began. More important, however, were the French army and air missions that were posted to Warsaw on 23–24 August, as soon as the signature of the Molotov–Ribbentrop Pact was announced. These missions were assigned to liaise with and provide counsel to the Polish general headquarters, to Rydz-Smigly and Stachiewicz, the supreme commander and the chief of staff. The French army's mission was led by General Faury, who had been on the reserve list since 1937 but was a recognised Polish specialist. Gamelin hand-picked Faury on the strength of the latter's long service in the 1920s in charge of instruction at the staff college in Warsaw. Command of the air mission was entrusted to General Armengaud, an inspector-general of the Armée de l'Air whom Pierre Cot had driven into early retirement in 1936.[107] Given minimal instructions by Vuillemin and Gamelin, Armengaud found himself – like Faury – sent to Warsaw just one week before the German invasion commenced. Gamelin charged Armengaud with providing technical advice and 'moral support' to the Polish high command. But he had 'not a word to say about Poland's plan of campaign, the strategic conduct of the war or the varied eventualities that might be envisaged'.[108]

The detailed history of the adventurous month spent by these missions in Poland in August–September 1939 lies, like the details of the German–Polish war, outside this study's compass. A number of points, however, call for remark. The first is that the Polish mobilisation in the last days of August was delayed, with damaging results for Polish defensive readiness, at Franco-British behest. The reasons for thus deferring the military precautions that French and Polish intelligence, through Asché's warnings, knew to be essential varied from the dishonourable to the purely cynical. In the case of Bonnet, at the Quai d'Orsay, the motive was the chance to give life to the Italian notion of another great power conference – a 'new Munich', to forestall war again, this time at the price of partitioning Poland.[109] In Gamelin's case, the thinking was that last-ditch attempts at conciliation would doubtless fail but would gain extra time for the French armed forces to reach full readiness, with maximum *couverture* strength in place, leaving only general mobilisation itself to be decreed by the government when German operations began. Polish readiness to delay full mobilisation owed itself to their determination to appear the aggrieved party and thereby to compel Franco-British intervention at their side. In leaning over to avoid provoking German invasion, they implemented Franco-British advice not to give Germany the pretext of Polish mobilisation as a basis for hostilities. In the afternoon of 31 August, the eve of Germany's attack, France's ambassador in Warsaw wired Bonnet that 'Yesterday General Stachiewicz congratulated himself in front of General Faury for having agreed to delay general mobilisation. He understood perfectly the political considerations which militated in favour of this and recognised that the drawbacks of a technical kind [sic] which resulted were of only secondary import.'[110]

A second point about the Polish–German campaign concerns the enduring effects of Russophobia in Warsaw. Not only did this, for valid reasons from Poland's viewpoint, pose insurmountable obstacles in July and August 1939 to the negotiation of an Anglo-Franco-Polish-Soviet pact and military agreement. It continued to haunt Polish thinking and strategy at the moment of German invasion. For, though Rydz-Smigly was unaware of the secret protocol to the 23 August Russo-German pact which provided for Soviet military participation in dismembering Poland, he still disposed some 20 per cent of Poland's mobilised forces along or behind the frontier with Russia. Therefore, not simply was Polish deployment weakened on 1 September 1939 by the absence from its order-of-battle of the eight divisions whose mobilisation had been postponed by Stachiewicz; it was further handicapped in the first week of desperate fighting against the Wehrmacht by the unavailability of the forces (equivalent to about eight divisions) that were left standing watch in the east over the Red Army.[111]

The third point of note about the start of German–Polish hostilities is the existence of sharply divergent views, about the situation of the Poles, among the French military missions in Warsaw. According to Armengaud, the air mission's chief, Faury and Musse 'believed Poland's resistance might extend till the spring'. They apparently expressed 'confidence' in the calibre of Polish generalship and in the effectiveness of the Polish war plan. For his own part, however, Armengaud claimed to have been dismayed by the dilatoriness – as well as by the secretiveness – that attended the Poles' military preparations. The optimism of the French army officers was supposedly based on the encouraging impressions of Polish defensive capabilities that Ironside's British military mission had circulated, after its visit to Warsaw in July 1939. Armengaud had only five or six days, following his own arrival in Warsaw, in which to judge for himself the quality of Poland's military resources, before the German invasion began. What he saw, though, discouraged him so deeply that he forecast very presciently to Noël, the French ambassador, 'that the Polish army would be annihilated in a fortnight'.[112]

As the Polish defences crumbled during September, in accordance with this prediction, the French missions had to play a difficult cat and mouse game, staying close enough to the front to gauge the nature of the battle, yet avoiding becoming prisoners of the Germans as the Poles retreated. Trying to offer guidance to the Polish generals, at the same time as wiring interim reports to Gamelin, the French liaison officers displayed no little personal courage under the fluid and frightening conditions of a military collapse. Armengaud's own deputy chief of staff was shot down outside Warsaw on 2 September, whilst flying to join one of the Polish headquarters. In the circumstances, the quantity and accuracy of the information reported to Paris was outstanding. As a result the French higher commanders were alerted very early and very fully to the methods and devastating consequences of the German operations in the east.[113]

By means of Gamelin's headquarters diary, the extent of French attention to the German operational techniques is apparent. As early as 9 September enough was known for Gamelin to instruct his staff to tell Georges 'To alert the armies as to the predominant role played in the attack as well as in exploitation by tanks. Hence, to erect anti-tank obstacles not just on a line but also in depth (minefields, prepared destructions . . .).' Two days later, the Belgian military attaché in Paris reported being informed by the 2e Bureau that the 'cooperation of German airpower in the [land] battles is proving a considerable difficulty for the Poles'.[114] On 12 September Gamelin's staff received a report from Faury which told them that the 'Germans are attacking with one hundred tanks per kilometre of front'. This, it was noted at Vincennes, 'is the Guderian theory'; it was the concentration of massed armour for the offensive *schwerpunkt*. Faury advised that a density of thirty anti-tank guns per kilometre would have to be achieved by defending forces in order to prevent breakthroughs by panzers employing these tactics. Gamelin attended closely to the character of the developing campaign, demanding that 'Faury be requested, by telegram, to relay the teachings . . . of the initial operations on the Polish front'. The next day, too, Gamelin showed concern about attack from low-flying aircraft 'which have, in Poland, had tremendous moral as well as material effectiveness. "They must [he said] be taught a good lesson whenever they attempt to operate boldly at low altitude."' Another day later, on 14 September, he instructed his staff to repeat to Georges that 'the fight against the aviation [threat] must be prepared most urgently and thoroughly, with the object of ensuring that Germany's air force, emboldened by its success in Poland, receives a good drubbing when it first tries conclusions against us'. Besides this injunction, Dufieux, the inspector of infantry, was charged that day with visiting all the French armies on the frontiers 'to check himself that precautions against air power, and anti-aircraft defence, are really receiving the full attention of our units'.[115]

14 September also brought a first-hand account of the fighting, when Major Choisy, an officer of Faury's mission, arrived from Poland and reported in person to Vincennes. Three days after that came a despatch from Armengaud 'very heavily stressing the primary role played in

Poland by German aviation, which almost immediately deprived the [Polish] command of all means of action'.[116] This warning came, in fact, from a long report by Armengaud, dated 16 September, the first of two which he filed via Romania. This one was chiefly devoted to the activities of the Luftwaffe. Although it was of an interim nature, taking its analysis only through the first ten days of operations, it nevertheless illuminated the impact of German air superiority on the Polish leadership's attempts to keep control over its forces. The Polish command, warned Armengaud, 'has been blinded, deprived of liaison, shorn of communications'; the supremacy of the Luftwaffe was 'perhaps the first and foremost cause of the Polish defeat because it has all but eliminated the [functioning of the] high command and the arteries of the nation'. Furthermore, added Armengaud, the German air force 'had attacked only military objectives'; it had not been diverted into anything resembling strategic warfare against industrial or civilian targets.[117]

A second report, dated 23 September, was also sent by Armengaud from neutral Romania (where the French missions, shortly joined by the Polish government, took refuge from the closing jaws of the German and Soviet vice). This report discussed the German ground operations. In particular, it analysed the combined actions staged by the panzer divisions and the Luftwaffe. Such cooperation 'was massive in scale', stressed Armengaud, 'principally during the breakthrough battles (from Silesia and Pomerania) in the first days of the war'. The German air force had assisted 'to the army's direct benefit' in four phases: prior to battle, through reconnaissance; during battle, by 'pinning down frontline Polish units and destroying counterattacks'; in the exploitation process, by 'forcing Polish formations to ground and restricting them to moving only by night'; and in harassing rear areas, paralysing communications and hindering concentration of reserves. Armengaud judged that it was its inferiority in armour and aircraft that had led Poland to defeat in under three weeks 'and without even completing her mobilisation or fielding all her reserves'.

If Armengaud was perceptive in recognising the importance of German air–armour coordination he was equally alive to the unprecedented concentrations of tanks which characterised the German successes. Here, he warned, was the emergence of a redoubtable new concept: 'the tendency of the Germans to form groups for exploitation, consisting of two panzer divisions with one motorised (or light infantry) division . . . which seek to outstrip their enemy's withdrawal and then lay armoured detachments across his line of retreat'. The novelty lay partly in the massing of such large amounts of mobile forces. But an equally menacing innovation, emphasised Armengaud, was the roaming of the panzers some 30 kilometres ahead of their supporting non-motorised infantry divisions and the advance of the light elements of the armoured divisions themselves up to another 50 kilometres forward of the main unit. This was deep penetration of a truly revolutionary kind, such as to challenge all conventional defensive doctrine and calculations as to the meaning of 'breakthrough'. This was a forecast of what came to be called blitzkrieg.[118]

Meanwhile Faury's main report, containing the army mission's observations on the Polish campaign, was also filed from Romania. It reached Gamelin in October 1939. Like the warnings from Armengaud, it was emphatic about the perils that the new German operational techniques represented for the Allies. It underlined the effects produced by the combination of shock and speed in the German method of attack. It stressed the single-mindedness with which the Wehrmacht pursued the aim of destroying its adversary's ability to continue organised military resistance. It highlighted the spearhead role given to armour and tactical aviation.[119]

It was not only by means of telegrams and written reports that Gamelin obtained these graphic descriptions of blitzkrieg. Corroboration came from face-to-face briefings. On 4 October Gamelin saw Musse, the former military attaché in Warsaw, who had returned to France. Likewise, both Faury and Armengaud, after their own circuitous escapes through the Balkans, were summoned to present their first-hand impressions about the defeat of the Poles to Gamelin. So struck was Gamelin by what he heard that he immediately despatched Armengaud to London, from 2 to 5 October, to share his analysis of blitzkrieg with the British military authorities.[120] In discussion with the British chief of air staff, Air Chief Marshal Sir Cyril Newall, and with the CIGS, Ironside, Armengaud pressed for an urgent increase in the number of RAF squadrons based in France, in order to help compensate for the incompleteness of French air rearmament. But the British took Armengaud's warnings to justify maintenance of their priority in deploying RAF fighters in Britain, for direct home defence. The French entreaties – as well as later requests in the same vein from Vuillemin and Gamelin – went largely unanswered. Armengaud complained that this was because the French service chiefs failed to insist that Daladier press the issue directly with Chamberlain.[121]

Justly, it is stressed that Germany's military command possessed what one historian has called the 'integrity to recognise that the operational success in Poland had revealed major flaws'. The German army has been credited for learning by its experiences in Poland and then instituting 'a vast training program to correct deficiencies'.[122] Yet Gamelin strove mightily to see that the French army also absorbed lessons from its ally's collapse. Hitherto, however, few scholars have acknowledged this.[123] Yet it is the case, as we have seen, that Gamelin received accurate intelligence about the nature of the war in the east, even as it unfolded in September 1939. He worked untiringly to make his senior subordinate generals recognise the dangers to the west posed by German capabilities. By mid-October he was regularly employing staff command-conferences to impress upon Georges, Dufieux and Prételat, in particular, the importance of ordering specialised training and practice for defence against low-level air attacks, as well as preparing the means of counterattacking German panzer assaults. The effect of Luftwaffe support of the German ground operations was also stressed repeatedly. 'Concerning the Stukas', Gamelin justifiably wrote later, 'we took steps before the war, after distributing regulations, as regards measures to take to counter them. These were completed following the campaign in Poland. I myself often drew attention to the question.'[124] And, of the Anglo-French conference at Vincennes on 6 October, Ironside's military assistant, Colonel Roderick Macleod, noted that 'Gamelin said . . . the chief lesson to be learnt from the Polish campaign was the penetrative power of the speedy and hard-hitting German armoured formations and the close cooperation of their Air Force.'[125]

During the autumn of 1939, Gamelin and his *cabinet* plainly showed outstanding diligence in their endeavours to improve the preparedness of the French and British armies in France. Indeed, in their attention to detail they surpassed what might normally be expected of such a high level of command (where the principal duties lay with inter-service coordination, liaison with French allies, national mobilisation and grand strategic planning).

It is not at Gamelin's door, then, that should be laid the shortcomings in the functioning of subordinate headquarters, the incomplete equipment or the flawed combat-effectiveness that blemished the Franco-British defensive performance in 1940. Rather, future campaign historians must address questions about the reasons for failures lower down the chain of command – among corps and divisional generals and staffs, and even at the regimental level.[126]

Since this study has documented the prescient warnings issued by Gamelin, it has to be asked what became of them after responsibility for their transmission had shifted to Georges and Dufieux, at theatre level, to Huntziger, Corap, Giraud and Blanchard in command of the armies that later did most of the fighting, and to the divisional generals in charge of the building block formations of the army? Were there too many intermediate layers of authority, as some commentators argue, muffling the urgent message of danger that left Vincennes till it became inaudible down the long line of command?[127] Or were the Allied troubles of 1940 rooted in other – only distantly related – problems? Did they stem from units having to receive the German offensive whilst handicapped by the unresolved shortages of anti-aircraft guns, anti-tank weapons and mines? Did they arise from the impossibility in the harsh winter of early 1940 of giving revised training – incorporating lessons learned from Poland – to the many divisions required for forward frontier defence?[128]

It would be misleading to imply that no improvements sprang from French observation of the Polish campaign. One positive outcome was to end the protracted debate in the French high command over the merits and drawbacks of establishing heavy armoured divisions. It will be recalled that this had been discussed indecisively by the CSG in December 1937, and in December 1938. Gamelin and Héring had favoured the creation of such divisions. But other CSG generals had resisted. At the time Gamelin had not pressed to overcome this, since the inadequate output of heavy Char B tanks at that juncture provided real enough grounds for not forcing the issue. It was the destruction of Poland's defences by the German panzers that compelled the French to reconsider their lack of heavy armoured divisions.[129]

The Wehrmacht's triumph in the east highlighted what might be accomplished when tanks were concentrated, led boldly and unleashed behind enemy lines. Poland demonstrated that operations of rupture were not only possible but offered a means to achieve a strategic decision. The French needed to look afresh at their methods of riposte. They concluded, belatedly, that massing their own heavy armour into divisions for *colmatage* was the key requirement to enable them to crush any German breakthrough in France.

The crucial advocate for French heavy tank divisions was General Gaston Billotte. In October he had been appointed commander of the French First Army Group concentrated on the border with Belgium. On 6 December 1939 Billotte sent a study of the use of armour to Gamelin and Georges. This first argued that almost indefensible terrain, the paucity of Polish fortifications and the shortage of Polish anti-tank weapons had given Germany victory in the east. It then warned that Belgium reproduced many of the conditions which the Germans had exploited in Poland. Billotte accurately estimated the tank strength available to the Germans ('about two thousand'). He warned that: 'Technically and numerically our superiority over the five German armoured divisions is undoubted. Tactically the same is not true, since we have only three [mechanised] divisions with which to oppose the

German five.' (Unknown to Billotte, the Germans at this point were reorganising their armour and establishing ten panzer divisions – each more manoeuvrable, though with a smaller tank complement.)

By this persuasive paper Billotte finally put an end to French prevarication about forming heavy armoured divisions. With some improvisation, he insisted, the means existed: the four available Char B battalions could be joined to an equivalent number of light tank battalions and two armoured reconnaissance groups, the whole being divided into two DCRs (Divisions Cuirassées de Réserve). 'These major units', he urged, 'ought to be constituted at the earliest moment ... to give them the cohesion they need and train leaders capable of manoeuvring them.' Increasing the number of French large mechanised units was essential, affirmed Billotte, in order to 'be sure of retaining a superiority over our adversary in the event of the battle beginning in Belgium by an onrush of German armour ...'.[130] This note antedated by seven weeks the more celebrated memorandum about the tank forces that de Gaulle sent Gamelin and other leaders in early 1940.[131] It led the French army to take a big step forward, for on 16 December 1939 the army staff decreed the constitution of the first DCR. Headquartered at Poissy in the Seine-et-Oise, it was formed from four Char B battalions, motorised infantry and supporting arms. The new division embarked on the task of weapons training and the search for tactical cohesion. It was a race against time that Hitler would not permit it to win.[132]

Why were the French not taught more by the calamity that had befallen their ally? After all, as a postwar analysis of Polish strategy written by a senior French officer closely implicated in the Sedan disaster of 1940 ruefully concluded: 'we did no better than them, in spite of the lessons that we drew out of their defeat'.[133] Doubtless a gamut of considerations, some psychological and others physical, contributed to a deadening of the impact of the events in the east on the French and British forces.

One factor was the perennial difficulty of changing cumbersome organisations set in traditional ways and subject to hierarchical habits. In revealing itself to be prone to this institutional inertia, this *conformisme militaire*, the French army was not exceptional among defence organisations, but it was exacerbating the peril suspended over it in 1939–40. Its problems, as the general who commanded the Paris air region in the phoney war conceded later, lay with its 'bureaucratic ways, division and fear of responsibilities, personal rivalries, disagreements between the army and air staffs'; with its 'byzantinism instead of simplicity in the organisation of the hierarchy ... [with] a sort of comfortable way of settling in to the war'.[134]

A second impediment to radical change was the widespread belief among the western Allied generals that the Poles had invited their own destruction by their imprudent dispositions and their naïve defensive plans. Both in his August 1936 talks with Rydz-Smigly in Warsaw and in the May 1939 discussions with Kasprzycki in Paris, Gamelin ascertained only the 'main outlines' (*les grandes lignes*) of the Polish war plan.[135] On both occasions he counselled the Poles to avoid concentrating forces too far to the west, close to the German border. For all the pre-war consultations, the French, according to Armengaud, lacked any clear idea of Polish plans when the conflict commenced. The Polish generals had not heeded French advice to deploy circumspectly, maintaining reserves in depth. Equally, as one military commentator later lamented, the French, when the guarantees were given in the spring of 1939, 'had not required our ally to adopt a coherent plan of operations, one fashioned through complete liaison with our general staff'.[136] Indeed, according to Armengaud, it was only after the chiefs of the French missions angrily remonstrated with the Polish command that the latter disclosed the Polish plans once the German invasion had begun.[137]

Criticism – even disparagement – of the Poles was thus an important factor in dispelling the anxieties that their swift collapse had caused, fleetingly, among the French and British. The immaturity of Rydz-Smigly, Kasprzycki and Stachiewicz as strategists was a *leitmotiv* of Franco-Britsh analyses. Allegations that the Polish ideas possessed a puerile *naïveté* were commonplace. The 'Poles are fighting very courageously', wrote Britain's military attaché in Paris in mid-September 1939, 'but their initial plan was quite "enfantin". And they were so secret about it.' A month later Daladier visited Gamelin's headquarters and warmed to the same theme, exclaiming: 'God knows the Poles had their warnings! But they're childlike in their national behaviour.'[138] Such strictures were turned against the French when they did no better the following year. With Paris about to fall to the Germans, the US ambassador wrote to the State Department in Washington on 7 June 1940:

The truth about Gamelin is that neither he nor any of his associates in the High Command drew any lessons whatsoever from the German invasion of Poland. In Paris at that time it was popular to regard the Poles with contempt, and the wish being father to the thought, Gamelin and his associates announced their certainty that Germany could never employ such tactics with success against the French army. No training whatsoever was given to the French troops in methods of resisting combined attack by airplanes and tanks. The Germans employed against the French exactly the same tactics that they had employed against the Poles and with exactly the same results.[139]

This reaction by the American may have been natural in the context of the bewildering calamity that was overtaking France as he wrote. But the evidence now reveals that there was not such a neat link as this between the Polish and French defeats. There may indeed have been some complacency among French and British leaders that their own plans and deployments would never be as unwise as had been those of the Poles. Yet it seemed an irrefutable point that France would pose a more difficult proposition to the Wehrmacht than had Poland. French officers reflected, not incorrectly, that almost half of the western front benefited from defence by fortifications or other prepared positions. Poland, in contrast, had possessed few fixed defences. Furthermore, it had borders that were some 3,000 kilometres long and which it had insufficient troops to hold securely. Much was also made, in French after-action analyses, of the way the unusually dry weather and clear atmospheric conditions in Poland in September 1939 had facilitated the German mobile and air operations. And these were not the only sources of comfort for western analysts. A further reassurance was drawn from the successes enjoyed by Polish anti-tank weapons against the lightly armoured Panzer I and Panzer II tanks that formed the bulk of the Wehrmacht's mechanised forces. Another, still, was the fact that the Germans suffered some 43,000 casualties even in as one-sided a campaign as this and that French intelligence reported the infliction of extensive material attrition on German air and ground formations.[140]

These were, to most western observers, sufficient indication that Germany would not prove capable of repeating its easy triumph in the east. Poland had been surprised in the act of mobilising and concentrating. The Franco-British armies were deployed, their training could only improve. Moreover, Gamelin estimated that the Poles had made mistakes; for example, a corps had taken the offensive into the Danzig corridor and fallen into the trap laid by the Germans. Pownall, the BEF chief of staff, reflected the prevalent view when he noted on 21 September 1939 'that only on the Western front can the war be lost on land – But it won't be!'[141] The refrain was shortly taken up by the politicians. On trying to press in London, early in October, for more RAF strength to be based in France, Armengaud met the rejoinder from Kingsley Wood, the British secretary of state for air: 'France was not Poland; the French army was the foremost in the world; it was strong enough to . . . defy German assaults.'[142] Their belief that the broken terrain of northwest Europe afforded inherent advantages to the Franco-British defences that the Poles had not possessed gave the Allied commanders further confidence. Another factor was the ability of the Franco-British armies to surpass the force-to-space density that the Poles had managed.

Gamelin remarked in this sense on 9 October, to Reynaud (who was visiting Vincennes), that:

> The Polish example cannot be held up as a rule offering conclusive teachings: Poland fielded one division for every thirty or forty kilometres against the German. We, for our part, are deploying seventy-five infantry divisions along the 750 kilometre front from Dunkerque to the Rhône, or one division every ten kilometres ... [whilst in] aviation, German superiority is only very minimal over the whole of the Franco-British air fleet.[143]

A belief that a campaign in the west would be waged in conditions quite different from those in Poland was a comfort to the Allies. By 12 October Pownall was contentedly confiding in his diary that Franco-British preparations 'make [German] victory in the spring most improbable'.[144] As the twilight war stretched into the unusually severe winter of 1939–40, the Allies in the west felt less and less reason to conduct a radical review of their assumptions. Too many French and British military chiefs 'wore the smile', in the words of Armengaud (now commanding the air defences of Paris), 'of men who knew the worth of our Command ... who had faith in France's lucky star'. Armengaud claimed that he strove to keep western weaknesses in the forefront of attention, but found his powerlessness in the face of the widespread optimism 'grew greater the more that the battle of Poland receded into the past'.[145]

As will be seen, Gamelin was less prone than most to such creeping complacency. He did not flinch from the work that remained to be done, striving to improve the levels of equipment and training among the unevenly battle-worthy divisions of the French army. This required time. However, the respite offered by the *sitzkrieg* after the fall of Poland seemed to promise that time; it had been axiomatic for so long among Franco-British strategists that time would work on their side that it was no longer questioned. Gort reportedly mused, just three weeks after hostilities began, that 'the war may be lost in France, even though it cannot be won there'. Struck by the inactivity of the Allies in October 1939, Oliver Harvey, private secretary to Lord Halifax, wondered in his diary: 'I suppose this strategy is all right?'[146] Such concern as this found little echo, however, beside the din that was now coming from the increasingly busy Franco-British war machine.

12 The Twilight War: military stagnation and political conflict, 1939–1940

Gamelin stood firm against any precipitate offensive action against Germany in the autumn of 1939. In spite of Poland's desperate plight he maintained that France needed to complete its own move onto a war footing before it attempted to bring assistance to an ally. This conversion from conditions of peace to general mobilisation necessitated complex transformations in both the French armed forces and the French economy. Judgements have differed sharply as to the efficiency with which French arrangements for mobilisation functioned in 1939–40. This chapter will discuss not just the narrowly military, but also the military-economic, dimensions to the process. In particular it will examine Gamelin's estimation of how successfully France went to war. It will consider Gamelin's familiarity with the condition of the French armies in 1939–40 and explore his endeavours to employ the respite of the phoney war profitably by expanding and reinforcing French combat resources. It will close by recounting how demoralising civil-military strife resurfaced at the highest levels of war policy-making; and how Gamelin's confidence in Daladier waned, bringing back the bad old days to French defence politics which became blighted once again by open political-military hostility on the eve of the shooting war on the western front.

The first French concern when war began was with strictly military mobilisation. As already discussed, each of the peacetime twenty-one infantry divisions – the army's backbone – underwent temporary dislocation in order to convert to a war strength. This reorganisation merged the mobilised reservists at their regimental depots with the professional cadres and serving conscripts. Out of this melting pot emerged the A and B series reservist divisions that tripled the field strength of the army.[1]

In the short term, however, the process caused immense disturbance. It left Gamelin and his senior theatre commanders facing Germany,

General Georges and General Prételat, few formations immediately able to engage the enemy. General mobilisation was mandatory before the French army could risk a war (as Gamelin had insisted when Germany remilitarised the Rhineland in 1936).² In September 1939 the mobilisation itself, once underway, prevented more than a token show of force by the French in front of the Siegfried Line. Until completion of mobilisation, and the arrival of all major units at the concentration points prescribed in Gamelin's war plan (Plan E, of 1938), even the defence of France itself remained precarious.³ This initial insecurity had been the reason, after all, for the insurance that the French had taken out on their inter-war security system – an insurance elaborately provided through the Maginot fortifications, the *frontalier* units that gave locally resident reinforcements to the fortress garrisons, and the *couverture* to strengthen border defence in any emergency short of war itself.

Gamelin attached prime importance to setting in place each of these elements of French security in their prescribed order. He abhorred the prospect of any disruption – whether by a German *attaque brusquée* (which he told the CSG in March 1939 was becoming a considerable danger), or by pressure from sections of the French government for an early offensive.⁴ Above all, Gamelin sought, in September–October 1939, to change gear smoothly from peace to war. He wanted to set the French war machine in motion without a hitch. Convinced that the road ahead was a long one, Gamelin attached overriding importance to making a trouble-free start to the journey.

For these reasons – and because of his apprenticeship under Joffre in 1914–18 – Gamelin always held the strategic outlook of the 'westerner'. During the phoney war of 1939–40 he opposed the diversion of military resources from the build-up in western Europe. He blocked plans for adventures in distant theatres that he regarded as secondary.⁵

The first such proposal that the Allies embark on a peripheral strategy arose as early as the second meeting of the Franco-British supreme war council (SWC), at Brighton, on 22 September 1939. What was mooted was the constitution of a Balkan front by means of a landing of a French expeditionary corps at Salonika.⁶ Those in Paris who favoured the venture hailed, not surprisingly, from military quarters with a vested interest in imperial and overseas operations. New fronts far away from Gamelin's oversight at Vincennes held the promise of glory and greater autonomy for Georges Mandel, the minister for the colonies, General Bührer, chief of staff of the colonial forces, and Darlan, head of the navy. The former pair, as Gamelin noted in connection with the Norwegian adventure of April 1940, were 'always in favour of energetic solutions'.[7] The Balkan project first surfaced on 15 September 1939, when rumours reached Gamelin's Vincennes headquarters not only that the Soviet Union was threatening Poland (a warning borne out two days later), but that Romania was mobilising and that Yugoslavia was 'agitating over Salonika', in a search for an Aegean port. Gamelin's headquarters speculated whether these were indications that 'the hoped-for extension of the [eastern] theatre of operations will come about?'[8] What attracted Gamelin was not the pretext to despatch French or British forces to the Balkans but the possibility of widening the war in the east by proxy – of using the blood of others to prolong the breathing space before the Wehrmacht turned west in earnest. It was a calculation that did Gamelin little honour, based as it was on a 'cut price war on the peripheries' in which other countries fought France's battle for it. (Till the Soviet invasion of Poland on 17 September 1939, Gamelin 'forecast that, even if it found no support in the east, the Polish army's agony would stretch out until the spring [of 1940]'.)[9]

In preparation for the second SWC meeting the situation in the Balkans was discussed by French military leaders at two conferences on 20 September. At the first the service chiefs convened without any diplomats or politicians. At the second meeting they were joined by Daladier, Coulondre (whom Daladier, on taking charge of the Quai d'Orsay personally a week before, had appointed *chef de cabinet* for foreign policy), Léger, and Champetier de Ribes (named under-secretary at the Quai in the 13 September reshuffle).[10] The naval and colonial commanders immediately applied pressure to commit French forces into an eastern European–Balkan theatre. Bührer was 'extremely worked up about getting a decision taken in this sense' – presumably so that a *fait accompli* could be presented to the British at the SWC. Gamelin, however, rejected such adventurism. It would, he said, be 'premature'. From his headquarters diary it is plain that he would have been content if an enlargement of the eastern war zone had occurred through German action. But, though eager to see major Wehrmacht commitment in the east for as long as possible, Gamelin was unwilling to engage Franco-British forces to bring this about.[11]

Daladier gave his backing to Gamelin's strategy. It emerged at the Brighton SWC, in any case, that the British had misgivings of their own about a Salonika operation.[12] The episode nevertheless marked the beginning rather than the end of a winter-long struggle for Gamelin to preserve the forces he was accumulating in France from detachment to a succession of strategic *projets* on the peripheries of Europe. After Salonika the next of these schemes to rear its head was a plan to fly bomber aircraft from French bases in Syria and the Lebanon to attack

Soviet oil installations at Baku. Fortunately for the Allied cause, the scheme was dropped because of its technical impracticability with the available aircraft.[13] This fantasy was followed by debates over whether to mount an expedition through Scandinavia to assist Finland, after the latter was attacked by the Soviet Union in November 1939.[14] Finally, there was the Franco-British intervention in Norway after Germany moved north in April 1940 – a gesture by the Allies that proved as ineffectual as Gamelin had feared but which, with Reynaud's rise to the prime ministership in March, he could not prevent.[15]

In striving to maintain the build-up of Franco-British resources in France itself, Gamelin faced an uphill task. Pressure mounted from the press, politicians and some military quarters to 'do something', the longer the phoney war continued. As a French general responsible for air defence of Paris later recalled: 'The high command was criticised because – with good reason – it viewed with repugnance the dispersal of forces away from the front in eastern France, the principal front in the global struggle. It was accused of being soft; its authority was undermined. Yet confidence should either have been shown in it or its leaders changed without further ado.'[16]

Gamelin needed a determination that is not always associated with his name in order to keep control over this first phase of the Allied war effort. Not everyone approved the French and British decision to renounce the strategic initiative. It was difficult for the Allied propaganda machines to make much out of the inactivity in the autumn of 1939 not just in the Mediterranean but also on the western front. Above all, Gamelin would do nothing hasty. 'Like a bather marching down to the sea and finding the water cold, remaining to paddle but not to swim, the French army stayed where it was.'[17]

In return, France was supposed to benefit from an orderly and undisturbed national mobilisation. 'The important thing', as John Colville, Chamberlain's private secretary, noted, 'is that every day's delay is so much gain to us as far as war production is concerned.'[18] Certainly this was an advantage by which Gamelin set great store. He regarded the partial mobilisation conducted in 1938 at the time of the Sudeten crisis as a trial run that smoothed the transition to war the following year. To the wartime Vichyite court at Riom, Gamelin claimed that the 'vast military measures' France undertook in the month of Munich 'served as excellent practice for our general mobilisation of 1939'.[19]

Other sources, however, present a more complicated picture. Some indicate that the economic as well as the military conversion to a war footing in France was bedevilled with difficulties. For every sector where the transition was trouble-free there was another in which scenes of chaos prevailed. French mobilisation stuttered and spluttered. It was not a well-oiled process. The problems are attested by war ministry archives and by the complaints sent to Gamelin and Georges by army and corps commanders struggling to put combat-ready formations into the field on the Maginot Line and the Belgian border. They are documented, too, by the reports of the parliamentary army commissioners who travelled on inspections to most subordinate headquarters at the front after the autumn rains arrived in November 1939 and made serious operations in France unlikely till the spring. Gamelin, indeed, witnessed the deficiencies at first hand in a series of visits he made to front-line corps and divisions during the 1939–40 winter.

What was wrong? Why was the underlying condition of the French war economy less satisfactory than the undisturbed mobilisation led the authorities in Paris to suppose? At last it is possible to take stock of the way France went to war in 1939. The archives of industrial companies, the ministries of commerce and industry, and of labour, as well as those of the parliamentary commissions, are available. There is, too, a masterly published dissection of France's mobilisation of 1939 by Jean-Louis Crémieux-Brilhac – a monumental work comparable to Jean-Jacques Becker's acclaimed treatment of 1914.[20]

A reading of Crémieux-Brilhac and a sampling of the primary sources make it possible to suggest an explanation for what otherwise appears a paradox. On the one hand, the mobilisation and concentration of the French fighting forces proceeded quite efficiently. Yet, on the other hand, the economy and the home front experienced widespread and serious disruption as they changed to a war regime. Grave shortcomings, moreover, were exposed in the armament and general equipment of many mobilised formations.

Completing the military mobilisation without a serious hitch raised morale in the French high command. In early September 1939 Gamelin's staff rejoiced that the 'concentration was proceeding under ideal conditions, the Germans not deigning to disturb it'.[21] This seemed confirmed when Gamelin travelled to Abbeville for the first meeting of the SWC on 12 September 1939. Besides holding discussions with the British at the *sous-préfecture* of the Somme *département*, Gamelin encountered the local French commander of the 2nd military region, based on Amiens. This general reported that, for the divisions brought onto a war footing in his area, 'the mobilisation was conducted very well'. The 'lessons of September 1938 and the repetition in April 1939 had born fruit'. Cadres and administrators, he added, 'had been called up before the effectives themselves . . . Everything occurred in a most well-ordered fashion'.[22] Apparently corroborating this view was the satisfied comment of Gauché, of the 2e Bureau, to Belgium's military attaché in Paris, that 'the French mobilisation was carried out extremely well'.[23]

Yet it was also evident that muddle and disorganisation plagued many of the French arrangements. Gauché admitted that nearly 30 per cent of civilian motor vehicles listed for compulsory delivery to the army had not materialised at the requisition depots.[24] So far as the front-line forces were concerned, the autumn call-up of 1939 may have avoided a descent into chaos. But the economic heart of the French total war effort definitely skipped several beats. Particularly in industry and agriculture, the mobilisation acted like a giant spanner thrown into the works of the economic machine. 'General mobilisation', reported the US naval attaché in Paris, 'dislocated industry necessitating closing of many industries as well as expansion of others, to such an extent that the reorganisation was far beyond the power of the Ministry of Armaments to handle . . .'.[25]

France's economic recovery – most apparent during the first half of 1939 in manufacturing industry and capital repatriation – ground almost to a halt. At factories and farms throughout the country economic output fell sharply as men were drafted into uniform. Skilled industrial employees were called up just like anyone else. Technicians, engineers and managers were needed in the workplace to keep the machine of the war economy turning purposefully. Instead they were mobilised as indiscriminately as unskilled blue-collar workers. There was no register of reserved occupations. Skilled labour was treated simply as fodder for the army, whose gargantuan appetite for manpower seemed insatiable. In some plants almost everyone of military age was mobilised in September 1939. As one historian has reflected:

Once the politicians and commanders decided to mobilize their male populations, in one sense they overshot the mark. In 1914, and to a lesser extent in 1939, the instinctive reaction of the military . . . was to put everything and everybody into uniform. As war dragged on it became increasingly clear that this was a mistake. The same technology that made military mobilisation possible also demanded that it remain incomplete.[26]

In the countryside of France the damage done by the call-up was, if anything, even more noticeable. The German invasion of Poland began on the eve of the 1939 harvest season. Mobilisation of agricultural labour threatened to cost France the bulk of the year's home-grown foodstuffs, along with animal feed required for the army's horsed transport and cavalry. The rural exodus that resulted occasioned one of the earliest confrontations between Daladier and Gamelin and started to erode the latter's confidence in Daladier's qualities as a wartime leader.

It was during lunch at the opening SWC meeting, on 12 September, that Daladier first made the question a matter of contention with Gamelin. That morning, said the French prime minister, whilst flying from Villacoublay air base over the fields of the Aisne and Somme to Abbeville for the conference, he 'had been heartbroken at seeing the countryside deserted and the harvests not yet gathered in: "Don't ask me to call up the old [reservist] classes", he said to General Gamelin.'[27]

The sight of how severely agriculture had been disrupted by the onset of war made a great impression on Daladier, whose concern over the fate of rural and small-town France went back to his own roots among the peasantry and shopkeepers of the Vaucluse. The realisation that mobilisation had denuded farms of their workforce prompted him to follow his lunchtime lament at Abbeville by writing 'in rather sharp terms' to Gamelin on 17 September, asking the general 'to grant leave to the agriculturalists so as to let them harvest their crops, and also to certain categories of workers in order to avoid the absence of qualified labour completely dislocating the economic life of the country'. Gamelin's reply argued, likewise 'very pointedly', that France faced 'the possibility in a very short time, of Germany swinging back [west] with all her forces'; it therefore opposed 'any radical measure' of the kind favoured by Daladier.[28]

According to his headquarters war diary, this incident left Gamelin 'genuinely tormented'. What Daladier had sought appeared, to Gamelin, to be symptomatic of a complacency that lurked beneath the surface of French civilian opinion.[29] It was a relaxed self-confidence that bordered on underestimation of the enemy. Gamelin knew that this was one of the most dangerous states of mind that could take hold in wartime. Yet, as the phoney war continued, he detected growing evidence, from conversations that his staff reported and from what he heard and read for himself, of a belief in Paris that Germany might be defeated by inexorable Franco-British economic pressure, without recourse to military engagements and the risks that they entailed.[30] The most notorious piece of early wartime Allied propaganda was a poster that showed a map of the world, coloured red with the vast expanses of the Franco-British colonial empires, and bearing the slogan: 'We shall win because we are the strongest' (*Nous vaincrons parce que nous sommes les plus forts*).[31] The substance behind the poster did not elicit any disagreement from Gamelin, but the style troubled him. It seemed to him that, from the war's outset, Allied politicians were closing their minds to the potent dangers facing them in the short term, before great but latent French and British resources were converted into raw military power.[32]

In manufacturing industry – and especially in the armaments sector – the mismanaged mobilisation presented France with still more serious problems. For one thing, it generated competition for manpower between the army and business. For another, the mobilisation of skilled as well as semi-skilled workers led to the military being forced to pay dearly, as measured in terms of sharply reduced production of weapons, munitions and general equipment. This proved to be all the more damaging because, for all its impressive recovery in the first half of 1939, the French economy had not caught up the backlogs in manufacture and delivery of material to units and depots at the moment the war began.[33] According to General Colson, who on mobilisation became responsible for all military resources in the French interior (as distinct from those at and directly behind the front in the 'zone of the armies'), 'the listed complements [of equipment] on the eve of general mobilisation ... looked as though they were going to be almost complete in respect of older material that had been in service for several years ... But the position over new armaments was different altogether.'[34] This is a judgement corroborated by Colonel Minart, a member of Gamelin's personal staff in 1939–40. Evidently French military production could ill afford the severe hiccup it suffered in the poorly administered transition from peace to war. In respect of some categories of munitions, said Minart, the situation was little short of 'tragic'. One example of this came in the Saar in September when the armour of Requin's Fourth Army expended fully one-third of its ammunition stocks during its limited offensive, even though each tank fired no more than thirty rounds.[35]

It is these deficiencies that account for the apparent paradox that Gamelin could proclaim the French army ready to go to war – without meaning, in any sense, that the army was ready to attempt to win the war.[36] Gamelin was too conscious of the manifold shortcomings of French military preparedness, of its incomplete rearmament, of its unready British ally, to recommend any assumption of large-scale offensive action by the west before 1941 or 1942.

As early as the first month of the war, the French defence chiefs registered the severity of the shortfalls in the levels of modern and competitive weapons actually with the combat formations. Supply of the best tanks, the Somua S35, the B1 bis and the Hotchkiss H39 dwindled to a trickle as the call-up of factory workers strangled industrial output. Likewise, delivery of modern artillery flagged seriously. This crippled the army's re-equipment with the Schneider 90mm dual-purpose cannon and with the 47mm anti-tank gun (effective, at combat ranges, against the defensive plating of almost all German tanks). Senior French commanders as well as Gamelin's staff learned that only sixteen of the divisional anti-tank batteries possessed the 47mm weapon, out of sixty-seven mobilised infantry divisions. Furthermore, only twenty-four of the other divisions had been allocated 75mm batteries instead. The remaining divisions had only the older and far less penetrative 25mm gun (to which, under most conditions, German Panzer IIIs and IVs were impervious). And only ten French divisions possessed a complete complement of even these inferior weapons.[37]

It was a threefold shortage, therefore, that confronted the French armies during and after the 1939 mobilisation. There were shortages of armaments with the mobilised units, shortages of munitions manufacture on the home front, and shortages of more general military supplies (from greatcoats and boots to blankets and waterproof capes). So much that should have been precisely organised in advance became subject to makeshift arrangements and improvisation. The unifying element, the factor that bound together all three types of shortage, was the failure to have a properly structured, equitable and commonly understood plan for distributing manpower. It was not to be expected that the French generals themselves would refrain from calling up entire classes of reservists once war appeared to be unavoidable at the beginning of September. Commanders responsible for assuring the integrity of the metropolitan frontiers were not the people to hold back from putting as many units as possible onto a war footing by trawling the civilian population's reservist classes.

From the narrow military perspective of military strategists, the overriding concern was the German demographic superiority over France and the way in which this translated into readily deployable armed forces. Germany had a population of some 70 million against 39 million French; a trained military manpower pool of some 8 million against the French 4.5 million; and about 110 mobilised divisions, according to French intelligence at the end of August 1939, against about 80 French divisions (some of which were required in North Africa and to watch Italy). But the headlong rush of the French to put the maximum number of divisions as possible into the field proved counterproductive, because so many of the soldiers of September had been the artisans and agriculturalists of August.[38] In a note produced by Colson on 22 September, with the purpose of briefing Dautry as the latter set the new armaments ministry in place, the army staff conceded that the manufacture of warlike supplies had almost come to a halt and that the reason was 'the mobilisation into the armies of a part [sic] of the specialist personnel of certain factories'.[39]

In truth the disruption that faced Dautry as he hastily put together his infant ministry was so widespread that it belied the existence of pre-war procedures for the transition of the economy onto a war footing. The task before Dautry was one of Herculean proportions.[40] In conjunction with Charles Pomaret, the minister of labour, he launched himself into the job of reclaiming essential skilled workers from the clutches of the generals. This required the civilian authorities to apply to the general staff for an *affectation spéciale* – a certificate of reserved occupation for vital war work. A certificate was needed for every individual whom they wished to be released to return to a job in industry or agriculture. In some cases the task was one on a daunting scale: at Renault's principal factory, at Boulogne-Billancourt, no fewer than 20,000 of the 32,000 workers had been mobilised. Car and truck assembly lines lay idle. Vehicle production, much of it destined for immediate requisition for military transport, was at a standstill.[41]

Ministers, officials and generals only understood after the damage had been done that there had been a calamitous failure to implement the provisions of the law of 11 July 1938 for the organisation of the nation for time of war. Yet this was legislation which had been purposely framed in order to ensure the distribution of manpower according to universally understood, rational and equitable principles in the event of national mobilisation. It had been conceived and enacted precisely to avoid the occurrence of the damaging competition for effectives between the armed forces and the economy that so blighted the way in which France went to war in 1939.[42]

So severe was the disruption of armaments production by the call-up that Dautry felt compelled to appeal for special efforts to redress the situation when he appeared before the army commission of the Chamber of Deputies, on 27 September.[43] The minister's anxiety had been fed by a report furnished to him by Colson. This listed the output levels in critical sectors of armaments one week earlier. It confirmed the need for a major effort to make up the serious shortages of 25mm anti-tank guns, light machine-guns (*fusils-mitrailleurs*) and 105mm artillery. Mechanised equipment, too, was rolling from the factories in worryingly short supply, according to the statistics Colson gave Dautry (see Table 6):

Table 6. *Estimated French tank production during the phoney war*

	Light tanks	Chars Bl	Somuas
Sept. 1939	80	7	12
Oct. 1939	90	10	12
Nov. 1939	120	20	?
Dec. 1939	135	20	?
Mar./Apr. 1940	200	50	30

Yet, compared with these estimates, it was calculated that 275 light tanks and 30 Chars B1 would need to be produced each month if the armoured forces were to be able to sustain a monthly combat attrition of 22 per cent (a level expected by the staff if significant operations began in the west). Indeed Colson offered the stark warning that the 'number of our tank battalions would therefore diminish until springtime if the armour were to be employed other than in limited actions'; 'if we want to have a major mass of tanks at our disposal in the spring', he concluded, 'we virtually have to hold back in reserve the tank units that we've mobilised, until then.'[44]

Nor were the emerging deficiencies in the French army confined to different types of weapons. Formidable shortcomings were also exposed in the area of communications gear. Colson's report, just cited, told Dautry of the severe dislocation of the manufacture of radio transmission equipment as a result of the mobilisation of inordinate numbers of radio-electrical engineers. This only served to exacerbate inherent problems that originated in the French army's doctrinal emphasis on fighting slow-moving and methodical *batailles de conduite*, under tight high command control. Doctrinal preparation and staff exercises of this sort, throughout the inter-war years, had deprived the development of field radio and modern signals technology of any impetus in France. 'The extremely low priority for communications', Robert Doughty has justly remarked, 'perhaps is best reflected in the French having spent only 0.15 per cent of their military budget for the purchase of communications equipment from 1923 to 1939.'[45] Little or no importance had been attached to providing headquarters with alternative communications systems, in case of damage to primary networks by enemy action or sabotage. In peacetime the permanent regional headquarters and military bases communicated principally by means of the army's own telephone exchanges. After mobilisation, however, the army had to improvise many more subordinate command posts. It commonly installed them in requisitioned country houses, or commandeered office space from local government bureaucrats in the many *mairies* and *sous-préfectures* of the towns of north and north-east France. The establishment of GQG under Georges at Les Bondons, a château at La Ferté-sous-Jouarre, and Lord Gort's BEF headquarters at the Château du Kergorlay, near Denain, were but two examples of this commonplace intrusion of the army into the timelessly elegant world of the French landed gentry. The sense of timelessness, however, was hardly disturbed by the arrival of these military staffs. They were ill-equipped with modern and rapid communications and instead relied on the existing land lines of the civilian PTT telephone network. Though this was adequate during the immobile winter of 1939–40, it proved to be disastrous once fast-moving operations commenced. Then, reliant on an over-centralised and static system, the rigid French arrangements for command and control 'found themselves unable to react or regain the initiative once the Germans forced their unwieldy headquarters to move and severed their lines of communications'.[46]

The more the autumn of 1939 wore on, however, the longer became the catalogue of embarrassing and dangerous deficiencies uncovered by the inquiries and inspections of the French authorities. The shortcomings that came to light went far beyond the signals and telephone systems. Disquieting revelations appeared in regard both to the equipment of the armies at the front and the performance of the war economy in the interior.

Much of the information was obtained through the investigations conducted by the Senate and Chamber army commissions. These bodies, even in wartime, remained responsible for scrutinising the government's military policies on behalf of parliament. They were a tangible expression of the principle of democratic control over the military authorities and of the accountability of government ministers. The commissioners enjoyed statutory rights to inspect munitions manufacturing firms and the depots which stockpiled military supplies in the interior. They also possessed the authority to visit the soldiers serving with the armies in the field.

The army commissioners exercised considerable influence in wartime, as they did under conditions of peace. Their extensive powers and prerogatives derived in part from legislation and in part from well-entrenched precedent. During the First World War, and particularly whilst Joffre's prestige was at its zenith in 1914–16, the French parliament had vigorously defended the remit of its commissions, maintaining that they were a key element in preserving the supremacy of the civilians over the direction and conduct of the war effort. After the conclusion of the conflict the importance of the Chamber army commission, in particular, had grown even greater. In the 1920s and 1930s it had commonly exercised its right not only to interrogate war ministers but also to require the most senior officers in the army to appear before it to answer commissioners' questions. Especially during 1934, 1935 and 1936, when anxiety over German rearmament intensified parliamentary attention to French defensive countermeasures, Pétain, Weygand and Gamelin, as well as technical specialists such as Happich, the director of armaments, found themselves quizzed under the glare of the commissions.

The activities and documentation that the commissions generated in the autumn of 1939 have, however, elucidated the shortcomings of the

French war effort more clearly for later historians than they did for contemporary authorities. The reason for this was largely to be found in the way in which the commissions acted as a catalyst of fresh civil-military strains. The prominence and intrusiveness of the commissioners during their visits to front-line headquarters and units in 1914–18 had already been a source of bitter protests from French generals in the earlier war. Since 1918 the position of these bodies had been consolidated, to the point where the presidents of the commissions (particularly those of the Chamber) behaved and were treated as major players in French defence policy-making. Since they exercised great influence over the size of military appropriations and the fate of procurement programmes, these presidents were courted by war ministers, generals and the defence bureaucrats with a mixture of fear, respect and resentment. From the late-1920s onwards the presidency of the Chamber army commission became elevated to the status of an unofficial anteroom to the office of the war minister. And in the case of Maginot in 1928 and Fabry in 1935, tenure of the Chamber army commission's presidency was a direct stepping stone into the rue Saint-Dominique, whilst for Guy La Chambre it led to appointment as air minister in 1938. It was the Chamber army commission which fulfilled the role of burial-ground for Reynaud's bill to create a professional army in 1935. French military chiefs, such as Gamelin, knew full well that taking account of these defence specialists in parliament was a sure source of frustration, a likely source of friction but something that they could not avoid.[47]

The scope of the activities of the parliamentary commissions in the 1939–40 winter aroused increasing irritation among the generals, who abhorred the high level of security clearance enjoyed by these politicians. The latter used this to roam and snoop in the jurisdiction of the 'zone of the armies' (areas that the military wished to see brought exclusively under their own control for the duration of the war). Their freedom of movement in front-line sectors and the nuisance factor that they represented to harassed commanders provoked a growing discontent about their functions and liberties among the commanders of the French armies, with Georges at GQG and even on the part of Gamelin.[48]

At least in part, the problem arose out of the sense of unreality that the phoney war engendered, for French generals could not even invoke the occurrence of active military operations to restrict the incursions of the commissioners. Indeed the frequency of parliamentary missions, after September 1939, appeared to become inversely proportionate to the decline in activity on the north-east front. The mobilised reservists gradually accustomed themselves to the peculiarity of 'war without war'; they settled into it and began to adopt it as their routine. 'Ici on s'installe dans la guerre' was a phrase heard more and more widely in border towns, billets and the estaminets where off-duty soldiers mingled socially with the remaining local population behind the lines. The saying appeared to express the resignation that came over the French troops as the autumn of 1939 stretched on towards winter. The optimism, bravado and even gaity that had characterised August 1914 was nowhere in evidence. Then the call-up had been greeted with patriotic songs. Then the French infantry had entrained to bellicose cries of 'vers Berlin', the grim greyness of their rifles relieved by colourful late-summer flowers pressed into the barrels by sweethearts, wives and mothers.[49]

In 1939, however, it was all a more sombre scene. The soldiers faced the dangers of the new war with a cold and stoical resolve. They had lost their illusions about quick victories won with negligible casualties. There was a resignation about the way in which most reacted to the start of one more round of blood-letting with the perennial enemy over the Rhine: *les salauds, les Boches*.[50] 'Il faut en finir' was the most enthusiastic remark that was summoned at the prospect.[51] French headquarters realised the challenge of motivation and protection of morale that lay ahead. The 'overriding preoccupation' of the troops deployed in France that autumn and winter, recollected an officer of Gamelin's staff, 'was to ensure their immediate security and to shelter themselves from the inclemencies of the weather'.[52] Another sensitive observer who noticed the distinctive and unfamiliar nature that the war took on was Jean-Paul Sartre, who had been mobilised into a division assigned to Alsace. Lunching with a chasseur, on temporary leave from the front in mid-November 1939, Sartre noted his companion ruing the precariousness of informal front-line truces:

He says: 'The Germans are two hundred and fifty metres away . . . During the first days they used to play . . . accordians and harmonicas. But a week ago, a Moroccan from our side brought down one of their lads with his rifle, and since then there's no way of leaving cover any more . . .'. He concludes gloomily: 'There's always some bloody idiot, and it's the others who have to pay for it' – a stock phrase here, but one that I usually hear pronounced when some drunken soldier has caused a rumpus and the cafés have been put out of bounds.[53]

The state of the soldiers' morale, let alone their zest for the perilous missions before them, therefore gave Gamelin cause for concern. Likewise a worry to Gamelin from the very outset was the steadiness of purpose among French civilian leaders. The *union sacrée* of 1914, intended to set aside partisan parliamentary disputes whilst France warded off the German invasion, had proved itself to be a notoriously imperfect guarantee of political unity in the First World War. But in

1939 there was not even an attempt to reconstruct that flawed instrument of French national cohesion. Instead, as Alfred Sauvy's memorable imagery would have it, France edged into the war 'like a reluctant bather, chilled to the bone, toes first, slowly lowering herself in, inch by inch, teeth chattering'.[54] A fluid cabal in favour of an early compromise peace with Germany was working discreetly in parliament to dampen down any tendencies by Daladier to invigorate the Allied war effort. Gamelin himself believed that Laval, Chautemps and Flandin formed the closet leadership of these unrepentant and unreconstructed appeasers. As Britain's military attaché in Paris, Colonel Fraser, wrote to his wife in England in October: 'German propaganda is very active here and their broadcast in French is often quite clever.' Fraser kept a clear head as to the risk of the 'worst thing . . . a premature patched-up peace', and confessed to his periodic 'misgivings' because 'silly stuff sometimes catches people'.[55]

Against this backdrop it was not surprising that hostility mounted between the generals and the parliamentary commissioners. The difficulties first loomed into view as early as September 1939 when Gamelin complained to his staff that 'our burdens come not from the military operations nor from the hard work we do, but from this government of hesitant, nervous fainthearts. That is what weighs down on us. Joffre did not have all these problems in 1914.' Later in the month he returned to the theme, confiding that the 'military operations are really as nothing; what is hard to endure is the government, the politicians and their cliques.'[56] Of course Gamelin was practising his use of selective memory, and not for the first or last time, in claiming that Joffre had been left undisturbed by politicians in the early years of the First World War. Indeed, Joffre had been party to long-running political guerrilla struggles over the contentious question of parliamentary control over the French war effort. Minart, one of Gamelin's personal staff in 1939–40, subsequently attested that the general 'in fact had a very vivid recollection of the backstairs manoeuvres which had so obstructed the action of Joffre'.[57]

Gamelin was only discovering anew that one of the greatest difficulties for a democracy at war is simultaneously to allay the phobias of politicians about a 'dictatorship of the army' and dispel the military's fears of disruptive meddling in strategic planning by 'incompetent' civilians. Moreover, Gamelin's venting of frustrations in this vein in the war's opening month actually antedated the beginning of a flow of complaints to him from his army commanders about the intrusions of the parliamentary commissioners. It was not a promising omen for the future course of civil-military relations.[58]

As the French front remained quiet, so the commissioners seized their opportunity to pry and peer into the functioning of the nation-in-arms. They exercised their authority to inquire into the relations between the frontier populations and the vast influx of military personnel which the mobilisation had brought among them. In the commissioners' purview, too, was the checking of the standards of the soldiers' barracks, rations, leave and medical arrangements, along with observation of the levels of weaponry, transport, training facilities, fortifications and air support. And the more the arrival of winter drove military operations into a hibernation, the more the parliamentarians plunged into an ever more feverish regime of inquiries, inspections and investigations. At its first wartime meeting, on 7 September, the Chamber army commission divided itself into seven working sub-committees, to deal with questions as varied as the organisation of the front-line armies, arms manufacture and industrial mobilisation, and the monitoring of colonial troops in France. The heightened inquisitiveness and sense of self-importance of this commission was reflected in the increase in the frequency with which it convened. Ten meetings of the full commission between January 1939 and the July summer recess grew to eighteen meetings from the outbreak of war till the end of April 1940.[59]

It was a highly uneven state of readiness that the parliamentarians uncovered, both among the field armies and in the factories, as their investigations progressed through the autumn and winter. In the case of the soldiers, the first reports of conditions among troops in the front line were presented at the Chamber army commission's meeting of 25 October 1939. At the next meeting, on 15 November, the first dossiers were to hand from members who had returned from inspections in the zone of the armies. Three deputies had visited units at Verdun and Metz, whilst the commission's president, Edmond Miellet, had been to the vast training camps and manoeuvre grounds at Bitche and Sarreguemines. All drew attention to shortages of weapons and equipment. They particularly emphasised the need to expedite production of anti-personnel mines and anti-tank guns and to raise the number of tracked carriers (*chenillettes*) in each infantry regiment from nine to twenty-seven to increase mobility.[60]

Meanwhile, mid-November also saw the first mission to an army in contact with the enemy – Condé's Third – by Charles des Isnards. The deputy spent time not only asking questions at the army commander's headquarters but also in touring the 32nd infantry division and its front-line sector. This formation was one of the first reserve category, of the A-Series, which meant that it could not be expected to have the complete inventory of up-to-date equipment that an active division would possess. Moreover, the report on the division, and the Third Army as a whole, has to be read with the bias of its author in view. For des Isnards was not only a die-hard right-winger, affiliated in the Chamber to one of the two principal conservative parties, Louis Marin's Republican Federation. He was, at the same time, a chief lieutenant of Pierre Taittinger on the executive committee of the far-right authoritarian 'action group', the Jeunesses Patriotes. In this second capacity, des Isnards had been a leading organiser of and participant in the rioting by the Jeunesses, along with other extra-parliamentary paramilitaries, on the streets of Paris on 6 February 1934. Nor should it be forgotten that the target of the demonstrations on that night of violence was none other than the prime minister who was now, in late 1939, leading France in war against Germany – the same Daladier, the same Radical incarnation of the Republic, against whom the rightist *manifestants* had directed their ire more than five years earlier.[61] Probably it would be unwarranted to read too much even into these striking coincidences. There is no evidence even of a circumstantial kind to suggest that the right was engaged in anything as organised as a plot or conspiracy, through the institution of the army commission, to force Daladier out of office a second time. Prudent plotters keep few written records of their intentions and the possibility of discovering any incriminating documentation in this case probably went up in smoke when the papers of the Jeunesses Patriotes were incinerated at the group's Paris headquarters just before the Germans reached the French capital on 14 June 1940.[62] Yet, even without a conspiracy of an explicit and organised kind, it was the case that the Chamber army commission counted among its members not merely des Isnards but also Taittinger himself. These men not only opposed Daladier, they were inveterate adversaries of Gamelin, whom they had long despised for his intimacy with Radical and socialist political leaders and for his alleged masonic connections. They had, it will be remembered, gone so far as to mount an unsuccessful attempt in the winter of 1934–5 to prevent him from succeeding Weygand – their favourite conservative general – at the head of the army.[63]

All that can be said with certainty is that the visits to the front by the right-wingers of the commissions, just like their tours of armaments factories, were not without an element of partisan political motivation. Indeed, the missions provided the right with a windfall: the opportunity to garner information about deficiencies in military equipment and war production which could then substantiate a *réquisitoire* against Daladier's administration beneath a conveniently 'patriotic' guise of concern for the interests of the troops.

In the case of des Isnards' visit to the Third Army in November 1939, he reported that the health of the rank-and-file was good, an average of only eighty to one hundred soldiers per day for the entire army being absent on account of sickness. The troops' food, too, was of acceptable standard and no complaints were filed. Regarding equipment, on the other hand, the situation was alarming. There were severe shortages, disclosed des Isnards, of boots, greatcoats and leather saddlery. Transport was another worry. The army was 32 per cent short of the number of lorries it required: 2,000 had been returned to workshops and garages in the interior of France for repairs in September and had not returned. Only eighty replacements had been received. Meanwhile equine diseases and accidents had seen the deaths of 1,545 of the army's horses since the war began. The most serious deficiencies of all, however, were in weaponry. As a whole, the army had a deficit of 325 25mm anti-tank guns against nominal establishment; where these weapons did exist they had been allotted to the active divisions at the expense of both the A and B Series reserves. The improved 47mm anti-tank gun was only just beginning to reach a very few units; there was a widespread lack of 50mm mortars (which des Isnards was told were highly valued by the troops for close-quarters fighting); and anti-aircraft artillery was 'missing, just as it is everywhere'.[64]

Concerned by this disclosure of so many material shortcomings, another commissioner was despatched almost immediately to make further investigations among the units of Condé's army (and also in General Edouard Requin's Fourth Army on its right flank). This second visitor was another conservative deputy, Camille Fernand-Laurent. He, too, had crossed swords previously with Daladier, having headed an inquiry that presented a highly critical report in October 1938 on the bottlenecks in rearmament which had left the French forces unready to fight at the time of Munich. What Fernand-Laurent found in December 1939 served to confirm des Isnards' report. Requisitioned motor transport, he said, was of low quality and breakdown-prone; anti-aircraft artillery was in short supply; the Third Army's A-Series divisions had only 50 per cent of their complement of anti-tank guns, whilst the B-Series divisions had none. The reports were, it appears, forwarded with an expression of the deputies' dissatisfaction to Daladier's military *cabinet* for comment. However, when the full commission met on 20 December to discuss these and other similar dossiers, it was irritated to find that no information had been furnished by Daladier in response to the criticisms. Des Isnards, particularly angered at the wall of silence from the ministry, 'insisted that it be made known to the Commission who was responsible for the truly catastrophic situation that had come to light after the mobilisation'.[65] The right had got the start it needed for a witchhunt against the Daladier government and the high command; the internecine wars that the French political class was so content to wage among itself under the looming shadow of a Wehrmacht attack were about to become intensified.

The second phase of investigations into the state of the front-line formations opened when parliamentary sessions resumed after the New Year recess. Meeting on 10 January 1940, the Chamber army commission received a further report from des Isnards. This one detailed a tour that he had made just after Christmas to the Seventh Army of General Henri Giraud.[66] When first mobilised, this was the army which Gamelin had designated as the strategic reserve for the whole north-eastern theatre. It had been held back throughout September and October 1939, its formations cantoned centrally in the quadrilateral between Rheims, Laon, Soissons and Châlons-sur-Marne. Since mid-November and the adoption of the Dyle plan it had been redeployed onto the far left flank of the Allied line, along the border with Belgium from the Channel coast to Armentières. Under its firebrand commander, Giraud (who had been commander of the 6th military region and military governor of Metz from 1936 till the war's outbreak), the army was assigned a challenging mission. This was to hustle forward in an arcing left hook to shore up the Belgians from the south of Antwerp to Brussels, in the event of the German invasion of Belgium that Gamelin thought was sure to come about as part and parcel of Hitler's attack against the West.[67]

With such a difficult and exacting role before it, one whose successful accomplishment would demand not only the dashing leadership expected from Giraud but also a fast advance by road and across country, the Seventh Army might have been expected to be fully armoured and motorised. More than this, it might have been expected that the component formations would all be the best-trained and most lavishly encadred active type. This was not the case. The Seventh Army's divisions were the 1st DLM, the 9th and 25th motorised infantry, the 21st infantry (all active formations), the 4th infantry (A-Series reserve), the 60th and 68th infantry (both B-Series reserve). For a mission in which speed and mobile fire-power would be of the essence this army was allocated two-thirds of its infantry without motor transport and unable to move faster than the heavily laden *poilu* could march. When des Isnards made his inspection late in December 1939, he found the formations occupied in strengthening their positions along the frontier itself, digging anti-tank ditches, laying barbed wire and finishing the construction of 'several concrete casemates'. Morale was 'good', he reported, although 'a certain disillusion' appeared 'to have shown itself when the hope of moving forward faded'. The heart of his report, however, was a catalogue of the army's shortcomings in equipment. There were 'massive gaps' in the weapons inventories, the shortages being notably severe in respect of anti-tank and anti-aircraft artillery. The 21st infantry division had only forty-eight of its establishment of sixty 25mm guns, the 9th infantry division just three anti-aircraft pieces. Neither motorised division yet possessed its reconnaissance group of armoured cars (AMDs) or its tractor-drawn light artillery. The two B-Series infantry divisions were utterly without anti-tank guns as well as anti-aircraft guns.[68] Only the 1st DLM, a powerful armoured division with two brigades of SOMUA and H.39 tanks as well as motorised dragoons, 'well-led, well-trained, well-armed and well-equipped' as Marcel Lerecouvreux has described it, was fit for the demanding job expected of Giraud.[69]

A week after this report on the weaknesses of the Seventh Army, the commission found a more encouraging dossier before it at its next meeting on 17 January 1940. This detailed a mission by three deputies, five weeks earlier, to the commander of the Ninth Army, General André Corap, and the subsequent inspection of front-line positions of that army and of General Georges Blanchard's First Army on its left, in the environs of Rocroi and Valenciennes. Overall, a 'noticeable improvement' had occurred in the provision of uniforms and personal kit since the commission's first visit to these sectors in October 1939. Morale was reportedly high and relations between the officers and men good. As a case in point, the deputies singled out the care and attention devoted by the commander of the 3rd corps, General de la Laurencie, to the comfort and contentedness of his troops. In the main the report praised the extent to which the frontier positions had been reinforced by the erection of field works and concreted emplacements over the course of the autumn, though it noted the paucity of shell-proof underground accommodation 'as a result of the lack of a sufficient labour force and the difficulty of excavating a land saturated with water'. Generally, however, the commissioners had gained a 'reassuring impression' about this zone.[70] Also encouraging was the report made at the same meeting by Taittinger on a visit he had paid in mid-December to one of the new tank divisions that Gamelin had ordered to be constituted. The formation, the 3rd DLM, was one of the additional large armoured units that Gamelin had realised were required in response to the massed panzer forces that the French knew had been employed so effectively in Poland. Taittinger found the new division in the process of formation, its units billeted in buildings adjoining the cavalry school at Saumur, around the celebrated medieval abbey of Fontevrault and in villages around St-Cyr. He was greatly impressed by the sight of the 'youthful and energetic' General de Laffond's work with the combat group of the division to bring it to fighting pitch, and by the well-maintained SOMUAs with which one of the tank regiments had just been equipped. On the negative side, however, the brand-new Hotchkiss tanks of the second armoured regiment were mostly lacking their 37mm turret armament. Taittinger noted that 138 of the guns in its long-barrelled version, along with ammunition, were urgently needed before the unit would have any fighting capability. There were serious shortages, also, of many items of uniform and personal kit for the men, even though morale, once again, was reportedly 'excellent'.[71]

As a last example of reports by commissioners on visits to the armies on the frontiers, it is worth considering the one presented on 28 February 1940. This related a five-day tour at the beginning of that month to the Third and Fourth Army sectors of Thionville-Faulquemont-Sarralbe, along and behind the Maginot Line. The mission was a follow-up to the inspections of these same armies in November and December by des Isnards and Fernand-Laurent – inspections which had brought alarming shortages of armaments and motor transport to the commission's attention. The February visit suggested that little or no improvement had been effected in the meantime. The deputies, this time Marcel Camel and Robert Lazurich, reported that whereas the prescribed complement of 25mm anti-tank guns was fifty-two per division, one of the divisions of the 9th corps had only twenty-one guns and the other division just eighteen. A 'very significant effort', they judged, 'ought to be made in this area'. Also problematic was the motor transport, just as it had been three months previously. Requisitioning had rarely produced vehicles capable of giving reliable service in military hands. Both the number of lorries and their carrying-capacity were invariably inadequate. The 57th colonial infantry regiment was found struggling with only thirty-four vehicles (its motor transport pool, according to regulation war strength, being seventy-one). The shortfall in tonnage capacity varied among units but reportedly averaged between 10 and 30 per cent per regiment. These difficulties were aggravated by the inadequate vehicle repair facilities and the slow rate of return of reconditioned lorries from the army motor transport parks in the rear. Shortages of spare parts and an insufficient number of specialist mechanics in these depots were cited as the chief causes of slow repairs – and of the need to send many vehicles with major defects back to better-equipped workshops far behind the lines. The great diversity of lorry marques – Berliet, Renault, Panhard, Citroën, Peugeot – rendered it difficult to maintain comprehensive spare-parts stocks. And there was a new twist to the apparently intractable problem of the *affectés spéciaux*, the soldiers who had been released for reserved industrial occupations: their departure to strengthen the workforce in essential war industries was easing the production bottlenecks which Dautry and the armaments ministry were seeking to loosen, but at the cost of taking the most qualified motor engineers away from the army's vehicle maintenance sections. The deputies recommended at the end of their report that the solving of transport problems of the scale plaguing Third and Fourth Armies needed more than achieving a faster rate of repair – it demanded 'the replacement of requisitioned equipment with new material whose type and marque best meets the needs of the armies'.[72]

The competition for skilled manpower between the front and the factories which this inspection highlighted was a constant source of concern to the Chamber army commission in the phoney war. The shortage of skilled labour in industries vital to the war effort proved, indeed, to be the major preoccupation of the second group of missions which the deputies organised after hostilities began. Some of the earliest visits by commissioners, during the conflict's opening weeks, were to investigate how the mobilisation was implemented at Schneider's great artillery works at Le Creusot and at the munitions' establishments at Toulouse and Tarbes. From these very first reports, the commission had no doubt of the seriousness of the deficiencies in the qualified workforce. 'For a long time now', remarked the president, Miellet, on 11 October 1939, France had 'been short of skilled labour.' It was 'astonishing', he added, 'that in the light of this, no real effort had been agreed to develop schools for apprenticeships'. Only at this rather belated juncture did the commission unanimously agree 'to representations to the government to insist that this be done'.[73]

As the phoney war lengthened the commission systematically set about monitoring conditions and productivity in the most important plants engaged in manufacturing armaments and military supplies. The extent of the disturbance of production by the mobilisation of the reservists was bluntly brought home as early as September 1939 when the commission heard at first hand from Dautry about the disruption with which the new ministry of armaments was having to cope. Examples of mismanagement – as well as conservative political paranoia – abounded. Where workers had not been mobilised without regard for the need of their skills to the continued operation of their factory, they fell under intense suspicion as possible communist agitators and saboteurs. Indeed, Dautry's first appearance before the Chamber army commission coincided with Daladier's drive against the PCF.[74] In this the French communist organisations were outlawed, the party newspaper, *L'Humanité*, closed down, forty-four PCF deputies arrested and tried for unpatriotic activities, and the remainder forced to flee abroad (in the case of the general-secretary, Maurice Thorez, to exile in the Soviet Union for the war's duration).[75]

The issues of personnel shortages and political sensibilities converged most notoriously in the case of the Renault main works, at Billancourt. Taittinger, accompanied by Armand Chouffet, deputy for the Rhône, visited the plant in the autumn and their report was considered by the Chamber army commission on 20 December 1939 and again on 17 January 1940.[76] Of the 32,000 Renault workers at the plant at the beginning of September 1939, 22,000 had been mobilised which 'it hardly needed to be said . . . did not exactly facilitate the Renault production'. The commissioners praised the patriotism of Louis Renault himself who had agreed to the government's request that he convert all his firm's productive capacity to military orders, however much this would jeopardise his market share in civilian automobiles once the war was over. But they censured the 'grave deficiency in the preparation of civilian mobilisation' which had not only brought about such a disruptive call-up of Renault workers but had also seen the company start the war without having its order-books filled even with immediate work from the military authorities. At the moment the deputies compiled their report, at the beginning of December 1939, the entire Renault workforce had recovered somewhat from the ravages of the mobilisation and was some 21–22,000 strong. Skilled men were returning from the armies at a rate of seventy-five per day, but to reach its war production targets the firm needed to attain a strength of 40,000 employees altogether at its factories (Billancourt, Issy-les-Moulineaux, Le Mans, Gannat in the Allier and St Etienne-sur-Loire). Output had, 'in a general way, diminished considerably at Renault'. This was ascribed to the temporary dislocation resulting from altering civilian auto assembly lines to military work and to the labour shortage. The 'individual productivity of the workers cannot be called into question', the commissioners reported, even though they warned that security measures were required as a precaution against the political agitation which they feared from having so many men of 'progressive ideas' together. Coordination of the Renault production plans and timetables with the ministry of armaments was reportedly improved vastly since the introduction of daily meetings between one of Dautry's senior lieutenants and the Renault top management. Dautry's own appointment was said to have resulted in 'a notable improvement over the existing state of affairs'. The commissioners 'regretted only . . . that the new regime had not been constituted fifteen months earlier'.[77] Certainly Dautry's endeavours met with wide approval. 'The consensus of opinion re the appointment of Mr. Raoul Dautry as Minister of Armaments' was, according to the US military attaché in Paris, 'that he is the Right Man in the Right Place. Mr. Dautry is well known for his abilities as an organizer and enjoys the reputation of being a thoroughly honest man with no political ambition.'[78]

Other politicians were, however, readily suspected by the command of using wartime conditions to help their own climb up the greasy pole.[79] The probing of the parliamentary commissioners was especially resented. Front-line commanders argued that all matters in the zone of the armies fell into the category of technical questions. These, the soldiers contended, should be reserved to the service specialists. As noted earlier, Gamelin freely acknowledged the respect in which he held Clemenceau for the latter's energetic and inspirational national leadership in the black days of 1917–18. But he had no patience for the Tiger's celebrated axiom that war had become 'too serious a business to be left to the generals'. Many officers suspected visiting parliamentarians of having no real interest in the army and of being concerned only to gain information with which to score political points back in Paris. At the same time, the sheer number of inspections led to the diversion of many hours of staff time into preparation of documents with which to answer inquiries, and into the escorting of VIPs around the front line.[80] Unit commanders argued that their staffs and their men needed to devote this time to training and to familiarisation with new equipment or new allies.

Parliamentarians complained in return about the military's obstruction of their duties and statutory powers. Charles Reibel, a conservative senator, asserted during the wartime Riom trial that the Senate army commission had been hindered by Jacomet, the secretary-general of the defence ministry, and not allowed to send its first mission to the front until December 1939.[81]

Certainly, from November onwards, protests about the commissioners were streaming into higher headquarters from commanders in the field. Gamelin was moved to object to Daladier that, though the parliamentarians had the force of the law (*droits de contrôle*) on their side:

the commissions, making their appearance all at the same time in the zone of the armies, are too numerous . . . this is resulting in the commands and staffs being overworked and distracted by the practicalities of the visits. From the standpoint of morale there are penalties to be faced when the troops are too frequently the object of such missions, the real purpose of which is not always understood by the soldier. Moreover . . . a demand for a 30 day long inspection in a front-line sector to inquire, for example, about its organisation and command does not seem to me to accord with the spirit of the law.

Over and above reservations of this sort, Gamelin was also alarmed about the danger of leakage of military secrets or even espionage as a result of such uninhibited civilian movements close to the front. 'Too often', he protested, 'one finds commission reports bulging with the most precise statistics about the state of our armaments. Yet ... it is dangerous in this area to allow dissemination of exact figures, even under cover of a stamp of secrecy.'[82]

Daladier sympathised with Gamelin. He wrote to the presidents of the Senate and Chamber army commissions in mid-November, asking each to apply strict restraint to the size and frequency of their inspections. Replies were returned within the week, assuring the government and high command of cooperation and good will.[83] Yet the problem persisted and, if anything, worsened as winter dragged on. By February 1940 Georges felt moved to tabulate, for Gamelin, the intrusiveness of political visits. 'Some [armies]', he explained, 'have been visited by five or even six missions, the majority of these staying several days each. It will not escape you how very heavy a burden this represents, to which is adding the work resulting from other inspections by journalists, as well as by French and foreign VIPs.' Georges asked that each Assembly be limited to not more than one visit per month to each of the eight French armies deployed in the north-east theatre. Gamelin supported this request and once again interceded with Daladier, whom he increasingly suspected of lacking sufficient resolution to defend the command's wishes against parliamentary pressures. At the start of March 1940, Gamelin, backing Georges's recommendation, wrote to demand fresh endeavours by Daladier to restrict the liberties of the commissioners. However, this letter was unceremoniously consigned to the files in Daladier's office, marked only with the stamp of General Decamp, his military *chef de cabinet*, and as 'Seen by the Minister'.[84] Doubtless it was buried by the avalanche of parliamentary censure which in March 1940 was falling on Daladier for his procrastination on the question of aiding the Finns in their struggle against Soviet invasion, and which on the 20th would cost him the prime ministership.[85]

When considering the attitude of the military to the missions of the deputies and senators it must also be remembered that the conditions of the front-line armies were investigated at first hand by France's top generals. It may seem surprising that this was so, for a great deal has been written, especially against Gamelin, purporting to show that he spent the phoney war in a kind of academic isolation, cloistered in the Château de Vincennes, devoid of direct contact with his field commanders let alone with the rank-and-file *poilus*. To fill out the caricature of a monastic recluse, a man utterly out of touch, writers have fastened eagerly onto contemporary complaints of Gamelin's invisibility. Authors have embraced the strictures in the war memoirs of de Gaulle, whose one meeting with Gamelin at Vincennes in the phoney war inspired a graphic characterisation of him as a remote ivory-towered savant. Further grist to this mill was supplied in the 'phoney war' diaries of Sartre who, mobilised in a reservist division stationed in Alsace, noted in February 1940: 'I've never heard anybody mention Gamelin, here. Never – not even to say something bad about him. He doesn't exist at all.'[86]

Of course, in any organisation measured in millions of men the majority would not be personally acquainted with the highest-ranking executives or leaders. Few of the US military personnel in the Pacific in 1942–5 would have had individual encounters with Chester Nimitz or Douglas MacArthur. Likewise few of the Wehrmacht rank-and-file can have set eyes on field marshals such as von Brauchitsch, von Bock or von Rundstedt. A genuinely intimate style of command from the front has, in modern war, become increasingly practicable only when unusually small forces are involved as in the case of Rommel's generalship over the two or three divisions of the Afrika Korps in 1941–2.

As for the visibility of France's senior generals in the phoney war, the record demands revision. Georges got out of La Ferté to visit Huntziger's Second Army, holding the Meuse between Montmédy and the confluence of the Bar River downstream from Sedan, on 21 November 1939.[87] Gamelin was even more active and took pains to work his way steadily through a programme of inspections to the armies of the northeast. His first tour, as early as 27 September 1939, was to Alsace. There, accompanied by Prételat, the Army Group No. 2 commander, he was met at Saverne, headquarters of the Fifth Army. After conferring with Bourret, the army's commander, de Lattre de Tassigny, his chief of staff, and Generals Aubert Frère and Georges Bloch, commanders of the army's 13th and 5th corps, Gamelin moved north to visit Fourth Army positions in Lorraine and the Saar. At Bonnefontaine he stopped at the command post of the 20th corps and then proceeded to that of the 9th corps at Faulquemont, receiving reports on the limited September offensive in the Saar from Generals Hubert and Laure, the respective corps commanders. After exchanging views over lunch with Generals Requin and Dame, the commander and chief of staff of Fourth Army, at their headquarters at Vic-sur-Seille, Gamelin continued on to Remilly. There he inspected elements of the 5th North African infantry division, followed by a visit to the 26th infantry division and a talk with General Condé, Third Army commander, at his headquarters at Fort Jeanne d'Arc. That evening, at Metz, Gamelin's path crossed with Lebrun, the president of the republic, who was making his own separate tour to units of the Third and Fourth Armies that had been engaged in the first actions of the war on the western front. Judging by the formations that he had seen, Gamelin observed in his diary that morale seemed 'excellent', despite some 1,500 French casualties – more than half suffered in the Saarland operations between 10 and 15 September.[88]

Ten days later, on 7 October, Gamelin travelled to the Ardennes–Meuse sector to inspect the Second and Ninth Armies under Huntziger and Corap. Huntziger, recorded Gamelin's diary, 'demanded anti-tank mines' and pointed out that the Second Army was 250 guns short of its regulation complement of 25mm anti-tank artillery. Gamelin also noted Huntziger's report that his 20th infantry division and his North African division were of 'very good' quality, whereas a 'mediocre' mark was given to the 55th infantry division of General Lafontaine, which broke when trying to defend the Meuse crossings at Sedan against the panzer and Luftwaffe onslaught, seven months later. At the 20th division's headquarters Gamelin held a briefing with generals Billotte, the Army Group No. 1 commander, Huntziger, Flavigny (the pioneering proponent of armour and commander, in 1933–6, of the first French light mechanised division, now leading the 21st corps), and four of the Second Army's divisional commanders. Belying his reputation for being taciturn and uncommunicative, Gamelin gave an overview of the situation of the war and led an animated exchange that ranged over questions of tactics as well as strategy. Trying to avoid complacency among his generals about the nature of Poland's defeat, he emphasised the importance of 'separating the elements that make up the German attack'. He also spoke of 'the role and employment of anti-tank and anti-aircraft defence and of the need for precautions against enemy air action', requiring the articulation and disposal of French forces with this threat in mind. Above all, Gamelin strove to focus on imbuing subordinates with effective concepts for 'the conduct of the defensive battle'. This, he told Huntziger's generals, meant the use of aggressive rather than passive methods of tactical defence. In terms of the strategic defence, he insisted that it meant prepositioning of local reserves and possession of a 'general reserve for motorised strategic manoeuvre'. Elsewhere on the Second Army front Gamelin was assured that the 7th colonial division was 'making great progress' and that the 71st infantry division of General Baudet (the other major formation broken around Sedan on 13–15 May 1940) was 'improving'. New concrete defensive works were reportedly under construction.

Leaving behind the Second Army, Gamelin drove north-west to Corap's Ninth Army deployed behind the Ardennes and the Givet salient into Belgium. At the headquarters of the 4th corps he conferred with its commander, General Boris, Corap and the generals of the 7th and 52nd infantry divisions. Gamelin talked of the need to familiarise units with the use of 75mm artillery in an anti-tank role because of the shortages of more specialist weapons. Air defence of military cantonments, the effects of blast from bombs and the defence of industrial plants located in advance of the main defensive lines were also discussed. In the afternoon the inspection was completed by a meeting at Vervins with the 11th corps commander, General Martin, and the commanding officers of the 1st cavalry division and 4th, 6th and 19th infantry divisions. Here, again, Gamelin took pains to make clear his awareness that these divisions were short of anti-tank guns and he warned the assembled generals 'not to count on the resistance of the Belgians' when serious operations began.[89]

Both in what he observed and in what he said during these tours, Gamelin was led to an ever-closer attention to the Belgian flank. He was more convinced than hitherto about the danger to Anglo-French security that was implicit in a German flanking attack through the Low Countries. It was not so much that his inspections in September and October 1939 filled him with special foreboding about the reliability of the Second or Ninth Armies or about the calibre of their generals. Indeed, driving from Mouzay, via Stenay, Sedan, Mézières and Charleville, en route from Huntziger to meet Corap, Gamelin noted with satisfaction that the encampments they crossed were 'as orderly as could possibly be, in every case: the men well turned-out, vehicles camouflaged. And, in the fields, many soldiers helping the farmers.'[90] Nonetheless, Gamelin was greatly impressed by the deficiencies in equipment that were commonplace among the divisions behind Luxembourg and southern Belgium. It became increasingly apparent to him that more divisions had to be sought from Britain and that plans had to be accelerated to put even more French units into the field.[91]

In the autumn, Gamelin paid one further visit to the troops on the frontiers. This mission, on 16 October, took him to Blanchard's First Army and to the BEF. It turned out to be an abbreviated inspection, interrupted by the intelligence reports which indicated the imminence of Germany's main offensive in the west and prompted Gamelin to make an early return to his headquarters.[92] Yet, even truncated, this tour afforded Gamelin the chance for meetings with Blanchard, Prioux, the commander of the mechanised cavalry corps, and with the corps and divisional generals of the 3rd and 5th corps.[93] Later still in the phoney war, Gamelin made two final visits to his armies. In the first, on 8–9 March 1940, he toured the major headquarters of Giraud's Seventh

Army, which by that time had been stationed on the Channel coast in readiness to execute the Dyle Plan. He met the commanders of the 9th, 60th, 53rd and 21st infantry divisions, Generals Didelet (formerly military attaché in Berlin in 1938–9), Deslaurens, Etcheberrigaray and Lanquetot. He also revisited the BEF, talking with Gort, the commander, Pownall, the chief of staff and Mason-Macfarlane, the chief of intelligence (and formerly British military attaché in Berlin from 1937 to 1939).[94] On 22 March, accompanied by Ironside, British chief of the Imperial General Staff, Gamelin inspected the forward and rear defensive positions of the Second and Third Armies. He was briefed by engineer officers about the emplacements under construction and had talks with Huntziger and Condé, as well as with three corps commanders and six divisional commanders. Gamelin's headquarters diary, which records the itinerary and names the generals who were visited, makes no mention of any particular problems or weaknesses ascertained on these inspections two months before the blitzkrieg.[95] If Gamelin was quietly growing in confidence as the spring of 1940 beckoned, he was not alone. Pownall, as has been discussed earlier, was convinced that Allied improvements in numbers of troops and quality of equipment during the winter made it difficult to imagine a successful German offensive from the springtime onwards. Ironside, too, was more optimistic by the time of his March 1940 tour with Gamelin. He noted in his diary that 'perhaps the bad winter had paralysed them [the French]'. But now he found 'Officers and men were working like beavers' and added his voice to a rising chorus of opinion that 'the Germans had missed their opportunity in not attacking when the French were concentrating', in September 1939.[96]

Conclusion

The French military performance came as a shocking disappointment when it was put to the test at last in the campaign of 1940. It not only failed to provide a platform for a French and Allied victory, it failed to deny an important, if transitory, triumph to the Germans. To be sure, the stigma of defeat was not borne by the French army alone. It also attached itself to the French air force, to the navy (to a lesser degree), and to the other armed forces beaten in the blitzkrieg: the British, the Belgians, the Dutch and the Luxembourgers. As Jeffery Gunsburg has properly emphasised, the misnamed 'Fall of France' was actually the disintegration of a flimsy western alliance.[1]

Nonetheless, the abiding images of 1940 are ones of military disaster in France. Newsreels, memoirs and documentary television have impressed on a collective consciousness the pictures that perpetuate the ignominy for France. They are images of forlorn soldiers – a third of them French – shuffling down the Dunkerque beaches to the 'little ships'; of roads jammed with carts, piled high with the pathetic impedimenta of the exodus from Belgium and the Nord; of abandoned Allied armour – mostly French because the other Allied armies had had so little. Scenes of this sort have not encouraged a charitable evaluation of the beaten commanders, of the *généraux de débâcle*.[2]

Reynaud's recall of Weygand to assume command on 19 May 1940 was not enough to save Gamelin from being branded as 'the man who lost the Battle of France'. The label has stuck to him. Indeed it has been Gamelin's misfortune over the decades since 1940 that this epithet has remained his principal and unenviable claim to notoriety, if not to fame. Gamelin's departure from the command spared him any part in the politically controversial liquidation of France's war effort at Bordeaux in mid-June – an imbroglio which ensnared Weygand, Huntziger, Noguès and Colson, to the lasting detriment of their reputations. All the same, Gamelin's was a considerable stigma. By his contemporaries as well as by subsequent generations, he was disparaged as the commander in whom the government and the country lost confidence when the going became tough. To rehabilitate Gamelin as a field commander in 1940 will be the uphill task of a more Quixotic study than this one.[3]

There seems no such obstacle, on the other hand, to a sympathetic reappraisal of his competence and professionalism in the direction of French rearmament down to – and even after – September 1939. Such an objective is attainable once the distinction is correctly drawn between, on the one hand, Gamelin as military commander and, on the other, Gamelin as architect of a programme of unprecedented peacetime defensive preparation. The general was the ring-master of an attempt by an assortment of the western powers to make common cause against Hitler. A differentiation between Gamelin's peacetime and wartime roles is fundamental to the conception, shape and argument of the present work. It has been convenient – even commonplace – to pass one single negative judgement on Gamelin's performance in 1940 and his proficiency in prewar high command. But to do this is analytically confusing as well as interpretatively misleading. For, since time immemorial, history tells of military chiefs who were renowned as penetrating strategic thinkers, or as innovative doctrinal and tactical reformers, or perhaps as outstanding peacetime administrators. Yet the skills of such men in these domains often did nothing whatsoever to suit them for the radically different challenges of wartime command. Indeed, the attributes for success in these different fields of military endeavour have been judged – by the light of modern management theory – to diverge significantly. This makes it exceptional when a senior officer in the twentieth century does display all the qualities of the warrior as well as those of the manager.[4]

What, then, is to form the basis of a revised and non-partisan verdict on Gamelin's record in the 1930s? The first step towards a summation must be to ensure that the playing field is level – that the grounds for judgement are neither anachronistic nor inappropriate. This requires a scrupulous accuracy in recognising the limitations on Gamelin's authority, before conclusions are formed as to his accomplishments and shortcomings. It is, for instance, invalid to characterise his responsibilities for the defeat of 1940 as 'crushing', in the way asserted by Jean Doise and Maurice Vaïsse, by pretending as they do that Gamelin had 'directed the entire French war machine' since 1935.[5] As we have seen, Gamelin never had the hold on the levers of military power that a statement of this sort implies. He lacked the authority to supervise, still less command, the air force and the navy down to January 1938. Even when designated chief of national defence staff, on 21 January 1938, Gamelin's remit was not to control but merely to coordinate the policies and strategies of the air, maritime and colonial forces. Ironically, the supreme command over all the services and over every theatre of war was only ever invested in Weygand, on 19 May 1940. Yet by that time most could see that it was too late to alter the outcome of the Battle of France. Albeit in circumstances of unparalleled desperation, therefore, the dying Republic placed unprecedented military powers in the lap not of the unimpeachably republican Gamelin but with the soldier from whom the régime had, in 1931, withheld undivided authority even over the army.[6]

The fact is that Gamelin never controlled the French war machine as a whole. He had to struggle, as we have witnessed, to shape a compatible air policy and avoid destructive inter-service competition over resources. This raises the question of his decision not to resign in protest or in frustration. An exploration of his reasons for refraining from such a course is proper in the light of the exasperation that he experienced and the fears that he voiced before 1939. Why did he not dramatise his view of the inadequacies which he believed were compromising French diplomatic and military security? Why did he hesitate to expose the disparities between his personal responsibility and France's strategic condition in the public auditorium of parliament or the press? Why, instead, did he grouse about them only in the cloistered world of command–government consultations?

Questions of this order are not simply academic. More than once, before and after the outbreak of war, Gamelin toyed with resignation. In the spring of 1939, Raoul Dautry, then semi-retired from his railway management career and not yet appointed to create an armaments ministry (as he was in September), spoke on the subject with Prételat. The latter had confided some disquiet about the Ardennes sector's defences under his charge. Dautry advised him that resignation was the honourable course under the circumstances for a disaffected military chief. If someone 'charged with providing leadership' found that he judged himself to be without the means to meet his responsibilities or was 'obstructed in what he was trying to do', he should quit, counselled Dautry.[7]

It is unclear whether Gamelin himself was ever given this advice about the circumstances in which a commander was justified in resigning. However, it is wholly plausible that he was. For Gamelin had met Dautry before the war and respected his business achievements. In the phoney war Gamelin commented approvingly to the officers of his *cabinet* how Dautry and his writings on modern business management had been an inspiration to the younger generation of French industrialists.[8] Though occasionally disagreeing during the 1939–40 winter over allocation of manpower between the armies at the front and the factories to the rear, in essentials Gamelin and Dautry found themselves in the same camp.

Gamelin's wartime trial by the Vichyites at Riom offers insight into his thinking about the propriety and professionalism of resignation. One witness was General Héring, commander-designate of the Fifth Army and military governor of Strasbourg in 1936–9 and an ally of Gamelin in the prewar struggles in the CSG with the conservatives for armoured divisions. During the Riom hearings Héring testified that 'one day, in an inspection in Alsace, Gamelin unburdened his mind to me'. In the courtroom Héring asked rhetorically whether Gamelin's reluctance to resign was 'proof that he had lacked character?' Answering himself, Héring argued the opposite: that Gamelin had interpreted his duty in the later 1930s as a mission to strive ceaselessly to build a stronger army, a more cohesive coalition of allies to contain German ambitions. In trying to attain these objectives, asserted Héring, Gamelin had judged it best to proceed 'by persuasion and by manoeuvre . . . [and] one cannot reproach him for having carried the struggle on to the end'.[9]

In his reluctance to quit, despite the difficulties he encountered, Gamelin demonstrated that some of the differences between him and Weygand were more of style than of substance. Weygand did not step down either, when confronted by the frustrations of command in the Cartel years of 1932–4. Rather, he played the part of Cassandra in the controversies over disarmament and declining defence appropriations. Furthermore, in retirement after January 1935, Weygand reasssuringly praised the army's battle-readiness, in articles, prefaces and, most notoriously, in a widely publicised speech at Lille in July 1939.[10] On close inspection it appears that Weygand and Gamelin had much in common in their conception of the duty involved in discharging high military office. Too often, historical accounts emphasise the more glaring contrasts between the personalities of the two commanders and underestimate this ethic that they shared.[11]

Apparently, too, it was judged to be 'no longer admissible' from 1938 onwards for one of France's most senior commanders to abandon his post with the international 'storm . . . starting to rumble'.[12] The years of anxiety of the early 1930s were linked to the years of peril of 1936–9 by this concept of responsible generalship. Resignation by Gamelin would – so it was feared by high-ranking French officers – have rocked French society to its very foundations. His departure would have shattered the French army's reputation abroad. This reputation was still considerable and it was an asset that French leaders urged Gamelin not to throw away. A resignation by Gamelin, it was felt, could scarcely have avoided injurious post-mortems in the press and parliament. No-one in positions of authority in Paris saw any advantage likely to accrue from laundering the dirty linen of French defence preparations in public. Gamelin felt himself to be caught in a dilemma. As he explained it afterwards:

> I often felt an anguish in my heart: that of knowing that French power was not in a condition to match up to all the often excessive hopes I felt were depending on it. It was not that I doubted our final victory. But how many people even in France . . . still harboured illusions, believed in the possibility of swift successes, were ignorant of the difficulties we were confronting in our endeavours to increase our war materials, did not sufficiently gauge the seriousness of the dangers . . . *Those of us who knew these things could not, however, run the risk of discouraging our allies [by admitting them], not even to press them more insistently on the effort that they needed to make on their own account*[13]

From 1934–5 onwards senior French figures such as Gamelin knew that the image of France was in trouble abroad. They knew that among powers whose friendship was essential – powers such as Britain, the USA, Belgium and the Little Entente – there was growing unease about France's political stability. They knew, too, that there was concern for France's social cohesiveness. There was disquiet over its economic stagnation. At a time of growing debate as to whether France was a power in irreversible decline, French military leaders tended to close ranks. They sought to maintain the image of the army as a disciplined, powerful and authoritative representation of *la vraie France*. French generals knew their army was still something in which outside observers felt France could justly take pride. They perceived that although foreigners now thought that France did many things badly, they still believed that France was rather good at soldiering. The French army, the Maginot Line, French military power and professionalism – these appeared to be the only surviving certainties in an era of uncertainty.

Therefore Gamelin contemplated resignation but never carried it through. He was persuaded that it could not be done without messy public recriminations. He judged, furthermore, that it would destroy foreign as well as French confidence in the French military machine – the last support of French power. The high command readily united behind Gamelin. To a man the generals turned their backs on their terrible difficulties. They opted instead to assure onlookers that the French army was in fine fettle and remained a sure shield for all who would accept French friendship. That the course chosen would be the one of braggadoccio and bluff emerged early on. This was apparent in March 1935, whilst Maurin was the war minister. Replying to an accusation in the Chamber army commission that France possessed merely the 'façade' of the defences it required, Maurin admitted: 'In my heart I agree with you. If I avoided elaborating on the state of our army before the Chamber it was because I thought it would be inopportune for any sort of weakness to be admitted to the outside world.'[14]

This behaviour in closing ranks rather than making a clean breast of problems was a characteristic tendency of the senior French military. Indeed it helps indicate how the higher commanders defined responsible generalship in the 1930s. Even so disaffected an officer as Weygand extolled the fitness of the army for war. The pattern of an outward display of confidence connected the Weygand and Gamelin eras. The entire high command was permeated by a sense, as Héring put it, that resignation had 'to be recognised for what it really is: an abdication'.[15] In this respect it was significant that Weygand heaped praise on Gamelin in 1931, when the latter was appointed chief of the general staff. In his last report as Gamelin's superior officer, and thus the last entry in Gamelin's confidential file, Weygand testified eloquently that Gamelin possessed the 'knowledge, the experience and all the qualities of thought and action to enable him to be of the greatest service to French national defence'.[16]

During their service together, then, the two officers were at least as drawn together by their patriotism and their shared professional code as they were pushed apart by their divergent styles and differing political sympathies. For many observers, however, this fact has been obscured. One cause of this was Weygand's moves after 1935 to distance himself from Gamelin and the regime. Another was the radically opposed responses of each man to the crisis of 1940.[17]

It is not to be denied that a rift occurred between them. But it must be averred that the rupture happened not in 1933, when Weygand clashed with Daladier over conscription, but only in the years after 1935. Only then, in the later-1930s, did Weygand throw in his lot once and for all with the political elements hostile to Gamelin's whole strategy of accommodation between the defence forces and the Republic. Weygand waged an ideological guerrilla war against the left and centre after 1936. He progressed from disparaging the Popular Front and the agenda of its *chambre rouge horizon*, to condemning the character and legitimacy of the Republic itself. It was in these later years, through his conservative prejudices and reactionary associations, that Weygand – the general who professed to take pride in 'never playing politics' – in fact turned into a political soldier.[18] Once this had happened, though not before, it could accurately be said that Weygand looked on Gamelin 'as a man eternally seeking a compromise and always ready to bow to the decisions of politicians, even when they went against the interests of the army'.[19] What Weygand proved unable to recognise, however, was the way in which his own diatribes and ultra-conservative fulminations eroded confidence in and respect for France's legitimately constituted regime. He failed to see how his own rhetoric and writings were a form of political interference – and one which only complicated the task of national defence that faced the state authorities in general and his successor in particular.[20] But almost to the end most observers misjudged Weygand. By the time they perceived the hollowness of his military reputation and the narrow conservativeness of his political objectives, it was too late. For example, R. Walton Moore, counsellor at the US State Department in Washington, wrote to Ambassador William C. Bullitt in Paris on 27 May 1940 to complain that he 'was bitterly disappointed when General Gamelin proved inadequate'. Yet Moore expressed himself 'now hopeful that his successor [Weygand] is the very best soldier who can be found in Europe for the mighty task assigned him'.[21] An embittered Daladier, imprisoned by the Vichy regime that Weygand helped establish, noted in 1941 that there seemed to be two Weygands: 'Which was the real one? The narrow reactionary? Or the man of war? ... His was a leading role in forcing the departure of Reynaud and the capitulation at Bordeaux, with Pétain, Baudouin, Bouthillier ... He was a prefect dressed as a general ... A fine example of political, military and moral tricksterism.'[22]

Weygand's step by step descent into the quagmire of political intervention affords an opportunity for concluding reflections on the condition of French civil-military relations when war began in September 1939. Héring's point that resignation, to a soldier, amounted to an abdication – something close to desertion – explains why Gamelin opted to discharge his responsibilities in the later 1930s as best he could. In western European democracies, by the mid-twentieth century, the threat to quit had ceased to be an acceptable option for those military chiefs who were required to deal with elected political authorities. For Gamelin, as for his British counterparts, resignation in the face of difficulties would have been dishonourable. It would have connoted an unwillingness to see a job through. Gamelin knew that the British army's leaders of his era – Montgomery-Massingberd, Deverell and Gort – had also experienced problems with their governments, foreign office and sister services. Just as surely, he understood why none of them had decided to step down from command, despite extraordinary friction with ministers over cuts in army estimates and disputed rearmament priorities.

For Gamelin, as for each British CIGS, the notion of resigning for a theatrical effect conflicted too fundamentally with the military ethic. That ethic or code demanded that the chiefs of the armed forces loyally serve an elected civilian leadership, without regard to its political label.

To this code of conduct Gamelin added a tenet of his own, which was not to call into question the patriotism of his political superiors, whatever their location in the French ideological spectrum. This outlook, however, had its reverse side: an unswerving belief that policy-making was the business of government. It was Gamelin's conviction that the military professional or civilian functionary, no matter how senior, was responsible for informing ministerial decisions but not for making them. This philosophy was most strikingly embodied in the title of Gamelin's memoirs: *Servir*, 'To Serve'.

Unhappily for Gamelin as well as for France, functional politics in the later Third Republic bore scant resemblance to such a straightforward hierarchy. Over matters of national defence, in Gamelin's idealisation, the advice of the military was supposed to elucidate but not supplant the reaching of conclusions by the government. The latter alone was empowered to make policy and alone stood electorally accountable for it. In practice, however, authority in the republic had, for too long, been confusingly diffused and political responsibilities shirked.[23] This was obscured from sight for much of the 1930s by Gamelin's extraordinary partnership with Daladier.

In practice, the defects of the French governmental and administrative system placed too heavy a burden on this pairing. This was especially so after April 1938 when Daladier added the prime minister's office to his responsibilities for national defence. The 'very fact that moderate and conservative leaders should turn to the left-wing Radical chief as a man capable of assuring "public safety" exposed their own bankruptcy'.[24] As contemporaries remarked, the forbidding nature of the challenges before him obliged Daladier by 1938–9 to act – despite himself – as a latter-day Jacobin. He turned into a 'democratic dictator'.[25] Uncertain of the trustworthiness of even his Radical colleagues, particularly Bonnet, his energies tended to be fruitlessly dissipated. From time to time, moreover, even his courage deserted him. With the noteworthy exceptions of their disagreement in late 1936 over whether to change tack on the non-fortification of the Franco-Belgian border and in 1938 over the merit in creating an armaments ministry in peacetime, Daladier and Gamelin thought alike on defence policy. Furthermore, at least until September 1939, they shared a genuine mutual respect. 'Indeed Gamelin was, and remained, Daladier's "man", and the Premier was always eager to defend his general against critics.' To try to 'distinguish between the basic military policies' of the two has been said to be as futile as 'trying to distinguish between Tweedledee and Tweedledum'.[26]

This is not the place where the much-needed full-scale study of Daladier can be essayed. 'Sooner or later', noted the former prime minister in the diary he kept as a wartime prisoner of Vichy, 'French justice must place on record that, between 1919 and 1939, no war minister did as much as I for national defence.'[27] And, without doubt, the formidable qualities which he brought to bear as architect and organiser of France's truly outstanding rearmament effort from 1936 to 1939 demand acknowledgement. 'The urgency with which an often maligned Daladier expanded the armed forces, developed new weapons and prepared for a war that he . . . looked upon with loathing . . . has seldom been recognised.'[28]

How melancholy it is, therefore, to have to record the decline of Daladier's personal and political authority once the war started. In September 1939 he tinkered with his government, most significantly by at last creating the ministry of armaments under Dautry. He also added the Quai d'Orsay to his individual burdens when he transferred the discredited Bonnet to the ministry of justice. This, however, only established a situation where there 'were too many hats for any man to wear – certainly too many for Daladier'.[29] Worse, it did not remove the prime minister's sense of vulnerability. The sympathetic American ambassador in France, Bullitt, whose accreditation to Paris since 1936 had enabled him to get to know and like Daladier, reported him a prey to fear of being toppled by political adversaries. In the autumn of 1939, by the US envoy's account, Daladier felt 'that his political life . . . could not last more than three months'.[30]

Gamelin's diary offers persuasive additional evidence that, with the onset of hostilities, the management of national defence and the operation of civil-military consensus underwent grave deterioration. After the war's outset – indeed down to the dramatic confrontations in the French war cabinet on the very eve of the German western offensive, as Reynaud sought to force Gamelin's dismissal – Daladier showed Gamelin uncommon loyalty. From the minister's perspective, their partnership remained very much in business. Explaining his fidelity, Daladier wrote later that 'If I disapproved of the general being relieved of his command, in the meeting on the morning of 9 May 1940, that was because he had my confidence. And I thought that, when the German attack was imminent, General Gamelin had taken the military measures that were necessary.'[31] The record of the phoney war reveals, however, that Daladier's regard for Gamelin was not a compliment that the general any longer returned.

The process of disillusionment on Gamelin's part began at the very first session of the French war cabinet, the *comité de guerre*, on 8 September 1939. Leaving this meeting (where the politicians present included Lebrun, the president of the Republic, Daladier, Mandel, the colonial minister and La Chambre, air minister), Gamelin complained scornfully to his adjutant:

> We don't have a single statesman among them. In times such as those in which we're living at the moment, one is really aware of what their absence means. M. Lebrun talked of the recent declaration by Germany giving us the assurance that she will respect Belgian neutrality. He believes in this guarantee and thinks that because of it we are relieved of an onerous uncertainty. Will history never correct the credulousness – to put it no more strongly – of the French?[32]

On 19 September Gamelin noted how Daladier was 'nervous, anxious about the domestic situation . . . wanting to re-assemble parliament but afraid of being overturned if he did so'. Although there was nothing as dramatic as an open rupture between them, the passage of the months of phoney war saw Daladier's stock as a war leader steadily sinking with Gamelin. In a further criticism, recorded in the journal of Gamelin's *cabinet* on 3 October, the general disparaged the prime minister as 'a waverer, changing his mind according to what he hears from the last person to have his ear'.[33]

Evidence of this kind supports the argument that the 'reproach to which Daladier . . . exposed himself' was that at a moment when his popularity was undeniable 'he failed to grasp the need to form a *gouvernement solidaire*' which no defeatist clique in or outside parliament would have dared defy.[34] At least one senior general recalled the 'atmosphere of political or military intrigues' of this period. This officer reflected that what 'was required was a government of Public Safety composed of a few men with energy and great will-power, enjoying the confidence of everyone; instead the Cabinet was an [unwieldy] crowd of ministers'.[35] Gamelin was bemused and exasperated as early as mid-September 1939 by Daladier's worry over his domestic position, for the general judged that Daladier 'could do anything he wished at the present time'.[36] Small wonder, when this was his own assessment of the political balance of power, that Gamelin was shocked at the absence of French statesmanship. Small wonder that he was unimpressed by the contrast to the Poincaré–Clemenceau duo offered by Lebrun and Daladier. The 'Tiger', said Gamelin to his staff in mid-October 1939, 'undoubtedly had some unattractive features'; but these were offset by his 'sterling qualities as a fighter'. France had been 'fortunate to have him with us against the Boche'. Equally, the 1914–18 war had been the making of Clemenceau, providing a cause worthy of him 'in the service of the nation'. It was impossible, reflected Gamelin, 'not to sense how much we are missing him now'.[37]

As the autumn continued, Gamelin felt that the waging of the war suffered because of the way Daladier always kept an eye on the weathervane of home-front politics. It was, the general complained to his staff in mid-September 1939, 'not the military operations that are our worry . . . but this government of irresolute and nervous fainthearts. They're the weight on our shoulders.'[38] Gamelin thought Daladier devoted undue attention in wartime to accommodating newspaper columnists and to placating the leading (as well as not-so-leading) lights in public life. Thus Daladier allowed Pétain to brow-beat him into dropping a planned inclusion of Herriot as foreign minister in place of Bonnet, in the September 1939 cabinet reshuffle. (The marshal, then serving as French ambassador in Madrid, argued that the former Radical Party leader was so overtly anti-fascist that his appointment might provoke Franco into entering the war against the Allies.) In the same vein, at the end of September a US attaché in Paris reported hearing that Daladier's ministerial reconstruction had been such a damp squib because 'no-one can agree on former Premier Flandin being in any Cabinet'.[39]

This excessive deference by Daladier to the egos of political rivals was seen at its worst after October 1939. Then, instead of completely remodelling the executive into a stripped-down and smoothly oiled machine concerned exclusively with the most resolute prosecution of the war, Daladier limited his reforms to placing Dautry at the new armaments ministry and taking personal charge at the Quai d'Orsay in place of Bonnet. As a result Daladier became rapidly swamped by paperwork, propelled with insufficient briefing from one meeting to another. He retreated more than ever behind a screen of advisors and assistants from his civil and military *cabinets* – men such as Roger Génébrier, Marcel Clapier, Robert Coulondre, Hyppolyte Ducos, the junior minister for foreign affairs, and General Decamp. The protectiveness of these aides was probably essential to avoid Daladier collapsing completely, so great were the pressures under which he had elected to put himself. He had become a factotum, the Figaro of the French war administration.

In taking so many roles, however, Daladier badly overestimated his own reserves of energy and managerial talent. Gamelin, on the other hand, appreciated the dangers. He confided to his own adjutant at the time of the reshuffle that 'Daladier has too much to do to accumulate the presidency of the council, national defence and war; he should lighten his load and keep for himself the presidency of the council and foreign affairs.'[40] On 27 September 1939 the emasculated nature of Daladier's governmental reorganisation was the subject of a well-informed despatch to the Office of Naval Intelligence in Washington from the US naval attaché in Paris. The latter reported a journalist's story:

that Daladier himself was known, by his close friends, as a 'weakling' and that he never did anything without asking the advice of people weaker than himself – Bonnet, Sarraut etc. . . . It was stated that the present war called for a 'military' man in the form of a dictator at the head of the government and that such weaklings as Bonnet, Sarraut etc. should be put aside. Daladier being a major in the reserve, was even suggested for promotion to a high rank and, conjointly with General Gamelin, to take over the government for the duration of the war. The newspaperman stated that this plan was pending and that this was the real reason why the War Cabinet was not formed.[41]

The sense of Daladier's own insecurity reflected here was accurate. The prime minister spent the autumn glancing nervously over his shoulder at the intrigues of his parliamentary rivals. He was particularly rattled by the former appeasers or *Munichois* whom Gamelin termed, on 3 October 1939, 'the peace-offensive brigade . . . Chautemps, Laval, Flandin, who draw support from the attitude of Pétain: "Let's proceed in softly-softly fashion for the moment; in the spring we'll be ready and the diplomatic position, particularly in respect of Italy, will be improved if not completely transformed in our favour."'

As this indicates, it was quite erroneous to speculate that Daladier and Gamelin thought of forming a double-act and appointing themselves as civil-military 'strongmen' to suspend the normal practice of government. On the contrary: Daladier responded to the pressures on him by the expedient of piling office upon office. In turn, Gamelin became increasingly discontented. Daladier's situation became preposterous as, in Richard Challener's deliciously Gilbertian description, he 'became a sort of Gallic Pooh Bah', the 'Lord High Everything Else of France.'[42]

When urged by fellow officers to use the influence that he was imagined to have over Daladier in the interests of military concerns, Gamelin denied that he had any special leverage if a question of national defence or army policy became entangled with considerations of domestic party politics. Such a state of affairs, Gamelin implied, was an all-too-common occurrence. If political calculation entered the reckoning, he lamented, 'Then all that counts are friendships, factions, debts to be repaid, ties from bygone days.'[43] Some weeks later, on 18 October 1939, Gamelin was reflecting over lunch with officers of his *cabinet* on the traits of a number of French war leaders and high officials. One of the staff interjected that the position of Jacomet, the secretary-general at the rue Saint-Dominique, appeared to be growing precarious. 'No', demurred Gamelin, 'his position is solid, M. Daladier will not cast him adrift.' The general concluded ruefully that Daladier had 'the weakness of staying faithful to his friends, no matter what they contrive to get up to'. By mid-March 1940 Gamelin was even more discontented with the prime minister when he heard that Daladier thought the Allies might win the war merely by dint of their economic superiority, so 'that there won't be a real battle, and everyone can be detached to duties in the interior'.[44]

This gradual estrangement in the course of the phoney war doomed the Daladier–Gamelin duumvirate. This was tragic because it was their work together in 1936–9 that had sufficiently strengthened French forces to make possible the decision to fight Hitler over Poland. As has been shown, Gamelin had played a central part in determining the issue and the moment on which to challenge and seek to halt the German drive for European hegemony. He had 'supported . . . Daladier in the foreign policy that brought France into the Second World War . . . in spite of German numerical superiority, French weakness in the air and limited support from Britain'.[45] Excessively academic in his strategic analyses, exaggeratedly qualified and cautious in his prescriptions, Gamelin shared at least some of Daladier's intellectual traits of lucidity and capacity for self-criticism. Both of them tended to see all sides to any situation, to discern the drawback that invariably had to be traded off in any way of solving a problem.

It was not so much that the general was indecisive or lacking in character. It was more that he perceived how an unguarded recommendation for a particular course of action might fill the decision-taking vacuum that periodically opened up in political waverers such as Daladier. He was 'quite intelligent enough to realize that his opinions might be treated as decisive arguments and he was both too hesitant and too scrupulous to orient . . . governments along the lines of a personal policy'. As has been pointed out, Gamelin had evolved a cardinal rule 'about respecting the superior authority of the political arm'; this carried with it the conviction that ministers should at all times be left the masters of their own decisions. Clearly, the general 'hesitated between forcing the government's hand and an unwillingness to encourage dangerous illusions'.[46] This attitude of 'correctness', as Gamelin would doubtless have described it, was most in evidence during March 1936, immediately before and after Germany's remilitarisation of the Rhineland. As discussed earlier, Gamelin then pointedly told Schweisguth and the army staff that the soldiers were 'not to put obstacles in the way of virile [political] decisions', though they were within their rights – indeed were duty bound – to 'resist madcap solutions' which might arise from the civilians.[47] But there was a basic problem that Gamelin failed to grasp sufficiently, then or later: this was just how difficult it had become for *any* government of the Republic to unite around *any* initiatives that were robust, dynamic and virile.

As Sir Denis Brogan discerned shortly after 1940, the mass of French parliamentarians 'feared great, dominant personalities'. They placed a premium instead on the style and conduct of the wheeling-dealing machine politicians. The men of party had 'succeeded only too well in taking personality out of politics'.[48] They had engineered a situation in which those who flourished were increasingly those with the methods made notorious by Laval, who reportedly said as early as 1925 'that in French politics it . . . [had become] more important to conciliate men than principles'.[49] It had become almost impossible for anyone, whether of the left, centre or right, to further a political career if they flew in the face of the influence-peddling and party machinations that had become 'the system' by the 1930s. The marginalisation and comparative impotence of mavericks such as Paul-Boncour and Cot, Reynaud and Mandel, was the proof.

In the place of the domineering and rather daunting giants of the past, the institutions of the French state were now in the hands of average and relatively anonymous 'system politicians'. This shift filled a growing clutch of offstage, retired conservative officers – such as Pétain, d'Esperey, de Castelnau, Weygand and Pujo – with anger and revulsion. Weygand was the most severe and ultimately significant case of military alienation. He 'felt himself to be the last representative of the old order of "strong men" – the Poincarés, the Maginots, the Barthous – all of whom had disappeared by the end of 1934'. Their places, as the best study of Weygand points out, had been taken 'by the political jugglers, the *uomini di combinazione* he despised: the Lavals, the Flandins, the Gamelins'.[50]

Once Reynaud replaced Daladier as prime minister on 21 March 1940 the direction of the French war effort became even more prey to intrigue, even more distracted by squabbles over prerogatives, even more poisoned by clashes of personality. Oliver Harvey, then private secretary to Lord Halifax, the British foreign secretary, had hoped in November 1938 that Reynaud (just appointed finance minister) might 'prove a cuckoo in the nest' for Daladier's government, stiffening its stance against Germany. 'He seems [added Harvey] to understand the nature of the threat and the need for real action. He is something of a French Winston.' The trouble was that Harvey's analogy was apt in more ways than its author intended. For Reynaud, like Churchill during the latter's 'wilderness years', lacked a sufficient parliamentary power-base. This prevented him from pursuing a truly independent war policy. Consequently, as prime minister in 1940, Reynaud remained the prisoner of the bloc of Radicals controlled by Daladier – who retained the ministry of national defence and war. Reynaud's eagerness to divert French troops to Norway to counter Hitler's invasion of Scandinavia in April 1940 was motivated chiefly by his need to find and prosecute a strategy manifestly different from the defence and blockade identified with Gamelin and Daladier. On the eve of the German blitzkrieg in the west, French war decisions were increasingly being shaped on grounds of private vendetta rather than strategic vision. 'If the Norwegian affair should develop favourably for the Allies', wrote US ambassador Bullitt on 18 April 1940 to R. Walton Moore of the State Department in Washington:

> the Reynaud government probably will remain in power for some time. If not, Daladier will return soon. It is too bad that there should be anything but close friendship between Reynaud and Daladier, since . . . they are both able men; but the lady love of each hates the lady love of the other, and . . . venom distilled in a horizontal position is always fatal.[51]

Reynaud jibbed against 'the system', but he was unable to break free from it. Furthermore – and a key point for this study – it was the case that Gamelin himself was a product of, and a believer in, the late Third Republic's 'system'. This fact prevented Gamelin, just as it prevented Reynaud, from perceiving either the extent of the problem of diminished authority among the civilian institutions, or its possible consequences.[52]

Gamelin full well knew how he himself had prospered through political alliance-building, from patience, from taking the line of least resistance. Nevertheless, even Gamelin underestimated how the pervasiveness of these habits throughout the political class might jeopardise the Republic in the event of grave national crisis. The political formations of the late-1930s were splintered and inward-looking, especially on the centre and right. Neither these parties – the Republican Federation, the Democratic Alliance, the PSF – nor their leaders such as Louis Marin, Flandin and de La Rocque were consciously seeking to subvert the Republic. Nor were they deliberately trying to steer France to defeat and humiliation.[53] But in their self-indulgent and internecine struggles between themselves and with each other, at a time of deepening national peril from German military power, they lost sight of the external wood because of their fixation on the internal trees.

The system spawned political leaders devoid of vision. 'What a pity there is no strong Frenchman now, a Clemenceau, a Poincaré or a Barthou' complained Harvey in his diary during January 1939.[54] But the French political class had grown averse to risks: by the late 1930s it sought to advance only conformists whom it had made in its own mould.

Conclusion

The increasing organisation of party – largely absent for much of the Third Republic – was eradicating the free spirits. It could be seen at work: it had made obstacles in the career path of the Cots, the Zays, the Mendès-France and 'did not breed Clemenceaus or even Poincarés any longer'.[55] To a general of Weygand's ilk, who had always regarded the régime with scepticism and suspicion, the decline in the quality of civilian leadership translated into a shirking of political responsibility and a shocking evaporation of the power of political decision.[56] Moreover, as noted above, even the republican Gamelin was mortified by the dearth of strong political direction under the disorientating conditions of phoney war that followed the defeat of Poland.

The decline in national leadership was considered so serious that any political father-figure still living found himself touted as a putative 'strongman'. On 19 September 1939 the director of the paper *L'Ere Nouvelle* visited Gamelin. 'All of a sudden', the latter's diary recounts, the journalist said to the general: 'Do you know that the government is going to fall? – People's minds are turning towards a personality from an unexpected quarter . . . towards M. Tardieu . . . You understand, don't you: M. Daladier doesn't have the stature required.' The proposal must have smacked of desperation: Gamelin reflected that only two months previously Tardieu had suffered a stroke.[57] Yet, bizarre as it appears, this episode did occur. Confirmation is offered by the US naval attaché in Paris, from whom a report at the end of September 1939 recorded 'that General Gamelin stated that France must find a Clemenceau as well as a Foch and that pressure was being brought to bear on Daladier by military men to act before the fighting commences'. It was remarked, the American continued, 'that the only candidate for Clemenceau's job was André Tardieu, who was at present near death in a hospital, but that [anyway] Tardieu so despised the group of "weaklings" in the Chamber that he would not accept the job under any conditions'.[58]

Thus, just when it most needed one, France could find no universally respected civilian *chef*. Since views as jaundiced as these were apparently voiced even by régime loyalists like Gamelin, it remains a persuasive argument that the mischief-makers in Paris in 1939–40 'would have been as relatively impotent as were the Caillaux, Malvys, Lavals of 1914–18 had there [still] been a central political authority to impose obedience'.[59]

Was Gamelin's very limited discernment of this 'fatal decline in the authority of the French State' a result, then, of un-worldliness on his part? Put another way, was Gamelin misplaced in the profession of a senior general, as some have charged?[60] De Gaulle, for one, offered an oft-quoted description in his war memoirs of visiting Gamelin's headquarters early in 1940. The account conveys a memorable image of the convent-like solitude and the Spartan conditions under which Gamelin worked. De Gaulle said they were reminiscent more of a religious recluse than of a military leader. Later in the same passage, employing another image intended to reinforce his criticism, de Gaulle likened Gamelin to an academic research scientist who had converted Vincennes into an ivory-towered laboratory for his experiments in search of a magic formula for victory.[61] Mme Jouhaux, one of Gamelin's companions during the incarceration at the Schloss Itter in 1943–4, noted that there she 'got to the point ... of wondering whether he was not more cut out for the career of an intellectual or ecclesiastic rather than for that of a *militaire*'. Francois-Ponçet, another of the French captives to keep a journal, recalled how in Gamelin's room at the castle 'there was always a little crucifix on his bedside table' and how 'chatting with him, one was astonished that he had chosen a military career, for which it did not seem his nature suited him'.[62] Nor were many historians for a long time inclined to contradict these wartime estimations. A. J. P. Taylor, for one, condemned Gamelin as a 'political soldier ... standing by in philosophical detachment' whilst France hurtled out of control down a road to military disaster and national disgrace.[63]

Yet there is another, more charitable, way in which to interpret Gamelin's behaviour during his years of command. This way may indeed explain his outlook on the civilian powers in the last phase of the Republic. This interpretation would begin by eschewing a hard and fast distinction between the general as peacetime defence organiser and as wartime army chief. For one thing, a separation of this sort is artificial: it has only been made with hindsight. Prior to the Battle of France, contemporaries were confident Gamelin would perform impressively as a commander. An informed British commentator, Brigadier Gordon Heywood (who had served in Paris from 1933 to 1936 as military attaché), ventured in 1938, after Gamelin was appointed chief of staff for national defence, that he was 'a born leader'.[64] Similarly, in July 1939, Britain's assistant military attaché in Paris reported the assurance of the editor of the newspaper *L'Epoque*, that Gamelin 'would, in war, more than fulfil the high expectations the nation had of him', adding that 'if anything his military virtues were more those of a wartime leader than a peacetime trainer'.[65]

With the exception of de Gaulle, others who visited Vincennes during the phoney war similarly expressed confidence in Gamelin. One was A. J. Liebling, the Paris correspondent of the *New Yorker* magazine. He used the good offices of Bullitt, the US ambassador, with Petibon, to gain an interview with Gamelin early in December 1939. The evidence of Liebling, who assiduously cultivated contacts with French generals, suggests that observers were mistaken if they read a boredom with his military career into Gamelin's love for philosophy, art, literature and history. Gamelin had not grown disenchanted with his life as France's most senior serving general; his readiness to turn conversations to cultural and scholarly topics simply betokened the authenticity of his reputation as an educated soldier. Liebling recounted how he had elicited from some of the general's contemporary military academicians 'that Gamelin from the moment of his first arrival at St. Cyr had made the same impression as an ambitious young seminarist who his colleagues at once feel is destined for a high place in the hierarchy. They had said, "He would rather be generalissimo than anything else in the world."' And after France's defeat, Liebling refused to follow the scribes who unselfconsciously forswore their earlier adulation of Gamelin and hunted him as if he were an outlaw with a price on his head. He simply reflected instead how it was 'hard for me to associate the calm little man ... with omissions in the most elementary parts of war. It is as if I had had a long conversation with a novelist – perhaps M. Jules Romains – and a couple of years later somebody came to me and said, "You remember M. Romains? He was an illiterate."'[66]

Coincidentally, Romains himself was another who obtained an interview with Gamelin at Vincennes in that same month of December 1939. In his novel *Les Hommes de Bonne Volonté*, set in the First World War, Romains had modelled one of his fictional officers on the younger Gamelin, at the side of Joffre on the Marne. Relating their meeting in 1939 after the Fall of France, Romains took pains to emphasise how sharp Gamelin's mind had still seemed and how impressively he was 'devoted to the problems of war [and] to their most recent development'. Critics who pointed to the catastrophe of 1940, using hindsight to conclude that Gamelin had to be adjudged 'an imbecile or a *baderne*' only demonstrated that they 'did not know what they were talking about'.[67]

It would be perverse indeed to argue that the political adroitness continually displayed by Gamelin actually handicapped French defensive preparations. In 1935, when Gamelin assumed command, the French defences in general, and the French army and its re-equipment in particular, were in poor shape. Weygand, certainly, had begun an important motorisation programme for part of the infantry and had initiated the cavalry's mechanisation. He was able to plead an adverse climate of arms control and financial constraint as an alibi for not accomplishing more. But these extenuating circumstances do not satisfactorily explain the barrenness of the achievement in the Weygand years. The estrangement between Weygand and the centre–left which governed France in 1932–4 had brought no political favour on the cause of national defence. Difficult though it is to quantify the degree to which military modernisation was hindered by the civil-military confrontations of that period, such quarrels can have done nothing to help give France the defences it required.[68] Without doubt Gamelin had to attend in 1935–6 before anything else – indeed in order to make anything else possible – to urgent political fence-mending.

It was not simply because it came naturally to him that Gamelin, from the outset, exercised his gifts as a conciliator, remained loyal to civilian ministers and tried to smooth their paths. Such an approach was made essential. Compromises had to be reached in order to eradicate the confrontational atmosphere that Weygand bequeathed to Gamelin in 1935–6. It is facile – and too redolent of history populated simply by heroes and villains – to concur with A. J. P. Taylor that Gamelin's outlook 'made him a good politician and diplomatist' but was 'hardly the most suitable' for high military command.[69] This is to neglect the fundamental changes that the twentieth century had wrought in the very nature of command.

The First World War – let alone the Second – demonstrated that the direction of defence forces still required leaders to show resourcefulness, guile and courage. But the demonstration of courage no longer meant generals mounting their horses and riding for the front line. Well before 1939–40, command had come to be exercised chiefly through the technology of the telephone, telegraph and radio set – as it would soon afterwards be through the satellite and computer. The higher an officer in the twentieth century found himself in the chain of command, the further removed he became from battle itself. This was a transformation with which generals and admirals steeped in traditions and sometimes personal experience of more direct physical command had to come to terms.[70] At the summit, the conduct of defence policy and the waging of war was a process located at the junction of politics and strategy. This was understood by Jules Romains at the time of his talk to Gamelin at Vincennes in December 1939. 'There are those', wrote the novelist, 'who tell you that Gamelin has made his career thanks to politicians he has flattered. Such people forget, for a start, that to attain the highest ranks military men always have to take account of politicians and win their support to a greater or lesser extent. This, however, proves nothing for or against the technical worth of these officers as technicians.'[71]

Criticisms usually made of Gamelin's adroitness as a military politician originate from the tendency of the winners to write the history of their times. Once the history is written its authors then mythologise their own part in it. The senior Allied military leaders of the later years of the Second World War – those who enjoyed success over the Axis – have not been systematically disparaged for possessing political acumen and diplomatic ability. The Anglo-American combined chiefs of staff, men such as Eisenhower, Marshall, King, Dill, Portal and Alanbrooke, have not had their reputations relentlessly run down because they were not, in an old-fashioned sense, 'fighting commanders'. Quite the contrary: these officers have, in the main, been lauded by history as outstanding military statesmen.[72] Yet each of them was a supremely political soldier, sailor or airman. On pondering the vicissitudes of reputation, therefore, it is hard not to conclude that the tributes heaped on these Allied caesars for their political skills were first and foremost the result of their finishing as winners.

Gamelin did not wear any laurel crown of victory. Yet he shared with these later Allied commanders an understanding of the task that faced the military leaders of the alliances against Hitler in 1939–45. The task, of course, was to manage the human and economic warlike resources of a multi-national coalition and to persuade diverse political systems to pull together so as to attain common objectives. Because he was farsighted about what high command in the Second World War would be like, Gamelin took to heart the fact that he was so prominently ensnared in the early débâcle of 1940. In a deeply personal sense, he was distraught at his own failure and at the failure of the Allied armies. Three days after his dismissal, false rumours circulated among the press corps in Paris that he had taken his own life.[73] In fact Gamelin was not the type for the melodramatic suicide *à la* Samsonov, who shot himself in the East Prussian woods after losing the Battle of Tannenberg in 1914. But Gamelin's written offer to Weygand in early June 1940 to serve wherever he could be of use to France was ignored. Purposeless, he remained like a marooned sailor in his Avenue Foch apartment, to await the German entry into Paris. He was, wrote the US ambassador, Bullitt, 'a crushed and broken man' who subsequently became prone to melancholy in prison at Itter in 1943–4, 'as if pursued by the very thought of the defeat'.[74]

Certainly there were strategic decisions with an adverse effect on the fortunes of France and her Allies in 1940 which were either Gamelin's alone, or his in significant measure. By far the most critical was his imposition on subordinates – some of whom had serious reservations – of the April 1940 Breda variant to Plan D, the defensive intervention into Belgium. The late addition of the Breda extension to the long-agreed forward defence of the north demanded the deployment of a

French light mechanised division along with motorised infantry formations into southern Holland. It also led to the movement of two more mechanised divisions, French motorised infantry and the motorised British forces into central Belgium. This manoeuvre attempted to incorporate the Dutch as well as Belgian armies into Allied defensive strength for the expected long war. It was intended to show that, in spite of its passivity during the fall of Poland, France possessed the ability and determination to rescue small friendly nations subjected to German aggression. However, the plan involved taking a gamble on temporarily depleting the French strategic reserves. The coastal dash to Breda required Gamelin to redispose Giraud's mobile Seventh Army, the *masse de manoeuvre* or general reserve, from its central counterattack position between Rheims and Châlons-sur-Marne to the Allied extreme left. In doing this, for reasons that made sense purely in their own terms, Gamelin stuck the necks of the Allies into the hanging noose of Germany's Manstein Plan. The latter, adopted in February 1940, involved a feint attack in strength into the Low Countries. This diversion served to lure forward the Allied left wing, whilst the main onslaught with seven panzer divisions was developed through the Ardennes. It was this latter operation which ruptured the Allied centre and subsequently permitted the decisive defeat of the Allied armies both north and south of the breakthrough.[75]

Gamelin has also been criticised for a supposedly harmful reluctance to take direct command in the critical days from 12 to 19 May. He has been accused of unwillingness to override or dismiss intermediate subordinate generals such as Georges, Billotte, Prételat and Huntziger.[76] Yet armchair strategy, though a seductive pastime, has little to offer to the process of understanding Gamelin's conduct during the Battle of France. He was dealing with a war in which the widespread availability of telegraphic and telephonic communications offered the temptation to any generalissimo to interfere in the dispositions of individual company commanders. Hitler's incorrigible meddling in the minutiae of the eastern front battles in 1941–5 is just the most striking Second World War example of this trait. It is far from the only one. In the later twentieth century the lure of command by remote control has, of course, increased still further. Satellites and micro-electronics offer a national leader the technology to direct a single nuclear-armed submarine of unprecedented destructive capability, half a world away from the leader's command rooms in the home country.

These temptations to interfere and override his subordinate generals were ones that Gamelin resisted for the first nine days of the battle for France. Yet, because France lost in 1940, such restraint has been fashioned into another stricture against Gamelin. He has been accused of displaying damaging passivity, one study claiming that there 'is no doubt that once the fighting began, Gamelin's inertia deprived his subordinates of the guidance they needed'.[77]

The present reappraisal has endeavoured to suggest that responsibility for the military defeat of the west – and blame for the fall of the Third Republic – is much more widely spread than is admitted by critics who have made Gamelin a scapegoat. In the end, 'when the decisive hour came', during the two critical months between Reynaud's assumption of the premiership in March and the end of May, 'the structure of civil-military relations in France was in complete disarray'.[78] Unforgivingly exposed, though not in the first instance by the Pétainist authoritarians, were the imperfections of the consensus between the armed services and the Third Republic that Gamelin valued so highly. Irreparable damage was done by a better-intentioned political operator: Reynaud himself. Parliamentarian though he was, Reynaud was a 'gravedigger' nevertheless. His conflict with Daladier and Gamelin had the character of a personal feud, *en pleine guerre*. It provoked pettiness and prevarication at the summit of war policy-making. At the same time it revealed the limits to what could be accomplished by the Daladier–Gamelin partnership. The exposure of these limits then encouraged moves fatal to the careers of the two individuals, to confidence in the continuing legitimacy of the liberal Republic and to the brand of sturdy Jacobin patriotism from which they had become indistinguishable.[79]

Gamelin's real failure, then, was not in his preparation of French rearmament or in his organisation of the Allied grand strategy. He had laid farsighted plans for a long war and knew that victory would require a welding together of a heterogenous Allied coalition. With its long opening defensive phase for the Allies and the eventual triumph of the latter's fully mobilised economies, the Second World War eventually followed a pattern remarkably akin to Gamelin's blueprint of 1938–40. Where Gamelin did not succeed was in transforming or sufficiently remodelling the ideology of the French military caste. The measure of his lack of success was the refusal of the officers, and especially the generals, to stay shoulder-to-shoulder with the regime in France's hour of supreme crisis.[80] 'Still there lurked beneath the surface a military suspicion of the republic and its works. There was loyalty to the nation, loyalty to France, but not loyalty to the Republic.' Least of all was there any loyalty to Reynaud's government of the moment.[81]

It should not perhaps be a surprise that Gamelin had not dispelled the anti-republicanism and the political opportunism of Pétain and Weygand. They, after all, were his own one-time superiors. Nor had

Gamelin ever been given effective authority over the navy and air force – from which prominent officers rallied to Pétain at the first possible opportunity in June 1940. Languishing in Vichy's prisons from 1940 to 1942, Daladier rued his failure between 1936 and 1939 to exert his political authority and cleanse the Augean stables of the armed forces' high commands. With hindsight, and quite correctly, Daladier acknowledged that the undertaking of such a purge had to come from government ministers such as himself. As one postwar commentator remarked, the 'extraordinary system of command', 'relieves . . . Gamelin of much of the responsibility for France's disasters'.[82]

In the event, what placed the Third Republic in mortal danger in 1940 was the fact that Gamelin's reassurances on the dependability of the high command had gone unquestioned. Gamelin did not deliberately dupe Daladier, nor even Reynaud. But he was himself deceived as to how superficially he had embedded in his fellow generals a republican ethos – an ethos of complete military-civil integration. This meant that, in the controversy about an armistice or an evacuation of the state authorities to North Africa, the upper echelons of the defence services proved 'ready to ditch the Third Republic, replacing it with a structure that would approximate Pétain's idea of a political order based on *patrie*, *famille* and *travail*'. To those who had never followed Gamelin in embracing the regime unreservedly, the republic's symbol, Marianne, 'was threadbare, and a slattern'.[83] For these elements, 1940 was to be seized as an apparently providential opportunity for a divorce and a fresh start. Perhaps by this analogy with a failed marriage we may come closest to comprehending how far Gamelin himself – as much as the Republic with which he was identified – became a victim in the wider crisis of 1940. Indeed, in Gamelin's estrangement from 'his' Daladier during the phoney war may be seen the harbinger of the separation between command and government which culminated in the political agony of Reynaud at Cangé, Briare and Bordeaux between 11 and 16 June 1940.

In the final analysis the charge laid against Gamelin by his critics has been one of military failure, not one of political conspiracy. It cannot be doubted that Gamelin devoted his career to the task of defending the French state in its particular incarnation as the Third Republic. He did so against enemies of the Republic within just as much as against foes of France without. For Gamelin, the Third Republic and France were one and the same, coterminous and indivisible. That his endeavours did not meet with sufficient success does not belittle him for making the attempt. For Gamelin, to defend France was to defend the Republic; to defend the Republic was to defend France. France's undoing resulted from military defeat in the field – a defeat in which Gamelin's deployments and his incomplete understanding of the quickened pace of land warfare played a major part. Even so, there 'is much to admire in the way Gamelin built a smaller and industrially weaker France into a powerful military machine to oppose Germany'.[84]

It was the military failure that made possible the interment of the Republic and Vichy's right-wing 'national revolution'. The defeat was a necessary and crucial condition for the birth of the Pétainist *Etat Français*. But it was not, itself, a sufficient condition for such far-reaching political change. The overthrow of the Republic was conceived in circumstances and by factors that were not as contingent or directly reversible as the course of one six-week campaign. Deeper malaises were required to turn the military setbacks into the full-scale national crisis witnessed in 1940. Foremost among these considerations were the civil-military prejudices and antipathies which had eaten away at the support for the Third Republic among its own institutions. The regime had been slowly but surely debilitated from within, as if by a recurring viral illness. The youthful Gamelin had seen these malignancies deep inside the French body politic at the turn of the century. Then they had provoked the disorders and convulsions of the Dreyfus affair. He had seen their recurrence in 1913–14 during the three-year service controversy, in 1917 in the mutinies crisis, and in 1919 at the time of the struggle between Foch and Clemenceau over the peace terms.

Throughout his own time in high military command, Gamelin concentrated his best efforts on treating the symptoms of recurrent civil-military malady. He understood that France itself was placed in danger by this periodic relapse into ill-will and quarrelling that dogged the relationship between the civilian authorities and their military officers. But, though Gamelin attended to the problem, he evidently did not get to the root of it. He was successful in making explicit anti-republicanism a taboo amongst his fellow generals and subordinate officers between 1935 and May 1940, but he was not successful in eradicating it. In making the problem less visible he came to underestimate its resilience and its gravity. He also overestimated his own ability to manage the mentality, the modes of thought, the prejudices, of his officers.[85]

Once the war had begun, this system of close ties between politicians and military men made any commander's position difficult. The supreme irony was that Gamelin, who had prospered for so long by adroit manipulation of political-military relationships, should have found himself brought down by his own methods, once these were employed against him by Reynaud, Baudouin and de Villelume. Gamelin had not protested sufficiently, or effectively, at the way

Daladier had placed sweeping responsibilities on him whilst at the same time hobbling his powers. Complaining about this mismatch at Riom and in his memoirs, at Gamelin did, was like shutting the gate after the horse had bolted.

Ultimately, Gamelin fell prey to hubris. He had acquired an overweaning confidence in his own ability as a broker, a fixer and a mediator. He exaggerated his own capacity to smooth away or circumvent difficulties affecting the French defence forces and the commanders who led them. Too late, in May–June 1940, Gamelin awoke to the seriousness of the challenge represented by the military and political reactionaries – the Pétains, Weygands, Baudouins, Huntzigers, Colsons, Pujos and Darlans – who lurked behind the purely vindictive or tactical intriguers, Reynaud and de Villelume. Gamelin and Daladier, between them, had failed to give French generalship the mental toughness and strategical imagination to prevent the conquest of the metropolitan territory. Nor had they implanted sufficient republican loyalty among the conservative generals to deter these from settling with the German invaders and unleashing the hunt for scapegoats on their own side. As a result, during the summer of 1940, those who were culpable threw themselves with unseemly enthusiasm into a search for those who could be held responsible.

Once his own authority was broken by the success of the blitzkrieg, Gamelin could not prevent his reactionary colleagues destroying the republican–military compromise. The compromise had always been a fragile thing, ever since the earliest days of the *Troisième*, seventy years before. It was Gamelin's achievement that this compromise was nonetheless held together throughout the turbulent years of fascism within and without in the 1930s, and could be demolished only *after* his armies had been defeated and he had been disgraced.

Appendix 1

Diagrammatic organisation of the French high command

Appendices

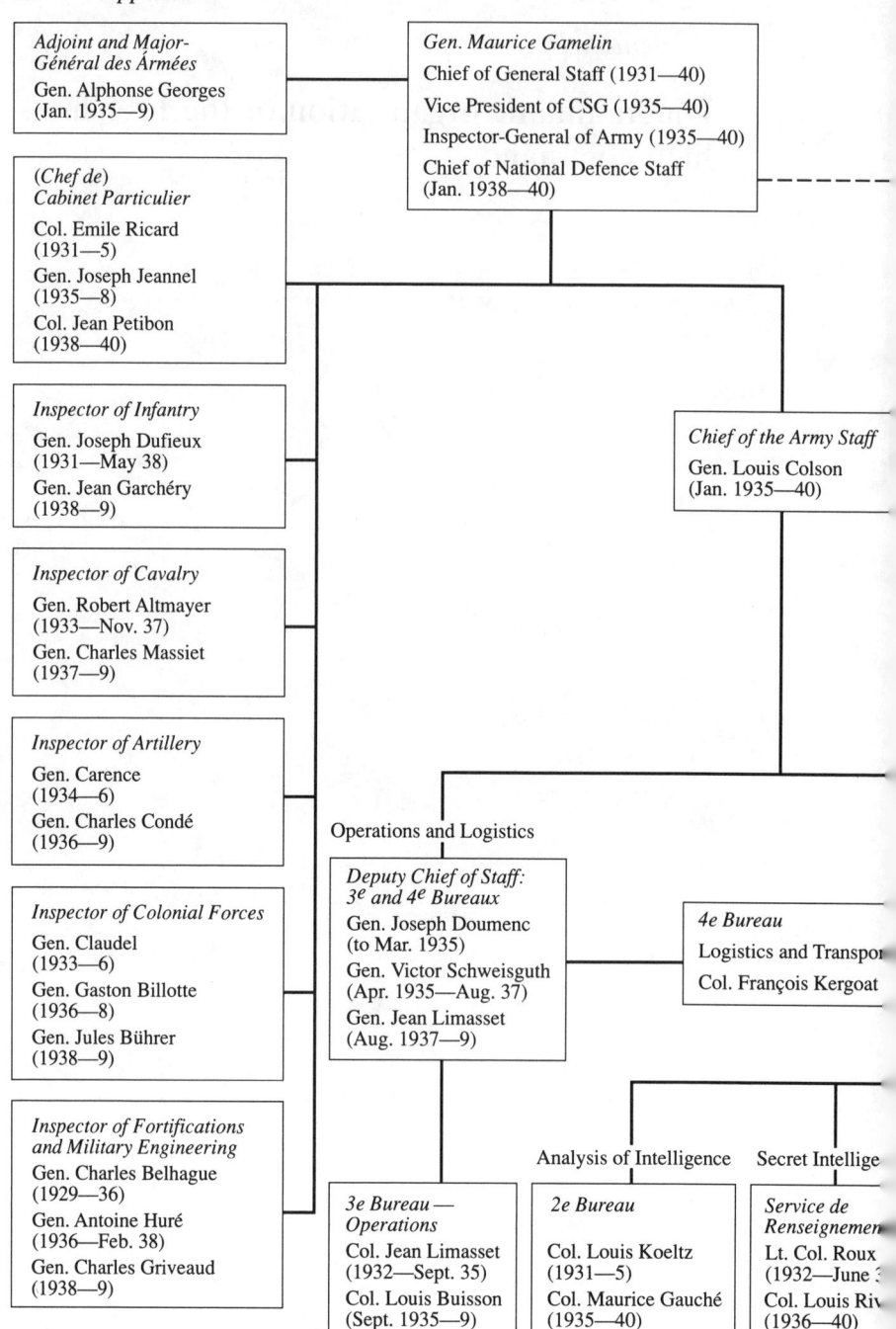

Adjoint and Major-Général des Armées
Gen. Alphonse Georges (Jan. 1935—9)

Gen. Maurice Gamelin
Chief of General Staff (1931—40)
Vice President of CSG (1935—40)
Inspector-General of Army (1935—40)
Chief of National Defence Staff (Jan. 1938—40)

(Chef de) Cabinet Particulier
Col. Emile Ricard (1931—5)
Gen. Joseph Jeannel (1935—8)
Col. Jean Petibon (1938—40)

Inspector of Infantry
Gen. Joseph Dufieux (1931—May 38)
Gen. Jean Garchéry (1938—9)

Inspector of Cavalry
Gen. Robert Altmayer (1933—Nov. 37)
Gen. Charles Massiet (1937—9)

Inspector of Artillery
Gen. Carence (1934—6)
Gen. Charles Condé (1936—9)

Inspector of Colonial Forces
Gen. Claudel (1933—6)
Gen. Gaston Billotte (1936—8)
Gen. Jules Bührer (1938—9)

Inspector of Fortifications and Military Engineering
Gen. Charles Belhague (1929—36)
Gen. Antoine Huré (1936—Feb. 38)
Gen. Charles Griveaud (1938—9)

Chief of the Army Staff
Gen. Louis Colson (Jan. 1935—40)

Operations and Logistics

Deputy Chief of Staff: 3ᵉ and 4ᵉ Bureaux
Gen. Joseph Doumenc (to Mar. 1935)
Gen. Victor Schweisguth (Apr. 1935—Aug. 37)
Gen. Jean Limasset (Aug. 1937—9)

4ᵉ Bureau
Logistics and Transport
Col. François Kergoat

3e Bureau — Operations
Col. Jean Limasset (1932—Sept. 35)
Col. Louis Buisson (Sept. 1935—9)

Analysis of Intelligence

2e Bureau
Col. Louis Koeltz (1931—5)
Col. Maurice Gauché (1935—40)

Secret Intelligence

Service de Renseignement
Lt. Col. Roux (1932—June ?)
Col. Louis Riv... (1936—40)

1 The French high command

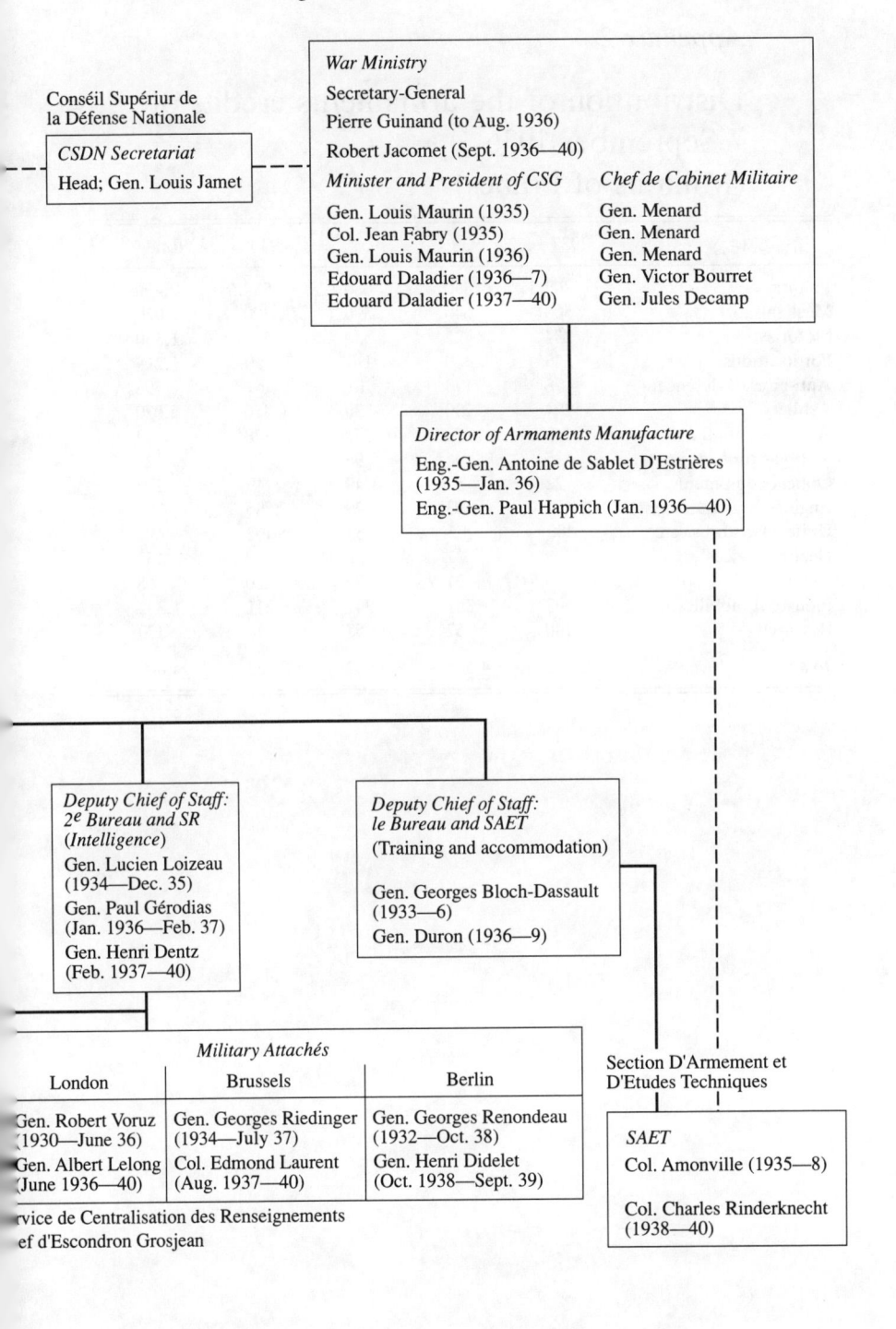

Conséil Supériur de la Défense Nationale

CSDN Secretariat
Head; Gen. Louis Jamet

War Ministry
Secretary-General
Pierre Guinand (to Aug. 1936)
Robert Jacomet (Sept. 1936—40)

Minister and President of CSG	*Chef de Cabinet Militaire*
Gen. Louis Maurin (1935)	Gen. Menard
Col. Jean Fabry (1935)	Gen. Menard
Gen. Louis Maurin (1936)	Gen. Menard
Edouard Daladier (1936—7)	Gen. Victor Bourret
Edouard Daladier (1937—40)	Gen. Jules Decamp

Director of Armaments Manufacture
Eng.-Gen. Antoine de Sablet D'Estrières (1935—Jan. 36)
Eng.-Gen. Paul Happich (Jan. 1936—40)

Deputy Chief of Staff: 2ᵉ Bureau and SR (Intelligence)
Gen. Lucien Loizeau (1934—Dec. 35)
Gen. Paul Gérodias (Jan. 1936—Feb. 37)
Gen. Henri Dentz (Feb. 1937—40)

Deputy Chief of Staff: 1e Bureau and SAET (Training and accommodation)
Gen. Georges Bloch-Dassault (1933—6)
Gen. Duron (1936—9)

Military Attachés

London	Brussels	Berlin
Gen. Robert Voruz (1930—June 36)	Gen. Georges Riedinger (1934—July 37)	Gen. Georges Renondeau (1932—Oct. 38)
Gen. Albert Lelong (June 1936—40)	Col. Edmond Laurent (Aug. 1937—40)	Gen. Henri Didelet (Oct. 1938—Sept. 39)

rvice de Centralisation des Renseignements
ef d'Escondron Grosjean

Section D'Armement et D'Etudes Techniques

SAET
Col. Amonville (1935—8)

Col. Charles Rinderknecht (1938—40)

Appendix 2

Distribution of the armaments credits of 7 September 1936 (Millions of Francs)

	1937	1938	1939	1940	Total
Infantry	300.5	830	680	589.5	2,400
Mechanisation	500	640	390	390	1,920
Motorisation	234	425	350	351	1,360
Fortifications	555	460	110	90	1,215
Anti-aircraft defence	78	198	161	161	598
Artillery	204	730	730	356	2,020
Artillery munitions	245.8	378	378	378	1,379
Anti-gas protection	35	96	96	97	324
Optical equipment	22	50	49	49	170
Engineering equipment	50	93	79	86	308
Uniforms, stores, etc.	100	175	163	162	600
Health services	20	37	38	37	132
Saddlery	6.5	21.5	20	20	68
Industrial mobilisation	302	381	341	311	1,335
Research	(40)	57	57	56	170
Totals	2,652	4,571	3,642	3,133	14,000

Notes

INTRODUCTION: MAURICE GAMELIN, THE DEFENCE OF FRANCE AND THE DECLINE OF THE THIRD REPUBLIC

1. See, for example, J. Gooch and E. Cohen, *Military Misfortunes. The anatomy of failure in war* (New York, 1990), ch. 8, 'Catastrophic Failure. The French army and air force, May–June 1940', pp. 197–230. A vast literature has concerned itself with modern French civil–military relations. Among the most illuminating studies are R. Holmes, *The Road to Sedan. The French army, 1866–1870* (Woodbridge, Suffolk, 1984); D. B. Ralston, *The Army of the Republic. The place of the military in the political evolution of France, 1871–1914* (Cambridge, MA, 1967); 'From Boulanger to Pétain: the 3rd Republic and the republican generals', in B. J. Bond and I. Roy (eds.), *War and Society. A Yearbook of Military History*, I (London, 1976), pp. 178–201; D. Porch, *The March to the Marne: the French Army, 1871–1914* (Cambridge, 1981); 'Bugeaud, Galliéni, Lyautey: the development of French colonial warfare', in P. Paret (ed.), *Makers of Modern Strategy. From Machiavelli to the Nuclear Age* (Princeton, NJ, 1986), pp. 376–407; J. Monteilhet, *Les Institutions militaires de la France, 1814–1932* (Paris, 1932); R. D. Challener, *The French Theory of the Nation-in-Arms, 1866–1939* (New York, 1955); 'The Third Republic and the generals: the gravediggers revisited', in H. Coles (ed.), *Total War and Cold War. Problems in civilian control of the military* (Columbus, OH, 1962), pp. 91–107; 'The military defeat of 1940 in retrospect', in E. M. Earle (ed.), *Modern France. Problems of the Third and Fourth Republics* (Princeton, NJ, 1951), pp. 405–20; P.-M. de La Gorce, *La République et son armée* (Paris, 1963) (English edn., *The French Army. A political-military history*, trans. K. Douglas, London, 1963); P. C. F. Bankwitz, *Maxime Weygand and Civil-Military Relations in Modern France* (Cambridge, MA, 1967); 'Maxime Weygand and the army–nation concept in the modern French army', *French Historical Studies*, 2 (Fall, 1961), pp. 157–88 (reprinted in J. C. Cairns (ed.), *Contemporary France. Illusion, conflict and regeneration* (New York, 1978), pp. 168–99); 'Maxime Weygand and the fall of France: a study in civil-military relations', *Journal of Modern History*, 31 (Sept. 1959), pp. 225–42; R. O. Paxton, *Parades and Politics at Vichy. The French officer corps under Marshal Pétain* (Princeton, NJ, 1966); J. S. Ambler, *Soldiers against the state. The French army in politics, 1945–1962* (New York, 1966); G. A. Kelly, *Lost Soldiers.*

The French army and empire in crisis, 1947–1962 (Cambridge, MA, 1965); R. Girardet, La Société militaire dans la France contemporaine, 1815–1939 (Paris, 1953); Girardet (ed.), La Crise militaire française, 1945–1962. Aspects sociologiques et idéologiques (Paris, 1964); A. Horne, The French Army and Politics, 1870–1970 (Basingstoke and London, 1984); E. S. Furniss, Jr, De Gaulle and the French Army. A crisis in civil–military relations (New York, 1964); M. Martin, Warriors into Managers. The French military establishment since 1945 (Chapel Hill, NC, 1981); H. Dutailly, Les Problèmes de l'Armée de Terre française, 1935–1939 (Vincennes, 1980); J. Doise and M. Vaïsse, Politique étrangère de la France, 1871–1969. Diplomatie et outil militaire (Paris, 1987); J. Bonnemaison, Pouvoirs. Revue française d'études constitutionnelles et politiques, 38 (1986) (L'Armée); J. Guisnel, Les Généraux. Enquête sur le pouvoir militaire en France (Paris, 1990); P. Boniface, L'Armée. Enquête sur 300,000 soldats méconnus (Paris, 1990).
2. See Bankwitz, Weygand and Civil-Military Relations, pp. 8–11; Gen. L. André, Cinq ans de ministère (Paris, 1907); Porch, March to the Marne, pp. 74–104; de La Gorce, La République et son armée, pp. 70–8.
3. Imprisoned by Vichy in Oct. 1940, Gamelin's former political master, Edouard Daladier (minister for national defence and war, 1936–40), bitterly wondered in his diary 'How I could have placed confidence in men of this kind ... salon reactionaries and political intriguers, militarists and not soldiers. Where Weygand trod, others would follow. How did I not remove these lamentable *badernes* like Dufieux, Prételat, Requin and many more? Poor Gamelin, who defended them to me during that period from 36 to 39. He's repaid today by having his heart ripped out by the attacks of these same gentlemen' (J. Daladier and J. Daridan, eds., *Edouard Daladier. Journal de captivité, 1940–1945* (Paris, 1991), pp. 49–50).
4. An excellent introduction to French experiences under the Vichy regime of 1940–4 is H. R. Kedward, *Occupied France. Collaboration and resistance, 1940–1944* (Oxford, 1985). See also P. Farmer, *Vichy. Political dilemma* (New York, 1955); R. Aron, *The Vichy Regime, 1940–44* (London, 1958); R. O. Paxton, *Vichy France. Old guard and new order* (New York, 1972); J.-P. Azéma, *1940. L'Année terrible* (Paris, 1990); M. Cointet-Labrousse, *Vichy et le fascisme. Les Hommes, les structures et les pouvoirs* (Brussels, 1987); P. Laborie, *L'Opinion française sous Vichy* (Paris, 1990); H. Rousso, *Le Syndrome de Vichy, 1944–198...* (Paris, 1987).
5. See Bankwitz, *Weygand and Civil-Military Relations*, pp. 290–334. The metaphor of the 'gravediggers' formed the basis of the indictment of civilian and military leaders of the Republic advanced in Pertinax (pseud. A. Géraud), *Les Fossoyeurs. Défaite militaire de la France. Armistice. Contre-révolution* (New York, 1944, 2 vols.).
6. Quotation from Bankwitz, *Weygand and Civil-Military Relations*, p. 271. For Vichy ideology and Pétain's objectives see R. Griffiths, *Pétain* (London, 1970); M. Ferro, *Pétain* (Paris, 1987); J.-R. Tournoux, *Le Royaume d'Otto. La France allemande, 1940–1944* (Paris, 1982), which reproduces extensive excerpts from the diary of another collaborationist soldier and Vichy minister, General Georges Bridoux; W. D. Halls, *The*

Youth of Vichy France (Oxford, 1981), which investigates Pétain's nationalistic youth movement, the Chantiers de la Jeunesse, led by another retired senior officer, General J. de La Porte du Theil; D. Rossignol, *Vichy et les Franc-Maçons* (Paris, 1980); M. R. Marrus and R. O. Paxton, *Vichy France and the Jews* (New York, 1981), *Vichy et les Juifs*, Paris, 1981; M. Cointet, *Le Conseil national de Vichy, 1940–1944* (Paris, 1989); C. Faure, *Le Projet culturel de Vichy. Folklore et révolution nationale, 1940–1944* (Lyon and Paris, 1989). For the politics of the French army during the Occupation, see Paxton, *Parades and Politics*; Bankwitz, *Weygand and Civil-Military Relations*, pp. 336–53; E. Anthérieu, *Le Drame de l'armée de l'armistice* (Paris, 1946); M. Lerecouvreux, *Résurrection de l'armée française. De Weygand à Giraud* (Paris, 1955). On the Riom Trial see H. Michel, *Le Procès de Riom* (Paris, 1979); P. Mazé and R. Génébrier, *Les Grandes Journées du procès de Riom* (Paris, 1945); P. Tissier, *The Riom Trial* (London, 1944); M. Ribet, *Le Procès de Riom* (Paris, 1945). The charges against Gamelin are found in G. Cassagnau, Procureur-Général à la Cour suprême de justice de l'état français, 'Réquisitoire définitif du procès de Riom', 15 Oct. 1941, Fonds Gamelin 1K 224/1, dr. 3 ('Riom'), SHAT.
7. Daladier, *Journal de captivité*, pp. 133, 177.
8. Gamelin's co-defendants at Riom were Daladier, Léon Blum, Pierre Cot (tried *in absentia*), Guy La Chambre, Robert Jacomet. The statement by Gamelin of his intention to remain silent is published in P. Soupiron, *Bazaine contre Gambetta ou le Procès de Riom* (Lyon, 1944), pp. 67–9, 179–88. Cf. P. Le Goyet, *Le Mystère Gamelin* (Paris, 1975), pp. 353–61; Gen. M.-G. Gamelin, *Servir* (Paris, 1946–7, 3 vols.), I, *Les Armées françaises de 1940*, pp. 348–57. For Blum's and Daladier's eloquent self-defence, see *L'Oeuvre de Léon Blum: Mémoires. La Prison et le procès. A l'échelle humaine, 1940–1945* (Paris, 1955); J. Colton, *Léon Blum, Humanist in Politics* (New York, 1966, reprinted 1986), esp. pp. 385–427 (1986 edn); J. Lacouture, *Léon Blum* (Paris, 1977) (trans. G. Holoch, New York, 1987), pp. 430–40; J. Joll, *Intellectuals in Politics. Three biographical essays* (London, 1962), pp. 43–6, 48–52; Michel, *Procès de Riom*, pp. 107–246.
9. A. Werth, *The Last Days of Paris. A journalist's diary* (London, 1940), p. 86; Daladier, *Journal de captivité*, pp. 35, 211. Cf. Le Goyet, *Mystère Gamelin*, pp. 360–1.
10. Daladier, *Journal de captivité*, pp. 114–15.
11. Gamelin, *Servir*, I, p. 223. Cf. de La Gorce, *French Army*, p. 293. Weygand's boast of possessing Foch's prescriptions to ward off disaster in 1940 is affirmed in Gamelin, *Servir*, III, *La Guerre. Septembre 1939 au 19 mai 1940*, p. 435. See also Bankwitz, *Weygand and Civil-Military Relations*, pp. 290–2, where the evidence for and against attribution to Weygand of a calculated promotion of Pétain as putative national saviour after 1935 is analysed, pp. 197–207, 233–7, 245–8, 262–4, 273–7. For indications of Laval's greater importance in this promotion, see G. Warner, *Pierre Laval and the Eclipse of France* (London, 1968), pp. 135–9, 145, 194–212.

12. Quotations from, respectively, A. Léon-Jouhaux, *Prison pour hommes d'état, 1943–1945* (Paris, 1973), p. 47; A. François-Poncet, *Carnets d'un captif, 1943–1945* (Paris, 1946), p. 34. Cf. Daladier, *Journal de captivité*, pp. 49–50, 133, 151–2, 177, 211; Le Goyet, *Mystère Gamelin*, pp. 361–8; Bankwitz, *Weygand and Civil-Military Relations*, pp. 353–5.
13. Cf. François-Poncet, *Carnets*, pp. 40–1.
14. Ibid., pp. 32, 34, 40–1; Léon-Jouhaux, *Prison*, pp. 33, 46–7, 52–3; Daladier, *Journal de captivité*, p. 211. See, however, Gamelin's criticisms during the Battle of France of the morale and preparation of French soldiers as well as civilians in the report he tendered at the request of Daladier on 16 May 1940, but which was received by Reynaud when the latter assumed personal charge of the defence ministry two days later: 'Lettre à M. le Ministre de la Défense nationale et de la Guerre, no. 1011 CAB./F.T., 18 mai 1940', in Gamelin, *Servir*, III, pp. 421–6; also the general's later elaboration of these allegations of poor discipline, lack of patriotism and fighting spirit in *Servir*, I, pp. 354–7. Cf. discussion of the 18 May 1940 report in Bankwitz, *Weygand and Civil-Military Relations*, pp. 157–9; Le Goyet, *Mystère Gamelin*, pp. 332–7; C. Paillat, *Dossiers secrets de la France contemporaine*, V, *Le Désastre de 1940. La Guerre éclair (10 mai au 24 juin 1940)* (Paris, 1985), pp. 358–61; Col. J. Minart, *P. C. Vincennes. Secteur 4* (Paris, 1945, 2 vols.), II, pp. 169–74.
15. See the sympathetic contemporary observation of the incarcerated Gamelin by his fellow detainee and erstwhile superior, Daladier, during the autumn of 1940, in the latter's *Journal de captivité*, pp. 32–5.
16. Reynaud in the diary for 9 Apr. 1940 of the secretary to the French war cabinet, P. Baudouin: *Neuf mois au gouvernement. Avril–décembre 1940* (Paris, 1948), p. 24; Jeanneney's formulation in his diary for 19 Mar. 1940: J.-N. Jeanneney (ed.), *Jules Jeanneney. Journal politique. Septembre 1939–juillet 1942* (Paris, 1972), p. 35. Ironically, however, for Daladier, it was Weygand who was 'a prefect dressed up as a general', who had 'built up the illusions of French patriots' (Daladier, *Journal de captivité*, p. 115, 22 Nov. 1941).
17. See, respectively, 'General Gamelin, or how to lose', in A. J. P. Taylor, *Europe: Grandeur and Decline* (London, 1977), pp. 289–94 (Penguin edn); de La Gorce, *French Army*, p. 293; J.-B. Duroselle, *Politique étrangère de la France. La Décadence, 1932–1939* (Paris, 1979), esp. pp. 13–27, 112–21, 181–209, 355–66.
18. J. C. Cairns, 'Some recent historians and the "strange defeat" of 1940', *JMH*, 46:1 (March 1974), pp. 60–85 (quotation from p. 81).
19. Quotations from Taylor, 'General Gamelin', p. 289. Conversation between Col. P. Le Goyet and the present author, Saint-Maur-des-Fossés, Val-de-Marne, France, 29 July 1982.
20. Besides Bankwitz's study of Weygand and the works on Pétain cited above (n. 5), see J. Weygand, *Weygand, mon père* (Paris, 1970); G. Raïssac, *Un soldat dans la tourmente. Le général Weygand* (Paris, 1963); C. Fouvez, *Le Mystère Weygand. Etude d'un dossier historique du 19e siècle* (Paris, 1967); B. Destremau, *Weygand* (Paris, 1989); H. R. Lottman, *Pétain: Hero or Traitor?* (New York and London, 1984); J. Lacouture, *Charles de*

Gaulle (Paris, 1984–88, 3 vols.; English edn, New York and London, 1990–1, 2 vols.); B. Ledwidge, *De Gaulle* (London, 1983); H. de Wailly, *De Gaulle sous la casque: Abbeville 1940* (Paris, 1990); B. Crozier, *De Gaulle. The Warrior* (London, 1967); P. Huard, *Le colonel de Gaulle et ses blindés. Laon, 15–20 mai 1940* (Paris, 1980).

21. R. J. Young, *In Command of France. French foreign policy and military planning, 1933–1940* (Cambridge, MA, 1978); J. A. Gunsburg, *Divided and Conquered. The French high command and the defeat of the West, 1940* (Westport, CT, 1979).
22. J. Gooch, *Armies in Europe* (London, 1980), p. 215; D. Porch, 'French Intelligence and the Fall of France, 1930–1940', *Intelligence and National Security*, 4:1 (Jan. 1989), pp. 28–58 (quotations from pp. 45, 52).
23. See, however, J. A. Gunsburg, 'Coupable ou non? Le Role du général Gamelin dans la défaite de 1940', *Revue historique des armées*, 4 (1979), pp. 145–63; 'Maurice-Gustave Gamelin, 1872–1958', in P. H. Hutton (ed.), *Historical Dictionary of the Third Republic* (Westport, CT, 1986, 2 vols.), I, pp. 412–13.
24. Cairns, 'Some recent historians', p. 81.
25. See, however, the present author's re-evaluation of Gamelin's actions in the campaign of 1940: 'Maurice Gamelin and the defeat of France, 1939–1940', in B. J. Bond (ed.), *Fallen Stars. Eleven Studies of Twentieth Century Military Disasters* (London and Oxford, 1991), pp. 107–40; for a reappraisal of Gamelin's role in the Allied intervention in Scandinavia during the spring of 1940, see M. S. Alexander, 'The Fall of France, 1940', *Journal of Strategic Studies*, 13:1 (Mar. 1990), pp. 10–44 (also published as J. Gooch (ed.), *Decisive Campaigns of the Second World War*, London, 1990).
26. At the improvised meetings of service chiefs and ministers convened by Edouard Daladier, French prime minister, on 23 Aug. 1939, to consider French responses to the Nazi–Soviet non-aggression pact announced earlier that day. See Gamelin, *Servir*, I, pp. 22–43; Le Goyet, *Mystère Gamelin*, pp. 225–6; Daladier, *Journal de captivité*, p. 88. Cf. criticism of Gamelin's claims for the army's 'readiness' in C. Paillat, *Dossiers secrets*, IV, *La Guerre immobile (avril 1939 au 10 mai 1940)* (Paris, 1984), pp. 100–14, 142–3; Dutailly, *Les Problèmes de l'Armée de Terre*, pp. 287–90; Doise and Vaïsse, *Diplomatie et outil militaire*, pp. 334–7; Duroselle, *La Décadence*, pp. 472–93; *Politique étrangère de la France. L'Abîme, 1939–1945* (Paris, 1982), pp. 19–26.
27. See Le Goyet, *Mystère Gamelin*, pp. 298ff; Taylor, 'General Gamelin', p. 294.
28. An impression that provides the sub-title of the important study by U. Bialer, *The Shadow of the Bomber. The British Government and the fear of bombardment from the air, 1932–1939* (London, 1980). Cf. R. J. Young, 'The use and abuse of fear: France and the air menace in the 1930s', *Intelligence and National Security*, 2:4 (Oct. 1987), pp. 88–109; D. Boussard, *Un problème de défense nationale. L'Aéronautique militaire au parlement (1928–1940)* (Vincennes, 1983).

29. See the measured tone of the obituary of Gamelin in *The Times* (London), 19 Apr. 1958. Cf. Gunsburg, 'Gamelin', in Hutton (ed.), *Historical Dictionary of the Third Republic*, I, pp. 412–13.

1 THE MAKING OF A REPUBLICAN GENERAL

1. The building still stands, two doors west of the junction of the rue de Solférino and the Bd. Saint-Germain, and is today sandwiched between the brasserie Le Solférino and a travel agency. Information on Gamelin's ancestry kindly supplied to the author by M. Pierre Uhrich, Lt. Col. Jacques Uhrich and the late M. Paul Gamelin, great-nephews of the general (correspondence and conversations, Apr., June 1978, Apr. 1983, Jan. 1988). Details of Gamelin's early life in République Française, Ville de Paris: Mairie du 7e arrondissement. Actes de Naissance, No. 1209, 21 Sept. 1872; Gamelin, *Servir*, II, *Le Prologue du drame, 1930–août 1939*, pp. v–xx, 338; Le Goyet, *Mystère Gamelin*, pp. 13–21; Paillat, *Dossiers secrets*, IV/I, *Le Désastre de 1940. La Répétition générale*, hereafter Paillat, *Répétition générale* (Paris, 1983), pp. 177–89; J.-L. Crémieux-Brilhac, *Les Français de l'an 40* (Paris, 1990, 2 vols.), II, *Ouvriers et soldats*, pp. 374–8.
2. See A. Mitchell, 'A situation of inferiority: France's military organisation after the defeat of 1870', *American Historical Review*, 86:1 (Feb. 1981), pp. 49–63; *Victors and Vanquished. The German Influence in France after 1870. Army and church in the Third Republic* (Chapel Hill, NC, 1982); A. Clayton, *France, Soldiers and Africa* (London, Oxford, Washington DC, 1988), pp. 65–92; Porch, *March to the Marne*, pp. 23–53, 136–68; M. Michel, *Galliéni* (Paris, 1990), pp. 40–56, 156–64, 175–246.
3. Quoted in de La Gorce, *French Army*, p. 294.
4. Quoted in Le Goyet, *Mystère Gamelin*, p. 15.
5. Appraisals of Gamelin from his confidential file in République Française, Ministère de la Guerre, 'Etats de service et notes de promotion: Maurice-Gustave Gamelin', SHAT. Cf. Le Goyet, *Mystère Gamelin*, pp. 16–17; Duroselle, *La Décadence*, pp. 25–6, 258–60, 266; *L'Abîme*, pp. 51–6; Pertinax, *Fossoyeurs*, I, pp. 47–51. On the 'colonial tradition' that emerged in part of the officer corps during the Belle Epoque, see Porch, 'Bugeaud, Galliéni, Lyautey', in Paret (ed.), *Makers of Modern Strategy*, pp. 376–407.
6. 'Etats de Service ... Gamelin', SHAT.
7. Ibid.; also Le Goyet, *Mystère Gamelin*, pp. 17–18.
8. Quoted in de La Gorce, *French Army*, p. 293.
9. Quoted in M. Percheron, *Gamelin* (Paris, 1938), p. 15.
10. Cabinet particulier du général Gamelin – Journal de marche, Fonds Gamelin 1K 224/9, SHAT (hereafter cited as Gamelin, Journal de marche), 18 Oct. 1939. More generally on Clemenceau see D. R. Watson, *Georges Clemenceau. A Political Biography* (London, 1974); E. Holt, *The Tiger* (London, 1980); J. Hampden-Jackson, *Clemenceau and the Third Republic* (London, 1946); J.-B. Duroselle, *Clemenceau* (Paris, 1989).
11. On Thomas see J. F. Godfrey, *Capitalism at War. Industrial policy and bureaucracy in France, 1914–1918* (Leamington Spa, 1987). For Tardieu,

see R. Binion, *Defeated Leaders. The political fate of Caillaux, Jouvenel and Tardieu* (New York, 1960); M. Clague, 'Vision and myopia in the "New Politics" of André Tardieu', *FHS*, 8:1 (Spring 1973), pp. 105–29.

12. Citations in 'Etats de Service ... Gamelin', SHAT; also Le Goyet, *Mystère Gamelin*, p. 20.
13. See M.-G. Gamelin, *Manoeuvre et victoire de la Marne* (Paris, 1954); *Servir*, II, pp. xiv–xvi; R.-G. Nobécourt, 'Gamelin et la bataille de la Marne (septembre 1914)', *Bulletin de la Société d'Histoire de Rouen*, 10 Nov. 1973, pp. 181–7; Le Goyet, *Mystère Gamelin*, pp. 22–34; Gen. P. Alexandre, *Avec Joffre d'Agadir à Verdun* (Paris, 1932); Marshal J. C. J. Joffre, *Mémoires du Maréchal Joffre, 1910–1917* (Paris, 1932, 2 vols.), II, pp. 141–50, 386–8, 390–3; P. Varillon, *Joffre* (Paris, 1956), pp. 365–83.
14. 'Etats de Service ... Gamelin', SHAT.
15. See M. M. Farrar, 'Politics versus patriotism: Alexandre Millerand as French minister of war', *FHS*, 11:4 (Fall 1980), pp. 577–609; Lt. Col. C. Bugnet, 'Joffre et M. Millerand', *Revue des deux mondes*, 8:151:32 (15 Apr. 1936), pp. 785–819; Minart, *P. C. Vincennes*, I, p. 69.
16. This account of Gamelin's First World War career is based on a detailed but unpublished study by R.-G. Nobécourt ('Maurice Gamelin, 1914–1918'), for a copy of which the author is indebted to M. Nobécourt. On Joffre's dismissal and its effect on Gamelin see R.-G. Nobécourt, 'La Disgrace du général Joffre en décembre 1916', *Bulletin de la Société d'Histoire de Rouen*, 15 May 1976, pp. 99–114; Le Goyet, *Mystère Gamelin*, pp. 34–8; Gamelin, *Servir*, II, pp. v–vi; Col. E. E. Herbillon, *Le général Alfred Micheler, 1914–1918. D'après ses notes, sa correspondance et les souvenirs personnels de l'auteur* (Paris, 1934).
17. See list of Gamelin's orders and decorations in Fonds Gamelin 1K 224/6, dr. 'Notices biographiques', SHAT. Among important recent work on the French army in the First World War is S. R. Williamson, 'Joffre reshapes French strategy, 1911–1913', in P. M. Kennedy (ed.), *The War Plans of the Great Powers, 1880–1914* (Boston and London, 1979; 2nd edn 1985), pp. 133–54; D. Porch, 'The French army in the First World War', in A. R. Millett and W. Murray (eds.), *Military Effectiveness* (Winchester, MA, and London, 1988), pp. 190–228; D. Englander, 'The French soldier, 1914–18', *French History*, 1:1 (May 1987), pp. 49–67; G. Pedroncini, *Pétain, général-en-chef, 1917–1918* (Paris, 1974).
18. Quotations about Gamelin and Weygand from de La Gorce, *French Army*, p. 293; Gamelin's views on the staff/command relationship in *Servir*, II, p. xiii.
19. Obituary of Weygand, *The Times* (London), 29 Jan. 1965. Cf. more sympathetic assessments in Bankwitz, *Weygand and Civil-Military Relations*, pp. 12–14, 190–2; Destremau, *Weygand*, pp. 92–8, 112–17, 128, 131–3; J. Planchais, 'Il y a vingt ans: la mort de Weygand, soldat conservateur', *Le Monde*, 27–28 Jan. 1985.
20. Quotations from, respectively, British Embassy (Paris), report for 1932 on leading personalities in France, Foreign Office, General Correspondence, FO 371, 16362, W66/66/17, PRO; Le Goyet, *Mystère Gamelin*, p. 44.

21. République Française. Ville de Paris. Mairie du 7e arrondissement: 'Etat civil. Actes de mariage: Gamelin–Marchand', 20 Sept. 1927.
22. See Bankwitz, *Weygand and Civil-Military Relations*, pp. 24–6; Gen. M. Weygand, *Mémoires* (Paris, 1950–7, 3 vols), II, *Mirages et réalité*, pp. 307–9.
23. The late Major-Gen. Sir Guy Salisbury-Jones, letter to the author, 16 Dec. 1977. The foregoing account of French military politics in the Levant during the 1920s is indebted to the unpublished memoirs of Guy Salisbury-Jones, 'My friends the French', which were generously made available to the present author. The primary sources for French military operations against the Druzes are found in Carton 15H 25, drs. 1–3, SHAT. See also Gamelin, *Servir*, II, pp. viii–xi; Destremau, *Weygand*, pp. 159–74; J. K. Tanenbaum, *General Maurice Sarrail, 1856–1929. The French army and left-wing politics* (Chapel Hill, NC, 1974), pp. 188–214, 220–1; Weygand, *Mirages et réalité*, pp. 207–96; Le Goyet, *Mystère Gamelin*, pp. 44–51; Gen. Andréa, *La Révolte Druze et l'insurrection de Damas, 1925–26* (Paris, 1937). Generally, on post-1918 French colonialism, see C. M. Andrew and A. S. Kanya-Forstner, *The Climax of French Imperial Expansion, 1914–1924* (London and Stanford, CA, 1981); Clayton, *France, Soldiers and Africa*, pp. 98–119.
24. Gamelin, Journal de marche, 18 Oct. 1939, 1K 224/9, SHAT. Sarrail's most recent biographer did not have the benefit of access to this diary and presents an overdrawn picture of competition and rivalry between the two generals (Tanenbaum, *Sarrail*, p. 208).
25. See Tanenbaum, *Sarrail*, pp. 51–74, 188–221. Cf. P. Coblentz, *Le Silence de Sarrail* (Paris, 1930), pp. 196–280; J. C. King, *Generals and Politicians. Conflict between France's high command, parliament and government, 1914–1918* (Berkeley, CA, 1951); M. Soulié, *La Vie politique d'Edouard Herriot* (Paris, 1962), pp. 190–1; Bankwitz, *Weygand and Civil-Military Relations*, pp. 24–6.
26. Gamelin, Journal de marche, 18 Oct. 1939, 1K 224/9, SHAT.
27. 'Etats de Service . . . Gamelin', SHAT.
28. See Gamelin, *Servir*, II, pp. xii–xiii; Bankwitz, *Weygand and Civil-Military Relations*, pp. 15–21, 35–9, 76. The epithet 'bureaucrates en képi' was Anatole France's. (See M. Corday, *Dernières pages inédites d'Anatole France*, Paris, 1925, p. 153.)
29. The phrase quoted is Gamelin's (*Servir*, II, p. 34), cf. pp. xxviii–xxxii, 75–6, 156–9; Bankwitz, *Weygand and Civil-Military Relations*, pp. 43–8, 87. France's decision to build the Maginot Line is analysed in J. M. Hughes, *To the Maginot Line. The politics of French military preparation in the 1920s* (Cambridge, MA, 1971); Gen. P.-E. Tournoux, 'Les Origines de la Ligne Maginot', *Revue d'histoire de la Deuxième Guerre Mondiale* (henceforth *RHDGM*), 9:33 (Jan. 1959), pp. 3–14; *Haut commandement, gouvernement et défense des frontières du nord et de l'est, 1919–1939* (Paris, 1960); V. Rowe, *The Great Wall of France. The triumph of the Maginot Line* (London, 1959); A. Kemp, *The Maginot Line. Myth and reality* (London, 1986; New York, 1988); P. Belperron, *Maginot of the Line* (Paris, 1940).

30. MacDonald's phrase may be found in Great Britain, *Statement Relating to Defence*, 11 Mar. 1935 (London, 1935), p. 4; Gamelin's description of the period from 1932 to 1934 occurs in his *Servir*, II, p. 72.
31. Weygand, *Weygand mon père*, pp. 225–33; Destremau, *Weygand*, pp. 230–77; Weygand, *Mirages et réalité*, pp. 381–401 and testimony of 25 July 1947 to the French National Assembly's investigating committee of 1947–51: République Française – *Commission chargée d'enquêter sur les événements survenus en France de 1933 à 1945, Annexes: Dépositions. Témoignages et documents recueillis par la commission d'enquête parlementaire* (Paris, 1951–2; 2 vols of report, 9 vols of testimony), I, pp. 231–45, hereafter *C. E. Témoignages*, with vol. no.). For the demographic origins of the 'lean years' see D. Kirk, 'Population and population trends in modern France' in Earle (ed.), *Modern France*, pp. 313–33; R. Tomlinson, 'The "Disappearance" of France: the politics of *dénatalité* under the Third Republic, 1890–1940', *Historical Journal*, 28:2 (June 1985), pp. 405–15. Knowledge of German military expansion before 1935 is explored in G. Castellan, *Le Réarmement clandestin du Reich, 1930–1935, vu par le 2e Bureau de L'Etat-major français* (Paris, 1954).
32. Gamelin, *Servir*, II, pp. 34, 57, 74, 88, 92.
33. Brig. T. G. G. Heywood (British military attaché, Paris, 1933–6), 'General Gamelin, Chief of the French General Staff of National Defence', *Journal of the Royal United Services' Institute* (Aug. 1938), pp. 607–13, quotations from pp. 611–12 (hereafter *RUSI Journal*).
34. Heywood, Jan. 1934 despatch to London, FO 371, 17652, C1085/85/17, PRO.
35. Gamelin, *Servir*, II, pp. 143–7.
36. Quotations from, respectively, 'Etats de service . . . Gamelin', SHAT; de La Gorce, *French Army*, p. 293. For Taittinger's intervention see CAC, 'Séance du 19 décembre 1934', 15th Leg. (1932–1936), Carton 5 bis, dr. VI, AAN; A. Le Révérend, *Un Lyautey inconnu. Correspondance et journal inédits, 1874–1934* (Paris, 1980), pp. 344–8; Bankwitz, *Weygand and Civil-Military Relations*, pp. 116–17, 174–81; Destremau, *Weygand*, pp. 287–305. Cf. the account of Pétain's sometime *chef de cabinet*, Gen. A. Conquet, *Auprès du Maréchal Pétain. Le Chef. Le Politique. L'Homme* (Paris, 1970), pp. 84–6, 127. The 1935 command reorganisation is analysed in Col. F.-A. Paoli, *L'Armée française de 1919 à 1939* (Vincennes, 1974–7, 4 vols.), IV, *La Fin des illusions, 1930–1935*, pp. 92–4; Gunsburg, *Divided and Conquered*, pp. 25–6; Dutailly, *Les Problèmes de L'Armée de Terre*, pp. 28–39; Duroselle, *La Décadence*, pp. 256–60; Col. R. A. Doughty, *The Seeds of Disaster. The development of French army doctrine, 1919–1939* (Hamden, CT, 1985), pp. 116–28.
37. The aphorism was Foch's, from his *Des principes de la guerre* (Paris, 1903), p. 272 (quoted in Bankwitz, *Weygand and Civil-Military Relations*, p. 294).
38. Quotations, respectively, from Heywood, 'General Gamelin', *RUSI Journal* (Aug. 1938), p. 612; British Embassy (Paris), report for 1932 on leading French personalities, FO 371, 16362, W66/66/17, PRO.
39. Heywood, 'General Gamelin', p. 612. Gamelin's 1935 exchange with Weygand is recounted in J. Weygand, *Weygand mon Père*, p. 239; also

Weygand, *Mirages et réalité*, p. 434. Cf. Bankwitz, *Weygand and Civil-Military Relations*, pp. 118–19; Gamelin, *Servir*, II, pp. 141–7; Le Goyet, *Mystère Gamelin*, pp. 63–4, 68–9, 71. The incident rankled Weygand, to judge from his pointed spurning of Gamelin's offer of assistance at the time of the former's reinstatement as French commander-in-chief on 20 May 1940. See Gamelin, *Servir*, III, pp. 434–8; Le Goyet, *Mystère Gamelin*, pp. 348–50; Gamelin, Journal de marche, 19–20 May 1940; Paillat, *Dossiers secrets*, V, *La Guerre éclair*, pp. 358, 366; Weygand, *Mémoires*, III, *Rappelé au service* (Paris, 1950), pp. 82–3 (English edn, *Recalled to Service*, trans. E. W. Dickes, London, 1952, pp. 48–52).
40. British Embassy (Paris), report for 1932 on leading French personalities, FO 371, 16362, W66/66/17, PRO.
41. F. Sieburg, 'General Gamelin', *Frankfurter Zeitung*, 3 Feb. 1935 (French trans. in Fonds Gamelin 1K 224/7, dr. 'Notices et renseignements biographiques', SHAT). Weygand's bellicosity towards Germany in 1933 and rumoured support for a preventive war in conjunction with Poland was reported not just by Sieburg but also by Col. T. G. G. Heywood, enc. of 25 Oct. 1933 (reporting a conversation with Weygand), in E. L. Woodward, R. Butler and others (eds.), *Documents on British Foreign Policy, 1919–1939* (London, 1946–85, 3 series), ser. 2, vol. V, doc. no. 508, p. 737 (hereafter *DBFP*). Cf. discussion of the episode in Bankwitz, *Weygand and Civil-Military Relations*, pp. 62–9, 77; Z. J. Gasiorowski, 'Did Pilsudski attempt to initiate a preventive war in 1933?', *JMH*, 28 (June 1955), pp. 135–52; H. Roos, 'Die Präventivkriegsplane Pilsudskis von 1933', *Vierteljahrshefte für Zeitgeschichte*, 5 (Oct. 1955), pp. 344–63; P. S. Wandycz, *The Twilight of France's Eastern Alliances, 1926–1936. French-Czechoslovak-Polish relations from Locarno to the remilitarization of the Rhineland* (Princeton, NJ, 1988), pp. 260–73.
42. Challener, 'Gravediggers revisited', p. 103.
43. Kühlenthal to Col. F. G. Beaumont-Nesbitt, British military attaché (Paris), in the latter's despatch of 11 Mar. 1937, FO 371, 20693, C2085/122/17, PRO.
44. Gamelin's prediction may be found in his Journal de marche, 9 Oct. 1939.

2 GAMELIN AND THE REBIRTH OF GERMAN POWER

1. See Bankwitz, *Weygand and Civil-Military Relations*, pp. 41–8, 83–135; Destremau, *Weygand*, pp. 208–12, 218–29, 254–63; Doughty, *Seeds of Disaster*, pp. 120–2, 129–32, 143–9; 'The French armed forces, 1918–40', in Millett and Murray (eds.), *Military Effectiveness*, II, pp. 39–69; J. J. Clarke, *Military Technology in Republican France. The evolution of the French armored force, 1917–1940*, Ph.D. dissertation, Duke University, 1969 (refs. to University Microforms International edn, Ann Arbor, MI, 1973), pp. 108–27.
2. 'Position générale de l'Armée française: memento des points de vue exposés par le général Gamelin au cours des conversations intérieures, en délégation', Jan. 1934, p. 2, Fonds Gamelin 1K 224/8, dr. 'Réunions du CSG, 1932–38', SHAT; also Gamelin, *Servir*, II, pp. 133–4.

3. See record of a conversation between Gamelin and Col. T. G. G. Heywood, British military attaché, Paris, 17 Jan. 1935, FO 371, 18823, C557/55/18, PRO. Cf. Gamelin, *Servir*, II, pp. 152–5. According to one recent study, 'Colson lived, without any apparent difficulties, in the shadow of the chief of general staff. He [Colson] is little-known. He has left neither papers nor testimony to show us how he would have wished to be seen ... He was, however, more than a mere intermediary between Gamelin and the EMA ... he knew how to dispose gently of projects and reports which displeased him. ... an enthusiast of fortifications, he had little interest in the offensive; a conservative by conviction ... he curbed [the staff's] imagination and spirit of initiative.' (Dutailly, *Problèmes de l'Armée de Terre*, p. 35.)
4. 'Communication du gouvernement français au gouvernement britannique: memorandum', 17 Apr. 1934, *Documents Diplomatiques Français, 1932–1939* (Paris, 1963 et seq.), 1st ser. (1932–5), vol. VI, doc. no. 104, hereafter *DDF*. Military influences on the preparation of this note are discussed in Bankwitz, *Weygand and Civil-Military Relations*, pp. 63–75; diplomatic context in Duroselle, *La Décadence*, pp. 89–112; M. Vaïsse, *Sécurité d'abord. La Politique française en matière de désarmement, 9 décembre 1930 au 17 avril 1934* (Paris, 1981), pp. 583–94. Gamelin's view of his mission is found in *Servir*, II, p. 190.
5. See G. Castellan, 'Le Réarmement clandestin de l'Allemagne dans l'entre-deux-guerres', in *Les Relations franco-allemandes de 1933 à 1939: Travaux du colloque d'historiens français et allemands* (Paris, 1976), pp. 277–96. Cf. Gen. M. Gauché, *Le Deuxième Bureau au travail, 1935–1940* (Paris, 1953), pp. 38–41, 110–27.
6. Manoeuvres at divisional level and higher were cancelled as an economy measure in 1932 and 1933. See Doughty, 'The French armed forces', pp. 42–4, 49, 53–5, 59–64; CAC, 'Séance du 6 juin 1934: audience du Maréchal Pétain, ministre de la guerre, sur les armements allemands', procès-verbal, pp. 2–8 and 'Séance du 3 juillet 1934: audience du Maréchal Pétain, ministre de la guerre, relative à l'aménagement des effectifs', procès-verbal, pp. 4–8, both in 15th Leg. (1932–6), Carton XV/739/48 bis, AAN. Cf. Bankwitz, *Weygand and Civil-Military Relations*, pp. 113–15, 152–3; B. A. Lee, 'Strategy, arms and the collapse of France, 1930–40', in R. T. B. Langhorne (ed.), *Diplomacy and Intelligence during the Second World War. Essays in honour of F. H. Hinsley* (Cambridge, 1985), pp. 43–67.
7. See Gen. A. Laffargue, *Fantassin de Gascogne. De mon jardin à la Marne et au Danube* (Paris, 1962), pp. 184–6; 'Contre l'attaque brusquée', *RDM*, 8:24 (15 Dec. 1934), pp. 742–64; H. Lémery, *D'une république à l'autre. Souvenirs de la mêlée politique, 1894–1944* (Paris, 1964), pp. 165–6; CAC, 'Séance du 7 novembre 1934: communication de M. le président [Jean Fabry]', pp. 4–5; 'Séance du 28 novembre 1934: communication de M. le président sur l'organisation et l'emploi des divisions de réserve', pp. 10–12; 'Séance du 4 décembre 1934: audience de M. le général Maurin, ministre de la guerre', pp. 18–23; 'Séance du 5 décembre 1934: audience de M. le général Maurin ... (suite)', pp. 8–10, 15th Leg., Carton XV/739/48 bis, AAN.

8. See C. de Gaulle, *Lettres, notes et carnets*, II, *1919–juin 1940* (Paris, 1980), pp. 367–452; *Mémoires de guerre*, I, *L'Appel: 1940–1942* (Paris, 1954), Livre de Poche edn, pp. 8–30; J. Lacouture, *Charles de Gaulle* (Paris, 1984–8, 3 vols.), I, *Le Rebelle, 1890–1944*, pp. 226–40; J.-N. Jeanneney, 'De Gaulle avant de Gaulle', *Le Point*, no. 424, 3 Nov. 1980, pp. 64–9.
9. It eventually appeared in the *Revue Hebdomadaire*, 1 June 1935 and was reprinted in C. de Gaulle, *Trois études* (Paris, 1945; Livre de Poche edn, 1973), pp. 165–88.
10. Colson, letter to de Gaulle, 17 Dec. 1934, Archives Reynaud, Carton 74 AP/12, AN. See also reports by Sir G. Clerk (British ambassador, Paris), 18–19 Dec. 1934, on the Senate debate and Flandin's subsequent statement in the Chamber, FO 371, 17654, C8696/85/17 and C8717/85/17, PRO. Cf. Bankwitz, *Weygand and Civil-Military Relations*, pp. 111–13.
11. Lacouture, *De Gaulle*, I, pp. 241–5. Cf. A. Sauvy, *De Paul Reynaud à Charles de Gaulle. Scènes, tableaux et souvenirs* (Paris, 1972), p. 13.
12. A full appraisal of Reynaud awaits the forthcoming biography by Dr Julian Jackson, of University College Swansea. Details of his early contacts with de Gaulle are found in the latter's letters of 17 Dec. 1934, 14 Jan., 14 Mar. 1935, in de Gaulle, *Lettres, notes et carnets*, II, pp. 376–81.
13. See R. A. Doughty, 'De Gaulle's concept of a mobile, professional army. Genesis of French defeat?', in L. J. Matthews and D. E. Brown (eds.), *The Parameters of War* (London and McLean, VA, 1987), pp. 243–56; B. J. Bond and M. S. Alexander, 'Liddell Hart and de Gaulle: prophets of limited liability and mobile defense', in Paret (ed.), *Makers of Modern Strategy*, pp. 598–623; Bankwitz, *Weygand and Civil-Military Relations*, pp. 124–66; Duroselle, *La Décadence*, pp. 263–6; Destremau, *Weygand*, pp. 137–8, 278–86.
14. C. de Gaulle, *Le Fil de l'épée* (Paris, 1932), Livre de Poche edn, 1973, pp. 7–12, 57–66, 82–98, 120–35; *Vers l'armée de métier* (Paris, 1934), Livre de Poche edn, 1972, pp. 11–15, 31–3, 46–51, 65–6, 87–92, 116–18.
15. See Gamelin, letter to Reynaud, 1 June 1937 in P. Reynaud, *La France a sauvé l'Europe* (Paris, 1947, 2 vols.), I, pp. 427–8; EMA (Cabinet) [Gen. Colson], 'Note pour le Cabinet militaire du ministre: réponses aux questions posées . . . au sujet du corps spécialisé . . .', 11 July 1936, in Gamelin, *Servir*, III, pp. 516–27.
16. Bankwitz, *Weygand and Civil-Military Relations*, pp. 125–43 (esp. bibliographical refs. in fns. 30, 34, 85, 86, 87 therein). Cf. Doughty, *Seeds of Disaster*, pp. 138–9, 141, 149–50, 159, 161, 174; Doise and Vaïsse, *Diplomatie et outil militaire*, pp. 301–2; Clarke, *Military Technology*, pp. 18–31, 47–79.
17. Gamelin, testimony, 2 Dec. 1947, *C. E. Témoignages*, II, p. 385.
18. Ibid., p. 384. Cf. Gamelin, *Servir*, III, p. 515; EMA, 'Etude sommaire sur la constitution d'un corps spécialisé', (n.d.), Archives Reynaud, Carton 74 AP/12, AN. Gen. A. Conquet, *L'Enigme des blindés, 1932–1940* (Paris, 1956), pp. 153–6, discusses contradictions between de Gaulle's offensively structured corps and the defensive cast of inter-war French grand strategy. Gamelin's response to de Gaulle is skilfully defended in Challener, 'The military defeat of 1940', pp. 414–18.

19. Gamelin, testimony, 2 Dec. 1947, *C. E. Témoignages*, II, p. 385.
20. De Gaulle, *Vers l'armée de métier* (Livre de Poche, 1972), pp. 25–33, 40–51. See also Bankwitz, *Weygand and Civil-Military Relations*, pp. 121–5, 129–32. On French *guerre de coalition* planning see R. J. Young, 'Preparations for defeat: French war doctrine in the interwar period', *Journal of European Studies*, 2 (1972), pp. 155–72 (esp. pp. 156–64); 'La Guerre de longue durée: some reflections on French strategy and diplomacy in the 1930s', in A. Preston (ed.), *General Staffs and Diplomacy before the Second World War* (London and Totowa, NJ, 1978), pp. 41–64.
21. Cf. Altmayer's successful opposition to Gamelin's attempt to expand from one to three DLMs at the 29 Apr. 1936 CSG (CSG Carton 1N 22, vol. 17, procès-verbal pp. 84–6, SHAT); Dufieux's campaign to retain infantry control of heavy armour, in Gamelin, *Servir*, II, pp. 82–3. See also Clarke, *Military Technology*, pp. 115–16, 132–5; Doughty, *Seeds of Disaster*, pp. 124–5, 153–6.
22. French armour's training difficulties are thoroughly documented in Clarke, *Military Technology*, pp. 66–72, 92–3, 101–2, 132–7, 139–40.
23. See letter to Reynaud, 14 Jan. 1935, in de Gaulle, *Lettres, notes et carnets*, II, pp. 379–80.
24. Art. 40 permitted the government, in exceptional circumstances, to keep conscripts with their units beyond their discharge date. On its application amid great controversy in 1935 see Marshal H.-P. Pétain, 'La Sécurité de la France au cours des années creuses', *RDM*, 8:26 (1 Mar. 1935), pp. i–xx; Sir G. Clerk (British ambassador, Paris), to Sir J. Simon (foreign secretary), 4 Mar. 1935, FO 371, 18800 C1751/227/17, PRO; Gamelin, *Servir*, II, pp. 152–60; Paoli, *L'Armée française de 1919 à 1939*, III, *Le Temps des compromis, 1924–30*, pp. 51–92 (with texts of the 1927–8 Laws on Army Organisation, Recruitment and Cadres); Bankwitz, *Weygand and Civil-Military Relations*, pp. 113–15; Dutailly, *Problèmes de l'Armée de Terre*, pp. 207–15; Doughty, *Seeds of Disaster*, pp. 20–4.
25. *Journal Officiel de la République Française: Chambre des Députés: Débats* (hereafter *JOC Débats*), 16 Mar. 1935, p. 1042. Cf. Flandin's attempt in this debate to direct attention to France's wider security problem (pp. 1021–2). For the command's achievements see Gamelin, *Servir*, II, pp. 41–3, 81–3; Gamelin, testimony, 2 Dec. 1947, *C. E. Témoignages*, II, pp. 383–4; Weygand, testimony, 25 July 1947, ibid., I, p. 241; Gunsburg, *Divided and Conquered*, pp. 15–17, 26–7.
26. [Colson] 'Note pour le Cabinet militaire du ministre . . .', 11 July 1936, in Gamelin, *Servir*, III, p. 522. Cf. Dutailly, *Problèmes de L'Armée de Terre*, pp. 214–17; Doughty, *Seeds of Disaster*, pp. 38–9.
27. Amendement par M. Paul Reynaud, député, au Projet de Loi portant modification à la Loi du 31 mars 1928 sur le recrutement de l'armée (Paris, 28 Mar. 1935), p. 2. Cf. Lacouture, *De Gaulle*, I, pp. 247–51; Doughty, *Seeds of Disaster*, pp. 28–32.
28. Amendement par M. Paul Reynaud, 28 Mar. 1935, p. 5.
29. Gamelin, testimony, 2 Dec. 1947, *C. E. Témoignages*, II, p. 385; Gauché, *Le Deuxième Bureau*, pp. 123–32, 236–7.

30. Gamelin, testimony, 2 Dec. 1947, *C. E. Témoignages*, II, pp. 371–2, 385; *Servir*, II, pp. 153, 186, 217.
31. See de Gaulle, letters to Reynaud, 8 May 1935, 25 Mar., 1 July 1936, in E. Demey, *Paul Reynaud, mon père* (Paris, 1980), pp. 292–3, 300, 302; also Gunsburg, *Divided and Conquered*, pp. 39–40; Dutailly, *Problèmes de L'Armée de Terre*, pp. 222–6. Weygand, too, asserted that the barrier of a recruitment 'ceiling' prevented formation of an all-professional tank corps. See Weygand, testimony, 25 July 1947, *C. E. Témoignages*, I, pp. 241–2; *En Lisant les mémoires de guerre du Général de Gaulle* (Paris, 1955), p. 13. Also upholding this *credo* was Gen. Marie-Eugène Debeney (chief of general staff, 1923–30), in his 'Encore l'armée de métier', *RDM*, 8:28 (15 July 1935), pp. 279–95.
32. *JOC Débats*, 16 Mar. 1935, pp. 1022–7. Cf. Joll, *Intellectuals in Politics*, pp. 43–4; noteworthy, however, is the interest of the Radical Senator C. Chautemps (prime minister, Nov. 1933–Jan. 1934 and June 1937–Mar. 1938), in de Gaulle's professional corps for internal police duties (disclosed in de Gaulle, letter to Reynaud, 23 Sept. 1936, in Demey, *Reynaud, mon père*, p. 305).
33. CAC, 'Séance du 5 juin 1935', procès-verbal, p. 4, 15th Leg., Carton XV/739/48 bis, AAN.
34. Ibid., 'Séance du 6 juin 1935: rapport de M. Jean Sénac sur le Projet de Loi No. 4996 portant modification à la Loi du 28 mars 1928 sur le recrutement de l'Armée', procès-verbal, pp. 2–3; *Rapport No. 5410, fait au nom de la Commission de l'Armée chargée d'examiner le Projet de Loi sur le recrutement de l'Armée* (Paris, 7 June 1935), esp. pp. 15–24.
35. CSG, 'Séance du 15 janvier 1935: exposé fait par M. le général Weygand à propos de certaines considérations relatives à l'état présent et futur de l'armée française', procès-verbal, pp. 60–7, Carton CSG 1N 22, vol. XVII, SHAT. Cf. Weygand, *Mirages et réalité*, pp. 431–3; Destremau, *Weygand*, pp. 290–1; Bankwitz, *Weygand and Civil-Military Relations*, pp. 83–98, 108–14, 145–6, 157–8; Dutailly, *Problèmes de L'Armée de Terre*, pp. 295–7 (Annexe 1: 'Conseil Supérieur de la Guerre, le général Weygand, vice-président, à M. le ministre de la guerre, no. 151/S', 11 Jan. 1935).
36. Figures on French army strengths from War Office (MI3), memorandum, 'The French army during the "années creuses"', 14 Mar. 1935, FO 371, 18800, C2193/227/17, PRO. Cf. Clerk (Paris) to Simon (Foreign Office), 4 Mar. 1935 in C1751/227/17; Pétain, 'La Sécurité de la France', *RDM*, 8:105:26 (1 Mar. 1935), pp. i–xx; Dutailly, *Problèmes de L'Armée de Terre*, pp. 222–3.
37. Dutailly, *Problèmes de L'Armée de Terre*, pp. 298–302 (Annexe 2: EMA, 'Etude faite par le 3e Bureau pour fournir des éléments de réponse aux lettres nos. 50–51–52 a/s du général Parisot, attaché militaire à Rome, en date du 28 mars 1935' (original ref. Carton 7N 3449/1, SHAT)); Col. T. G. G. Heywood (British military attaché, Paris), despatch dated 22 Oct. 1935, Section H, FO 371, 18800, C7342/227/17, PRO.
38. See Bond and Alexander, 'Liddell Hart and de Gaulle', pp. 614–20. Cf. Lee, 'Strategy, arms and the collapse of France', pp. 56–8, 60–5; Doughty,

'French armed forces', in Millett and Murray, *Military Effectiveness*, II, pp. 42–5, 49, 52–3.
39. 'Note sur la situation relative des forces allemandes et françaises et sur les conséquences à en tirer aux points de vue national et international' (n.d.), HCM Carton 2N 19, SHAT. For the EMA's manipulation of fears about Germany see Young, 'The use and abuse of fear', pp. 88–109.
40. HCM, 22 Mar. 1935, procès-verbal, Carton 2N 19, SHAT.
41. Ibid.; see also D. C. Watt, 'The secret Laval–Mussolini agreement of 1935 on Ethiopia', *The Middle East Journal*, 15 (Winter 1961), pp. 69–78.
42. The texts of the 27 June 1935 Gamelin–Badoglio accord and Denain's agreement with Gen. Valle (Italian under-secretary for air) appear in L. Noël, *Les Illusions de Stresa. L'Italie abandonnée à Hitler* (Paris, 1975), pp. 183–7, 201–3. See also Gamelin, *Servir*, II, p. 161; J. Fabry, *De la Place de la Concorde au Cours de l'Intendance* (Paris, 1942), pp. 66–70. The accords are analysed critically in Duroselle, *La Décadence*, pp. 130–9.
43. See R. J. Young, 'Soldiers and diplomats: the French embassy and Franco-Italian relations, 1935–6', *JSS*, 7:1 (Mar. 1984), pp. 74–91; 'French military intelligence and the Franco-Italian alliance, 1933–1939', *HJ*, 28:1 (1985), pp. 143–68; *In Command of France*, pp. 81–5, 88–92. Cf. E. M. Robertson, *Mussolini as Empire-Builder* (London, 1977), pp. 114–16, 130–1; 'Hitler and sanctions: Mussolini and the Rhineland', *European Studies Review*, 7 (1977), pp. 409–35.
44. Col. A. Thorne (Berlin), despatch, 19 Mar. 1935, FO 371, 18831, C2348/55/18, PRO.
45. War Office (MI3), memorandum, 20 Mar. 1935, p. 3, FO 371, 18831, C2295/55/18; FO memorandum, 26 Mar. 1935, section III, FO 371, 18832, C2539/55/18, PRO.
46. HCM, 23 Jan. 1935, procès-verbal, pp. 2–3, Carton 2N 19, SHAT. Cf. 'Rapport politique de l'année 1934 sur la Grande-Bretagne', 11 Dec. 1934, p. 87; Voruz to war ministry (Paris), 25 Apr. 1935, EMA/2, Grande-Bretagne, Carton 7N 2804, SHAT.
47. See Macgregor Knox, *Mussolini Unleashed, 1939–1941* (Cambridge, 1982), pp. 6–7, 14–30; Robertson, *Mussolini as Empire-Builder*, pp. 54–5, 161, 177–9; D. Mack Smith, *Mussolini's Roman Empire* (London, 1976), pp. 54–5 and esp. 169–82.
48. Col. T. G. G. Heywood, despatch, 9 Apr. 1935, reporting conversation with Maurin, FO 371, 18800, C3080/227/17, PRO.
49. Cf. Gauché, *Deuxième Bureau*, pp. 31–6, 40–51, 124–32.
50. See Paillat, *Répétition Générale*, pp. 36–45 ('Le travail de premier plan des services secrets français.')
51. Cf. Porch, 'French intelligence and the fall of France', pp. 28–58; A. P. Adamthwaite, 'French military intelligence and the coming of war, 1935–1939', in C. M. Andrew and J. Noakes (eds.), *Intelligence and International Relations, 1900–1945* (Exeter, 1987), pp. 191–208.
52. See Gamelin, *Servir*, II, p. 316; III, pp. 291–2. Cf. testimony of Gen. Paul de Villelume to the postwar parliamentary inquiry, *C. E. Témoignages*, IX, pp. 2765–99; 'Liaisons . . . auprès du ministère des affaires étrangères

(mars 1938–mai 1939)', Carton 7N 2525, SHAT. See also Duroselle, *La Décadence*, pp. 288–9; Gauché, *Deuxième Bureau*, p. 106.
53. See Schweisguth, 'Mementos', 8, 16 Nov. 1935, 9 Mar. 1936, 8 Feb. 1937, Papiers Schweisguth 351 AP Carton 2, dr. 6; Carton 3, dr. 8; Carton 3, dr. 11, AN.
54. See R. J. Young, 'French military intelligence and Nazi Germany, 1938–1939', in E. R. May (ed.), *Knowing One's Enemies: Intelligence Assessment before the Two World Wars* (Princeton, NJ, 1984), pp. 271–309; cf. A. Bérard, *Un Ambassadeur se souvient*, I, *Au temps du danger allemand* (Paris, 1976), pp. 94–9, 153–5.
55. Gamelin, *Servir*, II, p. 276.
56. See Duroselle, *La Décadence*, pp. 281–7.
57. Cf. testimony of Villelume, *C. E. Témoignages*, IX, pp. 2765–99; 'Mementos', Schweisguth, 27 Feb. 1936, 9–10 Mar. 1936, 8 Feb., 26 May 1937, Papiers Schweisguth, 351 AP Carton 3, drs. 7, 8, 11, 12, AN.
58. Minart, *P. C. Vincennes*, II, p. 27.
59. Gamelin, Journal de marche, 18 Sept. 1939.
60. Ibid., 21 Sept. 1939.
61. Vansittart, minute, 15 Apr. 1935 on Heywood despatch of 9 Apr. 1935, FO 371, 18800, C3080/227/17, PRO.
62. Baron de Gaiffier, ambassadeur de Belgique en France, à M. Paul Hymans (ministre des affaires étrangères, Bruxelles), 8 Feb. 1935, Carton 11.185 (2–3), sdr. 'Belgique: défense nationale, 1935', AMBAE.
63. 'Memento', Schweisguth, 19 Mar. 1935, Papiers Schweisguth, 351 AP Carton 2, dr. 3, AN.
64. Koeltz quoted in Col. T. G. G. Heywood, despatch, 22 Mar. 1935, FO 371, 18832, C2543/55/18, PRO.
65. Note prepared by the French foreign ministry, p. 4, FO 371, 18832, C2483/55/18, PRO. Cf. N. Rostow, *Anglo-French Relations, 1934–1936* (London, 1983), pp. 233–237; J. T. Emmerson, *The Rhineland Crisis, 7 March 1936. A study in multilateral diplomacy* (London, 1977), pp. 39–41, 63–4.
66. Foreign Office memorandum, 9 July 1935, FO 371, 18848, C5454/55/18, PRO.
67. Gauché, *Deuxième Bureau*, pp. 126–9.
68. Col. T. G. G. Heywood, report on a conversation with Gen. Georges, 8 May 1935, FO 371, 18840, C3907/55/18, PRO.
69. See Gauché, *Deuxième Bureau*, pp. 32–5, 54–5; 'Mementos', 12 Sept. 1935, 17 Sept. 1935, Papiers Schweisguth, 351 AP, Carton 2, dr. 5, AN.
70. See the sources cited at n. 43 above.
71. Description of Fabry from British Embassy (Paris), report for 1932 on leading personalities in France, FO 371, 16362, W66/66/17, PRO. An important source is the *journal de marche* of the war ministry during Fabry's tenure from June 1935 to Jan. 1936. This 185 page diary was maintained daily by Controller-General Lachenaud of Fabry's *cabinet ministériel*. Originally part of the Fonds Fabry (series 1K 93, SHAT), it is now held in Carton 5N 581 (Cabinet du ministre de la guerre), dr. 2, SHAT. On Fabry's political milieu see D. G. Wileman, 'P.-E. Flandin and the Alliance Démocratique, 1929–1939', *French History*, 4:2 (June 1990),

pp. 139–73; R. Sanson, 'La Perception de la puissance par l'Alliance Démocratique', *Revue d'Histoire Moderne*, 31 (1984), pp. 327–39. A more far-reaching exploration is likely in Julian Jackson's forthcoming study of Reynaud.
72. See talk between Schweisguth and Debeney recorded in the former's diary: 'Memento', 25 Mar. 1935, Papiers Schweisguth, 351 AP, Carton 2, dr. 3, AN.
73. See W. I. Shorrock, *From Ally to Enemy. The Enigma of Fascist Italy in French Diplomacy, 1920–1940* (Kent, OH, 1988); Young, 'French military intelligence and the Franco-Italian Alliance', pp. 158–61.
74. F.-M. Sir A. A. Montgomery-Massingberd to Viscount Halifax (secretary of state for war), 'Report on ... the French Army', 17 Aug. 1935, pp. 2–3, Montgomery-Massingberd Papers 158/5, LHCMA.
75. Ibid.; cf. Gamelin, *Servir*, II, p. 172.
76. 'Memento', 25 May 1935, Papiers Schweisguth, 351 AP, Carton 2, dr. 4, AN.
77. 'Report on ... the French Army', 17 Aug. 1935, p. 7, Montgomery-Massingberd Papers 158/5, LHCMA.
78. Ibid., pp. 2–3.
79. Gamelin, *Servir*, II, pp. 174–5. Cf. 'mementos', 6, 8, 9, 15, 16, 19 Nov. 1935, Papiers Schweisguth, 351 AP, Carton 2, dr. 6, AN.; Gamelin, Riom deposition, 'La Politique étrangère de la France, 1930–9, au point de vue militaire', pp. 6–8, Papiers Blum, 3BL3, dr. 1, FNSP.
80. 'Mementos', 6, 8, 9, 15 Nov. 1935, Papiers Schweisguth, 351 AP, Carton 2, dr. 6, AN. Cf. P. Masson, 'La Marine française et la crise de mars 1936', in *La France et L'Allemagne, 1932–1936* (Paris, 1980), pp. 333–72.
81. 'Memento', 15 Nov. 1935, Papiers Schweisguth, 351 AP, Carton 2, dr. 6, AN. Cf. Le Goyet, *Mystère Gamelin*, pp. 104–9; Duroselle, *La Décadence*, pp. 145–52; R. A. C. Parker, 'Great Britain, France and the Ethiopian crisis, 1935–1936', *English Historical Review*, 89:351 (Apr. 1974), pp. 293–332 (esp. pp. 302, 308–10, 315, 319–20).
82. Papiers Schweisguth, 'Rapport', 19 Nov. 1935; 'memento', 9 Dec. 1935, 351 AP, Carton 2, dr. 6, AN.
83. See P. Masson, 'La Marine française et la crise de mars 1936', in *La France et L'Allemagne, 1932–1936. Travaux d'un colloque d'historiens français et allemands* (Paris, 1980), pp. 333–72; Baron Aloisi, *Journal, 25 juillet 1932–14 juin 1936*, trans. from Italian by M. Vaussard (Paris, 1957), p. 317 (entry for 26 Oct. 1935). Cf. Young, 'Soldiers and diplomats', pp. 82–4, 85–6; W. I. Shorrock, 'Pierre Laval: diplomacy of realism or decadence?', unpub. paper read to the XIVth annual meeting of the Western Society for French History, 19–22 Nov. 1986, Baltimore MD, esp. pp. 8–10.
84. Papiers Schweisguth, 'Rapport', 19 Nov. 1935, 351 AP Carton 2, dr. 6, AN. Cf. Gamelin, *Servir*, II, pp. 173–5.
85. Gen. Sir Ronald F. Adam, letters to the author, 26 Nov. 1977, 15 Mar. 1979.
86. 'Report on ... the French Army', 17 Aug. 1935, p. 4, Montgomery-Massingberd Papers, 158/5, LHCMA.
87. Papiers Schweisguth, 'memento', 12 Dec. 1935, 351 AP, Carton 2, dr. 6, AN.

88. Quotations from, respectively, ibid., 12, 11 Dec. 1935. The official record of the Anglo-French army and air staff talks from the British side is found in *DBFP*, 2nd ser., vol. XV, appendix II ('Anglo-French Staff Discussions, December 9–10 1935: Report by Colonel T. G. G. Heywood . . . 18 December 1935'; 'Précis of a report by Air Vice-Marshal P. B. Joubert de La Ferté, on the air . . . conversations', 10 Jan. 1936). On the naval talks, 29 Oct.–9 Nov. 1935, see *DBFP*, 2nd ser. vol. XV, docs. nos. 148, 330, 338; also P. Masson, 'Les Conversations militaires franco-britanniques, 1935–8', in *Les Relations Franco-Britanniques de 1935 à 1939* (Paris, 1975), pp. 120–3. Cf. P. B. Joubert de la Ferté, *The Fated Sky* (London, 1952), p. 122; Fabry, *De la Place de la Concorde*, pp. 72–3; Viscount Templewood [Sir Samuel Hoare], *Nine Troubled Years* (London, 1954), pp. 173–82.
89. Gamelin, 'Réflexions d'une mauvaise nuit au sortir d'un haut comité militaire – déclaration grave de M. Laval, nuit du 21 au 22 novembre 1935', Fonds Gamelin, 1K 224/7, SHAT. Cf. Le Goyet, *Mystère Gamelin*, pp. 109–13, for an accurate published version of the document. Gamelin, *Servir*, II, pp. 178–81, provides a rather clumsily retouched version. Conquet, *Auprès du Maréchal Pétain*, pp. 216–20, purports to offer a second eye-witness account of the meeting and, from a Pétainist standpoint, criticises the accuracy of Gamelin's record. There is no surviving *procès-verbal* in the relevant HCM archive, Carton 2N 19, SHAT. Laval's démarches through François-Poncet and de Brinon may be followed in *Documents on German Foreign Policy, 1918–1945* (*DGFP*), ser. C, vol. IV (London, 1962), docs. nos. 373, 384, 404, 412, 415, 416, 419, 421, 423, 425, 435, 440, 467; A. François-Poncet, *Souvenirs d'une Ambassade à Berlin, septembre 1931–octobre 1938* (Paris, 1946), pp. 247–8; Bérard, *Un Ambassadeur se souvient*, I, pp. 285–6; E. Herriot, *Jadis*, II (Paris, 1952), pp. 613–14; F. Kupferman, *Laval* (Paris, 1976), pp. 51–2.

3 FIRST RESPONSES – DEFENCE VERSUS DETENTE IN THE LAVAL ERA

1. See G. Warner, *Pierre Laval*, pp. 85–91; Kupferman, *Laval*, pp. 45–8; military comment on the new ministry in Papiers Schweisguth, 'memento', 28 May 1935, 351 AP, Carton 2, dr. 4, AN.
2. Papiers Schweisguth, 'mementos', 16 Mar., 19 Apr., 22 May 1935, 351 AP, Carton 2, drs. 3 and 4, AN; cf. 'Note du 25 octobre 1934 justifiant le Projet de Loi ouvrant un compte spécial de 800 million francs au titre "Installation et Matériel d'armement"', Carton 5N 581, Cabinet du ministre de la guerre, 'Dossier du général Conquet', SHAT.
3. Papiers Schweisguth, 'mementos', 25, 27 May 1935, 351 AP, Carton 2, dr. 4, AN.
4. See above, ch. 2, n. 71.
5. Fabry, Journal, 12–13 June 1935. Cf. Papiers Schweisguth, 'mementos', 28 May, 8 June 1935, 351 AP, Carton 2, dr. 4, AN; Herriot, *Jadis*, II, pp. 558–9.

6. See R. Frankenstein, 'A propos des aspects financiers du réarmement français, 1935–39', *RHDGM*, 26:102 (Apr. 1976), pp. 4–7. Cf. Kupferman, *Laval*, pp. 53–4.
7. A disjunction identified at this time by de Gaulle: see his letters to Reynaud, 24 May and 27 Dec. 1935, 22 July and 9 Oct. 1936, 23 Apr. 1937, in Demey, *Reynaud mon père*, pp. 295, 298–9, 303, 306–7, 311.
8. See R. Frankenstein, 'Réarmement français, finances publiques et conjoncture internationale, 1935–39', *Bulletin de la Société d'Histoire Moderne*, 28:1 (Jan.–Mar. 1981), pp. 7–13 (esp. p. 8, table 2).
9. CAC, minutes, 'Séance du 18 mars 1936, présidence de M. Jean Sénac: audience de M. le général Maurin, ministre de la guerre, sur la situation nouvelle résultant de la rémilitarisation de la zone rhénane', p. 26, 15th Leg., Carton 5 bis, dr. IX, AAN.
10. Frankenstein, 'Réarmement français', pp. 9–10; cf. 'Aspects financiers du réarmement', p. 6.
11. Papiers Schweisguth, 'memento', 24 June 1935, 351 AP, Carton 2, dr. 4, AN. Cf. Fabry, Journal, 15 June 1935, 17–18 June 1935.
12. Fabry, Journal, 27 June 1935. Fabry's argument to the army and finance commissions in ibid., 25–26 June 1935. Total war ministry rearmament spending for 1935–7 was set at 2,629 million francs: see Fabry, Journal, 21 June 1935; CAC, 'Séance du 25 juin 1935: audience de M. Jean Fabry, ministre de la guerre, sur le Projet de Loi no. 5484 tendant à autoriser des dépenses pour les besoins exceptionnels du département de la guerre', pp. 3–12, 15th Leg., Carton 5 bis, dr. IX, AAN.
13. Fabry, Journal, 28 June 1935. Cf. Papiers Schweisguth, 'memento', 28 June 1935, 351 AP, Carton 2, dr. 4, AN.
14. Fabry, Journal, 2 July 1935; Gamelin, *Servir*, II, pp. 167–71. Cf. Duroselle, *La Décadence*, pp. 138–9.
15. Fabry, Journal, 9 July 1935, cf. 5 July 1935; Herriot, *Jadis*, II, p. 566.
16. Fabry, Journal, 24 July 1935, 8 Aug. 1935. Cf. Herriot, *Jadis*, II, pp. 567–71, 574.
17. Fabry, Journal, 5 Aug. 1935.
18. See Bankwitz, *Weygand and Civil-Military Relations*, pp. 148–67; the description of Pétain's tenure of the war ministry in 1934 as a 'truce' in Gen. E. Requin, *D'une guerre à l'autre, 1919 à 1939* (Paris, 1949), p. 182.
19. See P. Fridenson, *Histoire des Usines Renault*, I, *Naissance de la Grande Entreprise, 1898–1939* (Paris, 1972), pp. 235–55.
20. Frankenstein, 'Aspects financiers du réarmement', p. 18.
21. See Gamelin, *Servir*, I, pp. 112–13; also letters, Daladier to Gamelin, no. 80/D.N., 20 Apr. 1938; Gamelin to Daladier no. 2633/S, 8 June 1938, in ibid., pp. 122–4. Cf. 'Note du secrétariat général du Conseil Supérieur de la Défense Nationale: les données actuelles du problème militaire français', no. 68 D.N./3, 8 Feb. 1938, in *DDF*, 2nd ser., vol. VIII, doc. no. 127.
22. Deposition of Germain-Martin, 17 Feb. 1948, *C. E. Témoignages*, III–IV, p. 703; confirmed in Frankenstein, 'Aspects financiers du réarmement', pp. 2–5.
23. See Frankenstein, 'Réarmement français', p. 11.

24. Papiers Schweisguth, 'memento', 8 Apr. 1935, 351 AP, Carton 2, dr. 3, AN. On the Vincennes trials: 'Rapport de présentation au Conseil Supérieur de la Guerre sur l'adoption des Chars B1 et D2', 24 Mar. 1934, CSG Carton 1N22, vol. 17, SHAT; also Fridenson, *Usines Renault*, I, p. 203.
25. Papiers Schweisguth, 'Rapports et conférences: Conseil Consultatif de l'Armement: séance du 9 avril 1935', 351 AP, Carton 2, dr. 3, AN.
26. Ibid. Cf. Fabry, *De la Place de la Concorde*, p. 81; Gamelin, *Servir*, II, p. 149; Clarke, *Military Technology*, pp. 77–80, 151–3.
27. J. J. Clarke, 'The nationalisation of war industries in France, 1936–37: a case study', *JMH*, 49:3 (Sept. 1977), pp. 417–18. Cf. *Military Technology*, pp. 164–70; Fridenson, *Usines Renault*, I, pp. 201–44.
28. See Fridenson, *Usines Renault*, I, pp. 196–203, 213–30.
29. Ibid., p. 229.
30. Papiers Schweisguth, 'memento', 11 May 1935, 351 AP, Carton 2, dr. 4, AN. Cf. Clarke, *Military Technology*, p. 173.
31. Fridenson, *Usines Renault*, I, p. 229, n. 5.
32. CAC, minutes, 'Séance du 18 mars 1936 . . . audience de M. le général Maurin . . .', pp. 23–4, 15th Leg., Carton 5 bis, dr. IX, AAN.
33. Commission de l'Armée du Sénat (CAS), 'Séance du 25 mars 1936, présidence de M. Daniel Vincent: audience de MM. les généraux Colson et Happich', 15th Leg., Carton 5 bis, AAN.
34. Deposition of Germain-Martin, 17 Feb. 1948, *C. E. Témoignages*, III–IV, pp. 705–6.
35. CAS, minutes, 'Séance du 25 mars 1936 . . .', pp. 48–53, 15e Lég., Carton 5 bis, AAN. (Chéron had been finance minister, 1932–3; Jacquy was an independent senator for the Marne, 1933–41; Neyret a Union Démocratique et Radical senator for the Loire, 1933–41; Le Moignic a Gauche Démocratique senator for L'Inde française, 1928–44.)
36. CAS, minutes, 'Séance du 25 mars 1936 . . .', p. 50.
37. See Frankenstein, 'Aspects financiers du réarmement', p. 6; quotations from pp. 16, 17.
38. Fabry, Journal, 5 Aug. 1935; quotation from Fabry, *De la Place de la Concorde*, p. 85.
39. Attention is drawn to this point in Michel, *Procès de Riom*, pp. 162–7.
40. See Clarke, 'Nationalisation of war industries in France', pp. 416–22; Fridenson, *Usines Renault*, I, p. 227.
41. Papiers Schweisguth, 'Rapports et conférences: Conseil Consultatif de l'Armement, séance du 24 juin 1935', 351 AP, Carton 2, dr. 4, AN.
42. Fabry, Journal, 6 Aug. 1935; quotation from Fridenson, *Usines Renault*, I, pp. 203–4.
43. Gen. G. Bloch-Dassault, 'Examen du bilan des fabrications d'armement à la date du 1er janvier 1936', in Fabry, Journal, 8 Jan. 1936.
44. The cost of each Char B1 was 1.8–2 million francs, according to Col. T. G. G. Heywood (British military attaché, Paris), despatch, 4 Apr. 1935, FO 371, 18800, C2927/227/17, PRO. Cf. Clarke, *Military Technology*, pp. 151–3. On the 1931 *automitrailleuses* programme, see P. Touzin, *Les Véhicules*

blindés français, 1900–1944 (Paris, 1977), pp. 60–71; Clarke, 'Nationalisation of war industries', p. 417.
45. See Clarke, *Military Technology*, pp. 148–9.
46. Fridenson, *Usines Renault*, I, p. 211.
47. CAC, minutes, 'Séance du 25 juin 1935: audience de M. Fabry . . .', pp. 11–12, 15th Leg., Carton 5 bis, dr. IX, AAN. (Besset was the Indépendant de Gauche deputy for Paris, 11e arrondissement, 1928–36.)
48. Bloch-Dassault, 'Examen du bilan des fabrications', in Fabry, Journal, 8 Jan. 1936. For war ministry suspicions about Renault's practices see Fabry, Journal, 3 Sept. 1935; *De la Place de la Concorde*, p. 85.
49. CAS, minutes, 'Séance du 26 février 1936, présidence de M. Daniel Vincent: audience de MM. les généraux Maurin, ministre de la guerre et Colson, chef d'Etat-Major de l'Armée', p. 49, 15th Leg., Carton 5 bis, AAN. (De La Grandière was an independent senator for the Maine-et-Loire, 1934–41.)
50. Clarke, 'Nationalisation of war industries', p. 422. On the order for 200 H35s, see Fabry, Journal, 20 Sept. 1935; *De la Place de la Concorde*, p. 84.
51. See Fabry, Journal, 22 Oct. 1935; Fridenson, *Usines Renault*, I, p. 227 n. 5.
52. CAS, minutes, 'Séance du 26 février 1936 . . . audience de MM. les généraux Maurin . . .', pp. 49–50, 15th Leg., Carton 5 bis, AAN.
53. Fabry, Journal, 25 Nov. 1935.
54. Ibid., 11, 12, 17, 20 Sept. 1935.
55. Gamelin, *Servir*, II, p. 183; Fabry, Journal, 3–4 Oct. 1935.
56. HCM, minutes, 23 Jan., 22 Mar., 5 Apr. 1935 mtgs., HCM, Carton 2N19, SHAT. Cf. Gamelin, *Servir*, II, pp. 155, 159–60, 165–6; Conquet, *Auprès du Maréchal Pétain*, pp. 157–63.
57. Contemporary views on Laval's policy over the Abyssinian dispute in Fabry, Journal, 28 Aug., 26 Sept. 1935; Herriot, *Jadis*, II, pp. 574–608. Cf. historians' interpretations in Le Goyet, *Mystère Gamelin*, pp. 104–8; Young, *In Command of France*, pp. 82–90, 100–10; Parker, 'Great Britain, France and the Ethiopian crisis', pp. 293–332.
58. Fabry, *De la Place de la Concorde*, pp. 70–2; Italian enmity, the French general staff estimated, would demand the deployment of thirteen divisions in the Alpine-Riviera theatre, to the detriment of French concentrations facing Germany. (Le Goyet, *Mystère Gamelin*, p. 108.)
59. Description of the British army in Fabry, Journal, 29 July 1935; cf. *De la Place de la Concorde*, p. 69. Gamelin's views on Italy and Britain in his *Servir*, II, pp. 174–5.
60. Papiers Schweisguth, 'mementos', 12, 17 Sept. 1935, 351 AP, Carton 2, dr. 5, AN; Gamelin, 'Réflexions . . . au sortir d'un Haut Comité Militaire', 21–22 Nov. 1935, pp. 4–8, Fonds Gamelin, 1K 224 Carton 7, SHAT.
61. Gamelin, *Servir*, II, pp. 194–5; prior knowledge in Paris of the likelihood of German remilitarisation of the Rhineland in 1936 in Papiers Schweisguth, 'memento', 15 Jan. 1936, 351 AP, Carton 3, dr. 7, AN; *DDF*, 2nd ser., vol. I, docs. nos. 82 ('Note de l'Etat-Major de l'Armée pour le Haut Comité Militaire', 18 Jan. 1936); 83 ('Compte-rendu de séance du Haut Comité Militaire: séance du 18 janvier 1936'); 154 (François-Poncet (French Ambassador, Berlin) to Flandin, Minister for

Foreign Affairs, 8 Feb. 1936); 155 ('Compte-rendu du réunion des ministres de la Défense Nationale ... 7 février 1936'); François-Poncet, *Souvenirs*, pp. 248–51; P. Stehlin (asst. French air attaché, Berlin, 1936–9), *Témoignage pour l'histoire* (Paris, 1964), pp. 35–40.
62. Cf. Gamelin, *Servir*, II, pp. 176–7, 181–2, 197–214.
63. Ibid., pp. 173, 176; cf. Fabry, Journal, 3 Oct. 1935.
64. Fabry, Journal, 17 Oct. 1935; cf. Young, 'La Guerre de longue durée', esp. pp. 46–50; Bankwitz, *Weygand and Civil-Military Relations*, pp. 121–4, 129–32.
65. Fabry, Journal, 6 Nov. 1935; cf. Herriot, *Jadis*, II, pp. 611–12.
66. Gamelin, 'Réflexions ... au sortir d'un Haut Comité Militaire', 21–22 Nov. 1935, p. 6 (cited above, n. 60). Cf. Le Goyet, *Mystère Gamelin*, pp. 109–13; Gamelin, *Servir*, II, pp. 178–81; Conquet, *Auprès du Maréchal Pétain*, pp. 216–20.
67. See *DGFP*, ser. C, vol. IV, docs. nos. 373, 384, 404, 412, 415, 416, 419, 421, 423, 425; François-Poncet, *Souvenirs*, pp. 247–8; Bérard, *Un ambassadeur se souvient*, pp. 285–6; Herriot, *Jadis*, II, pp. 613–14.
68. Gamelin, 'Réflexions ... au sortir d'un Haut Comité Militaire', 21–22 Nov. 1935, p. 6 (cited above, n. 60); *DGFP*, ser. C, vol. IV, docs. nos. 435, 440, 467.
69. Kupferman, *Laval*, p. 52.
70. Gamelin, 'Réflexions ... au sortir d'un Haut Comité Militaire', 21–22 Nov. 1935, p. 7 (cited above, n. 60).
71. See Herriot, *Jadis*, II, pp. 623–35; G. Bonnet, *Vingt ans de vie politique, 1918–1938: de Clemenceau à Daladier* (Paris, 1969), pp. 234–6, 239–40. (Bonnet was minister for commerce and industry in the 1935–6 Laval and Sarraut governments.) For modern historians' interpretations of Sarraut's transitional administration cf. J. Delperrié de Bayac, *Histoire du Front Populaire* (Paris: 1972), pp. 159–93.
72. Cf. S. A. Schuker, 'France and the remilitarisation of the Rhineland in 1936', *FHS*, 14:3 (Spring 1986), p. 338. Cf. Young, *In Command of France*, pp. 130–1. The description of the French army's re-equipment occurs in Bankwitz, *Weygand and Civil-Military Relations*, p. 135. On March 1936 as a lost opportunity see Stehlin, *Témoignage*, pp. 39–41. Cf. L. Noël, *La Guerre de 1939 a commencé quatre ans plus tot* (Paris, 1979), pp. 46–58; A. Horne, *To Lose a Battle: France 1940* (London, 1969), pp. 34–7; G. Chapman, *Why France Collapsed* (London, 1968), pp. 23–5. The most persuasive exposition of the French command's grounds for rejecting a military response by France alone remains Emmerson, *Rhineland Crisis*, pp. 104–17.
73. See Gamelin, *Servir*, II, pp. 212–14.
74. See Col. F. G. Beaumont-Nesbitt (British military attaché, Paris, 1936–8) and Sir G. Clerk (British ambassador, Paris, 1934–7), despatches, 17 Mar. 1936, FO 371, 19870, C234/172/17, C654/172/17, C2014/172/17, PRO. Cf. Frankenstein, 'Aspects financiers du réarmement', pp. 4–7.
75. Papiers Schweisguth, 'memento', 27 Feb. 1936, 351 AP, Carton 3, dr. 7, AN.
76. Gamelin, deposition, 2 Dec. 1947, *C. E. Témoignages*, II, p. 370.

77. Fabry, Journal, 22 Oct., 25 Nov., 20 Dec. 1935, 2, 4 Jan. 1936. The powers of the Direction des Fabrications d'Armement by its establishment Law of 3 July 1935 and by Fabry's measures – which were alleged to deny the CSG any oversight of equipment under construction – are criticised in Gamelin, *Servir*, I, p. 207; II, pp. 111–15, 188–90.
78. See Gamelin, *Servir*, I, pp. 210–11; Bloch-Dassault, 'Examen du bilan des fabrications', in Fabry, Journal, 8 Jan. 1936; Colson, statement to the Senate that, under the existing organisation of armoured vehicle manufacture, 'le rythme des fabrications ne peut pas être accéléré' (CAS, minutes, 'Séance du 26 février 1936', p. 49, 15th Leg., Carton 5 bis, AAN).
79. CSG, minutes 29 Apr. 1936 mtg., CSG Carton 1N22, vol. XVII, p. 86, SHAT; Flavigny's views in his letter to Reynaud, 24 Apr. 1936, Archives Reynaud, Carton 74 AP 12, AN. Cf. Papiers Schweisguth, 'Rapport', 24 Dec. 1935; 'memento', 8 Jan. 1936, in, respectively, 351 AP, Carton 2, dr. 6 and Carton 3, dr. 7, AN; Gamelin, deposition, 2 Dec. 1947, *C. E. Témoignages*, II, p. 384; *Servir*, II, pp. 187–8.
80. See Gen. M.-E. Debeney, 'La Motorisation des armées modernes', *RDM*, 8:32 (15 Mar. 1936), pp. 273–91. Cf. illuminating analysis of bureaucratic rivalry between the army inspectorates, the armaments' directorate and Gamelin's *cabinet* in Clarke, *Military Technology*, pp. 142–7, 191–3; also Maurin's naive belief that the civilian automobile market's depression would suffice, by itself, to ensure that military requirements became 'très rapidement servis' (CAS, minutes, 'Séance du 26 février 1936', p. 50, 15th Leg., Carton 5 bis, AAN).

4 THE POPULAR FRONT, THE ARMY AND POLITICS

1. Gamelin, *Servir*, II, pp. 220–1.
2. Gamelin, written submission to the Vichy Supreme Court at Riom: 'La politique étrangère de la France 1930–9 au point de vue militaire', p. 21, Blum Archives, 3BL3, dr. 1, FNSP. I am grateful to Dr N. T. N. Jordan, University of Illinois, Chicago, for this reference.
3. CPDN, 29 July 1936, procès-verbal, p. 25, Carton 2N 24, SHAT.
4. Gamelin, *Servir*, II, pp. 222–4. The encounter is not related in *L'Oeuvre de Léon Blum: Mémoires. La Prison et le procès. A l'Échelle humaine, 1940–1945* (Paris, 1955). Cf. Colton, *Léon Blum*, pp. 198–203.
5. Gamelin, *Servir*, II, pp. 57, 75, 253; appreciation by Col. Kühlenthal in Col. F. G. Beaumont-Nesbitt (Paris), despatch to War Office, 11 Mar. 1937, FO 371, 20693, C2085/122/17, PRO.
6. Gamelin, Riom submission p. 12, Blum Archives, 3BL3, dr. 1, FNSP.
7. On Daladier see Gamelin, *Servir*, II, pp. 88–92, 95–109, 221; 298; Pertinax, *Fossoyeurs*, I, pp. 107–99; de Monzie, *Ci-devant*, pp. 99–100; G. Bonnet, *Dans la tourmente, 1938–1948* (Paris, 1971), pp. 15–16; J. Daridan, *Le Chemin de la défaite, 1938–1940* (Paris, 1980), pp. 43–4; J. Monnet, *Mémoires* (Paris, 1976), p. 138; Léon-Jouhaux, *Prison*, pp. 34–6; Bankwitz, *Weygand and Civil-Military Relations*, pp. 94–105. On Delbos see Duroselle, *La Décadence*, pp. 293–4; J. E. Dreifort, *Yvon Delbos at*

the Quai d'Orsay. French Foreign Policy during the Popular Front, 1936–1938 (Lawrence, Kansas, 1973).
8. Weygand, 'L'État militaire de la France', *RDM*, 8:106:35 (15 Oct. 1936), p. 735. Cf. Griffiths, *Pétain*, pp. 161–4; Bankwitz, *Weygand and Civil-Military Relations*, p. 273; B. Singer, 'From patriots to pacifists: the French primary school teachers, 1880–1940', *Journal of Contemporary History*, 12:3 (July 1977), pp. 413–34.
9. Lt. Col. S. Waite (assistant military attaché, Paris) to Dept. of the Army (G2), Washington DC, 30 Oct. 1936: 'France (Political) – Subject: Change in M. Blum's policy', Record Group 165, Box no. 1643, doc. file no. 2657-c-301/1, USNARA.
10. Young, 'French military intelligence', p. 163.
11. Gamelin, Journal de marche, 6 Oct. 1939, Fonds Gamelin 1K 224/9, SHAT; Blum's judgement of Gamelin in Pertinax, *Fossoyeurs*, I, p. 51, n. 2.
12. Quoted in Young, 'Soldiers and diplomats', p. 85.
13. Quoted in Young, 'French military intelligence', p. 149.
14. On Noguès see W. Hoisington, *The Casablanca Connection. French Colonial Policy, 1936–1943* (Chapel Hill, NC, 1984). On Dentz see G. London, *Le général Dentz et l'amiral Esteva devant la Haute Cour de Justice* (Paris, 1947). On Decoux see Admiral J. Decoux, *A la barre de l'Indochine* (Paris, 1949). Cf. Duroselle, *L'Abîme*, pp. 220–1, 238–56.
15. Fabry, *Place de la Concorde*, p. 63.
16. Papiers Schweisguth, 'mementos', 16 July 1935, 12, 16 Sept. 1935, 351 AP, Carton 2, dr. 5, AN. Langeron's memoir-diary, *Paris, juin 40* (Paris, 1946), is uninformative about the 1930s.
17. Sir E. Phipps to FO, London, 5 July 1937, FO 371, 20696, C4888/822/17, PRO. On Gallifet's part in the military repression of the 1871 Paris Commune, see R. Tombs, *The War against Paris 1871* (Cambridge, 1981), pp. 176, 179, 186; also J. P. T. Bury and R. Tombs, *Thiers: A political life, 1797–1873* (Cambridge, 1986).
18. Papiers Schweisguth, 'memento', 28 May 1936, 351 AP, Carton 3, dr. 9, AN. Cf. Gamelin, *Servir*, II, pp. 219–20.
19. De Gaulle, *Lettres, notes et carnets*, II, pp. 393, 411–14.
20. G. Chapman, 'The French army and politics', in M. E. Howard (ed.), *Soldiers and Governments. Nine studies in civil-military relations* (London, 1957) p. 69.
21. Chautemps twice resigned the premiership to avoid responsibility during major crises – firstly that of February 1934, and then the German Anschluss with Austria of March 1938. His memoirs, *Cahiers secrets de l'armistice* (Paris, 1963), discuss only the period 1939–40.
22. See Salengro's Denain speech, 7 Sept. 1936, reported in Sir G. Clerk to FO, in FO 371, 19859, C6327/1/17, PRO. For Daladier's statement see Clerk despatch to FO, 24 Feb. 1937, FO 371, 20693, C1597/122/17, PRO. Cf. P. Faure, *De Munich à la 5e République* (Paris, n.d.).
23. République Française, *JOC Débats*, 24 May 1927, p. 1597; Gamelin, *Servir*, II, p. 221.
24. See de Monzie, *Ci-devant*, p. 218; Daridan, *Chemin de la défaite*, pp. 196–7, 201, 205–6; D. Leca, *La Rupture de 1940* (Paris, 1978), pp. 126–8; P. de

Villelume, *Journal d'une défaite: août 1939–juillet 1940* (Paris, 1976), pp. 328–9; M. S. Alexander, 'The Fall of France, 1940', cited above, Introduction, n. 25.
25. CAC, 'Séance du 6 février 1938: audition de M. Daladier, ministre de la défense nationale et de la guerre', p. 10, 16th Leg., Carton 17, AAN.
26. Pertinax, *Fossoyeurs*, I, pp. 111–12.
27. Gamelin, *Servir*, II, pp. 91–2, 222, 298. Cf. A. P. Adamthwaite, *France and the Coming of the Second World War* (London, 1977), pp. 114–16, 169–70; Duroselle, *La Décadence*, pp. 332–4.
28. De Gaulle, *Mémoires de guerre*, I, pp. 27–9; cf. Joll, *Intellectuals in Politics*, pp. 44–5.
29. Gamelin, Journal de marche, 11 Oct. 1939, Fonds Gamelin 1K 224 Carton 9, SHAT.
30. Beaumont-Nesbitt despatch, 9 June 1936, in FO 371, 19871, C4183/172/17. PRO. Reynaud in *JOC Débats*, 27 Jan. 1937, pp. 171–2. For the 6 June 1936 decree that established the coordinating role of the war minister over national defence and turned the HCM into the CPDN see Gamelin, *Servir*, II, pp. 251–2; also Lt. Col. J. Vial, 'La Défense nationale: son organisation entre les deux guerres', *RHDGM*, 5:18 (Apr. 1955), pp. 11–32; E. C. Kiesling, 'A Staff College for the nation-in-arms: The Collège des Hautes Etudes de Défense Nationale, 1936–1939' (Ph.D. diss., Stanford University, 1988), pp. 67–72.
31. Challener, 'Gravediggers revisited', pp. 97–8.
32. See M. S. Alexander, 'Soldiers and Socialists. The French officer corps and leftist government, 1935–7', in M. S. Alexander and H. Graham (eds.), *The French and Spanish Popular Fronts. Comparative perspectives* (Cambridge, 1989), pp. 63–78.
33. Papiers Schweisguth, 'memento', 28 May 1936, 351 AP, Carton 3, dr. 9, AN.
34. Daladier to Chamber of Deputies, reported by Gp. Capt. D. Colyer (British air attaché, Paris), 24 Feb. 1937, FO 371, 20693, C1114/122/17, PRO.
35. Challener, 'Gravediggers revisited', p. 98. On the politics of *la marine* and French army–navy rivalry, see Pertinax, *Fossoyeurs*, I, pp. 55–6; J. Raphaël-Leygues, *Georges Leygues, le 'père' de la marine* (Paris, 1983); H. Coutau-Bégarie, C. Huan, *Darlan* (Paris, 1989); J. Raphaël-Leygues, F. Flohic, *Darlan* (Paris, 1986); H. Coutau-Bégarie, *Castex. Le Stratège inconnu* (Paris, 1985); C. W. Koburger, *The Cyrano Fleet. France and its navy, 1940–42* (London, 1989); R. C. Hood III, *Royal Republicans. The French naval dynasties between the world wars* (Baton Rouge and London, 1985).
36. Gamelin, *Servir*, III, p. 53; cf. II, pp. 378–9, 409–10.
37. See Gunsburg, *Divided and Conquered*, pp. 46–54.
38. Beaumont-Nesbitt to Clerk, enc. in Clerk (Paris) to Eden, 11 June 1936, FO 371, 19857, C4248/1/17, PRO.
39. Eden, telegram to FO reporting conversation with Chautemps, Paris, 25 Jan. 1938, FO 371, 21593, C534/36/17, PRO; Phipps to FO, 24 Jan. 1938, C479/36/17. For the 21 Jan. 1938 decree see Gamelin, *Servir*, II, pp. 306–12. Cf. Kiesling, 'Staff College for the nation-in-arms', pp. 72–4.

40. Cour Suprême de Justice à Riom: Commission rogatoire de Me. Emile Leseuer: déposition de M. Robert Jacomet, 8 Jan. 1941, Fonds Gamelin 1K 224/5, dr. 1, SHAT. Cf. Pertinax, *Fossoyeurs*, I, pp. 146–7; R. Jacomet, *L'Armement de la France, 1936–1939* (Paris, 1946), pp. 27–42, 77–83, 157–9.
41. See Gamelin, *Servir*, I, pp. 53–4.
42. Ibid., pp. 207–10; II, pp. 306–8; Gamelin's testimony, 2 Dec. 1947, *C. E. Témoignages*, II, pp. 369–70; E. du Réau, 'Edouard Daladier et les problèmes posés pas la mobilisation industrielle au moment de la crise de Munich', *Revue des Etudes Slaves*, 52:1–2 (1979), pp. 71–90.
43. Gamelin, *Servir*, II, pp. 52–3, 309. References to the maintenance of this diary occur in *Servir*, I, p. ii; II, pp. 51 n. 1, 92, 118 n. 1, 159, 165, 203–4, 263, 317 n. 1, 389, 460 n. 2; III, pp. 109, 125, 293, 303, 337. On the odyssey of Gamelin's *journal de marche*, see J. Vanwelkenhuyzen, *Les Avertissements qui venaient de Berlin. 9 octobre 1939–10 mai 1940* (Paris-Gembloux, 1982), pp. 215–16, 377 n. 84; 'Un éclairage nouveau sur la débâcle de 40? Les archives secrètes de Gamelin sauvées', in *Dernières nouvelles d'Alsace*, 27 Mar. 1988. (I am grateful to Prof. Serge Berstein of the Institut d'Etudes Politiques, Paris, for drawing this discovery to my attention.)
44. Gamelin, *Servir*, II, p. 456; interview with Gen. O. Poydenot, Versailles, 27 July 1982.
45. Gamelin, *Servir*, II, pp. 159, 167, 169; interviews and correspondence with Petibon's son, Guy Petibon, Paris, 14 June 1978, 1982–3; Pertinax, *Fossoyeurs*, I, p. 51. According to André Géraud, Petibon boasted to the head of the British military mission to Vincennes in 1939–40 that 'Everything has to pass through my hands.' Géraud added that Petibon 'had the reputation of throwing a spanner in the works, if need be, to emphasize the authority of his big boss,' p. 53 n. 6.
46. A. J. Liebling, *The Road back to Paris* (New York, 1988), pp. 31–2.
47. Gamelin, *Servir*, III, p. 39 n. 1.
48. Fraser, despatch of 17 Sept. 1938, FO 371, 21596, C10082/36/17, PRO.
49. Minart, *P. C. Vincennes*, I, p. 73.
50. Gen. O. Poydenot, letter to the author, 3 Apr. 1983.
51. Gamelin, *Servir*, III, p. 39 n. 1.
52. Papiers Schweisguth, 'memento', 3 June 1937, 351 AP, Carton 3, dr. 13, AN; Pertinax, *Fossoyeurs*, I, p. 109; Gunsburg, *Divided and Conquered*, p. 54.
53. Gamelin, *Servir*, II, pp. 309–11; III, pp. 222–3. Cf. J. M. Sherwood, *Georges Mandel and the Third Republic* (Stanford, CA, 1970), pp. 217–21; G. Wormser, *Georges Mandel. L'Homme politique* (Paris, 1967), pp. 210–17; F. Varenne, *Georges Mandel, mon patron* (Paris, 1947), pp. 155–63; Duroselle, *La Décadence*, pp. 237–9; Kiesling, 'Staff College for the nation-in-arms', pp. 72–4.
54. Maj. C. A. de Linde, assistant British military attaché, Paris, reporting talk with André Pironneau, despatch no. 1089, July 1939, FO 371, 22917, C10869/130/17, PRO.
55. Gamelin, *Servir*, II, p. 89; cf. pp. 222, 259–65.

56. Gamelin, Journal de marche, 18 Oct. 1939, Fonds Gamelin 1K 224/9, SHAT.
57. See the magnificently cynical exposure of the foibles of the *Troisième* by R. de Jouvenel, *La République des camarades* (Paris, 1914).
58. Pertinax, *Fossoyeurs*, I, pp. 48–50, 102–4. Cf. Gamelin, *Servir*, II, pp. xxiii–xxxi, 141–8, for evidence of the general's self-awareness on this score.
59. Daridan, *Chemin de la défaite*, p. 170; Gamelin, *Servir*, II, pp. 89–90.
60. 'Note sur le général Georges', 9 Dec. 1943, Fonds Gamelin 1K 224/7, SHAT.
61. Gamelin, *Servir*, I, pp. 60–1; II, pp. 143–4, 306.
62. See Bankwitz, *Weygand and Civil-Military Relations*, pp. 118–19.
63. Papiers Schweisguth, 'mementos', 21 May 1935, 15 May 1936, 351 AP, Carton 2, drs. 4, 9, AN.
64. Daladier quoted in Gamelin, *Servir*, I, pp. 61–2. Cf. *Servir*, II, pp. 383–8; Gamelin, testimony, 11 Dec. 1947, *C. E. Témoignages*, I, pp. 413–14.
65. Blum, *Oeuvre*, pp. 112–13; *JOC Débats*, 15 Mar. 1935, pp. 1022–53. Cf. Bankwitz, *Weygand and Civil-Military Relations*, pp. 126–7.
66. De Gaulle, *Mémoires de guerre*, I, pp. 18–20; Blum, *Oeuvre*, pp. 113–15; Colton, *Léon Blum*, pp. 225–30; Lacouture, *Léon Blum*, pp. 335–7 and *De Gaulle. Le Rebelle*, pp. 252–7; Georges Lefranc, *Histoire du Front Populaire* (Paris, 1974 edn), pp. 396–8.
67. Lacouture, *Léon Blum*, p. 357; J. Nobécourt, *Une Histoire politique de l'armée*, I, *De Pétain à Pétain, 1919–1942* (Paris, 1967), pp. 153–67, 203, 221ff.
68. Gamelin, Riom submission, p. 13, Blum Archives, 3BL3, dr. 1, FNSP.
69. Bankwitz, *Weygand and Civil-Military Relations*, pp. 276–7, and pp. 266–75; G. Loustaunau-Lacau, *Mémoires d'un français rebelle* (Paris, 1948), pp. 108–28; J.-R. Tournoux, *L'Histoire secrète. La Cagoule. Le Front Populaire. Vichy* (Paris, 1962), pp. 16ff; Gamelin, *Servir*, II, pp. 253–66, 303–4; Jeanneney (ed.), *Journal politique*, p. 184.
70. R. Allen, minute, 25 Sept. 1936, FO 371, 19871, C6616/172/17, PRO.
71. Gauché reported in Beaumont-Nesbitt to War Office, London, FO 371, 19871, C6616/172/17, PRO.
72. Col. H. Fuller, US military attaché, Paris, to Dept. of the Army (G2), Washington DC, 6 Oct. 1936: 'Communistic influence in the French Army', Record Group 165, Box no. 1643, doc. file no. 2657-c-298/3, USNARA.
73. See E. Weber, *Peasants into Frenchmen. The modernisation of rural France* (Stanford, CA, 1976), pp. 293, 298–302, 474–5.
74. Lyautey's essay was first published in the *Revue des deux mondes*. It was reissued wth a preface by Weygand in 1935, by Plon, and has been reprinted again as Maréchal Hubert Lyautey, *Le Rôle social de l'officier* (Paris, 1984).
75. Fuller to Dept. of the Army (G2), Washington DC, 6 Oct. 1936, cited above, n. 72 (emphasis added); Pironneau quoted in Beaumont-Nesbitt to War Office, London, FO 371, 20702, C3753/532/62, PRO.

76. Papiers Schweisguth, 'memento', 8 June 1935, 351 AP, Carton 2, dr. 4, AN; Gamelin, Journal de marche, 10 Sept. 1939, Fonds Gamelin 1K 224/9, SHAT.
77. Daladier at Versailles, reported in Clerk despatch to Foreign Office, London, 25 June 1936, FO 371, 19857, C4683/1/17, PRO; cf. Beaumont-Nesbitt enc., Clerk to FO, 11 June 1936, in C4248/1/17.
78. Cf. Gamelin: 'thanks to M. Daladier's influence we began to secure very important finances . . . for our armaments' (Riom submission, p. 14, Blum Archives, 3BL3, dr.1, FNSP); Colton, *Léon Blum*, pp. 224–5; R. Frankenstein, *Le Prix du réarmement français, 1935–39* (Paris, 1982).
79. Daladier clung to his personal experiences of 1914–18. In a Gallic counterpoint to the British army's 'Old Bill' of trench cartoonist Bruce Bairnsfather ('if you knows of a better 'ole, go to it!'), he reportedly held that 'The first and last word in the art of war is knowing how to dig and hold a trench. Everything else is twaddle.' (Pertinax, *Fossoyeurs*, I, pp. 111–12.)
80. Gamelin, *Servir*, II, pp. 220–1; Fuller to Dept. of the Army (G2), Washington DC, 6 Oct. 1936, cited above, n. 72.
81. D. Attruia, 'Le Prolétariat et la lutte contre la guerre et le fascisme', *Le Libertaire*, 7 Apr. 1936. Cf., more generally, D. N. Baker, 'The surveillance of subversion in interwar France: the Carnet B in the Seine, 1922–1940', *FHS*, 10:3 (Spring 1978), pp. 486–516; J.-J. Becker, *Le Carnet B. Les Pouvoirs publics et l'antimilitarisme avant la guerre de 1914* (Paris, 1973).
82. Army commission debate, 12–13 Nov. 1936, reported by Clerk to Foreign Office, London, FO 371, 19872, C8231/172/17, PRO; Gamelin, Riom submission, (cited above, n. 2), p. 14.
83. Gamelin, Journal de marche, 11 Oct. 1939, Fonds Gamelin 1K 224/9, SHAT.
84. See S. Berstein, *Histoire du Parti Radical* (Paris, 2 vols. 1980–2), II, *Crise du Radicalisme*; P. J. Larmour, *The French Radical Party in the 1930s. History of a decline* (Stanford, CA, 1962); S. B. Butterworth, 'Daladier and the Munich Crisis: a reappraisal', *JCH*, 9:3 (July 1974), pp. 191–216; E. du Réau, 'Edouard Daladier et la mobilisation industrielle à l'epoque de la crise de munich', *Munich. Mythes et réalités* (Paris, 1979), pp. 71–91; 'Edouard Daladier et l'image de la puissance française en 1938', *RHA* (Oct. 1983), pp. 26–39.
85. Le Col. G. Raquez, attaché militaire près l'Ambassade de Belgique en France à M. le Ministre de la Défense nationale, Cabinet; au Chef d'Etat-Major de l'Armée, Bruxelles: 'Le débat à la Chambre française sur la Défense Nationale et la conduite de la guerre éventuelle', no. 2 R.P./627, Feb. 1937, AMBAE.
86. Beaumont-Nesbitt, despatch, 7 Dec. 1937, FO 371, 20694, C8572/122/17, PRO. Cf. CAC, 'Séance du 17 novembre 1937: exposé de M. Georges Potut sur le budget de la défense nationale de 1938', p. 6, 16th Leg., Carton 15, AAN; F. Boudot, 'Sur les problèmes du financement de la défense nationale, 1936–1940', *RHDGM*, 21:81 (Jan. 1971), pp. 49–72 (esp. 62–3).

87. Lt. Col. S. Waite to Dept. of the Army (G2), Washington DC, 30 Oct. 1936, 'France (Political): Change in M. Blum's policy', Record Group 165, Box no. 1643, doc. file no. 2657-c-301/1, USNARA.
88. Lacouture, *Léon Blum*, p. 357.
89. Gen. A. Beaufre, *1940. The Fall of France* (London, 1967; New York, 1968), pp. 43–5, 57–8, 163; M. Bloch, *L'Etrange Défaite. Témoignage écrit en 1940* (Paris, 1946), pp. 47–9, 52–3, 77–81, 108–19, 125–6, 132–5, 140–4.

5 THE ROAD TO REARMAMENT: GAMELIN, DALADIER AND POPULAR FRONT DEFENCE POLICY

1. 'Programmes d'armement français: histoire et situation actuelle, juin 1936', pp. 4–5, CPDN, Carton 1, SHAT.
2. Daladier in *DDF*, 2nd ser., II, doc. no. 369 (CPDN, minutes, 26 June 1936); Gamelin's priorities in his *Servir*, II, pp. 243–4 ('Programme établi par le général Gamelin et remis au général Colson', Aug. 1936).
3. Statistics from Colson, 'Coup d'oeil rétrospectif sur les armements français de 1919 à 1939', Fonds Gamelin, 1K 224, Carton 7, SHAT. Cf. deposition of Robert Jacomet (secretary-general, war and defence ministry, 1936–40), 18 July 1947, *C. E. Témoignages*, I, pp. 199–200; Gamelin, *Servir*, I, pp. 220–2; R. Frank[enstein], 'Le Front Populaire, a-t-il perdu la guerre?', *L'Histoire*, 58 (July–Aug. 1983), pp. 58–66; *Le Prix du réarmement*.
4. *DDF*, 2nd ser., II, doc. no. 369 (CPDN, minutes, 26 June 1936).
5. Gamelin, *Servir*, I, pp. 211–13; cf. Papiers Schweisguth, 'mementos', 8 June 1936, 351 AP, Carton 3, dr. 9, AN.
6. Petibon's views as reported by Col. F. G. Beaumont-Nesbitt (British military attaché, Paris), in Sir G. Clerk (British ambassador, Paris) to A. Eden (foreign secretary), 11 June 1936, FO 371, 19857, C4248/1/17, PRO. For Daladier's position: CAC, 'Séance du 12 février 1936 ... Ve partie: exposé de M. Marc Rucart sur la nationalisation du commerce et de la fabrication des armes de guerre', pp. 12–15, 15th Leg., Carton 5 bis, dr. IX; 'Séance du 8 juillet 1936: rapport de M. Armand Chouffet sur le Projet de Loi No. 465 sur la nationalisation de la fabrication des matériels de guerre, suivi d'une audience de M. Daladier, ministre de la défense nationale et de la guerre', pp. 3–13, 14–51, 16th Leg., Carton 15, AAN.
7. Gamelin, *Servir*, II, pp. 240–3 (letter to Daladier no. 2444/S, 25 June 1936 and annexed 'Note'); *DDF*, 2nd ser., II, doc. no. 375 ('Chambre des Députés, Commission de l'Armée: "séance du 1er juillet 1936 – audience de M. Daladier, ministre de la défense nationale et de la guerre"').
8. CAC, 'Séance du 15 juillet 1936', 16th Leg., Carton 15, AAN. 484 deputies voted in favour of the Bill, 85 against. (See British Embassy, Paris, to Foreign Office, London, 17 July 1936, FO 371, 19871, C5255/172/17, PRO.) Cf. Clarke, 'Nationalisation of war industries', pp. 423–5.
9. Fabry–Daladier exchange in the Senate, 29 Dec. 1936, in Etat Français: Cour Suprême de Justice à Riom. Commission rogatoire de Me. René Baraveau – déposition de M. Jean Fabry le 2 octobre 1941, Pt. II, pp. 3, 5, 10–12, Fonds Fabry, 1K 93, Carton 2, SHAT. For accusations by right-wing deputies that Blum was 'playing class politics' over nationalisation,

see *JOC Débats*, 31 July 1936, pp. 7–8, 12. Characteristic charges on the issue at Riom may be found in Cour Suprême de Justice: Réquisitoire définitif dressé par M. le procureur-général Georges Cassagnau, le 15 octobre 1941 . . . Xe partie – les responsabilités de M. Daladier . . . XIIe partie – les responsabilités du général Gamelin, pp. 110–12, 150–2 respectively, Fonds Gamelin, 1K 224, Carton 1, dr. 1, SHAT.
10. Description of the decrees in Clarke, 'Nationalisation of war industries', p. 427, statistics pp. 425–6. Hotchkiss's other factories, at Gennevilliers and Clichy, which undertook predominantly civilian work, escaped nationalisation. See Riom deposition of Eugène Boyer (chairman, Société Hotchkiss, 1932–7), 3 Dec. 1940, Archives Daladier, 4 DA 24, dr. 2, FNSP. On Hotchkiss's activities in the early 1930s see L. Launay and J. Sennac, *Les Relations internationales des industries de guerre* (Paris, 1932), pp.93–7.
11. Michel, *Procès de Riom*, pp. 168–9.
12. Col. Beaumont-Nesbitt (British military attaché, Paris), despatch, 5 Nov. 1936, reporting Daladier's meeting the previous day with the CAC, FO 371, 19872, C7891/172/17, PRO. Jacomet's statistics from his deposition, 18 July 1947, to the postwar parliamentary inquiry: *C. E. Témoignages*, I, p. 200. Cf. the figure of 7,409 firms working in some capacity for the French service ministries on 1 Jan. 1937 and 11,474 by 1 Jan. 1939 in du Réau, 'Edouard Daladier et . . . la mobilisation industrielle', *Revue des Etudes Slaves*, 52:1–2 (1979), p. 80. Cost of the Chars B and D2 programmes in excerpts from Daladier's meeting with the Senate Finance Commission, 27 Nov. 1936, Archives Daladier, 1 DA 7, dr. 3, sub-dr. a, FNSP; Fridenson, *Usines Renault*, I, p. 292; Clarke, 'Nationalisation of war industries', p. 426; R. Jacomet, *L'Armement de la France, 1936–1939* (Paris, 1945), pp. 192–4.
13. See Jacomet, deposition, 18 July 1947, *C. E. Témoignages*, I, p. 208; Gamelin, *Servir*, I, p. 213; Clarke, 'Nationalisation of war industries', p. 426.
14. Quotations from Fabry, Riom deposition, 2 Oct. 1941, Pt. II, p. 3, Fonds Fabry, 1K 93, Carton 2, SHAT; Fabry, *Place de la Concorde*, pp. 116–17. Entrepreneurs' criticism at Riom of the nationalisations in depositions of Edgar Brandt, 29 Nov. and 5 Dec. 1940 (Fonds Gamelin, 1K 224, Carton 5, dr. 1, 'Procédure René Baraveau', SHAT); 17 Oct. and 30 Oct. 1940 (in Archives Daladier, 4 DA 12, dr. 5, entry no. 48, FNSP); of Armaments-Engineer Emile Carré, 21–22 Nov. 1940, specifically concerning nationalisation at Hotchkiss-Levallois, Archives Daladier, 4 DA 13, dr. 1, entry no. 66, FNSP; CAC, 'Contrôle des fabrications d'armement: rapport de M. Camille Fernand-Laurent' (concerning R35 and Renault *chenillette* output in 1936–7), 16th Leg., séance no. 49, 25 Oct. 1938, pp. 24–6, Carton 17, AAN.
15. R. Dautry, Riom deposition, 9 Oct. 1940, pp. 7–8, Archives Daladier, 4 DA 13, dr. 5, entry no. 95, FNSP.
16. See Paillat, *Dossiers Secrets*, III, *La Guerre à l'horizon*, pp. 328–33, 363–6, 397–400; Delperrié de Bayac, *Histoire du Front Populaire*, pp. 427–40.
17. A. Prost, 'Le Climat social', in R. Rémond and J. Bourdin (eds.), *Edouard Daladier, chef de gouvernement, avril 1938–septembre 1939* (Paris,

1977), pp. 99–100. Cf. Rémond and Bourdin, 'Les Grèves de juin 1936: essai d'interprétation', in J. Bourdin (ed.), *Léon Blum, chef de gouvernement* (Paris: 1967), pp. 69–87; Delperrié de Bayac, *Histoire du Front Populaire*, pp. 221–60; A. Rossiter, 'Popular Front economic policy and the Matignon negotiations', *HJ*, 30:3 (1987), pp. 663–84; 'The Blum government, the Conseil National Economique and economic policy', in Alexander and Graham (eds.), *The French and Spanish Popular Fronts*, pp. 156–170; H. Dubief, *Le Déclin de la Troisième République* (Paris, 1979), pp. 179–92. The euphoria over possibilities for socio-economic transformation in May–June 1936 and the rapid onset of disillusionment is vividly recalled in the memoirs of Blum's former political secretary, Jules Moch, *Rencontres avec Léon Blum* (Paris, 1970), pp. 159–82.
18. EMA/Section d'Armement et d'Etudes Techniques, 'Situation actuelle de l'armée française – défense contre les engins mécaniques et les divisions blindées', 26 June 1936, Archives Daladier, 4 DA 1, dr. 3, FNSP. Cf. Papiers Schweisguth, 'mementos', 21 July 1936, 351 AP, Carton 3, dr. 9, AN.
19. Happich accusations in his Riom deposition, 20 Dec. 1940, Fonds Gamelin, 1K 224, Carton 5, dr. 1, SHAT; Daladier's declaration reported in Beaumont-Nesbitt (British military attaché, Paris), despatch to London, 5 Nov. 1936, FO 371, 19872, C7891/172/17, PRO. For the labour arbitration and collective bargaining arrangements instituted by the Blum and Chautemps governments in 1936–7, see J. Colton, *Compulsory Labor Arbitration in France, 1936–1939* (New York, 1951); A. Mitzman, 'The French working class and the Blum government, 1936–37' in Cairns (ed.), *Contemporary France*, pp. 110–38, esp. pp. 120–7; Rossiter, 'The Blum government, the Conseil National Economique and economic policy', in Alexander and Graham (eds.), *French and Spanish Popular Fronts*, pp. 156–70. On the 'revenge of the bosses', cf. I. Kolboom, *La Revanche des patrons. Le Patronat français face au front populaire* (Paris, 1986); P. Fridenson, 'Le Patronat français', in J. Bourdin and R. Rémond (eds.), *La France et les Français en 1938–1939* (Paris, 1978), pp. 139–57.
20. Cour Suprême de Justice à Riom, 'Commission rogatoire du 8 novembre 1940 de Me. Emile Lesueur – déposition de M. Paul Panhard, le 2 décembre 1940'; 'Commission rogatoire de Me. René Baraveau – déposition de M. Paul Panhard, le 5 septembre 1941', both in Archives Daladier, respectively 4 DA 24, dr. 2, sub-dr. P and 4 DA 17, dr. 3, entry no. 242B, FNSP.
21. Contract and output statistics from Panhard's Riom deposition, 5 Sept. 1941, cited above, n. 20.
22. Ibid. Apparently Panhard et Levassor was deterred from expanding capacity to build AMDs after the war ministry's initial order in 1935 because of erratic payments for equipment the firm delivered. By September 1936 the French army owed the company 100 million francs. (Testimony of Jacomet to the postwar parliamentary inquiry, 18 July 1947: *C. E. Témoignages*, I, p. 197.)
23. Panhard, Riom deposition, 5 Sept. 1941, cited above, n. 20; censure of the army inspectorates in CAC, 'Séance du 7 mai 1937: audience de M. Daladier, ministre de la défense nationale et de la guerre', Archives

Daladier, 4 DA 2, dr. 4, sub-dr. c, FNSP; Dautry's criticism in his Riom deposition, 24 July 1941, p. 3, 4 DA 13, dr. 5; Gamelin's complaints in 'Note du général Gamelin pour le secrétaire-général Jacomet', EMA/ SAET, no. 1914, 7 May 1937, p. 5, in Fonds Gamelin, 1 K 224, Carton 4, dr. 'Procès de Riom: enquêtes et notes', sub-dr. 4, SHAT. Jacomet, however, emphasised problems in controlling the land forces' armaments programme owing to the dearth of Ingénieurs de fabrications d'armement – a technical corps only formed in July 1935 and, at the end of 1936, still consisting of only 190 engineers and 35 administrative assistants. See Jacomet, testimony to the postwar parliamentary inquiry, 18 July 1947, *C. E. Témoignages*, I, pp. 196–7, 203; Gamelin, *Servir*, II, pp. 188–90, 290; Clarke, 'Nationalisation of war industries', pp. 422–3; Young, *In Command of France*, pp. 187–90; Touzin, *Les Véhicules blindés français*, pp. 64–71.

24. Panhard, Riom deposition, 5 Sept. 1941, cited above, n. 20.
25. Dufieux's recommendations as well as comment on the deficit of skilled labour in CSG, 'Séance d'études du 14 octobre 1936: étude du programme d'armement', minutes, pp. 4–5, Fonds Gamelin, 1K 224, Carton 8, dr. 'Réunions du CSG, 1932–38', SHAT; statistics on R35 output in ibid., pp. 2–3 and Papiers Schweisguth, 'Rapport du 27 avril 1937', 351 AP, Carton 3, dr. 12, AN.
26. On retention of a peace economy see Colson's remarks on the opposition of Popular Front finance minister, Vincent Auriol, to the scale of military credits for 1937–8 in the four-year armament plan of 7 Sept. 1936, in Papiers Schweisguth, 'mementos', 13 Feb. 1937, 351 AP, Carton 3, dr. 11, AN; Jacomet's testimony to the postwar parliamentary inquiry, 18 July 1947, *C. E. Témoignages*, I, pp. 200–3. Happich quoted in 'Note du général Gamelin', 7 May 1937, p. 4, cited above n. 23. Cf. historians' treatment of these issues in F. Boudot, 'Sur les problèmes du financement de la défense nationale', *RHDGM*, 21 (Jan. 1971), pp. 61–5; Frankenstein, 'Aspects financiers du réarmement', *RHDGM*, 102, pp. 7–10; 'Réarmement français, finances publiques', pp. 9–11.
27. Fridenson, *Usines Renault*, I, pp. 291–2. On stockpiling of warlike stores, see Gamelin, 'Réflexions . . . au sortir d'un Haut Comité Militaire, 21–22 novembre 1935', pp. 2, 6, Fonds Gamelin, 1K 224, Carton 7; CSDN minutes: 22 Nov. 1925, Carton 2N 12, dr. 14 (48), both SHAT; Herriot, *Jadis*, II, pp. 611–12. Quotations on French neglect to seek help abroad in Dautry, Riom deposition, 24 July 1941, pp. 4–5, Archives Daladier, 4 DA 13, dr. 5, entry no. 95, FNSP. Raw material importing and devaluation discussed in CPDN, 5 Dec. 1936, 9 July 1937, 3 Nov. 1937, minutes in CPDN Carton 1, SHAT; also du Réau, 'Edouard Daladier et . . . la mobilisation industrielle' (cited above, n. 12) pp. 73, 82–5; R. Nayberg, 'La Problématique du ravitaillement de la France en carburant dans l'entre-deux-guerres: naissance d'une perspective géo-stratégique', *RHA*, 4 (1979), pp. 5–27.
28. Cf. Gunsburg, *Divided and Conquered*, pp. 40–4; Clarke, *Military Technology*, pp. 184–96; Dutailly, *Les Problèmes de L'Armée de Terre*, pp. 227–44, 249–60, 264–8; Doughty, *Seeds of Disaster*, pp. 10–12, 31–5, 91–4;

'The French armed forces, 1918–1940', in Millett and Murray (eds.), *Military Effectiveness*, II, pp. 59–61, 63–5.

29. Salengro's pledge came in a speech at Denain, reported in Sir G. Clerk (British ambassador, Paris), despatch to London (Foreign Office), 7 Sept. 1936, FO 371, 19859, C6327/1/17, PRO; missions of the DIMs prescribed in the 1936 *IGU*, excerpts in Archives Daladier, 4 DA 6, dr. 5, sub-dr. a, FNSP; description of infantry's refusal to assault without accompanying tanks from de Gaulle, letter to Reynaud, 15 Oct. 1937, in Demey, *Paul Reynaud: mon père*, p. 315 (corroborated in war minister Maurin's admission in 1934 that it had become 'impossible to launch an infantry unit into attack unless it's preceded by tanks', CAC, 'Séance du 5 décembre 1934: audience de M. le général Maurin', procès-verbal, p. 8, 15th Leg., Carton 5 bis, dr. VI, AAN); Gamelin warning in CSG, 'Séance d'études du 14 octobre 1936, soir: la division cuirassée', p. 1, Fonds Gamelin, 1K 224, Carton 8, dr. 'Réunions du CSG, 1932–8', SHAT; diversion of infantry tanks to new cavalry armoured formations detailed in Gamelin, *Servir*, I, pp. 261–3; Clarke, *Military Technology*, p. 123.

30. Quotations from, respectively, CSG, 'Séance d'études du 14 octobre', pp. 2–3, cited above; Gamelin, *Servir*, II, p. 289. On Char B output cf. *Servir*, I, pp. 262–70; R. H. S. Stolfi, 'Equipment for victory in France, 1940', *History*, 55:183 (Feb. 1970), pp. 1–20 (esp. pp. 2–3); for definitive establishment of French heavy tank divisions (Divisions Cuirassées de Réserve) in Dec. 1939 see Clarke, *Military Technology*, pp. 205–8.

31. Daladier's opposition to the Char B – crystallised, he confessed, by advice from his *chef de cabinet militaire* in 1936–7, Gen. Victor Bourret – in Papiers Schweisguth, 'mementos', 4 July 1936, 351 AP Carton 3, dr. 9, AN; CAC, 'Séance du 1er décembre 1937: audience de M. Daladier, ministre de la défense nationale et de la guerre', pp. 15–16, 16th Leg., Carton XV, dr. '1937', AAN; 'Cour Suprême de Justice à Riom: procès-verbal in extenso de l'audience du 27 février 1942', pp. 191–7, Fonds Gamelin, 1K 224, Carton 1, dr. 3, SHAT; Velpry to the Conseil Consultatif de l'Armement, 4 May 1936 (Papiers Schweisguth, 'Rapports et conférences', 351 AP, Carton 3, dr. 9, AN); views of the commander of 511th Tank Regt, partially equipped with Char Bs, in Col. Christian Bruneau (commander, 1st DCR, May–June 1940), memorandum, 16 July 1936, Archives Daladier, 4 DA 7, dr. 2, sub-dr. b, FNSP; de Gaulle's experience recounted in his letter to Reynaud, 15 Oct. 1937, in Demey, *Paul Reynaud: mon père*, pp. 314–16. Gamelin's views on brigades in CSG minutes, 15 Dec. 1937, 2 Dec. 1938, Carton 1N 22, vol. 17, pp. 100–3, 120–9, Annex, pp. 133–4 (a note by Gen. Pierre Héring, proposing establishment of armoured combat commands each of two tank battalions, rather than the heavier four or six battalion DCR favoured by Gamelin), SHAT. This crucial debate on structures for French armoured forces may also be followed in Papiers Schweisguth, 'Rapport du 17 novembre 1936', 351 AP, Carton 3, dr. 10, AN; and EMA, 'Note sur la division cuirassée et les manoeuvres de Barrois', 13 Feb. 1937, Carton 1N 37, sub-dr. 4, SHAT; Doughty, *Seeds of Disaster*, pp. 163–77.

32. Praise of Gamelin in de La Gorce, *The French Army*, p. 294; Besson remark in 'Considérations ... sur la division cuirassée', 10 Dec. 1937, Carton 1N 37, sub-dr. 5, SHAT.
33. See Gamelin, *Servir*, II, pp. 289–90. In *Servir*, I, p. 265, Gamelin lists D2 strength in Sept. 1939 as one battalion (the forty-five tanks built in 1936–7), and claims he requested production to be resumed 'from the start of the war'. One historian has asserted – without substantiating evidence – that a second D2 contract was placed in June 1938 (Stolfi, 'Equipment for victory', pp. 4–5).
34. Quotations from CSG, 'Rapport de présentation de la question de la constitution d'une troisième DLM', 6 Dec. 1937; 'Note du général Besson au sujet de la création d'une troisième DLM', 10 Dec. 1937, Carton 1N 37, sub-drs. 2 and 5 respectively, SHAT. On cancellation of exercises cf. Gamelin, testimony to the postwar parliamentary inquiry, 2 Dec. 1947, *C. E. Témoignages*, II, p. 387; Jacomet, testimony, 11 July 1947, in ibid., I, p. 200; Gamelin, *Servir*, I, pp. 262–6; II, pp. 290–1, 342; Clarke, *Military Technology*, pp. 199–201.
35. Statement attributed to Daladier by Sir G. Clerk (British ambassador, Paris), report on the Chamber of Deputies debate over Blum's rearmament plan, 24 Feb. 1937, FO 371, 20693, C1597/122/17, PRO. Reynaud's return to the *armée de métier* issue at this time is seen in his Chamber speech (*JOC Débats*, 27 Jan. 1937, pp. 168–72) and his *Le Problème militaire français* (Paris, 1937). Cf. M. S. Alexander, 'Soldiers and Socialists', in Alexander and Graham (eds.), *French and Spanish Popular Fronts*, pp. 70–3, 74–6; Doughty, 'De Gaulle's concept of a mobile, professional army: genesis of French defeat?', in Matthews and Brown, *The Parameters of War*, pp. 243–56.
36. Ministère de la défense nationale et de la guerre (Cabinet du ministre): 'Analyse d'interpellation de M. Paul Reynaud sur la politique militaire du gouvernement', Archives Daladier, 4 DA 3, dr. 4, sub-dr. b, FNSP; de Gaulle's linkage of recruitment and unemployment in his 'Mémorandum sur le recrutement d'un corps spécialisé', Archives Reynaud, 74 AP, Carton 12, AN. Cf. Gamelin, *Servir*, I, pp. 257–8.
37. Statistics from Paul Ramadier (Minister of Labour), to the 1938 ILO conference, cited in the CGT newspaper *La Voix du Peuple*, June 1938 (annex to Robert Bothereau – CGT assistant-secretary, 1936–40 – Riom deposition, 27 Dec. 1940, Archives Daladier, 4 DA 24, dr. 2, FNSP).
38. EMA Cabinet, 'Note pour le cabinet militaire du ministre' [drafted by Gen. Colson], 11 July 1936, in Gamelin, *Servir*, III, pp. 516–27. Cf. 'Note complémentaire au sujet des difficultés de recrutement d'une armée de métier', 21 July 1936, Archives Daladier, 4 DA 3, dr. 4, sub-dr. b, FNSP.
39. On British experience see R. A. C. Parker, 'British rearmament, 1936–9: Treasury, trade unions and skilled labour', *EHR*, 96:379 (Apr. 1981), pp. 306–43; G. C. Peden, *British Rearmament and the Treasury, 1932–39* (Edinburgh, 1979), pp. 81–4, 180; J. D. Scott, *Vickers: A History* (London, 1962), pp. 209–10, 217–26.
40. Pierre Chaumié (Senator, Gauche Démocratique, Lot-et-Garonne, 1935–41), in CAS, minutes, 'Séance du 26 février 1936: audience de M. le

général Maurin, ministre de la guerre', p. 44, 15th Leg., Carton 5 bis, AAN; background to the issue of meeting labour shortages by encouraging migrant workers in G. S. Cross, 'Toward social peace and prosperity: the politics of immigration in France during the era of World War I', *FHS*, 11:4 (Fall 1980), pp. 610–32. Important archival losses or destructions hamper analysis of these questions today. Especially frustrating is the disappearance of the minutes and documentation of the Commerce and Industry Commission of the Chamber of Deputies between 9 July 1936 and 17 Oct. 1939. Surviving papers from the 16e Législature comprise only six *procès-verbaux* (from 16 June to 8 July 1936), none of which discuss rearmament, and minutes of an 18 Oct. 1939 meeting. (See Commission du Commerce et de l'Industrie, 16th Leg., Carton 58, AAN.)

41. CAC, 'Séance du 18 mars 1936: audience de M. le général Maurin, ministre de la guerre', pp. 23–4, 15th Leg., Carton 5 bis, dr. IX, AAN.
42. Cf. Fridenson, 'Le Patronat', in Bourdin and Rémond (eds.), *La France et les Français*, esp. pp. 145–52; Kolboom, *Revanche des patrons*, passim; J. Colton, 'Politics and economics in the 1930s: the balance sheets of the "Blum New Deal"', in C. K. Warner (ed.), *From the Ancien Régime to the Popular Front. Essays in honor of Shepard B. Clough* (New York, 1968), pp. 181–208; J. K. Munholland, 'Between Popular Front and Vichy: the decree laws of the Daladier ministry, 1938–40', unpublished paper read at the XIVth annual meeting, Western Society for French History, Baltimore, 19–22 Nov. 1986; Jeanneney, 'La Politique économique de Léon Blum'; Mendès-France, 'La Politique économique du gouvernement Léon Blum'; Gout, Juvigny and Mousel, 'La Politique sociale du Front Populaire', in Bourdin (ed.), *Léon Blum*, pp. 207–40; Duroselle, *La Décadence*, pp. 305–10.
43. Gen. L. Colson, 'Coup d'oeil . . . sur les armements français', Fonds Gamelin, 1K 224, Carton 7, SHAT.
44. Miellet (CAC chairman after the appointment of his predecessor, Guy La Chambre, as air minister in Jan. 1938), in 'Séance du 11 octobre 1939: rapports sur les Etablissements du Creusot, de Toulouse et de Tarbes', p. 3, 16th Leg., Carton 17, AAN; armaments council warnings in EMA/SAET, no. 1914, 'Note du général Gamelin', 7 May 1937, p. 1, Fonds Gamelin, 1K 224, Carton 4, dr. 'Procès de Riom: enquêtes et notes', sub-dr. 4, SHAT.
45. 'Cour Suprême de Justice à Riom: commission rogatoire de Me. Lemaire – rapport de M. le controleur de l'administration de l'armée Edmond Briat sur la mobilisation industrielle des Usines Schneider et Creusot', 21 Dec. 1940, conclusions, p. 4, Archives Daladier, 4 DA 12, dr. 6, entry no. 51, FNSP. See also Chambre des Députés: Commission du Travail (hereafter: CTC), 'Séance du 6 mars 1940: audience de M. Charles Pomaret, ministre du travail', pp. 35–7, Folder B102, dr. 3, AAN.
46. See Moch, *Rencontres*, pp. 229–31. Cf. Colton, 'The balance sheets of the "Blum New Deal"', pp. 194–8, 200–1, 203–4.
47. Gamelin to Blum, no. 296/EMA, 11 July 1936; Gamelin to Daladier, no. 7C/EMA, 9 Jan. 1937, both in EMA/SAET, no. 1914, 7 May 1937, p. 4,

Fonds Gamelin, 1K 224, Carton 4, dr. 'Procès de Riom: enquêtes et notes', sub-dr. 4, SHAT.
48. CTC, 'Séance du 17 novembre 1937: rapport de M. Doussin sur la proposition de résolution no. 2164 tendant à inviter le gouvernement à faciliter la rééducation des chomeurs et des manoeuvres de l'industrie', p. 2, Folder B102, dr. 1, AAN.
49. EMA/SAET, no. 1914, 7 May 1937, pp. 4–5, cited above, n.47. Cf. Gamelin, *Servir*, II, pp. 288–9.
50. E. Bonnefous, *Histoire politique de la IIIe République*, VI, *Vers la guerre: du Front Populaire à la conférence de Munich, 1936–1938* (Paris, 1965), pp. 211–14; J.-P. Rioux, 'La Conciliation et l'arbitrage obligatoire des conflits du travail', in Bourdin and Rémond (eds.), *Edouard Daladier*, pp. 112–28; Colton, *Compulsory Labor Arbitration*, pp. 58–70, 120–4; Delperrié de Bayac, *Histoire du Front Populaire*, pp. 427–8.
51. Delperrié de Bayac, *Histoire du Front Populaire*, pp. 416–26.
52. On the *Caisse*, despatches of Sir E. Phipps (British ambassador, Paris), 7 Mar. 1938, FO 371, 21594, C1569/36/17; 5 July 1939, FO 371, 22917, C9674/130/17, PRO; defence expenditure percentages in Frankenstein, 'Aspects financiers du réarmement', p. 11. Cf. Frankenstein, *Le Prix du réarmement*, pp. 86–8, 177–82; G. Bonnet, *Dans la tourmente, 1938–1948* (Paris, 1971), pp. 46, 56–8.
53. Bonnefous, *Histoire politique*, VI, p. 272.
54. English trans. of communiqué issued after the Blum–CGT talks, FO 371, 21594, C1795/36/17, PRO. Similar sentiments were expressed by the *patronat* in the statement released on 21 Mar. 1938 after Blum met representatives of the CGPF and the Metallurgical and Mining Employers (trans. in FO 371, 21594, C1950/36/17, PRO).
55. Duroselle, *La Décadence*, p. 329. Cf. J.-D. Bredin, *Joseph Caillaux* (Paris, 1980), pp. 287–93; P. J. Larmour, *The French Radical Party in the 1930s. The history of a decline* (Stanford CA, 1964), pp. 235–8; S. Berstein, *Histoire du Parti Radical*, II, *Crise du Radicalisme* (Paris, 1982), pp. 495–504, 528–34.
56. E. du Réau, 'L'Aménagement de la loi instituant la semaine des quarante heures', in Bourdin and Rémond (eds.), *Edouard Daladier*, pp. 129–30, 133–8 (quotation p. 138); on Daladier's use of decree powers I have benefited greatly from the unpublished paper of J. Kim Munholland of the University of Minnesota, cited above, n. 42.
57. Delperrié de Bayac, *Histoire du Front Populaire*, pp. 453–62; Larmour, *French Radical Party*, pp. 239–43; Bonnefous, *Histoire politique*, VI, pp. 354–6.
58. CAC, 'Contrôle des fabrications d'armement: rapport de M. Camille Fernand-Laurent', 25 Oct. 1938, p. 3, 16th Leg., Carton 17, AAN; Daladier's announcement on the 48-hour week quoted in du Réau, 'L'aménagement . . . des quarante heures', p. 137. Cf. Colton, *Compulsory Labor Arbitration*, pp. 131–7.
59. CAC, 'rapport . . . Fernand-Laurent', 25 Oct. 1938, cited above, pp. 15, 40.

60. Gamelin, *Servir*, II, pp. 363–4, cf. I, pp. 203–4; F. Varenne, *Mon patron, Georges Mandel* (Paris, 1947), p. 149; O. Wormser, *Georges Mandel, l'homme politique* (Paris, 1967), pp. 209–10.
61. Gamelin, *Servir*, I, pp. 200–3. On the 11 July 1938 Law, see E. C. Kiesling, 'A Staff College for the nation-in-arms: The Collège des Hautes Etudes de Défense Nationale, 1936–1939' (Ph.D. diss., Stanford University, 1988), pp. 73–4.
62. J. Rueff, *De L'Aube au crépuscule. Autobiographie* (Paris, 1977), p. 159. Cf. M. Debré, *Mémoires*, I, *Trois Républiques pour une France* (Paris, 1984), pp. 141–53, 154–9; A. Sauvy, *De Paul Reynaud à Charles de Gaulle. Scènes, tableaux et souvenirs* (Paris, 1972), pp. 70–8.
63. Colton, *Compulsory Labor Arbitration*, pp. 138–41; Fridenson, *Usines Renault*, I, pp. 255–60, 267–71. Cf. the view of the general secretary of the employers' federation, the CGPF, in C.-J. Gignoux, *L'Economie française entre les deux guerres, 1919–1939* (Paris, n.d. (1942?)), pp. 280–2, 307–10; text of Reynaud's radio broadcast of 12 Nov. 1938 and speeches of 26 Nov. and 1 Dec. in P. Reynaud, *Courage de la France* (Paris, 1939), pp. 23–39, 49–59, 61–6.
64. Monmousseau in CTC, 'Séance du 16 décembre 1938: audience de M. Pomaret ... sur les décrets-lois relatifs à la législation sociale', pp. 2–4, 16th Leg., Folder B102, dr. 1, AAN; Pomaret in ibid., pp. 5, 9, 11.
65. R. F. Kuisel, 'Technocrats and public economic policy: from the Third to the Fourth Republic', in Cairns (ed.), *Contemporary France*, p. 239.
66. Larmour, *French Radical Party*, p. 254. This interpretation is supported and developed in Munholland, 'Between Popular Front and Vichy: the decree laws of the Daladier Ministry', cited above, n. 42.
67. See Sauvy, *De Paul Reynaud à Charles de Gaulle*, pp. 80–1.
68. Reynaud, *La France a sauvé L'Europe*, I, pp. 509–15; Sauvy, *De Paul Reynaud à Charles de Gaulle*, p. 80. Cf. a fellow minister's contemporary criticism of Reynaud's plans to finance war in de Monzie, *Ci-devant*, pp. 57–60, 93, 97–8, 120; historical analysis in Duroselle, *La Décadence*, pp. 443–5.
69. Cf. Reynaud's emphasis on revitalising French exports of civilian manufactures in his radio broadcast, 17 Nov. 1938; Chamber speech, 9 Dec. 1938; Senate speech, 28 Dec. 1938 (texts reprinted in Reynaud, *Courage de la France*, pp. 42–7, 68–83, 113–22).
70. CTC, 'Séance du 28 juin 1939: audience de M. Charles Pomaret, ministre du travail', procès-verbal, p. 12, 16th Leg., Folder B102, dr. 2, AAN. For the British parallel cf. Peden, *British Rearmament and the Treasury*, pp. 82–3.
71. Tom Kemp, 'The French economy under the Franc Poincaré', in Cairns (ed.), *Contemporary France*, pp. 66–91 (quotation p. 78). Pomaret's disclosures in CTC, 'Séance du 28 juin 1939 ...', procès-verbal, pp. 5–6; cf. corroborative remarks in Dautry's Riom deposition, 9 Oct. 1940, p. 3, Archives Daladier, 4 DA 13, dr. 5, entry no. 95, FNSP.
72. Boudot, 'Sur les problèmes du financement de la défense nationale'.
73. See Adamthwaite, *France and the Coming of the Second World War*, p. 342.

74. The aborted negotiation may be followed in O. H. Bullitt (ed.), *For the President, Personal and Secret. Correspondence between Franklin D. Roosevelt and William C. Bullitt* (London, 1973), pp. 315–19, 323, 334–6, 353. Cf. its discussion in Peden, *British Rearmament and the Treasury*, p. 86; Duroselle, *La Décadence*, p. 456.
75. De Monzie, *Ci-devant*, p. 120.
76. Sauvy, *De Paul Reynaud à Charles de Gaulle*, p. 80; Duroselle, *La Décadence*, pp. 443–5.
77. CPDN procès-verbal, 5 Dec. 1938 in Gamelin, *Servir*, II, pp. 371–8. Also testimony of air minister La Chambre to the postwar parliamentary inquiry, 25 Nov., 27 Nov. 1947, *C. E. Témoignages*, II, pp. 307–9, 328–335; Jacomet testimony, 18 July 1947, I, p. 210; Monnet, *Mémoires*, pp. 139–57. Cf. discussion by modern historians in Duroselle, *La Décadence*, pp. 447–57; Michel, *Le Procès de Riom*, pp. 220–4; P. Facon, 'Le Plan V (1938–1939)', *RHA*, 4 (1979), pp. 115–18, 121–3.
78. Bouthillier's views reported in Col. Rinderknecht (director, SAET), note on a meeting between Jacomet, Bouthillier and the SAET, 24 July 1939, in Gamelin, *Servir*, II, pp. 435–6. Cf. Commission du Commerce et de l'Industrie: Chambre des Députés. Audience de M. Fernand Gentin, ministre, le 18 octobre 1939, procès-verbal, pp. 13–14, AAN; also Daladier's injunction to husband financial reserves in Présidence du Conseil, 'Directives de la politique économique française: Programmes de production et d'achat pour 1940', 24 Feb. 1940, pp. 2–4, Archives Daladier, 3 DA 5, dr. 2, sub-dr. c, FNSP.
79. See Reynaud, *La France a sauvé l'Europe*, I, pp. 538–40; *Courage de la France*, pp. 145–6, 161, 195–7 (radio broadcasts, 28 Jan., 6 Mar., 21 Apr. 1939); Sauvy, *De Paul Reynaud à Charles de Gaulle*, p. 81.
80. Gamelin's fears of an early, all-out, German western offensive in the autumn of 1939 in his Journal de marche, 9 Sept. 1939, 9 and 14 Oct. 1939, Fonds Gamelin, 1K 224, Carton 9, SHAT; corroborated in Minart, *P. C. Vincennes*, I, p. 45; II, p. 29.
81. CSG, 'Procès-verbal de la séance d'études, 13 mars 1939', p. 5, Carton 1N22, CSG vol. 17, annex no. 1, SHAT.
82. CSG, 'Procès-verbal de la séance d'études, 10 juillet 1939', pp. 2–3, Carton 1N22, CSG vol. 17, annex no. 2, SHAT.
83. Gamelin, *Servir*, I, pp. 289–90; II, p. 434.
84. Weapons' output from Dautry, Riom deposition, 9 Oct. 1940, Archives Daladier, 4 DA 13, dr. 5, FNSP; cf. Colson, briefing paper for Dautry on the latter's appointment as armaments' minister: 'Note sur la situation des fabrications d'armement', 22 Sept. 1939, Fonds Gamelin, 1K 224, Carton 7, SHAT. Warning on continuing French air weakness in Le général, chef d'état-major général de l'Armée de l'Air à M. le ministre de l'air, no. 167/EMGAA, 26 Aug. 1939 (reproduced in La Chambre, testimony to the postwar parliamentary inquiry, 25 Nov. 1947, *C. E. Témoignages*, II, pp. 331–2). Cf. the French air chiefs' confessions of impotence even after six months of respite in the phoney war: 'Guy La Chambre et Vuillemin ont dit que l'aviation était incapable de faire quoi que ce soit avant 2 mois'

(Gamelin, Journal de marche, 11 Mar. 1940, Fonds Gamelin, 1K 224, Carton 9, SHAT).
85. De La Gorce, *The French Army*, p. 294.
86. The key passage from Weygand's speech is reproduced in de Monzie, *Ci-devant*, pp. 125–6. Cf. discussion in Bankwitz, *Weygand and Civil-Military Relations*, pp. 146–8, 261–4; Destremau, *Weygand*, pp. 363–5.
87. De Gaulle, letter to Reynaud, 26 Aug. 1936, in Demey, *Paul Reynaud. Mon père*, p. 304.
88. Sauvy, *De Paul Reynaud à Charles de Gaulle*, pp. 66–7. Cf. Gamelin's counter-complaint of the finance ministry's 'tendances à toujours restreindre les horizons' (*Servir*, II, p. 435).
89. Michel, *Le Procès de Riom*, p. 232.
90. De La Gorce, *The French Army*, p. 294.

6 GAMELIN AND AIR SUPPORT OF THE ARMY

1. See P. Cot, *Le Procès de la République* (New York, 1944, 2 vols.), I, pp. 78–9. Cf. La Chambre's testimony to the post-1945 French parliamentary inquiry, 25 Nov. 1947, *C. E. Témoignages*, II, pp. 295–359; also that of Cot, 1 Aug. 1947, in I, pp. 263–86.
2. Cour Suprême de Justice à Riom. Exécution d'une commission rogatoire: 'Audition de M. Edouard Frédéric-Dupont, le 7 janvier 1941', Fonds Gamelin 1K 224/4, dr. labelled 'Procès de Riom: enquêtes et notes', sub-dr. 2, 'Interrogatoires de Mes. Lagarde et Maillefaud', SHAT.
3. J. A. Gunsburg, 'L'Armée de l'air versus the Luftwaffe, 1940', *Defence Update International*, 45 (1984), pp. 44–53; Gen. C. Christienne, 'La RAF dans la Bataille de France au travers les rapports Vuillemin de juillet 1940', *Service Historique de l'armée de l'air. Recueil d'articles et études (1981–1983)* (Vincennes, 1987), pp. 314–33; J. Millet, 'Un exemple de lutte pour la supériorité aérienne: la Bataille de France', *Histoire de la Guerre Aérienne. Hommage au capitaine Georges Guynemer à l'occasion du 70e anniversaire de sa disparition* (Colloque International Air 1987, Paris, 10–11 Sept. 1987, published Vincennes, 1988), pp. 93–113; Gen. L. Robineau, 'L'Armée de l'air dans la bataille de France', *Les Armées françaises pendant la Seconde Guerre Mondiale, 1939–1945* (Colloque International, Paris, 7–10 May 1985, published Paris 1986), pp. 41–52.
4. Le Goyet, *Mystère Gamelin*, p. 101.
5. See Gen. C. de Cossé-Brissac, 'Combien d'avions allemands contre combien d'avions français le 10 mai 1940?', *Revue de Défense Nationale*, 4 (June 1948), pp. 741–59; Duroselle, *La Décadence*, pp. 251–3, 447–58; *L'Abîme*, pp. 20–2, 62–3.
6. The outstanding study of the French aviation industry is H. E. Chapman, *Reshaping French Industrial Politics. Workers, employers, state officials and the struggle for control in the aircraft industry, 1928–1950* (Ph.D. dissertation, University of California, Berkeley, 1983; Ann Arbor, University Microfilms International, 1984).

7. See E. C. Kiesling, 'A Staff College for the nation-in-arms: the Collège des Hautes Etudes de Défense Nationale, 1936–1939' (Ph.D. dissertation, Stanford University, 1988); Coutau-Bégarie, *Castex*, pp. 114–83.
8. See de La Gorce, *French Army*, pp. 186–7, 244–5, 276–7; Nobécourt, *Histoire politique de l'armée*, I, pp. 183–96; B. J. Bond, *War and Society in Europe, 1870–1970* (London, 1984; Fontana pbk. edn, 1986), pp. 138–58.
9. De Gaulle, undated letter to Paul Reynaud, c. Dec. 1936, Archives Reynaud 74 AP, Carton 20, AN; Reynaud's assertions occurred during the 1937 Chamber debate on the military budget, in *JOC Débats*, 27 Jan. 1937, p. 169.
10. De Gaulle, *Vers l'armée de métier* (Livre de Poche edn, 1973), pp. 88–91. The failure of de Gaulle to champion air–armour combination in this, his most famous book, is overlooked by most of his subsequent admirers and by some critical analysts. See, among others, Doughty, 'De Gaulle's concept of a mobile professional army', in Matthews and Brown (eds.), *The Parameters of War*, pp. 243–56. De Gaulle's oversight is discussed in Bankwitz, *Weygand and Civil-Military Relations*, pp. 124–50.
11. De Gaulle, 'Memorandum adressé aux généraux Gamelin, Weygand et Georges et à MM. Daladier et Reynaud, le 26 janvier 1940', in C. de Gaulle, *Trois études* (Paris, 1973, Livre de Poche edn, 1973), pp. 54–5, 59–60, 68–9; Gamelin, Journal de marche, 14 Sept. 1939, Fonds Gamelin 1K 224/9, SHAT. Cf. discussion of de Gaulle's military writings in A. C. Robertson, *La Doctrine du général de Gaulle* (Paris, 1959), pp. 109–53.
12. See the entry on Laurent Eynac, France's first air minister in British Embassy (Paris), 'Report on leading personalities in France, 1932', FO 371, 16362, W66/66/17, PRO; Boussard, *L'Aéronautique militaire au parlement*, pp. 19–77.
13. See Gen. J.-H. Jauneaud, *J'Accuse le Maréchal Pétain* (Paris, 1977), pp. 13–35; Gunsburg, *Divided and Conquered*, pp. 19–20.
14. See P. Cot, *L'Armée de l'air* (Paris, 1939). On Douhet's influence in interwar French army and air force circles see P. Facon, 'Douhet et sa doctrine à travers la littérature militaire et aéronautique française de l'entre-deux-guerres: une étude de perception', *RHA*, 170 (Mar. 1988), pp. 94–103. For the armée de l'air's strategic thought in its infant years see P. Buffotot, 'La Doctrine aérienne du haut commandement français pendant l'entre-deux-guerres', in Gen. C. Christienne (ed.), *Le Haut Commandement français face au progrès technique entre les deux guerres. Etudes présentées par les membres de la Commission française d'Histoire militaire à l'occasion du Colloque International d'histoire militaire de Bucarest (août 1980)* (Vincennes, 1980), esp. pp. 19–28; Col. P. Le Goyet, 'L'Evolution de la doctrine d'emploi de l'aviation française entre 1919 et 1939', *RHDGM*, 73 (Jan. 1969), pp. 1–41.
15. *Projet de Loi de Défense Nationale: Chambre des Députés*, 15th Leg., no. 3146 (Paris, June 1934). Cf. Boussard, *L'Aéronautique militaire*, pp. 67–81; R. J. Young, 'The strategic dream: French air doctrine in the inter-war period', *JCH*, 9:4 (Oct. 1974), pp. 59–76; Gunsburg, *Divided and Conquered*, p. 20.

16. See M.-E. Debeney, *La Guerre et les hommes. Réflexions d'après-guerre* (Paris, 1937), pp. 87–9; Estienne's preface to G. Murray Wilson, *Les Chars d'assaut au combat, 1916–1919* (Paris, 1931), p. 15. Cf. Griffiths, *Pétain*, pp. 143–9.
17. See R. A. Doughty, 'The French armed forces, 1918–1940', in Murray and Millett, *Military Effectiveness*, II, pp. 49–54; Gunsburg, *Divided and Conquered*, pp. 29–30.
18. See Young, 'Use and abuse of fear', *Intelligence and National Security*, 2, 4 (Oct. 1987), pp. 88–109. For a discussion of similar British perceptions in the mid-1930s as to the intentions behind the Luftwaffe expansion see Bialer, *Shadow of the Bomber*, passim; 'British elite opinion and the influence of the fear of bombardment from the air, 1932–1939', *British Journal of International Studies*, 6 (1980), pp. 32–51. For German perspectives see W. Murray, *Luftwaffe. A history, 1933–1945* (Baltimore, MD, 1985), pp. xi–xiv, 1–27; R. J. Overy, 'The German pre-war aircraft production plans, November 1936–April 1939', *EHR*, 357 (1975), pp. 778–97; 'From "Uralbomber" to "Amerikabomber": the Luftwaffe and strategic bombing', *JSS*, 1:2 (Apr. 1978), pp. 154–78.
19. CAC, 15th Leg., séance du 21 mars 1935: 'Audition de M. le général Maurin, ministre de la guerre', pp. 16–18, 25, Carton 5 bis, dr. VIII, AAN.
20. M. S. Alexander, 'Did the Deuxième Bureau work? The role of intelligence in French defence policy and strategy, 1919–39', *Intelligence and National Security*, 6:2 (Apr. 1991), pp. 293–333.
21. Georges' prediction reported in despatch from Col. T. G. G. Heywood to War Office, London, 8 May 1935, FO 371, 18840, PRO.
22. Gamelin to the CPDN meeting of 26 June 1936, *DDF*, 2nd ser., vol. II (Paris, 1964), doc. no. 369, pp. 553–61.
23. Capt. Townshend Griffiss, assistant military attaché (Paris) for air, to Dept. of the Army (G2), Washington DC, 9 June 1936, 'France: Aviation. Subject: Air Ministry – New Air Minister', Record Group 165, Box no. 844, doc. file no. 2081–846/115, USNARA.
24. The outstanding analysis of inter-war French Radicalism is Berstein, *Histoire du Parti Radical* (2 vols.). Still useful is Larmour, *French Radical Party*. On Zay, a Popular Frontist who was education minister from 1936 to 1939, see his own memoir-diaries, *Carnets secrets de Jean Zay* (Paris, 1942, preface by P. Henriot); *Souvenirs et solitude* (Paris, 1944, reprinted Paris 1987). Cf. P. Morris, 'Two Frenchmen: Henri Queuille and Jean Zay. A review article', in *Review of the Association for the Study of Modern and Contemporary France*, 32 (Jan. 1988), pp. 27–9; M. Ruby, *La Vie et l'oeuvre de Jean Zay* (Paris, 1969). On Mendès-France see J. Lacouture, *Pierre Mendès-France* (Paris, 1981; English trans. G. Holoch, New York, 1984); P. Mendès-France, *Oeuvres complètes* (Paris, 1985 to date).
25. See Cot's enthusiastic report, 14 Oct. 1933, after returning from the USSR, *DDF*, 1st ser., vol. IV (Paris 1968), doc. no. 308, pp. 569–72; Cot, *Procès*, I, pp. 52–6, 63–9, 84–94; II, pp. 218–20, 338–50; evidence to the post-1945 parliamentary inquiry, 1 Aug. 1947, *C. E. Témoignages*, I, pp. 268–77; Duroselle, *La Décadence*, pp. 77–8.

26. Daladier alerted ministers and service chiefs that 'our attitude on 7 March [1936], when Germany reoccupied the Rhineland, has shaken the Little Entente'. CPDN, 29 July 1936, procès-verbal, p. 25, Carton 2N 24, SHAT. Cf. Paillat, *La Guerre à l'horizon*, p. 251.
27. Procès-verbal, CPDN, 29 July 1936, esp. pp. 22–5, Carton 2N 24, SHAT. Cf. Jauneaud, *J'Accuse le Maréchal Pétain*, pp. 29–63; Gunsburg, *Divided and Conquered*, pp. 19–20, 29, 45–53.
28. For the initial compliance of the air force generals in post towards Cot in 1936, and the resulting 'honeymoon' that summer, see Gen. J. Armengaud (bomber fleet commander and air force inspector-general, 1932–6), *Batailles politiques et militaires sur l'Europe. Témoignages, 1932–1940* (Paris, 1948), pp. 35–6.
29. See Paillat, *La Guerre à l'horizon*, pp. 288–93; Jauneaud, *J'Accuse le Maréchal Pétain*, pp. 51–7; L. Moulin, *Jean Moulin* (Paris, 1982), pp. 106–8, 115–27; H. Frenay, *L'Enigme Jean Moulin* (Paris, 1977), pp. 21–30; H. Michel, *Jean Moulin, l'Unificateur* (Paris, 2nd edn, 1970); F. Bédarida, *Jean Moulin et le Conseil National de la Résistance* (Paris, 1984).
30. The description is by Jauneaud, in his *J'Accuse le Maréchal Pétain*, p. 31.
31. Quotations from Cot in CPDN, procès-verbal, 29 July 1936, p. 22, Carton 2N 24, SHAT. The rise of French political opposition to the *marchands des canons*, accused of profiteering through private manufacture and trade in arms, is beyond the purview of this study. Useful exploration of the issue in respect of the aviation industry occurs in Paillat, *La Guerre à l'horizon*, pp. 293–9. The growth of parliamentary concern which led to Cot's and Daladier's legislation of 11 Aug. 1936, may be traced in the minutes of the Chamber army commission, meetings of 23, 30 Jan., 13 Feb., 21 Mar. 1935, 12, 19 Feb., 4 Mar. 1936, in 15th Leg., Carton 5 bis, drs. VII, VIII, IX, AAN; also meeting of 1 July 1936 (audience of Daladier) in *DDF*, 2nd ser., vol. II, doc. no. 375, pp. 569–78; meeting of 8 July 1936 (esp. report by deputy Armand Chouffet on *Projet de Loi no. 465 tendant à la nationalisation des fabrications de matériaux de guerre*, pp. 3–13); audience of Daladier, pp. 14–51; meetings of 15 July, 5, 8 Aug. 1936, all in CAC 16th Leg., Carton 15, AAN.
32. See Clarke, 'Nationalisation of war industries', pp. 411–30; Alexander and Graham (eds.), *French and Spanish Popular Fronts*, pp. 6–7; Cot, *Procès*, I, pp. 270–3, 279–87; II, pp. 272–89; Boussard, *L'Aéronautique militaire*, pp. 112–17; Chapman, *Reshaping French Industrial Politics*, pp. 27–59, 88–156.
33. Armengaud, *Batailles politiques et militaires*, pp. 35–8.
34. See Gunsburg, *Divided and Conquered*, pp. 45–8 for an excellent summary of Cot's objectives and innovations at the air ministry in 1936–7.
35. Quotations from CPDN, procès-verbal, meeting of 26 June 1936, *DDF*, 2nd ser., vol. II, doc. no. 369, pp. 553–61; cf. Cot, *Procès*, II, pp. 226–9, 338–45, 348–54; Jauneaud, *J'Accuse le Maréchal Pétain*, pp. 52–3.
36. See Boussard, *L'Aéronautique militaire*, pp. 109–10; Chapman, *Reshaping French Industrial Politics*, pp. 147–9; Gunsburg, *Divided and Conquered*, pp. 49–50; 'Armée de l'air versus the Luftwaffe', pp. 44–5; French air industry output figures from Frankenstein, *Le Prix du réarmement*, pp.

265–6; Adamthwaite, *France and the Coming of the Second World War*, pp. 162–3.
37. Papiers Schweisguth, 'mementos', 3, 4 Apr. 1936, 351 AP, Carton 3, dr. 8, AN (respectively, meeting between Schweisguth and Gen. Mouchard, Armée de l'Air deputy chief of staff, to discuss air cooperation with Britain; meeting between Gamelin, Schweisguth, Georges, Pujo to prepare an appreciation for Premier Sarraut of the comparative state of French and German armed forces.)
38. Cot to CPDN, 29 July 1936, procès-verbal p. 22, Carton 2N 24, SHAT.
39. Ibid., p. 23.
40. Gamelin, Riom submission: 'La Politique étrangère de la France, 1930–9, au point de vue militaire', Papiers Blum, Carton 3BL3, dr. 1, FNSP.
41. See Chapman, *Reshaping French Industrial Politics*, pp. 157–230 for the most comprehensive and judicious investigation of these and other problems dogging French aviation in 1936–7. Cf. Boussard, *L'Aéronautique militaire*, pp. 103–25.
42. Gunsburg, *Divided and Conquered*, pp. 46–9; Jauneaud, *J'Accuse le Maréchal Pétain*, pp. 54–8, 63–75; Young, 'Strategic dream', pp. 68–70.
43. See Gamelin, *Servir*, II, pp. 247, 277, 319–20.
44. See Frenay, *L'Enigme Jean Moulin*, pp. 23–6, 31–53, 63–75, 213–25; Maurice Duverger, 'Le Mystère Pierre Cot', *Le Monde*, 27 Nov. 1979; obituary of Cot in *The Times*, 23 Aug. 1977. *Pierre Cot (1895–1977). Livre de témoignages* (Paris, 1979); Moulin, *Jean Moulin*, pp. 83, 105–7, 115–16, 126, present favourable portraits of Cot by admirers and former colleagues. Cot fully realised that he aroused extremes of hatred or devotion: see his *Procès*, I, pp. 16–29, 48–75 (esp. p. 75, where he concludes that 'In a French proverb, people are said to have the friends they deserve; if this is equally true of one's enemies, I'm proud of mine.'); also Cot, evidence to the postwar French parliamentary inquiry, 1 Aug. 1947, *C. E. Témoignages*, I, pp. 273–4, 285–6. Cf. appraisals by modern historians in Duroselle, *La Décadence*, pp. 254–5; Young, *In Command of France*, pp. 174–7; Chapman, *Reshaping French Industrial Politics*, pp. 27–33, 146–50, 231–7.
45. Le Col. G. Raquez, attaché militaire près l'Ambassade de Belgique en France à M. le Ministre de la Défense Nationale, Cabinet; au Chef d'Etat-Major de l'Armée, Bruxelles: 'Le débat à la Chambre française sur la Défense Nationale et la conduite de la guerre éventuelle', no. 2 R.P./627, Feb. 1937, AMBAE.
46. Sir Eric Phipps to Foreign Office, London, 4 Sept. 1938, FO 371, 21595, C9239/36/17, PRO.
47. Gamelin, Journal de marche, 18 Sept. 1939, Fonds Gamelin 1K 224, Carton 9, SHAT.
48. Gamelin, Riom submission (cited above, n. 40), p. 14.
49. Gamelin, *Servir*, I, p. 277.
50. EMA/2e Bureau, Note no. 511, 10 Apr. 1936, quoted in 'Note sur le problème militaire français', 1 June 1936, Archives Daladier 4 DA 1, dr. 4, sdr. a, FNSP.
51. Young, 'Strategic dream' (cited above, n. 15), p. 67.

52. P. Buffotot, 'Le Réarmement aérien allemand et l'approche de la guerre vus par le 2e Bureau Air français, 1936–1939', unpublished paper read to the Franco-German Colloquium, Bonn, Sept. 1978, pp. 21, 26–30.
53. Gen. H. Navarre, *Le Temps des vérités* (Paris, 1979), pp. 33–9, 50–5, 60–1; P. Stehlin, *Témoignage pour l'histoire* (Paris, 1964), pp. 55–8, 106–9.
54. Gen. J. Armengaud, 'Les Leçons de la Guerre d'Espagne', *RDM*, CVIIe année, Per. 8, 40 (15 Aug. 1937); H. Niessel, 'Chars, anti-chars et motorisation dans la guerre d'Espagne', *Revue Militaire Générale*, 3 (1938); Gen. J. Duval, *Les Leçons de la Guerre d'Espagne* (Paris, 1938).
55. Madeleine Astorkia, 'L'Aviation et la Guerre d'Espagne: la cinqième arme face aux expériences de la guerre moderne', unpublished paper read to the Franco-German Colloquium, Bonn, Sept. 1978, esp. pp. 19–23. Cf. Dominique de Corta, 'Le Rôle de l'attaché militaire français pendant la guerre civile espagnole', unpublished *mémoire de maîtrise*, Université de Paris I Panthéon-Sorbonne (1981); P. Le Goyet, *Missions de Liaison* (Paris, 1978), pp. 207–58; Duroselle, *La Décadence*, pp. 283–6.
56. Duval, *Leçons de la Guerre d'Espagne*, pp. 82–3, 153–4, 180–1, 228–39.
57. See Gamelin, Journal de marche, 13 Sept., 14 Oct. 1939, Fonds Gamelin 1K 224 Carton 9, SHAT; Young, 'Strategic dream', pp. 67, 76; Gunsburg, *Divided and Conquered*, pp. 52–3.
58. Gamelin, *Servir*, II, pp. 280–1.
59. For the extent of British intelligence about the Armée de l'Air see RAF Intelligence Summaries (France), 1936 and 1938 in AIR 8/210, AIR 8/252, AIR 8/287, PRO; also Group Capt. D. Colyer, British air attaché, Paris: 'Exchange of information between British and French Air Staffs', no. 331/556/35, 20 Mar. 1937; A[ir] I[ntelligence] 3b. 213, 'Comments on the French order-of-battle for the German Air Force', 2 Apr. 1937; 'Exchange of information between British and French Air Staffs, March–April 1937' (minute sheet signed by Group Capt. L. C. H. Medhurst, Deputy Director of Air Intelligence, Air Ministry, London), 21 Apr. 1937, all in AIR 40/186, PRO.
60. Air Ministry memorandum, 26 Apr. 1934 and minute by M. J. Creswell of the Foreign Office, 28 Apr. 1934: 'French Air Force reserves and re-equipment', FO 371, 17653, C2653/85/17, PRO.
61. Report by Group Capt. D. Colyer on an interview with M. Pierre Cot and minute by Ralph Wigram of the Foreign Office, 12 June 1936, FO 371, 19871, C4182/172/17, PRO.
62. Strang, minute of 6 July 1937 on report by Phipps of a conversation with Gamelin, 5 July 1937, FO 371, 20696, C4888/822/17, PRO.
63. See Chapman, *Reshaping French Industrial Politics*, pp. 231–4. Cf. Gunsburg, *Divided and Conquered*, pp. 49–50.
64. See Bullitt, *For the President*, pp. 256–60.
65. 'The reorganization of the French defence ministries', telegram recording talks in Paris between Eden and Chautemps, 25 Jan. 1938, FO 371, 21593, C534/36/17, PRO.
66. Gamelin, 'Les Causes de nos revers en 1940', unpublished signed typescript (n.d. but internal evidence suggests c. 1956–7), p. 7, Fonds Gamelin

1K 224 Carton 7, SHAT. For modern scholarly assessments of La Chambre's ministry cf. Chapman, *Reshaping French Industrial Politics*, pp. 242–56; Duroselle, *La Décadence*, pp. 447–58.
67. See Cot's evidence to the postwar French parliamentary inquiry, 1 Aug. 1947, *C. E. Témoignages*, I, p. 273; also Cot, *Procès*, II, pp. 220, 223–4; 'Exchange of information between British and French Air Staffs, March–April 1937' (minute sheet signed by Group Capt. Medhurst, Deputy Director of Air Intelligence), 21 Apr. 1937, AIR 40/186, PRO; P. Fridenson and J. Lecuir, *La France et la Grande-Bretagne face aux problèmes aériens (1935–mai 1940)* (Paris, 1976), pp. 81–2.
68. Cited in Boussard, *L'Aéronautique militaire*, p. 132; cf. Gen. C. Christienne, 'L'Industrie aéronautique française de septembre 1939 à juin 1940', in *Français et Britanniques dans la Drôle de Guerre. Actes du Colloque franco-britannique tenu à Paris du 8 au 12 décembre 1975* (Paris, 1979), pp. 389–410 (esp. pp. 391–2).
69. CPDN 8 Dec. 1937, procès-verbal, p. 69, Carton 2N 24, SHAT. Cf. Boussard, *L'Aéronautique militaire*, p. 133; Fridenson and Lecuir, *La France et la Grande-Bretagne*, pp. 82–3; Cot, *Procès*, II, pp. 252–62.
70. Vuillemin's letter of 15 Jan. 1938, reproduced in La Chambre's evidence to the postwar French parliamentary inquiry, *C. E. Témoignages*, II, séance du 25 novembre 1947, pp. 300–2. See also Chapman, *Reshaping French Industrial Politics*, pp. 231–2.
71. Commission de l'aéronautique (Chambre des Députés), 16 Feb. 1938, procès-verbal, quoted in Boussard, *L'Aéronautique militaire*, p. 131.
72. Joint session of Senate armed forces' commissions, 9 Feb. 1938, cited in Boussard, *L'Aéronautique militaire*, p. 132.
73. *DDF*, 2nd ser., vol. VIII, doc. no. 447 (Réunion du Conseil Supérieur de l'Air, 15 Mar. 1938), pp. 832–49; La Chambre, testimony to postwar French parliamentary inquiry, 25 Nov. 1947, *C. E. Témoignages*, II, pp. 302–3; Chapman, *Reshaping French Industrial Politics*, pp. 245–8.
74. CPDN 15 Mar. 1938, procès-verbal reproduced in Gamelin, *Servir*, II, pp. 322–8 (statement by Vuillemin quoted at p. 326).
75. Supplementary French defences expenditure 1938, reported by the British military attaché, Paris, 17 Mar. 1938, FO 371, 21594, C1869/36/17, PRO.
76. Table and other statistics cited taken from Boussard, *L'Aéronautique militaire*, pp. 132, 134; cf. pp. 82, 85, 110, 112; Gunsburg, *Divided and Conquered*, pp. 51–3; Christienne, 'L'Industrie aéronautique' (cited above, n. 68), pp. 392–3.
77. Phipps (Paris) to Foreign Office, London, reporting a conversation with Alexis Léger, 4 Sept. 1938, FO 371, 21595, C9239/36/17, PRO.
78. Facon, 'Le Plan V', pp. 102–23. See also La Chambre, evidence to the postwar French parliamentary inquiry, 25 Nov. 1947, *C. E. Témoignages*, II, pp. 303–12.
79. Quoted in Boussard, *L'Aéronautique militaire*, p. 134.
80. *DDF*, 2nd ser., vol. VIII, doc. no. 462 ('Note du Général Gamelin, Chef d'Etat-Major Général de la Défense Nationale', no. 1777/S, 16 Mar. 1938), pp. 864–5.

81. British Industrial Intelligence Centre report, Apr. 1938, quoted in Committee of Imperial Defence Paper no. 1417-B on the French aircraft industry 1937-8, CAB. 53, PRO.
82. Gamelin, *Servir*, I, pp. 277–80.
83. See Chapman, *Reshaping French Industrial Politics*, pp. 253–362; Boussard, *L'Aéronautique militaire*, pp. 135–40; J. Truelle, 'La Production aéronautique militaire française jusqu'en juin 1940', *RHDGM*, 19:73 (Jan. 1969), pp. 75–110.
84. Maj. E. Wouters, attaché de l'air près l'Ambassade de Belgique en Grande-Bretagne à M. le Ministre de la Défense Nationale (Cabinet); au Chef d'Etat-Major de l'Armée: 'Objet – Forces aériennes des Grandes Puissances', no. XVII/AI/5047, 11 Jan. 1939, AMBAE.
85. Boussard, *L'Aéronautique militaire*, p. 139.
86. See P. Facon, 'La Visite du général Vuillemin en Allemagne (16–21 août 1938)', *Service Historique de l'Armée de l'Air. Recueil d'articles et études (1981–1983)*, pp. 221–62. Cf. Gauché, *Deuxième Bureau*, p. 52.
87. Gamelin, *Servir*, II, p. 341. Cf. Adamthwaite, *France and the Coming of the Second World War*, pp. 238–9.
88. P. Facon, 'Le Haut Commandement aérien français et la crise de Munich (1938)', *SHAA. Recueil d'articles et études 1981–1983*, pp. 169–95 (quotation from p. 188). Cf. Duroselle, *La Décadence*, pp. 341–2, 448.
89. 'Le Général chef d'Etat-major général de l'Armée de l'air à M. le Ministre de l'Air', no. 127/EMGAA, 26 Sept. 1938, reproduced in La Chambre's testimony to the postwar French parliamentary inquiry, 25 Nov. 1947, *C. E. Témoignages*, II, p. 313. Cf. Adamthwaite, *France and the Coming of the Second World War*, pp. 239–42.
90. Facon, 'Le Haut Commandement aérien français et la crise de Munich', p. 189.
91. Young, 'Strategic dream', pp. 71–6.
92. Gamelin, *Servir*, I, pp. 281–4.
93. *JOC Débats*, 27 Jan. 1937, pp. 171–2.
94. See this study, ch. 4, p. 97.
95. 'Attributions en temps de paix du Chef d'Etat-Major Général de la Défense Nationale', decree of 21 Jan. 1938, art. 1, reproduced in Gamelin, *Servir*, II, pp. 308–9.
96. Ibid., pp. 309–12.
97. See Gunsburg, *Divided and Conquered*, pp. 54–6, 67–8.
98. Le général Vuillemin, chef d'Etat-Major général de l'armée de l'air à M. le général Gamelin, chef d'Etat-major général de la Défense nationale, 25 Oct. 1938, Carton Z 12964, SHAA, discussed in Facon, 'Le Haut Commandement aérien français et la crise de Munich', pp. 185–9.
99. 'Extrait du procès-verbal de la réunion des chefs d'Etat-Major généraux', 25 Nov. 1938, reproduced in Gamelin, *Servir*, II, pp. 366–9. For the Franco-US air negotiations see J. McVickar Haight, Jr. *American Aid to France, 1938–1940* (New York, 1970); 'Jean Monnet and the American arsenal after the beginning of the war', in E. M. Acomb and M. L. Brown (eds.), *French Society and Culture since the Old Regime* (New York, 1966),

pp. 269–83; 'France, the United States and the Munich Crisis', *JMH*, 32:4 (Dec. 1960), pp. 340–58.
100. CPDN, 5 Dec. 1938, procès-verbal reproduced in Gamelin, *Servir*, II, pp. 371–8 (quotation from p. 373). See also J. Monnet, *Mémoires* (Paris, 1976), pp. 13–36, 59–89, 137–78; Bullitt, *For the President*, pp. 372–3, 382; Chapman, *Reshaping French Industrial Politics*, pp. 244–5, 248, 347.
101. Gen. A. Lelong (French military attaché, London), 'Etude sur la participation de l'Angleterre dans l'éventualité d'une action commune franco-britannique en cas de guerre', 8 Nov. 1938, Papiers Daladier 4 DA 8, dr. 3, sdr. b, FNSP; CSDN Paper no. CU/1 for Daladier, 'La puissance des forces armées franco-britanniques', 22 Nov. 1938, Carton 5N579, dr. 2, SHAT. Cf. Young, *In Command of France*, pp. 218–19; Fridenson and Lecuir, *La France et la Grande-Bretagne*, pp. 101–13.
102. See Arnaud Teyssier, 'L'Appui aux forces de surface: l'armée de l'air à la recherche d'une doctrine (1933–1939)', *Histoire de la Guerre Aérienne* (see above, n. 3), pp. 247–77; Gamelin, *Servir*, I, pp. 278–84.
103. See Fridenson and Lecuir, *La France et la Grande-Bretagne*, pp. 115–62.
104. Obituary of Gamelin in *The Times*, 19 Apr. 1958. See also Fridenson and Lecuir, *La France et la Grande-Bretagne*, pp. 163–78; Christienne, 'L'Industrie aéronautique française', pp. 394–410.

7 GAMELIN, THE MAGINOT LINE AND BELGIUM

1. Useful interpretative studies of inter-war Franco-Belgian relations include J. C. Helmreich, *Belgium and Europe. A study in small power diplomacy* (The Hague, 1976); D. O. Kieft, *Belgium's Return to Neutrality. An essay in the frustrations of small power diplomacy* (Oxford, 1972); J. K. Miller, *Belgian foreign policy between two wars, 1919–1940* (New York, 1951); F. Vanlangenhove, *La Belgique en quête de sécurité, 1920–1940* (Brussels, 1969); *L'Élaboration de la politique extérieure de la Belgique entre les deux guerres* (Brussels, 1983).
2. See Commission de Défense du Territoire (hereafter: CDT), 'memorandum par le général Guillaumat', 23 Oct. 1922, p. 3; CDT, 'séance du 30 octobre 1922: procès-verbal', p. 16; 'rapport au ministre de la guerre sur les principes de l'organisation défensive du territoire', 27 Mar. 1923, all in EMA/3e Bureau, Carton 154, SHAT. Cf. 'La question du système fortifié à créer sur notre frontière de Belgique: notice historique du général Gamelin', pp. 2–3, Fonds Gamelin, 1K224 Carton 7, SHAT.
3. J. C. Helmreich, 'The negotiation of the Franco-Belgian military accord of 1920', *FHS*, 3:3 (Spring 1964), pp. 360–78. The accord's text is found in the documentary collection, *Les Relations militaires franco-belges. Mars 1936 au 10 Mai 1940. Travaux d'un colloque d'historiens belges et français* (Paris, 1968), pp. 43–5 (hereafter: *RMFB*). Cf. J. Willequet, *Albert Ier, roi des Belges* (Brussels, 1979), pp. 185–7.
4. See Kieft, *Belgium's Return to Neutrality*, pp. 41–3; Gamelin, *Servir*, II, p. 25; Gen. P.-E. Tournoux, *Défense des Frontières. Haut Commandement-Gouvernement, 1919–1939* (Paris, 1960), pp. 178–82.

5. J. Vanwelkenhuyzen, *Neutralité armée. La Politique militaire de la Belgique pendant la 'drôle de guerre'* (Brussels, 1979), pp. 101–2.
6. Maginot speech reported in *The Times* (London), 18 Feb. 1930; cf. Rowe, *The Great Wall of France*, p. 52.
7. See Vanwelkenhuyzen, *Neutralité armée*, p. 102; Willequet, *Albert Ier*, pp. 227–30; Gen. R. F. C. van Overstraeten, *Au Service de la Belgique. I, Dans l'étau* (Paris, 1960), pp. 27–37.
8. French mobilisation Plan A bis, operative from 1926 to 1929, is summarised in Tournoux, *Défense des frontières*, p. 335.
9. Cf. treatment of French fortifications' policy in J. Williams, *The Ides of May. The defeat of France, May–June 1940* (London, 1968), pp. 60–75; Horne, *To Lose a Battle*, pp. 26–9. The issue is ably analysed, however, in J.-L. Gentile, 'Le Parlement français et la montée du nazisme, 1919–1933' (Université de Paris IV Sorbonne: unpub. thèse de doctorat de 3e cycle, 1976), pp. 117–61.
10. Reynaud, *Le Problème militaire français*, pp. 66–70.
11. See Gen. G. Riedinger (French military attaché, Brussels, 1934–7), despatches to EMA/2e Bureau dated 9 Apr., 17 Oct. 1934, 6 Nov. 1935; Col. E. Laurent (French military attaché, Brussels, 1937–40), despatches to EMA/2e Bureau, 14, 21 Sept. 1937, 27 Apr. 1939, in EMA/2e Bureau (Belgique), Cartons 7N 2729, 7N 2730, 7N 2731, SHAT.
12. For a penetrating discussion of this predicament's outcome see D. W. Alexander, 'Repercussions of the Breda Variant', *FHS*, 8:3 (Spring 1974), pp. 459–88.
13. Gamelin, 'La Question du système fortifié', p. 5 (cited above, n. 2).
14. See Gamelin, *Servir*, I, pp. 330–3.
15. Gamelin, 'La Question du système fortifié', p. 1.
16. The final report of the Commission de Défense des Frontières, of 6 Nov. 1926, outlined a recommended optimal defensive line inside northern France for the 'eventuality where political or military events prevent us from undertaking the advance ... we envisage' (quoted in 'Rapport de présentation au CSG relatif au programme de défense de la région du Nord: avril 1932', p. 2, in Fonds Gamelin, 1K 224, Carton 8, dr. labelled 'Réunions du CSG, 1932–8', SHAT).
17. See CSG, 'procès-verbal', 28 May 1932; CSG 'procès-verbal', 4 June 1932, Carton 1N 21, vol. 16, pp. 189–202, 203–17, SHAT. Cf. Gamelin, 'La Question du système fortifié', pp. 6–7.
18. See minutes: CSG, 15 Dec. 1925, Carton 1N 20, vol. 15, pp. 103–21; 17 Dec. 1926, Carton 1N 21, vol. 16, pp. 16–33; 18 Jan., 4 July, 12 Oct. 1927, Carton 1N 21, vol. 16, pp. 37–56, 64–79, 87–102, SHAT. Cf. 'Memorandum sur l'état d'avancement des études et des travaux d'organisation des frontières', n.d. for presidents of the Senate and Chamber army commissions, in Papiers Paul Painlevé, 313 AP, Carton 230, AN.
19. See Rowe, *The Great Wall of France*, pp. 26–60; Hughes, *To the Maginot Line*, pp. 195–215; Tournoux, *Défense des frontières*, pp. 50–217 *passim*; Jordan, 'The cut-price war on the peripheries', *passim*.
20. Details of Tardieu's proposals in CSG, 'Procès-verbal de la séance du 4 juin 1932', Carton 1N 21, vol. 16, pp. 204, 208, SHAT; Gamelin, written

submission for the Vichy Supreme Court of Justice at Riom: 'La politique étrangère de la France 1930–9 au point de vue militaire', p. 4, Papiers Blum, 3 BL 3, dr. 1, FNSP; 'La Question du système fortifié', pp. 3, 7; *Servir*, II, pp. 69, 71.
21. Lucien Lamoureux, unpublished 'Souvenirs politiques, 1919–1940', ch. 7, 'Le Cabinet Doumergue, 1934', section entitled 'Autres accords – Belgique', Microfilm 31, Bibliothèque de Documentation Internationale Contemporaine, Université de Paris X Nanterre. For the history of the customs' agreements see G.-H. Soutou, 'La Politique économique de la France à l'égard de la Belgique, 1914–24', in *Les Relations franco-belges de 1830 à 1934* (Metz, 1975).
22. See Gamelin, *Servir*, II, p. 84; CSG, 'Séance du 4 juin 1932: procès-verbal', Carton 1N 21, vol. 16, p. 205, SHAT.
23. Gen. R. F. C. van Overstraeten, *Albert Ier, Léopold III. Vingt ans de Politique militaire belge, 1920–1940* (Bruges, 1946), pp. 191–2.
24. See Gamelin, *Servir*, II, pp. 124–7, 130, 137–40. Cf. the vigorous defence of the Marshal by his one-time military *chef de cabinet* in Conquet, *Auprès du Maréchal Pétain*, pp. 47–56, 80–1, 84–6, 177, 231.
25. See Gen. M. Weygand, 'L'Etat militaire de la France', *RDM*, 8:151:35 (15 Oct. 1936), p. 735; J. Carcopino, *Souvenirs de sept ans, 1937–1944* (Paris, 1953), p. 189; Warner, *Pierre Laval*, pp. 135–9, 150–5; Bankwitz, *Weygand and Civil-Military Relations*, pp. 204–20, 234–9, 243–5, 263–4, 273–81. Cf. more generally, B. Singer, 'From patriots to pacifists: The French primary school teachers, 1880–1940', *JCH*, 12:3 (July 1977), pp. 413–34; R. Martin, *Idéologie et action syndicale. Les instituteurs de l'entre-deux-guerres* (Lyon, 1982), pp. 176–211, 266–75, 299–335, 355–74.
26. Description of Pétain in Gamelin, 'Les Causes de nos revers en 1940' (a 16pp. signed but undated typescript, attributable from internal evidence to the years 1956 or 1957), p. 10, Fonds Gamelin, 1K 224, Carton 7, SHAT. Cf. Griffiths, *Pétain*, pp. 161–4.
27. A wish discussed in Jordan, 'The cut-price war on the peripheries', *passim*; generally, on fortifications as a force-multiplier in French high command calculations see Lee, 'Strategy, arms and the collapse of France', esp. pp. 56–8.
28. CAC, 'Séance du 21 mars 1935: audience de M. le général Maurin, ministre de la guerre, et du général Colson, relative aux effectifs français et allemands', pp. 15, 38–40, in 15th Leg. (1932–6), Carton 5 bis, dr. VIII, AAN.
29. On the April 1935 Gamelin–Cumont conversations and Maurin's contacts with the Belgians see van Overstraeten, *Albert Ier, Léopold III*, pp. 156–7, 162–6, 214–15.
30. See Gentile, 'Le Parlement français et la montée du Nazisme', pp. 117–61.
31. Most of these criticisms are explicit or implicit in the essay by Lee, 'Strategy, arms and the collapse of France', esp. at pp. 56–9, 63–7. Lee argues (p. 67) 'that financial constraints, by delaying the onset of French rearmament in the first half of the 1930s, left France short of what she needed to have in 1940'. This overlooks the two central problems facing French strategic planners in the early 1930s: firstly, that parliamentary

support for major new weaponry, munitions and military vehicle programmes was unobtainable in the politico-economic context of the Geneva disarmament conference; and, secondly, that war material produced by a French rearmament drive between 1930 and 1935 would have been largely obsolete by 1940.

32. Cf. Maurin's remarks in CAC, 'Séance du 21 mars 1935', pp. 15, 38–40, 15th Leg., Carton 5 bis, dr. VIII, AAN; Gamelin's remarks in CSG, 'Procès-verbal de la séance d'études du 14 octobre 1936: soir: la division cuirassée)', pp. 1–3, in Fonds Gamelin, 1K 224, Carton 8, dr. labelled 'Réunions du Conseil Supérieur de la Guerre, 1932–8', SHAT.

33. See the argument of Griffiths (*Pétain*, pp. 136–7), that France's devotion of financial resources on a large scale to the Maginot Line was disproportionate to the security that this investment could purchase and, on this account, was detrimental to the amount of military security procured by France between the wars. Bankwitz (*Weygand and Civil-Military Relations*, p. 139), argues that 'armaments programs made way only gradually and grudgingly for the matériel and the units which gave the army ... mobility. The admission of these elements was especially impeded during the early part of Weygand's command by *the looming presence of the Maginot Line. The great defensive network not only monopolized the credits appropriated to the Army for purposes other than maintenance in a proportion roughly equivalent to two thirds; it also reinforced the defensive orientation of the average military mind*' (emphasis added).

34. See Gentile, 'Le Parlement français et la montée du Nazisme', pp. 139–41.

35. The point appeared through such remarks as those of Pétain, then minister for war, who emphasised in a debate in the Chamber of Deputies over supplementary fortifications' finance, on 14 June 1934: 'I insist on the immediate voting of these credits. They correspond to the profound feeling of the population which wishes to live in peace behind solid frontiers. The fortifications are the inscription on the ground of that will.' (Report in the conservative newspaper *L'Echo de Paris*, 15 June 1934, quoted in Griffiths, *Pétain*, p. 136.)

36. The French military establishment's repudiation of any 'policy of adventurism' was most authoritatively expounded in the intervention of General Louis Maurin, then war minister, during the debate in the Chamber of Deputies on 15 Mar. 1935 over restoration of two-year conscript service. 'How [asked Maurin] could anyone believe that we contemplate the offensive when we have spent billions to establish a fortified barrier? Would we be mad enough to go beyond this barrier to I don't know what kind of adventure?' (in République Française: *JOC Débats*, 15 Mar. 1935, p. 1045).

37. Cf., however, the contention of Lee ('Strategy, arms and the collapse of France', p. 59) that 'From the end of 1927 to the middle of 1936, France spent 5,000 million francs on fortifications and only 3,400 million francs on weaponry. The expense of the Maginot Line thus cut across the simultaneous effort to substitute firepower for manpower.' See also above, n. 33.

38. On Tardieu's *Plan d'outillage national* of 1930, see R. F. Kuisel, *Capitalism and the State in Modern France. Renovation and Economic Management in the Twentieth Century* (Cambridge, 1981), pp. 90–2; also Clague, 'Vision and myopia in the new politics of André Tardieu', pp. 105–29. On Popular Front proto-Keynesianism and strategies for demand management, see Colton, 'The balance sheets of the "Blum New Deal"', pp. 181–208. Cf., on Blum's *politique du pouvoir d'achat* and the discrepancy between the Popular Front's domestic agenda and France's need to rearm, Jackson, *Defending Democracy*, pp. 160–83, 190–201.
39. An inkling of awareness that such a dimension to the Maginot Line existed appears in Kuisel, *Capitalism and the State* (pp. 69–71), but is not explored in any depth. It is ignored completely in the analysis by Caron (*An Economic History of Modern France*, pp. 248–58) of the French economy and public finances in the inter-war years. Interestingly, Rowe has written (*The Great Wall of France*, p. 57), that André Maginot's 'fault was an obsession with the defence of his ancestral province ... His greatness was bounded by his deep-rooted local patriotism'. Is this a suggestion that even Maginot – a deputy whose constituency lay in the frontier département of the Meuse – may not have been blind to the 'pork-barrelling' advantages that he might personally derive at election-time from construction of the fortifications in his own locality?
40. CSG, 'Séance du 4 juin 1932: procès-verbal', Carton 1N 21, vol. 16, pp. 207–10, SHAT. Four years later Daladier, as minister for war and national defence, revealed to parliamentarians that French intelligence judged the Belgian army to be improving as an effective fighting force, its peacetime strength being assessed as 25,000 volunteer professionals and 44,000 militia undergoing eight to thirteen months service, organised into six infantry and two cavalry divisions, one army artillery brigade, two anti-aircraft artillery regiments, three aircraft regiments, one corps of Chasseurs Ardennais and five battalions of frontier cyclists ('Audience de M. Daladier devant la Commission des Finances: aperçu général de la situation de l'Europe au point de vue des armements militaires de divers pays', 27 Nov. 1936, Archives Daladier, 1 DA 7, dr. 3, sdr. a, FNSP).
41. On French command and control doctrine embodied in the concept of the rigidly controlled *bataille de conduite*, and the inhibitions this fostered, see the excellent summary in Doughty, 'The French armed forces, 1919–1940', in Murray and Millett (eds.), *Military Effectiveness*, II, pp. 54–8. Cf. Doughty, *Seeds of Disaster*, pp. 74–5, 83, 89–90, 93–111; Bankwitz, *Weygand and Civil-Military Relations*, pp. 126, 131, 133–6, 139–40, 144–5; Dutailly, *Les Problèmes de l'Armée de Terre*, pp. 180–96.
42. See Rowe, *The Great Wall of France*, pp. 44–6, 52–7, 82–5.
43. Gamelin, *Servir*, II, p. 184, n. 1.
44. 'Réunions des 6e, 16e et 20e Régions militaires', 16 Feb. 1935; 'Réunion de la CORF', 14 Mar. 1935; 'Réunion des commandants de Régions frontières', 15 Apr. 1935; 'memento', 13 Mar. 1935, all in Papiers Schweisguth, 351 AP 2, dr. 3, AN; see also official minutes of the CORF, 55th meeting, 14 Mar. 1935, EMA/3e Bureau, unnumbered carton labelled 'CORF, 1927–35', SHAT; Gamelin, 'La Question du système fortifié à

créer sur notre frontière du nord', p. 2, n. 3, Fonds Gamelin, 1K 224, Carton 7, SHAT. Cf. Hughes, *To the Maginot Line*, pp. 195–7, 203–5, 244–5.

45. Gamelin, 'La question du système fortifié', p. 3, cited above; more generally, on French anxieties about surprise attack by Germany, see R. J. Young, 'L'Attaque brusquée and its use as myth in inter-war France', *Historical Reflections/Réflexions Historiques*, 8:1 (Spring 1981), pp. 93–113.
46. Papiers Schweisguth, 'mementos', 8, 12 Aug. 1935, 351 AP 2, dr. 5, AN.
47. Jean Fabry, Maginot's successor as president of the Chamber's army commission, warned fellow deputies in 1933 that the *frontalier* system depended upon 'the sense of military duty which motivates the peoples of the frontier localities'. (CAC, 'Communication du président sur l'organisation défensive de la frontière du Nord-Est', 18 Jan. 1933, 15th Leg., Carton 738/48 bis, AAN.) War Plan D – operative from Apr. 1933 to Apr. 1935 – designated the French Third, Fourth and Fifth Armies for the Saar–Lorraine front with the 'general mission' of '*the defence, whatever the cost* [emphasis added], of the fortified position' (Archives Daladier, 'Les Plans de mobilisation', 4 DA 3, dr. 4, sub-dr. c, pp. 85–6, FNSP).
48. CSG, 'Séance du 28 mai 1932: procès-verbal', Carton 1N 21, vol. 16, p. 196, SHAT.
49. Gamelin: 'Memento sur la position générale de l'armée française', Jan. 1934, Fonds Gamelin 1K 224, Carton 8, dr. labelled 'Réunions du Conseil Supérieur de la Guerre, 1932–8', SHAT.
50. CAC, 'Séance du 21 mars 1935: audience de M. le général Maurin, ministre de la guerre, et du général Colson, relative aux effectifs français et allemands', pp. 19–20, 15th Leg., Carton 5 bis, dr. VIII, AAN.
51. CSG, 'Séance du 28 mai 1932: procès-verbal', Carton 1N 21, vol. 16, p. 190, SHAT. Cf. Gamelin, *Servir*, II, pp. 68–9.
52. According to Gamelin (*Servir*, II, p. 69), the timing of the CSG discussion of this credit resulted from collusion between Tardieu and the president of the Senate army commission, General Adolphe Messimy (who had been war minister himself in 1911–12). These politicians wished to resolve the issue during the parliamentary recess brought about by the May 1932 Chamber elections, without a public debate that might exacerbate Belgian suspicions of French defensive plans for the northern frontier.
53. Gamelin and Tardieu, when both were on Joffre's staff in 1915, had jointly studied possible postwar frontier defences, enabling Gamelin to claim in 1932 (*Servir*, II, pp. 66–7, 69) that he was striving to profit from Tardieu's premiership to accomplish a pre-arranged defence programme. Cf. Le Goyet, *Mystère Gamelin*, pp. 22–36. On Maubeuge's value in 1914 and its potential in the early 1930s, see: le général H. Gouraud à M. le général Weygand, lettre, 29 Sept. 1931; rapport de M. le colonel Larcher sur la déclassification des forts de Maubeuge, Sept. 1931; le général C. Belhague, inspecteur-général du génie, à M. François Piétri, ministre de la défense nationale, 12 Apr. 1931, all in CSG Carton no. 45 labelled 'Défense des frontières, 1930–9' (Folders '1931' and '1932'), SHAT; Le Goyet, *Missions de liaison*, pp. 131–2.

54. 'Rapport de présentation au Conseil Supérieur de la Guerre: Région du Nord', Apr. 1932, pp. 6, 9–10, Fonds Gamelin, 1K 224, Carton 8, dr. labelled 'Réunions du CSG, 1932–8', SHAT (emphasis in original).
55. CSG, 'Séance du 28 mai 1932: procès-verbal', Carton 1N 21, vol. 16, pp. 190–1, SHAT.
56. Pétain, *avis écrit* to 28 May 1932 CSG, in Gamelin, *Servir*, II, p. 70.
57. Guillaumat in, respectively, CSG, 'Séance du 28 mai 1932: procès-verbal', Carton 1N 21, vol. 16, p. 197, SHAT; Gentile, 'Le Parlement français et la montée du Nazisme', p. 127.
58. CSG, 'Séance du 28 mai 1932: procès-verbal', p. 191. Pétain's new-found concern with air forces stemmed from his nomination in Feb. 1931 as inspector of the DAT (Défense Aérienne du Territoire), France's newly established metropolitan air-defence programme (a post he held until he accepted appointment as war minister in the government formed by Gaston Doumergue after the 6 Feb. 1934 riots). See Paoli, *La Fin des illusions*, pp. 84–90; Conquet, *Auprès du Maréchal Pétain*, pp. 61–3, 109–10, 231–2; Griffiths, *Pétain*, pp. 143–7, 153–4.
59. Gamelin, *Servir*, II, p. 71.
60. CSG, 'Séance du 28 mai 1932: procès-verbal', Carton 1N 21, vol. 16, p. 198; Piétri's observation is repeated in Gamelin, *Servir*, II, p. 71.
61. Gamelin, *Servir*, II, p. 71.
62. Sources on the 1933 split within the CSG include the minutes of its meetings of 25 Jan. 1933, Carton 1N 21, vol. 16, pp. 225–40; 15 May 1933 and 18 Dec. 1933, Carton 1N 22, vol. 17, pp. 8–30, 34–47; also Gamelin, *Servir*, II, pp. 98–109; Weygand, *Mémoires*, II, pp. 397–405. Cf. interpretations in Bankwitz, *Weygand and Civil-Military Relations*, pp. 95–105; Doise and Vaïsse, *Diplomatie et outil militaire*, p. 305; de La Gorce, *La République et son armée*, pp. 325–8.
63. Foch quoted in Capitaine de frégate J. Rouch, 'Souvenirs sur le maréchal Foch', *RDM*, 8:9 (15 May 1932), p. 354.
64. Gamelin, *Servir*, II, p. 71.
65. Ibid., p. 72; also 'La Question du système fortifié à créer sur notre frontière du nord', pp. 6–7, Fonds Gamelin, 1K 224, Carton 7, SHAT.
66. CSG, 'Séance du 4 juin 1932: procès-verbal', Carton 1N 21, vol. 16, pp. 205–16 *passim*; Gamelin, *Servir*, I, pp. 81–108. With Weygand and Gamelin in the minority at the vote were Generals Gouraud, Dufieux, Belhague and Mittelhauser; their opponents were Generals Guillaumat, Debeney, Maurin, Brécard, Ragueneau, Walch and Hergault. None of the marshals attended.
67. A major concern of both Weygand and Gamelin was the doubtful combat-fitness of French reservist divisions which would, however, have to be risked in operations at the start of a war to provide sufficient large units for the bound forward into Belgium. See Weygand in CSG, 'Séance du 4 juin 1932: procès-verbal', Carton 1N 21, vol. 16, p. 217, SHAT. Cf. Pétain's criticism of the poor value of French reserve formations in 1914, in CSG, 'Séance du 18 décembre 1933: procès-verbal', Carton 1N 22, vol. 17, p. 42, SHAT; also discussed in Bankwitz, *Weygand and Civil-Military Relations*,

pp. 103–4, 157–9, 248; de La Gorce, *La République et son Armée*, pp. 326–7; Doughty, *Seeds of Disaster*, pp. 28–9, 31–2.
68. CSG, 'Séance du 4 juin 1932: procès-verbal', Carton 1N 21, vol. 16, p. 217.
69. Born in 1881 at Ypres, Devèze made his political career in Brussels. From 1939 to 1946 he represented the Walloon constituency of Verviers.
70. CSG report on additional frontier defences (undated but c. 1933), p. 16, EMA/3e Bureau, CORF Carton labelled 'CORF, 1927–35', SHAT. Cf. the conclusion of the historian Judith Hughes (*To the Maginot Line*, p. 223), that 'the Belgians viewed France's failure to construct concrete bastions in the north as primarily a danger to themselves; the unfortified frontier constituted an invitation to the Germans to repeat their strategy of 1914'.
71. See *Les Relations militaires franco-belges*, pp. 19–20; for evidence that Chardigny, French military attaché in Brussels till 1933, may have exacerbated Belgian suspicions of the military accord, see van Overstraeten, *Albert Ier, Léopold III*, p. 82.
72. See British Foreign Office paper: 'Post-war developments in general staff conversations between Britain and France', May 1935 (which records Belgian requests for a British military guarantee in May 1934, during a visit to London by the Belgian foreign minister, Paul Hymans – requests repeated in the autumn of 1934 by Devèze to the British ambassador in Brussels, Sir Esmond Ovey), FO 371, 18840, C3944/55/18, PRO. Cf. Vanlangenhove, 'La Belgique en quête de sécurité', pp. 13–15, 29–40; also historians' interpretations of the question in D. Stevenson, 'Belgium, Luxembourg and the defence of Western Europe, 1914–1920', *International History Review*, 4:4 (Nov. 1982), pp. 502–23; S. Marks, '*Ménage à trois*. The negotiations for an Anglo-Franco-Belgian alliance in 1922', ibid., pp. 524–53; Willequet, *Albert Ier*, pp. 186–90; Kieft, *Belgium's Return to Neutrality*, pp. 20–4.
73. See Kieft, *Belgium's Return to Neutrality*, pp. 50–4.
74. See van Overstraeten, *Dans l'étau*, pp. 10–16, 18–44.
75. Kieft, *Belgium's Return to Neutrality*, p. 42.
76. See van Overstraeten, *Albert Ier, Léopold III*, pp. 42–3, 46–7.
77. See Willequet, *Albert Ier*, pp. 153–9, 210–17; R. Aron, *Léopold III ou le choix impossible, février 1934–juillet 1940* (Paris, 1977), pp. 155–61; Kieft, *Belgium's Return to Neutrality*, pp. 33–4, 45–7.
78. See the memoirs of the director of political affairs at the Belgian foreign ministry, Baron P. van Zuylen, *Les Mains libres. Politique extérieure de la Belgique, 1914–1940* (Brussels, 1950), pp. 331–5; also van Overstraeten, *Albert Ier, Léopold III*, pp. 177–84, 189–91, 194–9.
79. See report of 5 Feb. 1936 by the French ambassador in Brussels, Jules Laroche, to French foreign minister Flandin, on talks with Vandervelde, *DDF*, 2nd ser., vol. 1, docs. nos. 136, 137; also 'memento', 16–17 July 1936, Papiers Schweisguth, 351 AP, Carton 3, dr. 9, AN.
80. See van Zuylen, *Les Mains libres*, pp. 334–8; van Overstraeten, *Dans l'étau*, pp. 54–5.
81. See *DDB*, vol. III, docs. nos. 159, 160 (both Devèze to van Zeeland, reporting talks in Brussels with the French military attaché, Gen.

Riedinger, 17, 24 Jan. 1936), 171 (Vanlangenhove's record of his conversations at the Quai d'Orsay). Cf. Vanlangenhove, *La Belgique en quête de sécurité*, pp. 83–5.

82. The letters are reproduced in *Les Relations militaires franco-belges*, pp. 46–7; also in *DDB*, vol. III, doc. no. 176.

83. The elections gave the Flemish Nationalists 16 seats, the Rexists 21 and the Communists 9, in a Chamber of 202 representatives. On the heated politics of the summer of 1936 in Belgium, see Laroche, despatch to Flandin, 28 May 1936, EMA/2e Bureau (Belgique), Carton 7N 2733, SHAT; also informative are the memoirs of the Belgian minister of transport from June 1936 to Oct. 1937 (later minister for health, Apr. 1939–May 1940), M.-H. Jaspar, *Souvenirs sans retouche* (Paris, 1968), pp. 182–94, 204–21, 231–4, 263–4.

84. 'Rapport', 30 June 1936, Papiers Schweisguth, 351 AP, Carton 3, dr. 9, AN; report by F. Sarrien (French Consul, Liège), to Ambassador Laroche (forwarded by Riedinger to Daladier), 17 June 1936, in EMA/2e Bureau (Belgique), Carton 7N 2733, dr. 1, SHAT.

85. *DDB*, vol. IV, doc. no. 128 (circular to Belgian diplomatic posts carrying the text of Leopold's statement), 15 Oct. 1936. Cf. the memoirs of the foreign minister in van Zeeland's second government, P.-H. Spaak, *Combats inachevés*, I, *De l'indépendance à l'alliance* (Paris, 1969), pp. 42–53; and J. Willequet, *Paul-Henri Spaak. Un homme, des combats* (Brussels, 1975), pp. 55–9.

86. See *DDF*, 2nd ser., vol. III, docs. nos. 358, 359, pp. 547–59; Laroche, the French ambassador in Brussels, anticipated both the furore in the French newspapers and Belgian discomfiture at this. Accompanying his report of Leopold's declaration on 14 Oct. 1936, Laroche requested the Quai – presumably via Pierre Comert's press liaison office and the Quai's *fonds secrets* – to encourage 'the press to behave prudently in its commentaries' on the policy of Belgium (p. 521, n. 1). Note the tendency of some modern historians to perpetuate the myth of Belgium's pre-1936 'alliance' with France, as in R. Doughty's comment (*The Seeds of Disaster*, p. 65), that 'The [French] High Command ... clung to its original intention to rush forward into Belgium ... and it became particularly problematic *when that uncertain ally defected from her alliance with France*' (emphasis added).

87. CSG, 'Séances d'études: procès-verbaux des réunions du 14 octobre 1936; 15 octobre 1936', in Fonds Gamelin, 1K 224, Carton 8, dr. 'Réunions du CSG, 1932-8', SHAT.

88. See Kieft, *Belgium's Return to Neutrality*, pp. 148–54; van Overstraeten, *Dans l'étau*, p. 69.

89. Text of the Anglo-French declaration in *DDB*, vol. IV, doc. no. 227. Cf. *Les Relations militaires franco-belges*, pp. 29–33, 59; van Overstraeten, *Albert Ier, Léopold III*, pp. 257–9.

90. See Riedinger (French military attaché, Brussels), report on meeting with Devèze, 29 Oct. 1934, in EMA/2e Bureau (Belgique), Carton 7N 2729, SHAT; van Overstraeten, *Albert Ier, Léopold III*, pp. 137–9.

91. Cumont's report of the talks in van Overstraeten, *Albert Ier, Léopold III*, pp. 141–3. Cf. Gunsburg, *Divided and Conquered*, pp. 21–2. Cumont had

become Belgian army chief of staff in October 1934 and remained in post until succeeded by General Edouard van den Bergen in September 1935.
92. See Riedinger, despatch to war ministry (2e Bureau), 16 Jan. 1935, EMA/ 2e Bureau (Belgique), Carton 7N 2729, SHAT; Loizeau's report of his meeting with Cumont, 22 Feb. 1935; 'Grand Rapport', Papiers Schweisguth, 351 AP, Carton 2, dr. 3, AN; Gamelin, *Servir*, II, p. 165; van Overstraeten, *Albert Ier, Léopold III*, pp. 144–6.
93. Details of Bineau's career in CSG, Carton 1N 22, vol. 17, pp. 72–3, SHAT.
94. *Les Relations militaires franco-belges*, pp. 47–51 (text of 5 Apr. 1935 Cumont–Gamelin talks); van Overstraeten, *Albert Ier, Léopold III*, pp. 162–4; *Dans l'étau*, pp. 50–1 (mistakenly dating the talks to 25 April); 'Rapport', 23 July 1935, Papiers Schweisguth, 351 AP, Carton 2, dr. 5, AN. Cf. Le Goyet, *Mystère Gamelin*, pp. 218–19; Gunsburg, *Divided and Conquered*, p. 28.
95. Van Overstraeten, *Albert Ier, Léopold III*, pp. 173–4; *Dans l'étau*, pp. 51–2; Gamelin, *Servir*, II, p. 186; Fabry, *De La Place de la Concorde*, p. 68; Journal, 6–7 Sept. 1935, Cabinet du ministre de la guerre, Carton 5N 581, dr. 2, SHAT. Cf. criticism of the DLM in the report on these manoeuvres to Pétain from his *chef de cabinet militaire* (Conquet, *Auprès du Maréchal Pétain*, pp. 208–9).
96. 'Rapport', 21 Jan. 1936, Papiers Schweisguth, 351 AP, Carton 3, dr. 7, AN.
97. 'Memento', 22 Feb. 1936, Papiers Schweisguth, 351 AP, Carton 3, dr. 7, AN; cf. the report on this talk by the Belgian attaché, Col. Raquez, in *DDB*, vol. III, doc. no. 170 (Count de Kerchove de Denterghem [Belgian ambassador, Paris], to Van Zeeland, 26 Feb. 1936).
98. See B. J. Bond, *British Military Policy between the Wars* (Oxford, 1980), pp. 227–8; Emmerson, *The Rhineland Crisis*, pp. 193–96.
99. 'Compte-rendu d'une mission à Londres, 17–23 mars 1936', Papiers Schweisguth, 351 AP 3, dr. 8, AN. Van Overstraeten records (*Albert Ier, Léopold III*, p. 191), that Belgium's military attaché in London, General Nyssens 'had pressed [at the completion of his posting in Dec. 1935] the British general staff to agree to an eventual meeting with the Belgian staff . . . But the reply had been . . . that this suggestion could not be acted upon for the moment.'
100. 'Memento', 21 Apr. 1936, Papiers Schweisguth, 351 AP, Carton 3, dr. 8, AN.
101. *Les Relations militaires franco-belges*, pp. 52–8 (procès-verbal, 15 May 1936 conference); 'mementos', 14–15 May 1936, Papiers Schweisguth, 351 AP, Carton 3, dr. 9, AN; report from French ambassador Laroche to Flandin, 20 May 1936, on reaction in Brussels to the conference, in EMA/ 2e Bureau (Belgique), Carton 7N 2733, dr. 1, SHAT. Cf. van Overstraeten, *Albert Ier, Léopold III*, pp. 206, 220; Gamelin, *Servir*, II, p. 216.
102. *DDF*, 2nd ser., vol. II, doc. no. 480 (Schweisguth, report, 18 July 1936); Dufieux's report of 20 July 1936, in EMA/2e Bureau (Belgique), Carton 7N 2733, dr. 5, SHAT; 'mementos', 3 July, 16–17 July, 28–31 July 1936, Papiers Schweisguth, 351 AP, Carton 3, dr. 9, AN.

103. CSG, 'Séance d'études du 15 octobre 1936 . . . missions des armées: procès-verbal', p. 2, Fonds Gamelin 1K 224, Carton 8, dr. labelled 'Réunions du CSG, 1932–8', SHAT.
104. 'Rapport', 20 Oct. 1936, Papiers Schweisguth, 351 AP, Carton 3, dr. 10, AN.
105. 'Compte-rendu d'une mission à Londres, 17–23 mars 1936', Papiers Schweisguth, 351 AP, Carton 3, dr. 8, AN.
106. Col. F. G. Beaumont-Nesbitt to War Office (London), 28 Oct. 1936, FO 371, 19872, C7762/172/17, PRO.
107. Hughes, *To the Maginot Line*, p. 216.
108. 'La Question du système fortifié à créer sur notre frontière du nord', p. 8, Fonds Gamelin, 1K 224, Carton 7, SHAT.
109. E. Daladier, ministre de la guerre (cabinet du ministre) à l'EMA: 'Note sur la fortification des frontières', 15 June 1933; also a note of the same title, no. 6954, 16 Sept. 1933, both in Archives Daladier, 4 DA 7, dr. 7, sdr. a, FNSP; CAC, 'Séance du 24 mai 1934 pour considérer un Projet de Loi no. 3146 tendant à l'approbation d'un programme de travaux concernant la défense nationale', p. 3, 15th Leg., Carton XV/739/48bis, AAN; *JOC Débats*, 16 June 1934, p. 1529; *JO Sénat: Débats*, 28 June 1934, p. 849. Cf. Gamelin, *Servir*, II, pp. 109–10.
110. The well-connected Parisian journalist André Géraud recorded how Daladier punctured the pretensions of strategists (Pertinax, *Les Fossoyeurs*, I, p. 112).
111. Daladier to Auriol, letter, no. 10,733, 21 Oct. 1936, Archives Daladier, 4 DA 7, dr. 7, sdr. b, FNSP.
112. Quoted in Rowe, *The Great Wall of France*, p. 93. Cf. Gamelin, *Servir*, II, pp. 249–50.
113. Bankwitz adds that 'These fears . . . were epitomised by Daladier's opposition to early offensives in Belgium which, in his words, would "kill one or two million of [France's] sons without the allies assuming their share of the common sacrifice"' (*Weygand and Civil-Military Relations*, p. 163, quoting Daladier, testimony, 21 May 1947, to the postwar French parliamentary inquiry, *C. E. Témoignages*, I, p. 22).
114. EMA/3e Bureau: 'Note sur les régions fortifiées. 2e partie – état d'avancement des travaux et de l'armement des ouvrages', 23 June 1936, Archives Daladier, 4 DA 7, dr. 7, sdr. b, FNSP. Cf. Tournoux, *Défense des frontières*, pp. 265–6.
115. See Frankenstein, *Le Prix du réarmement français*, pp. 46–9, 53–4, 57–8.
116. Papiers Schweisguth, 'Grand Rapport', 7 July 1936 and 'memento', 8 July 1936, 351 AP, Carton 3, dr. 9, AN.
117. Daladier, Cassell speech of 31 Oct. 1936 cited in Rowe, *The Great Wall of France*, p. 93.
118. Gamelin, 'La Question du système fortifié à créer sur notre frontière du nord', p. 6, Fonds Gamelin, 1K 224, Carton 7, SHAT.
119. CSG, 'Séance d'études du 15 octobre 1936 . . . missions des armées: procès-verbal', pp. 4–5, Fonds Gamelin, 1K 224, Carton 8, dr. labelled 'Réunions du CSG, 1932–8', SHAT.
120. Gamelin, *Servir*, II, p. 250.

121. 'Note sur les crédits alloués aux régions frontières de 1935 à 1938', 9 Sept. 1938, Archives Daladier, 4 DA 7, dr. 7, sdr. c, FNSP; also CSG, 'Séance d'études du 14 octobre 1936 . . . armement: procès-verbal', p. 4, Fonds Gamelin, 1K 224, Carton 8, dr. labelled 'Réunions du CSG, 1932–8', SHAT.
122. A point underlined by Bankwitz (*Weygand and Civil-Military Relations*, p. 150), who stresses that 'Weygand's and Gamelin's policy was to concentrate attention on modernising the army once the main Maginot fortifications in Alsace and Lorraine had been completed'.
123. Etat Français: Cour Suprême de Justice à Riom, 'Commission rogatoire de Me. René Baraveau. Déposition du général Emile Ricard, le 9 décembre 1940. Annexe: "Note sur l'importance des travaux d'organisation défensive exécutés par les armées françaises de septembre 1939 à mai 1940"', Fonds Gamelin, 1K 224, Carton 5, dr. 1, SHAT.
124. Gamelin, *Servir*, II, p. 316 (Gamelin noting here that his request 'resulted in practically no action. We had to continue simply . . . on the basis of credits that we already expected.')
125. Hughes, *To the Maginot Line*, p. 218.
126. Van Overstraeten, *Albert Ier, Léopold III*, p. 242.
127. Prételat, letter to Gamelin, 19 Dec. 1938, Archives Daladier, 4 DA 7, dr. 7, sdr. c, FNSP; copy also annexed to 'Commission rogatoire de Me. René Baraveau. Déposition du général Colson, le 23 juin 1941', Fonds Gamelin, 1K 224, Carton 5, dr. 1, SHAT.
128. Gen. G. Prételat, *Le Destin tragique de la Ligne Maginot* (Paris, 1950), pp. 12–13.
129. See official doctrine regarding operational use of the Ardennes as codified in the army's *Instruction sur l'organisation défensive du territoire* (Paris, 1929), pp. 1–2, copy in EMA/3e Bureau, unnumbered carton labelled 'CORF, 1927–35', SHAT.
130. Reproduced in Gamelin, *Servir*, II, p. 128. Cf. Conquet, *Auprès du Maréchal Pétain*, pp. 56–7; *L'Enigme des blindés, 1932–40* (Paris, 1956), pp. 178–81.
131. Gamelin quoted in P.-E. Tournoux, *Défense des frontières*, p. 271; see also analysis of how this outlook bred French military complacency in the face of parliamentary warnings of the Ardennes' vulnerability in early 1940 in M. S. Alexander, 'Prophet without honour? The French High Command and Pierre Taittinger's report on the Ardennes defences, March 1940', *War and Society*, 4:1 (May 1986), pp. 53–77.
132. Van Overstraeten, *Albert Ier, Léopold III*, p. 186 (citing report from Capt. Gierst of the Belgian general staff).
133. Ibid. (citing report from Col. Georges Raquez, Belgian military attaché, Paris).
134. CSG, 'Séance d'études du 15 octobre 1936 . . . missions des armées: procès-verbal', pp. 5–6, Fonds Gamelin, 1K 224, Carton 8, dr. labelled 'Réunions du CSG, 1932–8', SHAT.
135. Gamelin, *Servir*, I, pp. 245, 94. Cf. a description of the post-1934 preparations in the Ardennes sector by the chief of staff of the Second Army,

deployed to defend it after war's outbreak, in Gen. Edmond Ruby, *Sedan: Terre d'épreuve. Avec la IIe armée, mai–juin 1940* (Paris, 1948), pp. 17–37.
136. EMA/3e Bureau, 'Le problème militaire français', 1 June 1936, pp. 7–9, Archives Daladier, 4 DA 1, dr. 4, sdr. a, FNSP.
137. Ibid., pp. 6–7. Cf., on the evolution of French doctrines of *colmatage* and armoured counter-stroke: Bankwitz, *Weygand and Civil-Military Relations*, pp. 123–4, 129–34, 154–5, 158–9; Doughty, *Seeds of Disaster*, pp. 92–4, 98–9, 102–5, 110–11, 154–5, 182.
138. See Gamelin, *Servir*, II, pp. 290–1, 342; also EMA, 'Note sur la division cuirassée et les manoeuvres de Barrois', 13 Feb. 1937, CSG Carton 1N37, sdr. 4, SHAT; de Gaulle (commanding 507th tank regiment at Metz, part of the experimental *Groupement d'instruction des chars lourds*), letter to Reynaud, 15 Oct. 1937, in Demey, *Paul Reynaud, mon père*, pp. 314–16; Clarke, *Military Technology in Republican France*, pp. 191–7.
139. Cf. the assessment that 'Gamelin was undoubtedly one of the French generals most favourably disposed to the offensive organisation of the army through the use of mechanical power' in de La Gorce, *The French Army*, p. 294; and the view that 'General Héring ... at least partially understood the value of tanks' in Doughty, *Seeds of Disaster*, p. 181.
140. In CSG, 'Séance d'études du 14 octobre 1936, soir: la division cuirassée, procès-verbal', p. 2, Fonds Gamelin, 1K 224, Carton 8, dr. labelled 'Réunions du CSG, 1932–8', SHAT.
141. For his awareness of Belgian deployments and defensive measures in Belgium's Luxembourg province in 1937–9, see Le Goyet, *Missions de Liaison*, pp. 276–80.
142. His contacts are explored in M. S. Alexander, 'In lieu of alliance: the French general staff's secret cooperation with neutral Belgium, 1936–40', *JSS*, 14:4 (Dec. 1991), pp. 413–27.
143. Ibid.
144. See D. W. Alexander, 'Repercussions of the Breda variant'.
145. 'Edmond Joseph Louis Jules Laurent (Général de Brigade), Etats de Service et notes de promotion', dr. 493 Gx: 5e série, SHAT; cf. M. S. Alexander, 'Did the Deuxième Bureau work?' pp. 315–16, 320–1.
146. Papiers Schweisguth, 'Compte-rendu au retour d'une permission en Hollande, 22–31 juillet 1937', 351 AP, Carton 3, dr. 13, AN; Le Goyet, *Missions de liaison*, pp. 274–5, 276–80.
147. Van den Bergen finally went too far and was removed as chief of staff in mid-January 1940. His downfall occurred during the invasion scare produced by the capture from a German aircraft that crashed at Mechelen-sur-Meuse of Wehrmacht plans for a western offensive, when the Belgian government repudiated his issue of orders to raise the frontier barriers and admit French forces. See Willequet, *Paul-Henri Spaak*, pp. 94–7; Spaak, *Combats inachevés*, pp. 71–80; Vanwelkenhuyzen, *Les Avertissements*, pp. 64–122.
148. In his despatch from Brussels of 17 March 1938, in the aftermath of Germany's Anschluss with Austria, Laurent reported that 'The [Belgian] high command has remained calm ... but at the same time General Van den Bergen has spoken very confidentially to me of the need for French

support of the Belgian army and of the absolute requirement for secrecy to surround such conversations.' (EMA/2e Bureau – Belgique, Carton 7N 2731, SHAT.)
149. Le Col. E. Laurent, attaché militaire près l'Ambassade de France en Belgique, à M. le ministre de la Défense Nationale et de la Guerre (Paris), no. 260/5, 16 Dec. 1937, EMA/2e Bureau (Belgique) Carton 7N 2730, SHAT.
150. Le Col. E. Laurent, attaché militaire près l'Ambassade de France en Belgique, à M. le ministre de la Défense Nationale et de la Guerre (Paris), 24 Mar. 1938, EMA/2e Bureau (Belgique), Carton 7N 2731, SHAT.
151. Annual appraisals in Laurent, 'Etats de Service et notes de promotion', dr. 493 Gx, 5e série, SHAT.
152. Le Goyet, *Le Mystère Gamelin*, pp. 229–31.
153. *DDF*, 2nd ser., vol. XIX, doc. no. 353, pp. 357–8 (Le général Gamelin, chef d'état-major général de la défense nationale, commandant-en-chef les forces terrestres, à M. Daladier, ministre de la défense nationale et de la guerre, D. no. 4/Cab. F. T., 1 Sept. 1939). Cf. Le Goyet, *Mystère Gamelin*, pp. 229–31; J. R. Colville, *Man of Valour*, (London, 1972) p. 152.
154. Le colonel M. Delvoie, attaché militaire près l'Ambassade de Belgique en France, au lieut.-gén., adjutant-général du Roi et à M. le ministre de la Défense nationale, le général chef d'Etat-major de l'armée: no. 1 OD/5390/169c, AMBAE (Brussels).
155. Ibid., no. 1 OD/5603/194c (2 Oct. 1939). Cf. Gauché, *Le Deuxième Bureau*, pp. 53, 55, 231; also Belgian ministers' justification for their country's continued neutrality after Sept. 1939 in Spaak, *Combats inachevés*, pp. 57–8, 68–70; Willequet, *Paul-Henri Spaak*, pp. 91–3.
156. Le colonel M. Delvoie, attaché militaire près l'Ambassade de Belgique en France, au lieut.-gén., adjutant-général du roi et à M. le ministre de la Défense nationale et de la Guerre, le général chef de l'Etat-major de l'armée, no. 1 OD/5649/195c (3 Oct. 1939), AMBAE.
157. Le conseiller de l'Ambassade de Belgique en France, Carlo de Radigues, à M. P.-H. Spaak, ministre des affaires étrangères et du commerce extérieur, no. 16.779/5259/P.10 (4 Oct. 1939), AMBAE.
158. Gamelin, Journal de marche, 21 Sept. 1939, Fonds Gamelin, 1K 224, Carton 9, SHAT.
159. Ibid., 9 Oct. 1939. Cf. Vanwelkenhuyzen, *Neutralité armée*, pp. 25–6; *Les Relations militaires franco-belges*, pp. 79–84.
160. J. Néré, *The Foreign Policy of France from 1914 to 1945* (London, 1975), pp. 97–8.

8 GAMELIN, YUGOSLAVIA AND EASTERN ALLIANCES: ASSETS OR EMBARRASSMENTS?

1. Cf. Lee, 'Strategy, arms and the collapse of France', pp. 60–6; Jordan, 'The cut-price war on the peripheries', pp. 128–66; G.-H. Soutou, 'L'Impérialisme du pauvre: la politique économique du gouvernement français en Europe Centrale et Orientale de 1918 à 1929. Essai

d'interprétation', *Relations Internationales*, 7 (1976), pp. 216–39; Duroselle, *La Décadence*, pp. 99–104, 220–33.
2. See P. S. Wandycz, *France and her Eastern Allies, 1919–1925. French-Czechoslovak-Polish relations from the Paris Peace Conference to Locarno* (Minneapolis, MN, 1962); *Twilight* passim.
3. Wandycz, *Twilight*, p. 16; cf. Weygand, *Mirages et réalité*, pp. 178–82, 185–91, 202–4.
4. See, however, J. B. Hoptner, *Yugoslavia in Crisis, 1934–1941* (New York and London, 1962), pp. 12–13, 35, 55–6, 149; A. Breccia, *Jugoslavia, 1939–1941. Diplomazia della Neutralita* (Rome, 1978), pp. 36, 154–6, 191–2, 206–8.
5. See P. S. Wandycz, 'L'Alliance franco-tchécoslovaque de 1924: un échange de lettres Poincaré-Beneš', *Revue d'Histoire Diplomatique*, 3–4 (1984), pp. 328–33; *Twilight*, pp. 29–36, 63 (n. 70), 98–105.
6. R. J. Young, 'The aftermath of Munich: the course of French diplomacy, October 1938 to March 1939', *FHS*, 8:2 (Fall 1973), pp. 305–22 (quotations p. 307, p. 308).
7. See Wandycz, *Twilight*, pp. 4–5, 9–12, 32–6, 55–6, 75–8, 86, 98–101; Le Goyet, *Mystère Gamelin*, pp. 173–5, 193, 235.
8. See A. Marès, 'Mission militaire et relations internationales: L'exemple franco-tchécoslovaque, 1918–1925', *RHMC*, 30 (Oct.–Dec. 1982), pp. 559–86; 'La Faillite des relations franco-tchécoslovaques: la mission militaire française à Prague (1926–1939)', *RHDGM*, 28:3 (July 1978), pp. 45–71; Wandycz, *Twilight*, pp. 10–11, 29–30, 83–4, 154–5, 196–8, 379, 462; Faucher testimony to the French postwar parliamentary inquiry, 20 July 1948, *C. E. Témoignages*, V, pp. 1191–1211; Duroselle, *La Décadence*, p. 364.
9. 'Note de L'Etat-major de l'armée: Obligations d'assistance mutuelle pouvant incomber à la France', 9 July 1936, in *DDF*, 2nd ser., vol. II, no. 419, p. 642.
10. See Shorrock, *From Ally to Enemy*; 'France, Italy and the Eastern Mediterranean in the 1920s', *International History Review*, 8:1 (Feb. 1986), pp. 70–82. Cf. Duroselle, *La Décadence*, pp. 91–2, 99–112, 130–52; Warner, *Pierre Laval*, pp. 64–72, 94ff.
11. See Gen. A. Béthouart, *Des Hécatombes glorieuses au désastre, 1914–1940* (Paris, 1972), pp. 147–52.
12. Ibid., pp. 174–83.
13. Gamelin, *Servir*, II, p. 278.
14. Béthouart, *Des Hécatombes glorieuses*, pp. 166–7.
15. Ibid., p. 168.
16. Ibid., pp. 169, 154, 172–3.
17. 'Position générale de l'Armée française (memento des points de vue exposés par le Général Gamelin au cours des conversations intérieures, en délégation)', Jan. 1934, Fonds Gamelin 1K 224, Carton 8, dr. 'Réunions du CSG, 1932–8', SHAT.
18. HCM, séance du 23 janvier 1935, Carton 2N 19, SHAT.
19. Papiers Schweisguth, memento, 22 Mar. 1935, 351 AP, Carton 2, dr. 3, AN; HCM, 'Note sur la situation relative des forces allemandes et

françaises et sur les conséquences à en tirer aux points de vue national et international' (apparently a briefing paper for the 22 Mar. 1935 HCM), Carton 2N 19, SHAT.
20. See, for instance, Gamelin, *Servir*, II, pp. 153–5, 161–75; cf. Young, *In Command*, pp. 76–91; 'French military intelligence and the Franco-Italian alliance', pp. 143–68; 'Soldiers and diplomats', pp. 74–91.
21. See French military attaché, Belgrade: reports to Paris, 27 Apr., 21 May 1935, in EMA/2e Bureau: Yugoslavie, Carton 7N 3192, SHAT; Gamelin, *Servir*, II, pp. 171–3; Béthouart, *Des Hécatombes glorieuses*, pp. 188–9.
22. See Young, *In Command*, pp. 89–92; Adamthwaite, *France and the Coming of the Second World War*, pp. 31–6; Warner, *Pierre Laval*, pp. 63–73, 94–110.
23. Etat-major du général Gamelin, 'Rapport du Commandant Petibon sur la situation dans les Balkans', Carton 1N 43, dr. 1 – 1935, SHAT; Papiers Schweisguth, memento, 29 Oct. 1935, 351 AP, Carton 2, dr. 6, AN.
24. CPDN, séance du 29 juillet 1936: procès-verbal, p. 25, Carton 2N 24, SHAT.
25. Lt.-Col. Béthouart, attaché militaire (Belgrade), à M. le Ministre de la Guerre, EMA, 2e Bureau, Paris: séjour du Maréchal Franchet d'Esperey à Belgrade (received in Colson's *cabinet*, 20 May 1936), in Carton 7N 3195, dr. 3, sdr. c, SHAT; cf. Bordereau d'envoi, 4 June 1936, containing reports from Yugoslav newspapers of d'Esperey's tour of provincial Yugoslav cities, in Carton 7N 3195, dr. 1, SHAT; and Etat-majors divers, Carton 1N 45, dr. 3, Correspondance du Maréchal Franchet d'Esperey: lettre au général Gamelin, sur la force croissante de l'Allemagne dans les rapports internationaux, 19 June 1936, SHAT; Gen. Paul Azan, *Franchet d'Esperey* (Paris, 1949), p. 275.
26. See below, ch. 10.
27. Gamelin, *Servir*, II, p. 238.
28. 'Extrait d'une lettre datée du 14 avril 1937 adressée par le Lt.-Col. Béthouart, attaché militaire à Belgrade, au Lt.-Col. Gauché', EMA/2e Bureau, Section des Affaires Etrangères, Carton 7N 3198, SHAT.
29. *DDF*, 2nd ser., vol. I, docs. nos. 136, 137 (reports of 5 Feb. 1936 from J. Laroche, French ambassador in Brussels, to French foreign minister Flandin on talks with Belgian socialist party leader E. Vandervelde); Hoptner, *Yugoslavia in Crisis*, pp. 56, 61–2, 85–7, 91–2; Dreifort, *Yvon Delbos*, pp. 120–33, 136–7, 138–44.
30. Béthouart to 2e Bureau, Paris, 14 Apr. 1937 (cited above, n. 28).
31. Légation de France en Yougoslavie: Le chef de bataillon Molle, stagiaire à l'Ecole d'Infanterie de Sarajevo à M. le Lt.-Col. Béthouart, attaché militaire à Belgrade (enc. in: Béthouart au ministère de la Déf. Natle. et de la Guerre, no. 138/2), 7 July 1937, EMA/2e Bureau, Carton 7N 3195, dr. 3, sdr. 1, SHAT.
32. Le ministre de la défense nationale et de la guerre à M. le ministre des affaires étrangères (Direction des Affaires politiques et commerciales: Europe). 'Objet: Yougoslavie – collaboration sur le plan militaire' (n.d.: internal evidence indicates mid-1937), in EMA/2e Bureau, Carton 7N 3195, dr. 3, sdr. 1, SHAT.

33. Béthouart to 2e Bureau, Paris, no. 44/SC, 7 Feb. 1938: 'Demande de documentation pour des conférences à faire sur l'Armée française', EMA/ 2e Bureau, Carton 7N 3195, dr. 3, sdr. 1, SHAT.
34. Le colonel Merson, attaché militaire (Belgrade), à M. le Président du Conseil, ministre de la Déf. natle. et de la Guerre – EMA/2e Bureau, no. 281/SC, 5 Nov. 1938, Carton 7N 3195, dr. 3, sdr. 1, SHAT.
35. Béthouart, *Des hécatombes glorieuses*, pp. 175, 191–2.
36. Ibid., p. 195.
37. Dreifort, *Yvon Delbos*, pp. 138–40.
38. Béthouart, *Des hécatombes glorieuses*, pp. 175–6, 185, 187–8, 193–5.
39. Béthouart to EMA/2e Bureau: 'Rapport général', no. 130/SC, 9 June 1937, pp. 1–5, in Carton 7N 3198, SHAT.
40. Ibid., p. 6.
41. EMA/2e Bureau (SAE): 'Note sur le voyage de M. de Neurath en Europe centrale et dans les Balkans' (n.d., June 1937 according to internal evidence); also 'Note sur les conséquences du rapprochement de la Yougoslavie avec la Bulgarie, l'Italie et la Hongrie' (n.d.), both in EMA/2 Yougoslavie, Carton 7N 3198, SHAT.
42. See Béthouart, 'Rapport général', 9 June 1937, cited above (n. 39).
43. 'Extrait d'une lettre datée du 14 avril 1937 adressée par le Lt.-Col. Béthouart au Lt.-Col. Gauché', in EMA/2e Bureau (SAE), in Carton 7N 3198, SHAT. Cf. EMA/2e Bureau – Missions: 'Note pour L'Etat-Major de l'Armée (3e Bureau): séjour des Généraux Chefs d'Etat-Major Généraux des armées Roumaine et Yougoslave' no. 2414, 7 May 1937 (enclosing Gamelin's invitation to Nedić and the latter's acceptance), in Carton 7N 3195, dr. 3, sdr. c, SHAT.
44. 'Notice sur le Général de Division Miliutin Neditch, Chef d'Etat-Major Général de l'Armée Yougoslave', 7 July 1937, in Carton 7N 3195, dr. 3, sdr. c, SHAT.
45. Article from *L'Echo de Paris*, 12 July 1937, in ibid.
46. EMA/2e Bureau (SAE): 'Compte-rendu d'une conversation entre le Maréchal Franchet d'Esperey et le Général Neditch entendue par le Capitaine Defrasne du 2e Bureau', 15 July 1937, in Carton 7N 3195, dr. 3, sdr. c, SHAT.
47. Deverell, 'Note to the Minister for Coordination of Defence after a visit to French manoeuvres', 15 Oct. 1937, CAB. 21/575, PRO; cf. Gamelin, *Servir*, II, pp. 276–7.
48. Gamelin, *Servir*, II, pp. 277–80.
49. Ibid.; cf. Béthouart to 2e Bureau, no. 91/1, 'Note de Renseignements: Objet: grandes manoeuvres yougoslaves en 1937', 20 May 1937; EMA/2e Bureau, telegram no. 1607, 15 Sept. 1937 to att. mil., Belgrade; 'Compte-rendu de l'officier de liaison de l'Etat-Major de l'Armée (2e Bureau) auprès des Affaires Etrangères', no. Y9/22, 24 Sept. 1937; EMA/2e Bureau – SAE, 'Note du 2e Bureau concernant des inexactitudes et des omissions constatées dans un document officiel yougoslave. Objet: Collaboration militaire et rapports politiques franco-yougoslave (fin septembre 1937)'; cutting from *L'Echo de Belgrade*: 'Le général Gamelin à Belgrade'; P/a no. 27. 946 Y9/22c: 'Yougoslavie – Note au sujet du passage

du Général Gamelin a Belgrade', 7 Oct. 1937, all in Carton 7N 3195, dr. 3, sdr. c, SHAT.
50. See Dreifort, *Yvon Delbos*, pp. 139–41.
51. Ibid., pp. 145–6; Duroselle, *La Décadence*, pp. 321–3; records of the London talks of 29–30 Nov. 1937 in *DDF*, 2nd ser., vol. VII, doc. no. 287, pp. 518–45; also *DBFP*, 2nd ser., vol. XIX, doc. no. 354, pp. 590–620.
52. Béthouart to EMA/2e Bureau, 'Rapport sur l'aide éventuelle à apporter à l'armée yougoslave', no. 43/S, 8 Nov. 1937, Carton 7N 3195, dr. 2, SHAT.
53. Le ministre de la déf. natle. et de la guerre à M. le ministre des affaires étrangères (Direction des Affaires Politiques et Commerciales – Europe), EMA/2e Bureau (SAE): 'Objet: Yougoslavie – collaboration sur le plan militaire', 21 Nov. 1937, Carton 7N 3195, dr. 2, SHAT. Cf. Gauché, *Deuxième Bureau*, p. 53.
54. 'Communiqué officiel publié à la suite du voyage à Belgrade de M. Yvon Delbos', annex no. 3 to Béthouart's report on Delbos's tour, Dec. 1937, Carton 7N 3198, SHAT. Cf. Dreifort, *Yvon Delbos*, pp. 144–5.
55. EMA/2e Bureau (Section Midi), 'Yougoslavie: rapport au sujet de la visite de M. Delbos: D'un informateur très bien placé', no. 28.463, 21 Dec. 1937, Carton 7N 3198, SHAT.
56. Béthouart to EMA/2e Bureau, 'Rapport général', no. 262/SC, 21 Dec. 1937, Carton 7N 3195, dr. 2, SHAT. Cf. Dreifort, *Yvon Delbos*, pp. 147–50.
57. EMA/2e Bureau (SAE), 'Note sur la collaboration militaire franco-yougoslave' (n.d.: presumed Dec. 1937), Carton 7N 3195, dr. 2, SHAT. Cf. Duroselle, *La Décadence*, pp. 321–3.
58. Cited in Hoptner, *Yugoslavia*, p. 88; Cf. Béthouart, *Des hécatombes glorieuses*, pp. 197–8; Dreifort, *Yvon Delbos*, pp. 148–9.
59. Béthouart to EMA/2e Bureau: Rapport général, no. 58/SC, 16 Feb. 1938, Carton 7N 3195, dr. 2, SHAT.
60. EMA/2e Bureau (SAE), 'Compte-rendu du Lt. Col. Gauché au sujet de la visite du Col. Popovitch, Chef du 2e Bureau yougoslave', no. 909 bis, 24 July 1937, Carton 7N 3195, dr. 1, SHAT.
61. Brugère to Bonnet, lettre au sujet des conversations entre Etat-Majors français et yougoslave, no. 232/100, 16 May 1938, copy to EMA/2e Bureau in Carton 7N 3195, dr. 1, SHAT. Unfortunately Brugère's memoirs, *Veni, Vidi, Vichy* (Paris, 1944), begin in April 1940 and neglect to discuss the early years of his Belgrade posting.
62. MAE (Direction des affaires politiques et commerciales: Europe), Massigli to Daladier, no. 1796: 'Liaison entre Etats-Majors français et yougoslave', 18 June 1938, Carton 7N 3195, dr. 1, SHAT; cf. Béthouart, *Des hécatombes glorieuses*, pp. 200–4.
63. Entertaining Reynaud to lunch at Vincennes during the phoney war, Gamelin had to listen to the minister telling him how he 'shuddered when he thought of the stupidities that France had committed over the last few years' and how the mistake had been 'not to have stifled the German menace at birth, in 1936, when it could have been done at minimal cost. We had everyone else with us then [at which point in the diary Gamelin's ordnance officer had entered a question-mark] and Poland had made a fine

gesture.' (Gamelin, Journal de marche, 18 Oct. 1939, Fonds Gamelin, 1K 224, Carton 9, SHAT.
64. See Duroselle, *La Décadence*, p. 274; R. Massigli, *La Turquie devant la guerre* (Paris, 1965); *DDF*, 2nd ser. vol. XV, doc. no. 443 (Massigli [Ankara] to Bonnet, 19 Apr. 1939), pp. 711–12. More generally see M. Vaïsse, 'Against appeasement: French advocates of firmness, 1933–8', in Mommsen and Kettenacker (eds.), *Fascist Challenge*, pp. 227–35; Pertinax, *Fossoyeurs*, I, p. 61 n. 2.
65. Wandycz, *Twilight*, p. 453.
66. Ibid., p. 462; cf. B. R. Posen, *The Sources of Military Doctrine. France, Britain and Germany between the World Wars* (Ithaca, New York, 1984), pp. 123–7.
67. EMA/2e Bureau: 'Yougoslavie – commandes d'armements', Carton 7N 3195, dr. 2, SHAT.
68. Cf. *DDF*, 2nd ser. vol. XVI, doc. no. 457 ('Procès-verbal de la réunion des chefs d'Etats-Major généraux', 16 June 1939), pp. 867–71; vol. XV, docs, nos. 416 (Gamelin to Daladier, 15 Apr. 1939), 438 ('Note du Cabinet du Ministre de la Déf. Natle. et de la guerre: aide à la Pologne', 18 Apr. 1939), pp. 672–3, 703–4.
69. EMA/2e Bureau, Section de renseignements, no. 336, 'Yougoslavie, Renseignements, d'un observateur compétent et généralement très bien renseigné: Objet – la reconnaissance de l'Union soviétique', 15 Feb. 1938, Carton 7N 3198, SHAT.
70. Béthouart to Président du Conseil, Ministre de la Défense Nationale et de la Guerre, EMA/2e Bureau, no. 123/30: Rapport général, 23 May 1938, Carton 7N 3198, SHAT.
71. CPDN, séance du 29 juillet 1936: procès-verbal, p. 24, Carton 2N 24, SHAT.
72. Posen, *Sources of Military Doctrine*, p. 127; cf. Young, 'Aftermath of Munich', pp. 308–9.
73. Col. F. G. Beaumont-Nesbitt, Enc. no. 1 reporting conversations between Giraud, Winston Churchill and Lord Lloyd at Verdun and Metz, in Clerk to Eden, 22 Sept. 1936, FO 371, 19871, C6616/172/17, PRO. On Loizeau and the USSR see Gen. L. Loizeau, 'Une mission militaire en URSS', *RDM*, 8 (15 Sept. 1955), pp. 252–76. Cf. Young, *In Command of France*, pp. 145–9; R. R. Rader, 'Anglo-French estimates of the Red Army, 1936–1937', *Soviet Armed Forces Review Annual*, 3 (1981), pp. 265–80; J. S. Herndon, 'British perceptions of Soviet military capability, 1935–9' in Mommsen and Kettenacker (eds.), *Fascist Challenge*, pp. 297–319.
74. See Gamelin, *Servir*, II, pp. 280–1.
75. Cf. Duroselle, *La Décadence*, pp. 329–39; Young, *In Command of France*, pp. 192–209; Adamthwaite, *France and the Coming of the Second World War*, pp. 98–106, 141–3, 175–99; Jordan, 'The cut-price war on the peripheries', pp. 149–54; J.-M. d'Hoop, 'La France, la Grande-Bretagne et les pays balkaniques de 1936 à 1939', and F. W. Deakin, 'Anglo-French policy in relation to South-East Europe, 1936–1939', both in *Les Relations Franco-Britanniques, 1935–1939* (Paris 1975), pp. 53–61 and 63–90.
76. See Duroselle, *La Décadence*, pp. 341–53.

77. De Monzie, *Ci-devant*, p. 100.
78. See D. Wingeate Pike, *Les Français et la Guerre d'Espagne, 1936–1939* (Paris, 1975); Duroselle, *La Décadence*, pp. 301–5, 315–23.
79. Clerk to Eden, 22 Sept. 1936, FO 371, 19871, C6616/172/17, PRO; cf. Duroselle, *La Décadence*, pp. 355–64.
80. Gamelin to Daladier, no. 5494/S, 3 Dec. 1938; no. 5705, 19 Dec. 1938; no. 5808/S, 27 Dec. 1938, all in *Servir*, I, pp. 133–7. Cf. Young, *In Command of France*, pp. 208, 218; 'Aftermath of Munich', pp. 311–13, 320–1.
81. Cf. Jordan, 'The cut-price war on the peripheries', pp. 155–7; Anita J. Prazmowska, *Britain, Poland and the Eastern Front, 1939* (Cambridge, 1987), esp. pp. 24–30, 43–4, 80–4.
82. Fraser, 'The French military position after Munich', 5 Dec. 1938, CAB. 21/510, C15175/36/17, PRO.
83. On disillusionment with France after Munich see Duroselle, *La Décadence*, pp. 364–6.

9 MEN OR MATERIAL? GAMELIN AND BRITISH SUPPORT FOR FRANCE

1. *DDF*, 2nd ser., vol. VII, docs. nos. 287, 291; *DBFP*, 2nd ser., vol. XIX, doc. no. 354, pp. 590–620; cf. interpretation in Adamthwaite, *France and the Coming of the Second World War*, pp. 66–70.
2. See Col. H. Ismay, 'Note on the role of a field force' (to Sir M. Hankey, secretary to the Cabinet and CID), 1 Dec. 1937, CAB. 21/510, PRO; Peden, *British Rearmament*, pp. 129–44; Bond, *British Military Policy*, pp. 257–9.
3. D. Johnson and J.-B. Duroselle, 'Les Ententes cordiales', in F. Bédarida, F. Crouzet, D. Johnson (eds.), *Dix siècles d'histoire franco-britannique. De Guillaume le conquérant au Marché commun* (Paris, 1979), pp. 304–21.
4. J. C. Cairns, 'Great Britain and the Fall of France: a study in allied disunity', *JMH*, 27 (Dec. 1955), pp. 365–409. Cf. D. W. J. Johnson, 'Britain and France in 1940', *Trans. of the Royal Historical Soc.*, 5th ser., vol. 22 (1972), pp. 141–57; A. Shlaim, 'Prelude to downfall: the British offer of Union to France, June 1940', *JCH*, 9:3 (July 1974), pp. 27–63; E. M. Gates, *End of the Affair. The collapse of the Anglo-French alliance, 1939–40* (London, 1981).
5. P. M. H. Bell, 'Shooting the rapids: British reactions to the Fall of France, 1940', *Modern and Contemporary France. Review of the Association for the Study of Modern and Contemporary France*, no. 42 (July 1990), pp. 16–28; *A Certain Eventuality: Britain and the Fall of France* (Farnborough, Hants., 1974).
6. See, respectively, S. R. Williamson, *The Politics of Grand Strategy: Britain and France prepare for War, 1904–1914* (Cambridge, MA, 1969); J. Gooch, *The Plans of War. The General Staff and British military strategy, c. 1900–1916* (London, 1974); also W. J. Philpott, 'The strategic ideas of Sir John French', *JSS*, 12:4 (Dec. 1989), pp. 458–78.
7. Williamson, 'Joffre reshapes French strategy', in Kennedy (ed.), *War Plans*, pp. 133–54; R. A. Prete, 'French strategic planning and the

deployment of the BEF in 1914', in *Proceedings of the Western Society for French History*, XIVth annual mtg., Baltimore, MD (19–22 Nov. 1986). Cf. J. C. Cairns, 'International politics and the military mind: the case of the French Republic, 1911–1914', *JMH*, 25:3 (Sept. 1953), pp. 272–85.

8. See J. C. Cairns, 'A nation of shopkeepers in search of a suitable France, 1919–40', *AHR*, 79 (1974), pp. 710–43.
9. See M. S. Alexander, 'Did the Deuxième Bureau work?' pp. 293–333.
10. The expression is taken from Wesley K. Wark, 'Three Military attachés at Berlin in the 1930s: soldier-statesmen and the limits of ambiguity', *IHR*, 9:4 (Nov. 1987), pp. 586–611.
11. CSG, 'Procès-verbal de la séance tenue le 15 janvier 1935, au ministère de la Guerre, sous la présidence de M. le ministre de la Guerre: exposé par M. le général Weygand, vice-président du CSG, Inspecteur Général de l'Armée, de certaines considérations relatives à l'état présent et futur de l'Armée française', Carton 1N 22, pp. 60–7, SHAT. Cf. Bankwitz, *Weygand and Civil-Military Relations*, pp. 113–14.
12. HCM, 'Séance du 23 janvier 1935: procès-verbal', pp. 2–3, Carton 2N 19, SHAT. Cf. Gamelin, *Servir*, II, p. 155.
13. See Bond and Alexander, 'Liddell Hart and de Gaulle', in Paret (ed.), *Makers of Modern Strategy*, pp. 600–3.
14. Ibid., pp. 605–6.
15. Gen. R. Voruz, French military attaché (London), Report for 1930, pp. 80–1, EMA/2 Grande-Bretagne, Carton 7N 2798, SHAT.
16. Col. H. Needham, report on Lorraine manoeuvres, 8 Sept. 1930, FO 371, 14902, W9268/38/17, PRO. Cf. Weygand, *Mémoires*, II, pp. 313, 340–60; Gamelin, *Servir*, II, pp. 11–53; Col. F.-A. Paoli, *L'Armée française de 1919 à 1939*, III, *Le Temps des compromis, 1924–30* (Vincennes, 1974), pp. 155–69, 188–92; Bond and Alexander, 'Liddell Hart and de Gaulle', pp. 607–8.
17. See Bond and Alexander, 'Liddell Hart and de Gaulle', pp. 606, 610–11; Bond, *British Military Policy*, pp. 158–62.
18. The cuts, as well as public attitudes towards the army in Britain, are lucidly analysed in Bond, *British Military Policy*, pp. 6–34, 72–97; M. E. Howard, *The Continental Commitment. The dilemma of British Defence policy in the era of two world wars* (London, 1972; pbk. edn. 1974, refs. to latter edn.), pp. 75–104; P. J. Dennis, *Decision by Default. Peacetime conscription and British defence, 1919–1939* (London, 1972), pp. 1–27.
19. For example, Voruz: 'Rapport sur le budget militaire britannique, 1934–35', 5 Apr. 1934; to 2e Bureau 21 June 1934 (EMA/2 Grande-Bretagne, Carton 7N 2805); Cuny to 2e Bureau, 10 Apr. 1935, pp. 1–2, 4–5 (EMA/2 Grande-Bretagne, Carton 7N 2804) SHAT.
20. On the DRC and the British army, see Peden, *British Rearmament and the Treasury*, pp. 107–12, 121–3; J. P. Harris, 'The British General Staff and the coming of war, 1933–9', *Bulletin of the Institute of Historical Research*, 59:140 (Nov. 1986), pp. 196–211 (esp. pp. 199–202).
21. Gen. R. Voruz: 'Rapport politique sur la Grande-Bretagne pour l'année 1934', 11 Dec. 1934, p. 87, EMA/2 Grande-Bretagne, Carton 7N 2804, SHAT.

22. 'Position générale de l'Armée française: point de vue du général Gamelin', Jan. 1934, Fonds Gamelin, 1K 224, Carton 8, dr. labelled 'Réunions du CSG, 1932–8', SHAT.
23. The description of the Pétain era at the war ministry as a 'truce' is found in Requin, *D'une guerre à l'autre*, p. 182. See also Bankwitz, *Weygand and Civil-Military Relations*, pp. 110–11.
24. Unpublished memoirs of Gen. Sir J. Burnett-Stuart, quoted in Bond, *British Military Policy*, p. 181. Cf., on Weygand's visit, the summary of an unpublished report from the Counsellor of the US Embassy in London, in A. Furnia, *The Diplomacy of Appeasement* (Washington, 1960), p. 117; Weygand, *Mémoires*, II, pp. 408, 424–5; Bankwitz, *Weygand and Civil-Military Relations*, p. 253.
25. Viscount Hailsham (secretary of state for war, Nov. 1931–June 1935), in July 1934 (quoted in Bond, *British Military Policy*, p. 206).
26. Gamelin, *Servir*, II, p. 110; cf. p. 276.
27. See letters, Voruz to EMA/2e Bureau, 13 Apr. 1933, 12 May 1933; Gen. Moyrand (deputy chief of French army staff), letter to Voruz, 25 April 1933; itinerary of Montgomery-Massingberd's visit, 12–13 July 1933, all in EMA/2e Bureau – Grande-Bretagne, Carton 7N 2802, SHAT.
28. Gen. R. Voruz, 'Rapport sur le budget militaire britannique, 1934–5', 5 Apr. 1934, EMA/2e Bureau – Grande-Bretagne, Carton 7N 2805, SHAT.
29. Gen. R. Voruz, 'Rapport politique sur la Grande-Bretagne pour l'année 1934', 11 Dec. 1934, p. 87, EMA/2e Bureau – Grande-Bretagne, Carton 7N 2804, SHAT.
30. Cdt. Cuny, despatch, 10 Apr. 1935, esp. pp. 1–2, 4–5, EMA/2e Bureau – Grande-Bretagne, Carton 7N 2804, SHAT.
31. *Daily Herald*, 15 June 1934, quoted in Gen. R. Voruz to 2e Bureau, 21 June 1934, EMA/2e Bureau – Grande-Bretagne, Carton 7N 2805, SHAT.
32. 'Compte-rendu par le général Weygand d'un voyage à Bruxelles et à Londres', 11 May 1935, Cabinet du ministre de la guerre, Carton 5N 579, dr. 1, SHAT. Cf. Weygand, *Mémoires*, II, pp. 454–5.
33. These remarks rest on consultation of a selection of Senate army commission materials and on a comprehensive reading of the unpublished minutes, ministerial *audiences* and appearances by senior military officers and functionaries of the Chamber army commission in the 14th, 15th and 16th legislatures of the Third Republic (1928–32, 1932–6, 1936–40), at the Archives de l'Assemblée Nationale [AAN], Paris. Cf. P. Géroudet, *Le Parlement et l'armée. La Commission de l'armée de la Chambre des députés (1928–1936)* (Paris, 1990); and, for comparison with the work and status of the foreign affairs commissions, J. E. Howard, *Parliament and Foreign Policy in France. A study of the origins, nature and methods of the parliamentary control of foreign policy in France during the Third Republic, with special reference to the period from 1919 to 1939* (London, 1948), pp. 61–80, 90–112. See also the analysis of France's leading inter-war professor of jurisprudence, and member of the Chamber foreign affairs commission from 1920–38 (who was later Vichy's minister of justice, 1941–3): J. Barthélemy, *Essai sur le travail parlementaire et le système des commissions* (Paris, 1937).

34. CAC, 'Procès-verbal de la séance du 21 mars 1935: audience de M. le général Maurin, ministre de la Guerre', pp. 29–30, 15th Leg., Carton 5 bis, dr. VIII, AAN.
35. Proposition no. 4233 de M. Pierre Taittinger, député, tendant à inviter le gouvernement à ne pas changer le haut commandement à la fin de l'année, *JOC Débats*, 10 Dec. 1934, p. 3022. Cf. M. S. Alexander, 'Taittinger, Pierre (1887–1967)', in D. S. Bell, D. Johnson, P. Morris (eds.), *Biographical Dictionary of the Third, Fourth and Fifth Republics* (Brighton, 1989), pp. 406–8; Bankwitz, *Weygand and Civil-Military Relations*, pp. 116–18.
36. CAC, 'Procès-verbal . . . 21 mars 1935', pp. 29–30, cited above, n. 34.
37. 'Note sur la situation relative des forces allemandes et françaises', HCM, Carton 2N 19, SHAT.
38. Ibid.; cf. Young, *In Command of France*, pp. 88–96.
39. Gen. Baratier, letter to Reynaud, 3 Apr. 1935, Papiers Reynaud, 74 AP, Carton 12, AN. See also Cdt. Cuny, report on the Royal Tank Corps, 1 Jan. 1935, pp. 1–3, EMA/2e Bureau – Grande-Bretagne, Carton 7N 2808, SHAT.
40. CID, paper no. 1181-B: COS 372, 'Annual Review by the Chiefs of Staff', 29 Apr. 1935, paras. 13, 35–6, CAB. 53/24, PRO.
41. See Bond and Alexander, 'Liddell Hart and de Gaulle', pp. 611–12; Bond, *British Military Policy*, pp. 162–3, 172–5, 189–90; *Liddell Hart. A study of his military thought* (London, 1977), pp. 78, 106–7. Cf. J. P. Harris, 'Two war ministers: A reassessment of Duff Cooper and Hore-Belisha', *War and Society*, 6:1 (May 1988), pp. 65–78.
42. Col. T. G. G. Heywood, memorandum, 26 Oct. 1934, FO 371, 17653, C7158/85/17, PRO.
43. Sir E. Ovey, paper no. 632: 'The security of Belgium', 27 Nov. 1934, FO 371, 17653, C8034/85/17, PRO.
44. FO memorandum, 26 March 1935 (section III), FO 371, 18832, C2539/55/18, PRO.
45. Gen. R. Voruz to war ministry, 25 Apr. 1935, EMA/2e Bureau – Grande-Bretagne, Carton 7N 2804, SHAT.
46. Col. T. G. G. Heywood, memorandum of a conversation with General Georges, 8 May 1935, pp. 5–6, FO 371, 18840, C3907/55/18, PRO.
47. For French fear by this time of such an offensive, see war minister Maurin's warning to parliamentarians of the German development of combined air-land tactics capable of 'knocking out an adversary in just a few weeks', in CAC, 'Procès-verbal . . . 21 mars 1935', p. 18 (cited above, n. 34).
48. After a meeting of army commanders at the beginning of 1936, Schweisguth noted that Gamelin, in conclusion 'drew out that . . . the evolution of the Italian situation could lead us once again to leave a dozen [French] divisions in the south-east, taking account of the weakening of Italy. The German danger continues to grow. Germany's air and armoured efforts give her a considerable force for sudden aggressive action either in the east or in Holland-Belgium. It is probable that she will complete this by a reoccupation and subsequent fortification of the demilitarised zone in

such a way as to immobilise us cheaply. The Belgians, moreover, have accomplished very little in regard to fortification and screening troops.' Papiers Schweisguth, 'memento', 15 Jan. 1936, 351 AP, Carton 3, dr. 7, AN.
49. Fabry, Journal de marche, 29 July 1935, Cabinet du ministre de la Guerre, Carton 5N 581, dr. 2, SHAT; *Place de la Concorde*, p. 69.
50. Gamelin, *Servir*, II, p. 173.
51. Montgomery-Massingberd to Viscount Halifax: 'Report on a visit by the CIGS to the French Army', 17 Aug. 1935, pp. 2–3, Field Marshal Sir Archibald Montgomery-Massingberd Papers, 158/5, LHCMA. Cf. Gamelin, *Servir*, II, p. 172.
52. Gamelin, *Servir*, II, pp. 174–5.
53. R. J. Young, 'Reason and madness: France, the Axis powers and the politics of economic disorder, 1938–39', *Canadian Journal of History*, 20 (Apr. 1985), pp. 65–83; on Italy's strategic and economic vulnerabilities see M. Knox, *Mussolini Unleashed*, pp. 12–35.
54. For evidence of French manipulation of the naval talks of 29 Oct. to 9 Nov. 1935 as an *entrée* to wider air and army conversations see *DBFP*, 2nd ser., vol. XV, docs. nos. 148, 330, 338. Cf. recent historical interpretations in A. Reussner, *Les Conversations franco-britanniques d'état-major, 1935–1939* (Vincennes, 1969); P. Masson, 'Conversations militaires franco-britanniques, 1935–38', pp. 120–3; Young, *In Command of France*, pp. 105–6, 108–13; Parker, 'Great Britain, France and the Ethiopian crisis', pp. 308–20.
55. Sir R. Adam, letters to the author, 26 Nov. 1977, 15 Mar. 1979. There was a sense of pessimism at this time among at least some seasoned French observers, General Voruz, the military attaché in London, reporting his perception that British sentiments 'had refrozen in regard to France' ('Rapport politique sur la Grande-Bretagne: 1935', p. 78, EMA/2e Bureau – Grande-Bretagne, Carton 7N 2807, SHAT.) See also the sources listed at ch. 2 above, n. 88.
56. Papiers Schweisguth, 'memento', 12 Dec. 1935, 351 AP, Carton 2, dr. 6, AN. Cf. Gamelin, *Servir*, II, p. 176.
57. Even though, in the autumn of 1935, French intelligence 'was already revealing to us that the general staff in Berlin was studying the possibility of reoccupying the demilitarised zone', as was subsequently conceded by Gamelin (*Servir*, II, pp. 194–5). Cf. confirmation in Papiers Schweisguth, 'memento', 15 Jan. 1936, 351 AP, Carton 3, dr. 7, AN. French unpreparedness and indecision, such prior signals notwithstanding, is convincingly demonstrated in Emmerson, *The Rhineland Crisis*, pp. 68–9, 104–6, 108, 111–14. Cf. Robertson, 'Hitler and sanctions', pp. 409–35.
58. *DDF*, 2nd ser., vol. I, docs. nos. 82 ('Note de l'Etat-major de l'Armée pour le Haut Comité Militaire', 18 Jan. 1936); 83 ('Compte-rendu de séance du Haut Comité Militaire: séance du 18 janvier 1936'); 154 (François-Ponçet (French ambassador, Berlin) to P.-E. Flandin (French foreign minister), 8 Feb. 1936); 155 ('Compte-rendu d'un réunion des ministres de la Défense nationale', 7 Feb. 1936); 186 (Flandin, letter to Maurin, 14 Feb. 1936); 187 ('Compte-rendu du Cdt. Petibon d'une conversation avec le Colonel Beaumont-Nesbitt', 13 Feb. 1936); also Papiers

Schweisguth, 'mementos', 30 Jan., 14 Feb. 1936, 351 AP, Carton 3, dr. 7, AN; Gen. P. Stehlin (French asst. air attaché, Berlin, 1936–9), *Témoignage pour l'histoire* (Paris, 1964), pp. 35–40; and, for the condition of French aviation at the time of the remilitarisation, Gen. C. Christienne and P. Buffotot, 'L'Armée de l'air française et la crise du 7 mars 1936', in *La France et L'Allemagne, 1932–1936*, pp. 315–31.

59. See Emmerson, *The Rhineland Crisis*, pp. 62–70. Cf. R. Meyers, 'Das Ende des Systems von Locarno. Die Remilitarisierung des Rheinlandes in Britischer Sicht', in *Les Relations franco-allemandes, 1933–1939*, pp. 299–334.

60. Baron de Gaiffier to Paul Hymans (Belgian foreign minister), 8 Feb. 1935, Carton 11.185 (2–3), sdr. labelled 'Belgique: défense militaire, 1935', AMBAE.

61. Papiers Schweisguth, 'mementos', 12, 17 Sept. 1935, 351 AP, Carton 2, dr. 5, 15 Jan. 1936, 351 AP, Carton 3, dr. 7. AN; Cf. Gauché, *Deuxième Bureau*, pp. 42–3; Paillat, *Dossiers secrets*, III, pp. 241–2.

62. See Bankwitz, *Weygand and Civil-Military Relations*, pp. 249–55, 258–61. Cf. the signalling to the Quai d'Orsay of the prospect of Germany seizing the pretext of the Chamber's ratification of the Franco-Soviet pact to reoccupy the Rhineland recounted in Gamelin, *Servir*, II, p. 198. The issue is ably analysed in W. E. Scott, *Alliance against Hitler. The Franco-Soviet Pact* (Durham, NC, 1963).

63. For example, in Horne, *To Lose a Battle*, p. 35; Williams, *Ides of May*, p. 71.

64. See Wileman, 'P.-E. Flandin and the Alliance Démocratique', pp. 139–73; R. Sanson, 'L'Alliance Démocratique', in Rémond and Bourdin (eds.), *La France et les Français*, pp. 327–39. Flandin's apologia for his record as foreign minister from Jan.–May 1936 is found in his *Politique française, 1919–1940* (Paris, 1947), pp. 193–211.

65. See Berstein, *Histoire du Parti Radical*, II, pp. 333–418; Larmour, *The French Radical Party*, pp. 200–2; D. A. L. Levy, 'The French Popular Front, 1936–37', in H. Graham and P. Preston (eds.), *The Popular Front in Europe* (London, 1987), pp. 58–83.

66. 'One of the most striking features of the [party election] manifestos as a whole [in the spring of 1936]' notes one historian, 'is the paucity of comment on foreign affairs. Only a matter of weeks after Hitler's invasion of the Rhineland, most candidates confined their comments to vague gestures of support for the League of Nations and for France's "traditional" alliances.' (A. W. H. Shennan, 'The parliamentary opposition to the Front Populaire and the elections of 1936', *HJ*, 27:3 (1984), pp. 677–95, quotation from pp. 691–2.)

67. Papiers Schweisguth, 'memento', 9 Mar. 1936, 'Rapport', 10 Mar. 1936, 351 AP, Carton 3, dr. 8, AN; Gamelin, *Servir*, II, pp. 203–4. Thirteen months after the remilitarisation, Schweisguth recorded that François-Poncet, France's ambassador in Berlin 'was accusing the military of not having wanted to march on 7 March last' – evidence that the differences which surfaced among the French policy-making elite during the crisis dragged on in long-term internal recriminations ('memento', 27 Apr. 1937,

351 AP Carton 3, dr. 12). See also Schuker, 'France and the remilitarization of the Rhineland', pp. 329–30; M. Müller, 'Frankreich und die Rheinlandbesetzung, 1936: Die Reaktion von Diplomaten, Politikern und Militärs', *Geschichte im Westen*, 1:1 (1986), pp. 15–30.

68. *DDF*, 2nd ser., vol. I, doc. no. 334, pp. 444–5 ('Compte-rendu: Réunion chez le général Gamelin, 4 bis, Boulevard des Invalides', 8 Mar. 1936).
69. Ibid., doc. no. 392, pp. 504–6 ('Note de l'état-major de l'armée relative à une opération de prise de gages face à l'Allemagne', 11 Mar. 1936); cf. Gamelin, *Servir*, II, pp. 208–11.
70. Less than three weeks before Hitler's coup, Gamelin explained to his air and navy counterparts that there was 'no prospect of envisaging that France alone could [re]occupy the demilitarised zone' (*DDF*, 2nd ser., vol. I, doc. no. 203, 'Compte-rendu: conférence des chefs d'état-majors du 19 février 1936'); cf. Navarre, *Service de Renseignements*, p. 79.
71. An interpretation most persuasively argued in Young, *In Command of France*, pp. 119–24. Cf. Reussner, *Conversations franco-britanniques*, pp. 105–11, 115–20. A critical assessment that indicts the French high command for vacillation and passivity, charging that the 'new fact brought out by the *Documents Diplomatiques Français* is the extent of the responsibility of the military chiefs, especially Maurin and Gamelin', is J.-B. Duroselle, 'France and the crisis of March 1936', in E. M. Acomb and M. L. Brown (eds.), *French Society and Culture since the Old Regime* (New York, 1966), pp. 244–67 (quotation p. 257); also, in similar vein, R. A. C. Parker, 'The first capitulation: France and the Rhineland Crisis of 1936', *World Politics*, 8:3 (1956), pp. 355–73. Writing more recently, however, Schuker ('France and the remilitarisation of the Rhineland', p. 338) adopts a view close to that of Reussner and Young, concurring that, the '1936 remilitarisation of the Rhineland appears as a manufactured crisis . . . It figured in no sense as a turning point of the 1930s.' His conclusion, however, is that 'The chance to "stop" Hitler was already lost. Historians would do well to shift their attention to an earlier period.'
72. Papiers Schweisguth, 'memento', 14 Feb. 1936, 351 AP, Carton 3, dr. 7, AN.
73. *DDF*, 2nd ser., vol. I, doc. no. 203.
74. 'Note du 2e Bureau sur la coopération franco-britannique en cas de réoccupation par le Reich de la zone démilitarisée', 18 Feb. 1936, EMA/2e Bureau – Grande-Bretagne, Carton 7N 2810, SHAT.
75. Ibid. Cf. Paillat, *Dossiers secrets*, III, pp. 242–3.
76. Gen. R. Voruz, despatch, 11 Mar. 1936, esp. pp. 4–6, EMA/2e Bureau – Grande-Bretagne, Carton 7N 2810, SHAT. French newspaper reactions to the coup are usefully surveyed in Paillat, *La Guerre à l'horizon*, pp. 250–1.
77. Papiers Schweisguth, 'memento', 9 Mar. 1936, 351 AP, Carton 3, dr. 8, AN. American military envoys in Paris reported the next day to Washington, the assistant military attaché commenting that 'French officers . . . stated that no whole or partial mobilisation would be undertaken by France alone . . . The official reaction of the English government . . . is somewhat disappointing to French opinion.' His superior, Col. Horace Fuller, confirmed in a minute on this despatch that 'All [French] officers

Notes to pages 261–4 479

who have been interviewed insist that France will not do anything alone.' (Major J. A. Lester to War Department, G-2, doc. no. 2657-C-25/54, 10 Mar. 1936, RG 165: Military Intelligence Division, Correspondence, 1917–41, Box no. 1643, USNARA, Washington DC.)

78. Papiers Schweisguth, 'Compte-rendu d'une visite par le général Schweisguth à Londres, 17–23 mars 1936', 351 AP, Carton 3, dr. 8, AN.
79. Ibid., letter to Colson, 18 Mar. 1936, 351 AP, Carton 6, dr. 11, sdr. a.
80. Ibid., 'Compte-rendu . . . Londres, 17–23 mars 1936'.
81. Ibid., 351 AP, Carton 6, dr. 11, sdr. b (copy of Flandin's Chamber of Deputies speech, 20 Mar. 1936, p. 5); cf. Flandin's own pretentious retrospective claims on behalf of the 19 Mar. declaration, and his 1936 tenure of the Quai d'Orsay in general, in his *Politique française*, pp. 209–12.
82. Reussner, *Conversations franco-britanniques*, p. 137.
83. Beaumont-Nesbitt, report on conversations with Gamelin and Petibon, Paris, 20 Mar. 1936, FO 371, 19896, C2203/4/18, PRO.
84. *Statement Relating to Defence*, Cmd. 5107 (London, 3 Mar. 1936), paras. 9, 30. See also Bond (ed.), *Chief of Staff*, I, pp. 104–6.
85. Cf. Gen. R. Voruz, 'Rapport sur l'armée britannique, 1935–6', esp. ch. 6, EMA/2e Bureau – Grande-Bretagne, Carton 7N 2807, SHAT; Cdt. Cuny to EMA (2e Bureau), 16 Mar. 1936, in Carton 7N 2810.
86. CAC, 'Séance du 18 mars 1936. Audience de M. le général Maurin, ministre de la guerre: procès-verbal', pp. 30–1, 15th Leg, Carton 5 bis, dr. IX, AAN. Cf. the similarly pessimistic assessment of the British armed forces that Maurin offered Belgium's ambassador in Paris on 31 Mar. 1936, recorded in van Overstraeten, *Albert Ier, Léopold III*, p. 214.
87. Papiers Schweisguth, letter from Debeney, 12 Apr. 1936, 351 AP, Carton 6, dr. 13, sdr. b, AN.
88. See Reussner, *Conversations franco-britanniques*, pp. 151–60.
89. Gen. Sir Ronald Adam, letter to the author, 15 Mar. 1979.
90. *DDF*, 2nd ser., vol. II, doc. no. 97 ('Rapport du général Schweisguth sur les conversation d'Etat-majors tenues à Londres du 15 au 16 avril 1936' [incl. 1 Annex]). A further four annexes to the official French record of the talks are conserved in Papiers Schweisguth, 351 AP, Carton 6, dr. 12, sdr. b, AN.
91. Sir G. Clerk (Paris), telegram to A. Eden [Foreign Secretary], London, 1 Apr. 1936, FO 371, 19899, C2577/4/18, PRO.
92. Voruz to EMA, Paris, 2 Apr. 1936, EMA/2e Bureau – Grande-Bretagne, Carton 7N 2810, SHAT.
93. Voruz to EMA, despatch no. 9/S: 'Conversations d'état-major', 7 May 1936, EMA/2e Bureau – Grande-Bretagne, Carton 7N 2810, SHAT.
94. Papiers Schweisguth, 'memento', 27 May 1936, 351 AP, Carton 3, dr. 9, AN.
95. See the excellent survey of these issues in Peden, *British Rearmament and the Treasury*, pp. 123–8.
96. See R. J. Minney, *The Private Papers of Hore-Belisha* (London, 1960), pp. 35–54; Bond, *Liddell Hart*, pp. 91–101, 104–5.

97. War Office memorandum on the despatch of a Field Force to the Continent in the event of war with Germany, July 1936, CAB. 64/22, PRO (quotations from, respectively, paras. 284, 287).
98. For contemporary thinking see, for example, Col. H. Pownall, 'The role of the army in a major continental war', June 1936, CAB. 21/509, PRO.
99. War Office memorandum (cited above n. 97), paras. 278, 285–6.
100. Sir B. H. Liddell Hart, *The Memoirs of Captain Liddell Hart*, II (London, 1965), p. 22 (letter to Hore-Belisha, 24 Sept. 1937). Cf., however, the vigorous and effective defence of the consistency of the soldiers in the War Office in adhering to a 'Continentalist' stance from 1933 to 1939 in Harris, 'The British general staff and the coming of war', pp. 203–7, 210–11.
101. *Relations militaires franco-belges*, p. 66 (Gamelin, 'Note au sujet de la question belge', 16 Oct. 1936); see also CSG, 'Séance d'études du 15 octobre 1936 . . . missions des armées', p. 2, Fonds Gamelin, 1K 224/8, dr. labelled 'Réunions du CSG, 1932–8', SHAT.
102. EMA/2e Bureau, 'Note sur la défense de la Belgique', 1 Feb. 1937, EMA/2e Bureau – Belgique, Carton 7N 2733, dr. 5, SHAT.
103. Papiers Schweisguth, 'Grand rapport du 5 janvier 1937'; 'memento', 27 Jan. 1937, both 351 AP, Carton 3, dr. 11, AN.
104. *DBFP*, 2nd ser., vol. XVIII, doc. no. 103 (Mr Edmond, Geneva, to Eden, 22 Jan. 1937).
105. Ibid., doc. no. 126 (Record by Mr Baxter of a conversation with Col. Clark, 29 Jan. 1937).
106. Ibid.
107. See Dennis, *Decision by Default*, p. 96.
108. *DBFP*, 2nd ser., vol. XVIII, doc. no. 103 n. 3 (minutes by Vansittart, 26 Jan., 1 Feb. 1937; by Eden, 31 Jan. 1937).
109. The best modern study of Vansittart remains N. Rose, *Vansittart: Portrait of a Diplomat* (London, 1982); see also D. Boadle, 'Vansittart's administration of the Foreign Office in the 1930s', in Langhorne (ed.), *Diplomacy and Intelligence*, pp. 68–84.
110. Vansittart, 'Notes on a conversation with M. Reynaud', 8 Dec. 1936; minute to Eden, 11 Dec. 1936 (both quoted in Dennis, *Decision by Default*, pp. 86–7), emphasis in original.
111. Vansittart memorandum, 1 Feb. 1937, quoted in Dennis, *Decision by Default*, p. 94. It should be noted that, the next month, Eden's private secretary remarked how his secretary of state had developed a 'lack of confidence in Van's judgement' and thought it likely, once Neville Chamberlain became prime minister, that Vansittart would 'quite likely' be retired (*Harvey Diaries*, p. 22, 7 Mar. 1937). In the event, after turning down an offer of the Paris Embassy, Vansittart was replaced as permanent under-secretary by Sir Alexander Cadogan, in January 1938, and sidetracked into the new and purely titular position of chief diplomatic advisor to His Majesty's government.
112. COS Paper, CP 41 (37), 'The role of the British army', 28 Jan. 1937 (quoted in Dennis, *Decision by Default*, pp. 92–3).
113. See Bond, *British Military Policy*, pp. 236–41; Peden, *British Rearmament and the Treasury*, pp. 128–35, 152–7.

114. *DBFP*, 2nd ser., vol. XVIII, doc. no. 103, n. 3 (Harvey minute, 1 Feb. 1937).
115. Papiers Schweisguth, 'Compte-rendu du général Schweisguth sur sa mission en Angleterre, 2 au 5 mars 1937', and annex: 'Renseignements recueillis à l'Ambassade de France', 351 AP, Carton 6, dr. 14, sdr. a, AN.
116. Ibid., 'memento', 12 Apr. 1937, 351 AP, Carton 3, dr. 12, AN. Cf. the report of Col. Beaumont-Nesbitt, Britain's military attaché in Paris, on this visit that he and Col. Clark of the War Office paid to Gamelin on 12 Apr. 1937, in FO 371, 20693, C2834/122/17, PRO.
117. Reynaud, letter to B. H. Liddell Hart, 12 Mar. 1949, Liddell Hart Papers, Individual Correspondence 1/594, LHCMA.
118. The visit is reported in *DDF*, 2nd ser., vol. V (20 Feb. 1937–31 May 1937) (Paris, 1968), doc. no. 335 (M. Charles Corbin, ambassadeur de France à Londres à M. Delbos, ministre des Affaires Etrangères, 24 Apr. 1937); also in le général Lelong [French military attaché, London] au ministère de la Défense nationale et de la Guerre, EMA (2e Bureau), D. no. 305, 29 Apr. 1937 ('Objet – la visite de M. Daladier à Londres et à Manchester'), EMA/2e Bureau – Grande-Bretagne, Carton 7N 2812, SHAT.
119. For evidence supporting these conclusions see Harris, 'The British general staff', pp. 209–11; M. Smith, '"A matter of faith": British strategic air doctrine before 1939', *JCH*, 15:3 (1980), pp. 423–42; 'Rearmament and deterrence in Britain in the 1930s', *JSS*, 1:3 (Dec. 1978), pp. 313–37; Bond, *British Military Policy*, pp. 248–65; Peden, *British Rearmament and the Treasury*, pp. 129–44.
120. Clerk to Eden, 11 June 1936, FO 371, 19857, C4248/1/17, PRO.
121. Col. F. G. Beaumont-Nesbitt (Paris): 'Report on the French army', 5 July 1937, FO 371, 20694, C5048/122/17, PRO.
122. See J. Charmley, *Chamberlain and the Lost Peace* (London, 1989), pp. 4–31, 66–7.
123. Inskip's Dec. 1937 report quoted in Bond, *British Military Policy*, p. 258.
124. Field Marshal Sir C. Deverell, 'Note to the Minister for coordination of defence after a visit to French manoeuvres', 15 Oct. 1937, CAB. 21/575, PRO.
125. Ibid., general staff minutes on pp. 6–8, 9.
126. Gort to B. H. Liddell Hart, 31 Oct. 1937, Liddell Hart Papers 1/322/52, LHCMA. For Deverell's concern, see his paper to Hore-Belisha and Inskip, 'The strategy of the French army in a future war', 1 Nov. 1937, CAB. 21/509, PRO; also notes on his conversation with Gen. Sir Edmund Ironside, GOC Eastern Command, 1 Dec. 1937 (the day Hore-Belisha replaced him with Gort), in R. Macleod and D. Kelly (eds.), *The Ironside Diaries, 1937–1940* (London, 1962), pp. 37–8. Another worried about Britain's wilful adoption of force-structures that would leave it unable to assist the French on land was Ismay: see his 'Note on the role of a Field Force' (to Hankey), 1 Dec. 1937, CAB. 21/510, PRO.
127. General staff minute on Deverell's 'Note ... after a visit to French manoeuvres', 15 Oct. 1937, p. 8, CAB. 21/575, PRO.
128. Quotations from, respectively, Cab. Conclusions 35 (37), 29 Sept. 1937, FO 371, 20694, C6821/122/17, PRO; notes by Hore-Belisha in Minney, *Private Papers of Hore-Belisha*, p. 59.

129. 'Notes on a telephone conversation with Hore-Belisha', 15 Oct. 1937, Liddell Hart Papers, 11/H-B 1937/56b, LHCMA. Cf. Liddell Hart, *Memoirs*, II, pp. 37–8; Macleod and Kelly (eds.), *Ironside Diaries*, pp. 26–33.
130. See Bond, *Liddell Hart*, pp. 76–8, 94–5, 100, 104. Cf. J. J. Mearsheimer, *Liddell Hart and the Weight of History* (Ithaca, NY 1988), pp. 111–12, 121–3.
131. Liddell Hart, 'Note on the question of the Channel Ports and the need of a British Field Force', 28 Aug. 1937, Liddell Hart Papers, 11/H-B 1937/23, LHCMA.
132. See Bond, *Liddell Hart*, pp. 96, 98, 113–14; *British Military Policy*, pp. 246, 255. Cf. Mearsheimer, *Liddell Hart and the Weight of History*, pp. 122–3, 124, 158–60, 183.
133. See Liddell Hart, *Memoirs*, II, pp. 18, 110, 199–205. For the correspondence between Liddell Hart and Weygand, and its acrimonious rupture after publication of the former's *Foch*, see Liddell Hart Papers, Correspondence File 1/742, LHCMA. Cf. Mearsheimer, *Liddell Hart and the Weight of History*, pp. 96–7.
134. Liddell Hart, *Memoirs*, II, p. 244.
135. Ibid., pp. 244–5.
136. Letter to Chamberlain, 23 Nov. 1937, in Minney, *Private Papers of Hore-Belisha*, p. 69. For Liddell Hart's recommendations in this respect, see his *Memoirs*, II, pp. 53–7.
137. See Bond (ed.), *Chief of Staff*, I, pp. 134–6, 142–4 (Pownall diary: 14, 25 Feb., 4, 11, 25 Apr. 1938). Cf. Dennis, *Decision by Default*, pp. 117–18; Sir J. R. Colville, *Man of Valour. The Life of Field-Marshal the Viscount Gort* (London, 1972), pp. 89–90, 93–4.
138. Macleod and Kelly (eds.), *Ironside Diaries*, p. 51 (25 Mar. 1938).
139. CPDN, 'Séance du 8 décembre 1937: procès-verbal', p. 70, CPDN Carton 1, 2N 20, SHAT. Cf. Adamthwaite, *France and the Coming of the Second World War*, p. 72.
140. *DDF*, 2nd ser., vol. VIII, doc. no. 206 (Le général Lelong, attaché militaire à Londres, à M. Daladier, ministre de la Défense Nationale et de la Guerre, 18 Feb. 1938).
141. Consideration of the effect on French morale of British strategic decisions in Eden's 'Memorandum on the chiefs of staff's comparison of the strength of Great Britain with that of other powers as at January 1938', CID Paper 1373-B, CAB. 23/90A, PRO. Cf. Bond (ed.), *Chief of Staff*, I, pp. 135–6 (Pownall diary, 21, 25 Feb. 1938). More generally on Eden's departure from Chamberlain's government see N. Rose, 'The resignation of Anthony Eden', *HJ*, 25:4 (1982), pp. 911–31.
142. *DDF*, 2nd ser., vol. VIII, doc. no. 206.
143. 'Report by the COS sub-committee on a comparison of the strength of Great Britain with that of certain other Powers as at January 1938', CID Paper 1366-B, Nov. 1937, CAB. 23/90A, PRO.
144. Gort to Liddell Hart, 31 Oct. 1937, Liddell Hart Papers 1/322/52, LHCMA.
145. 'Report by the COS', CID Paper 1366-B, CAB. 23/90A, PRO.

146. Beaumont-Nesbitt report on a conversation with Gen. Dentz, 8 Apr. 1938, FO 371, 21594, C2947/36/17, PRO. On the ministerial talks, see R. A. C. Parker, 'Anglo-French conversations, April and September 1938', in *Les Relations Franco-Allemandes, 1933–1939. Actes du Colloque international des historiens français et allemands no. 563 (Strasbourg, 7–10 octobre 1975)* (Paris, 1976), pp. 371–9.
147. Quotations from Hore-Belisha's report on these talks in Paris, CAB. 21/574, PRO. The French record is in *DDF*, 2nd ser., vol. IX, doc. no. 238 ('Note du général Gamelin, vice-président du CSG: conversation avec M. Hore-Belisha', 25 Apr. 1938). See also Minney, *Private Papers of Hore-Belisha*, pp. 120–1; Gamelin, *Servir*, II, pp. 317–18.
148. As the British historian Norman Gibbs perceptively observed, long before the opening of the French military archives, 'at least before Munich there is no clear evidence of French pressure upon Britain to provide a large expeditionary force', N. H. Gibbs, 'British strategic doctrine, 1919–1939', in M. E. Howard (ed.), *The Theory and Practice of War. Essays in honour of B. H. Liddell Hart* (London, 1965), p. 209.
149. *DDF*, 2nd ser., vol. IX, doc. no. 131 (Corbin to Paul-Boncour, 7 Apr. 1938); Corbin to Daladier, 18 Oct. 1939, Archives Daladier, 3 DA 2, dr. 3, sdr. c, FNSP.
150. Ismay, minute, 26 Apr. 1938, CAB. 21/554, PRO. See also Maj. C. A. de Linde (assistant British military attaché, Paris): 'Notes on the present state of the French Army', 23 Apr. 1938, FO 371, 21594, C3388/55/17, PRO.
151. Hankey note to Chamberlain, 28 Apr. 1938, CAB. 21/554, PRO.
152. For the French military's briefs to Daladier on the eve of the ministerial talks with Chamberlain, see *DDF*, 2nd ser., vol. IX, doc. no. 73 ('Note du général Gamelin, vice-président du CSG, sur la situation militaire actuelle', 29 Mar. 1938); doc. no. 144 (annex: 'Note du CSDN sur les accords d'états-majors dont la conclusion serait à rechercher par la France', 4 Apr. 1938); doc. no. 121 ('Note du vice-président du CSG relative aux possibilités de l'axe Rome-Berlin', 6 Apr. 1938); doc. no. 237 ('Note: conversations militaires franco-britanniques – accords d'Etats-majors', 25 Apr. 1938); lettre du général Gamelin à M. Daladier, ministre de la Défense nationale et de la Guerre, 4 Apr. 1938, Cabinet du ministre, Carton 5N 579, dr. 2, SHAT; Gamelin, *Servir*, II, pp. 315–16.
153. Parker, 'Anglo-French conversations', esp. pp. 375–9. Cf. Duroselle, *La Décadence*, pp. 335–7. The British record of the talks is in *DBFP*, 3rd ser., vol. I, doc. no. 164 ('Anglo-French conversations, 28–29 April 1938'); the French account in *DDF*, 2nd ser., vol. IX, doc. no. 258, annexes. A good, up-to-date, scholarly appraisal of British policy towards Germany and the Czech–Sudeten problem is Charmley, *Chamberlain*, pp. 72–142.
154. *DDF*, 2nd ser., vol. IX, doc. no. 444 (Lelong to Daladier, 24 May 1938). See also Beaumont-Nesbitt's account of talks with Petibon, Gamelin's *chef de cabinet*, 4 May 1938, FO 371, 21591, C4095/13/17, PRO; Bond (ed.), *Chief of Staff*, I, pp. 149–50 (Pownall diary, 30 May, 13 June 1938).

155. Liddell Hart, *Memoirs*, II, p. 193; Gamelin, *Servir*, II, pp. 338–9. Cf. Bond, *Liddell Hart*, p. 103. More generally, on the attempt to use the Royal visit to express Anglo-French solidarity, see R. Dubreuil, 'La Visite des souverains britanniques', in Rémond and Bourdin (eds.), *La France et les français*, pp. 77–94.
156. See *DDF*, 2nd ser., vol. VIII, doc. no. 316 ('Note du 2e Bureau de l'Armée de l'Air sur les conversations franco-britanniques des 3–4 mars 1938'); Fridenson and Lecuir, *La France et la Grande-Bretagne face aux problèmes aériens*, pp. 90–8; Major-Gen. L. A. Hawes, 'The story of the "W Plan": the move of our forces to France in 1939', *The Army Quarterly*, 101 (1970–1), pp. 445–56.
157. Major-Generals H. Pownall and P. Hobart had been invited to attend the French tank manoeuvres, scheduled for 26–31 Aug. 1938 (Beaumont-Nesbitt, despatch, 19 July 1938, FO 371, 21654, C7250/37/18, PRO).
158. Col. W. Fraser, despatch, 10 Oct. 1938, FO 371, 21596, C12021/36/17, PRO. (Fraser had relieved Beaumont-Nesbitt in Paris at the beginning of September 1938.) Cf. Gamelin, *Servir*, II, p. 362.

10 CZECHOSLOVAKIA, POLAND, THE SOVIET UNION: FROM APPEASEMENT TO WAR

1. The influence of Gamelin's counsel on the French government's response to the German–Czech dispute in 1938 is analysed in R. J. Young, 'Le Haut Commandement français au moment de Munich', *RHMC*, 24 (Jan.–Mar. 1977), pp. 110–29. Cf. W. K. Wark, 'Military attaché in Berlin', *Military History*, 12:3:122 (Mar. 1984), pp. 136–43; M. Hauner, 'Czechoslovakia as a military factor in British considerations of 1938', *JSS*, 1:2 (Sept. 1978), pp. 194–222; W. Murray, 'Munich 1938: the military confrontation', *JSS*, 2:3 (Dec. 1979), pp. 282–302.
2. Quoted in Jordan, 'The cut-price war on the peripheries', p. 154.
3. See the excellent modern study of Britain's guarantee to Poland by Prazmowska, *Britain, Poland and the Eastern Front*; 'Poland's foreign policy: September 1938–September 1939', *HJ*, 29:4 (1986), pp. 853–73; 'War over Danzig? The dilemma of Anglo-Polish relations in the months preceding the outbreak of the Second World War', *HJ*, 26:1 (Mar. 1983), pp. 177–83.
4. A development analysed in R. J. Young, 'The aftermath of Munich: The course of French diplomacy, October 1938 to March 1939', *FHS*, 8:2 (Fall 1973), pp. 305–22; and E. du Réau, 'Enjeux stratégiques et redéploiement diplomatique français: novembre 1938, septembre 1939', *Relations internationales*, 35 (Autumn 1983), pp. 319–35. Cf. Adamthwaite, *France and the Coming of the Second World War*, pp. 275–9, 303–34.
5. See M. S. Alexander, 'Les Réactions à la menace stratégique allemande en Europe occidentale: La Grande-Bretagne, la Belgique et le "cas Hollande", décembre 1938–février 1939', *Cahiers d'Histoire de la Seconde Guerre Mondiale*, 7 (Apr. 1982), pp. 5–38; F. H. Hinsley, E. E. Thomas, C. F. G. Ransom, R. C. Knight, *British Intelligence in the Second World War*, I (London, 1979), pp. 54–9, 68–9 and esp. 82–4. Cf. discussion of the

Jan. 1939 war scare and the way it led to British commitments to upholding the integrity of the western European states in D. C. Watt, *How War Came. The immediate origins of the Second World War, 1938–1939* (New York: Pantheon, 1989), pp. 99–107; 'Misinformation, misconception, mistrust: episodes in British policy and the approach of war, 1938–1939', in M. Bentley and J. Stevenson (eds.), *High and Low Politics in Modern Britain. Ten studies* (Oxford, 1983), pp. 215–54; C. M. Andrew, *Secret Service. The making of the British intelligence community* (London, 1985), pp. 412–19.

6. 'Situation militaire de l'Allemagne, début 1939', p. 2 (typescript memorandum probably from 2e Bureau), Archives Daladier, 4 DA 8, dr. 1, sdr. a, FNSP.
7. Gamelin, *Servir*, II, pp. 380, 401–2.
8. Gen. A. Lelong (French military attaché, London), to Gamelin: 'Compte-rendu des conversations d'Etats-Majors franco-britanniques: 1ère phase: Londres, 29 mars–4 avril 1939', 5 Apr. 1939, EMA/2e Bureau – Grande-Bretagne, Carton 7N 2816, SHAT.
9. 'Position générale de l'armée française: memento des points de vue exposés par le général Gamelin au cours des conversations intérieures, en délégation', Jan. 1934, Fonds Gamelin, 1K 224, Carton 8, dr. 'Réunions du CSG, 1932–8', SHAT.
10. 'The Czechoslovakian crisis: notes on a meeting of the CID with General Gamelin in London', 26 Sept. 1938, FO 371, 21782, C10722/10722/18, PRO. Accompanying Gamelin was Lelong, French military attaché in London, whilst those present on the British side were: Sir Thomas Inskip, minister for coordination of defence; Hore-Belisha, secretary of state for war; Kingsley Wood, secretary of state for air; Sir Hastings Ismay, secretary, CID; Lord Gort, CIGS; Sir Cyril Newall, chief of the air staff; Brig.-Gen. Beaumont-Nesbitt, deputy director of military intelligence. Cf. copy of French record of the meeting in CAB. 21/595, File 14/36/22, PRO.
11. Gamelin, 'Position générale de l'armée française'.
12. Ibid.
13. Young, 'Aftermath of Munich', p. 308. Cf. discussion of the commitments and implications for France of the political accord of 19 Feb. 1921 and the accompanying military convention of 21 Feb. 1921, in Paillat, *Le Désastre de 1940*, pp. 65–79.
14. See, for example, Sir H. Kennard (British ambassador, Warsaw), to Viscount Halifax (foreign secretary), 30 June 1939: enc. 'Leading personalities in Poland', entry on Rydz-Smigly, pp. 21–2, FO 371, C10430/10430/55, PRO. Cf. the portrayal of Rydz-Smigly in Paillat, *Le Désastre de 1940*, pp. 79–81, where he is characterised as 'the Polish Gamelin'.
15. See Conquet, *Auprès du Maréchal Pétain*, p. 168; Griffiths, *Pétain*, pp. 167, 179; Warner, *Pierre Laval*, pp. 82–4.
16. Papiers Schweisguth, 'Rapport du 26 novembre 1935', 351 AP, Carton 2, dr. 6, AN.
17. *DDF*, 2nd ser., vol. II, doc. no. 23, pp. 46–9.
18. Ibid., vol. II, doc. no. 369 (CPDN procès-verbal, 26 June 1936). Le Goyet (*Mystère Gamelin*, pp. 177–8) claims that Gamelin was well satisfied with

the outcome of Rydz-Smigly's autumn 1936 visit to France and the ensuing Rambouillet agreements, and 'still secretly harboured the hope of reconciling the Czechs and Poles.'

19. In Oct. 1938 Bonnet, the French foreign minister, was approached by a delegation of fellow *Munichois* Radical parliamentarians, led by Jean Montigny, with a plea to denounce the French pacts with Poland and the Soviet Union. After listening 'approvingly', Bonnet 'sadly' replied that he would pursue such a policy if he could, but that he would find a cabinet majority against him and 'could not count on Daladier, *for Gamelin believes that the assistance of the Polish army would be indispensable in the event of war.*' J. Montigny, *Le Complot contre la paix, 1935–1939* (Paris, 1966), pp. 206–7 (emphasis added).

20. For Gamelin's cordial relations with Rydz-Smigly see *Servir*, II, pp. 227–8; cf. the decline of the friendship and its reduction to 'strictly official' relations after Munich, pp. 356–7; also Le Govet, *Mystère Gamelin*, pp. 175–8, 183–7. On the background to French preferences for alliance with Poland rather than the Soviet Union, see M. J. Carley, 'Anti-Bolshevism in French foreign policy: the crisis in Poland in 1920', *IHR*, 11:3 (July 1980), pp. 410–31.

21. EMA (3e Bureau) note, 'Le Problème militaire français', 1 June 1936, p. 3, Archives Daladier, 4 DA 1, dr. 4, sdr. a, FNSP.

22. Watt, *How War Came*, p. 332.

23. See Dutailly, *Problèmes de l'armée de terre*, pp. 56, 109–11.

24. 'Aperçu général de la situation de l'Europe au point de vue des armements militaires de divers pays: audition de M. Daladier, ministre de la Défense nationale et de la Guerre devant la commission des finances, le 27 novembre 1936', Archives Daladier, 1 DA 7, dr. 3, sdr. a, FNSP; cf. confirmation of Czech military improvements from 1933–7 in testimony of Faucher to the postwar French parliamentary inquiry, 20 July 1948, *C. E. Témoignages*, V, pp. 1191–1211 (esp. pp. 1195–6).

25. On these missions see A. Marès, 'Mission militaire et relations internationales: L'exemple franco-tchécoslovaque, 1918–1925', *RHMC*, 30 (Oct.–Dec. 1982), pp. 559–86; Faucher's testimony before the postwar French parliamentary inquiry, 20 July 1948, *C. E. Témoignages*, V, pp. 1191–1211; ibid., testimony of de Villelume (12 Apr. 1951), IX, pp. 2741–64 (esp. pp. 2750–2).

26. Delbos to Noël, conveying instructions for Gamelin's mission to Poland, 30 July 1936, Archives Daladier, 1 DA 7, dr. 2, sdr. e, FNSP. See the attempt to interpret Polish foreign policy in the 1930s with some sympathy for Polish purposes and difficulties in H. L. Roberts, 'The diplomacy of Colonel Beck', in Craig and Gilbert (eds.), *The Diplomats*, pp. 579–614.

27. Gamelin, report from Warsaw to Daladier, 14 Aug. 1936 (detailing the general's first two conversations with Rydz-Smigly, 12–13 Aug. 1936), in Archives Daladier 1 DA 7, dr. 2, sdr. e, FNSP; also *DDF*, 2nd ser. vol. III, doc. no. 153, Léon Noël to Delbos, pp. 226–7.

28. Gamelin report to Daladier on talks with Rydz-Smigly and Stakiewicz in France, Sept.–Oct. 1936, 'Les Accords de Rambouillet', in Archives Daladier, 1 DA 7, dr. 2, sdr. e, FNSP; also French official record of the

Rambouillet agreement, 6 Sept. 1936 in *DDF*, 2nd ser. vol. III, doc. no. 259, pp. 377–8. Cf. evaluation of Rambouillet in Le Goyet, *Mystère Gamelin*, pp. 177–8; Paillat, *Le Désastre de 1940*, pp. 82–3; Jordan, 'The cut-price war on the peripheries', p. 148.
29. Wandycz, *Twilight*, p. 453.
30. Ibid. (quoting d'Arbonneau despatch, 3 Feb. 1936). Poland had in fact received French credits to help equip the army in earlier years: 400 million francs, by a law of 8 Jan. 1924, in four tranches. The final tranche had been released on 24 Feb. 1931, the last of the equipment being delivered on 31 Oct. 1935 (Le Goyet, *Mystère Gamelin*, p. 174, n. 1).
31. Weygand memorandum, 11 Jan. 1935, cited in Dutailly, *Problèmes de l'armée de terre*, p. 296.
32. See Armengaud, *Batailles politiques et militaires*, pp. 68–71, 93–8, 106–9, 112–17, 119.
33. See Watt, *How War Came*, pp. 188–98. Cf. Charmley, *Chamberlain*, pp. 178–84.
34. Statement by Chamberlain in the House of Commons concerning the guarantee to Poland, 31 Mar. 1939, in J. A. S. Grenville (ed.), *The Major International Treaties, 1914–1973. A history and guide with texts* (London, 1974), p. 189. Cf. the excellent analysis of British policy in giving the guarantee in Prazmowska, *Britain, Poland and the Eastern Front*, pp. 40–60.
35. Prazmowska, *Britain, Poland and the Eastern Front*, pp. 89–92. Poland's military weakness is well assessed in Murray, *Change in the European Balance of Power*, pp. 122–3, 163, 323–6.
36. For example, the visits to Warsaw of a British joint staff mission led by Brig. Clayton of the War Office and Captain Rawlings of the Royal Navy from 23–30 May 1939, and of Gen. Ironside, Inspector-Gen. of British Overseas Forces, in July. See Bond, *British Military Policy*, pp. 314–18; Prazmowska, *Britain, Poland and the Eastern Front*, pp. 94–8; Watt, *How War Came*, pp. 331–2.
37. Gamelin, *Servir*, II, pp. 413–25.
38. Macleod and Kelly (eds.), *Ironside Diaries*, pp. 76, 80–2.
39. See John Herman, 'Soviet peace efforts on the eve of World War Two: a review of the Soviet documents', *JCH*, 15:3 (July 1980), pp. 577–602 (esp. pp. 582, 588, 592).
40. Anglo-French Staff Conversations: Report on Second Stage, AFC(J); 56, 4 May 1939, CAB. 29/160, PRO; Lelong, report to Gamelin: 'Conversations d'Etats-Major franco-britanniques: 2e phase (Londres, 24 avril–4 mai 1939)', 5 May 1939, EMA 2e Bureau – Grande-Bretagne, Carton 7N 2816, SHAT. Cf. Watt, *How War Came*, p. 331.
41. Col. F. N. Mason-Macfarlane to Sir N. Henderson, FO 371, 22994, C3473/19/18, PRO. At least some Polish envoys in the western capitals saw through the Franco-British deceit, the Belgian military attaché in Paris reporting in Feb. 1939 that his Polish counterpart was showing a 'lack of confidence in France which, one might wonder, perhaps reflects the feelings of the Polish people and leads one to ask if, in the event of war in western Europe, Poland would not attempt to get herself out of her treaty

with France'. (Le col. M. Delvoie au lieut.-gén., chef d'état-major de l'armée, 2e section; au cabinet militaire du roi, no. 2 OD/710/9c, 2 Feb. 1939, AMBAE.)
42. Watt, *How War Came*, pp. 330, 332–5; Prazmowska, *Britain, Poland and the Eastern Front*, pp. 91–6, 122–8.
43. R. Woytak, *On the Border of War and Peace. Polish intelligence and diplomacy in 1937–39 and the origins of the Ultra Secret* (New York, 1979), p. 79.
44. Ibid.
45. See P. S. Wandycz, 'Colonel Beck and the French: the roots of animosity?', *IHR*, 3:1 (Jan. 1981), pp. 115–27; letters of Mendras to War Ministry in Castellan, *Réarmement*, pp. 490–1; also Castellan, 'Reichswehr et armée rouge', in J.-B. Duroselle (ed.), *Les relations germano-soviétiques de 1933 à 1939* (Paris, 1954), pp. 139–41, 204–5, 209–14; Chef de Bataillon André Bach, 'Le colonel Mendras et les relations militaires franco-soviétiques (1932–35)', unpub. mémoire de maîtrise, Université de Paris IV (Sorbonne), 1981, pp. 2–129 *passim*.
46. The only specialist study of the French *rapprochement* with Moscow remains Scott, *Alliance against Hitler*. But there is much perceptive analysis of the issues involved in Duroselle, *La Décadence*, pp. 43–9, 75–9, 91–2, 104–7, 111–21, 139–42. On the military contacts see Bankwitz, *Weygand and Civil-Military Relations*, pp. 249–61; Bach, 'Le colonel Mendras', pp. 133–51, 175–89.
47. On this earlier treaty, of 1894, see G. F. Kennan, *The Fateful Alliance. France, Russia and the coming of the First World War* (New York, 1984); J. F. V. Keiger, *France and the Origins of the First World War* (London and Basingstoke, 1983), esp. pp. 11–13, 88–102, 125–8, 150–61.
48. CAC, 15th Leg. (1932–6), 'Séance du 21 mars 1935 sous la présidence de M. Jean Fabry: audience de M. le général Maurin, ministre de la guerre, relative aux effectifs français et allemands: procès-verbal', pp. 29, 30, 32, 35, Carton 5 bis, dr. VIII, AAN. Cf. the similar conclusions of the British chiefs of staff two years later, that 'The intervention of the USSR, while Poland and Czechoslovakia remained neutral, would confer little immediate benefit in the Allies' cause. If Germany and Italy believed themselves justified in counting upon a quick decisive success against France or Great Britain the fear of Soviet intervention would not therefore necessarily deter them from war.' ('Comparison of the strength of Great Britain with that of certain other nations as at May 1937', COS paper no. 551, 9 Feb. 1937, para. 40 (iv), CAB. 4/26, PRO.)
49. For the roots of the anti-communism displayed by the Quai d'Orsay and French officer corps, see Carley, 'Anti-Bolshevism in French foreign policy', pp. 410–31; de La Gorce, *La République et son armée*, pp. 259–80, 305–14, 330–3; J. Delmas, 'L'Alliance militaire franco-russe et la révolution bolchévique: stratégie et idéologie', in A. Martel (ed.), *Forces Armées et Systèmes d'Alliances. Colloque International d'Histoire militaire et d'Etudes de Défense nationale, Montpellier, 2–6 septembre 1981* (Paris, 1983, 3 vols.), II, pp. 673–88; and Nobécourt, *Histoire politique de l'armée*, I, pp. 59–75, 169–79.

50. *DDF*, 2nd ser., vol. I, doc. no. 106 ('Note sur les répercussions possibles du Pacte Franco-Soviétique' [from the Archives de la Guerre] 27 Jan. 1936). 'Our Intelligence services', Gamelin asserted later, 'had advised us that the Germans were going to make a pretext [for remilitarising the Rhineland] of the imminent ratification by the Chamber of Deputies of the Franco-Soviet Pact.' (Gamelin written deposition at Riom: 'La Politique étrangère de la France 1930–9, au point de vue militaire', p. 9, Papiers Blum, 3 BL 3, dr. 1, FNSP. See also Bankwitz, *Weygand and Civil-Military Relations*, pp. 249–58.
51. Recording the deliberations of an *ad hoc* meeting of the Conseil Supérieur de la Guerre two days after Hitler's coup in the Rhineland, Schweisguth noted in his diary that the French military had 'not been consulted [by the Quai d'Orsay] over the Pact, but over a *rapprochement* with Russia within the framework of an eastern pact; we have always said that this could be useful to France from a negative point of view'. (Papiers Schweisguth: 'Réunion improvisée du CSG, le 9 mars 1936: 2e partie', 351 AP, Carton 3, dr. 8, AN.)
52. M. Vaïsse, 'Les Militaires français et l'alliance franco-soviétique au cours des années 1930', in Martel (ed.), *Forces armées*, pp. 689–703. Cf. P. Buffotot, 'The French High Command and the Franco-Soviet Alliance, 1933–1939', *JSS*, 5:4 (Dec. 1982), pp. 546–59.
53. Dutailly, *Problèmes de l'armée de terre*, pp. 35, 41, 44–5.
54. CAC, 'Séance du 21 mars 1935 . . . procès-verbal', p. 35, Carton 5 bis, dr. VIII, AAN.
55. Belgian Ambassador Baron de Gaiffier (Paris) to P. Hymans (Belgian foreign minister), 8 Feb. 1935, Carton 11.185 (2–3), sdr. 'Belgique: défense militaire, 1935', AMBAE, Brussels. Cf. Weygand's dismissive remark that 'The Red Army is a gendarmerie that will not be able to leave the soil of the Soviet Union' (quoted in Pertinax, *Les Fossoyeurs*, I, p. 16, n. 12). Discussing Weygand's attitude to French *rapprochement* with the Soviet Union, the general's most recent biographer notes that he 'never took up a position that was hostile to a pact which could be a support for the [French] army. But, after the [Soviet] purges of 1937 . . . he had little remaining faith in the Soviet army's ability to deliver any effective aid.' (Destremau, *Weygand*, p. 367, n.2.)
56. Papiers Schweisguth, 'memento', 13 Sept. 1935, 351 AP Carton 2, dr. 5, AN.
57. Dutailly, *Problèmes de l'armée de terre*, p. 41; Bach, 'Le colonel Mendras', pp. 23–37, 76–84, 101–29, 146–51, 175–9.
58. Gen. L. Loizeau, 'Une mission militaire en URSS', *RDM*, 8 (15 Sept. 1955), pp. 256–76; also the subsequent lecture by Mendras at the French Ecole de Guerre on Soviet air drops of troops, in Papiers Schweisguth, 'memento', 18 Nov. 1935, 351 AP, Carton 2, dr. 6, AN; and discussion of the French military attaché's role in engineering the Loizeau mission in Bach, 'Le colonel Mendras', pp. 190–3, 208–17. A perceptive analysis of the West's observation of these manoeuvres occurs in Rader, 'Anglo-French estimates of the Red Army, 1936–1937', pp. 265–80. Cf. shrewd discussion of the subordination of the French military assessments to

anti-Soviet political prejudices in Jordan, 'The cut-price war on the peripheries', pp. 146–7, 149–52.
59. Fabry, *De la Place de la Concorde*, pp. 67, 75–8.
60. Papiers Schweisguth, 'memento', 20 Sept. 1935, 351 AP, Carton 2, dr. 5, AN.
61. Gamelin, Journal de marche, 11 Oct. 1939, Fonds Gamelin 1K 224, Carton 9, SHAT.
62. Gamelin, 'La Politique étrangère de la France', p. 3, Papiers Blum, 3 BL 3, dr. 1, FNSP; cf. Gamelin's remark about the Red Army, after Stalin's purge of the Soviet high command in 1937: 'It's the old Russian Army but with some equipment. But what can one expect of it after its generals and field-grade officers have been put to death in their thousands?' (quoted in Pertinax, *Les Fossoyeurs*, I, p. 16, n. 12). Cf. Weygand's comments on the Red Army, quoted above, n. 55.
63. Ibid.
64. Gamelin, *Servir*, II, p. 196.
65. Gamelin, 'La Politique étrangère de la France', p. 5, Papiers Blum, 3 BL 3, dr. 1, FNSP.
66. Ibid. Cf. evidence that Gamelin prided himself on having eliminated 'the communist virus' among the nco's and other ranks of the French army, in Pertinax, *Les Fossoyeurs*, I, p. 16, n. 11, pp. 89–90, n. 16.
67. Andrew and Gordievsky, *KGB*, pp. 370–1.
68. E. Daladier, 'Les négociations franco-soviétiques de 1936–37', typescript draft memoirs in Archives Daladier, 1 DA 7, dr. 5, sdr. c, FNSP.
69. CAC, 15th Leg. (1932–6), 'Séance du 19 février 1936: procès-verbal', pp. 3–4, Carton XV/739/48 bis, AAN.
70. Papiers Schweisguth, 'mementos', 8 Oct. 1936 ('Conversation avec M. Léger'), 351 AP Carton 3, dr. 10, AN.
71. Col. F. G. Beaumont-Nesbitt to Sir G. Clerk (British ambassador, Paris), enc. no. 2 in Clerk to A. Eden (Foreign Office, London), 22 Sept. 1936, FO 371, 19871, C6616/172/17, PRO.
72. Clerk to Eden, 11 June 1936, FO 371, 19857, C4248/1/17, PRO.
73. Clerk to Eden, 22 Sept. 1936, FO 371, 19871, C6616/172/17, PRO.
74. Papiers Schweisguth, 'memento', 4 Nov. 1936, 351 AP, Carton 3, dr. 10, AN.
75. Ibid., 7 Nov. 1936. Cf. discussion of the resurgent French interest during late 1936 in contacts with the Red Army in Young, *In Command of France*, pp. 147–8.
76. Daladier, typescript memoir: 'Les négociations franco-soviétiques', Archives Daladier 1 DA 7, dr. 5, sdr. c, FNSP; also de Villelume, testimony to the French postwar parliamentary inquiry, 12 Apr. 1951, *C. E. Témoignages*, IX, pp. 2742–4.
77. Beaumont-Nesbitt to Clerk: report on Gen. Henri Giraud, enc. no 1 in Clerk to Eden, 22 Sept. 1936, FO 371, 19871, C6616/172/17, PRO.
78. Ibid., report by Beaumont-Nesbitt on a conversation with Col. M.-H. Gauché.
79. Clerk to Eden, 22 Sept. 1936 (cited above, n. 71).
80. Gamelin, Riom written deposition: 'La Politique étrangère de la France', pp. 12, 13, Papiers Blum, 3 BL 3, dr. 1, FNSP.

81. Beaumont-Nesbitt, report in FO 371, 20702, C3753/532/62, PRO.
82. Daladier, typescript memoir: 'Les négociations franco-soviétiques', Archives Daladier 1 DA 7, dr. 5, sdr. c, FNSP. Also Dutailly, *Problèmes de l'Armée de Terre*, p. 56. Cf. Young, *In Command of France*, p. 148.
83. 'Manoeuvres de Russie Blanche (Région de Minsk): rapport du général Schweisguth, chef de mission française', in Archives Daladier, 1 DA 7, dr. 5, sdr. b, FNSP. Also *DDF*, 2nd ser., vol. III, docs. nos. 343 (annex), 513 ('La mission en URSS, 5–23 septembre 1936'); Dutailly, *Problèmes de l'Armée de Terre*, pp. 54–5; Pertinax, *Les Fossoyeurs*, I, pp. 15–16. Young, *In Command of France*, pp. 145–7. Cf. the evaluations of the Red Army by British officers who also attended these 1936 Soviet exercises, in Lt.-Gen. Sir G. Le Q. Martel, *The Russian Outlook* (London, 1947), pp. 13–33; J. Connell, *Wavell, Scholar and Soldier* (London, 1964), pp. 182–3; and discussion of their reports in Herndon, 'British perceptions of Soviet military capability', in Mommsen and Kettenacker (eds.), *The Fascist Challenge*, pp. 297–319.
84. Gamelin, Riom written deposition: 'La Politique étrangère de la France', pp. 12, 13, Papiers Blum, 3 BL 3, dr. 1, FNSP.
85. Papiers Schweisguth, 'memento', 8 Feb. 1937, 351 AP, Carton 3, dr. 11, AN.
86. Daladier typescript memoir: 'Les négociations franco-soviétiques', Archives Daladier, 1 DA 7, dr. 5, sdr. c, FNSP.
87. Ibid.
88. Papiers Schweisguth, 'memento', 9 Apr. 1937, 351 AP, Carton 3, dr. 12, AN.
89. Ibid., 25 Apr. 1937. Daladier's visit to Britain, 21–24 Apr. 1937, is recounted in *DDF*, 2nd ser., vol. V, doc. no. 335 ('M. Corbin, ambassadeur de France à Londres à M. Delbos, ministre des Affaires étrangères, Paris', 24 Apr. 1937); also in 'le général Lelong, attaché militaire près l'Ambassade de France à Londres, au Ministère de la Défense nationale et de la Guerre, Etat-major de l'Armée, D. no. 305: Objet: La visite de M. Daladier à Londres et à Manchester', 29 Apr. 1937, EMA/2 Grande-Bretagne, Carton 7N 2812, dr. 'correspondance de l'attaché militaire en Grande-Bretagne, janvier–juin 1937', SHAT.
90. Papiers Schweisguth, 'memento', 27 Apr. 1937, 351 AP, Carton 3, dr. 12, AN.
91. See J. Erickson, *The Road to Stalingrad: Stalin's War with Germany* I (London, 1975; pbk. edn. 1985), pp. 12–20, 30–1, 44–9 (1985 edn); also M. Mackintosh, *Juggernaut: The Russian Forces, 1918–1966* (New York, 1967), pp. 84–95; and discussion of pre-1937 leadership and strategic thought in the Red Army in C. Rice, 'The making of Soviet strategy', in Paret (ed.), *Makers of Modern Strategy*, pp. 648–68.
92. Daladier typescript memoir: 'Les négociations franco-soviétiques', Archives Daladier, 1 DA 7, dr. 5, sdr. c, FNSP.
93. Emile Naggiar, French ambassador in Moscow, wired in July 1939 that he 'felt duty bound' to warn Bonnet that 'In support of Poland and Rumania . . . we must provide for the eastern front through as great a Russian participation as possible . . . The arrangement of present frontiers in the

East is such that the success or prolongation of Polish or Rumanian resistance [to Germany] depends on the attitude of Russia . . . The greatest danger lies . . . in the USSR . . . withholding any commitment on our side over Poland or Rumania because the Soviets would then retain a free hand for a policy of neutrality or an entente with Germany. Since we have guaranteed Poland and Rumania without a preliminary agreement with Moscow, the gravity of the situation becomes readily apparent.' (*DDF*, 2nd ser., vol. XVII, doc. no. 131 [L'ambassadeur de France à Moscou à M. Georges Bonnet, ministre des Affaires étrangères, 7 July 1939].) See the history of the 1939 negotiations in A. Read and D. Fisher, *The Deadly Embrace. Hitler, Stalin and the Nazi–Soviet Pact, 1939–1941* (New York and London, 1988).

94. Carl E. Schorske, 'Two German Ambassadors: Dirksen and Schulenburg', Craig and Gilbert (eds.), *The Diplomats*, pp. 477–510; H. von Herwarth (with S. Frederick Starr), *Against Two Evils. Memoirs of a diplomat-soldier during the Third Reich* (London, 1981), pp. 142–65. Cf. Craig, *Germany, 1866–1945*, pp. 710–13 (Oxford pbk. edn, 1985). There is an extensive debate over the date at which the French and British first received clear indication that German–Soviet negotiations had commenced. According to Gamelin's notes on a lunch in the spring of 1940 with the US ambassador to France, Bullitt, and Robert Coulondre (French ambassador to Germany, 1938–9), 'Bullitt asked Coulondre at what point he had known *with certainty* of the existence of Russo-German overtures; From 6 May [1939] [replied Coulondre]. I was kept informed hour-by-hour about these conversations. I succeeded in convincing Daladier of their occurrence.' (Gamelin, Journal de marche, 29 Apr. 1940, Fonds Gamelin, 1K 224, Carton 9, SHAT, emphasis added.) Two weeks earlier, however, Coulondre's senior lieutenant in the Berlin embassy wired Bonnet that 'Certain Nazi personalities' had gone as far as 'to affirm, in front of one of my colleagues, that Germany could, after all, seek an understanding with Russia to the detriment of Poland, and suggest to the Soviets a partition of that country'. (*DDF*, 2nd ser., vol. XV, doc. no. 473, p. 775 [M. de Vaux Saint-Cyr, chargé d'affaires de France à Berlin à M. le ministre des Affaires étrangères, 22 Apr. 1939].)

95. *DDF*, 2nd ser., vol. I, doc. no. 106 ('Note sur les répercussions possibles du Pacte Franco-Soviétique', 27 Jan. 1936).

96. Gamelin, Riom written deposition: 'La Politique étrangère de la France', p. 12, Papiers Blum, 3 BL 3, dr. 1, FNSP.

97. Gamelin, *Servir*, II, p. 461. Cf. similar views of Weygand cited above, n. 55; and of Gamelin, above, n. 62.

98. Musse quoted in Turlotte, 'Relations militaires franco-polonaises', p. 62.

99. See the masterful explication of this tangled diplomacy in Watt, *How War Came*, esp. pp. 361–84. Williamson Murray (*Change in the European Balance of Power*, p. 305) concludes that 'failure to reach an agreement with the Soviet Union and the resulting Nazi–Soviet pact . . . helped Germany to defeat Poland and concentrate against the West . . . cooperation between the West and Russia would have been a difficult task in the best of circumstances. Germany could and did offer Stalin concessions that no

democracy could match, while Eastern Europe refused to consider Soviet help, even when threatened by Germany.' On the British role, see R. Manne, 'The British decision for alliance with Russia, May 1939', *JCH*, 9:3 (July, 1974), pp. 3–26. Cf. the interpretation developed by Professor Duroselle (*La Décadence*, pp. 416–35), that, throughout the Anglo-Franco-Soviet negotiations of 1939, France alone genuinely sought to reach agreement and pressed her diplomacy vigorously, in an endeavour to conclude one.

100. Extracts from Sikorski's diary quoted in A. Polonsky, 'Wladyslaw Sikorski as opposition politician, 1928–1939', pp. 31–3 (unpub. paper read at the symposium on the occasion of the 40th anniversary of Sikorski's death, 26–27 Sept. 1983, School of Slavonic and East European Studies, University of London). Cf. Prazmowska, *Britain, Poland and the Eastern Front*, pp. 144–7, 149, 177–8.
101. 'Comparison of the strength of Great Britain with that of certain other nations as at January 1938', CID Paper 1366-B, 12 Nov. 1937, CAB, 4/26, PRO.
102. An expression attributed to Beck, the Polish foreign minister.
103. Prazmowska, *Britain, Poland and the Eastern front*, pp. 67–9. Cf. Roberts, 'The diplomacy of Colonel Beck', pp. 605–6, 608–10.
104. Quoted in Turlotte, 'Relations militaires franco-polonaises', p. 42.
105. Ibid. Cf. *DDF*, 2nd ser. vol. XVI, doc. no. 233, pp. 461–2; Gamelin, *Servir*, II, p. 413.
106. Gamelin, *Servir*, II, p. 415.
107. Musse despatch, 19 July 1939, quoted in Turlotte, 'Relations militaires franco-polonaises', p. 62. Cf. Prazmowska, *Britain, Poland and the Eastern Front*, pp. 141–5, 147–9.
108. Official minutes of the military and air talks in CSG Carton 2N 235, dr. 2, SHAT; discussion in Turlotte, 'Relations militaires franco-polonaises', pp. 42–9; Le Goyet, *Mystère Gamelin*, pp. 187–92.
109. Text in Gamelin, *Servir*, II, pp. 424–5; also Turlotte, 'Relations militaires franco-polonaises', pp. 73–5.
110. Dutailly, *Problèmes de l'armée de terre*, pp. 67–8, 105–14.
111. 'Directive pour le général commandant sur le théatre d'opérations du Nord-Est en vue des opérations initiales à conduire éventuellement entre Rhin et Moselle', 31 May 1939, in Gamelin, *Servir*, II, pp. 426–7. Cf. Turlotte, 'Relations militaires franco-polonaises', pp. 50–1.
112. 'Le général Georges, major-général, au général Prételat, commandant le groupe d'armées no. 2: Instruction personnelle et secrète du 24 juillet 1939', Carton 7N 3715, SHAT (quoted in Turlotte, 'Relations militaires franco-polonaises', pp. 51–2). Cf. Gamelin, *Servir*, II, pp. 427–8.
113. For example, Gamelin's self-justification in his *Servir*, II, p. 428.
114. This account of Franco-Polish air conversations follows Turlotte, 'Relations militaires franco-polonaises', pp. 47–9. The chronic inability of French air rearmament to attain promised states of readiness received a final underlining when, as Gamelin noted in his diary in March 1940: 'Guy La Chambre and Vuillemin have said that our aviation was incapable of doing anything at all for another two months.' (Journal de marche, 11

Mar. 1940, Fonds Gamelin, 1K 224, Carton 9, SHAT.) See also the sources cited below, ch. 11, n. 38.
115. Gamelin, *Servir*, II, pp. 428–9.
116. See P. R. Stafford, 'The French government and the Danzig crisis: the Italian dimension', *IHR*, 6:1 (Feb. 1984), pp. 48–87.
117. Gamelin, *Servir*, II, pp. 421–3.
118. Ibid., pp. 423–4.
119. Ibid., pp. 425–6.
120. See Stafford, 'The French government and the Danzig crisis', esp. pp. 53–87.
121. Young, 'Aftermath of Munich', p. 322. Cf. the later complaint of one leading Radical Party appeaser, the president of the Chamber of Deputies' foreign affairs commission, that 'a few men who held key positions, Lebrun [President of the Republic], Daladier, Gamelin, made us slide towards the catastrophe [of declaring war over Poland], against the wishes of the nation' (Montigny, *Complot contre la paix*, p. 207).
122. See Armengaud, *Batailles politiques et militaires*, pp. 117, 123–4, 126–7.
123. On the second day of Kasprzycki's visit, the British military attaché in Paris reported a talk with Petibon in which the latter, speaking with Gamelin's authority, 'agreed there should be complete frankness between ourselves and the French as to the nature of our respective conversations with the Poles, in order to avoid talking at cross purposes. *On the other hand, conversations between the French and ourselves are in another category and do not affect the Poles.*' Col. W. Fraser to Sir E. Phipps, no. 706, 18 May 1939, enc. in Group-Capt. D. Colyer, air attaché, Paris: 'Anglo-Polish Staff Conversations', D1638/955. P/1, 22 May 1939, AIR 40/2032, file labelled 'Interchange of information between British and French air staffs: August 1938 to September 1939', PRO (emphasis added).
124. Compare this cynically relaxed view of Poland's fate with the similar complacency shown by Gamelin in the spring of 1938 when he contemplated how little need be done to succour Czechoslovakia in the event of German attack. Then the general wrote that 'even if Czechoslovakia found itself in an initially difficult situation [sic], everything would be put to rights at the peace treaty, as it was for Serbia or for Rumania [in 1919]' (*DDF*, 2nd ser., vol. VIII, doc. no. 462, pp. 864–5: Note du général, chef d'Etat-Major général de la Défense nationale et de l'Armée, no. 1777/S, 16 Mar. 1938 [a paper not surprisingly marked 'très secret']).
125. 'Germany and Italy cannot hope to increase their resources appreciably in the course of the war: they will therefore stake their chances of success on a short war. The UK and France, on the other hand, are in a position to increase their war potential from one month to another ... Anglo-French strategy should therefore be adapted to a long war implying i) a defensive strategy at the outset ... ii) the building up of our military strength to a point at which we can adopt an offensive strategy.' (Anglo-French Staff Conversations: UK Delegation. Report on Stage 1: Part One, 'Broad Strategic Policy for the Allied Conduct of the War', COS Paper no. 877, 11 Apr. 1939, CAB. 53/47, PRO.)

126. 'Conversations militaires franco-britanniques: résumé des conversations du 13 juillet 1939', pp. 4, 6 in CSDN, Carton 136, SHAT. Gamelin's *chef de cabinet*, Petibon, had told Britain's military attaché in Paris at the close of 1938 'that in effect Germany was already engaged in a war in which the strategy was the same which she had employed in the last war . . . securing her position in the east before turning to strike westwards' (Col. W. Fraser, enc. to Sir E. Phipps [British ambassador, Paris], no. 1252, 23 Dec. 1938, FO 371, 22915, C16038/132/18, PRO). Cf. the reflection of the head of the French air mission to Warsaw on the eve of war in 1939, in his memoirs, that 'Our leaders knew full well that the effectiveness of French support for Poland, in the air as well as by land, would be negligible . . . Our general staff without doubt wished to maintain the alliance because, if Germany attacked Poland first, France could carry out her mobilisation and concentrate her armies without disturbance.' (Armengaud, *Batailles politiques et militaires*, p. 93.)
127. Armengaud, *Batailles politiques et militaires*, pp. 115–16.
128. J.-L. Crémieux-Brilhac, 'La France devant l'Allemagne et devant la guerre au début de septembre 1939', p. 12, unpub. paper read to the Franco-German historians' colloquium, Bonn, Sept. 1978; cf. Bonnet's statement in Oct. 1938 to a fellow *Munichois* Radical deputy that 'Gamelin thinks she [Poland] will hold out for six months, the delay that he says we require to complete the organisation of our own front', in Montigny, *Complot contre la paix*, p. 207.
129. Fraser (British military attaché), to Phipps (British ambassador, Paris): 'French action in the event of a German invasion of Poland', 4 Jan. 1939, p. 4, CAB. 21/555, File 14/5/18, PRO.
130. In Col. F. N. Mason-Macfarlane (British military attaché, Berlin), to Foreign Office, 18 Mar. 1939, FO 371, 22994, C3473/19/18, PRO.
131. Gamelin, *Servir*, II, p. 428.
132. Turlotte, 'Relations militaires franco-polonaises', p. 55.
133. Ibid., p. 56.
134. Ibid., pp. 54–7; Le Goyet, *Mystère Gamelin*, pp. 192–3, 235–6.
135. Text of the Protocol of Mutual Assistance between Poland and France, 4 Sept. 1939, in Grenville (ed.), *Major International Treaties, 1914–1973*, p. 192; cf. text of the Agreement of Mutual Assistance between Britain and Poland, 25 Aug. 1939, pp. 190–1.
136. For the text of the 23 Aug. Paris meeting of French ministers and military chiefs, see Gamelin, *Servir*, I, pp. 22–43; also retrospective reflections of Daladier in his *Journal de captivité*, p. 88. Cf. discussion of the conference and criticism of Gamelin's declaration of the army's readiness to mobilise in Le Goyet, *Mystère Gamelin*, pp. 225–6; Paillat, *La Guerre immobile*, pp. 100–14, 142–3; Dutailly, *Problèmes de l'armée de terre*, pp. 287–90; Duroselle, *La Décadence*, pp. 472–93; *L'Abîme*, pp. 19–26.
137. This was not the same as to claim that France was in a position immediately – or even for two-three years – to mount a war-winning offensive and overthrow Hitler's Reich. The dilemma of the inter-war French strategic posture thus came home to roost with the failure of successive governments to decide whether their aim was, in the words of one historian of the

civil-military problem, 'to make war – or to defend France?' (Nobécourt, *Histoire politique de l'armée*, I, pp. 188–9).
138. Daladier, *Journal de captivité*, pp. 34, 88.
139. Gamelin, Riom written deposition: 'La Politique étrangère de la France', p. 21, Papiers Blum, 3 BL 3, dr. 1, FNSP. See identical sentiments in Daladier, *Journal de captivité*, p. 205 and p. 88 (the former prime minister noting on 1 June 1941 that Gamelin had 'said to me personally [in 1939] that if France did not go to the rescue of Poland, she would be dishonouring herself'); also the reflection in the diary of a junior Quai d'Orsay diplomat (Hervé Alphand, *L'Etonnement d'être, 1939–1973* (Paris, 1977)), for 27 Aug. 1939: 'If war breaks out, how will we come out of it? And if it doesn't break out, can we hope for any future except as a province of Germany?' (Charles Alphand, this diarist's father, had been France's first ambassador to the Soviet Union on the restoration of diplomatic relations in 1932.) Cf., however, the bleak conclusion of Professor Duroselle (*La Décadence*, p. 493): 'Let it be noted that, for this peaceable people [the French], *war itself was a first defeat*.' (Emphasis added.)

11 GAMELIN AND THE FALL OF POLAND

1. Quotation from Harvey, *Diplomatic Diaries*, p. 318 (entry for 11 Sept. 1939). For the spring 1939 planning see 'Anglo-French Staff Conversations: UK delegation. Report on Stage One', DP (P) 56, 11 Apr. 1939, CAB. 53/49, PRO; Lelong, report to Gamelin, 5 Apr. 1939: 'Conversations d'Etats-Major franco-britanniques, 1ère phase (Londres, 29 mars–4 avril 1939)', EMA/2 Grande-Bretagne, Carton 7N2816, SHAT; Bond, *British Military Policy*, pp. 299–313.
2. See, in particular, Gamelin's remarks in this sense to Gort when the latter visited Paris for the 1939 Bastille Day parade: 'Conversations militaires franco-britanniques – résumé des conversations du 13 juillet 1939', p. 2, CSDN Carton 136, SHAT.
3. See Young, 'Guerre de longue durée', in Preston (ed.), *General Staffs and Diplomacy*, pp. 41–64 (esp. pp. 46–52).
4. Hughes, *To the Maginot Line*, p. 228.
5. Armengaud, *Batailles politiques et militaires*, pp. 133–4, 138; cf. Gen. Maxime Weygand, *Recalled to Service* (London, 1952), pp. v–vi; Challener, 'Gravediggers revisited', p. 92; also the reflection by John C. Cairns that the fall of France in 1940 'was, after all, only the collapse of the most exposed member of the wealthy Atlantic powers, not one of which had provided adequately for its defense after 1918' (Cairns, 'Some recent historians', p. 75).
6. For a highly polemical and skimpily documented interpretation in this vein see Jon Kimche, *The Unfought Battle* (London, 1968).
7. Harvey, *Diplomatic Diaries*, p. 318 (entry of 11 Sept. 1939).
8. Gamelin, Journal de marche, 18 Sept. 1939, Fonds Gamelin, 1K 224, Carton 9, SHAT.
9. Ibid., 9 Oct. 1939.
10. Ibid., 14 Oct. 1939.

11. Armengaud, *Batailles politiques et militaires*, pp. 93–4, 96, 111, 116–17, 138; Turlotte, 'Relations militaires franco-polonaises', pp. 54–7.
12. Gamelin, Journal de marche, 3 Sept. 1939, Fonds Gamelin, 1K 224, Carton 9, SHAT.
13. See Jean-Louis Crémieux-Brilhac, 'La France devant l'Allemagne et devant la guerre au début de septembre 1939', unpublished paper read to the Franco-German historians' colloquium, Bonn, Sept. 1978, p. 12.
14. Fraser, letter to his wife, 8 Sept. 1939 (emphasis in original). The text of the 4 Sept. 1939 Franco-Polish Treaty is in Grenville, *The Major International Treaties, 1914–1973*, p. 192; Jeanneney, *Journal politique*, p. 7.
15. Gamelin, Journal de marche, 6 Sept. 1939, Fonds Gamelin, 1K 224/9, SHAT; le colonel Delvoie, attaché militaire et de l'air près l'Ambassade de Belgique en France au Ministère de la Défense nationale (Bruxelles), no. 1 O.D./5453/182c, 16 Sept. 1939, microfilmed despatches of Belgian military attachés in France (1937–1940), AMBAE; Le Goyet, *Mystère Gamelin*, pp. 231–4.
16. Gamelin, *Servir*, III, pp. 50–3 (quotation from p. 50).
17. Gamelin, Journal de marche, 6 Sept. 1939 Fonds Gamelin, 1K 224/9, SHAT.
18. Ibid., 7, 8 Sept. 1939.
19. Ibid., 9 Sept. 1939.
20. 'Instruction Personnelle No. 1 pour le général adjoint au général commandant en chef les forces terrestres, commandant le théâtre d'opérations du Nord-Est; le général major-général', No. 27 CAB/FT, 9 Sept. 1939; 'Instruction Personnelle No. 2 . . .', No. 30 CAB/FT, 10 Sept. 1939, reproduced in Gamelin, *Servir*, III, pp. 62–4; Le Goyet, *Mystère Gamelin*, p. 240.
21. See Gamelin, *Servir*, III, pp. 60–1; Minart, *P. C. Vincennes*, I, pp. 19–21, 24, 26–9, 33–4. Cf. the meetings at this time between Julius Lukasiewicz, Polish ambassador in Paris, and Jeanneney, president of the French Senate, in Jeanneney, *Journal politique*, pp. 9–14.
22. Gamelin, Journal de marche, 12 Sept. 1939, Fonds Gamelin, 1K 224/9, SHAT; *Servir*, III, pp. 65–8; Le Goyet, *Mystère Gamelin*, pp. 232, 278; Minart, *P. C. Vincennes*, I, pp. 24–5. For the minutes of this first Anglo-French SWC meeting see F. Bédarida, *La Stratégie secrète de la drôle de guerre. Le Conseil Suprême Interallié, septembre 1939–avril 1940* (Paris, 1979), pp. 79–111.
23. Col. William Fraser, letter to his wife, 14 Sept. 1939 (emphasis in original).
24. Gamelin, Journal de marche, 12, 16 Sept. 1939, Fonds Gamelin, 1K 224, Carton 9, SHAT.
25. Col. W. Fraser, letter to his wife, 21 Sept. 1939.
26. Col. W. Fraser, letter to his wife, 27 Sept. 1939.
27. See Minart, *P. C. Vincennes*, I, pp. 31, 43; Gamelin, Journal de marche, 9, 15 Sept., 11 Oct. 1939, Fonds Gamelin, 1K 224, Carton 9, SHAT.
28. Le colonel Delvoie, attaché militaire et de l'air près l'Ambassade de Belgique en France au Ministère de la Défense nationale (Bruxelles), nos. 1 O.D./5375/168c, 7 Sept. 1939 and 1 O.D./5421/177c, 12 Sept. 1939, microfilm of despatches of Belgian military attachés in Paris (1937–1940), AMBAE; also Gauché, *Deuxième Bureau*, pp. 95–6, 162–3, 167–8.

29. See Murray, *Change in the European Balance of Power*, pp. 347–50, 359–60; J. J. Mearsheimer, *Conventional Deterrence* (Ithaca, NY; London, 1983), pp. 82–104.
30. Cf. Murray, *Change in the European Balance of Power*, pp. 312–13; 'The German response to victory in Poland: a case study in professionalism', *Armed Forces and Society*, 7:2 (Winter 1981), pp. 285–98; D. Irving, *The War Path, 1933–1939* (London, 1978), pp. 224–39, 252–3, 266.
31. See Gunsburg, *Divided and Conquered*, pp. 88–91, 100–109.
32. Gamelin, letter to Daladier, 1 Sept. 1939, in Fonds Gamelin, 1K 224/7, dr. 2, SHAT. See also Gamelin, *Servir*, III, pp. 16–17, 33–7, 74–5, 115–16; I, pp. 163–73, 175–94, 215–20; Minart, *P. C. Vincennes*, II, pp. 41–81 *passim*.
33. Le colonel Delvoie, attaché militaire et de l'air près l'Ambassade de Belgique en France, au Ministère de la Défense nationale (Bruxelles), no. 1 O.D./5375/168c, 7 Sept. 1939, in microfilm of despatches of Belgian military attachés in Paris (1937–40), AMBAE.
34. Gamelin, Journal de marche, 16 Sept. 1939, Fonds Gamelin, 1K 224, Carton 9, SHAT.
35. Cf. Young, 'The use and abuse of fear', pp. 88–109; Bialer, *Shadow of the Bomber, passim*.
36. Gamelin, Journal de marche, 1, 3, 5, 6 Sept. 1939, Fonds Gamelin, 1K 224, Carton 9, SHAT; Col. W. Fraser, letters to his wife, 15, 17 Sept. 1939.
37. 'Personally', wrote Gamelin later, 'I thought, on the contrary, that the Germans were holding back their aviation to act in conjunction with their land army in the battle as a whole and that, for us, this was the most dangerous hypothesis as far as the higher conduct of the war was concerned.' (*Servir*, III, p. 219.)
38. Le général, chef d'état-major général de l'Armée de l'Air à M. le Ministre de l'Air, No. 167/EMGAA, 26 Aug. 1939, reproduced in La Chambre's evidence to the post-1945 French parliamentary investigation, *C. E. Témoignages*, II, pp. 331–2 (séance du 25 novembre 1947); Gamelin, *Servir*, I, p. 281; cf. Paillat, *La Guerre immobile*, pp. 102–14.
39. See Le Goyet, *Mystère Gamelin*, pp. 266–8 ('General Gamelin maintained that, *a priori*, there was no interest [for the Allies] in bombing'); Gunsburg, *Divided and Conquered*, p. 89 ('Vuillemin reminded his units that civilian targets were strictly off limits').
40. Gamelin, *Servir*, III, p. 54 (Gamelin continued: 'There is no doubt that our inferiority in aviation weighed heavily on our decisions and on the fate of France.' ibid.) According to a report by General Mouchard, commander of 1st Air Army, on 23 Nov. 1939, the situation of the French air force was 'pitiful' and 'did not lend itself to any rapid improvement'. (Quoted in Minart, *P. C. Vincennes*, I, p. 61.)
41. It was therefore doubly disturbing to Gamelin when the six months demanded at the outbreak of war for overhauling the air force were up and he heard 'La Chambre and Vuillemin have said that our aviation will not be capable of doing anything at all for another two months.' (Gamelin, Journal de marche, 11 Mar. 1940, Fonds Gamelin, 1K 224, Carton 9, SHAT; cf. Gamelin, *Servir*, I, p. 284.)

42. Minart, *P. C. Vincennes*, I, p. 45. Cf. Gunsburg, *Divided and Conquered*, pp. 90–1.
43. *DDF*, 2nd ser., vol. XIX, doc. no. 353 (Le général Gamelin, chef d'Etat-Major général de la Défense nationale ... à M. Daladier, 1 septembre 1939), pp. 357–8. Cf. Le Goyet, *Mystère Gamelin*, pp. 229–30; Gunsburg, *Divided and Conquered*, pp. 89–90; Colville, *Man of Valour*, p. 152.
44. For contemporary assessments cf. Harvey, *Diplomatic Diaries*, pp. 324, 329 (entries for 3 Oct., 11 Nov. 1939); Gauché, *Deuxième Bureau*, pp. 178–9, 183–5; Minart, *P. C. Vincennes*, II, pp. 6–7, 9–17.
45. Gamelin, Journal de marche, 9, 10 Sept. 1939. Cf. Minart, *P. C. Vincennes*, I, pp. 23–4; Gamelin, *Servir*, III, pp. 51–65.
46. See Gamelin, Journal de marche, 11 Oct. 1939, Fonds Gamelin, 1K 224/9, SHAT ('The Service de Renseignement [Colonel Rivet] does not share the fears of General Prételat and of GQG about an imminent German attack.') Cf. Le colonel Delvoie, attaché militaire et de l'air près l'Ambassade de Belgique en France au Ministère de la Défense nationale (Bruxelles), No. 1 O.D./5453/182c, 16 Sept. 1939, microfilmed despatches of Belgian military attachés, Paris (1937–1940), AMBAE ('The head of the 2e Bureau [Col. Gauché] does not believe there will be important German operations in the West [until after the winter]').
47. See Gamelin, *Servir*, III, pp. 262–4; Gauché, *Deuxième Bureau*, pp. 164–214. Porch, 'French intelligence and the fall of France', esp. pp. 45–54, argues that 2e Bureau/SR cooperation in 1939–40 was deficient.
48. P. Paillole, *Notre espion chez Hitler* (Paris, 1985), p. 162; Paillat, *Répétition générale*, p. 38.
49. Gen. L. Rivet, 'Etions-nous renseignés en mai 1940? (II)', *Revue de Défense Nationale*, 11:6 (July 1950), pp. 24–39 (quotation from p. 31).
50. Paillole, *Notre espion*, p. 169; Gamelin was fully aware that much German armour had been destroyed or damaged in Poland (see *Servir*, III, p. 115).
51. Rivet, 'Etions-nous renseignés en mai 1940? (II)', p. 30.
52. Ibid., pp. 30, 37–8, notes 1 and 2; Paillole, *Notre espion*, pp. 170–2; Vanwelkenhuyzen, *Avertissements*, *passim*. Cf. Gen. L. Rivet, 'Le Camp allemand dans la fièvre des alertes (1939–1940)', *Revue de Défense Nationale*, (5e année), vol. 9 (1949), pp. 33–48 (on the Sas-Oster connection esp. pp. 43 n. 1, 46, 47 n. 1).
53. The above paragraphs are based on J. Stengers, 'ENIGMA, the French, the Poles and the British, 1931–1940', in C. M. Andrew and D. Dilks (eds.), *The Missing Dimension. Governments and intelligence communities in the 20th century* (London, 1981), pp. 126–37; G. Bloch, 'La Contribution française à la reconstitution et au décryptement de l'Enigma militaire allemande en 1931–32', *Revue historique des armées*, 4 (1985), pp. 17–25; Gen. G. Bertrand, *ENIGMA ou la plus grande enigme de la guerre, 1939–1945* (Paris, 1973); Hinsley *et al.*, *British Intelligence in the Second World War*, I, pp. 108–9, 138–9; L. Ribadeau-Dumas, 'Essai historique du chiffre de l'armée de terre: 4e partie (1919–39)', *Bulletin de l'Association des Réservistes du Chiffre*, new ser., 3 (1975), pp. 19–33; part 5 (1939–45), 4 (1976), pp. 33–47; Young, 'French military intelligence', pp. 275–7, 285–6;

C. M. Andrew, *Secret Service. The making of the British Intelligence Community* (London, 1985), pp. 448–51.
54. Minart, *P. C. Vincennes*, II, p. 7; cf. I, pp. 39–40, 43, 45.
55. Fraser, letter to his wife, 25 Sept. 1939; Bond, *Chief of Staff*, I, p. 240.
56. Minart, *P. C. Vincennes*, II, p. 7; Gauché, *Deuxième Bureau*, pp. 178–82.
57. Rivet, 'Etions-nous renseignés en mai 1940? (II)', p. 29.
58. Minart, *P. C. Vincennes*, II, p. 7; Rivet, 'Etions-nous renseignés en mai 1940? (II)', p. 35. Cf. Minart, *P. C. Vincennes*, I, pp. 43–4.
59. Le col. Delvoie, attaché militaire et de l'air près l'Ambassade de Belgique en France au Ministère de la Défense nationale (Cabinet) et au Lt. Gén. Chef d'Etat-major général de l'armée (2e Section), no. 1 O.D./5735/205c, 14 Oct. 1939 (Annexe 1: 'Formations allemandes à l'ouest selon le 2e Bureau français'), microfilmed Belgian military attaché despatches (Paris, 1937–40), AMBAE; Paillole, *Notre espion*, pp. 169–70.
60. Bond, *Chief of Staff*, I, p. 244.
61. Ibid., pp. 238, 245.
62. Gamelin, *Servir*, III, pp. 92, 113–14.
63. Minart, *P. C. Vincennes*, II, p. 6; le col. Delvoie . . . au Ministère de la Défense nationale (Cabinet) et au Lt. Gén., Chef d'Etat-major général de l'armée (2e Section), no. 1 O.D./5375/168c, 7 Sept. 1939, microfilmed Belgian military attaché despatches (Paris, 1937–40), AMBAE.
64. Fraser (Paris), letter to his wife, 9 Oct. 1939.
65. Bond, *Chief of Staff*, I, p. 244 (Pownall diary, 12 Oct. 1939).
66. Fraser (Paris), letter to his wife, 9 Oct. 1939; Gamelin, Journal de marche, 10 Oct. 1939, Fonds Gamelin, 1K 224, Carton 9, SHAT. Cf. Harvey, *Diplomatic Diaries*, p. 324 (5 Oct. 1939).
67. Rivet, 'Etions-nous renseignés en mai 1940? (II)', p. 29.
68. Gamelin, 'Instruction Personnelle no. 6', no. 69 CAB/FT, 29 Sept. 1939, reproduced in *Servir*, III, pp. 82–3; also 'Instruction Personnelle no. 7', no. 2223/SC (2) GQG, 30 Sept. 1939, *Servir*, III, pp. 83–4. Cf. Minart, *P. C. Vincennes*, I, pp. 29–30, 40–1.
69. Bond, *Chief of Staff*, I, pp. 242–3; Colville, *Man of Valour*, pp. 149–51; Minart, *P. C. Vincennes*, I, p. 43; Macleod and Kelly (eds.), *Ironside Diaries*, pp. 113–15, 122–4; Gunsburg, *Divided and Conquered*, pp. 93, 96.
70. Gamelin, Journal de marche, 9 Oct. 1939, Fonds Gamelin 1K 224, Carton 9, SHAT.
71. 'Great activity on the front between the Moselle and the Saar', noted Gamelin's adjutant; 'The General is expecting the battle.' (Gamelin, Journal de marche, 10 Oct. 1939, Fonds Gamelin, 1K 224/9, SHAT.) Cf. ibid., 11, 12, 13 Oct. 1939 entries. Cf. Macleod and Kelly (eds.), *Ironside Diaries*, pp. 124–5.
72. Order of the Day, 12 Oct. 1939, reproduced in Gamelin, *Servir*, III, p. 92; Minart, *P. C. Vincennes*, I, p. 46.
73. Col. W. Fraser (Paris), letter to his wife, 13 Oct. 1939.
74. Gamelin, Journal de marche, 14 Oct. 1939, Fonds Gamelin 1K 224, Carton 9, SHAT.
75. Col. Delvoie, attaché militaire et de l'air près l'Ambassade de Belgique en France au Ministère de la Défense nationale (Cabinet) . . . , no. 1 O.D./

5753/205c, 14 Oct. 1939, annex 2, microfilmed despatches of Belgian military attachés (Paris, 1937–40), AMBAE. Cf. Rivet, 'Etions-nous renseignés en mai 1940? (I)', pp. 637–43; (II), p. 35; 'Le camp allemand', pp. 35–9; Vanwelkenhuyzen, *Avertissements*, pp. 10–30; Mearsheimer, *Conventional Deterrence*, pp. 101–13.
76. Gamelin, Journal de marche, 15 Oct. 1939, Fonds Gamelin, 1K 224, Carton 9, SHAT; Bond, *Chief of Staff*, I, p. 246.
77. Gamelin, Journal de marche, 15 Oct. 1939; *Servir*, III, p. 93; Villelume, *Journal d'une défaite*, pp. 64, 67–8.
78. This account follows the detailed itinerary with timings and notes on Gamelin's meetings in 'Voyage à la 1ère Armée et à la B.E.F., 15–16 octobre [1939]', Journal de marche, Fonds Gamelin, 1K 224, Carton 9, SHAT. Cf. *Servir*, III, pp. 94–5; Minart, *P. C. Vincennes*, I, pp. 46–50.
79. Gamelin, Journal de marche, 17, 18, 19 Oct. 1939; Villelume, *Journal d'une défaite*, pp. 71–2; Minart, *P. C. Vincennes*, I, pp. 51–3.
80. Bond, *Chief of Staff*, I, pp. 247, 249 (Pownall diaries, 25, 29 Oct. 1939); Col. Delvoie, attaché militaire et de l'air près l'Ambassade de Belgique en France au Ministère de la Défense nationale (Cabinet) ... no. 1 O.D./5870/212c, 25 Oct. 1939, microfilmed despatches of Belgian military attachés (Paris, 1937–40), AMBAE (reporting the imperturbability of Gauché, chief of the French army 2e Bureau); Macleod and Kelly (eds.), *Ironside Diaries*, pp. 134–5 (24 Oct. 1939); Villelume, *Journal d'une défaite*, p. 77.
81. See Murray, 'German response to victory', pp. 287–92; *Change in the European Balance*, pp. 338–40.
82. This summary leans heavily on the skilful analysis in Mearsheimer, *Conventional Deterrence*, pp. 114–21. Cf. Vanwelkenhuyzen, *Avertissements*, pp. 33–62; G. Brausch, 'Sedan 1940. Deuxième Bureau und strategische Uberraschung', *Militärgeschichtliche Mitteilungen*, II, 1967, pp. 15–92 (esp. pp. 39–45 on the scares of Oct.–Nov. 1939).
83. For the seriousness with which the highest Allied military chiefs took the Oct. 1939 alert, see Gamelin, Journal de marche, 14 Oct. 1939, Fonds Gamelin, 1K 224/9, SHAT; Villelume, *Journal d'une défaite*, pp. 67, 71–2; Minart, *P. C. Vincennes*, I, p. 45; Macleod and Kelly (eds.), *Ironside Diaries*, pp. 115, 124–5; Sir J. Kennedy, *The Business of War. The War Narrative of Major-General Sir John Kennedy. Introduced by Brigadier Bernard Fergusson* (London, 1957), pp. 27–9.
84. See Mearsheimer, *Conventional Deterrence*, pp. 103–4, 113, 117; Bond, *France and Belgium*, pp. 50–2.
85. See Murray, *Change in the European Balance*, pp. 338–40.
86. Jodl's diary and Hitler's memorandum quoted in Mearsheimer, *Conventional Deterrence*, pp. 102, 241 (n. 32) respectively.
87. Cf. Reynaud's remark at Vincennes on 9 Oct. 1939 that the war was 'the "struggle of the petits-bourgeois against the gangsters" ... with the French army representing the world's final barrier against the predators' and Gamelin's reply that 'once again the Franco-German duel was going to decide the fate of the world'. Gamelin, Journal de marche, 9 Oct. 1939, Fonds Gamelin, 1K 224, Carton 9, SHAT.

88. Ibid., 14 Oct. 1939.
89. See B. J. Bond, 'Brauchitsch', in Correlli Barnett (ed.), *Hitler's Generals* (London, 1989), pp. 75–100.
90. Gamelin, Journal de marche, 10, 21 Sept. 1939, Fonds Gamelin, 1K 224, Carton 9, SHAT.
91. Ibid., 10 Oct. 1939; also on Bineau's scepticism about a major German autumn offensive in the West, Villelume, *Journal d'une défaite*, pp. 72, 77.
92. Gamelin, Journal de marche, 19 Oct. 1939, Fonds Gamelin, 1K 224, Carton 9, SHAT.
93. Col. Delvoie, attaché militaire et de l'air près l'Ambassade de Belgique en France au Ministère de la Défense nationale (Cabinet) ... no. 1 O.D./5375/168c, 7 Sept. 1939 and no. 1 O.D./5453/182c, 16 Sept. 1939, microfilmed Belgian military attaché despatches (Paris, 1937–1940), AMBAE.
94. Minart, *P. C. Vincennes*, II, pp. 6–7. Cf. Gamelin, *Servir*, III, pp. 115–16.
95. Gauché's intelligence reported in Col. Delvoie, attaché militaire et de l'air près l'Ambassade de Belgique en France, au Ministère de la Défense nationale (Cabinet) ... no. 1 O.D./5836/210c, 21 Oct. 1939 and no. 1 O.D./5870/212c, 25 Oct. 1939, microfilmed Belgian military attaché despatches (Paris, 1937–40), AMBAE.
96. Gamelin, Journal de marche, 11 Oct. 1939, Fonds Gamelin, 1K 224, Carton 9, SHAT.
97. Rivet, 'Etions-nous renseignés en mai 1940? (II)', p. 34; Delvoie despatch to Brussels, no. 1 O.D./5870/212c, 25 Oct. 1939 (cited above, n. 95).
98. Minart, *P. C. Vincennes*, II, p. 10 n. 1. Cf. Villelume, *Journal d'une défaite*, pp. 79, 87, 93–7.
99. Rivet diary, 2 Nov. 1939, quoted in Paillole, *Notre espion*, p. 170; 'Etions-nous renseignés en mai 1940? (II)', p. 35.
100. Rivet diary, in Paillole, *Notre espion*, pp. 170–1. Cf. Gauché, *Deuxième Bureau*, pp. 183–6, 191–3. Cf. modern scholarly analysis in Gunsburg, *Divided and Conquered*, pp. 119–27; Vanwelkenhuyzen, *Avertissements*, pp. 27–30, 34–8, 97.
101. Cf. Bond, *Chief of Staff*, I, pp. 246, 252–4; Colville, *Man of Valour*, pp. 152–4; Macleod and Kelly (eds.), *Ironside Diaries*, pp. 124–59; Mearsheimer, *Conventional Deterrence*, pp. 115–21; Bond, *France and Belgium*, pp. 51–8; Fergusson (ed.), *Business of War*, pp. 27–32.
102. Minart, *P. C. Vincennes*, II, p. 7.
103. See Gamelin, *Servir*, II, pp. 135–7; Bond, *Chief of Staff*, I, pp. 252–6; Duroselle, *L'Abîme*, pp. 77–82; Roger Keyes, *Outrageous Fortune*, pp. 115–26; Villelume, *Journal d'une défaite*, pp. 90–5.
104. The major sources for the Dyle Plan and the meetings that approved it are in Gamelin, *Servir*, I, pp. 82–3; III, pp. 138–48; Le Goyet, *Mystère Gamelin*, pp. 280–3; Macleod and Kelly (eds.), *Ironside Diaries*, pp. 145–58; Villelume, *Journal d'une défaite*, pp. 95–9; Bédarida, *La Stratégie secrète*, pp. 149–82; Minart, *P. C. Vincennes*, I, pp. 92–100. Excellent scholarly analysis occurs in Gunsburg, *Divided and Conquered*, pp. 124–31; Bond, *France and Belgium*, pp. 48–61; D. W. Alexander, 'Repercussions of the Breda Variant', pp. 459–88.

105. Gamelin's elaboration of a defence of the Dyle Plan may be followed in *Servir*, I, pp. 84–7, 89–107; III, pp. 148–52. Cf. the acknowledgement by modern historians of certain advantages to the strategy in Bond, *France and Belgium*, pp. 53–4, 60–1; Gunsburg, *Divided and Conquered*, pp. 131, 141–2.
106. Cf. Murray, 'German response to victory', pp. 285–98; *Change in the European Balance*, pp. 338–40. See also Charles W. Sydnor Jr, *Soldiers of Destruction. The S.S. Death's Head Division, 1933–1945* (Princeton, NJ, 1977), pp. 37–119.
107. Le Goyet, *Mystère Gamelin*, pp. 192–3, 235; Turlotte, 'Relations militaires franco-polonaises', pp. 54–8. Musse's service in Warsaw as military attaché is evaluated in Turlotte, pp. 59–63.
108. Armengaud, *Batailles politiques et militaires*, p. 96.
109. See Stafford, 'The French government and the Danzig crisis', pp. 48–87 *passim*.
110. *DDF*, 2nd ser., XIX, no. 247 (Noël to Bonnet, telegram no. 1351, 31 Aug. 1939), p. 251.
111. Armengaud, *Batailles politiques et militaires*, pp. 93–4, 97–8, 102–7, 111–15; Gen. E. Ruby, 'La Stratégie polonaise', *Revue de Défense Nationale*, 11:6 (Dec. 1950), pp. 558–69; Woytak, *On the Border of War and Peace*, pp. 76, 79, 86, 88, 114. Cf. Prazmowska, *Britain, Poland and the Eastern Front*, pp. 104–5, 143–9, 175–7.
112. Armengaud, *Batailles politiques et militaires*, pp. 116–17. For Ironside's upbeat report of July 1939 and the uncertainties it generated see Macleod and Kelly (eds.), *Ironside Diaries*, pp. 77–8, 80–2; Bond, *British Military Policy*, p. 318; Turlotte, 'Relations militaires franco-polonaises', pp. 56, 64. Cf. Prazmowska, *Britain, Poland and the Eastern Front*, pp. 97–8; 'The Eastern Front and the British guarantee to Poland' (unpublished paper, for sight of which I am grateful to Dr Prazmowska), pp. 23–35.
113. See Armengaud, *Batailles politiques et militaires*, pp. 119–22, 123–35 *passim*. The US Department of the Army (G2 Division) also received very complete intelligence on the fall of Poland from its military attaché there, Maj. William H. Colbern. His reports are preserved in Record Group 165, Military Intelligence Division, US National Archives and Records Administration, Washington DC and have been analysed in an unpublished paper by André Ausems of San Diego State University (for sight of which I am indebted to its author.) Cf. also Philip V. Cannistraro, Theodore P. Kovaleff, Edward R. Wynot (eds.), *Poland and the Coming of the Second World War. The Diplomatic Papers of Anthony J. Drexel Biddle Jr., U.S. Ambassador to Poland, 1937–1939* (Columbus, OH, 1976).
114. Gamelin, Journal de marche, 9 Sept. 1939, Fonds Gamelin 1K 224/9, SHAT; le col. Delvoie, attaché militaire et de l'air près l'Ambassade de Belgique en France, au Ministre de la Défense nationale (Cabinet), au Lt. Gén. Chef d'Etat-Major de l'Armée (2e Section), no. 1 O.D./5400/172c, 11 Sept. 1939, microfilmed despatches, Belgian military attachés (Paris, 1937–40), AMBAE.

115. Gamelin, Journal de marche, 12, 13, 14 Sept. 1939, Fonds Gamelin 1K 224, Carton 9, SHAT; *Servir*, III, pp. 69–92; Minart, *P. C. Vincennes*, I, pp. 30–1, 41–3, 45.
116. Gamelin, Journal de marche, 14, 17 Sept. 1939, Fonds Gamelin 1K 224/9, SHAT. Cf. Armengaud, *Batailles politiques et militaires*, pp. 154, 304–8.
117. 'Rapport du général Armengaud sur la situation en Pologne et sur les décisions consecutives à prendre (le 16 septembre 1939)', in Armengaud, *Batailles politiques et militaires*, pp. 304–11 (Annex VIII. Août et Septembre 1939: Rapports sur la mission en Europe); quotations pp. 307–8. Cf. Gamelin, *Servir*, III, pp. 61–2, n. 1; Gunsburg, *Divided and Conquered*, pp. 91–2.
118. 'Note sur les opérations de l'armée de terre allemande en Pologne et la coopération des grandes unités blindées et de l'aviation (du 23 septembre 1939)', in Armengaud, *Batailles politiques et militaires*, pp. 311–16 *passim*.
119. Faury's report is extensively quoted and paraphrased in Le Goyet, *Mystère Gamelin*, pp. 236–9. Cf. Ruby, 'La Stratégie polonaise', pp. 560–5, 568–9.
120. See Gamelin, Journal de marche, 1, 2, 4, 5 Oct. 1939, Fonds Gamelin 1K 224, Carton 9, SHAT. Cf. Gunsburg, *Divided and Conquered*, pp. 111–12.
121. Armengaud, *Batailles politiques et militaires*, pp. 160–8, 179, 181; Macleod and Kelly (eds.), *Ironside Diaries*, pp. 116–22; Bond, *Chief of Staff*, I, pp. 241–2.
122. Murray, 'German response to victory', pp. 294–5.
123. Jeffery Gunsburg has to be excepted from this stricture, however, for his recognition (*Divided and Conquered*, p. 93), that 'On the whole, the French command understood the Blitzkrieg system. This information was disseminated in October 1939, although the French were not certain that the enemy would try these tactics in the west ... The Polish campaign did not lead the French command to despair; the Poles had been out-generaled as well as overwhelmed by German superiority in equipment.'
124. Gamelin, *Servir*, I, p. 279. Cf. Gunsburg, *Divided and Conquered*, pp. 94–5.
125. Macleod and Kelly (eds.), *Ironside Diaries*, p. 117.
126. Cf. M. S. Alexander, 'The Fall of France, 1940', pp. 33–5; Lee, 'Strategy, arms and the collapse of France, 1930–40', pp. 56–63, 66–7; Gary D. Sheffield, 'Blitzkrieg and attrition: land operations Europe, 1914–45', in G. D. Sheffield, Colin McInnes (eds.), *Warfare in the Twentieth Century. Theory and practice* (London, 1988), pp. 51–79; Doughty, 'The French armed forces, 1918–40', in Murray and Millett (eds.), *Military Effectiveness*, II, pp. 53–66.
127. See, for example, Minart, *P. C. Vincennes*, I, p. 77; Armengaud, *Batailles politiques et militaires*, pp. 199–201, 205, 209.
128. See Bond, *Chief of Staff*, I, pp. 279, 283; Minart, *P. C. Vincennes*, I, pp. 48, 56; Gunsburg, *Divided and Conquered*, pp. 99–101.
129. See Gunsburg, *Divided and Conquered*, pp. 94–5, 102–4.
130. Gen. Gaston Billotte, 'Etude sur l'emploi des chars', no. 3748 S/3, 6 Dec. 1939, Archives Daladier 4 DA 7, dr. 1, sdr. a, FNSP. Cf. Gamelin, *Servir*, III, pp. 275–81.

131. 'Mémorandum du Colonel de Gaulle aux MM. Daladier et Reynaud, à MM. les généraux Gamelin, Weygand et Georges, le 26 janvier 1940', in de Gaulle, *Trois études* (Livre de Poche edn, 1973), pp. 49–70. Cf. de Gaulle, *Mémoires de guerre*, I (Livre de Poche edn, 1971), pp. 32–4; Doughty, 'De Gaulle's concept of a mobile, professional Army', in Matthews, Brown (eds.), *The Parameters of War*, pp. 253–4; Lacouture, *De Gaulle*, I, pp. 288–307 (the fullest discussion of the document).
132. See EMA 1er Bureau, Décret No. 13.080, 16 Dec. 1939, in Archives Daladier 4 DA 3, dr. 3, Piece No. C6. Cf. Gunsburg, *Divided and Conquered*, pp. 104, 106, 112–13.
133. Ruby, 'La Stratégie polonaise', p. 569. Ruby was chief of staff to Gen. Charles Huntziger, commander of Second Army defending Sedan in May 1940. See Ruby, *Sedan. Terre d'Epreuve*.
134. Armengaud, *Batailles politiques et militaires*, p. 199.
135. Ibid., pp. 111–15. Cf. Gamelin, *Servir*, II, pp. 228–30; Ruby, 'La Stratégie polonaise', pp. 562–3. A recent historian's appraisal of how much the French command knew about Polish plans is Turlotte, 'Relations militaires franco-polonaises', pp. 55–7.
136. Armengaud, *Batailles politiques et militaires*, pp. 69–70, 93–4, 102–8, 111–15, 126–7, 306–7; Ruby, 'La Stratégie polonaise', p. 563.
137. Armengaud, *Batailles politiques et militaires*, pp. 115, 122–6.
138. Col. W. Fraser, letter to his wife, 14 Sept. 1939; Gamelin, Journal de marche, 11 Oct. 1939, Fonds Gamelin 1K 224, Carton 9, SHAT.
139. W. C. Bullitt letter to R. Walton Moore, counsellor, State Department, 7 June 1940, Judge R. Walton Moore Papers, Group 55, Box 3, Franklin D. Roosevelt Presidential Library, Hyde Park, New York.
140. See Gamelin, *Servir*, III, p. 115; Gauché, *Deuxième Bureau*, pp. 162–3, 165–77.
141. Bond, *Chief of Staff*, I, p. 238 (emphasis in original).
142. Armengaud, *Batailles politiques et militaires*, pp. 171–2.
143. Gamelin, Journal de marche, 9 Oct. 1939, Fonds Gamelin 1K 224/9, SHAT. Cf. Macleod and Kelly (eds.), *Ironside Diaries*, pp. 117–22.
144. Bond, *Chief of Staff*, I, p. 245. Cf. the reflection by Jeffery Gunsburg that 'The Polish campaign did not lead the French command to despair ... Things would be different in the west.' (*Divided and Conquered*, p. 93.)
145. Armengaud, *Batailles politiques et militaires*, p. 200.
146. Harvey, *Diplomatic Diaries*, pp. 322, 324 (entries of 22 Sept., 3 Oct. 1939).

12 THE TWILIGHT WAR: MILITARY STAGNATION AND POLITICAL CONFLICT

1. Cf. First-hand accounts of the 1939 mobilisation by junior officers and other ranks in Bloch, *L'Etrange défaite*, pp. 25–30; G. Sadoul, *Journal de guerre, 1939–40* (Paris, 1977), pp. 14–42; R. Felsenhardt, *1939–1940 avec le 18e corps d'armée*, (Paris, 1973) pp. 7–29; D. Barlone, *A French Officer's Diary (23 August 1939 to 1 October 1940)* (Cambridge, 1942; trans. L. V. Cass), pp. 1–18.
2. See *DDF*, 2nd ser., vol. I, doc. no. 525, pp. 696–700.

3. For summaries of Plan E see Dutailly, *Les Problèmes de l'armée de terre*, pp. 100–14; P.-E. Tournoux, *Haut Commandement, gouvernement*, pp. 339–41.
4. For Gamelin's attaque brusquée warning see CSG, 'Procès-verbal: séance d'études du 13 mars 1939', p. 5, Carton 1N 22, vol. XVII, annex 1, SHAT; also discussion of the term's fluid meaning under EMA manipulation in Young, 'L'Attaque brusquée', pp. 93–113.
5. Cf. Armengaud, *Batailles politiques et militaires*, pp. 201, 205; Minart, *P. C. Vincennes*, I, pp. 45, 225; Macleod and Kelly (eds.), *Ironside Diaries*, p. 158 (18 Nov. 1939: 'It is all "wait and see" and a complete subservience to the French point of view that all our effort should be made in France.')
6. See minutes of 22 Sept. 1939 SWC meeting, with commentary, in Bédarida, *La Stratégie secrète*, pp. 115–46.
7. Gamelin, *Servir*, III, p. 315. Weygand, whom Gamelin had recalled from retirement at the end of August 1939, to take command over French forces in the Near East from headquarters at Beirut, was another prime mover of the Salonika project. He wrote to Gamelin, advocating an expedition, on 9 Sept. 1939. See Minart, *P. C. Vincennes*, I, p. 231, n. 1. Cf. Gamelin, *Servir*, III, pp. 110, 206–9; Weygand, *Recalled to Service*, pp. 12–19, 35–8; Destremau, *Weygand*, pp. 373–82; Bankwitz, *Weygand and Civil-Military Relations*, pp. 286–91; Pertinax, *Fossoyeurs*, I, pp. 17, 59–61.
8. Gamelin, Journal de marche, 15 Sept. 1939, Fonds Gamelin 1K 224, Carton 9, SHAT.
9. An interpretation convincingly developed in Jordan, 'The cut price war on the peripheries', pp. 140–1, 156–8.
10. See Gamelin, Journal de marche, 19, 20 Sept. 1939, Fonds Gamelin 1K 224, Carton 9, SHAT; Gamelin, *Servir*, III, p. 208.
11. Gamelin, Journal de marche, 20 Sept. 1939.
12. See Bédarida, *La Stratégie secrète*, pp. 124–31. Cf. text of the first S.W.C. meeting at Abbeville, 12 Sept. 1939, discussion concerning Allied options in the Balkans after Poland's defeat in ibid., pp. 99–100; also Villelume, *Journal d'une défaite*, p. 33 (13 Sept. 1939: 'L'Angleterre est opposée à un débarquement à Salonique.'); Macleod and Kelly (eds.), *Ironside Diaries*, pp. 104–5 (Paper: 'Strategy in the Middle East', 7 Sept. 1939: 'When I interviewed General Gamelin in France he drew me a picture of General Weygand commanding in what he called the Levant ... I put in this warning because I foresee that we may be led into a repetition of the unfortunate Salonika expedition of the late war'.)
13. See Le Goyet, *Mystère Gamelin*, pp. 260–5; F. G. Weber, *The Evasive Neutral. Germany, Britain and the quest for a Turkish alliance in the Second World War* (Columbia, MO, and London, 1979), pp. 32–50; C. O. Richardson, 'French plans for Allied attacks on the Caucasus oil fields, January–April 1940', *FHS*, 8:1 (Spring 1973), pp. 130–56; P. Buffotot, 'Le Projet de bombardement des pétroles soviétiques du Caucase en 1940, un exemple des projets alliés dans la drôle de guerre', *RHA*, 4 (1979), pp. 79–101; Gamelin, *Servir*, III, pp. 210–13.
14. See Gamelin, *Servir*, III, pp. 187–202; R. A. C. Parker, 'Britain, France and Scandinavia, 1939–1940', *History*, 61 (1976), pp. 369–87; J. Nevakivi,

The Appeal that was Never Made. The Allies, Scandinavia and the Finnish winter war, 1939–1940 (London, 1976).
15. The Reynaud–Gamelin showdown over Norway is fully explicated in M. S. Alexander, 'The Fall of France, 1940', in J. Gooch (ed.), *Decisive Campaigns of the Second World War* (*Journal of Strategic Studies*, Special Issue, 13:1 (Mar. 1990) pp. 10–44); cf. F. Kersaudy, *Stratèges et Norvège, 1940. Les Jeux de la guerre et du hasard* (Paris, 1977); *Norway, 1940* (London, 1990); Duroselle, *L'Abîme*, pp. 87–94, 108–16.
16. Armengaud, *Batailles politiques et militaires*, p. 201.
17. Rowe, *Great Wall of France*, p. 116.
18. Colville, *Fringes of Power*, p. 40.
19. Gamelin, 'La Politique étrangère de la France, 1930–39, au point de vue militaire', written deposition for the Riom Trial, p. 16, Archives Blum, 3 BL 3, dr. 1, FNSP.
20. Crémieux-Brilhac, *Les Français de l'an 40* (esp. II, pp. 21–173, 347–59, 363–70, 498–537). For the First World War mobilisation cf. J.-J. Becker, *1914: Comment les Français sont entrés en guerre* (Paris, 1977). For the unhappy precedent of 1870, see T. J. Adriance, *The Last Gaiter Button. A study of the mobilization and concentration of the French Army in the War of 1870* (Westport, CT, 1987).
21. Gamelin, Journal de marche, 6 Sept. 1939, Fonds Gamelin 1K 224, Carton 9, SHAT.
22. Ibid., 12 Sept. 1939.
23. Le col. Maurice Delvoie, attaché militaire et de l'air près l'Ambassade de Belgique en France au Ministère de la Défense nationale (Cabinet) . . . no. 1 O.D./5453/182c, 16 Sept. 1939, microfilmed despatches of Belgian military attachés (Paris and London, 1937–40), AMBAE.
24. Ibid.
25. US naval attaché, Paris, to Office of Naval Intelligence, Washington DC, no. 649, 20 Dec. 1939, President's Secretary's File, Box 196, Naval Attaché (Paris): 'Estimates of potential military strength', Documents B, vol. 1, doc. no. 54, Franklin D. Roosevelt Presidential Library, Hyde Park, New York.
26. Martin L. Van Creveld, *Technology and War, from 2000 BC to the Present* (New York and London, 1989), p. 163. Cf. Crémieux-Brilhac, *Les Français de l'an 40*, II, pp. 85–91, 143–53, 394–7.
27. Gamelin, Journal de marche, 12 Sept. 1939, Fonds Gamelin 1K 224/9, SHAT; Gamelin, *Servir*, I, pp. 215–20; III, pp. 65–8, 224–8; Minart, *P. C. Vincennes*, II, pp. 41–9, 64–70.
28. Gamelin, Journal de marche, 18 Sept. 1939; *Servir*, III, pp. 236–43.
29. Gamelin, Journal de marche, 18 Sept. 1939, Fonds Gamelin 1K 224, Carton 9, SHAT.
30. 'When the real war begins over here', Gamelin warned his staff on 18 Sept. 1939, 'it will come as a very rude awakening.' By 17 Jan. 1940 Gamelin was saying to Herriot: 'What's serious, in the times we're presently living through, is the way a lot of people believe we can wage and win the war without a battle.' On 11 Mar. 1940 he noted incredulously that 'Daladier no longer thought there'd be any fighting [that year] and that men could be returned to the interior for other duties.' On 3 May 1940 he forecast to his

adjutant that 'France is going to experience one of the hardest summers in her history.' (Gamelin, Journal de marche, 18 Sept. 1939, 11 Mar., 3 May 1940); *Servir*, III, p. 125 (warning to Herriot).
31. The poster is reproduced in S. Marchetti, *Affiches, 1939–1945. Images d'une certaine France* (Lausanne, 1982), p. 42. On French propaganda in the phoney war see Pertinax, *Fossoyeurs*, I, pp. 167–71; Gamelin, *Servir*, III, pp. 121–33; Duroselle, *L'Abîme*, pp. 67–70; P. Masson, 'Moral et propagande', in *Français et Britanniques dans la drôle de guerre*, pp. 163–71.
32. Another general who did worry was Ironside, British CIGS. He reflected, on 24 Oct. 1939: 'I cannot get people down to realities here. We are going to produce some 12 to 15 divisions in the spring and no more, and we must prepare for this ... It is all very well ordering the equipment ... it is a matter of getting it. We have to withstand an attack in the spring with what we have got ...' (Macleod and Kelly (eds.), *Ironside Diaries*, pp. 134–5).
33. See Duroselle, *L'Abîme*, pp. 61–7; Crémieux-Brilhac, *Les Français de l'an 40*, II, pp. 23–34, 42–52.
34. Colson, 'Coup d'oeil retrospectif sur les armements français de 1919 à 1939', Fonds Gamelin 1K 224, Carton 7, SHAT. Cf. Minart, *P. C. Vincennes*, II, pp. 70–1.
35. Minart, *P. C. Vincennes*, I, p. 64.
36. See Dutailly, *Les Problèmes de l'armée de terre*, pp. 287–90, for discussion of the differences between readiness for mobilisation and readiness to fight.
37. See Minart, *P. C. Vincennes*, II, pp. 70–5, 79–81; Colson, 'Note sur la situation des fabrications d'armement à la date du 20 septembre 1939' (sent to Dautry, 22 Sept. 1939), Fonds Gamelin 1K 224, Carton 7, SHAT.
38. See Minart, *P. C. Vincennes*, I, pp. 57–60; II, pp. 68–70; Gamelin, *Servir*, III, pp. 238–43.
39. Cited in Minart, *P. C. Vincennes*, II, p. 76.
40. The best modern investigation of the French war economy concludes that 'Dautry had taken on an impossible mission ... he succeeded better than the still-insufficient and badly-used armaments of May–June 1940 would lead one to suppose ... what's astonishing is not that the French army then had so few weapons but, as he said himself, that it had as many as it did.' Crémieux-Brilhac, *Les Français de l'an 40*, II, p. 114; on Dautry's achievements see pp. 105–14, 132–64; Pertinax, *Les Fossoyeurs*, I, pp. 154–63; Daridan, *Chemin de la défaite*, pp. 148, 163–5; de Monzie, *Ci-Devant*, p. 176; Dautry's testimony to the postwar parliamentary inquiry, 11 and 18 Jan. 1949, C. E. *Témoignages*, VII–VIII, pp. 1945–2015; Dautry's Riom Trial deposition of 9 Oct. 1940, Archives Daladier, 4 DA 13, dr. 5, entry no. 95, FNSP.
41. See CAC, 'Mission d'inspection portant sur les Usines Renault et sur l'Arsenal de Puteaux effectuée le 1er décembre [1939] pour le compte de la Commission de l'Armée par MM. Chouffet, Courson et Taittinger', 16th Leg., Carton 15, AAN; Fridenson, *Usines Renault*, I, pp. 289, 328. Cf. Clarke, *Military Technology*, pp. 211–13; Crémieux-Brilhac, *Les Français de l'an 40*, II, pp. 129–42.

42. See Kiesling, 'Staff College for the nation-in-arms', pp. 48–61; Gamelin, *Servir*, I, pp. 200–3. The text of the 11 July 1938 Law was discussed and amended by the Chamber army commission on 10, 24 Feb., 3, 10, 17 Mar. 1937. (See minutes of meetings on those dates in CAC, 16th Leg., Carton 15, AAN.) The Law's history was analysed for the British Foreign Office by Sir Eric Phipps, ambassador in Paris, in FO 371, 21594, C2201/36/17, PRO. For the text of the decree of 7 Sept 1938 on the higher direction of a war, see Archives Reynaud, 74 AP Carton 12, AN.
43. CAC, 'Séance no. 65 du 27 septembre 1939: audience de M. Raoul Dautry, ministre de l'armement, procès-verbal', 16th Leg., Carton XVII, AAN.
44. Colson, 'Note sur la situation des fabrications d'armement . . .', 22 Sept. 1939, Fonds Gamelin 1K 224, Carton 7, SHAT. Cf. Minart, *P. C. Vincennes*, II, p. 76.
45. Doughty, 'The French armed forces, 1918–40', in Murray and Millett (eds.), *Military Effectiveness*, II, p. 58.
46. Ibid. Doughty's essay has (pp. 54–7) an excellent explanation of the concept of *bataille de conduite*. See also Bankwitz, *Weygand and Civil-Military Relations*, pp. 121–33; Doughty, *Seeds of Disaster*, pp. 74–6, 81–6, 91–111; Dutailly, *Les Problèmes de l'armée de terre*, pp. 176–255 *passim*.
47. For the politics of the army commissions and their relations with the war ministry see Farrar, 'Politics versus patriotism', pp. 577–609. Cf. J. Barthélemy, *Le Travail parlementaire et le système des commissions* (Paris, 1937); Minart, *P. C. Vincennes*, I, p. 69.
48. See the complaints voiced in Gamelin, letter to Daladier, 3 Nov. 1939, and replies to Daladier from Edmond Miellet (president, Chamber army commission), 16 Nov. 1939, and Senator Valière (president, Senate army commission), 17 Nov. 1939, in Cabinet du Ministre Carton 5N 588, dr. 1, sdr. 'Exercice du droit de contrôle', SHAT. Cf. Georges, letter to Gamelin no. 91 CAB/NE, 29 Feb. 1940; Gamelin, letter to Daladier no. 546 CAB/FT, 3 Mar. 1940, in ibid., sdr. 'Lettres des autorités militaires'.
49. Cf. Duroselle, *L'Abîme*, p. 17 ('On ne parle pas de "fleur au fusil", le 3 septembre 1939. Les Français sont tristes et ont raison de l'être').
50. Minart's claim that there was 'chez tous une atmosphère de confiance en une victoire rapide' (*P. C. Vincennes*, I, p. 57), is at odds with most accounts. See the evocative exploration of the French people's mood of resigned existentialism in R. C. Cobb, *French and Germans, Germans and French. A personal account of France under two occupations, 1914–18, 1940–44* (Hanover and London, 1983).
51. See Colville, *Fringes of Power*, p. 26 (diary, 22 Sept. 1939). Cf. the report of Belgium's military attaché in London on Britain's mood: 'I must add to the words "calm and cold resolution" I used in my earlier reports that they [the English] seem minded to meet the situation as phlegmatically as possible.' (Lt. Gen. Baron Vinçotte, attaché militaire près L'Ambassade de Belgique à Londres à M. le Ministre de la Défense nationale [Cabinet], no. 6154, 9 Sept. 1939, AMBAE).
52. Minart, *P. C. Vincennes*, I, p. 48.
53. J. P. Sartre, *The War Diaries November 1939–March 1940* (London, 1984), p. 19 (17 Nov. 1939).

54. Sauvy, *De Paul Reynaud à Charles de Gaulle*, p. 97.
55. Col. W. Fraser, letter to his wife, 9 Oct. 1939. For the names of French politicians suspected of seeking a negotiated peace see Gamelin, Journal de marche, 3 Oct. 1939, Fonds Gamelin 1K 224, Carton 9, SHAT; *Servir*, III, p. 107; Jeanneney, *Journal Politique*, pp. 15–22.
56. Gamelin, Journal de marche, 20 Sept. 1939, 24 Sept. 1939.
57. Minart, *P. C. Vincennes*, I, p. 69.
58. See M. S. Alexander, 'Prophet without honour?' pp. 53–77.
59. CAC, 'séance no. 64 du 7 septembre 1939', 16th Leg., Carton XVII, AAN.
60. Ibid., 'séance no. 67 du 25 octobre 1939'; 'séance no. 68 du 15 novembre 1939'.
61. See Bankwitz, *Weygand and Civil-Military Relations*, pp. 178–201; R. J. Soucy, 'Centrist fascism: Pierre Taittinger and the Jeunesses Patriotes', *JCH*, 16:2 (Apr. 1981), pp. 349–68; W. D. Irvine, *Conservatism in Crisis. The Republican Federation in France in the 1930s* (Baton Rouge, 1979), pp. 115–19, 122, 197–9.
62. Claude Taittinger to the present author.
63. See ch. 1, pp. 29–30.
64. CAC, 'Mission de contrôle effectuée par M. Charles des Isnards à l'armée du Général Condé, le 17 novembre 1939', 16th Leg., Carton XV, dr. '1939', AAN.
65. CAC, 'Séance du 20 décembre 1939: rapport de M. Fernand-Laurent sur une mission de contrôle aux 3e et 4e armées', Archives Daladier, 4 DA 2, dr. 4, sdr. c, FNSP; CAC, 'Séance no. 72 du 20 décembre 1939', procès-verbal, p. 2 (des Isnards quotation), 16th Leg., Carton XVII, AAN.
66. CAC, 'Séance no. 73 du 10 janvier 1940', 16th Leg., Carton XVII, AAN.
67. See D. W. Alexander, 'Repercussions of the Breda Variant', pp. 459–88.
68. CAC, 'Rapport fait par M. des Isnards, député, membre de la Commission de l'Armée, sur une mission de contrôle à la 7e armée', 28 Dec. 1939, pp. 1, 2, 5, 16th Leg., Carton XV, dr. '1940', AAN. Cf. Archives Daladier 4 DA 2, dr. 4, sdr. c, FNSP.
69. M. Lerecouvreux, *L'Armée Giraud en Hollande (1939–1940)* (Paris, 1951), p. 29. Cf. Gunsburg, *Divided and Conquered*, pp. 99–100.
70. CAC, 'Rapport sur une mission de contrôle effectuée par MM. Ponsard, Rotinat et Thiébaut, députés, délégués de la Commission de l'Armée pour étudier la situation matérielle, le ravitaillement et l'installation des troupes dans la zone de l'avant (1ère et 9e armées), régions de Rocroi, Cambrai, Valenciennes, du 7 au 10 décembre 1939', 18 Dec. 1939, pp. 1, 4–7, 16th Leg., Carton XV, AAN.
71. CAC, 'Rapport de M. Pierre Taittinger, contrôleur de la Commission de l'Armée, sur la mission de contrôle qu'il a effectuée à la IIIe Division Légère Mécanique et à L'Ecole de Cavalerie de Saumur, le 15 décembre 1939', 16th Leg., Carton XV, AAN.
72. CAC, 'Rapport présenté par MM. Camel et Lazurich, députés, sur leur mission de contrôle auprès des troupes de la zone de l'avant dans la région

de Thionville-Faulquemont-Sarralbe (3e et 4e armées), du 31 janvier au 5 février 1940', pp. 10, 13, 14, 16th Leg., Carton XV, dr. '1940', AAN; also 'Séance no. 77, du 28 février 1940', procès-verbal, 16th Leg., Carton XVII, AAN. Cf. Crémieux-Brilhac, *Les Français de l'an 40*, II, pp. 428–32, 444–7, 451–5.

73. CAC, 'Séance no. 66, du 11 octobre 1939', procès-verbal, pp. 2–3, 16th Leg., Carton XVII, AAN. Cf. 'Commission rogatoire de Me. Lemaire, conseiller à la Cour Suprême de Justice à Riom: Conclusions d'un rapport du Contrôleur-Général de l'Administration de l'Armée Edmond Briat sur la mobilisation industrielle des Usines Schneider et Creusot', 21 Dec. 1940, pp. 1, 3, 4, Archives Daladier 4 DA 12, dr. 6, Déposition No. 51, FNSP. Cf. Crémieux-Brilhac, *Les Français de l'an 40*, II, pp. 76–82, 169–73, 331–4, 343–5.
74. CAC, 'Séance no. 65, du 27 septembre 1939: audience de M. Raoul Dautry, ministre de l'armement', 16th Leg., Carton XVII, AAN. Cf. Ibid., 'Séance no. 71, du 13 décembre 1939: audience de M. Albert Sarraut, ministre de l'intérieur, sur les mesures prises pour parer à la propagande communiste'.
75. See J. Kim Munholland, 'The Daladier Government and the "Red Scare" of 1938–1940', in John F. Sweets (ed.), *Proceedings of the Tenth Annual Meeting of the Western Society for French History*, 14–16 Oct. 1982 (Lawrence, KA, 1984), pp. 495–506; Crémieux-Brilhac, *Les Français de l'an 40*, II, pp. 236–53, 262–83, 285–303, 317–26, 477–97. Cf. J.-P. Azéma, A. Prost, J.-P. Rioux, *Le Parti Communiste français des années sombres, 1938–1941* (Paris, 1986).
76. See CAC, 'Séance no. 72, du 20 décembre 1939'; 'Séance no. 74, du 17 janvier 1940', both procès-verbaux in 16th Leg., Carton XVII, AAN.
77. CAC, 'Mission d'inspection effectuée le 1er décembre 1939 pour le compte de la Commission de l'Armée par MM. Chouffet, Courson et Taittinger, portant sur les Usines Renault et sur l'Arsenal de Puteaux', pp. 1–10, 16th Leg., Carton XV, AAN. Cf., however, the much more critical analysis of Renault's attitude towards war work in Crémieux-Brilhac, *Les Français de l'an 40*, II, pp. 125–42; also Fridenson, *Usines Renault*, I, pp. 292–4, 300–3.
78. Col. H. H. Fuller, US military attaché, Paris, to Dept. of the Army (G2), Washington DC, 29 Sept. 1939, MID, RG 165, Box No. 1793, File no. 2724-C-37/41, USNARA. According to André Géraud, however, 'Impartial judges were of the opinion that M. Dautry had a gift for motivating people but was not a good administrator ... he tended, if you will, to lose sight of the wood for the trees.' (Pertinax, *Fossoyeurs*, I, p. 155.) For Gamelin's view of Dautry see the former's *Servir*, III, p. 108.
79. See Gamelin, *Servir*, III, pp. 118–19.
80. One was the Duke of Windsor, who had been given the rank of a major-general and assigned to liaison duties between Gort and Gamelin. See M. Bloch, *The Duke of Windsor's War* (London, 1980), pp. 27–31, 36–7, 42–3.
81. Cour Suprême de Justice à Riom: déposition de M. Charles Reibel, sénateur, ancien ministre, 22 July and 22 Sept. 1941, Archives Daladier, 4 DA 17, dr. 5, FNSP.

82. Gamelin, letter to Daladier, 3 Nov. 1939, Cabinet du Ministre, Carton 5N 588, dr. 1, sdr. 'Exercice du droit de contrôle', SHAT.
83. Ibid., see correspondence between Daladier, Senator Valière and Edmond Miellet (presidents, Senate and Chamber army commissions), 10, 16, 17 Nov. 1939.
84. Georges letter to Gamelin, no. 91 CAB/NE, 29 Feb. 1940; Gamelin letter to Daladier, no. 546 CAB/FT, 3 Mar. 1940, ibid., sdr. 'Lettres des autorités militaires'.
85. See Jeanneney, *Journal politique*, pp. 34–9; Villelume, *Journal d'une défaite*, pp. 220–41; de Monzie, *Ci-devant*, pp. 198–206; Duroselle, *L'Abîme*, pp. 87–105.
86. Sartre, *The War Diaries*, p. 222. Cf. de Gaulle, *Mémoires de guerre*, I, pp. 38–9 (Livre de Poche edn. 1971). Examples of the use of such allegations by modern historians include, Horne, *To Lose a Battle*, pp. 93, 103–5, 224; Duroselle, *L'Abîme*, pp. 51–7; Crémieux-Brilhac, *Les Français de l'an 40*, II, pp. 374–82.
87. See Paillat, *La Guerre immobile*, pp. 348–51.
88. Gamelin, Journal de marche, 27–28 Sept. 1939, Fonds Gamelin 1K 224, Carton 9, SHAT.
89. Gamelin, Journal de marche, 7 Oct. 1939, Fonds Gamelin, 1K 224, Carton 9, SHAT.
90. Ibid. Cf. Gamelin, *Servir*, III, pp. 116–17.
91. See Macleod and Kelly (eds.), *Ironside Diaries*, pp. 113, 134–5, 137–8, 155, 163–4, 172; Bond, *Chief of Staff*, I, p. 278.
92. See above, ch. 11, pp. 329–30.
93. Gamelin, Journal de marche, 15–16 Oct. 1939, Fonds Gamelin 1K 224, Carton 9, SHAT.
94. Ibid., 8–9 Mar. 1940. Cf. Bond, *Chief of Staff*, I, pp. 288–93, for Pownall's diary on these dates, which makes no mention of Gamelin's visit.
95. Gamelin, Journal de marche, 22 Mar. 1940; *Servir*, III, p. 292.
96. Macleod and Kelly (eds.), *Ironside Diaries*, pp. 231–3.

CONCLUSION

1. Gunsburg, *Divided and Conquered*, pp. xxi–xxii. Cf. H. Dutailly, 'Faiblesses et potentialités de l'armée de terre (1939–1940)', in *Les Armées françaises pendant la Seconde Guerre Mondiale, 1939–1945. Colloque International à l'Ecole Nationale Supérieure de Techniques Avancées, Paris, du 7 au 10 mai 1985* (Paris, 1986), pp. 23–32.
2. The epithet, applied to an earlier generation of defeated and politicised French commanders, was that of Emile Terquem. See his *Généraux de débâcle et de coup d'état* (Paris, 1905).
3. See, however, M. S. Alexander, 'Maurice Gamelin and the defeat of France', in Bond (ed.), *Fallen Stars*, pp. 107–40.
4. This is a theme partially elaborated in Martin, *Warriors into Managers*, pp. 3–85 *passim*. Cf., however, the comments *à propos* the 1991 Gulf War by the defence correspondent of *The Times* of London that 'These days, with so much emphasis on management rather than leadership, the notion that

the man or woman in charge should have charismatic qualities has tended to be frowned on, at least in some intellectual circles ... military leaders have to be managers as well as leaders ... However ... the ability to inspire remains essential.' (M. Evans, 'Born to Run?', *The Times Saturday Review*, 29 June 1991, pp. 10–11.)

5. Doise and Vaïsse, *Diplomatie et outil militaire*, p. 341.
6. See Bankwitz, *Weygand and Civil-Military Relations*, pp. 290–327.
7. Dautry, Riom written deposition, 9 Oct. 1940, Archives Daladier, 4 DA 13, dr. 5, file no. 95, FNSP. Cf., for Dautry's views more generally on French rearmament and command-industry relations, his testimony to the postwar parliamentary inquiry, 11 Jan., 18 Jan. 1949, *C. E. Témoignages*, VII–VIII, pp. 1845–2015.
8. Gamelin, *Servir*, III, p. 108. Dautry, on retiring from the direction of the *Chemins de Fer de l'Etat* in 1937 (where he had laid the groundwork for the creation, that year, of the unified, nationalised French railway network, the SNCF), had published a well-received book of reflections and memoirs under the title, *Métier d'homme*.
9. Héring, 19 Mar. 1942 Riom deposition, reproduced in Soupiron, *Bazaine contre Gambetta*, p. 189.
10. On Weygand's encomium on the army at Lille and the misleading confidence it generated, see de Monzie, *Ci-devant*, pp. 125–6.
11. The most sustained and sophisticated examination of the relations between the two generals remains Bankwitz, *Weygand and Civil-Military Relations*, passim.
12. Héring, 19 Mar. 1942 Riom deposition, in Soupiron, *Bazaine contre Gambetta*, p. 189.
13. Gamelin, *Servir*, II, pp. 280–1 (emphasis added).
14. CAC, 'Séance du 21 mars 1935: audition de M. le général Maurin, ministre de la Guerre', pp. 52–3, 15th Leg., Carton 5 bis, dr. VIII, AAN. The accusation to which Maurin was responding had come from Albert Forcinal, *Républicain-Socialiste* deputy for the Eure, 1928–42.
15. Héring, 19 Mar. 1942 Riom deposition, in Soupiron, *Bazaine contre Gambetta*, p. 189. In the early summer of 1938, with the Sudeten storm-clouds gathering, Gamelin wrote to Daladier that 'If my higher duty requires me to remain silent, it nevertheless obliges me to lay before you once again, personally and respectfully, the import of the decisions you have felt pressed to take. Concealing none of my thinking from you is, for me, a question of loyalty towards you.' ('Lettre du général Gamelin au Ministre de la Défense Nationale et de la Guerre', no. 2633/S, 8 June 1938, Fonds Gamelin, 1K 224, Carton 8, dr. 'Organisation du Haut-Commandement: notes de principe, 1935–8', SHAT.)
16. Citation of Weygand, 20 Feb. 1931, in Gamelin, 'Etats de service', confidential personnel dossier, SHAT.
17. See Daladier, *Journal de captivité*, pp. 34–5, 114–15, 218–19.
18. See Nobécourt, *Histoire politique de l'armée*, pp. 221–4; Bankwitz, *Weygand and Civil-Military Relations*, pp. 195–207, 245–66, 276–89.
19. These issues are masterfully analysed in Bankwitz, *Weygand and Civil-Military Relations*, pp. 232–89.

20. de La Gorce, *The French Army*, p. 294.
21. See Bankwitz, *Weygand and Civil-Military Relations*, pp. 235ff; cf. Duroselle, *La Décadence*, pp. 251–67.
22. Moore letter to Bullitt, 27 May 1940, in R. Walton Moore Papers, Group 55, Box 3, FDR Presidential Library, Hyde Park, New York.
23. Daladier, *Journal de captivité*, pp. 49–50.
24. Pertinax, *Les Fossoyeurs*, I, pp. 117–18.
25. Hughes, *To the Maginot Line*, p. 263; cf. de Monzie, *Ci-devant*, pp. 99–100, 204–5, 276–8.
26. Pertinax, *Les Fossoyeurs*, I, pp. 113–16.
27. Challener, 'The gravediggers revisited', pp. 95–6.
28. Rowe, *Great Wall of France*, p. 94.
29. Challener, 'The gravediggers revisited', p. 99; Pertinax, *Les Fossoyeurs*, I, pp. 137–9.
30. Bullitt to FDR, 16 Sept. 1939, in O. H. Bullitt, *For the President*, p. 373.
31. Daladier, letter, 20 May 1966, in reply to Col. Adolphe Goutard's article, 'La Surprise du 10 mai' in *Revue de Paris*, 10 May 1966, Archives Daladier, 4 DA 7, dr. 1, sdr. a, FNSP.
32. Gamelin, Journal de marche, 8 Sept. 1939, 1K 224, Carton 9, SHAT.
33. Ibid., 19 Sept. 1939, 3 Oct. 1939.
34. Duroselle, *L'Abîme*, p. 49; also Pertinax, *Les Fossoyeurs*, I, pp. 140–1. Cf. discussion of government weaknesses and relations with the command by E. du Réau: 'Haut commandement et pouvoir politique', in *Les Armées françaises*, pp. 67–86.
35. Armengaud, *Batailles politiques et militaires*, pp. 200–1.
36. Gamelin, Journal de marche, 19 Sept. 1939, 1K 224, Carton 9, SHAT. What Daladier did do – partly out of his own anti-communism and partly to create a scapegoat around which to try to reunite the Radicals and Right – was to stage a witch-hunt against the French Communist Party. Its offices and its newspaper, *L'Humanité*, were closed down, forty-four of its deputies placed on trial and its general secretary, Maurice Thorez, forced to flee to the Soviet Union. See J. Kim Munholland, 'The Daladier government and the "Red Scare" of 1938–1940', in J. F. Sweets (ed.), *Proceedings of the Tenth Annual Meeting of the Western Society for French History, 14–16 October 1982* (Lawrence, KA, 1984), pp. 495–506.
37. Gamelin, Journal de marche, 18 Oct. 1939, 1K 224, Carton 9, SHAT; cf. Pertinax, *Les Fossoyeurs*, I, p. 97; Duroselle, *L'Abîme*, p. 51.
38. Gamelin, Journal de marche, 20 Sept. 1939, 1K 224, Carton 9, SHAT.
39. US naval attaché (Paris) to ONI (Washington), no. 521, 27 Sept. 1939: 'France – war mobilisation', in President's Secretary's File (PSF), Box 196: Estimates of potential military strength: Documents B, vol. 1, doc. no. 51, FDR Presidential Library, Hyde Park, New York; for Pétain's opposition to giving Herriot the Quai d'Orsay see Gamelin, Journal de marche, 13 Sept. 1939, 1K 224, Carton 9, SHAT; also Gamelin, *Servir*, III, p. 106.
40. Gamelin, Journal de marche, 11 Sept. 1939; Pertinax, *Les Fossoyeurs*, I, pp. 141–3.

41. US naval attaché (Paris) to ONI (Washington), no. 521, 27 Sept. 1939: 'France – war mobilisation', PSF, Box 196: Documents B, vol. 1, doc. no. 51, FDR Presidential Library, Hyde Park, New York.
42. Challener, 'The gravediggers revisited', p. 99; the quotation about the peace offensive occurs in Gamelin, Journal de marche, 3 Oct. 1939, 1K 224, Carton 9, SHAT; also in *Servir*, III, p. 107.
43. Gamelin, Journal de marche, 11 Sept. 1939, 1K 224, Carton 9, SHAT.
44. Ibid., 18 Oct. 1939, 11 Mar. 1940.
45. Gunsburg, 'Gamelin', in Hutton (ed.), *Historical Dictionary of the Third Republic*, I, pp. 412–13.
46. All three quotations from de La Gorce, *The French Army*, p. 294.
47. Papiers Schweisguth, 'Memento: réunion improvisée du Conseil Supérieur de la guerre, le 9 mars 1936', 351 AP Carton 3, dr. 8, AN. Cf. Young, *In Command of France*, pp. 122–3; Schuker, 'France and the remilitarization of the Rhineland', p. 329.
48. D. W. Brogan, *French Personalities and Problems* (London, 1946), p. 175.
49. 'Pierre Laval', in British Embassy, Paris, to the Secretary of State for Foreign Affairs (London): 'Report on leading personalities in France, 1932', FO 371, 16362, W66/66/17, PRO.
50. Bankwitz, *Weygand and Civil-Military Relations*, p. 206; cf. Pertinax, *Les Fossoyeurs*, I, p. 97.
51. Bullitt letter to Moore, 18 Apr. 1940, R. Walton Moore Papers, Group 55, Box 3, FDR Presidential Library, Hyde Park, New York; Harvey's appraisal of Reynaud occurs in Harvey, *Diplomatic Diaries*, pp. 218–19.
52. For an illuminating discussion of the problem and its *dénouement* in the showdown between Weygand and Reynaud in 1940 see Bankwitz, *Weygand and Civil-Military Relations*, pp. 223–327. Cf. the same author's 'Maxime Weygand and the Fall of France', pp. 225–42.
53. A recent general study which properly reiterates this essential but often overlooked point is R. A. C. Parker, *Struggle for Survival. The History of the Second World War* (Oxford, 1989), p. 50.
54. Harvey, *Diplomatic Diaries*, p. 238 (10 Jan. 1939).
55. Brogan, *French Personalities and Problems*, p. 154; cf. Duroselle, *L'Abîme*, pp. 45–6, 51.
56. See Bankwitz, *Weygand and Civil-Military Relations*, esp. pp. 220–39.
57. Gamelin, Journal de marche, 19 Sept. 1939, 1K 224, Carton 9, SHAT.
58. US naval attaché (Paris) to ONI (Washington) no. 521, 27 Sept. 1939: 'France – war mobilisation', PSF Box 196, Documents B, vol. 1, doc. no. 51, FDR Presidential Library, Hyde Park, New York.
59. The argument quoted occurs in Brogan, *French Personalities and Problems*, p. 154.
60. Quotation in ibid., p. 154. Cf. du Réau, 'Haut commandement et pouvoir politique', in *Les Armées françaises*, esp. pp. 75–80.
61. De Gaulle, *Mémoires de Guerre*, I (*Livre de Poche* edn, 1971), pp. 38–9; also Gamelin's version of this encounter in *Servir*, II, pp. 289–90.
62. Léon-Jouhaux, *Prison*, p. 53; François-Poncet, *Carnets*, p. 44. Cf., however, evidence of Gamelin's indifference towards religion before 1939

and his infrequent taking of holy communion during his wartime imprisonment in Daladier, *Journal de captivité*, p. 88.
63. Taylor, *Europe. Grandeur and decline*, p. 294.
64. Heywood, 'General Gamelin', in *RUSI Journal*, Aug. 1938, p. 612.
65. Maj. C. A. de Linde, record of conversation with André Pironneau, despatch no. 1089, FO 371, 22917, C10869/130/17, PRO.
66. Liebling, *The Road back to Paris*, pp. 25–33.
67. J. Romains, *Sept Mystères du destin de L'Europe* (New York, 1940), pp. 68–9, 80–99; cf. Nobécourt, *Histoire politique de l'armée*, p. 202.
68. See Bankwitz, *Weygand and Civil-Military Relations*, pp. 86, 135–6, 138–9, 145–6.
69. Taylor, *Europe. Grandeur and Decline*, p. 290.
70. The phenomenon has recently received attention in M. Van Creveld, *Command in War* (Cambridge, MA, 1985); J. Keegan, *The Mask of Command* (London and New York, 1987); *The Price of Admiralty* (London and New York, 1989); T. Travers, *The Killing Ground* (London, 1987).
71. Romains, *Sept mystères*, pp. 99–100.
72. See S. E. Ambrose, *Eisenhower*, I, *The Soldier* (London, 1984); F. C. Pogue, *George C. Marshall* (New York, 1963–73, 3 vols.); A. Danchev, *Very Special Relationship. Field Marshal Sir John Dill and the Anglo-American Alliance, 1941–44* (London, 1986); R. W. Love, 'Ernest Joseph King', in K. J. Hagan (ed.), *The Chiefs of Naval Operations* (Annapolis, 1980), pp. 137–79; D. Richards, *Portal* (London, 1977); D. Fraser, *Alanbrooke* (London, 1982).
73. See Werth, *The Last Days of Paris*, p. 71; Pertinax, *Les Fossoyeurs*, I, p. 96.
74. The American's description of Gamelin is in Bullitt, letter to Moore, 7 June 1940, R. Walton Moore Papers, Group 55, Box 3, FDR Presidential Library, Hyde Park, New York; that of Gamelin at Itter occurs in Léon-Jouhaux, *Prison*, p. 53.
75. The most satisfying analysis remains that of D. W. Alexander, 'Repercussions of the Breda Variant'. Cf. Gunsburg, *Divided and Conquered*, pp. 126–42; Duroselle, *L'Abîme*, pp. 77–87, 131–6; Bond, *France and Belgium 1939–40*, pp. 52–89.
76. Pertinax, *Les Fossoyeurs*, I, p. 57.
77. Gooch and Cohen, *Military Misfortunes*, p. 221.
78. Challener, 'The gravediggers revisited', p. 100.
79. See M. S. Alexander, 'The Fall of France, 1940', in Gooch (ed.), *Decisive Campaigns*, pp. 10–44; cf. Bankwitz, *Weygand and Civil-Military Relations*, pp. 299–314.
80. See Daladier, *Journal de captivité*, pp. 33–5, 49–50.
81. Challener, 'The gravediggers revisited', p. 104; cf. Porch, 'French intelligence and the Fall of France', pp. 39, 44; M. S. Alexander, 'Soldiers and Socialists', in Alexander and Graham (eds.), *The French and Spanish Popular Fronts*, pp. 63–78.
82. Rowe, *The Great Wall of France*, p. 106. Daladier's retrospective acknowledgement of – and remorse over – his own indulgence towards the military conservatives occurs in his *Journal de captivité*, pp. 34, 49–50.

83. Challener, 'The gravediggers revisited', pp. 103–4.
84. Gunsburg, 'Gamelin', in Hutton (ed.), *Historical Dictionary of the Third Republic*, I, p. 413.
85. See the remarks in Porch, 'French intelligence and the Fall of France', pp. 44–5, 52.

Select bibliography

ABBREVIATIONS
AHR   American Historical Review
EHR   English Historical Review
FHS   French Historical Studies
HJ   Historical Journal
IHR   International History Review
JCH   Journal of Contemporary History
JMH   Journal of Modern History
JSS   Journal of Strategic Studies
RDM   Revue des deux mondes
RHA   Revue historique des armées
RHDGM   Revue d'histoire de la Deuxième Guerre Mondiale
RHMC   Revue d'histoire moderne et contemporaine
RUSI   The Royal United Services Institute Journal
SHAA   Service Historique de l'armée de l'air
SHAT   Service Historique de l'armée de terre

Unless indicated otherwise, all works in English are published in London and all in French are published in Paris.

PRIMARY SOURCES

A. Unpublished archival collections

1. Belgium
Archives du Ministère des Affaires Etrangères et du Commerce Extérieur (*AMBAE*):
   Cartons 11.183 (II); 11.185 (I); 11.185 (2–3); 11.186; 11.188; 11.984
Archives du Service Historique des Forces Armées: Carton 14 E2G

2. France
Archives de l'Assemblée Nationale (*AAN*)
Commission de l'Armée de la Chambre des Députés, minutes and reports: 14th Legislature, 1928–32, Carton XIV/448; 15th Legislature, 1932–36, Cartons 739/48 bis; 5 bis; 16th Legislature, 1936–40, Cartons XV, XVII
Commission du Commerce et de l'Industrie de la Chambre des Députés: 16th Legislature, 1936–40, Carton 58
Commission du Travail de la Chambre des Députés, minutes and reports: 16th Legislature, Folder B102

Select bibliography 519

Archives Nationales (AN)
Papiers Paul Painlevé, series 313 AP, Cartons 217, 230, 233, 235–242
Papiers Joseph Paul-Boncour, Entrée 2699 (cote provisoire), Cartons 20/13, 20/20
Papiers Paul Reynaud, series 74 AP, Cartons 12, 20
Papiers Victor-Henri Schweisguth, series 351 AP, Cartons 2–7

Bibliothèque de Documentation Internationale Contemporaine (BDIC)
Papiers Lucien Lamoureux, microfilm 31

Fondation Nationale des Sciences Politiques (FNSP)
Archives Edouard Daladier

Ministère des Affaires Etrangères (MAE)
Papiers Maurice Gamelin, 2 Cartons

Service Historique de l'Armée de Terre, Vincennes (SHAT)
Cabinet du Ministre de la Guerre (et de la Défense Nationale), Cartons 5N 579; 5N 581; 5N 587; 5N 588
Comité Permanent de la Défense Nationale (incorporating Haut Comité Militaire), Cartons 2N 19–21
Conseil Supérieur de la Défense Nationale, Carton 2N 12; Dossiers 135, 136
Conseil Supérieur de la Guerre, Cartons 1N 20–22 (*procès-verbaux*, 1921–39); 1N 37 ('La division cuirassée'); 1N 43 ('Etat-Major Gamelin, 1935–9'); 1N 44 ('Etat-Majors divers [dr. 1 'Général Altmayer'; dr. 2 'Conseil Consultatif de l'Armement'; dr. 3 'Général Besson'; dr. 4 'Lettres du Général Besson'; dr. 5 'Lettres du Général Massiet'; dr. 6 'Général Billotte'; dr. 7 'Comptes-rendus des réunions des chefs d'Etat-majors'; dr. 8 'Général Claudel']); 1N 45 ('Etats-majors divers'); 1N 46 ('Etat-Major Georges, 28 mars 1933–20 novembre 1937'); 1N 47 ('Etat-Major Georges'); 1N 48 ('Projet d'Opération "Sarre", 1938–9'); 1N 49 ('Projets d'Opérations sur le Front Sud-Est'); 1N 50–1 ('Défense des Frontières'); 1N 52 ('Création d'une Commission d'Organisation des Régions Fortifiées'); 1N 53 ('Organisations défensives'); 1N 54 ('Régions Fortifiées, 1930–3, 1938–9'); 1N 55 ('Régions Fortifiées du Nord-Est'); 1N 57–8 ('Exercices du CSG, 1934–5'); 1N 59–60 ('Exercices du CSG, 1936–7'); 1N 61–2 ('Exercices du CSG, 1937–8'); 1N 78 ('Reconnaissances sur le terrain: Belgique, Jura, région de Givet, secteur fortifié de Montmédy'); 1N 98 ('Manoeuvres d'ensemble de 1938: emploi d'une brigade cuirassée dans une opération du rupture')
Etat-Major de l'Armée (EMA), 2e Bureau, Attachés militaires, Belgique: Cartons 7N 2729–2736
EMA, 2e Bureau, Attachés militaires, Grande-Bretagne: Cartons 7N 2798–2802; 7N 2804–5; 7N 2807–10; 7N 2815–20; 7N 2822
EMA, 2e Bureau, Attachés militaires, Yougoslavie: Cartons 7N 3191–3195; 7N 3198
EMA, 3e Bureau: Carton 154 ('Commission de Défense du Territoire')
EMA, 3e Bureau: unnumbered Cartons labelled 'Commission d'Organisation des Régions Fortifiées, 1927–35' and 'Commission d'Organisation des Régions Fortifiées, 1928–38')

Fonds Jean Fabry, series 1K 93
Fonds Maurice Gamelin, series 1K 224 (9 Cartons)

3. Great Britain
Liddell Hart Centre for Military Archives (LHCMA), King's College, London
Sir Basil Liddell Hart Papers
Field Marshal Sir Archibald Montgomery-Massingberd Papers

Public Record Office, London (PRO)
Air Ministry Papers, series AIR 8, AIR 40
Cabinet Office Papers, series CAB 4, CAB 21, CAB 23, CAB 53, CAB 64
Foreign Office General Correspondence, series FO 371

4. United States of America
Franklin D. Roosevelt Presidential Library, Hyde Park, New York
President's Secretary's File
President's Personal File
Judge R. Walton Moore Papers

US Army Military History Institute, Carlisle Barracks, Pennsylvania
Brig. Gen. Bradford Gethren Chynoweth Papers
Gen. Raymond E. Lee Papers

US National Archives, Washington DC (USNARA)
Record Group 165 (Military Intelligence Division), G2 papers and military attaché reports from London, Paris, Madrid, Moscow, Berlin, 1935–40

B. Published documentary collections
Commission d'enquête parlementaire sur les événements survenus en France de 1933 à 1945 (Presses Universitaires de France, 1951–2, 2 vols. of *Rapport de M. Charles Serre au nom de la Commission parlementaire*; 9 vols. of *Témoignages et documents*).
Documents on British Foreign Policy, 1919–1939 (*DBFP*) (ed. Sir E. L. Woodward, W. N. Medlicott and R. Butler) (HMSO, 2nd ser.; 3rd ser.: 1946 *et seq.*).
Documents Diplomatiques Belges, 1920–1940 (*DDB*) (ed. F. Vanlangenhove and C. de Visscher) (Brussels: Académie Royale de Belgique. Commission Royale d'Histoire, Palais des Académies, 1964–6, 5 vols.).
Documents Diplomatiques Français, 1932–1939 (*DDF*) (Sous la direction de MM. P. Renouvin, M. Baumont, J.-B. Duroselle, Y. Lacaze, J. Laloy, pour la Commission de publication des documents relatifs aux origines de la guerre de 1939–1945) (Imprimerie Nationale, 1963 *et seq.*).
Documents on German Foreign Policy, 1918–1945 (*DGFP*) series C (1933–7), vol. IV (HMSO, 1962).

C. Trial transcripts
Buttin, Batonnier Paul *Le Procès Pucheu* (Amiot-Dumont, 1947)
London, Géo *L'Amiral Estéva et le général Dentz devant la Haute Cour de Justice*. (Lyon: Roger Bonnefon, 1945).

Le Procès Flandin devant la Haute Cour de Justice, 23–26 Juillet 1946 (Librairie de Médicis: Editions Politiques, Economiques et Sociales, 1947).
Le Procès de Charles Maurras. Compte-rendu sténographique (Albin Michel, 1949, 2 vols.).
Le Procès du Maréchal Pétain. Compte-rendu sténographique (Albin Michel, 1949, 2 vols.).
Le Procès de Général Raoul Salan. Sténographie complète des audiences. Réquisitoire-plaidoiries-verdict (Nouvelles Editions Latines, 1962).
Ribet, Maurice: *Le Procès de Riom* (Ernest Flammarion, 1945).

SECONDARY SOURCES

A. Colloquia Papers and conference proceedings

Le Gouvernement de Vichy, 1940–1942 (Actes du colloque 'Le Gouvernement de Vichy et la Révolution Nationale', 6–7 mars 1970) (Presses de la Fondation Nationale des Sciences Politiques, 1972).
Les Relations Franco-Britanniques, 1935–1939 (Editions du Centre National de la Recherche Scientifique, 1975).
Les Relations Franco-Allemandes, 1933–1939 (Editions du Centre National de la Recherche Scientifique, 1976).
Français et Britanniques dans la drôle de guerre (Centre National de la Recherche Scientifique, 1977).
La France et L'Allemagne, 1932–1936 (Editions du Centre National de la Recherche Scientifique, 1980).
Sagnes, Jean and Caucanas, Sylvie: *Les Français et la Guerre d'Espagne* (Perpignan: Centre de Recherches sur les problèmes de la frontière, 1990).

B. Memoirs, personal accounts and diaries

Alphand, Hervé: *L'Etonnement d'être. Journal, 1939–1973* (Arthème Fayard, 1977).
Anon.: *The Diary of a Staff Officer (Air Intelligence Liaison Officer) at Advanced Headquarters North B.A.F.F. 1940* (Methuen, 1941).
Ardizzone, Edward: *Baggage to the Enemy. Experiences of an Official War Artist in Northern France* (1942).
Argoud, Col. Antoine: *La Décadence, l'imposture et la tragédie* (Arthème Fayard, 1974).
Armengaud, Gen. Jules: *Batailles politiques et militaires sur l'Europe. Témoignages, 1932–1940* (Editions du Myrte, 1948).
Barbey, Frédéric: *La Belgique d'Albert Ier et de Léopold III. Le Témoignage d'un diplomate de 1918 à 1948* (Librairie Académique Perrin, 1950).
Barlone, Capt. D: *A French Officer's Diary (23 August 1939 to 1 October 1940)*, preface by Gen. P. L. Legentilhomme (Cambridge University Press, 1942).
Baudouin, Paul: *Neuf mois au gouvernement. Avril–décembre 1940* (La Table Ronde, 1948).
Beaufre, Gen. André: *1940. The Fall of France* (trans. D. Flower, preface by Capt. Sir B. H. Liddell Hart: Cassell, 1967); French edn, *Le Drame de 1940* (Plon, 1965).

Beck, Col. Joseph: *Dernier rapport. Politique polonaise, 1926–1939* (Neuchatel: Editions de la Baconnière, 1951).
Belin, Commissaire: *Trente ans de sûreté nationale* (Bibliothèque France-Soir, 1950).
Belin, René: *Du Secrétariat de la CGT au gouvernement de Vichy. Mémoires, 1933–1942* (Editions Albatros, 1978).
Beneš, Edouard: *Munich* (trans. from the Czech original by Svatoplak Pacejka, Stock, 1969).
Bérard, Armand: *Un ambassadeur se souvient*, I, *Au temps du danger allemand* (Plon, 1976).
Béthouart, Gen. Antoine: *Cinq années d'espérance. Mémoires de guerre, 1939–1945* (Plon, 1968).
Des hécatombes glorieuses au désastre, 1914–1940 (Presses de Cité 1972).
Beuve-Méry, Hubert: *Réflexions politiques, 1932–1952* (Editions du Seuil, 1951).
Billotte, Gen. Pierre: *Le Temps des armes. Les Chemins de l'aventure* (Plon, 1972).
Bloch, Marc: *L'Etrange Défaite. Témoignage écrit en 1940* (Editions Franc-Tireur, 1946); *Strange Defeat. A statement of evidence written in 1940* (English-language edn trans. Gerald Hopkins, New York: W. W. Norton, 1968).
Bond, Brian J. (ed.): *Chief of Staff. The Diaries of Lieutenant General Sir Henry Pownall*, I, *1933–1940* (Leo Cooper, 1972).
Bonnet, Georges: *Vingt ans de vie politique, 1918–1938: de Clemenceau à Daladier* (Arthème Fayard, 1969).
Dans la tourmente, 1938–1948 (Fayard, 1971).
Bonte, Florimond: *Le Chemin de l'honneur. De la chambre de députés aux prisons de France et au bagne d'Afrique* (Les Editeurs Français Réunis, 1949).
Bourget, Gen. Paul-Alexandre: *De Beyrouth à Bordeaux: La Guerre de 1939–40 vue du P. C. Weygand* (Berger-Levrault, 1946).
de Brinon, Count Fernand: *Mémoires* (La Page Internationale, 1949).
Bruce-Lockhart, Sir Robert: *Friends, Foes and Foreigners* (Putnam, 1957).
The Diaries of Sir Robert Bruce-Lockhart, 1912–1938.
Brugère, Raymond: *Veni, vidi, Vichy. Témoignages, 1940–1945* (Deux-Rives, 1953).
Bryant, Sir Arthur: *The Turn of the Tide, 1939–1943. A study based on the diaries and autobiographical notes of Field Marshal the Viscount Alanbrooke, KG, OM* (William Collins, 1957; Reprint Society, 1958).
Bullitt, Orville H. (ed.): *For the President: Personal and Secret. Correspondence between Franklin D. Roosevelt and William C. Bullitt* (André Deutsch, 1973).
Callet, Gen. Jean: *L'Honneur de commander* (Charles-Lavauzelle, 1990).
Cammaerts, Emile: *The Prisoner at Laeken. King Leopold, legend and fact* (Preface by Admiral of the Fleet Sir Roger Keyes) (The Cresset Press, 1941).
Cannistraro, Philip V., Edward D. Wynot Jr., Theodore P. Kovaleff (eds.): *Poland and the Coming of the Second World War. The Diplomatic Papers of A. J. Drexel Biddle Jr., United States Ambassador to Poland, 1937–1939* (Columbus OH: Ohio State University Press, 1976).

Capelle, Baron Robert: *Dix huit ans auprès du Roi Léopold* (Arthème Fayard, 1970). *Au Service du Roi, 1934–1945* (Dessart, Brussels, 2 vols., 1949).
de Carbuccia, Horace: *Le Massacre de la Victoire, 1919–1934. Gringoire. L'Affaire Stavisky. 6 février 1934. Le Guignol parlementaire. Fascistes et nazis au pouvoir* (Plon, 1973).
Carcopino, Jérôme: *Souvenirs de sept ans, 1937–1944* (Ernest Flammarion, 1953).
Catroux, Gen. Georges: *Dans la bataille de Méditerranée. Egypte. Levant. Afrique du Nord. 1940–1944* (René Julliard, 1949).
Cerruti, Elizabeth: *Je les ai bien connus. Souvenirs d'ambassades* (trans. B. de Saint-Marceaux) (Hachette, 1950).
Chandos, Lord (Oliver Lyttelton): *The Memoirs of Lord Chandos* (The Bodley Head, 1957).
Charles-Roux, François: *Cinq mois tragiques aux Affaires Etrangères. 21 mai–1 novembre 1940* (Plon, 1949).
Chautemps, Camille: *Cahiers secrets de l'Armistice, 1939–1940* (Plon, 1963).
Chérau, Gaston: *Concorde! Le 6 février 1934* (Denoël and Steele, 1934).
Churchill, Winston S.: *The Second World War*, I, *The gathering storm* (Cassell, 1948).
Cockett, Richard (ed.): *My Dear Max. The letters of Brendan Bracken to Lord Beaverbrook, 1925–1958* (The Historians' Press, 1990).
Colville, Sir John R.: *The Fringes of Power. Downing Street Diaries, 1939–1955* (Hodder and Stoughton, 1985).
Conquet, Gen. Alfred: *Auprès de Maréchal Pétain. Le Chef. Le Politique. L'Homme* (Editions France-Empire, 1970).
Cooper, Alfred Duff, Lord Norwich: *Old Men Forget: The autobiography of Viscount Norwich* (Rupert Hart-Davis, 1953).
Cornil, Gen. Fernand: *Détresse et espérance. Les Responsabilités du commandement de l'armée et du gouvernement dans la tragédie de mai 1940* (Brussels: Les Editions Ferdinand Wellens-Pay, 1944).
Cot, Pierre: *Le Procès de la République* (New York: Editions de la Maison Française, 1944, 2 vols.; English edn, *Triumph of Treason*, trans. Sybil and Morton Crane, New York: Ziff-Davis, 1944).
Coulondre, Robert: *De Stalin à Hitler. Souvenirs de deux ambassades, 1936–1939* (Hachette, 1950).
Cox, Sir Geoffrey: *Countdown to War. A personal memoir of Europe, 1938–1940* (William Kimber, 1988; reprinted Coronet Books, 1990).
Daladier, J. and J. Daridan, eds.: *Edouard Daladier: Journal de captivité, 1940–1945* (Calmann-Lévy, 1991).
Daridan, Jean: *Le Chemin de la Défaite, 1938–1940* (Plon, 1980).
Daudet, Léon: *Souvenirs politiques* (Préface de Michael de Saint Pierre) (Editions Albatros, 1974).
Davignon, Vicomte Jacques: *Berlin, 1936–1940. Souvenirs d'une mission* (Paris and Brussels: Les Editions Universitaires, 1951).
Debeney, Gen. Marie-Eugène: *La Guerre et les hommes. Réflexions d'après-guerre* (Plon, 1937).
Debré, Michel: *Mémoires*, I, *Trois Républiques pour une France* (Plon, 1985).
Denuit, Désiré: *L'Eté ambigu de 1940. Carnets d'un journaliste* (Brussels: Louis Musin, 1978).

Dilks, David (ed.): *The Diaries of Sir Alexander Cadogan, 1938–1945* (Cassell, 1971).
Dodd, William E.: *Ambassador Dodd's Diary, 1933–1938*, ed. William E. Dodd Jr, and Martha Dodd, with an Introduction by Charles A. Beard (Victor Gollancz, 1942).
Dorgelès, Roland: *La Drôle de guerre, 1939–1940* (Albin Michel, 1957).
Doumenc, Gen. André: *Histoire de la neuvième armée, 10–18 mai 1940* (Paris and Grenoble: Arthaud, 1945).
Duclos, Jacques: *Mémoires*, I, *Le Chemin que j'ai choisi. De Verdun au Parti Communiste*, II, *1935–1939. Aux jours ensoleillés du Front Populaire* (Arthème Fayard, 1968, 1969).
Eden, Anthony (The Earl of Avon): *Another World, 1897–1917* (Allen Lane, 1976).
The Eden Memoirs, II, *Facing the Dictators* (1961).
Fabre-Luce, Alfred: *Journal de la France, mars 1939–juillet 1940* (Imprimerie JEP, 1941).
Journal de la France, 1939–1944 (Geneva: Les Editions du Cheval Ailé, 1946, 2 vols.).
Fabry, Jean: *Février 1934–juin 1940. De la Place de la Concorde au Cours de l'Intendance* (Les Editions de France, 1942).
Felsenhardt, Robert: *1939–40 avec le 18e corps d'armée* (La Tête de Feuilles, 1973).
Flandin, Pierre-Etienne: *Politique française, 1919–1940* (Les Editions Nouvelles, 1947).
Frachon, Benoît: *Pour la CGT. Mémoires de lutte, 1902–1939* (Messidor Editions Sociales, 1981).
François-Poncet, André: *Souvenirs d'une Ambassade à Berlin, septembre 1931–octobre 1938* (Ernest Flammarion, 1946).
Carnets d'un captif, 1943–1945 (Arthème Fayard, 1952).
De Versailles à Potsdam. La France et le problème allemand contemporain, 1919–1943 (Ernest Flammarion, 1948).
Au Palais Farnèse. Souvenirs d'une ambassade à Rome, 1938–1940 (Arthème Fayard, 1961).
Frossard, Ludovic-Oscar: *Sous le signe de Jaurès. Souvenirs d'un militant* (Ernest Flammarion, 1943).
Gafencu, Grigore: *The Last Days of Europe. A Diplomatic Journey in 1939* (trans. Fletcher Allen, Frederick Muller, 1947).
Gamelin, Gen. Maurice-Gustave: *Servir* (Plon, 1946–7, 3 vols.).
Manoeuvre et victoire de la Marne (Bernard Grasset, 1954).
de Gaulle, Charles: *Mémoires de guerre*, I, *L'Appel, 1940–1942* (Plon, 1954, Livre de Poche edn, 1954).
Lettres, notes et carnets, II, *1919–juin 1940* (Plon, 1980).
Génébrier, Roger: *Septembre 1939. La France entre en guerre. Quelques révélations sur ce qui s'est passé dans les derniers jours de la Paix* (Alta/Editions Philippine, 1982).
Gladwyn, Lord (formerly Gladwyn Jebb): *Memoirs of the Lord Gladwyn* (1972).
Grandsard, Gen. Charles: *Le 10e Corps d'Armée dans la bataille, 1939–1940* (Berger-Levrault, 1949).

Grigg, P. J.: *Prejudice and Judgment* (Jonathan Cape, 1948).
le Grix, François: *En écoutant Weygand* (Nouvelles Editions Latines, 1949).
Guderian, Gen. Heinz: *Panzer Leader* (trans. Constantine Fitzgibbons, Michael Joseph, 1952; Fontana, 1974).
Guillaume, Gen. Augustin: *Homme de guerre* (Editions France-Empire, 1977).
de Guingand, Major-Gen. Sir Francis: *Operation Victory* (Hodder and Stoughton, 1947).
Hailsham, Viscount (Hogg, Quintin): *A Sparrow's Flight: Memoirs* (Collins, 1990).
Halifax, the Earl of (Wood, Edward Lindley): *Fulness of Days* (Collins, 1957).
Harvey, John (ed.): *The Diplomatic Diaries of Oliver Harvey, 1937–1940* (Collins, 1970; New York: St Martin's Press, 1971).
von Hassell, Ulrich: *The Von Hassell Diaries, 1938–1944. The story of the forces against Hitler inside Germany as recorded by Ambassador Ulrich von Hassell a leader of the movement* (Hamish Hamilton, 1948).
Henderson, Sir Nevile: *Failure of a Mission. Berlin, 1937–1939* (Hodder and Stoughton, 1940).
  Water under the Bridges (Hodder and Stoughton, 1945).
Herriot, Edouard: *Jadis*, II, *D'une guerre à l'autre, 1914–1936* (Ernest Flammarion, 1948).
Herwarth, Hans von: *Against Two Evils. Memoirs of a diplomat-soldier during the Third Reich* (Collins, 1981).
Home, Lord (Douglas Home, Alec, formerly Lord Dunglass): *The Way the Wind Blows. An autobiography by Lord Home* (Collins, 1976).
Horrocks, Lieut.-Gen. Sir Brian: *A Full Life* (Leo Cooper, 1974).
Hossbach, Col. Friedrich: *Entre la Wehrmacht et Hitler, 1934–1938* (trans. of German original *Zwischen Wehrmacht und Hitler, 1934–1938*, Payot, 1951).
Ismay, Gen. Hastings (Lord Ismay): *The Memoirs of Lord Ismay* (Heinemann, 1960).
Jacomet, Robert: *L'Armement de la France, 1936–1939* (Les Editions Lajeunesse, 1945).
Jaspar, Marcel-Henri: *Souvenirs sans retouche* (Arthème Fayard, 1968).
Jauneaud, Gen. Jean-Henri: *J'accuse le Maréchal Pétain* (Pygmalion, 1977).
Jeanneney, J.-N. (ed.): *Jules Jeanneney: journal politique, septembre 1939–juillet 1942* (Librairie Armand Colin, 1972).
Jedrzejewicz, Waclaw (ed.): *Diplomat in Berlin, 1933–1939. Papers and Memoirs of Josef Lipski, Ambassador of Poland* (New York and London: Columbia University Press, 1968).
Joffre, Marshal Joseph Jacques Césare: *Mémoires du Maréchal Joffre, 1910–1917* (Plon, 1932, 2 vols.).
Jones, R. V.: *Most Secret War. British Scientific Intelligence, 1939–1945* (Hamish Hamilton, 1978).
Joubert de la Ferté, Air Chief Marshal Sir Philip B.: *The Fated Sky* (Hutchinson, 1952).
Jouhaud, Gen. Edmond: *La Vie est un combat* (Arthème Fayard, 1974).
Joxe, Louis: *Victoires sur la nuit. Mémoires, 1940–1946* (Flammarion, 1981).

Kammerer, Albert: *La Vérité sur l'armistice. Ephéméride de ce qui s'est réellement passé* (Editions Médicis, 1944).
Kennedy, Gen. Sir John: *The Business of War: the War Narrative of Major-General Sir John Kennedy. Introduction by Brigadier Sir Bernard Fergusson* (Hutchinson, 1957).
Kelly, Denis: see Macleod, Col. Roderick.
Kirkpatrick, Sir Ivone: *The Inner Circle. The Memoirs of Ivone Kirkpatrick* (Macmillan, 1959).
Koeltz, Gen. Louis: *Comment s'est joué notre destin. Hitler et l'offensive du 10 mai 1940* (Hachette, 1957).
Laffargue, Gen. André: *Fantassin de Gascogne. De mon jardin à la Marne et au Danube* (Ernest Flammarion, 1962).
Langeron, Roger: *Paris, juin 40* (Ernest Flammarion, 1946).
de Lattre de Tassigny, Marshal Jean: *Ne pas subir. Ecrits, 1914–1952. Textes rassemblés et présentés par Elizabeth du Réau, André Kaspi, Marc Michel, Guy Pedroncini et Maurice Redon* (Plon, 1984).
Laval, Pierre: *Laval Parle. Notes et mémoires redigés à Fresnes, d'août à octobre 1945* (La Diffusion du Livre, 1948; English edn, *The Unpublished Diary of Pierre Laval. With an introduction by Josée Laval, Countess R. de Chambrun*, The Falcon Press, 1948).
Leblanc, Raymond: *Dés pipés. Journal d'un Chasseur Ardennais* (Brussels: André Gilbert, 1942).
Lebrun, Albert: *Témoignage* (Plon, 1945).
Leca, Dominique: *La Rupture de 1940* (Arthème Fayard, 1978).
Lémery, Henry: *D'une République à l'autre. Souvenirs de la mêlée politique, 1894–1944* (La Table Ronde, 1964).
Léon-Jouhaux, Augusta: *Prison pour Hommes d'Etat* (Denoël Gonthier, 1973).
Lerecouvreux, Marcel: *L'Armée Giraud en Hollande, 1939–1940* (Nouvelles Editions Latines, 1951).
Leutze, James (ed.): *The London Observer. The Journal of General Raymond E. Lee, 1940–1941* (Hutchinson, 1971).
Liddell Hart, Sir Basil H.: *The Memoirs of Captain Liddell Hart*, II (Cassell, 1965).
Liddell Hart, Sir Basil H. (ed.): *The Rommel Papers* (William Collins, 1953).
Liebling, Abbott Joseph: *The Road back to Paris* (New York: Paragon Publishers, 1988).
Loucheur, Louis: *Carnets secrets, 1908–1932* (Editions Brepols, Brussels and Paris, 1962).
Macleod, Col. Roderick and Kelly, Denis (eds.): *The Ironside Diaries, 1937–1940* (Constable, 1962).
Maisky, Ivan M.: *Before the Storm: Recollections* (trans. G. Shelley, Hutchinson, nd).
Malaquais, J.: *Journal de guerre, 28 août 1939–15 juillet 1940* (New York: Editions de la Maison Française, nd).
von Manstein, Field Marshal Erich: *Lost Victories* (ed. and trans. Anthony G. Powell; foreword by B. H. Liddell Hart, Methuen, 1958; reprinted Novato, CA: Presidio Press, 1982).

Marshall-Cornwall, Gen. Sir James: *Wars and Rumours of Wars. A memoir* (Leo Cooper/Martin Secker and Warburg, 1984).
von Mellenthin, Major-Gen. F. W.: *Panzer Battles. A Study of the employment of armor in the second world war* (Norman, OK: University of Oklahoma Press, 1956; reprinted New York: Ballantine Books, 1971, 1990).
Mengin, Robert: *No Laurels for de Gaulle. A personal appraisal of the London years* (Michael Joseph, 1967).
Menu, Gen. Léon: *Lumière sur les ruines. Les Combattants de 1940 réhabilités* (Plon, 1953).
Michiels, Lieut.-Gen. Oscar: *Dix-huit jours de guerre en Belgique, 10–28 mai 1940* (Berger-Levrault, 1947).
Minart, Col. Jacques: *P. C. Vincennes. Secteur 4* (Berger-Levrault, 1945, 2 vols.).
Minney, Rubeigh J.: *The Private Papers of Hore-Belisha* (Collins, 1960).
Moch, Jules: *Rencontres avec Léon Blum* (Plon, 1970).
Monnet, Jean: *Mémoires* (Arthème Fayard, 1976) (English edn, *The Memoirs of Jean Monnet*, trans. Richard Mayne, William Collins, 1977).
Montigny, Jean: *Toute la vérité sur un mois dramatique de notre histoire. De l'Armistice à l'Assemblée Nationale, 15 juin–15 juillet 1940* (Editions Mont-Louis, 1940).
Heures tragiques de 1940. La Défaite (Bernard Grasset, 1941).
Le Complot contre la paix, 1935–1939 (La Table Ronde, 1966).
Mornet, Procureur-Général: *Quatre ans à rayer de notre histoire* (Editions SELF, 1949).
de Monzie, Anatole: *Ci-devant* (Ernest Flammarion, 1941).
Navarre, Gen. Henri: *L'Agonie de l'Indochine* (Plon, 1956).
Le Temps de vérités (Plon, 1979).
Nicolson, Harold: *Harold Nicolson Diaries and Letters, 1930–1964* (ed. and cond. Stanley Olson, Collins, 1980).
Noël, Léon: *L'Agression allemande contre la Pologne* (Ernest Flammarion, 1946).
Les Illusions de Stresa. L'Italie abandonnée à Hitler (Editions France-Empire, 1975).
La Guerre de 1939 a commencé quatre ans plus tôt (Editions France-Empire, 1979).
van Overstraeten, Gen. Raoul François Casimir: *Albert Ier. Léopold III. Vingt ans de politique militaire belge, 1920–1940* (Bruges: Desclée de Brouwer, 1946).
Au service de la Belgique, I, *Dans l'Etau* (Plon, 1960).
Léopold III prisonnier. Le Journal inédit de la vie quotidienne à Laeken du célèbre conseiller militaire du roi, 31 mai 1940–10 mai 1945 (Brussels: Didier Hatier, 1986).
Paillole, Paul: *Services spéciaux, 1935–1945* (Robert Laffont, 1975).
Paul Boncour, Joseph: *Entre deux guerres. Souvenirs sur la IIIe République* (Plon, 1946, 3 vols.).
Peyrouton, Marcel: *Du service public à la prison commune. Souvenirs. Tunis-Rabat-Buenos Aires-Vichy-Alger-Fresnes* (Plon, 1950).
Pomaret, Charles: *Le Dernier Témoin. Fin d'une république, juin et juillet 1940* (Presses de la Cité, 1968).

Prételat, Gen. Gaston: *Le Destin tragique de la Ligne Maginot* (Berger-Levrault, 1950).
Prieux, Jacques: *Grandeur nature. Carnet de mobilisation et de guerre* (Brussels: Editions Nossent, 1947).
Prioux, Gen. Jules: *Souvenirs de guerre, 1939–1943* (Ernest Flammarion, 1947).
Reid, Miles: *Last on the List* (Leo Cooper, 1974).
Requin, Gen. Edouard: *D'une guerre à l'autre, 1919–1939* (Charles Lavauzelle, 1949).
  Combats pour l'honneur, 1939–1940 (Charles Lavauzelle, 1946).
le Révérend, André: *Un Lyautey inconnu. Correspondance et journal inédits, 1874–1934* (Librairie Académique Perrin, 1980).
Reynaud, Paul: *La France a sauvé l'Europe* (Ernest Flammarion, 1947, 2 vols.).
Rhodes-James, Robert (ed.): *Chips. The Diaries of Sir Henry Channon* (Weidenfeld and Nicolson, 1967).
Rist, Charles: *Une saison gâtée. Journal de guerre et de l'occupation, 1939–1945* (Arthème Fayard, 1983).
Ritchie, Charles: *The Siren Years. A Canadian Diplomat Abroad, 1937–1945* (Toronto: Macmillan of Canada, 1974; Laurentian Library, 1977).
Ruby, Gen. Edmond: *Sedan. Terre d'épreuve: Avec la IIe Armée, mai–juin 1940* (Ernest Flammarion, 1948).
Rueff, Jacques: *De l'aube au crépuscule. Autobiographie* (Plon, 1977).
Sadoul, Georges: *Journal de Guerre, 1939–1940* (Les Editeurs français réunis, 1977).
Salter, Lord (formerly Sir Arthur Salter): *Memoirs of a Public Servant* (Faber and Faber, 1961).
Sartre, Jean-Paul: *Carnets de la drôle de guerre. Novembre 1939–mars 1940* (Gallimard, 1983) (English edn, *The War Diaries of Jean-Paul Sartre. November 1939–March 1940*, trans. Quintin Hoare. Verso, 1984).
Sauvy, Alfred: *De Paul Reynaud à Charles de Gaulle. Scènes, tableaux et souvenirs* (Casterman, 1972).
Serrigny, Gen. Bernard: *Trente ans avec Pétain* (Plon, 1959).
Simon, Sir John (Viscount Simon): *Retrospect* (Hutchinson, 1952).
Slessor, Marshal of the RAF Sir John: *The Central Blue. The Autobiography of Marshal of the RAF Sir John Slessor* (Cassell, 1956).
Spaak, Paul-Henri: *Combats inachevés. De l'indépendance à l'alliance* (Fayard, 1969).
Spears, Major-Gen. Sir Edward Louis: *Assignment to Catastrophe* (Heinemann, 1954).
Stehlin, Gen. Paul: *Témoignage pour l'histoire* (Robert Laffont, 1964).
Strang, Lord (William Strang): *Home and Abroad* (André Deutsch, 1956).
Swinton, Viscount (Cunliffe-Lister, Sir Philip): *I Remember* (Hutchinson, nd).
Tabouis, Geneviève: *Ils l'ont appelée Cassandre* (New York: Editions de la Maison Française, 1942).
Tardieu, André: *Notes de semaine, 1938: L'Année de Munich* (Ernest Flammarion, 1939).
Taylor, A. J. P. (ed.): *Off the Record. Political Interviews by W. P. Crozier, 1933–1943* (Hutchinson, 1973).
Templewood, Viscount (Hoare, Sir Samuel): *Nine Troubled Years* (William Collins, 1954).

Thorez, Maurice: *Fils du peuple* (Les Editions Sociales, 1949).
Tissier, Pierre: *The Riom Trial* (Harrap, 1943).
Vandervelde, Emile: *Carnets, 1934–1938* (Editions Internationales, 1966).
Varenne, Françisque: *Mon patron Georges Mandel* (Editions Défense de la France, 1947).
de Villelume, Gen. Paul: *Journal d'une défaite, août 1939–juillet 1940*, ed. and with an introduction by René Rémond (Fayard, 1976).
Werth, Alexander: *The Last Days of Paris. A journalist's diary* (Hamish Hamilton, 1940).
  The Twilight of France. A journalist's chronicle, 1933–1940 (Hamish Hamilton, 1942).
Weygand, Gen. Maxime: *Mémoires* (Ernest Flammarion, 1950–7, 3 vols.).
  En lisant les mémoires de guerre du Général de Gaulle (Ernest Flammarion, 1955).
Winterton, The Earl: *Orders of the Day. Memories of nearly fifty years of the House of Commons* (Cassell, 1953).
Zeller, Gen. André: *Dialogues avec un colonel* (Plon, 1972).
van Zuylen, Baron Pierre: *Les Mains libres. Politique extérieure de la Belgique, 1914–1940* (Brussels: Desclée de Brouwer, 1950).

C. Biographies

Assouline, Pierre: *Monsieur Dassault* (Balland, 1983).
Berstein, Serge: *Edouard Herriot, ou la République en personne* (Presses de la Fondation Nationale des Sciences Politiques, 1985).
Boulogne, Jean: *La Vie de Louis Renault* (Editions du Moulin d'Argent, 1931).
Charmley, John: *Duff Cooper. The authorised biography* (Weidenfeld and Nicolson, 1986).
Cole, Hubert: *Laval. A Biography* (William Heinemann, 1963).
Colton, Joel: *Léon Blum, Humanist in Politics* (New York: Alfred Knopf, 1966; reprinted 1986).
Cordier, Daniel: *Jean Moulin: L'Inconnu du Panthéon*, I, *Une ambition pour la République*, II, *Le Choix d'un destin* (Jean-Claude Lattès, 1989).
Droit, Michel: *De Lattre, Maréchal de France* (Editions de Flore, 1952).
Dutton, David: *Austen Chamberlain: Gentleman in Politics* (Bolton: Ross Anderson, 1985).
Farrar, Marjorie Milbank: *Principled Pragmatist. The political career of Alexandre Millerand* (Leamington Spa: Berg, 1991).
Feiling, Keith: *The Life of Neville Chamberlain* (Macmillan, 1946).
Ferro, Marc: *Pétain* (Arthème Fayard, 1987).
Fink, Carole: *Marc Bloch. A Life in History* (Cambridge University Press, 1989).
Fraser, Gen. Sir David: *Alanbrooke* (Collins, 1982).
Fraser, Geoffrey and Natanson, Thadee: *Léon Blum. Man and Statesman* (Victor Gollancz, 1937).
Hamilton, Nigel: *Monty*, I, *The Making of a General, 1887–1942* (Hamish Hamilton, 1981).
Keyes, Roger: *Outrageous Fortune. The Tragedy of Leopold III of the Belgians* (Secker and Warburg, 1984); (French language edn: *Un règne brisé. Léopold III, 1901–1941*, Paris and Gembloux: J. Duculot, 1985).

Echec au roi. Léopold III, 1940–1951 (Paris and Gembloux: J. Duculot, 1986).
Kuisel, Richard F.: *Ernest Mercier. French Technocrat* (Berkeley, CA: University of California Press, 1967).
Kupferman, Fred: *Pierre Laval* (Masson, 1976).
Laval (Arthème Fayard, 1987).
Lacouture, Jean: *De Gaulle* (Seuil, 1984–8, 3 vols.); (English edn, trans. Patrick O'Brian, 2 vols.), *De Gaulle: The Rebel, 1890–1944*; *De Gaulle: The Ruler, 1945–1970* (Collins Harvill, 1990–1).
Laure, Gen. A. M. E.: *Pétain* (Berger-Levrault, 1941).
Le Révérend, André: *Lyautey* (Arthème Fayard, 1983).
Logue, William: *Léon Blum: The Formative Years, 1872–1914* (De Kalb, ILL: Northern Illinois University Press, 1973).
Macleod, Iain: *Neville Chamberlain* (Frederick Muller, 1961).
Mallet, Alfred: *Pierre Laval* (Amiot-Dumont, 1955, 2 vols.)
Michel, Marc: *Galliéni* (Arthème Fayard, 1990).
Nicolson, Nigel: *Alex. The Life of Field Marshal Earl Alexander of Tunis* (Weidenfeld and Nicolson, 1973).
Noël, Léon: *Témoignage d'un chef. Le général Guillaumat* (Editions Alsatia, 1949).
Raphaël-Leygues, Jacques: *Georges Leygues, Le Père de la marine (ses carnets secrets de 1914 à 1934)* (France-Empire, 1983).
Raphaël-Leygues, Jacques and François Flohic: *Darlan* (Plon, 1986).
Rhodes, Anthony: *Louis Renault. A Biography* (Cassell, 1969).
Roberts, Andrew: *The Holy Fox. A Life of Lord Halifax* (Weidenfeld and Nicolson, 1991).
Salisbury-Jones, Major-Gen. Sir Guy: *So Full a Glory. A biography of Marshal de Lattre de Tassigny* (Weidenfeld and Nicolson, 1954).
Simiot, Bernard: *De Lattre* (Ernest Flammarion, 1953).
Torrès, Henry: *Pierre Laval* (Victor Gollancz, 1941).
Warner, Geoffrey: *Pierre Laval and the Eclipse of France* (Eyre and Spottiswoode, 1968).
Waterfield, Gordon: *Professional Diplomat. Sir Percy Loraine of Kirkharle Bt., 1880–1961* (John Murray, 1973).
Weygand, Gen. Maxime: *Foch* (Ernest Flammarion, 1947).
Le général Frère. Un chef. Un héros. Un martyr (Ernest Flammarion, 1949).

D. Contemporary studies
Alerme, Col. M.: *Stratégie anglaise* (Editions du Centre d'Etudes de l'Agence Inter-France, nd).
Les Causes militaires de notre défaite (Editions du Centre d'Etudes de l'Agence Inter-France, 1941).
Allard, Paul: *La Vérité sur les marchands de canons* (Bernard Grasset, 1935).
Les Responsables du désastre (Les Editions de France, 1941).
L'Enigme de la Meuse. La Vérité sur l'affaire Corap (Les Editions de France, 1941).
Les Plans secrets du G.Q.G. pendant la guerre (Les Editions de France, 1941).
Bainville, Jacques: *La Troisième République, 1870–1935* (Arthème Fayard, 1935).

Barthou, Louis: *Le Traité de paix* (Bibliothèque Charpentier, 1919).
Benjamin, René: *Le Printemps tragique* (Plon, 1941).
Benoîst-Méchin, Jacques: *La Moisson de quarante* (Albin Michel, 1941).
Blum, Léon: *La Réforme gouvernementale* (Editions Bernard Grasset, 1936).
Bois, Elie J.: *Truth on the Tragedy of France* (Hodder and Stoughton, 1941).
Bonnard, Abel: *Pensées dans l'action. Morale d'une défaite. Le Maréchal Pétain chef de l'Etat* (Editions Bernard Grasset, 1941).
Bordeaux, Henry: *Joffre ou l'art de commander* (Editions Bernard Grasset, 1933).
Buisson, Georges: *La Chambre et les Députés* (Hachette, 1924).
Cardinne-Petit, R.: *Les Soirées du Continental. Ce que j'ai vu à la censure, 1939–1940* (Jean-Renard, 1942).
Clemenceau, Georges: *Grandeur and Misery of Victory* (Harrap, 1930).
Habriou, C.: *La Déroute (1939–1940)* (Editions C.-L., 1941).
Henriot, Philippe: *Comment mourut la paix. Le Procès des responsables* (Editions de France, 1941).
De La Hire, J.: *Le Crime des évacuations* (Tallandier, 1940).
Jordan, W. M.: *Great Britain, France and the German Problem, 1918–1939. A study of Anglo-French relations in the making and the maintenance of the Versailles Settlement* (1943).
Jouvenel, Bertrand de: *Après la défaite* (Plon, 1941).
  La Dernière année. Choses vues de Munich à la guerre (A l'Enseigne du Cheval Ailé, 1947).
Kammerer, Albert: *La Vérité sur L'Armistice. Ephéméride de ce qui s'est réellement passé* (Editions Médicis, 1944).
de Kérillis, Henry: *Français, voici la vérité* (New York: Editions de la Maison Française, 1942).
Lazareff, Paul: *De Munich à Vichy* (New York: Brentano's, 1944).
Lévy, Louis: *Vérités sur la France* (Penguin, 1941).
  France is a Democracy (Victor Gollancz, 1943).
Lombard, P.: *Histoire de quarante-six jours (10 mai–15 juin 1940)* (Editions de France, 1941).
Nollet, Gen. Charles: *Une expérience de désarmement. Cinq ans de contrôle militaire en Allemagne* (Gallimard, 1932).
Patenôtre, Raymond: *La Crise et le drame monétaire* (Gallimard, 1932).
  Voulons-nous sortir de la crise? (Plon, 1934).
Pertinax (pseud. of Géraud, André): *Les Fossoyeurs. Défaite militaire de la France. Armistice. Contre-révolution* (New York: Editions de la Maison Française, 1943, 2 vols.).
Recouly, Raymond: *Les Causes de notre effondrement* (Editions de France, 1941).
Romains, Jules: *Sept Mystères du destin de l'Europe* (New York: Editions de la Maison Française, 1940).
Tardieu, André: *Avec Foch, août–novembre 1914* (Flammarion, 1939).
Thibaudet, Albert: *La République des professeurs* (Editions Bernard Grasset, 1927).
Walker-Smith, Derek: *Neville Chamberlain* (Robert Hale, 1939).

Weygand, Gen. Maxime: *Le Fauteuil du Maréchal Joffre. Discours de réception de M. le Général Weygand à l'Académie Française et réponse de M. Jules Cambon, ambassadeur de France* (Plon, 1932).

E. Contemporary articles
Anon.: 'Daladier', *Picture Post*, 5:9 (2 Dec. 1939), pp. 17–25.
Anon. [Werth, Alexander]: 'The life of General Gamelin', *Picture Post*, 4:13 (30 Sept. 1939), pp. 32–7.
Armengaud, Gen. Jules: 'La Neutralité volontaire de la Belgique et les progrès de l'armement aérien', *RDM*, 8:40 (1 July 1937).
 'La Tchécoslovaquie devant L'Allemagne', *RDM*, 8:44 (15 Apr. 1938), pp. 766–79.
Coudurier de Chassaigne, J.: 'Un nouveau premier ministre: M. Neville Chamberlain', *RDM*, 8:44 (Mar. 1938), pp. 442–52.
Debeney, Gen. Marie-Eugène: 'Nos fortifications du Nord-Est', *RDM*, 8:23 (15 Sept. 1934), pp. 241–64.
 'Encore l'armée de métier', *RDM*, 8:28 (15 July 1935), pp. 279–95.
 'La Motorisation des armées modernes', *RDM*, 8:32 (15 Mar. 1936), pp. 273–91.
 'Le Problème de la couverture', *RDM*, 8:36 (15 Nov. 1936), pp. 268–93.
Gibson, Irving M. (pseud. of Kovacs, Arpad V.): 'Military origins of the Fall of France', *Military Affairs*, 7:1 (Spring 1943), pp. 25–40.
Kraehe, Enno A.: 'Motives behind the Maginot Line', *Military Affairs*, 8:1 (Spring 1944), pp. 138–52.

F. Historical studies
Adamthwaite, Anthony P.: *France and the Coming of the Second World War* (Frank Cass, 1977).
 The Making of the Second World War (Unwin Hyman, 1977).
Adriance, Thomas J.: *The Last Gaiter Button: A Study of the mobilization and concentration of the French army in the war of 1870* (Westport, CT: Greenwood Press, 1987).
Alexander, Martin S., and Graham, Helen (eds.): *The French and Spanish Popular Fronts. Comparative Perspectives* (Cambridge University Press, 1989).
Amaury, P.: *Les Deux Premières Expériences d'un 'Ministère de l'Information' en France* (LGDJ, 1969).
Amouroux, Henri: *La Grande Histoire des français sous l'Occupation, 1939–1945* (Arthème Fayard, 1977–83, 6 vols.).
Andrew, Christopher M.: *Secret Service. The Making of the British Intelligence Community* (Heinemann, 1985).
Andrew, Christopher M. and Dilks, David (eds.): *The Missing Dimension. Governments and Intelligence Communities in the Twentieth Century* (Basingstoke and London: Macmillan, 1984).
Andrew, Christopher M. and Noakes, Jeremy (eds.): *Intelligence and International Relations, 1900–1945* (Exeter: Exeter University Publications, 1987).
Armengaud, Gen. Paul: *Le Drame de Dunkerque, mai–juin 1940* (Plon, 1948).

Aron, Robert: *Léopold III ou le choix impossible, février 1934–juillet 1940* (Plon, 1977).
Artaud, Denise: *La Reconstruction de l'Europe, 1919–1929* (Presses Universitaires de France, 1973).
La Question des dettes interalliées et la reconstruction de l'Europe, 1917–1929 (Lille: Presses de l'Université de Lille III, 1978).
Auvray, Michel: *Objecteurs, insoumis, déserteurs: une histoire des réfractaires en France* (Stock, 1983).
Azéma, Jean-Pierre: *1940. L'Année terrible* (Editions du Seuil, 1990).
Balfour, Michael: *Propaganda in War, 1939–1945. Organisations, Policies and Publics in Britain and Germany* (Routledge and Kegan Paul, 1979).
Bankwitz, Philip C. F.: *Maxime Weygand and Civil-Military Relations in Modern France* (Cambridge, MA: Harvard University Press, 1967).
Alsatian Autonomist Leaders, 1919–1947 (Lawrence, KA: The Regent's Press of Kansas, 1978).
Barber, Noel: *The Week France Fell: June 1940* (Macmillan, 1976).
Bariéty, Jacques: *Les Relations franco-allemandes après la Première Guerre Mondiale* (Publications de la Sorbonne, 1977).
Barnett, Correlli (ed.): *Hitler's Generals* (Weidenfeld and Nicolson, 1989).
Barros, James: *Betrayal from Within. Joseph Avenol, Secretary-General of the League of Nations, 1933–1940* (New Haven, CT and London: Yale University Press, 1969).
Becker, Jean-Jacques: *Le Carnet B. Les Pouvoirs publics et l'antimilitarisme avant la guerre de 1914* (Klinksieck, 1973).
Le Parti Communiste Français, veut-il prendre le pouvoir? La Stratégie du PCF de 1930 à nos jours (Seuil, 1981).
The Great War and the French People (Leamington Spa: Berg, 1985).
Bell, Philip M. H.: *A Certain Eventuality. Britain and the Fall of France* (Farnborough: Saxon House, 1974).
The Origins of the Second World War in Europe (Longman, 1986).
Bellanger, C. et al: *Histoire générale de la presse française*, III, *1871–1940* (Presses Universitaires de France, 1972).
Bernard, Henri: *Panorama d'une défaite. Bataille de Belgique-Dunkerque (10 mai–4 juin 1940)* (Gembloux: Editions Duculot, 1984).
Berstein, Serge: *Histoire du Parti Radical* (Editions de la Fondation Nationale des Sciences Politiques, 1980–2, 2 vols.).
Bialer, Uri: *The Shadow of the Bomber. The Fear of Air Attack and British Politics, 1932–1939* (Royal Historical Society, 1980).
Birn, Donald S.: *The League of Nations' Union* (Oxford University Press, 1981).
Bloch, Michael: *The Duke of Windsor's War* (Weidenfeld and Nicolson, 1982).
Bond, Brian J.: *Liddell Hart. A Study of his Military Thought* (Cassell, 1977).
British Military Policy between the Two World Wars (Oxford: Clarendon Press, 1980).
France and Belgium, 1939–40 (Davis-Poynter, 1975; reprinted, Brassey's, 1990).
Boussard, Dominique: *Un problème de défense nationale: L'Aéronautique militaire au parlement (1928–1940)* (Vincennes: Publications du Service Historique de l'Armée de l'Air, 1983).

Brogan, Sir Denis W.: *French Personalities and Problems* (Hamish Hamilton, 1946).
Bury, J. P. T.: *France, 1814–1940* (Methuen, 1949).
Caron, François: *An Economic History of Modern France* trans. from the French by Barbara Bray (Methuen, 1979).
Ceadel, Martin: *Pacifism in Britain, 1914–1945. The Defining of a Faith* (Oxford: Clarendon Press, 1980).
Chapman, Guy: *Why France Collapsed* (William Collins, 1968).
Charmley, John: *Chamberlain and the Lost Peace* (Hodder and Stoughton, 1989).
Chastenet, Jacques: *Vingt ans d'histoire diplomatique, 1919–1939* (Geneva: Editions du Milieu du Monde, 1945).
Clayton, Anthony: *The British Empire as Superpower, 1919–1939* (Basingstoke and London: Macmillan, 1986).
   France, Soldiers and Africa (Oxford: Brassey's, 1988).
Colton, Joel: *Compulsory Labor Arbitration in France, 1936–1939* (New York: King's Crown Press, Columbia University, 1951).
Cooke, J. J.: *New French Imperialism, 1880–1910. The Third Republic and Colonial Expansion* (Newton Abbot: David and Charles, 1973).
Cowling, Maurice: *The Impact of Hitler: British Politics and British Policy, 1933–1940* (Cambridge University Press, 1975).
Crémieux-Brilhac, Jean-Louis: *Les Français de l'an 40* (Gallimard 1990, 2 vols.).
Cruickshank, Charles: *The Fourth Arm. Psychological warfare, 1938–45* (Davis-Poynter, 1977).
Delperrié de Bayac, Jacques: *Histoire du Front Populaire* (Arthème Fayard, 1972).
Dennis, Peter J.: *Decision by Default. Peacetime conscription and British defence, 1919–39* (Routledge and Kegan Paul, 1972).
   The Territorial Army, 1906–1940 (Woodbridge, Suffolk: Boydell and Brewer for the Royal Historical Society, 1987).
Deutsch, Harold C.: *The Conspiracy against Hitler in the Twilight War* (Minneapolis, MN: University of Minnesota Press, 1968).
Doise, Jean, and Vaïsse, Maurice: *Politique étrangère de la France, 1871–1969. Diplomatie et outil militaire* (Imprimerie Nationale, 1987).
Doughty, Robert A.: *The Seeds of Disaster. The Development of French Army Doctrine, 1919–1939* (Hamden, CT: Archon Books, 1985).
   The Breaking Point. Sedan and the Fall of France, 1940 (Hamden, CT: Archon Books, 1990).
Douglas, Roy (ed.): *1939: A Retrospect After Forty Years* (Macmillan, 1981).
Draper, Theodore: *The Six Weeks' War. France, May 10–June 25 1940* (New York, Viking, 1944).
Dreifort, John E.: *Yvon Delbos at the Quai d'Orsay. French Foreign Policy during the Popular Front, 1936–1938* (Lawrence, Manhattan and Wichita, KA: The University Press of Kansas, 1973).
Duroselle, Jean-Baptiste: *Histoire diplomatique, de 1919 à nos jours* (1963 et seq.).
   Politique étrangère de la France, 1871–1969. La Décadence, 1932–1939 (Imprimerie Nationale, 1979).

Politique étrangère de la France, 1871–1969. L'Abîme, 1939–1945 (Imprimerie Nationale, 1982).
Emmerson, James T.: *The Rhineland Crisis, 7 March 1936. A study in multilateral diplomacy* (Maurice Temple Smith, 1977).
Faucier, Nicolas: *Pacifisme et anti-militarisme dans l'entre-deux-guerres, 1919–1939* (Spartacus, 1983).
Fauvet, Jacques: *Histoire du Parti Communiste français de la guerre à la guerre, 1917–1939* (Arthème Fayard, 1964).
Fauvet, Jacques and Planchais, Jean: *La Fronde des généraux* (Arthaud, 1961).
Flood, P. J.: *France, 1914–18. Public Opinion and the War Effort* (Macmillan, 1990).
Fonvieille-Alquier, François: *Les Français dans la drôle de guerre, 39–40* (Robert Laffont/Librairie Jules Tallandier, 1971); English edn: *The French and the Phoney War, 1939–40* (Garden City, NJ: Garden City Press, 1973).
Fouvez, Charles: *Le Mystère Weygand. Etude d'un dossier historique au XIXe siècle* (La Table Ronde, 1967).
Frankenstein, Robert: *Le Prix du réarmement français, 1935–39* (Publications de la Sorbonne, 1982).
Fridenson, Patrick: *Histoire des usines Renault, I, Naissance de la grande entreprise, 1898–1939* (Editions du Seuil, 1972).
Gates, Eleanor: *End of the Affair. The collapse of the Anglo-French Alliance, 1939–40* (Allen and Unwin, 1981).
Georges, Bernard, Renauld, Marie-Anne and Tintant, Denise: *Léon Jouhaux et le mouvement syndical français, 1921–1954* (Presses Universitaires de France, 1979).
Gilbert, Martin: *The Roots of Appeasement* (Weidenfeld and Nicolson, 1966).
Glover, Michael: *The Fight for the Channel Ports, Calais to Brest 1940. A study in confusion* (Leo Cooper with Martin Secker and Warburg, 1985).
Godfrey, John F.: *Capitalism at War. Industrial policy and bureaucracy in France, 1914–1918* (Leamington Spa: Berg, 1987).
Gooch, John: *Armies in Europe* (London, Boston and Henley: Routledge and Kegan Paul, 1980).
Gooch, John and Cohen, Eliot: *Military Misfortunes. The Anatomy of Failure in War* (New York: Free Press, 1991), ch. 8, 'Catastrophic failure: the French Army and Air Force, May–June 1940', pp. 197–230.
Gordon, M. R.: *Conflict and Consensus in Labour's Foreign Policy, 1914–1964* (Stanford, CA: Stanford University Press, 1968).
Goutard, Col. Adolphe: *1940, La Guerre des occasions perdues* (Hachette, 1956).
Graham, Helen and Preston, Paul (eds.): *The Popular Front in Europe* (Basingstoke and London: Macmillan, 1987).
Grando, René, Jacques Queralt, Xavier Febrés: *Vous avez la mémoire courte . . . 1939: 500,000 républicains venus du Sud 'indésirables' en Roussillon* (Marcevol: Editions du Chiendent, 1981).
Greene, Nathanael: *Crisis and Decline. The French Socialist Party in the Popular Front Era* (Ithaca, NY: Cornell University Press, 1969).
Griffith, Paddy: *Military Thought in the French Army, 1815–51* (Manchester: Manchester University Press, 1989).

Gunsburg, Jeffery A.: *Divided and Conquered: the French High Command and the Defeat of the West, 1940* (Westport, CT: Greenwood Press, 1979).
Haight, John McVickar, Jr: *American Aid to France, 1938–1940* (New York: Atheneum, 1970).
Hardie, Frank: *The Abyssinian Crisis* (Batsford, 1974).
Helmreich, Jonathan E.: *Belgium and Europe. A study in small power diplomacy* (The Hague: Mouton, 1976).
Hoisington, William A. Jr: *The Casablanca Connection. French colonial policy, 1936–1943* (Chapel Hill, NC and London: University of North Carolina Press, 1984).
Holmes, Richard: *The Road to Sedan. The French Army, 1866–1870* (Woodbridge, Suffolk: Boydell and Brewer, 1984).
Hood, Ronald Chalmers III: *Royal Republicans. The French Naval dynasties between the world wars* (Baton Rouge, LA and London: Louisiana State University Press, 1985).
Horne, Alistair A.: *To Lose a Battle. France 1940* (Macmillan, 1969; reprinted 1990).
  The French Army and Politics, 1870–1970 (Macmillan, 1984).
Howard, John Eldred: *Parliament and Foreign Policy in France. A study of the origins, nature and methods of parliamentary control of foreign policy in France during the Third Republic, with special reference to the period from 1919 to 1939* (The Cresset Press, 1948).
Howarth, Stephen: *August '39. The Last Four Weeks of Peace in Europe* (Hodder and Stoughton, 1989).
Huard, Paul: *Le colonel de Gaulle et ses blindés. Laon, 15–20 mai 1940* (Plon, 1980).
Jackson, Julian: *The Politics of Depression in France, 1932–1936* (Cambridge University Press, 1985).
  The Popular Front in France. Defending Democracy, 1934–38 (Cambridge University Press, 1988)
Jackson, Robert: *The Fall of France, May–June 1940* (Arthur Barker 1975).
Jones, Kenneth Paul (ed.): *US Diplomats in Europe, 1919–1941* (Santa Barbara, CA: and Oxford: ABC Clio Press, 1981).
Kaiser, David E.: *Economic Diplomacy and the Origins of the Second World War. Germany, Britain, France and Eastern Europe, 1930–39* (Princeton University Press, 1980).
Kedward, H. R.: *Occupied France. Collaboration and Resistance, 1940–1944* (Oxford: Basil Blackwell, 1985).
Kennedy, Paul M.: *The Realities behind Diplomacy. Background Influences on British External Policy, 1865–1980* (Allen and Unwin, 1981).
  Strategy and Diplomacy, 1870–1945 (Allen and Unwin, 1983).
  The Rise and Fall of the Great Powers. Economics and Military Strength, 1500–2000 (Unwin Hyman, 1988).
Kent, Bruce: *The Spoils of War. The politics, economics and diplomacy of reparations, 1918–1932* (Oxford: Oxford University Press, 1989).
Kersaudy, François: *Stratèges et Norvège, 1940. Les Jeux de la guerre et du hasard* (Hachette, 1977).
  Churchill and de Gaulle (Collins, 1981; reprinted 1990).

Norway, 1940 (Collins, 1990).

Ketchum, Richard M.: *The Borrowed Years, 1938–41: America on the way to war* (New York: Random House, 1989).

Keylor, William R.: *Jacques Bainville and the Renaissance of Royalist History in Twentieth-Century France* (Baton Rouge, LA and London: Louisiana State University Press, 1979).

Koburger, Charles W., Jr: *The Cyrano Fleet. France and its navy, 1940–42* (Praeger Publishers, 1989).

Kolboom, Ingo: *La Revanche des patrons. Le Patronat français face au Front Populaire* (Ernest Flammarion, 1986).

Kriegel, Annie: *Le Congrès de Tours (1920). Naissance du Parti Communiste Français* (Julliard, 1964).

Kuisel, Richard F.: *Capitalism and the State in Modern France. Renovation and economic management in the twentieth century* (Cambridge University Press, 1981).

Kyba, Patrick: *Covenants without the Sword. Public Opinion and British Defence Policy, 1931–1935* (Waterloo, Ontario: Wilfrid Laurier University Press, 1983).

La Gorce, de, P.-M.: *La République et son armée* (Arthème Fayard, 1963).

Lamb, Richard: *The Drift to War, 1922–1939* (W. H. Allen, 1989).

Lefranc, Georges: *Histoire du Front Populaire* (Payot, 1965; reprinted 1974).

Le Goyet, P.: *Le Mystère Gamelin* (Presses de la Cité, 1975).

Lentin, Anthony: *Guilt at Versailles. Lloyd George and the pre-history of Appeasement* (Leicester: Leicester University Press, 1984).

Lethève, Jacques: *La Caricature sous la IIIe République* (Armand Colin, 1986).

Leutze, James: *Bargaining for Supremacy: Anglo–American naval relations, 1937–1941* (Chapel Hill, NC: University of North Carolina Press, 1977).

Livian, Marcel: *Le Parti Socialiste et l'immigration: le gouvernement Blum, la main d'oeuvre immigré et les réfugiés politiques, 1920–1940* (Editions Anthropos, 1982).

Lloyd, Ian: *Rolls Royce: The Merlin at War* (Macmillan, 1978).

Lord, Walter: *The Miracle of Dunkirk* (New York: Viking Press, 1982).

Marchetti, Stephane: *Affiches, 1939–1945: Images d'une certaine France* (Lausanne: Edita, 1982).

Marcus, John T.: *French Socialism in the Crisis Years, 1933–1936. Fascism and the French Left* (New York and London: Stevens, 1958).

Marks, Sally: *Innocent Abroad. Belgium at the Paris Peace Conference of 1919* (Chapel Hill, NC: University of North Carolina Press, 1981).

Martel, Gordon (ed.): *The Origins of the Second World War reconsidered. The A. J. P. Taylor debate after twenty-five years* (Allen and Unwin, 1986).

Martin, Roger: *Idéologie et action syndicale. Les Instituteurs de l'entre-deux-guerres* (Lyon: Presses Universitaires de Lyon, 1982).

May, Ernest R. (ed.): *Knowing One's Enemies. Intelligence assessment before the two world wars* (Princeton University Press, 1984).

McInnes, Colin, and Sheffield, Gary D. (eds.): *Warfare in the Twentieth Century. Theory and practice* (Unwin Hyman, 1988).

McLaine, Ian: *Ministry of Morale. Home Front morale and the Ministry of Information in World War II* (Allen and Unwin, 1979).

MacNab, Roy: *For Honour Alone. The cadets of Saumur in the defence of the Cavalry School, France 1940* (Hale, 1988).
Mearsheimer, John J.: *Conventional Deterrence* (Ithaca, NY and London: Cornell University Press, 1983).
  Liddell Hart and the Weight of History (Ithaca, NY: Cornell University Press; and Oxford: Brassey's, 1988).
Michel, Henri: *Le Procès de Riom* (Albin Michel, 1979).
  La Défaite de la France. Septembre 1939–juin 1940 (Presses Universitaires de France, 1980).
Miller, Jane K.: *Belgian Foreign Policy between Two Wars, 1919–1940* (New York: Bookman Associates, 1951).
Mitchell, Allan: *The German Influence in France after 1870. The formation of the French Republic* (Chapel Hill, NC: University of North Carolina Press, 1979).
Mortimer, Edward: *The Rise of the French Communist Party, 1920–1947* (Faber and Faber, 1984).
Murray, Williamson: *The Change in the European Balance of Power, 1938–1939. The path to ruin* (Princeton, NJ: Princeton University Press, 1984).
  Luftwaffe: a history, 1933–1945 (Baltimore, MD: The Nautical and Aviation Publishing Company of America, 1985; Grafton, 1988).
Muselier, Vice-Admiral: *De Gaulle contre le Gaullisme* (Plon, 1946).
Mysyrowicz, Ladislas: *Autopsie d'une défaite. Origines de l'effondrement militaire français de 1940* (Lausanne: Editions l'Age d'Homme, 1973).
Naylor, John F.: *Labour's International Policy: the Labour Party in the 1930s* (Weidenfeld and Nicolson, 1969).
Néré, Jacques: *The Foreign Policy of France from 1914 to 1945* (Routledge and Kegan Paul, 1975).
Nevakivi, Jukka: *The Appeal that was Never Made. The Allies, Scandinavia and the Finnish Winter War, 1939–1940* (Christopher Hurst, 1976).
Nobécourt, Jacques: *Une histoire politique de l'armée*, I, *De Pétain à Pétain, 1919–1942* (Editions du Seuil, 1967).
Orde, Anne: *Great Britain and International Security, 1920–1926* (Royal Historical Society, 1978).
Osgood, Samuel M: *The Fall of France, 1940. Causes and responsibilities* (Boston: D. C. Heath and Company, 1965).
Overy, Richard, with Wheatcroft, Andrew: *The Road to War* (Macmillan for BBC Books, 1989).
Paillat, Claude: *Dossiers secrets de la France contemporaine* (Robert Laffont, 7 vols., 1979–86).
Paillole, Paul: *Notre espion chez Hitler* (Plon, 1985).
Parker, R. A. C.: *Struggle for Survival. The history of the second world war* (Oxford University Press, 1989).
Pike, David Wingeate: *Les Français et la guerre d'espagne, 1936–1939* (Presses Universitaires de France, 1975).
Pimlott, Ben: *Labour and the Left in the 1930s* (Cambridge University Press, 1977).
Posen, Barry R.: *The Sources of Military Doctrine. France, Britain and Germany between the world wars* (Ithaca, NY and London: Cornell University Press, 1984).

Postan, M. M., Denys Hay, J. D. Scott: *The Design and Development of Weapons: Studies in Government and Industrial Organisation* (HMSO and Longmans, Green and Co., 1964).
Prazmowska, Anita J.: *Britain, Poland and the Eastern Front, 1939* (Cambridge University Press, 1987).
Prost, Antoine: *Les Anciens Combattants et la société française (1914–1939)* (Presses de la Fondation Nationale des Sciences Politiques, 1977, 3 vols.).
Raïssac, Guy: *Un soldat dans la tourmente. Le général Weygand* (Editions Albin Michel, 1963).
Ralston, David B.: *The Army of the Republic. The place of the military in the political evolution of France, 1871–1914* (Cambridge, MA, Harvard University Press, 1967).
Read, Anthony and Fisher, David: *The Deadly Embrace. Hitler, Stalin and the Nazi–Soviet Pact, 1939–1941* (New York and London, W. W. Norton, 1988).
Reader, W. J.: *Architect of Air Power. The Life of the First Viscount Weir of Eastwood* (Collins, 1968).
ICI: A History, II, *The first quarter century, 1926–1952* (Oxford University Press, 1972).
Rémond, René: *Histoire de France*, VI, *Notre siècle, 1918–1988* (Arthème Fayard, 1988).
Pour une histoire politique (Editions du Seuil, 1988).
Rémy (pseud. of Renault-Roulier, Gilbert): *Le 18e jour. La Tragédie de Léopold III, Roi des belges* (France-Empire, 1976).
Chronique d'une guerre perdue (France-Empire, 1979–82, 5 vols.).
Reynolds, David: *The Creation of the Anglo-American Alliance, 1937–1941. A study in competitive cooperation* (Europa, 1981).
Rimbaud, Christiane: *L'Affaire du Massilia, été 1940* (Editions du Seuil, 1984).
Rimbaud, Christiane, en collaboration avec Pierre Béteille: *Le Procès de Riom* (Plon, 1973).
Robertson, Arthur Clendenin: *La Doctrine du général de Gaulle* (Arthème Fayard, 1959).
Robbins, Keith G.: *Appeasement* (Oxford: Basil Blackwell, 1988).
Rock, W. R.: *British Appeasement in the 1930s* (Edward Arnold, 1977).
Rossi-Landi, Guy: *La Drôle de Guerre. La Vie politique en France, 2 septembre 1939–10 mai 1940* (Pedone, 1971).
Rostow, Nicholas: *Anglo-French Relations, 1934–1936* (Macmillan, 1984).
Sauvy, Alfred: *Histoire économique de la France entre les deux guerres* (Arthème Fayard, 1965 et seq., 3 vols.).
La Vie économique des français de 1939 à 1945 (Ernest Flammarion, 1978).
Schuker, Stephen A.: *The End of French Predominance in Europe. The Ruhr occupation and the Dawes Plan, 1923–24* (Chapel Hill, NC: University of North Carolina Press, 1976).
Scott, William E.: *Alliance against Hitler. The Franco-Soviet Pact* (Durham, NC: Duke University Press, 1963).
Shirer, William L.: *The Collapse of the Third Republic. An inquiry into the Fall of France in 1940* (New York: Simon and Schuster, 1969).
Shorrock, William, I: *From Ally to Enemy. The enigma of Fascist Italy in French diplomacy, 1920–1940* (Kent, OH: Kent State University Press, 1988).

Singer, Barnett: *Village Notables in 19th Century France. Priests, mayors, schoolmasters* (Albany, NY: State University of New York Press, 1983).
Soutou, Georges-Henri: *L'Or et le sang. Les Buts de guerre économique de la première guerre mondiale* (Arthème Fayard, 1989).
Stein, Louis: *Beyond Death and Exile. The Spanish Republicans in France, 1939–1955* (Cambridge, MA: Harvard University Press, 1979).
Stengers, Jean: *Léopold III et le gouvernement. Aux origines de la question royale belge* (Paris and Gembloux: J. Duculot, 1980).
Tanenbaum, Jan Karl: *General Maurice Sarrail, 1856–1929. The French army and left-wing politics* (Chapel Hill, NC: The University of North Carolina Press, 1974).
Thomas, Daniel H.: *The Guarantee of Belgian Independence and Neutrality in European Diplomacy, 1830s–1930s* (Kingston, RI: D. H. Thomas Publishing, 1986).
Tint, Herbert: *France since 1918* (Batsford, 1970; reprinted 1980).
Van Creveld, Martin: *Supplying War. Logistics from Wallenstein to Patton* (Cambridge University Press, 1977).
   Technology and War, from 2000 BC to the Present (New York: Collier Macmillan, 1989).
   The Training of Officers. From military professionalism to irrelevance (New York and London: Collier Macmillan, 1990).
Vidalenc, Jean: *L'Exode de mai–juin 1940* (Presses Universitaires de France, 1957).
Waley, Daniel: *British Public Opinion and the Abyssinian War, 1935–6* (Maurice Temple Smith, 1975).
Wandycz, Piotr S.: *France and her Eastern Allies, 1919–1925. French-Czechoslovak-Polish relations from the Paris Peace Conference to Locarno* (Minneapolis, MN: University of Minnesota Press, 1962).
   The Twilight of French Eastern Alliances, 1926–1936. French-Czechoslovak-Polish relations from Locarno to the remilitarization of the Rhineland (Princeton, NJ: Princeton University Press, 1988).
Wark, Wesley K.: *The Ultimate Enemy. British Intelligence and Nazi Germany, 1933–1939* (Ithaca, NY: Cornell University Press, 1985).
Warner, Philip: *The Battle of France, 10 May–22 June 1940. Six weeks which changed the world* (New York: Simon and Schuster, 1990).
Watt, Donald Cameron: *Succeeding John Bull. America in Britain's place, 1900–1975* (Cambridge University Press, 1985).
   How War Came. The immediate origins of the Second World War, 1938–1939 (New York: Pantheon Books, 1989).
Weber, Frank G.: *The Evasive Neutral. Germany, Britain and the quest for a Turkish alliance in the Second World War* (Columbia MO and London: University of Missouri Press, 1979).
Weinberg, Gerhard L.: *The Foreign Policy of Hitler's Germany* (Chicago and London: University of Chicago Press, 1970, 1980, 2 vols.).
Williams, John: *The Ides of May. The Defeat of France, May–June 1940* (Constable, 1968).
Wohl, Robert: *French Communism in the Making, 1914–1924* (Stanford, CA: Stanford University Press, 1966).

Wolfers, Arnold: *Britain and France between Two Wars. Conflicting strategies of peace from Versailles to World War II* (New York, 1966).
Young, Robert J.: *In Command of France. French foreign policy and military planning, 1933–1939* (Cambridge MA: Harvard University Press, 1978).

G. Articles

Adamthwaite, Anthony P.: 'Le Facteur militaire dans la prise de décision franco-britannique avant Munich', in *Munich 1938: Revue des études slaves*, special edition, 52:1–2 (Paris, 1979), pp. 59–69.
'The British government and the media, 1937–1938', *JCH*, 18:2 (Apr. 1983), pp. 281–97.
Alexander, Don W.: 'Repercussions of the Breda Variant', *FHS*, 8:3 (Spring 1974), pp. 459–88.
Alexander, Martin S.: 'Les Réactions à la menace stratégique allemande en Europe occidentale. La Grande-Bretagne, la Belgique et le "cas Hollande", décembre 1938–février 1939', *Cahiers d'Histoire de la Second Guerre Mondiale*, 7 (Brussels, 1982), pp. 5–38.
'Force de Frappe ou feu de paille? Maurice Gamelin's appraisal of military aviation before the Blitzkrieg of 1940', in *Colloque International AIR 84. Adaptation de l'arme aérienne aux conflits contemporains et processus d'indépendance des armées de l'Air des origines à la fin de la Seconde Guerre mondiale* (Fondation pour les Etudes de Défense Nationale, 1985), pp. 65–80.
'Prophet without honour? The French High Command and Pierre Taittinger's report on the Ardennes defences, March 1940', *War and Society*, 4:1 (May 1986), pp. 53–77.
'The Fall of France, 1940', *JSS*, 13:1 (Mar. 1990), pp. 10–44; reprinted in Gooch, John (ed.): *Decisive Campaigns of the Second World War* (Frank Cass, 1990), pp. 10–44.
'Did the Deuxième Bureau work? The role of intelligence in French defence policy and strategy, 1919–39', *Intelligence and National Security*, 6:2 (Apr. 1991), pp. 293–333.
'In lieu of alliance. The French general staff's secret cooperation with neutral Belgium, 1936–1940', *JSS*, 14:4 (Dec. 1991), pp. 413–27.
'Safes and houses. William C. Bullitt, Embassy security and the shortcomings of the US Foreign Service in Europe before the Second World War', *Diplomacy and Statecraft*, 2:2 (July 1991), pp. 187–210.
'Maurice Gamelin and the defeat of France, 1939–1940', in Bond, Brian J. (ed.): *Fallen Stars. Eleven studies in twentieth century military disaster* (Oxford: Brassey's, 1991), pp. 107–40.
Alexander, Martin S. and Bond, Brian J.: 'Liddell Hart and de Gaulle. The doctrines of limited liability and mobile defense', in Paret, Peter (ed.), *Makers of Modern Strategy. From Machiavelli to the Nuclear Age* (Princeton NJ: Princeton University Press, 1986), pp. 597–623.
Allardyce, Gilbert D.: 'The political transition of Jacques Doriot, 1934–36', *JCH*, 1:1 (1966), pp. 56–74.
Amouroux, Henry: 'Il y a cinquante ans: Le Front Populaire', *Le Figaro-Magazine* (3 May 1986), pp. 21–8.

Ausems, André: 'The Netherlands Military Intelligence Summaries, 1939–1940, and the defeat in the Blitzkrieg of May 1940', *Military Affairs*, 50:4 (Oct. 1986), pp. 190–9.

Baker, Donald N.: 'The politics of Socialist protest in France. The left wing of the Socialist Party, 1921–39', *JMH*, 43:1 (Mar. 1971), pp. 10–41.

'Two paths to socialism: Marcel Déat and Marceau Pivert', *JCH*, 11:1 (Jan. 1976) pp. 107–28.

'The surveillance of subversion in interwar France: the Carnet B in the Seine, 1922–1940', *FHS*, 10:3 (Spring 1978), pp. 486–516.

'The Socialists and the workers of Paris: the Amicales Socialistes, 1936–1940', *International Review of Social History*, 24:3 (1974), pp. 1–33.

Bankwitz, Philip C. F.: 'Maxime Weygand and the Fall of France. A study in civil-military relations', *JMH*, 31:3 (Sept. 1959), pp. 225–42.

'Maxime Weygand and the army-nation concept in the modern French army', *FHS*, 2:2 (Fall 1961), pp. 157–88.

'Paris on the Sixth of February 1934. Riot, insurrection or revolution?', in Gooch, Brison D. (ed.), *Interpreting History* (Homewood, IL: Dorsey Press, 1967), pp. 337–68.

Batowski, Henryk: 'General Wladislaw Sikorski's foreign policy, 1939–1943', *Polish Western Affairs*, 23:1 (1982), pp. 66–82.

Beaufre, Gen. André: 'Liddell Hart and the French army, 1919–1939', in Howard, Michael E. (ed.), *The Theory and Practice of War. Essays in Honour of B. H. Liddell Hart* (Cassell, 1965).

Becker, Jean-Jacques: 'La Parti Communiste a-t-il contribué à la défaite?', *L'Evénement du jeudi*, 247 (27 July–2 Aug. 1989), pp. 50–2.

Bédarida, François: 'L'Armée et la République: les opinions politiques des officiers français en 1876–78', *Revue Historique*, 232 (1964), pp. 119–64.

'La Rupture franco-britannique de 1940. Le Conseil Suprême interallié, de l'invasion à la défaite de la France', *Vingtième siècle*, no. 25 (Jan.–Mar. 1990), pp. 37–48.

Bell, Philip M. H.: 'Prologue de Mers-el-Kébir', *RHDGM*, 9:33 (Jan. 1959), pp. 15–36.

'Shooting the rapids. British reactions to the Fall of France, 1940', *Modern and Contemporary France. Review of the Association for the Study of Modern and Contemporary France*, 42 (July 1990), pp. 16–28.

Beloff, Max: 'The Sixth of February', in Joll, James (ed.), *The Decline of the Third Republic* (Macmillan/St Antony's Papers no. 5, 1959), pp. 8–35.

Berstein, Serge and Jeanneney, Jean-Noël: 'Les Raisons de l'échec du Cartel des Gauches (1924)', *Bulletin de la Société d'Histoire Moderne*, 23:2 (Apr.–June, 1978), pp. 2–15.

Berstein, Serge: 'Il y a cinquante ans: la chute du premier gouvernement de Front Populaire', *Le Monde* (21–22 June 1987), p. 2.

Bialer, Uri: '"Humanization" of air warfare in British foreign policy on the eve of the Second World War', *JCH*, 13:1 (Jan. 1978), pp. 79–96.

'Elite opinion and defence policy: air power advocacy and British rearmament during the 1930s', *British Journal of International Studies*, 6 (Apr. 1980), pp. 32–51.

Binion, Rudolph: 'Repeat performance. A psychohistorical study of Leopold III and Belgian neutrality', *History and Theory. Studies in the Philosophy of History*, VIII (1969), pp. 213–59.

Birn, Donald S.: 'The League of Nations Union and collective security', *JCH*, 9:3 (July 1974), pp. 131–59.

Blatt, Joel: 'The parity that meant superiority: French naval policy towards Italy at the Washington Conference, 1921–1922, and interwar French foreign policy', *FHS*, 12:2 (Fall 1981), pp. 223–48.

Bloch, Charles: 'Great Britain, German rearmament and the Naval Agreement of 1935', in Gatzke, Hans W. (ed.), *European Diplomacy between Two Wars, 1919–1939* (Chicago: Quadrangle Books, 1972), pp. 125–51.

Bodinier, Capt. Gilbert: 'Gamelin, les fortifications et les chars, à travers les rapports de l'EMA, 1935–1939', *RHA*, 4 (1979), pp. 125–44.

Bonnemaison, Jacques: 'La Décision militaire', *Pouvoirs. Revue française d'études constitutionnelles et politiques*, no. 38, *L'Armée* (Sept. 1986), pp. 81–6.

Boudot, François: 'Sur les problèmes du financement de la défense nationale, 1936–1940', *RHDGM*, 21:81 (Jan. 1971), pp. 49–72.

Braddick, Henderson B.: 'The Hoare–Laval Plan: a study in international politics', in Gatzke, Hans. W. (ed.): *European Diplomacy between Two Wars, 1919–1939* (Chicago: Quadrangle Books, 1972), pp. 152–71.

Brausch, Gerd: 'Sedan 1940. Deuxième Bureau und strategische Uberraschung', *Militärgeschichtliche Mitteilungen*, 2 (1967), pp. 15–92.

Buffotot, Patrice: 'Le Projet de bombardement de pétroles soviétiques du Caucase en 1940: un exemple des projets alliés dans la drôle de guerre', *RHA*, 4 (1979), pp. 79–101.

'The French High Command and the Franco-Soviet Alliance, 1933–1939', *JSS*, 5:4 (Dec. 1982), pp. 546–59.

'L'Arme nucléaire et la modernisation de l'armée française', *Pouvoirs. Revue française d'études constitutionnelles et politiques*, no. 38, *L'Armée* (Sept. 1986), pp. 33–46.

Burdick, Charles B.: 'The American military attachés in the Spanish Civil War, 1936–1939', *Militärgeschichtliche Mitteilungen*, 45:2 (1989), pp. 61–77.

Butterworth, Susan Bindoff: 'Daladier and the Munich Crisis: a reappraisal', *JCH*, 9:3 (July 1974), pp. 191–216.

Cairns, John C.: 'International politics and the military mind: the case of the French Republic, 1911–1914', *JMH*, 25:3 (Sept. 1953), pp. 272–85.

'Along the road back to France, 1940', *AHR*, 64:3 (Apr. 1959), pp. 583–603.

'March 7, 1936, again: the view from Paris', *International Journal*, 20 (Spring 1965), pp. 230–46 (reprinted in Gatzke, Hans W. (ed.), *European Diplomacy between Two Wars, 1919–1939* (Chicago: Quadrangle Books, 1972), pp. 172–92).

'A nation of shopkeepers in search of a suitable France, 1919–40', *AHR*, 79:3 (June, 1974), pp. 710–43.

'Great Britain and the Fall of France: a study in allied disunity', *JMH*, 27:4 (Dec. 1955), pp. 365–409.

'Some recent historians and the "Strange Defeat" of 1940', *JMH*, 46:1 (Mar. 1974), pp. 60–85.

Calmy, Christophe: 'C'est la faute aux pacifistes', *L'Evénement du jeudi*, 247 (27 July–2 Aug. 1989), pp. 64–5.
Cameron, Elizabeth R.: 'Alexis Saint-Léger Léger', in Craig, Gordon A. and Gilbert, Felix (eds.), *The Diplomats* (Princeton, NJ: Princeton University Press, 1953), pp. 378–405.
Carlton, David: 'Eden, Blum and the origins of non-intervention', *JCH*, 6:3 (1971), pp. 40–55.
Challener, Richard D.: 'The military defeat of 1940 in retrospect', in Earle, Edward Mead (ed.), *Modern France. Problems of the Third and Fourth Republics* (Princeton NJ: Princeton University Press, 1951), pp. 405–20.
  'The Third Republic and the generals: the gravediggers revisited', in Coles, Harry C. (ed.), *Total War and Cold War. Problems in civilian control of the military* (Columbus, OH: Ohio State University Press, 1962), pp. 91–107.
Chapman, Guy: 'The French Army and politics', in Howard, Michael E. (ed.), *Soldiers and Governments. Nine studies in civil-military relations* (Eyre and Spottiswoode, 1957), pp. 53–72.
Christienne, Gen. Charles: 'L'Industrie aéronautique française de septembre 1939 à juin 1940', in *Service Historique de L'Armée de L'Air. Recueil d'articles et études, 1974–1975* (Vincennes: Publications du Service Historique de L'Armée de L'Air, 1977), pp. 227–38. Reprinted in *Français et Brittaniques dans la drôle de guerre* (Editions du CNRS, 1979), pp. 389–410.
  'La RAF dans la bataille de France au travers des rapports Vuillemin de juillet 1940', in *Service Historique de L'Armée de L'Air. Recueil d'articles et études (1981–1983)* (Vincennes: Publications du Service Historique de L'Armée de L'Air, 1987), pp. 313–33.
Clague, Monique: 'Vision and myopia in the new politics of André Tardieu', *FHS*, 8:1 (Spring 1973), pp. 104–29.
Clarke, Jeffery Johnstone: 'The nationalisation of war industries in France, 1936–37: a case study', *JMH*, 49:3 (Sept. 1977), pp. 411–30.
Cliadakis, Harry: 'Neutrality and war in Italian policy, 1939–40', *JCH*, 9:3 (July 1974), pp. 171–90.
Cockett, R. B.: 'Ball, Chamberlain and *Truth*', *HJ*, 33:1 (Mar. 1990), pp. 131–42.
Cohen, William B.: 'The colonial policy of the Popular Front', *FHS*, 8:3 (Spring 1972), pp. 368–93.
Cointet, Jean-Paul: 'Le Soldat et la politique: gouvernement et haut-commandement en France entre les deux guerres', *Bulletin de la Société d'Histoire Moderne*, 24:3 (July–Sept. 1978), pp. 8–23.
Colton, Joel: 'Politics and economics in the 1930s. The Balance sheets of the "Blum New Deal"', in Warner, Charles K. (ed.), *From the Ancien Régime to the Popular Front. Essays in honor of Shepard B. Clough* (New York: Columbia University Press, 1968), pp. 181–208.
Cornick, Martyn: 'The Fall of France, 1940. Bibliographical essay', *Modern and Contemporary France. Review of the Association for the Study of Modern and Contemporary France*, 42 (July 1990), pp. 37–44.
de Cossé-Brissac, Gen. Charles: 'L'Armée allemande dans la campagne de France de 1940', *RHDGM*, 14:53 (Jan. 1964).
  'Combien de chars français contre combien de chars allemands le 10 mai 1940?', *Revue de Défense Nationale*, 5 (July 1947), pp. 75–91.

'Combien d'avions allemands contre combien d'avions français le 10 mai 1940?' *Revue de Défense Nationale*, 4 (June 1948), pp. 741–59.

Coutrot, Aline: 'Youth movements in France in the 1930s', *JCH*, 5:1 (Jan. 1970), pp. 23–36.

Coutouvidis, J.: 'Government in exile. The transfer of Polish authority abroad, September 1939', *Review of International Studies*, 10:1 (Oct. 1984), pp. 285–96.

Coverdale, John F.: 'The Battle of Guadalajara, 8–22 March 1937', *JCH*, 9:1 (Jan. 1974), pp. 53–75.

Cross, Gary S.: 'Toward social peace and prosperity: the politics of immigration in France during the era of World War I', *FHS*, 11:4 (Fall 1980), pp. 610–32.

Crouzet, François: 'Recherches sur la production d'armements en France (1815–1913)', *Revue Historique*, 251 (1974), pp. 45–84.

Deist, Wilhelm: 'Die Deutsche Aufrüstung in Amerikanischer sicht: Berichte des US-militärattachés in Berlin aus den Jahren 1933–1939', *Frankfurter Historische Abhandlungen*, 17 (1978), pp. 279–95.

Delarue, Jacques: 'La Travail de sape de la cinquième colonne', *L'Evénement du jeudi*, 247 (27 July–2 Aug. 1989), pp. 61–3.

Delmas, Gen. Jean: 'Les Exercices du Conseil Supérieur de la Guerre: 1936–37 et 1937–38', *RHA*, 4 (1979), pp. 29–57.

Dilks, David: 'The Twilight War and the Fall of France: Chamberlain and Churchill in 1940', *Transactions of the Royal Historical Society*, 5th ser., 28 (1978), pp. 61–86.

Dobry, Michel: 'Le Jeu du consensus', *Pouvoirs. Revue française d'études constitutionnelles et politiques*, no. 38, *L'Armée* (Sept. 1986), pp. 47–66.

Dogan, Mattei: 'Militaires sans épée dans la politique', *Pouvoirs*, no. 38, *L'Armée*, pp. 113–25.

Douglas, Allen: 'Violence and fascism. The case of the Faisceau', *JCH*, 19:4 (Oct. 1984), pp. 689–712.

Douglas, Roy: 'Chamberlain and Eden, 1937–38', *JCH*, 13:1 (Jan. 1978), pp. 97–116.

Doughty, Col. Robert A.: 'De Gaulle's concept of a mobile, professional army: genesis of French defeat?', in Matthews, Lloyd J. and Brown, Dale E. (eds.): *The Parameters of War. Military History from the Journal of the U.S. Army War College* (McLean, VA and Oxford: Pergamon-Brassey's, 1987), pp. 243–56.

'The French Armed Forces, 1918–40', in Millett, Allan R. and Murray, Williamson (eds.), *Military Effectiveness*, II, *The inter-war years* (Boston: Allen and Unwin, 1988), pp. 39–69.

Duroselle, Jean-Baptiste: 'Les Incertitudes de notre politique militaire: La France et la crise de mars 1936', annex in Bonnefous, Georges, and Bonnefous, Edouard, *Histoire politique de la IIIe République*, VI, *vers la guerre. Du Front Populaire à la conférence de Munich, 1936–1938* (Presses Universitaires de France, 1965), pp. 387–92.

'France and the Crisis of March 1936', in Acomb, Evelyn M. and Brown, Marvin C. (eds.), *French Society and Culture since the Old Regime* (New York: Holt, Rinehart and Winston, 1966), pp. 244–67.

'Les Généraux se sont trompés de guerre', *L'Evénement du jeudi*, 247 (27 July–2 Aug. 1989), pp. 48–9.
Dutter, Gordon: 'Doing business with the fascists. French economic relations with Italy under the Popular Front', *French History*, 4:2 (June 1990), pp. 174–98.
Eichholtz, Dietrich: 'La Grande Industrie allemande et l'armement de 1933 à 1939', *Cahiers d'Histoire de l'Institut Maurice Thorez*, 24 (1978), pp. 90–122.
Englander, David: 'The French soldier, 1914–18', *French History*, 1:1 (Mar. 1987), pp. 49–67.
Facon, Patrick: 'Le Plan V (1938–1939)', *RHA*, 4 (1979), pp. 102–23.
  'Le Haut Commandement aérien français et la crise de Munich (1938)', in *Service Historique de l'Armée de l'Air. Recueil d'articles et études (1981–1983)* (Vincennes: Publications du Service Historique de l'Armée de l'Air, 1987), pp. 169–95.
  'L'Aviation populaire: entre les mythes et la réalité', in *Service historique de l'armée de l'air. Recueil . . . (1981–1983)*, pp. 197–219.
  'La Visite du général Vuillemin en Allemagne (16–21 août 1938)', in *Service historique de l'armée de l'air. Recueil . . . (1981–1983)*, pp. 221–62.
Fair, John D.: 'The Norwegian Campaign and Winston Churchill's rise to power in 1940: a study of perception and attribution', *IHR*, 9:3 (Aug. 1987), pp. 411–37.
Farrar, Marjorie M.: 'Politics versus patriotism: Alexandre Millerand as French Minister of War', *FHS*, 11:4 (Fall 1980), pp. 577–609.
Ferris, John R.: 'Treasury control, the ten year rule and British Service policies, 1919–1924', *HJ*, 30:4 (Dec. 1987), pp. 859–83.
Frank[enstein], Robert: 'A propos des aspects financiers du réarmement français, 1935–39', *RHDGM*, 26:102 (Apr. 1976), pp. 1–20.
  'Réarmement français, finances publiques et conjoncture internationale, 1935–39', *Bulletin de la Société d'Histoire Moderne*, 9:1 (Jan.–Mar. 1981), pp. 7–18.
  'Le Front Populaire a-t-il perdu la guerre?', *L'Histoire*, 58 (July–Aug. 1983), pp. 58–66.
  'La Gauche sait-elle gérer la France? (1936–1937/1981–1984)', *Vingtième Siècle: revue d'histoire*, 6 (Apr.–June 1985), pp. 3–21.
  'Est-ce le Front Populaire qui a perdu la guerre?', *L'Evénement du jeudi*, 247 (27 July–2 Aug. 1989), pp. 52–4.
Fridenson, Patrick: 'Le Patronat français', in Bourdin, Janine, and Rémond, René (eds.), *La France et les français en 1938–1939* (Presses de la Fondation Nationale des Sciences Politiques, 1978), pp. 139–57.
Gallagher, M. D.: 'Léon Blum and the Spanish Civil War', *JCH*, 6:3 (1971), pp. 56–65.
Gasiorowski, Zygmunt J.: 'Did Pilsudski attempt to initiate a preventive war in 1933?', *JMH*, 27:2 (June 1955), pp. 135–52.
Gatzke, Hans W.: 'Russo-German military collaboration during the Weimar Republic', *AHR*, 63:3 (Apr. 1958), pp. 565–97 (reprinted in Gatzke (ed.), *European Diplomacy between Two Wars, 1919–1939* [Chicago: Quadrangle Books, 1972], pp. 40–72).

Gibbs, N. H.: 'British strategic doctrine, 1919–1939', in Howard, Michael E. (ed.), *The Theory and Practice of War. Essays in honour of B. H. Liddell Hart* (Cassell, 1965), pp. 196–209.

Gibson, Irving M. (pseud. of Kovacs, Arpad V.): 'The Maginot Line', *JMH*, 17:2 (June 1945), pp. 130–46.

'Maginot and Liddell Hart: the doctrine of defense', in Earle, Edward Mead, *Makers of Modern Strategy. Military thought from Machiavelli to Hitler* (Princeton NJ: Princeton University Press, 1943; paperback reprint 1971), pp. 365–87 (1971 edn).

Ginsburg, Shaul, 'Du Wilsonisme au Communisme: l'itinéraire du pacifiste Raymond Lefèbvre en 1919', *RHMC*, 23 (Oct.–Dec., 1976), pp. 583–605.

Gunsburg, Jeffery A.: 'Coupable ou non? Le Rôle du général Gamelin dans la défaite de 1940', *RHA*, 4 (1979), pp. 145–63.

'L'Armée de l'air versus the Luftwaffe, 1940', *Defence Update International*, 45 (1984), pp. 44–53.

Haglund, David G.: 'George C. Marshall and the question of military aid to England, May–June 1940', *JCH*, 14:4 (Oct. 1980), pp. 745–60.

Haight, John McVickar, Jr: 'France, the United States and the Munich Crisis', *JMH*, 32:4 (Dec. 1960), pp. 340–58.

'Jean Monnet and the American arsenal after the beginning of the war', in Acomb, Evelyn M. and Brown, Marvin L. (eds.), *French Society and Culture since the Old Regime* (New York: Holt, Rinehart and Winston, 1966), pp. 269–83.

Hansen, Erik: 'Depression decade crisis: Social Democracy and Planisme in Belgium and the Netherlands, 1929–1939', *JCH*, 16:2 (Apr. 1981), pp. 293–322.

Harris, J. P.: 'The British General Staff and the coming of war, 1933–9', *Bulletin of the Institute of Historical Research*, 59:140 (Nov. 1986), pp. 196–211.

'Two war ministers: a reassessment of Duff Cooper and Hore-Belisha', *War and Society*, 6:1 (May 1988), pp. 65–78.

'British military intelligence and the rise of German mechanized forces, 1929–40', *Intelligence and National Security*, 6:2 (Apr. 1991), pp. 395–417.

Hauner, Milan: 'Did Hitler want a world dominion?', *JCH*, 13:1 (Jan. 1978), pp. 15–31.

'Czechoslovakia as a military factor in British considerations of 1938', *JSS*, 1:2 (Sept. 1978), pp. 194–222.

Helmreich, Jonathan E.: 'The negotiation of the Franco-Belgian military accord of 1920', *FHS*, 3:3 (Spring 1964), pp. 360–78.

Hillgruber, Andreas: 'England's place in Hitler's plans for world dominion', *JCH*, 9:1 (Jan. 1974), pp. 5–22.

Hood, Ronald Chalmers III: 'The French Navy and parliament between the wars', *IHR*, 6:3 (Aug. 1984), pp. 386–403.

'Bitter victory: French military effectiveness during the Second World War', in Millett, Allan R. and Murray, Williamson (eds.), *Military Effectiveness*, III, *The Second World War* (Boston: Allen and Unwin, 1988), pp. 221–55.

Irvine, William D.: 'French conservatives and the "New Right" during the 1930s', *FHS*, 8:4 (Fall 1974), pp. 534–62.

Jacobson, Jon: 'Is there a new international history of the 1920s?', *AHR*, 88:3 (June 1983), pp. 617–45.
Jauffret, Jean-Charles: 'Etudes sur l'armée française de 1870 à 1914', *Revue Historique*, 269 (1983), pp. 399–407.
  'Armée et pouvoir politique. La Question des troupes spéciales chargées du maintien de l'ordre en France de 1871 à 1914', *Revue Historique*, 270 (1984), pp. 97–144.
Johnson, Douglas W. J.: 'Léon Blum and the Popular Front', *History*, 55:180 (June 1970), pp. 199–206.
  'Britain and France in 1940', *Transactions of the Royal Historical Society*, 5th ser., 22 (1972), pp. 141–57.
Joll, James: 'The making of the Popular Front', in J. Joll (ed.), *The Decline of the Third Republic* (St Antony's Papers, no. 5, 1959), pp. 37–66.
  'The Front Populaire after thirty years', *JCH*, 1:2 (1966), pp. 27–42.
Judt, Tony: 'The French Socialists and the Cartel des Gauches of 1924', *JCH*, 11:2–3 (July 1976), pp. 199–216.
  'Une historiographie pas comme les autres: the French communists and their history', *European Studies Review*, 12:4 (Oct. 1982), pp. 445–78.
Kaspi, André: 'Les Américains et les Anglais nous ont-ils lâchés?', *L'Evénement du jeudi*, no. 247 (27 July–2 Aug. 1989), pp. 58–60.
Kaufmann, William W.: 'Two American ambassadors: Bullitt and Kennedy', in Craig, Gordon A. and Gilbert, Felix (eds.), *The Diplomats, 1919–1939* (Princeton, NJ: Princeton University Press, 1953), pp. 649–81.
Kelly, Michael: 'Aragon and the spirit of the Popular Front', *Quinquérème. New studies in modern languages*, 11:1 (Jan. 1988), pp. 3–13.
Kennedy, Paul M.: 'Strategy versus finance in twentieth-century Great Britain', *IHR*, 3:1 (Jan. 1981), pp. 44–61.
Kovacs, Arpad V.: see Gibson, Irving M.
Kriegel, Annie: 'The French Communist Party and the problem of power, 1920–1939', in Cairns, John C. (ed.), *Contemporary France. Illusion, conflict and regeneration* (New York, Franklin Watts, 1978), pp. 92–109.
Krumeich, Gerd: 'A propos de la politique d'armement de la France avant la première guerre mondiale', *RHMC*, 29 (Oct.–Dec. 1982), pp. 662–72.
Kupferman, Fred: 'De Léon Blum à François Mitterand. La Gauche, la crise et la vérité', *L'Express (Edition Internationale)*, no. 1629 (1 Oct. 1982), pp. 78–86.
Levey, Jules: 'Georges Valois and the Faisceau. The making and breaking of a fascist', *FHS*, 8:2 (Fall 1973), pp. 279–304.
Lowenthal, Mark M.: 'Roosevelt and the coming of the war: The search for United States policy 1937–42', *JCH*, 16:4 (Oct. 1981), pp. 413–40.
Lukacs, John: 'The Coming of the Second World War', *Foreign Affairs*, 68:4 (Fall 1989), pp. 165–72.
Lukowitz, David C.: 'British pacifists and appeasement: the Peace Pledge Union', *JCH*, 9:1 (Jan. 1974), pp. 115–27.
Manne, Robert: 'The British decision for alliance with Russia, May 1939', *JCH*, 9:3 (July 1974), pp. 3–26.
Marès, Antoine: 'La Faillite des relations franco-tchécoslovaques: la mission militaire française à Prague (1926–1939)', *RHDGM*, 28:3 (July 1978), pp. 45–71.

'Mission militaire et relations internationales: l'exemple franco-tchécoslovaque, 1918–1925', *RHMC*, 30 (Oct.–Dec. 1982), pp. 559–86.
Marks, Sally: '*Ménage à trois*. The negotiations for an Anglo-Franco-Belgian Alliance in 1922', *IHR*, 4:4 (Nov. 1982), pp. 524–53.
'Black Watch on the Rhine: a study in propaganda, prejudice and prurience', *European Studies Review*, 13:3 (July 1983), pp. 297–334.
Marquis, Alice Goldfarb: 'Written on the wind: the impact of radio during the 1930s', *JCH*, 19:3 (July 1984), pp. 385–415.
Marseille, Jacques: 'L'Investissement français dans l'empire colonial: l'enquête de Vichy (1943)', *Revue Historique*, 251 (1974), pp. 409–32.
Marshall-Cornwall, Gen. Sir James: 'The tragedy of Leopold III', *History Today*, 30 (Feb. 1980), pp. 28–33.
Millet, Jérôme: 'Un exemple de lutte pour la supériorité aérienne: la bataille de France', in *Histoire de la guerre aérienne. Hommage au capitaine Georges Guynemer à l'occasion du 70e anniversaire de sa disparition. Paris: 10–11 septembre 1987* (Vincennes: Publications du Service Historique de l'Armée de L'Air, 1988), pp. 93–113.
Mitchell, Allan: 'Thiers, Macmahon and the Conseil Supérieur de la Guerre', *FHS*, 6:2 (Fall 1969), pp. 232–52.
'The xenophobic style: French counterespionage and the emergence of the Dreyfus Affair', *JMH*, 52:3 (Sept. 1980), pp. 414–25.
'"A situation of inferiority": French military reorganisation after the defeat of 1870', *AHR*, 86:1 (Feb. 1981), pp. 49–62.
'The Freycinet reforms and the French Army, 1888–1893', *JSS*, 4:1 (Mar. 1981), pp. 19–28.
Mouré, Kenneth: '"Une éventualité absolument exclue": French reluctance to devalue, 1933–1936', *FHS*, 15:3 (Spring 1988), pp. 479–505.
Müller, Klaus-Jürgen: 'Protest-Modernisierung-Integration. Bemerkungen zum Problem Faschistischer Phänomene in Frankreich, 1924–1934', *Francia. Forschungen zur westeuropäischen Geschichte*, 8 (Munich and Zurich: Artemis Verlag, 1981), pp. 465–523.
'L'Armée allemande n'était pas invincible', *L'Evénement du jeudi*, 247 (27 July–2 Aug. 1989), pp. 46–8.
Müller, Michael: 'Frankreich und die Rheinlandbesetzung 1936. Die Reaktion von Diplomaten, Politikern und Militärs' *Geschichte im Westen*, 1:1 (1986), pp. 15–30.
Munholland, J. Kim: 'The Daladier government and the "Red Scare" of 1938–1940', in Sweets, John F. (ed.), *Proceedings of the Tenth Annual Meeting of the Western Society for French History*, 14–16 Oct. 1982 (Lawrence, KA: The Regents' Press of the University of Kansas, 1984), pp. 495–506.
Murray, W. J.: 'The French Workers' sports movement and the victory of the Popular Front in 1936', *The International Journal of the History of Sport*, 4:2 (Sept. 1987), pp. 203–30.
Murray, Williamson: 'Munich 1938: the military confrontation', *JSS*, 2:3 (Dec. 1979), pp. 282–302.
'The German response to victory in Poland: a case study in professionalism', *Armed Forces and Society*, 7:2 (Winter 1981), pp. 285–98.

'Appeasement and intelligence', *Intelligence and National Security*, 2:4 (Oct. 1987), pp. 47–64.

Neville, Peter: 'Why France fell. 50 years on', *Modern History Review*, 2:1 (Sept. 1990), pp. 20–1.

Noël, Léon: 'Souvenirs de la Conférence de la Haye, 5–30 août 1929', *Revue d'Histoire diplomatique*, 97 (1983), pp. 231–55.

Nouschi, Marc: 'La Marine française au début de la guerre d'Espagne', *Bulletin de la Société d'Histoire Moderne*, 25:4 (Oct.–Dec. 1978), pp. 15–36.

Overy, Richard J.: 'The German pre-war aircraft production plans, November 1936–April 1939', *EHR*, 90:357 (Oct. 1975), pp. 778–97.

'From "Uralbomber" to "Amerika bomber": the Luftwaffe and strategic bombing', *JSS*, 1:2 (Apr. 1978), pp. 154–78.

'Mobilisation for total war in Germany, 1939–1941', *EHR*, vol. 103:408 (July 1988), pp. 613–39.

'Did Hitler want total war?', *History Sixth*, 4 (May 1989), pp. 26–30.

Parker, R. A. C.: 'The first capitulation: France and the Rhineland Crisis of 1936', *World Politics*, 8:3 (1956), pp. 355–73.

'The British government and the coming of war with Germany, 1939', in Foot, M. R. D. (ed.), *War and Society. Historical essays in honour and memory of J. R. Western, 1928–1971* (Paul Elek, 1973), pp. 1–15.

'Great Britain, France and the Ethiopian crisis, 1935–1936', *EHR*, 89:351 (Apr. 1974), pp. 293–332.

'Economics, rearmament and foreign policy: the United Kingdom before 1939 – a preliminary study', *JCH*, 10:4 (Oct. 1975), pp. 637–47.

'Britain, France and Scandinavia, 1939–40', *History*, 61:20 (Oct. 1976), pp. 369–87.

'British rearmament, 1936–9: treasury, trade unions and skilled labour', *EHR* 96:379 (Apr. 1981), pp. 306–43.

'The pound sterling, the American Treasury and British preparations for war, 1938–1939', *EHR*, 98:387 (Apr. 1983), pp. 261–79.

Peden, George C.: 'Sir Warren Fisher and British rearmament against Germany', *EHR*, 94:370 (Jan. 1979), pp. 29–47.

'The burden of imperial defence and the continental commitment reconsidered', *HJ*, 27:2 (June 1984), pp. 405–23.

'A matter of timing. The economic background to British Foreign Policy, 1937–1939', *History*, 67:220 (Feb. 1984), pp. 15–28.

'Arms, government and businessmen, 1935–1945', in Turner, John (ed.), *Businessmen and Politics. Studies of business activity in British politics, 1900–1945* (Heinemann, 1984), pp. 130–45.

Philpott, William J.: 'The strategic ideas of Sir John French', *JSS*, 12:4 (Dec. 1989), pp. 458–78.

Pile, Gen. Sir Frederick: 'Liddell Hart and the British Army, 1919–1939', in Howard, Michael E. (ed.), *The Theory and Practice of War. Essays in honour of B. H. Liddell Hart* (Cassell, 1965), pp. 170–82.

Planchais, Jean: 'Il y a vingt ans: La Mort de Weygand, soldat conservateur', *Le Monde*, 27–8 Jan. 1985, p. 2.

'L'Armée et le tournant de 1958', *Pouvoirs. Revue française d'études constitutionnelles et politiques*, no. 38, *L'Armée* (Sept. 1986), pp. 5–12.

Ploquin, Jacques: 'Alliances militaires et marchés d'avions pendant l'entre-deux-guerres: le cas français (1936–1940)', in *Service Historique de l'armée de l'air. Recueil d'articles et études (1981–1983)* (Vincennes: Publications du Service Historique de L'Armée de L'Air, 1987), pp. 3–88.

Prazmowska, Anita J.: 'War over Danzig? The dilemma of Anglo-Polish relations in the months preceding the outbreak of the Second World War', *HJ*, 26:1 (Mar. 1983), pp. 177–83.

'Poland's foreign policy: September 1938–September 1939', *HJ*, 29:4 (Dec. 1986), pp. 853–73.

Pronay, Nicholas, and Taylor, Philip M.: '"An improper use of broadcasting ..." The British Government and clandestine Radio Propaganda Operations against Germany during the Munich Crisis and after', *JCH*, 19:3 (July 1984), pp. 357–84.

Pugh, Anthony Cheal: 'Defeat, May 1940: Claude Simon, Marc Bloch and the writing of disaster', in Higgins, Ian (ed.), *The Second World War in Literature. Eight essays* (Edinburgh and London: Scottish Academic Press, 1989), pp. 59–70.

Pugh, Michael C.: 'An international police force: Lord Davies and the British debate in the 1930s', *International Relations*, 9:4 (Nov. 1988), pp. 335–51.

Rader, R. R.: 'Anglo-French estimates of the Red Army, 1936–1937', *Soviet Armed Forces Review Annual*, 3 (1981), pp. 265–80.

du Réau, Elizabeth: 'L'Information du "décideur" et l'élaboration de la décision diplomatique française dans les dernières années de la IIIe République', *Relations internationales*, 32 (Winter 1982), pp. 525–41.

'Enjeux stratégiques et redéploiement diplomatique français: novembre 1938, septembre 1939', *Relations internationales*, 35 (Autumn 1983), pp. 319–35.

Reussner, André: 'La Réorganisation du Haut-Commandement au mois de mai 1940', *RHDGM*, 3:10–11 (June 1953), pp. 49–59.

Reynolds, David: 'Churchill and the British decision to fight on in 1940. Right policy, wrong reasons', in Langhorne, Richard T. B. (ed.), *Diplomacy and Intelligence during the Second World War. Essays in honour of F. H. Hinsley* (Cambridge University Press, 1985), pp. 150–77.

'Eden the diplomatist, 1931–56', *History*, 74:240 (Feb. 1989), pp. 64–84.

'1940. Fulcrum of the twentieth century', *International Affairs*, 66:2 (Apr. 1990), pp. 325–50.

Richardson, Charles O.: 'French plans for Allied attacks on the Caucasus oil fields, January–April 1940', *FHS*, 8:1 (Spring 1973), pp. 130–56.

Rioux, Jean-Pierre: 'La Médiocrité de nos chefs militaires', *L'Evénement du jeudi*, 247 (27 July–2 Aug. 1989), pp. 44–5.

Robertson, Esmonde M.: 'Hitler and sanctions: Mussolini and the Rhineland', *European Studies Review*, 7:4 (Oct. 1977), pp. 409–35.

Rollot, Gen.: 'Les Rapports franco-belges au moment de l'offensive allemande de Sedan, le 10 mai 1940', *RHDGM*, 10:38 (Apr. 1960), pp. 1–14.

Rose, Norman: 'The resignation of Anthony Eden', *HJ*, 25:4 (Dec. 1982), pp. 911–31.

Rousso, Henry: 'Comment la IIIe République s'est suicidée', *L'Evénement du jeudi*, 247 (27 July–2 Aug. 1989), pp. 55–7.

Rutkoff, Peter M.: 'The Ligue des Patriotes: the nature of the Radical right and the Dreyfus Affair', *FHS*, 8:4 (Fall 1974), pp. 585–603.

Schor, Ralph: 'Xénophobie et extrême-droite. L'Exemple de "l'Ami du Peuple" (1928–1937)', *RHMC*, 23 (Jan.–Mar. 1976), pp. 116–44.

Schuker, Stephen A.: 'France and the remilitarization of the Rhineland, 1936', *FHS*, 14:3 (Spring 1986), pp. 299–338.

Shennan, A. W. H.: 'The parliamentary opposition to the Front Populaire and the elections of 1936', *HJ*, 27:3 (Sept. 1984), pp. 677–95.

Shlaim, Avi: 'Prelude to downfall: the British offer of union to France, June 1940', *JCH*, 9:3 (July 1974), pp. 27–63.

Shorrock, William I.: 'France, Italy, and the Eastern Mediterranean in the 1920s', *IHR*, 8:1 (Feb. 1986), pp. 70–82.

Simard, Marc: 'Doumergue et la réforme de l'état en 1934: la dernière chance de la IIIe République?', *FHS*, 16:3 (Spring 1990), pp. 576–96.

Singer, Barnett: 'From patriots to pacifists: the French primary school teachers, 1880–1940', *JCH*, 12:3 (July 1977), pp. 413–34.

Smith, Malcolm S.: 'The RAF, air power and British foreign policy, 1932–1937', *JCH*, 12:1 (Jan. 1977), pp. 153–74.

'Rearmament and deterrence in Britain in the 1930s', *JSS*, 1:3 (Dec. 1978), pp. 313–37.

'"A Matter of Faith": British strategic air doctrine before 1939', *JCH*, 15:3 (July 1980), pp. 423–42.

Soucy, Robert J.: 'French Fascist intellectuals in the 1930s. An old new left?', *FHS*, 8:3 (Spring 1974), pp. 445–58.

'Centrist fascism. Pierre Taittinger and the Jeunesses Patriotes', *JCH*, 16:2 (Apr. 1981), pp. 349–68.

Soutou, Georges-Henri: 'La Politique économique de la France en Pologne (1920–1924)', *Revue Historique*, 251 (1974), pp. 85–116.

'La Politique économique de la France à l'égard de la Belgique, 1914–24', *Les Relations Franco-Belges de 1830 à 1934* (Presses Universitaires de Metz, 1975).

'L'Impérialisme du pauvre. La Politique économique du gouvernement français en Europe Centrale et Orientale de 1918 à 1929. Essai d'interprétation', *Relations Internationales*, 7 (1976), pp. 216–39.

Stafford, Paul M.: 'The Chamberlain-Halifax visit to Rome: a reappraisal', *EHR*, 98:386 (Jan. 1983), pp. 61–100.

'The French government and the Danzig crisis: The Italian dimension', *IHR*, 6:1 (Feb. 1984), pp. 48–87.

'Political autobiography and the art of the plausible: R. A. Butler at the Foreign Office', *HJ*, 28:4 (Dec. 1985), pp. 901–22.

Steinberg, Jonathan: 'A German plan for the invasion of Holland and Belgium, 1897', *HJ*, 6:1 (1963), pp. 107–17.

Stengers, Jean: 'Une lettre de Paul-Emile Janson sur la politique de neutralité', *Académie Royale de Belgique: Bulletin de la Classe des Lettres et des Sciences Morales et Politiques*, 5th ser., 64 (1978-4), pp. 173–88.

'A propos de l'étude de M. F. Vanlangenhove sur "L'élaboration de la politique étrangère de la Belgique entre les deux guerres mondiales"',

Académie Royale de Belgique: Bulletin de la Classe des Lettres et des Sciences Morales et Politiques, 5th ser., 68 (1981–3), pp. 115–27.

'L'Accord militaire franco-belge de 1920 et le Luxembourg', in Poidevin, Raymond and Trausch, Gilbert (eds.), *Les Relations franco-luxembourgeoises de Louis XIV à Robert Schuman. Actes du Colloque de Luxembourg (17–19 novembre 1977)* (Metz, Presses Universitaires de Metz, 1978).

Stevenson, David: 'Belgium, Luxembourg and the defence of Western Europe, 1914–1920', *IHR*, 4:4 (Nov. 1982), pp. 502–23.

Stolfi, R. H. S.: 'Equipment for victory in France in 1940', *History*, 55:183 (Feb. 1970), pp. 1–20.

Sumler, David E.: 'Domestic influences on the nationalist revival in France, 1909–1914', *FHS*, 6:4 (Fall 1970), pp. 517–37.

Taylor, Philip M.: '"If war should come": Preparing the fifth arm for total war, 1935–1939', *JCH*, 16:1 (Jan. 1981), pp. 27–51.

Teyssier, Arnaud: 'L'Appui aux forces de surface: l'armée de l'air à la recherche d'une doctrine (1933–1939)', in *Histoire de la Guerre aérienne. Hommage au capitaine Georges Guynemer à l'occasion du 70e anniversaire de sa disparition. Paris: 10–11 septembre 1987* (Vincennes: Publications du Service Historique de l'Armée de L'Air, 1988), pp. 247–77.

Thiéblemont, André: 'Les Traditions dans les armées. Le jeu de la contestation et de la conformité', *Pouvoirs. Revue française d'études constitutionnelles et politiques*, no. 38, *L'Armée* (Sept. 1986), pp. 99–112.

Tournoux, Gen. Paul-Emile: 'Les Origines de la Ligne Maginot', *RHDGM*, 9:33 (Jan. 1959), pp. 3–14.

Truelle, Jean: 'La Production aéronautique militaire française jusqu'en juin 1940', *RHDGM*, 19:73 (Jan. 1969), pp. 75–110.

various: 'Il y a 50 ans, le Front Populaire', *Le Monde: supplément du numéro 12, 852* (25–26 May 1986).

Vaïsse, Maurice: 'Le Mythe de l'or en France: les aspects monétaires du New Deal vus par les français', *RHMC*, 16 (July–Sept. 1969), pp. 463–79.

'Les Militaires français et l'Alliance franco-soviétique au cours des années 1930', Martel, André (ed.), *Forces armées et systèmes d'alliances. Colloque international d'histoire militaire et d'études de défense nationale tenu à Montpellier, 2–6 septembre 1981* (Cahiers de la Fondation pour les Etudes de Défense Nationale, 1982), III, pp. 689–703.

'Le Bureau d'Etudes des Affaires Etrangères et l'Italie, 1940–44', *Revue d'Histoire diplomatique*, 87 (1983), pp. 322–40.

Vanwelkenhuyzen, Jean: 'L'Alerte du 10 janvier 1940. Les documents de Mechelen-sur-Meuse', *RHDGM*, 3:12 (Sept. 1953), pp. 33–54.

'La Surprise du 10 mai 1940', *Le Monde*, no. 10,040 (11 May 1977), p. 10.

'La Belgique et la menace d'invasion, 1939–1940: les avertissements qui venaient de Berlin', *Revue Historique*, 264 (1980), pp. 375–98

'La Conférence diplomatique du 5 avril 1940', *Cahiers d'Histoire de la Seconde Guerre Mondiale* (Brussels), pp. 85–101.

'Le Haut Commandement belge et les Alliés en 1914–18 et en mai 1940', *Revue belge d'histoire militaire*, 25:1 (Mar. 1983), pp. 1–45.

'A propos d'un article écrit en 1936: Le problème belge vu par Charles de Gaulle', *Revue Générale* (Brussels, 1983), pp. 33–49.

'Regards nouveaux sur mai 1940', *Actes du Colloque d'Histoire militaire belge, 1830–1980* (Brussels: Musée Royal de l'Armée et d'Histoire Militaire, 1981), pp. 261–78.
Vial, Jean: 'La Défense Nationale. Son organisation entre les deux guerres', *RHDGM*, 5:18 (Apr. 1955), pp. 11–32.
Villatte, Robert: 'Le Changement de commandement de mai 1940. Etude critique de témoignages', *RHDGM*, 2:5 (Jan. 1952), pp. 27–36.
Vital, David: 'Czechoslovakia and the Powers, September 1938', *JCH*, 1:4 (1966), pp. 37–67 (reprinted in Gatzke, Hans W. (ed.), *European Diplomacy between Two Wars, 1919–1939* (Chicago: Quadrangle Books, 1972), pp. 193–220).
Wall, Irwin M.: 'French Socialism and the Popular Front in 1936', *JCH*, 5:3 (July 1970), pp. 3–20.
  'The resignation of the First Popular Front government of Léon Blum, June 1937', *FHS*, 6:4 (Fall 1970), pp. 538–54.
  'Socialists and bureaucrats. The Blum Government and the French administration, 1936–37', *International Review of Social History*, 14:3 (1974), pp. 325–46.
Wandycz, Piotr: 'L'Alliance franco-tchécoslovaque de 1924: un échange de lettres Poincaré-Benes', *Revue d'Histoire Diplomatique*, 3–4 (1984), pp. 328–33.
Wanty, Gen. Emile: 'Le Problème de la défense des Ardennes en 1940', *RHDGM*, 11:42 (1961), pp. 1–16.
  'Les Relations militaires franco-belges de 1936 à octobre 1939', *RHDGM*, 8:31 (1958), pp. 12–23.
Wark, Wesley K.: 'Three military attachés at Berlin in the 1930s: soldier-statesmen and the limits of ambiguity', *IHR*, 9:4 (Nov. 1987), pp. 586–611.
Warner, Geoffrey: 'The Stavisky Affair and the riots of February 6th 1934', *History Today*, 8 (June 1958), pp. 377–85.
Watt, Donald Cameron: 'German plans for the reoccupation of the Rhineland: a note', *JCH*, 1:4 (1966), pp. 193–99.
  'Misinformation, misconception, mistrust: episodes in British policy and the approach of war, 1938–1939', in Bentley, Michael and Stevenson, John (eds.), *High and Low Politics in Modern Britain. Ten studies* (Oxford: Clarendon Press, 1983), pp. 215–54.
  'The secret Laval–Mussolini agreement of 1935 on Ethiopia', *The Middle East Journal*, 15 (Winter 1961), pp. 69–78.
Weinberg, Gerhard L.: 'The Nazi-Soviet Pacts: a half-century later', *Foreign Affairs*, 68:4 (Fall 1989), pp. 175–89.
Wileman, Donald G.: 'P.-E. Flandin and the Alliance Démocratique, 1929–1939', *French History*, 4:2 (June 1990), pp. 139–73.
Willcox, Temple: 'Projection or publicity? Rival concepts in the pre-war planning of the British Ministry of Information', *JCH*, 18:1 (Jan. 1983), pp. 97–116.
Willequet, Jacques: 'Regards sur la politique belge d'indépendance, 1936–1940', *RHDGM*, 8:31 (1958), pp. 3–11.
Williamson, Samuel R.: 'Joffre reshapes French strategy, 1911–1913', in Kennedy, Paul M. (ed.), *The War Plans of the Great Powers, 1880–1914* (Boston, Allen and Unwin, 1979; reprinted 1985), pp. 133–54.

Winock, Michel: 'Aurait-on pu gagner la guerre de 39–40?', *L'Evénement du jeudi*, 247 (27 July–2 Aug. 1989), pp. 40–3.
Wright, Gordon: 'Ambassador Bullitt and the Fall of France', *World Politics*, 10 (Oct. 1957), pp. 63–90.
Wright, Jonathan and Stafford, Paul: 'Hitler and the Hossbach Memorandum', *History Today*, 38 (March 1988), pp. 11–17.
Yapou, Eliezer: 'The autonomy that never was: the autonomy plans for the Sudeten in 1938', in Dinstern, Y. (ed.), *Models of Autonomy* (New Brunswick and London: Transaction Books, 1981), pp. 97–122.
Young, Neil: 'Foundations of victory: the development of Britain's air defences, 1934–40', *RUSI Journal*, 135:3 (Autumn 1990), pp. 62–8.
Young, Robert J.: 'Preparation for defeat: French war doctrine in the inter-war period', *Journal of European Studies*, 2:2 (June 1972), pp. 155–72.
  'The aftermath of Munich: the course of French diplomacy, October 1938 to March 1939', *FHS*, 8:2 (Fall 1973), pp. 305–22.
  'The strategic dream: French air doctrine in the inter-war period, 1919–39', *JCH*, 9:4 (Oct. 1974), pp. 57–76.
  'Spokesmen for economic warfare: the industrial intelligence centre in the 1930s', *European Studies Review*, 6:4 (Oct. 1976), pp. 473–89.
  'Le Haut commandement français au moment de Munich', *RHMC*, 24 (Jan.–March 1977), pp. 110–29.
  'La guerre de longue durée: some reflections on French strategy and diplomacy in the 1930s', in Preston, Adrian (ed.), *General Staffs and Diplomacy before the Second World War* (London and Totowa, NJ: Croom Helm, 1978), pp. 41–64.
  'L'Attaque brusquée and its use as myth in inter-war France', *Historical Reflections/Réflexions Historiques*, 8:1 (Spring 1981), pp. 93–113.
  'Soldiers and diplomats: The French Embassy and Franco-Italian relations, 1935–6', *JSS*, 7:1 (Mar. 1984), pp. 74–91.
  'French military intelligence and the Franco-Italian Alliance, 1933–1939', *HJ*, 28:1 (Mar. 1985), pp. 143–68.
  'Reason and madness: France, the Axis powers and the politics of economic disorder, 1938–39', *Canadian Journal of History/Annales Canadiennes d'Histoire*, 20 (Apr. 1985), pp. 65–83.
  'The use and abuse of fear: France and the air menace in the 1930s', *Intelligence and National Security*, 2:4 (Oct. 1987), pp. 88–109.

H. Unpublished papers

Buffotot, Patrice: 'Le Réarmement aérien allemand et l'approche de la guerre vus par le 2e Bureau air français, 1936–1939', Franco-German Historians' Colloquium, Bonn, Sept. 1978.
Crémieux-Brilhac, Jean-Louis: 'La France devant l'Allemagne et devant la guerre au début de septembre 1939', Franco-German Historians' Colloquium, Bonn, Sept. 1978.
Duroselle, Jean-Baptiste: 'Les Négociations anglo-franco-soviétiques de 1939', History of International Relations Seminar, Université de Paris IV Sorbonne, 22 Nov. 1977.

Masson, Philippe: 'La Marine française et la stratégie alliée (1938–1939)', Franco-German Historians' Colloquium, Bonn, Sept. 1978.

I. Interviews

General Sir Ronald Adam: DDMO, 1935–6; Commandant, Staff College, Camberley, 1937; Deputy CIGS, 1937–9; GOC 3rd Corps, BEF, France and Belgium, 1939–40 (Sussex, Aug. 1978).

General Pierre Billotte: Char B company commander, 3rd DCR, France, 1940; son of General Gaston Billotte, GOC French 1st Army Group, 1940 (Paris, Mar. 1978).

Major-General the Viscount Bridgeman: GSO2, War Office, 1935–7; GSO1, BEF headquarters, France and Belgium, 1939–40 (Minsterley, Shropshire, Aug. 1978).

General Sir David Fraser: son of Brigadier-General William Fraser, British military attaché, Paris, 1938–40 (Isington, Hants., Sept. 1983).

Colonel Roger Gasser: adjutant to General Weygand, Beirut, 1924–5 and 1939–40; France, May–June 1940 (Paris, Apr. 1978).

General Augustin Guillaume: Chief of Intelligence (2e Bureau) 1936–9, then of the Bureau des Affaires politiques, 1939–40, at Rabat, headquarters of General Noguès, commander-in-chief and resident-general, French North Africa (Paris, Mar. 1978).

Major-General L. A. Hawes: Head of GS (Plans) section, responsible for preparing the transport to France of the BEF, 1938–9 (West Harting, Hants., July 1979).

General Sir James Marshall-Cornwall: Military attaché, Berlin, 1928–32; head of British Military Mission to Egypt, 1937–8; Deputy CIGS for anti-aircraft and coast defence, 1938–9; chief of British Staff, Anglo-French Military Committee, 1939–40 (Malton, Yorks., Aug. 1978; London, Mar. 1983).

Guy Petibon: son of General Jean Petibon, personal staff officer to Gamelin, 1919–37; *chef de cabinet* to Gamelin, 1937–40 (Paris, June 1978).

General Olivier Poydenot: Chief of section for liaison with Allied armies, *cabinet particulier* of Gamelin, 1939–40 (Versailles, July 1982).

General Sir Harold Redman: Staff of General Sir Richard Howard-Vyse, No. 1 British military mission, attached to Gamelin's headquarters, Nogent-sur-Marne, 1939–40 (Lulworth, Dorset, Aug. 1983).

Major-General Sir Guy Salisbury-Jones: British liaison officer, French Levant headquarters, Beirut, 1924–5; attached to Gamelin's headquarters during the Druze War in Syria, 1925–6; liaison officer at Weygand's Near-East headquarters, Beirut, 1939–40 (Hambledon, Hants., Aug. 1978 and Sept. 1983).

Index

Abbeville (Somme) 318, 353, 355
Abwehr (counter-intelligence) 325
Abyssinia (Ethiopia)
   Italy invades (1935) 46, 51, 53, 72–6, 217, 220, 255–6
Adam, Gen. Sir Ronald 256–7, 263
ADGB (air defence of Great Britain) 274
affectation spéciale 358, 369–70
Africa
   East, Italy and 255–6
   North 14, 41, 182, 308: army in, disaffection 85; Britain and 275; *and* Fall of France 85, 400; *and* Franco–Italian accord 52; popular rising feared 88; troops in France (1933–5) 44, 374; *see also* Algeria *etc.*
africains 15
agriculture 354–5, 376
aircraft 164, 164–7
   British 166
   German 159, 166
   imported 169–70
   types: Amiot 143, 306, 308; Curtiss P-36, 169; Dewoitine 520, 166; Glenn Martin 169; Hawker Hurricane 166; LéO 45, 166, 317; Messerschmitt 109, 166; Morane-Saulnier 406, 166; Stuka (Junker 87) 159, 343
air force 11–12, 96, 142–71
   administrative reforms 154
   aircraft imported 169–70
   aircraft numbers 143, 153, 155–6
   air superiority 164, 166–8, 307, 322
   armaments 111
   and army 154–5, 159, 163, 165
   autogyros 158
   autonomy 91–3, 97, 146–7, 152, 154–5, 168–9
   communications 143
   deficiencies 144, 156–7, 160–1, 162–3, 166–7: problems summarised 167–71; recovery (1939–40) 144
   expansion (1938) 139
   finance 61, 67, 138, 162–4
   Franco–British co-operation 162, 259
   Franco–Italian overtures 52
   ground control 143
   industrial problems 155–7, 162–7, 230
   industry reorganised 153–4, 156, 165–6, 168
   Instruction on . . . Major Air Units (1937) 157
   manpower 143
   mechanisation 180–1
   and mobilisation 150
   and nationalisation 113, 114
   origins 146–7
   paratroops 158
   Plan I (1934) 147, 148, 154, 161, 165
   Plan II/III/IV 155, 156, 163, 164
   Plan V (1938) 130, 138, 163–9, 164, 167–8
   and Poland 306, 307–8, 317
   political organisation 168
   'popular aviation' movement 158
   preparedness (1938–9) 130, 132, 167, 234, 307, 322
   preparedness, World War II 140, 317
   Renault and 63, 69
   role 142, 146; 'adjunct to army' 164, 169; *as* artillery 160; Blitzkrieg 159; contradictions 167–8; de Gaulle on 145–6; home defence priority 150; Reynaud on 145; strategic priority 147, 150, 152–3, 157, 159, 170; strategic-tactical 'proportionality' 163–5; tactical priority 159, 160, 170; World War II 167–8
   and Spanish Civil War 160
   training 143
   World War II 10, 142–4, 167–8, 307–8: achievements 143; Baku proposal 352; disadvantages 143; *and* Fall of France 378, 400

558   Index

Alanbrooke, 1st Viscount (Sir Alan F. Brooke) 397
Albert Canal (Belgium) 174, 175, 176, 191, 192, 194, 207, 323
Albert I, King of the Belgians 188
Alexander, King of Yugoslavia 212–13, 215, 218, 220
  assassinated (1934) 213
Algeria 15, 99
Alliance Démocratique (Democratic Alliance) 36, 51, 131, 258, 392
Alphand, Charles 291, 293
Alsace 44, 175, 181
  annexed by Prussia (1871) 13
  World War II 98, 326
Altmayer, Gen. Robert 39, 78
Amiens (Somme) 198, 353
André, Gen. Louis 1–2, 17
années creuses see army: manpower: 'lean years'
Antwerp (Belgium) 173, 194, 336, 367
Arbonneau, Gen. d' 287, 303
Ardennes plateau 194, 199–201, 204, 205
  World War II 375–6, 398
Arlon (Belgium) 176, 177, 191
armaments *see* army: mechanisation; Germany: rearmament *etc.*
Armée de l'Air *see* air force
armée de metier see army: professional
Armengaud, Gen. Jules 160, 287; *and* Poland 338, 339, 340–41, 346, 347, 348
armistice (1940) 2, 154, 378, 400
armoured cars 117–19, 118 *table*, 140
army
  affaire des fiches (1901–4) 2, 17
  and air force 143, 152, 154–5, 163, 165: 'air force as adjunct' 164, 169; army air force 146, 147, 148; early views of 148; problems summarised 167–71
  armoured corps 375
  army commissioners 360–1, 363–70
  and Belgium 172–209: logistic problems 174–5
  British on 271–3
  cavalry 118–19, 123–4, 376
  colonial infantry 369, 375
  communications 359–60, 396, 398
  concentration proposed 40–1
  conscription *see* military service *below*
  defence aims *see* strategy *below*
  deficiencies disguised 382–3
  demographic problems *see* manpower *below*
  DLMs (armoured divisions) 192, 367, 368–9
  and Dreyfus affair 1–2, 17, 108–9
  experience limitations 144–5
  Fifth Army 316–17, 374
  finance 107, 110–11, 111, 164
  First Army 174, 182, 192; World War II 329, 336, 368, 376
  Fourth Army 316–17, 328, 330, 356, 366, 369, 369–70, 374, 374–5
  frontalier battalions 183
  and generalship 396, 398
  horses 354, 366
  intelligence *see* intelligence
  internal problems 26–9, 184–6, 345
  and invasion threat (autumn 1939) 329
  Maginot Line garrisons 183
  manoeuvres 84, 103, 119, 122–3, 158, 192, 202, 247; British at 271–2, 297; E. Europeans at 223, 224; re-established (1930) 244; USSR at 293
  manpower 34–6, 107, 112, 140, 141; essential workers 358, 369–70, 371; Franco–Italian accord 52–3; inferiority (1939) 357; law of July 1938 358; 'lean years' (*années creuses*) 26, 28, 36, 40, 42–4, 43, 185, 244; training problems 125
  mechanisation 36, 44, 65, 71, 110–41, 119, 201–2, 251; (1939) 320; anti-tank guns 356–7; *and* British army 243; finance 56–61, 77, 174; *Fonds d'armement . . .* (1936) 77; de Gaulle on 37–42, 100–1; heavy divisions 122–3, 140, 201–2; industrial problems 58, 59, 61–72, 77, 202, 251; internal problems 42, 65, 77–9, 118–19; *and* Maginot Line 180–1; *at* manoeuvres (1935) 192; *and* nationalisation 113–15; *and* Polish campaign 340, 344–5; 'Provisional Notice on . . . Large Armoured Units' 140; research 114–15; shortfalls 110, 112, 140; strategic problems 120–2; training problems 120–2, 124
  military service 14, 28, 103, 105, 185; indefinite term (1939) 135; one-year term (1928) 173; Petain and 178; two-year term (1935–9) 36, 40, 43–4, 250; Weygand on 43
  mobilisation 150, 180, 190, 280; Law of 1938 133; Poland threatened 306–7; Sudetenland threatened (1938) 118, 124, 132, 202, 278, 280, 352; World War II 316, 320, 349–50, 352–6
  modernisation 9, 34, 36, 40, 44, 104–6, 99–100; *see also* mechanisation *above*

Index

morale 102–3, 104–5, 377
motorised infantry 367, 368
'nation-in-arms' concept 39, 100–1
Ninth Army 368, 375, 376
North African infantry 43–4, 374
outdated policy 35–6
overseas troops 43–4, 320, 321, 369, 374, 375
political administration 133, 135, 148–9, 185; army commissioners 360–1, 363–70; unified staff proposed 96–7
political position 1–4, 11, 17, 42, 99, 100–2, 384; *Corvignolles* 101–2; CSAR (Cagoule) 101, 102; Dreyfus affair 1–2, 17, 108–9; Fall of France 2–5, 109; 401; *grande muette* 85; Popular Front 81–6, 101–4, 107–9; *and* USSR 292–4, 295, 296
political relations 42, 61, 72, 76–8, 98–9; *and* Fall of France 399–402; Popular Front 80
preparedness 123, 138–41, 202, 289, 320–1, 343–8, 364; (1935–7) 62, 72, 74–5, 251, 252; (1938–9) 118, 130, 132, 138–41, 202, 356–9; Weygand on 141
professional 41, 42, 124–5, 361; Blum and 100–1; de Gaulle/Reynaud proposals 37–42, 87–8, 100–1, 124–5
reserves 112, 135, 192, 201–2, 214, 316–17, 320, 349
role/structure 14, 34–5, 103, 105–6, 152
Second Army 374, 375, 376, 377
Seventh Army 367, 376–7, 398
strategy 41, 58, 120, 148, 238
Third Army 316–17, 307, 328, 330, 364–6, 369–70, 374–5, 377
transport 119, 369–70
World War II 4, 6–7, 374–7; army commission reports 363–70; Fall of France (1940) 2–5; 378; morale 361–2, 367–8, 369, 375; zone of the armies 356, 361
artillery 71–2, 116, 140
World War II 356–7, 358, 366, 368, 369, 375, 376
for Yugoslavia 231
Asché (agent) *see* Schmidt
Astier de la Vigerie, Gen. François 157
Atelier de Construction de Rueil 120, 152
attaque brusquée 50, 252
Auriol, Vincent 121
Ausseur, Commander 329
Austria 216–17
Anschluss with Germany (1938) 130, 165, 199, 232, 262

Czechoslovakia threatened by 216
Italy supports 73
automitrailleuse see tanks: AMC/AMR
aviation *see* air force
Axis (Rome–Berlin) 220
see also Germany; Italy

Badoglio, Field Marshal Pietro 21, 74, 192
and Abyssinia invaded 53–4
Gamelin and Franco–Italian accord 52, 60, 73, 74, 216, 255–6
Balkans
World War II, front proposed 350–1
see also Yugoslavia; Europe: Eastern *etc.*
Baltic Republics 291, 300
see also Lithuania
Baril, Col. 324, 326
Barthou, Louis (Jean-Louis) 35, 293, 295, 391, 392
bataille de conduite 359
Baudet, Gen. 375
Baudouin, Paul 384, 401, 402
Beaumont-Nesbitt, Col. F. G. 91, 261, 263, 297
Beck, Col. Jozef 229, 283, 285, 288, 304, 305, 325
Belfort (Territoire de B.) 216
Belgium
access to/through 124, 172
army 41, 182, 189, 191
and Britain 187, 193, 195–6, 260, 265, 276–7
defence, Franco–Belgian 172–209; active/passive options 172–3; air power 166, 170; arms supply from France 230; Belgian 'independence' (1936) 190, 192, 195, 198, 202–3, 265; Belgian opposition to 176; Cumont meetings (1934–5) 191–2; dilemmas 12, 173, 203–4, 206–7, 209; finance 175–80, 184–6; fortifications 173–80; *ligne d'arrêt* 175; logistic problems 174–5; military (Foch–Maglinse) accord (1920) 173, 187, 188–9, 191, 192, 202; political problems 178, 184–5, 186–9; tripartite approach (1936) 193–4
and Franco–Soviet pact 218
French approaches to 49–50, 88, 92, 103
German advance to frontier (1939) 326
intelligence 205, 334
isolationism 173
Locarno treaties abrogated (1936–7) 190–1

Belgium (*cont.*)
  neutralism 188, 193, 195, 199, 203, 236
  non-belligerence (1939) 207, 208–9, 322–3
  and Rhineland 76, 78, 259, 260, 261–2
  World War II 317, 318, 321–1, 376; Breda Plan 397–8; Dyle Plan 336–7; French Seventh army and 367; invasion threatened 330, 333, 335, 336
Bellefon, Méric de 47
Bergen, Gen. Edouard van den 194, 199, 202–9, 283, 322
Berliet (truck company) 369
Bertrand, Col. Gustave 325
Besset, Lucien 70
Besson, Gen. 122–3
Béthouart, Col. Antoine 213–16, 218–21, 225–7
Billotte, Gen. Gaston 330, 344–5, 375, 398
Bineau, Gen. Henri 192, 204, 317, 328, 329, 333
Blanchard, Gen. Georges 174, 330, 343, 368, 376
Bletchley Park (Britain) 325
Bloch-Dassault, Gen. Georges 64, 65, 68, 69, 70, 72, 77, 112, 374
Blum, Léon 4, 79, 80–109, 113, 128, 131–63, 190, 258, 270
  and defence policy 42, 195
  and E. Europe 283
  and Gamelin 107, 159
  and de Gaulle 90, 100–1
  and industry 67, 115, 117, 131
  and Maginot Line 180
  popular rising feared 105
  and USSR 218, 296, 298, 300
Bonnet, Georges-Etienne 121, 129, 234, 276, 307, 338, 385, 386, 388, 389
  and E. Europe 229, 234
  foreign minister (1938–9) 229, 316
  and Poland 308–11, 312, 338
  von Ribbentrop accord (1938) 135
  and Yugoslavia 228
Boulanger, Gen. Georges-Ernest-Jean-Marie 13, 42
Bourret, Gen. Victor 97–8, 316, 374
Bouthillier, Yves 121, 137, 138, 384
Brandt, Edgar 67, 74, 113, 231
Brazil, 21–2, 95, 298
Breda (Netherlands) Plan 397–8
Briand, Aristide 180
Brinon, Count Fernand de 55
Britain
  air power 12, 238, 269–70, 274, 277; Franco–British relations 166, 169–71, 242, 261, 268; *and* Poland 317, 342; priorities 170–1, 247, 248; *and* Rhineland 259
  army 238, 261; Defence Requirements Committee (1933–4) 245; French assessments of 242–5, 246–7; leadership problems 253; mechanisation 242–5, 263, 266–8; political relations 261; Territorial Army 244, 245, 254; weakness (1935) 254
  and Austrian Anschluss 274–5
  and Belgium 186, 187, 191, 193–6, 207–8, 247, 22–4, 265
  see British Expeditionary Force
  and Czechoslovakia/Sudetenland 225, 275, 277
  defence policy, inter-war 193, 237, 238, 247–9, 253–4, 262–5, 268, 269–70, 271, 274; (1935) 50, 252–4; (1938) 274–8; 'factions' (1936) 298; French assessment of (1935) 45; *and* French policy 265, 268; limited liability 263–4; war by proxy 273–4, 277; *see also* Rhineland *etc.*
  economic affairs 244, 269, 271
  and E. Europe 224, 235, 237, 247
  Empire 238–9, 247, 248, 254, 271, 275, 355
  and France 35, 49, 236–78; Anglo–French agreements 141, 144, 162, 202, 237, 251, 270–1; Franco–British supreme war council (SWC) 318, 337, 350–1, 353, 355; *and* Franco–Soviet pacts 233, 297–301; *on* French air power 161, 164, 166; French approaches to (1935–6) 46, 49–50, 53–5, 73, 88; *on* French army 244, 270, 277, 278; French intelligence in 47, 241–2; *on* French morale (1936) 102, 103; French needs 103, 246–7, 280, 390; French reliance on 72–3, 76, 103, 252; *and* Popular Front 270, 297–8
  and German rearmament 246–7, 249, 254, 270, 276
  and Greece, integrity guaranteed (1939) 279
  industry 112, 125, 136
  intelligence, Enigma codes 325
  and Italy 53, 72, 256–7, 276
  and Low Countries 260, 264, 265, 268, 276–7, 280; *see also* Belgium *above and* Netherlands *below*
  navy 238, 247, 248, 261, 274; Anglo–

Index 561

French accords (1935–6) 53, 54, 256–7, 261, 268
  and Netherlands 195–6, 247, 252–3
  and Norway expedition 352, 392
  and Poland 389, 305, 311, 314–17, 342, 346–7; integrity guaranteed (1939) 279, 288, 305; Polish campaign 288–9, 337, 338, 342
  preparedness 193–4, 195–6, 261, 263, 280, 289, 343–4
  and Rhineland 76, 257, 259–62, 260, 262–3
  and Romania 279
  and Spanish Civil War 236
  Stresa Front 45
  and Sudetenland 225, 277
  and USSR 300–2, 312–13
British Expeditionary Force (BEF) 238, 259–60, 315, 328, 329, 330, 336, 359, 376
Brugère, Raymond 221, 227, 227–8, 229, 234
Buat, Gen. Edmond 21, 24
Bührer, Gen. Jules 350–1
Buisson, Col. Louis 51
Bullitt, William C. 162, 169, 384, 386, 392, 394, 397
Bureaux, Deuxième 46, 324

Cagoule/Cagoulards *see* CSAR
Caisse Autonome des Investissements de la Défense Nationale 130
Cambon, Roger 47
Camel, Marcel 369
Carence, Gen. Antoine 72, 185
Cartel des Gauches 22, 52
Castelnau, Gen. de 101, 391
Castex, Adml. Raoul 144, 145, 330
Catoire, Capt. Maurice 85
CE (contre-espionnage) 324
Centre des Hautes Etudes Aériennes 153
Centre des Hautes Etudes Militaires (CHEM) 121, 144, 192, 204
CGT *see* Confédération Générale du Travail
Chamberlain, (Arthur) Neville 141, 170–1, 253, 271, 322
  and Belgium 268, 277
  and Daladier 269
  defence policy 264, 268, 269–70, 272
  and E. Europe 237, 288, 342
  and France 276, 277
  and Germany 271, 275
  Munich agreement 279
  and USSR 303
Champetier de Ribes 351

Chautemps, Camille 87–8, 115, 117, 129, 130–1, 157, 162, 190, 389
  and appeasement 363, 389
  and Britain 237, 270, 275
  and defence investments 130
  and E. Europe 225
Chéron, Henri 66, 70
Churchill, Sir Winston Leonard Spencer 391
Ciano, Galeazzo, Conte di Cortellazzo 221, 225
Cinquième Bureau 324
Citroën, André 63, 121, 369
Clapier, Marcel 388
Clemenceau, Georges 17–18, 97, 131, 372, 387, 392–3, 401
Clerk, Sir George 270, 297, 298
Collège des Hautes Etudes de Défense Nationale (CHEDN) 144, 145
colmatage 201
Colson, Gen. Louis 4, 35, 40, 77, 86, 87, 97, 99, 206, 233
  and Britain 54, 259, 268
  and E. Europe 223, 224, 227, 228
  and Fall of France, 378, 402
  finance 60, 64, 127
  and de Gaulle 36–7, 38, 41, 125
  industry 65, 66, 111–12
  and Italy 233
  and mobilisation 356, 357, 358–9
  and USSR 233, 292–3, 294, 295, 301
Colyer, Grp. Capt. Douglas 161
Comité Secret d'Action Révolutionnaire (CSAR) 101, 102
Commission de Défense des Frontières 175
communists *see* Parti Communiste Français
Condé, Gen. Charles 316, 323, 364, 366, 374, 377
Confédération Générale du Travail (CGT) 83, 131, 134
  see also trade unions
Conseil Supérieur de la Défense Nationale (CSDN) 36, 94, 97
Conseil Supérieur de la Guerre (CSG) 14, 30
Conseil Supérieur de l'Air 147, 153, 157
Cooper, A. Duff *see* Duff Cooper
Corap, Gen. André 6, 343, 368, 375–6
Corbin, Charles 45, 47, 260, 261, 269, 277
Cot, Pierre 11, 85, 106, 139, 150–2, 157–8, 391, 393
  air force 147, 150, 152, 155–6, 159, 161, 162, 170
  air minister (1933–4) 146–7, 148

Cot, Pierre (*cont.*)
  air minister (1936–8) 150, 152, 156, 157–8, 161–2, 164, 165–6
  arraigned at Riom 113, 142
  and decentralisation 130
  and E. Europe 283
  and nationalisation 112, 113, 114
  political views 83, 151–2, 154
  and USSR 296, 300
Coulondre, Robert 351, 388
CPDN 97, 110, 163–4, 178
Croix de Feu organisation 104
Croizat, Ambroze 131
CSAR (Comité Secret d'Action Révolutionnaire) 101, 102
CSDN (Conseil Supérieur de la Défense Nationale) 36, 94, 97
CSG *see* Conseil Supérieur de la Guerre
Cumont, Gen. 179, 191, 192, 194
Cuny, Col. 47, 244–5
Czechoslovakia 135, 212, 222, 285, 319
  and Britain 225
  and France 152, 210–12, 212, 215, 216, 225, 232, 285
  German threat to 51–2, 118, 118, 164, 216, 262
  Munich agreement (1938) 118, 118, 169, 230, 234, 279, 303
  and Poland 281, 289
  and Rhineland 81
  Sudetenland 62, 124, 132, 133, 167, 202, 225, 229, 230, 234, 275, 279
  and USSR 215, 232
  and Yugoslavia 225

Daladier, Edouard 4, 28, 30, 81, 83, 89, 106–7, 110–41, 197, 234–5, 258, 385–92
  and air power 138, 146, 167, 169, 230, 322
  and appeasement 363, 389
  and army 28, 105–6, 185, 400
  and army commissions 365, 366, 372–3
  and Balkans 351
  and Belgium 196–8, 322
  and Bonnet 385, 386, 388, 389
  and Britain 269, 275, 276–7
  and communists 370–1
  and Czechoslovakia 285
  and Dautry 386, 388
  decree powers 138
  defence aims 88, 90, 123, 196–8, 233, 234, 280
  defence minister 40, 41, 82–3, 91–3, 140
  and E. Europe 217, 226, 283, 373
  fortifications 180, 196–8, 203, 234
  and Franco–German reconciliation 138
  and Gamelin 88–93, 100, 107–8, 133, 159, 385–90, 399, 400, 402
  and 'generalissimo' 168–9
  and Georges 100
  imprisoned (1940–45) 6, 384, 386, 400
  and industry 67, 110–14, 128–9, 131–3, 233
  and La Chambre 162
  Munich agreement 132, 133, 138, 167, 234, 279
  and Pétain 388
  and Poland 280–1, 342, 346
  popular rising feared 86, 87, 104
  prime minister (1934) 86, 87; (1938–40) 89, 90, 106–9, 131, 135, 386, 388, 391
  and Reynaud 138, 391–2
  and Sudetenland 277, 279
  and USSR 294–5, 296, 300–1
  and Weygand 384
  World War II 10, 313, 322, 327, 329, 351, 354–5, 365, 366–7, 386–90, 392
  and Yugoslavia 219–20, 229
Dampierre, Roger de 221
Daridan, Jean 98
Darlan, Adml. François 93, 97, 306, 350, 351, 402
Dautry, Raoul 115, 117, 119, 357–8, 370, 371–2, 380–1, 386, 388
DCR *see* Division Cuirassée de Réserve
DCR (Division Cuirassée de Réserve) 201–2, 345
Debeney, Gen. Marie-Eugène 24, 25, 52, 148, 262–3
Decamp, Gen. Jules 98, 329, 373, 388
Degrelle, Léon 189
Delbos, Yvon 82, 85, 190, 229
  and Britain 237, 266, 267, 275
  and E. Europe 225, 226, 227, 283
  and Poland 285–6
Delestraint, Col. Charles 123
Deleuze, Maj. Georges 328
Delvoie, Col. Maurice 205, 207–8, 316, 320–1
Democratic Alliance (Alliance Démocratique) 36, 51, 131, 258, 392
Denain, Gen. Victor 45, 46, 52, 147
Dentz, Gen. Henri 47, 85, 190, 206, 224, 306, 311
des Isnards, Charles 364–7, 369
Deverell, Field Marshal Sir Cyril 224, 266, 268, 271–3, 384
  Chief of Imperial General Staff 246
Devèze, Albert 187–8, 189–90
Didelet, Gen. Henri 377

Dill, Gen. Sir John Greer 194, 263, 330, 397
Douai (Nord), defence 175, 183
Douhet, Gen. Giulio 147
Doumenc, Gen. (André) Joseph 38
Doumergue, Gaston 84, 177, 178
Dreyfus, Capt. Alfred/Dreyfus affair 1, 2, 17, 42, 84, 108–9, 401
Ducos, Hippolyte 388
Duff Cooper, Alfred, 1st Viscount Norwich 266, 268
Dufieux, Gen. Joseph 15, 39, 72, 78, 120, 122, 194, 343; *and* Poland 340, 343; *and* subversion, right-wing 102
Dunkerque (Dunkirk) (Nord) 198, 378
Durand-Viel, Adml. Georges 93
Duroselle, Jean-Baptiste 8, 142–3
Duval, Gen. Jean 160
Dyle river 183, 336; Dyle Plan (1939–40) 336–7, 367, 377

Ecole de Guerre Aérienne 153
Ecole de l'Air 147
Ecole Supérieure de la Guerre 1, 15–16, 95, 121
Eden, Sir (Robert) Anthony, 1st Earl of Avon 49, 93, 162, 266–7, 269, 276
Egypt, Britain and 275
EMA 84, 201, 206
Enigma codes 325–6
Entente, Little *see* Little Entente
Esperey, Gen. de *see* Franchet d'Esperey
Estienne, Gen. Jean-Baptiste 38, 148
Etcheberrigaray, Gen. 377
Ethiopia *see* Abyssinia
Europe
  Eastern 50–1, 85, 152, 210–35, 215–16, 277, 281, 295; French policy for 210, 211–12, 225; German policy for 50–1, 222; *and* Rhineland 81; *and* Sudetenland 281; *and* USSR 290, 291, 294, 295, 295–6; *see also* Poland; Yugoslavia *etc.*
Evekink, Col. van Voorst tot Voorst 329

Fabry, Jean 25–6, 51–2, 57, 59, 60, 61, 63, 68–73, 77–8, 79, 99, 180, 250, 294
  and army commissions 42, 361
  on Bastille Day (1935) 86
  and Britain 255
  defence aims 74–6, 123
  defence minister 88, 89
  and Italy 46, 51, 53, 73, 74, 220, 256
  and nationalisation 67, 113, 115
  political position 104, 106
Faucher, Gen. Louis 212, 285

Faure, Paul 88
Faury, Gen. Louis 212, 312, 316, 338, 339, 340, 342
Favre, Jules (Gabriel-Claude-Jules) 13
FCM (Forges et Chantiers de la Méditerranée) 62
Féquant, Gen. Philippe 154, 157, 159, 162
Fernand-Laurent, Camille 132–3, 366, 369
Ferry, Jules-François-Camille 13
Ferté-sous-Jouarre, La (Seine) GQG, (WWII) 317, 359
Février, André 128
fiches, affaire des 2, 17
Finland, USSR invades (1939) 352, 373
Flandin, Pierre-Etienne 36, 40, 44, 131, 189, 388–9, 391
  and Alliance Démocratique 36, 51, 258, 392
  and appeasement 363, 389
  finance 56, 57, 59, 75
  prime minister (1934–5) 36, 82
  and Rhineland 257, 258, 259, 261, 262
Flavigny, Gen. Jean 78, 100–1, 375
Foch, Marshal Ferdinand 6, 16–17, 25, 31, 99, 185, 274, 401; Foch–Maglinse military accord (1920) 173, 187, 188–9, 191, 192, 202; *and* Weygand 5, 17, 21, 31, 274
Forschungsamt (German intelligence dept) 324
fortifications 172–209, 272–3, 347, 350, 368, 375
  and air power 272
  Ardennes gap 199–201
  Belgian 205
  Britain and 253–4, 272–3, 276, 277
  construction delays 197, 199
  as force-multiplier 178, 180
  Maginot Line *see* Maginot Line
  môles de résistance 184
  Poland 288, 290, 347
  political rationale 180–1
  Siegfried Line 316, 319, 328, 329, 331, 350
Four Power Pact (1933) 295
France
  alliances 45, 49–55, 72–3, 76, 88, 103, 215–16, 229, 233–4, 247, 282, 284–5, 289, 301–5, 378, 389
  and arms supply 230–3, 286–78; Belgium 172–209; Britain 141, 162, 236–78, 252; Czechoslovakia 212; E. Europe 210–35, 279–80; Four Power Pact (1933) 295; *and* Franco–Soviet pacts 218, 300–2; intelligence

France (*cont.*)
    assessments 240–1; *and* Italian–French *rapprochement* 216–17; *and* Italo–Yugoslav pact 222–3; *and* Italy in Abyssinia 217, 255–7; *and* Popular Front 218, 220–1, 270, 297–300; *and* Rhineland remilitarised 217, 259, 259–60, 261–2, 283–4
    army *see* army
    and Belgium 172–209, 230, 259
    and Britain 236–78, 297, 318
    defence policy, inter-war 26–8, 31–2, 35, 39, 42, 44–5, 49–52, 72, 74–5, 81, 133, 138–41, 151, 168–9, 230–1, 235, 236–7, 242–3, 305; administration 65–9, 91–4, 96–7, 135, 148, 156–7, 186–6, 395–6; air power 64, 155–6, 170; allies *see* alliances *above*; appeasement 55, 229, 279–80, 309–11, 338, 363, 389; armaments 67–8, 71, 110–41; Belgian frontier 172–209; contradictions 167–8; dilemmas 140, 249; fear of war 10, 12; finance 137–8, 174; fortifications 172–209; Fortress France 196–8; four-year plan 110–13; inter-service problems 91–3, 96–7, 152–3, 156–7; 'Law for organisation . . .' (1938) 133; long/short war concerns 139, 141; Maginot Line 179–83; mechanisation 110–41, 201–2; peripheral campaigns 350–2; Poland 279–90, 302–13, 306–7, 314–48; Rhineland evacuated (1930) 173, 174; *and* Rhineland remilitarised 76–7, 234, 257–8, 259–61; *and* Spanish Civil War 235, 236; strategic assumptions 121; 'use of fear' 44, 46; weakness disguised 250, 382–3
    demographic problems 36, 128
    disarmament 27, 35, 42
    economic policy 26–7, 56–79, 128–9, 130–1, 136–7, 138–9, 232–3, 353–4; depression 26, 27, 124–5, 181, 244; Popular Front 121–2, 125, 127, 128–32; Reynaud and 133–9; unemployment 124–9, 135, 136–7
    and E. Europe 236, 279–313
    empire overseas 14, 22, 97, 355, 369, 374; *see also* Algeria; Indo-China *etc.*
    Foreign Office (Quai d'Orsay) 9, 10, 46–9, 58, 85, 154, 169, 212, 213, 234, 241; Belgium 173, 187; Britain 169–71; E. Europe 81, 85, 152; Germany, reconciliation contemplated 31–2, 136, 138; Italy 21, 44–6, 51–2, 72–5, 215, 233, 255–6, 259–60; Munich agreement 167, 234; *and* Rhineland 257–8; USA 169–70; USSR 151–2; Yugoslavia 210–11, 213; *see also* alliances; defence policy *above*
    intelligence *see* intelligence
    internationalism, inter-war 26–7, 35, 101
    and Poland 229, 279–348, 390; intelligence co-operation 325; overestimation 280–1, 302, 303, 311, 311–13, 316; Rambouillet Agreements (1936) 286–7
    rearmament 110–31
    Third Republic 1–3, 8–9, 13–14, 42, 56, 86, 378–402; Alliance Démocratique 36, 258; Cartel des Gauches 22, 52; 'government by decree' 56, 60, 64; Popular Front 60, 79, 80–109, 153–4, 195, 197–8, 258; 'Republic of Pals' 91, 98, 158; 'Republic of the Radicals' 17, 106, 108; weaknesses 101–2, 365, 390–1
    and USSR 218, 232–3, 258, 282–4, 289–97, 295–6, 302–3
    Vichy govt. (1940–44) 2, 3–6, 8–9, 67, 85, 384, 401–2
    World War I 19–21, 387, 393
    World War II 347–8, 355, 357, 378, 386, 390, 398; command distribution 359–60; initial tactics 316, 319; morale 361–2; peace negotiations refused (1939) 327–8; peripheral campaigns 350–2, 392; political problems 366–7, 372, 386–402; war aims 314, 316, 320–23, 392
    and Yugoslavia 221, 227, 236–7
    see also individual topics and persons
Franchet d'Esperey, Marshal Louis 81, 102, 217, 224, 391
Franco, Generalissimo Francisco 101, 388
François-Poncet, André 6, 7, 47, 55, 75, 394
Franco–Prussian War (1870) 12, 13, 161
Fraser, Col. William 95, 207–8, 235, 316, 318–19, 327, 363
Frédéric-Dupont, Edouard 142–3
Frente Popular (Spanish Popular Front) 101, 108
Frère, Gen. Aubert 374
frontalier battalions 183
Frossard, Ludovic-Oscar 129, 132
Fuller, Maj.-Gen. John Frederick Charles 242, 253
Fyda, Col. 306, 316

Gaiffier, Baron de 49

Index

Galet, Gen. Emile 188
Gallifet, Gaston-Alexandre-Auguste de, Marquis 86
Gambetta, Léon-Michel 13, 104
Gamelin, Eugénie (*née* Marchand) (wife of Gamelin), marriage 22
Gamelin, Marguérite (sister of MG) 14
Gamelin, Gen. Maurice (Maurice-Gustave)
  achievement summarised 8, 9–12, 143, 378–402
  and air power 142–71
  and alliances 53, 88, 382, 399
  and appeasement (1939) 310–13
  and army: mechanisation 65, 71–2, 78, 122–3, 140, 243; modernisation 9, 34, 36, 40, 44, 104–6, 119
  and army commissions 360, 361, 372–3
  and attaque brusquée 139
  and Austrian Anschluss 262
  and Belgium 92, 172–209
  and Blum 80–1, 82, 85, 107, 159
  and Bonnet 308–11
  and Britain 53–5, 73, 92, 236–78, 298–9, 300–01, 376
  cabinet particulier 18, 94–6
  character 2, 14, 15, 16, 23, 30–1, 89, 390, 394, 402; artistic interests 14, 30, 395; attitude to politicians 17–18, 19, 20, 23–4, 28–9, 32, 44; duty, concept of 381, 384–5, 390; foreign assessments of 5, 23, 31–2, 55, 82, 86; philosophical interests 14, 30, 395; *and* Vichy government 5–6
  and Clemenceau 372, 387
  and Cot 158–9, 168
  and Czechoslovakia 262, 285
  and Daladier 82–3, 88–91, 92–3, 98, 100, 108–9, 133, 140, 313, 354–5, 372–3, 385–90, 400, 402
  defence aims 11, 44, 55, 63, 74–6, 139–41, 149–50, 169–70, 201, 230, 233, 235, 245, 399–402
  Ardennes 199–201
  armoured divisions 140, 201–2
  arms supply 230
  and disarmament 180
  E. Europe 215, 230, 233
  and E. Europe 210–35, 279–80
  and Fabry 55–60, 70–5, 104
  finance 57, 59, 60, 174
  and fortifications 184, 197, 198, 199–200, 203
  and de Gaulle 38–9, 146
  and Georges 99–100, 233, 398
  and Germany 49, 50, 73, 76
  honours, medals 19–21
  and industry 77, 111–12, 126, 128, 129, 133, 232
  and intelligence 9, 46, 336
  and Italy 46, 52–5, 73–4, 255–6
  and Jacomet 159
  and Joffre 350, 363, 395
  journal de marche 94
  and La Chambre 159, 162
  and Laurent 204
  and Laval 74–6
  and Maginot Line 180–3, 198
  and military service 185
  and mobilisation 353–4
  and Munich agreement 169, 279
  and neutralism 208
  opposition to 29–30, 365, 386
  overseas postings 15, 21–4, 95
  and Pétain 177–8, 246
  and Pironneau 103
  and Poland 235, 262, 280–1, 285–6, 301, 302, 305, 306–7, 311, 337–42, 375
  political position 9, 24, 25–6, 29, 56, 81, 82, 84–5, 86, 109, 296, 384–5, 400–1
  political relations 79, 98–9, 107–9, 138–41, 186, 396, 401
  popular rising feared 104, 106
  power constraints 96–7, 168–9, 171, 379–80, 400, 402
  promotions 16, 18, 19, 20, 22
  regiments (service with) 15, 16, 18, 19, 20, 24–5
  and Resignation 380–84
  and Reynaud 89
  and Rhineland remilitarised 154, 257, 258–9, 279, 283–4, 390
  and right-wing subversion 102
  in Romania 224
  and Rydz-Smigly 283, 285, 286, 287
  and Sarrail 23–4
  Servir (memoirs) 5, 8, 385
  and Spanish Civil War 160
  staff appointments 12, 17–18, 19, 25–6, 26–30, 82, 95, 96–7, 168–9, 242, 379, 297
  and Sudetenland crisis 132–3, 167, 279, 281–2
  and USSR 284, 294–5, 301, 302–3
  and Vuillemin 162, 169, 306–8, 321–2
  and Weygand 11, 26–30, 140, 391
  World War II 6–7, 317, 321–2, 328–30, 332–4, 336–7, 349, 351–5, 362–3, 373–4, 377–9, 387–8, 392, 394–9, 401
  and Yugoslavia 219, 224–5, 231

Gamelin, Pauline (*née* Uhrich) (mother of MG) 13
Gamelin, Zéphyrin (father of MG) 13
Garde Mobile, popular rising feared (1936) 87
Gasnier-Duparc, Alphonse 106
Gauché, Col. Maurice 46, 50, 103, 298–9, 316, 324, 327, 334–5, 353
  and Belgium 207, 320–21
  and Enigma 326
  and Yugoslavia 218, 225, 227, 228–9, 230
Gaulle, Gen. Charles-André-Marie-Joseph de 8, 12, 37–8, 374, 3293–4
  on air power 145–6
  army modernisation proposals 36–42, 86, 87–8, 90, 100–1, 123, 124–5, 141, 145–6, 252, 345
  political position 86, 87–8, 100–1
Génébrier, Roger 388
Geneva, disarmament conference (1932–4) 27, 35, 42, 180, 243, 244
Georges, Gen. Alphonse 6, 7, 73–4, 99–100, 102, 122, 183, 233, 307, 321, 323
  and air power 149, 155
  and army commissions 361, 373
  army modernisation 99–100, 146, 344
  and Belgium 193, 323
  and Britain 255, 259, 260, 329
  and German capabilities 50, 307, 319
  GQG 359
  and intelligence 46, 324
  and Poland 306–7, 317, 323, 340, 343
  and Rhineland 257
  World War II 6, 7, 317, 326, 328, 330, 332–3, 343, 350, 374, 398
  and Yugoslavia 227
Géraud, André (Pertinax) 5
Germain-Martin, Henri 62, 65
Germany
  air power 11, 143, 149; air superiority 153, 155–6, 162, 164, 166–7; Blitzkrieg 146, 159–60; Poland 146, 340–2
  Austria, Anschluss with (1938) 130, 165, 199, 232
  Belgian non-belligerence (1939) 207, 208
  Belgium invaded by (1914) 172
  Czechoslovakia 118, 124, 132–3, 135, 164, 167, 202, 229, 279, 305
  and E. Europe 50–1, 215, 222, 227, 232
  E. Prussia 290, 292
  France, invaded (1940) 398; Franco-German reconciliation 31, 32, 75, 135; French diplomats in 47, 75, 160
  frontier fortification (1936) 152
  on Gamelin 31–2
  and Geneva conferences 243
  as historic threat 12, 13
  intelligence 324, 325
  Italy 54, 220
  Lithuania, Memel annexed (1939) 279, 305
  Munich agreement (1938) 118, 132, 133, 135, 167, 169, 230, 234, 279, 295
  Norway invaded by (1940) 352
  Poland 118, 280, 288, 314–48, 337–42; Germany invades (1939) 10, 48, 171, 207, 208, 314–48; Polish–German pact (1934) 285, 305
  preparedness assessed 50, 252, 258–9, 319–20
  rearmament 25, 26, 28, 33, 45, 110; air force re-established (1935) 40
  arms limitation proposed 73, 75
  and Blitzkrieg 159
  clandestine 35, 46, 243, 297
  conscription/military service (1935–6) 41, 43, 44, 45, 49, 50, 122, 178, 254
  and E. Europe 215–16
  four-year plan 112
  French assessment of (1935) 49–51
  manpower, World War II 357
  mechanisation 38, 40, 44, 251
  Rhineland 45, 49–50, 55, 73–4
  Rhineland, allies evacuate (1926; 1930) 46, 173, 174, 179
  Rhineland, remilitarised (1936) 64, 76–8, 81, 154, 189, 217, 234, 257–63, 279, 390
  Scandinavia invaded by (1940) 392
  and Spanish Civil War 236
  Sudetenland *see* Czechoslovakia *above*
  USSR 151–2, 295, 302
  frontiers 291–2, 293, 297, 302
  Nazi–Soviet pact (1939) 10, 304, 312–13, 337, 339
  Versailles Treaty repudiated 35
  on Weygand 31–2
  World War II 282, 327–8, 331–2, 333
  Yugoslavia 221–2, 227, 232–3
Giraud, Gen. Henri-Honoré 148, 174, 233, 298, 343, 367, 376–7, 398
Gitton, Marcel 105, 132
Givet (Belgium) 199, 200, 336, 375–6
Glišić, Col. 228
Goering, Reichsmarschall Hermann 112, 324
Gort, 6th Viscount (John S.S.P. Vereker) 272, 275, 276, 311, 328, 330, 348, 359, 377, 384

Index

Grand Quartier Général (GQG) 19, 20, 317, 359
Great Britain *see* Britain
Greece, integrity guaranteed (1939) 279–80, 281
Grévy, Jules (François-Paul-Jules) 13
Groussard, Col. Georges 102
Guderian, Gen. Heinz Wilhelm 340
guerre d'attente 140
guerre de longue durée 139
Guillaumat, Gen. Adolphe 184
Guillaut, Lt.-Col. François 95
Guinand, Pierre 56–7, 60–1, 67, 93

Hailsham, 1st Viscount (Douglas McGarel Hogg) 247
Haining, Gen. Robert 266, 268
Halder, Gen. Franz 331
Halifax, Earl of (Edward F.L. Wood) 53, 256, 276, 391
Hankey, Maurice Pascal Alers, 1st Baron 112, 276
Happich, Engineer-Gen. Paul 65, 66, 77–8, 116, 119, 120, 126, 129, 132–3, 360
Hart, B.H. Liddell *see* Liddell Hart
Harvey, Oliver 268, 348, 391, 392
Haut Comité Militaire (HCM) 44, 110, 177–8, 250
Héring, Gen. Pierre 148, 202, 333, 344, 381, 383, 384
Herriot, Edouard 22, 28, 72, 76, 151, 300, 388
Heywood, Brig. T.G.G. (Gordon) 31, 149, 253, 261, 394
Hitler, Adolf 44, 167, 207, 237, 288, 329, 332–3
 and generals 331–2, 333, 398
 see also Germany
Holland *see* Netherlands
Hore-Belisha, (Isaac) Leslie 241, 264, 269, 272–3, 274, 275, 277
Hotchkiss company 62, 68, 69, 70, 111, 112, 113, 114, 126, 356, 369
Huet, Maj. François 94, 329
Hungary 216, 222, 224, 229
Huntziger, Gen. Charles 4, 6, 7, 343, 374, 375, 377, 378, 398, 402
Huré, Gen. Antoine 196

Indochina 14, 86
industry 56–79, 80, 120–1, 132–3, 138–9, 153
 and army bureaucracy 119–20
 aviation 130, 153–7, 165–6
 decentralisation 64–6, 68, 126, 130, 153–4, 156
 diplomatic problems 230–31, 286–8
 economic constraints 58, 59, 61–3, 119, 123
 labour problems 116–17, 119, 120, 126, 127–8, 129, 131, 134, 138–9, 166, 197; forty-hour week 127, 131–2, 135, 136–7; government remedies 116, 117, 125, 127, 128–9, 131–2, 134; skills shortages 116, 117, 120, 125–9, 136–7, 156, 354, 370, 371; unemployment 124–9, 132, 135, 136–7; unrest (1936–8) 86–7, 105, 116–17, 129
 market problems 61, 63, 64, 66, 59, 119
 and mobilisation 94, 110–11, 353, 354, 355, 356–7, 358; essential workers (*affectés spéciaux*) 135, 358, 369
 nationalisation 62, 66, 67, 111–15, 153
 output recovery (1939) 138
 production delays 112, 114, 116–20, 118
 production shortfalls 118, 155, 157, 165, 230–1
 profiteering alleged 59, 60, 69–70
 secondary suppliers 117, 120, 127–8
 sixty-hour week 135
 training 128–9, 136–7, 370
 World War II 135, 353, 354, 356–9, 370–1; *see also* army commissions
Inskip, Sir Thomas 237, 271
Instruction on ... Major Air Units (1937) 157
intelligence 28, 33, 46–9, 160, 213, 224, 229, 240–1, 323–6
 air force 149, 159–60
 Enigma codes 325–6
 Foreign Office (Quai d'Orsay) 47–9
 German rearmament 35, 40, 43–4, 50, 152, 159, 258, 321
 Germany 282, 350
 and invasion threatened 331–2, 334
 Italy 213, 228
 Laurent 204–8
 Poland 284, 285, 289
 Service de Renseignements ... (SR) 46, 204, 241, 324
 World War II 319, 323–6, 327, 328, 329–30
 Yugoslavia 213, 218, 226, 227, 228–9, 232
 see also Britain; Yugoslavia *etc.*
Ironside, Field Marshal William Edmund, 1st Baron 275, 377
 and Poland 289, 311, 317, 339, 342
Italy 73, 162, 166, 182–3, 222, 338
 Abyssinia invaded by (1935) 46, 51, 53, 72–6, 217, 220, 255–6

Italy (*cont.*)
  and France 21, 58, 126, 192, 261–2, 389; France repudiates 85, 215, 217; Franco–Italian accord (1935) 255–6; *rapprochement* 44–6, 51–5, 60, 72–5, 85, 211, 215, 216, 233
  and Germany 54, 220
  leaves League of Nations (1937) 220
  and Poland 317
  and Spanish Civil War 236
  and Yugoslavia 44, 211, 212–13, 214, 215, 216–17, 220–1, 225, 227, 232–3; Italo–Yugoslav pact (1937) 221, 222
Itter, Schloss 6, 394, 397

Jacomet, Robert 93–4, 111, 112, 113, 114, 119, 121, 129, 159, 372, 389
Jamet, Gen. Louis 94, 110, 170, 317
Jauneaud, Gen. Jean-Henri 153, 155, 157, 159, 170
Jaurès, Jean-Joseph-Marie-Auguste 105, 106
Jeannel, Gen. Joseph 94
Jeanneney, Jules 8
Jeunesses Patriotes 30, 250, 365
Jodl, Gen. Alfred 332
Joffre, Marshal Joseph-Jacques-Césaire 17, 19, 20, 23, 30, 32, 92, 238
  and army commissions 360, 363
  and Gamelin 12, 17–18, 19, 20, 96, 350
Jouhaux, Léon 131

Kasprzycki, Gen. 286, 288–9, 306, 306–7, 346
Keller, Gen. Louis 123, 157
Kerchove, Count André de 177
Koeltz, Col. Louis 46, 49, 50
Kühlenthal, Col. 32, 297

La Chambre, Guy 113, 142, 162–5, 230, 296–7, 329, 361, 387
  air force preparedness 140, 167, 169, 322
  and Gamelin, 159, 169
Laffargue, Col. André 36
Laffly company 66
Laffond, Gen. de 369
Lafontaine, Gen. 375
La Grandière, Palamède de 70, 71
La Laurencie, Gen. de 368
Lamoureux, Lucien 177
Langenhove, Fernand van 189
Langeron, Roger 86, 87
Laroche, Jules 189
La Rocque, Col. François Casimir de 104, 392

Lattre de Tassigny, Gen. Jean-Marie-Gabriel de 294, 374
Laure, Gen. Auguste Emile 374
Laurent, Col. Edmond 46, 187, 204–8, 329–30
Laval, Pierre 4, 26, 44, 49–54, 75–6, 77, 110, 389, 390, 391, 393
  and appeasement 55, 73, 75, 215, 363, 389
  economic policy 56–62
  and Italy 44–5, 51, 53, 54, 74, 75, 216, 220, 256
  prime minister (1935–6) 76, 77, 82
  and USSR 151–2, 218, 291, 292, 293
Lazurich, Robert 105, 132, 369
League of Nations 22, 45, 53, 72–3, 220, 239, 255
Lebanon 22, 351–2
Lebas, Jean 128, 136
Lebrun, Albert 60, 185, 374–5, 386–7
Léger, Alexis Saint-Léger 48, 158, 164, 257, 300, 351
Le Goyet, Col. Pierre 143; *Mystère Gamelin, Le* 8, 11
Lelong, Gen. Albert 47, 170, 266, 275, 276, 278, 298
Le Moignic, Eugène 66
Léon-Jouhaux, Augusta 6, 394
Leopold III, King of the Belgians 177, 188, 190, 192, 198, 203
Lerecouvreux, Marcel 368
Levant *see* Near East; Syria *etc.*
Leygues, Georges 92
Libya, Italy in (1935–6) 54
Liddell Hart, Sir Basil Henry 242, 263–4, 265, 273–4, 278
Liège (Belgium) 173, 174, 176, 177, 194, 205, 323
Lille (Nord) 172, 174, 175, 183, 198, 329
Lithuania, Memel annexed (1939) 279, 305
Little Entente (Czechoslovakia/Romania/Yugoslavia) 210, 232, 281
  weakened 222, 224, 225
  see also Europe, Eastern
Locarno, Treaties of (1925) 49, 190–1, 202, 212, 248, 261–2
  Belgium abrogates 190–1
  new version proposed (1936) 261–2
  and Rhineland 260, 261–2
Loizeau, Gen. Lucien 191, 233, 293–4
Lorraine
  annexed by Prussia (1871) 12, 13
  defence of 174, 175, 180, 181, 330
  Gamelin's connection with 12, 13, 25
Loustaunau-Lacau, Maj. Georges 101–2

Index

Low Countries *see* Belgium; Netherlands *etc.*
Luftwaffe (German air force) *see* Germany: air power
Luxembourg 172, 174, 200, 318, 329, 330, 376, 378; *see also* Belgium
Lyautey, Marshal Hubert (Louis-Hubert-Gonzalve) 15, 103

MacMahon, Marshal Patrice 13
Maginot, André 25, 51, 99, 182, 204, 243, 250, 361, 391
  and Belgian frontier 173, 174
  and Maginot Line 180, 182–3
Maginot Line 26, 36, 50, 53, 148, 179–83, 223, 242, 304, 328, 369
  Belgian gap 124, 199–201
  Britain and 247, 253–4, 256, 264, 272–3, 276, 277
  construction delays 44, 182–3, 198, 199
  extension considered 172, 173–4, 176–9, 183, 209
  finance 26, 179–80, 182–3, 198
Maglinse, Gen., military accord 173, 187, 188–9, 191, 192, 202
Mailly (Aube) 121, 122–3, 142, 223
Malvy, Louis-Jean 393
Mandel, Georges 97, 106, 131, 350–1, 386, 390
Manstein Plan (Feb. 1940) 398
Marchandeau, Paul 121, 133
Marchand, Eugénie *see* Gamelin, Eugénie
Margerie, Roland de 47
Marić, Gen. 217–18, 222, 223–5, 227–9, 231
Marin, Louis 365, 392
Marquet, Adrian 4
Martin, Gen. Louis 376
Mason-Macfarlane, Gen. F.N. [Frank Noel] 377
masse de manoeuvre 201, 398
Massigli, René 229, 234
Maubeuge (Nord) 184, 197, 199
Maurin, Gen. Louis 16, 29, 88, 89, 106, 119, 251
  and army 44, 56–7, 58, 75, 185, 382–3
  and Britain 45, 46, 242, 250–1, 262
  defence policy 68, 149, 178, 257
  and industry 64–5, 71, 79, 126
  and USSR 291–3, 294, 296–7
Maurras, Charles 2
Mediterranean sea 53, 54, 256–7, 275, 283
Mendès-France, Pierre 123–4, 151, 393
Mendras, Col. Edmond 291, 294
Menzies, Maj.-Gen. Sir Stewart ('C') 325
Metz (Moselle) 176, 223, 259, 364, 374

Région Fortifiée de 175, 182–3
Meuse river
  defence line on 175–6, 182, 191, 194, 200–1, 374–5; *and* Belgian non-belligerence 207, 323
Mézières (Ardennes) 199, 376
Micheler, Gen. Alfred 20
Michel, Henri 114
Miellet, Edmond 128, 364, 370
Millerand, Alexandre 19, 20, 92
Milne, Field Marshal Sir George 244
Minart, Col. Jacques 48, 335, 336, 356, 363
Mittelhauser, Gen. Charles 212, 215, 285
Moch, Jules 59
Monick, Emmanuel 47
Monmousseau, Gaston 134–5
Monnet, Jean 169
Montgomery-Massingberd, Field Marshal Sir Archibald 193, 244, 246, 247–8, 253, 261, 384
  and French defences 53, 55
  and Italy 52, 53, 256
Montmédy (Meuse) 174, 176, 181, 200, 328, 374
Monts de Flandre 184, 198
Monzie, Anatole de 132, 138, 234
Moore, R. Walton 384, 392
Moselle river 307, 328, 330
Moulin, Jean 153
Mourmelon (Marne) 121
Munich agreement *see under* Germany
Musse, Gen. Félix 303, 305–6, 337, 339, 342
Mussolini, Benito Amilcare Andrea 44–5, 73, 220, 222, 256, 279
  see also Italy

Naggiar, Emile 221
nationalisation *see under* industry
navy (French) 55–4, 65, 91–3, 97, 113, 168, 378, 400
Nazi–Soviet (Molotov–Ribbentrop) pact (1939) 10, 304, 312–13, 337, 339
Near East 22, 182, 257, 275, 308; *see also* Syria *etc.*
Nedić, Gen. Milutin 222, 223–4, 228, 283
Netherlands 170, 188, 191, 325–6, 334, 398
  and Britain 193, 195–6, 260
  threatened 118, 174, 194, 329
  World War II 143, 317–18, 333, 335, 336, 376, 378, 397–8
Neurath, Freiherr Konstantin von 221, 222, 223
Newall, Air Chief Marshal Sir Cyril 317, 342

Niessel, Gen. Henri 160, 282
Nivelle, Gen. Robert-Georges 20
Noël, Léon 285, 286, 339
Noguès, Gen. Auguste 85, 97, 168, 378
North Africa see Africa
Norway 350, 352, 392
Nyon (Switzerland), Conference at (1937) 236

OKW (Oberkommando Wehrmachts) 332
Oster, Col. Hans 325, 329, 334
Overstraeten, Gen. Raoul François Casimir van 177, 188, 192, 199, 203
Ovey, Sir Esmond 254

Painlevé, Paul 180
Panhard, Paul 117
Panhard company/Panhard & Levassor 117–20, 118, 124, 126, 140, 369
paratroops 158, 294
Parti Communiste Français (PCF) 83, 102, 105–6, 291, 292, 300, 370–1; see also Popular Front
Parti Ouvrier Belge 188–9
Parti Social Français (PSF) 104, 392; see also Popular Front
Paul-Boncour, Joseph 25, 28, 82, 163, 180, 277, 390
Paul, Prince (Regent of Yugoslavia) 217, 218–19, 220, 224–5, 228, 229
'PC Bruno' 325
PCF see Parti Communiste Français
Pellé, Gen. 16–17, 20, 212
Pertinax (André Géraud) 5
Pétain, Marshal Henri Philippe Omer 8, 25–6, 43, 62, 92, 99, 177–8, 180, 194, 242, 283, 360, 389, 391
 and alliances 242, 250
 and Belgium 177, 178, 184–5
 defence minister (1934) 245–6
 defence policy 35–6, 44, 52, 56–7, 68, 178, 184–5, 197, 200, 204
 and E. Europe 215, 224
 and Fall of France 109, 384, 400–2
 political views 81, 84, 100, 101, 178, 399
 Vichy govt. 3, 4, 5, 6, 142
Petibon, Col. Jean 94–6, 99, 112, 192
 and Britain 260, 261–2
 and E. Europe 216, 224, 311
 World War II 329–30, 394
Peugeot company 63, 121, 369
Phipps, Sir Eric 93, 161
Piétri, François 45, 59, 184, 185
Pilsudski, Josef Klemens 211, 283
Pironneau, André 103, 223, 299

Poincaré, Raymond 180, 387, 391, 392–3
Poland 81, 211, 279–90, 291, 302–13, 314–48
 air force 288, 306, 341
 and Czechoslovakia 216, 281, 290
 Danzig (Gdansk) Corridor 288, 306, 347
 and France 152, 210–12, 215, 217, 224, 229, 235, 282, 302–13; Franco–Polish treaties (1921; 1939) 212, 279–81, 282, 288, 305, 316, 390; French military missions in 282, 290, 312, 337–8; Rambouillet Agreements (1936) 286–7
 and Germany, Polish–German pact (1934) 285, 288, 305
 Germany invades (1939) 10, 48, 146, 171, 207, 208, 314–48
 governments-in-exile 325, 341
 and Munich agreement 303
 preparedness (1939) 287–8, 302, 303, 311, 339
 threatened 51–2, 118, 262, 302–13, 304–5
 and USSR 288, 289–90, 295, 300, 301, 302–3, 312, 318, 339
police, popular rising feared (1936) 86, 87
Pomaret, Charles 132, 135, 136–7, 138, 358
Popović, Col. 223, 228
Popular Front 60, 79, 80–109, 153–4, 195, 218, 270, 291, 296
Porch, Douglas 9
Portal, Air Chief Marshal Charles Frederick Algernon, 1st Viscount 397
Pownall, Gen. Sir Henry Royds 275, 326–9, 330, 347, 348, 377
Poydenot, Lt.-Col. Olivier 95
Prételat, Gen. Gaston 122, 199, 200, 202, 323, 328, 333, 334, 343, 380
 and German capabilities 307, 319
 World War II 319, 350, 374, 398
Prioux, Gen. Jules 376
PSF see Parti Social Français
Pujo, Gen. Bertrand 154, 155, 391, 402

Quai d'Orsay see France: Foreign Office

Radical party 17, 106–8, 151, 130–1, 258
RAF (Royal Air Force) see Britain: air power
Ramadier, Paul 60, 128, 132
Rambouillet Agreements (1936) 286–7
Raquez, Col. Georges 106, 194, 205
Red Army see Union of Soviet Socialist Republics: army

Régions Fortifiées 175, 182–3
Régnier, Marcel 57, 58, 59, 60–1, 67, 75, 77
Reibel, Charles 178–9, 372
Reichenau, Field Marshal Walther von 45
Renault company 61, 62–6, 68–71, 77, 78, 111, 112, 113, 114, 115, 121, 126, 358, 369, 371
Renault, Louis 66, 71, 78, 119, 121, 371
Renondeau, Gen. Georges 47
Republican Federation party 365, 392
Requin, Gen. Edouard 316, 323, 356, 366, 374
Revue des Deux Mondes 83–4
Revue Militaire Française 36–7
Reynaud, Paul 2, 37, 51, 106, 141, 168, 174, 185, 348, 352, 378, 390, 392
  and air power 145, 146, 170
  and army 315, 361, 399
  and Britain 252, 267, 269, 278
  and Daladier 91, 131, 133, 391–2, 399
  finance minister (1938–40) 133–7, 391
  and de Gaulle army proposals 37, 38–42, 44, 87, 88, 100–1, 124–5, 141, 145
  and Gamelin 7, 89, 141, 208, 386, 399, 401
  prime minister (1940) 352, 384, 391–2, 399, 400, 402
Rhineland *see* Germany: Rhineland
Rhine river 175, 182, 207, 307, 328, 333
Ribbentrop, Joachim von 135
  see also Nazi–Soviet pact
Ricard, Gen. Emile 94, 199
Riedinger, Gen. Georges 187, 203, 204
Riom (Cantal), trial at (1940–2) 3–4, 6–7, 67, 113, 114, 115, 142, 158–9, 313, 352, 372, 381
Rivet, Col. Louis 46, 324–6, 334–6
Romains, Jules (Louis-H.-J. Farigoule) 395, 396
Romania
  army 215, 216–17, 351
  and Britain (1939) 279–80, 281
  and France 152, 210–12, 216–17, 223–4, 305
  and Poland falling 341
  and USSR 232, 300
  see also Europe: Eastern
Rommel, Field Marshal Erwin Johannes Eugen 374
Rueff, Jacques 133–4
Rydz-Smigly, Marshal Eduard 283–6, 288, 305–6, 311, 316, 338
  Polish campaign 318, 339, 346
  and USSR 302, 339

Saar river 183, 328, 330

offensive (1939) 307, 316, 318, 323, 324, 356, 374, 375
Sablet d'Estrières, Engineer-Gen. Antoine de 71, 77
SAET (Section d'Armements et d'Etudes Techniques) *see under* army: mechanisation
St Cyr, military academy at 14–15, 95, 102, 106, 368, 395
Salengro, Roger 88, 122
Salonika (Greece) 283, 350–1
Sarrail, Gen. Maurice 22–4, 32, 82
Sarraut, Albert-Pierre 76, 82, 87, 92, 258, 389
  and Rhineland 258, 259
Sarraut, Maurice 18, 25, 82
Sartre, Jean-Paul 362, 374
Sas, Maj. 325, 329
Sauvy, Alfred 133, 135–6, 141, 363
Scandinavia 352, 392
  see also Norway *etc.*
Schacht, Hjalmar 221
Scheldt river 173, 193, 197, 198
Schmidt (Asché) (agent) 324–5, 326, 334, 335, 336, 338
Schneider company 67, 68, 71, 114, 356, 370
Schweisguth, Gen. Victor-Henri 47, 99–100, 155, 190, 197, 224
  and Belgium 193–4, 195, 205
  and Britain 54, 193–4, 195, 257, 259, 260, 261, 262–3, 266, 268, 268–9
  and E. Europe 50, 216, 228
  and Italy 46, 233
  and mechanisation/tanks 57, 62, 78
  popular rising feared 86, 87
  and Rhineland 73, 257, 259, 260, 390
  and USSR 233, 292–3, 294, 295, 297, 298–301
Section Française de l'Internationale Ouvrière (SFIO) 105–6, 107, 128–9
  see also Popular Front
Sedan (Ardennes) 199, 200, 345, 374, 375, 376
Semenov, Gen. 299, 300–1
Service de Renseignements et de Contre-Espionnage (SR) 46, 204, 241, 324
Servir (Gamelin) 5, 8, 385
SFIO *see* Section Française de l'Internationale ...
Sichitiu, Gen. 223–4
Sieburg, Friedrich 31–2
Siegfried Line 316, 319, 328, 329, 331, 350
Sikorski, Gen. Wladyslaw Eugeniusz 304, 325

Simon, Lt.-Col. Henri 95
Simon, Jules (Jules-François-Simon Suisse) 13
Sitzkrieg 348
SNCF (Société Nationale des Chemins de Fer Français) 115
SOMUA company 68, 123, 124, 201, 356, 358, 368, 369
Sosnkowski, Gen. 289
Souiéda (Syria) 22–3
Spaak, Paul-Henri 190
Spain 101, 108, 388
  Civil War (1936–9) 101, 108, 160, 235, 236
Stachiewicz, Gen. 286, 288, 305, 311, 338, 339, 346
Stalin, Joseph (I.V. Dzhugashvili)
  and army 293, 301, 303
  and foreign communists 291, 294
  see also Union of Soviet Socialist Republics
Stehlin, Capt. Paul 160
Stojadinović, Dr Milan 217, 218, 220–9, 232
Strang, William 161
Stresa Front 45, 295
Sudetenland *see under* Czechoslovakia
Swayne, Brigadier Jack 329
Switzerland 182–3, 329
Syria 22, 85, 351–2
  Druze rising (1925–7) 15, 22–3
  Gamelin in 15, 22–4, 95
Syrovy, Gen. 224
Szymanski, Col. 311

Taittinger, Pierre 30, 250–1, 291, 296, 365, 368–9, 371
tanks 38, 58, 61–72, 78, 110, 120, 266, 359, 375
  Britain 242–3, 266, 268–9
  cavalry 68–9, 122, 123
  German 159, 340, 344–5
  heavy divisions 344–5
  infantry dependence 122
  masse de manoeuvre 201
  at mobilisation 356, 358, 358–9, 368, 369
  Polish campaign 340, 341–2, 347
  production delays 116–20, 140
  types: AMC/AMR 69; [Char] B/B1 62–3, 68, 69, 71–2, 110, 114, 116, 123, 140, 201, 320, 345, 356, 358, 359; [Char] D/D2 62–3, 72, 114, 123; H.35 69, 70, 110, 116, 122, 124; H.39 356, 368, 369; R.35 62, 63, 64, 68–9, 110, 116, 120, 122, 123, 271; Renault FT 62; S.35 68, 122, 140, 201, 356, 358, 368, 369
  for Yugoslavia 231
  see also industry; army: mechanisation
Tarbes (Hautes-Pyrénées) 156, 370
Tardieu, André-Pierre-Gabriel-Amédée 18, 25, 51, 82, 107, 176, 180, 181, 185, 393
Teschen (Czechoslovakia/Poland) 281, 303
Thomas, Albert 18
Thorez, Maurice 258, 370
Thorne, Col. Andrew 45
'Tiger' *see* Clemenceau
Toulouse (Haute-Garonne) 154, 370
trade unions 105, 129, 131, 132, 134, 136
Tukachevski, Marshal Mikhail 293, 295, 301
Tunisia, Gamelin in 15

Uhrich *family* 13, 14
Uhrich, Pauline *see* Gamelin, Pauline
unemployment 124–9, 132, 135, 136–7
union sacrée 362
Union of Soviet Socialist Republics (USSR) 151–2, 290–1, 295, 300, 302, 352, 373
  air force 158, 293, 294, 300
  army 291–2, 293–5, 299, 301, 302, 303
  defence policy, inter-war 294, 299–300
  and E. Europe 152, 215
  and France 151–2, 210, 218, 233, 258, 290–303
  and Germany 10, 291–2, 293, 295, 297, 302, 304, 312–13, 337, 339
  and Poland 289–90, 295, 300–1, 302–3, 312, 318, 351
United Kingdom *see* Britain
United States of America (USA) 21, 107, 137, 150–1, 346–7, 354, 372, 384, 391
  and air power 138, 169–70
  arms supplied by 138, 230
  on French govt. 388–9, 392, 393
  on French morale 103, 105
USSR *see* Union of Soviet Socialist Republics

Valenciennes (Nord) 175, 368
van Overstraeten/van Zeeland *etc. see* Overstraeten/Zeeland *etc.*
Vandervelde, Emile 189
Vansittart, Sir Robert Gilbert, 1st Baron 49, 267, 269
Velpry, Col. Pol-Maurice 38, 123
Ventzov, Gen. 296, 298
Verdun (Meuse) 19, 182, 223, 364

Index

Versailles, Treaty of (1919) 31, 33, 35, 46, 149, 172, 239
Viénot, Pierre 266, 267
Vignolles, Château de 325
Villelume, Col. Paul de 46–7, 48, 298–9, 401, 402
Vincennes, Château de (defence HQ) 8, 95, 315
Voruz, Gen. Robert 45, 47, 244–5, 260, 261, 263, 266
Vuillemin, Gen. Joseph 97, 140, 157, 162, 299, 322, 329
  on air force preparedness 140, 163–4, 167, 169, 170, 230, 307–8, 322
  and Poland 289, 306–8, 317, 338, 342
  and Sudetenland threatened 234

war, aspects/theories
  aggressive defence 375
  air force strategic priority 147, 149, 152–100, 170
  air power 142, 150, 157
  attaque brusquée/surprise attack 149, 252
  attritional war 139
  bataille de conduite 182, 359
  Blitzkrieg 146, 149, 159, 341–2
  defensive as superior 178, 180
  fortifications 178, 180, 187
  masse de manoeuvre 201
  service interdependence 145–6
  tanks favour defender 201
  total industrialised war 144
  war by proxy 273–4
Wehrmacht *see* Germany: rearmament
Weir, William Douglas, 1st Viscount 264
Werth, Alexander 5
Weygand, Gen. Maxime 5–6, 8–9, 17, 21–2, 26–9, 141, 146, 180, 194, 215, 246, 251, 274, 287, 290, 360, 383, 391, 393
  and armistice 378, 384, 402
  and Belgium 186–7, 191, 199
  and Britain 243, 245, 246, 249
  character 21, 28, 29, 31–2, 42
  chief of the general staff 25, 26, 242
  and Daladier 83, 100
  defence policy 31–2, 34, 35–6, 40–8, 140, 174–5, 199, 204, 233, 243–4, 395–6
  and Flandin 391
  and Gamelin 30, 383, 391, 397
  and de Gaulle 146
  and Georges 99, 233
  political views 82, 83–4, 85, 100, 101, 107, 178, 365, 383–4, 396, 399

  reinstated (1940) 2–3, 378, 380, 381, 384
  and Rhineland 258
  and Spanish Civil War 160
  and USSR 258, 291, 294, 295
Wood, Sir (Howard) Kingsley 347
World War I 19–21, 25, 137, 159, 161, 184, 238–9, 249–50, 283, 292, 396
  army commissions 360, 361
  army policy affected by 35–6, 38
  Liddell Hart on 242, 273–4
  mobilisation 362
  Schlieffen plan 265, 276
  union sacrée 362
World War II 4, 6–7, 10, 94, 95, 345, 349–402
  air power 142–4
  Ardennes breached (1940) 199, 204
  Battle of France 378, 397–9
  Belgian non-belligerence (1939) 207–9
  Dyle-Breda manoeuvres 174, 397–8
  France falls (1940) 2, 10, 109, 185, 378, 398
  France, preparedness 74–5, 123, 140
  French military organisation 108–9, 406
  Norway campaign 352
  phoney war 322, 349–77
  Polish campaign 314–48

Ybarnégaray, Jean 4
Yugoslavia
  army 214–20, 222, 225, 226, 228
  and Britain 228
  and Czechoslovakia 225
  and France 52, 152, 210–35, 236–7; arms supplies 231–3; commercial support 221, 226, 227; Franco–Russian pact 232; French military advisers in 213–14; French policy for 215, 216–17; intelligence co-operation 223, 228–9, 232; security accords (1927; 1932) 211, 213
  Gamelin in 224–5
  and Germany 51–2, 218, 220, 221–2, 227–8, 229, 232
  and Hungary 222, 224, 229
  internal problems 214–15, 218, 220, 221, 224, 225, 231–2
  and Italy 44, 212–13, 214, 215, 216–17, 220–1, 227; Italo–Yugoslav pact (1937) 221, 222
  neutralism 220, 228

Zay, Jean 151, 393
Zeeland, Paul van 189, 190
Zuylen, Pierre van 203